THE BOOK OF ISAIAH

THE BOOK OF ISAIAH

The English Text, with Introduction, Exposition, and Notes

Edward J. Young

Volume 2
Chapters 19 to 39

William B. Eerdmans Publishing Company
Grand Rapids, Michigan / Cambridge, U.K.

© 1969 Wm. B. Eerdmans Publishing Co.

Wm. B. Eerdmans Publishing Co.
2140 Oak Industrial Drive N.E., Grand Rapids, Michigan 49505 /
P.O. Box 163, Cambridge CB3 9PU U.K.

Printed in the United States of America

17 16 15 14 13 12   14 13 12 11 10 9

Library of Congress catalog card number 63-17786

ISBN-13: 978-0-8028-9552-3

www.eerdmans.com

TABLE OF CONTENTS

Preface to Volume Two

The present volume carries on the exposition of Isaiah through chapter 39. Its purpose is to allow the prophet to speak for himself and, as much as possible, to expound his message for readers of the present day.

It seems best to reserve a discussion of the authorship of the prophecy for the third volume. Throughout the work, however, readers will discover various comments which support the position undergirding this commentary, namely, that Isaiah is the author of the entire work.

In publishing a series of commentaries both on the Old and the New Testaments written from the standpoint of those who believe in the absolute trustworthiness of the Bible, the Eerdmans Publishing Company has shown true vision; and the present author, in seeking to carry out a portion of this work, would pray that the Lord of all mercy will bless these efforts to His own glory.

There remains only the pleasant duty of expressing my gratitude to Mrs. Margaret Gregson and Mrs. Carl K. Spackman, for the care with which they have prepared the typescript; and to Mr. G. Lindsay Russell for his help in the translation of Sennacherib's account of his siege of Jerusalem.

—EDWARD J. YOUNG

We deeply regret the fact that Dr. Young did not live to see this second volume of his commentary on the Book of Isaiah published. Fortunately for those of us who remain behind, he had completed both this volume and the manuscript for Volume 3 before his death on February 14, 1968, and he had made arrangements with several authors for future volumes in the New International Commentary on the Old Testament, of which he was General Editor.

Dr. R. K. Harrison, Professor of Old Testament at Wycliffe College, University of Toronto, accepted the publisher's invitation to become the new General Editor of this series of Old Testament commentaries.

LIST OF ABBREVIATIONS

abs.   absolute
acc.   accusative
adj.   adjective
Akk.   Akkadian
ANEP   Pritchard: *Ancient Near Eastern Pictures*
ANET   Pritchard: *Ancient Near Eastern Texts* (1950)
Aq   Aquilla
Ar.   Arabic
Aram.   Aramaic
B   Codex Vaticanus
BA   *Biblical Archaeologist*
BASOR   *Bulletin American Schools of Oriental Research*
BDB   Brown, Driver, Briggs: *Hebrew Lexicon*
BH   *Biblia Hebraica*
BK   Baumgartner, Köhler: *Lexicon in Veteris Testamenti Libros* (1953)
Cas.   Plautus: *Casina*
CIS   *Corpus Inscriptionum Semiticarum*
col.   column
Com.   *Commentary*
cons.   consecutive
const.   construct
DOTT   *Documents of Old Testament Times*, ed. Winton Thomas
Egy.   Egyptian
Eth.   Ethiopic
f.   feminine
fut.   future
gen.   genitive
Gk.   Greek

GKC   Gesenius, Kautzsch, Cowley: *Hebrew Grammar* (1910)
Heb.   Hebrew
HTC   Mowinckel: *He That Cometh* (1956)
HUCA   *Hebrew Union College Annual*
IB   *Interpreter's Bible* (1952-1956)
imp.   imperfect
imper.   imperative
inf.   infinitive
in loc. on the passage being discussed
JAOS   *Journal of the American Oriental Society*
JBL   *Journal of Biblical Literature*
JCS   *Journal of Cuneiform Studies*
JNES   *Journal of Near Eastern Studies*
JQR   *Jewish Quarterly Review*
JTS   *Journal of Theological Studies*
KB   *Keilinschriftliche Bibliotek*
lit.   literally
m.   masculine
M   Masoretic Text
mss.   manuscripts
nom.   nominative
NSI   Cooke: *North Semitic Inscriptions* (1903)
NT   New Testament
obj.   object
OS   *Oudtestamentische Studiën*

9

OT	Old Testament	Targ.	Targum
part.	participle	*TT*	Driver: *A Treatise on the Use of the Tenses in Hebrew* (1892)
perf.	perfect		
PL	Migne: *Patrologia Latina*		
pl.	plural	*TWNT*	Kittel: *Theologisches Wörterbuch zum Neuen Testament*
pred.	predicate		
prep.	preposition		
pret.	preterite	Ug.	Ugaritic
1Q	First Isaiah Manuscript, Qumran	*VT*	*Vetus Testamentum*
		Vulg.	Vulgate
S	Symmachus	*WThJ*	*Westminster Theological Journal*
s.	singular		
subj.	subject	*ZAW*	*Zeitschrift für die alttestamentliche Wissenschaft*
Syr.	Syriac		
T	Theodotion		

Outline

The first volume of this three-volume commentary on the Book of Isaiah dealt with the following material:

I. THE CRISIS AND THE MESSIAH (1:1—12:6)

    A. INTRODUCTION TO THE ENTIRE PROPHECY (1:1-31)
        1. Judah's Sinful Condition (1:1-9)
        2. God's Judgment upon Judah (1:10-31)

    B. EARLY MESSAGES OF ISAIAH (2:1—5:30)
        1. God's Blessing and Judgment (2:1-22)
        2. Judah's Punishment and Glory (3:1—4:6)
        3. God and Judah (5:1-30)

    C. JUDAH'S TRUE HOPE: THE MESSIANIC KING (6:1—12:6)
        1. Isaiah's Vision of the Holy God (6:1-13)
        2. The Crisis and the Promise (7:1-25)
        3. The Assyrian Invader (8:1—9:7)
        4. The Threat of Assyria (9:8—10:34)
        5. Judah's Hope in the Messiah (11:1—12:6)

II. THE THEOCRACY AND THE NATIONS (13:1—39:8)

    A. JUDAH AND THE WORLD POWER (13:1—27:13)
        1. The Growth of the Mesopotamian Power (13:1—14:32)
        2. The Downfall of Moab, Syria, and Other Nations (15:1—18:7)

The present volume begins with point 3 under II A.

        3. Egypt in Confusion (19:1-25)
        4. Egypt and Ethiopia: a False Hope (20:1-6)
        5. Babylon (21:1-10)
        6. Edom (21:11-12)
        7. The Arabians (21:13-17)
        8. Jerusalem as One of the Nations (22:1-14)
        9. Shebna the Steward (22:15-25)
      10. Tyre, the Sea Power (23:1-18)

    B. GOD'S SOVEREIGNTY MANIFESTED IN SALVATION AND JUDGMENT; CONCLUSION TO CHAPTERS 13—23 (24:1—27:13)

Text and Commentary

3. EGYPT IN CONFUSION (19:1-25)

1 The burden[1] of Egypt. Behold! the LORD is riding upon a light
cloud, and coming to Egypt, and the idols of Egypt will shake
from before him, and the heart of Egypt will melt in its midst.
2 And I shall incite Egypt against Egypt, and a man will fight
against his brother, and a man against his neighbor, city against
city, kingdom against kingdom.
3 And the spirit of Egypt will fail in its midst, and its counsel I
shall swallow, and they will seek unto the idols and unto the sor-
cerers and unto the spirits and unto the familiar spirits.
4 And I shall shut up Egypt in the hand of hard masters, and a
strong king will rule over them, saith the Sovereign One, the LORD
of hosts.

1 In the days of Moses Egypt had been the great oppressor of
God's people, and God had punished her. He had shown in the
Exodus that He was the true God, supreme over all Egypt's idols.
Nevertheless, in times of need and crisis His people still turned to
the nation that had oppressed them in ancient times. If refuge was
needed, they would seek it in Egypt. Again therefore, God must
show that He is sovereign, that His own people may know the folly
of trusting in their enemy. Isaiah molds his description with a
figure taken from the storm, and depicts the Lord riding[2] upon a
light cloud, that He may speedily execute His work of judgment.

---

1 For a defense of the view that מַשָּׂא is an imposed burden, i.e. an argument or thesis, cf. P. A. H. De Boer, "An Inquiry into the Meaning of the
Term מַשָּׂא," OS, Vol. 5, 1948, pp. 197-214. See also H. S. Gehman, "The 'Burden'
of the Prophets," JQR, Vol. 31, No. 2, 1940. B reads ὅρασις, Aq ασμα αιγυπτου,
S T λημμα.

2 B has καθηται; Aq επιβαινει; 1Q here supports M. It is true, as Dillmann
states, the point of departure, whether heaven or Zion (8:18), is not mentioned.
Dillmann thinks that v. 17 points to the latter, but it is not necessary for the
prophet's purpose to mention God's point of departure. The picture presents
God in action, riding to Egypt, and is far more vivid than if all details had
been included. It is characteristic of the biblical writers that they concentrate
upon the essential and omit the nonessential. König takes the participle as expressing futurity. Grammatically, this is possible; but the picture is stronger
if the Lord is conceived as already riding the cloud.

13

The scene does not necessarily suggest that the Lord comes from the Temple at Jerusalem nor from heaven, but merely that He comes as a judge.

This is not the first time that God is represented as coming to fulfill a specific purpose. We are reminded of the song of Deborah, "Lord, when thou wentest out of Seir, when thou marched·t out of the field of Edom, etc." (Judg. 5:4).[3] And again in 2 Samuel 5:24 we have the words, "for then shall the LORD go out before thee." In Psalm 96:13 the Lord's coming is definitely associated with judgment, "for he cometh, for he cometh to judge the earth."

Elsewhere in Scripture also the clouds are represented as being His vehicles (cf. Ps. 18:10ff.; 104:3). Isaiah's figure prepares for the vision of Daniel in which the Son of Man is associated with the clouds of heaven (cf. Dan. 7:13; note also Matt. 24:30; 26:64; Acts 1:7; 14:14ff.). With this symbolism in mind, we are ready for the poetic description to follow.

It is to Egypt that the Lord comes, and Egypt—the word occurs four times in this verse—will feel the effect of His judgment. Isaiah begins his prophecy with an introductory *Behold!* and immediately focuses attention upon the Lord, who is the true subject of the prophecy. We are to behold Him riding upon a light[4] cloud and coming to Egypt. In the second half of the verse Isaiah states what the consequences of the Lord's coming will be. He begins with a verb, *and there will shake,*[5] the root of which is the same that had described the swaying of the heart of Ahaz and his court. When one hears the voice of the Lord he will sway, as did the people at Mt. Sinai when they saw the theophany and heard the Lord's voice (cf. Ex. 20:18). Fear fills the hearts of the idols and they sway because of the Lord, for His coming means their complete destruction.

Is Isaiah here predicting a real and genuine existence for the idols, or is he merely engaging in sarcasm and ridicule? Perhaps neither of these alternatives really gets at the heart of the matter. Isaiah nowhere suggests that the idols have a real existence. They are dumb idols, mere statues, and cannot do those things that a god

---

[3] Duhm engages in overrefinement in holding that in ancient times Yahweh marched (e.g., Judg. 5:4; 2 Sam. 5:24). Isaiah, he claims, only looks into the distance; here Yahweh Himself comes to Egypt, but no results follow. This is thought to betray a non-Isaianic authorship.

[4] I.e., swiftly. Cf. Ps. 104:3.

[5] ונעו — the accent is *Milra,* possibly because of the *waw* consecutive.

14

should do. Nothing in the book of Isaiah would lead to the conclusion that the prophet believed in the existence of real gods apart from the one true God. On the other hand it will not do to say that the prophet is merely engaging in ridicule. Rather, he is using poetic language to express the thought that the coming of the Lord means the complete destruction of the idols. For this reason he represents them as acting as though they were alive. Jeremiah later describes the destruction of the idols in more prosaic fashion (cf. 43:12,13; 46:25; Ezek. 30:13).

Not only will the idols sway, but, personifying the nation, Isaiah declares that the very heart of Egypt will melt.[6] The judgment is to affect the whole country, so that its heart will melt, not being able to withstand, and being terrified by fear of the oncoming Lord. It is a figure that Isaiah has used previously when speaking of the Day of the Lord (cf. 13:7). The heart is said to be in the midst of the nation, a statement that adds intensity to the description. When in the very midst of the nation the heart has melted there is nothing left to withstand the coming of the Lord.

2 Having in a general utterance proclaimed the coming of the Lord for judgment and the results of that coming, the prophet now introduces the Lord as speaking in the first person, and announcing that He will bring about a civil war in Egypt. The word which Yahweh employs to describe His activity is forceful, meaning *to prick* or *to excite*.[7] The Lord will stir up Egypt so that it will be set in opposition to itself. In this verse the word *Egypt* occurs twice. It is not to be rendered *Egyptian*, nor does it necessarily refer to Upper as over against Lower Egypt, even though at this time Upper Egypt was completely under the domination of an Ethiopian king. Nor is the reference to nome rising against nome. It is simply that Egypt will be turned against itself and wholly disunified.

True unity, we may learn from this passage, comes from the Lord; and when He sets a nation against itself, there can be no unity. Only when a nation repents and turns to Him can true unity be found. The Lord, therefore, is the source of unity.

The result of Egypt's disunity appears in that a man will fight against his brother.[8] There is no reason why this statement should

---

6 Note the gradation of emphasis in these clauses.
7 The root is סוך. Cf. Isa. 9:10.
8 An interesting illustration of this thought is found in the admonitions of

15

not be taken in a literal sense. Must not that be a greatly disunited land, wherein men fight their brothers? When households are divided, how great the disunity must be! We are reminded of the words of Jesus Christ, "And the brother shall deliver up the brother to death..." (Matt. 10:21a). The coming of the Lord brings division; here, it is not necessarily a division between believer and unbeliever, but one caused when, feeling the effects of judgment, men turn even against their own brothers.

Leaving the family, the prophet goes on to point out that the division will extend to all men. A man will be set against his neighbor, as well as against his brother. Likewise the various cities of Egypt will fight one against another and the smaller kingdoms which existed in lower Egypt will also turn against each other, with the result that there will be a civil war. It is a general description of internal strife, caused by the approach of God in judgment.

Herodotus (ii.141-147) states that there were civil wars in the days of Psammetichus, who finally succeeded in uniting Egypt.[9] At earlier periods also, namely during the 23rd and .24th dynasties, there were disorders and uprisings. Is it these to which Isaiah refers? Some commentators think so, but more likely he is presenting a general picture of a period of disorders caused by the judgment of God. His intention is not so much to depict one particular epoch of civil war as it is to show that when God acts in judgment, the nation will lose its unity. This interpretation would seem to be substantiated by the fact that the picture of salvation which follows does not have reference merely to the presence of the Coptic Church in Egypt insofar as that church represents Him, but rather to the fact that even nations which once had been

---

Ipu-wer, who describes civil strife in Egypt. The question is asked how it is that every man kills his own brother. Even the winds are said to oppose one another. Cf. *ANET,* pp. 443d, 445c. The period of the 23rd and the 24th dynasties was characterized by revolutions and uprisings. With the advent of the Ethiopian Piankhi and the accession of Shabaka (715 B.C.?) a strong, central authority was established. The second verb (imp.) expresses the consequences that follow the first (perf. with *waw* cons.). God acts, and men are set at variance one with another.

[9] Note the statement (Herodotus ii.147) that the Egyptians could not continue for any time without a king (οὐδένα γὰρ χρόνον οἷοί τε ἦσαν ἄνευ βασιλέος διαιτᾶσθαι), so they divided Egypt into twelve districts (δώδεκα μοίρας) and set twelve kings over them. Cf. Diodorus i.66.

alienated from God and were His enemies will one day be brought to worship Him (see comments on v. 18).

3 The external confusion with which Egypt is to be characterized could possibly be controlled if the heart of the land were itself sound. That heart is not sound, however, for it will melt, and the very spirit of the land will fail. The external confusion is to be accompanied by an internal one so that in its entirety, the country will fall to pieces. Egypt is to be overcome and subdued. She will have no strength left to resist the Lord or in any way to assert herself in opposition to Him.

The verb which describes the failing of the spirit means basically "to lay waste."[10] In Jeremiah 19:7 it is used figuratively of God's laying waste, and so making void, the counsel of Judah and Jerusalem. In our present verse it is passive. The spirit[11] of Egypt is laid waste, i.e., rendered bewildered or confused. It is an internal failing, and Isaiah repeats the words "in its midst" calling to mind the phrase of verse 1, "and the heart of Egypt shall melt in its midst."

The failure of the spirit of Egypt appears in that Egypt no longer has any counsel. The counsel which it would devise for its own deliverance is one which cannot stand. No strong voice of wisdom can be raised, for God Himself will bring to mishap any advice or counsel proposed.[12] This is a vigorous way of stating that Egypt's counsel is to be completely destroyed. Whatever advice is proposed comes to distress by God and so exists no more; it is completely gone.

The tragic result is that, inasmuch as there is no sound voice, the people engage in that most foolish of all follies, the turning to spiritualistic media. When man acts thus unwisely, surely true counsel has disappeared! The prophet lists the objects of the

10 The verbal form is *Niphal* perfect, for *nā-baq-qāh*, from בקק. Occasionally, the strengthening does not occur in *Ayin-Ayin* verbs (cf. Ezek. 41:7; Judg. 5:5; Gen. 17:11; Jer. 8:14); hence, the text is not in need of emendation.

11 רוח is the principle of self-consciousness, the spirit that directs the person, and gives him the will to act as he should (cf. 1 Kings 10:5). As employed in this passage it is about equivalent to our use of *heart* in expressions such as, "he has no heart for it." Note that in this verse Egypt is still personified.

12 The rendering *to swallow* does not seem applicable, and *to confuse* or *confound* is not justifiable. A. Guillaume (*JTS*, Vol. 13, Part 2, Oct. 1962, pp. 320-322) has made a convincing plea for deriving the root from Ar. *balagha* (with *Ghain*) in the sense of bringing *injury* or *distress*.

people's inquiry, and at the head of all stand the idols.[13] A wise nation seeks the source of wisdom, namely God; a foolish people whom wisdom has forsaken looks for advice and help from those who have no counsel or wisdom. When God abandons us, we are left to search for wisdom where it cannot be found.

4 The climax of the Lord's judging action is seen in that He gives Egypt over to hard rulers. Isaiah employs an expressive word which suggests the locking up of Egypt so that there will be no escape.[14] It is as though he said, "I shall lock up or shut up Egypt to hard masters." This is God's intention and He is fully able to carry it out, for unlike the shaking gods of Egypt, He has true power. The hard ruler[15] was probably a foreigner who would not have true love of the country at heart, and so would deal with it in a cruel manner, being concerned only with his own welfare. He would be like the rich who "answer roughly" (Prov. 18:23b). Until this time the priestly caste had dominated the scene. All was to be changed, however, and the priestly caste, representing the gods of Egypt, would have to give way to a hard ruler.

In particular, a strong or cruel king was to appear upon the scene, and Egypt would be subject to his hard reign. When, however, was the prophecy to be fulfilled? And who is the strong king and the hard ruler? Several answers have been given to these questions. In line with his general dispensational interpretation, Bultema believes that the king will be the little horn mentioned in

---

[13] The word אטים is *hapax legomenon*. Sumerian gives *edimmu* and *etimmu*, hence the word probably refers to the spirit of a dead person. Note the frequency of the conjunction. Those without counsel turn to every possible source and cannot find sufficient advice. For secular references to the superstitions of Egypt cf. Herodotus ii.54ff., 82, 83, 139, 152, who denies that men have the gift (τέχνη) of prophecy. Isaiah describes the Egyptian superstitions with Hebrew terms, and his language is reminiscent of Deut. 18.

Duhm declares that only a Jew of later times could reproach the Egyptians for seeking counsel of their gods; the writer, he thinks, is already regarding heathendom as a fall from monotheism. That monotheism appeared only late in Israel's history, however, is a thesis which cannot be established.

[14] Lit., *And I shall shut up*. B παραδώσω; the verb suggests full abandonment.

[15] The plural is that of excellence and is used with an attribute in the singular.

[16] "*Het is met het oog op het begin en het eind van dit hoofdstuk misschien het veiligst om hier te willen denken aan den koning van het hersteld Romeinsche Rijk, den kleinen hoorn van Daniël 7 of aan Gog, den koning van het Nooirden*" (p. 237).

Daniel 7.[16] Gesenius thinks that it is Psammetichus,[17] and Penna suggests that it may be the Ethiopian Piankhi or the Assyrian Sargon II.[18] Fischer thinks that the prophecy was fulfilled through Esarhaddon who conquered Egypt about 670,[19] and Duhm claims that it was Ochus.[20] What may be said of these suggestions?

In the first place it is probably correct, as Duhm observes, that the severe rule of a native ruler was so commonplace that the threat of a hard native ruler would not necessarily inspire terror. The hard ruler would likely be an outsider. Who was this outsider, however, and when did he rule? Perhaps something may be said in favor of each of the views presented, save that Ochus would be too far in the future, and the position that the strong king is the little horn of Daniel 7 is ruled out on other grounds. Nevertheless, none of these identifications seems entirely to satisfy.

Isaiah is picturing an age when great changes were to come, and such a time was just beginning. Assyria was now upon the horizon of world history. For a time the appearance of the Assyrian power did put Egypt into a position of secondary importance, but it is difficult to limit Isaiah's reference to one particular Assyrian ruler. It would seem more in keeping with the general emphasis of the prophecy to see here the rise of the Assyrian power as such, and to find the fulfillment of the passage in the period of the four world monarchies. It is thus a general picture of the political vicissitudes that are to come over Egypt. The certainty of the fulfillment is attested by the mention of the Lord as the Sovereign One who has all power, and so can fulfill all His threats.

> 5 And the waters from the sea will dry up, and the river will be wasted and dry.

[17] "Der strenge Herr und harte König, welchem Jehova Aegypten übergibt, ist nun Psammetichus, den die Geschichte gerade nicht als einen solchen, aber doch als einen bey seinen Unterthanen wenig beliebten Fürsten schildert" (Commentar, in loc.).

[18] "Se si ammette che il v. 8 si referisce al periodo che precedette l'affermarsi della xxv dinastia etiope, il padrone duro potrebbe essere Sargon II, che vinse gli Egiziani a Rafia, certamente trattandoli non troppo con i guanti, secondo le consuetudini militari dell'Assiria. Ma potrebbe essere anche qualche otro, come — par essempio — l'etiope Piankhi che, partendo da Napata, estese il suo dominio quasi su tutto l'Egitto" (Com. in loc.).

[19] "Erfüllt wurde seine Voraussage allerdings erst durch Asarhaddon (681-688), der um 670 Ägypten eroberte und zum assyrischen Reiche schlug" (Com. in loc.).

[20] "Der harte Herr ist ein ausländischer Eroberer, nach unserer Annahme Artax. Ochus" (in loc.). Cf. Cheyne in ZAW, Vol. 13, 1893, pp. 125-128.

6 And the rivers will stink, the brooks of defense shall be empty
and dry, the reed and rush shall become sick.

7 The meadows by the river, by the mouth of the river, and all the
sown ground of the river, it shall wither, driven away, and it is not.

8 And the fishermen shall mourn, and they shall lament, all who cast
a hook into the river, and those who spread a net upon the surface
of the water languish.

9 And the workers of combed flax will be ashamed, and the weavers
of white cloth.

10 And her pillars are broken down, all the laborers for hire are
grieved at heart.

5 In line with the political disturbances that will come to Egypt,
the basic conditions for human existence also disappear. This is
not necessarily a consequent of the hostile rulers which are
promised, nor will it necessarily be temporally subsequent to what
had been mentioned in verses 1-4; but this threat is also a result of
the Lord's coming in judgment, and may be realized concurrently
with what is predicted in the first strophe (vv. 1-4). There is,
however, a gradation introduced into the statement of the threat;
for whereas at first (vv. 1-4) dire calamities were predicted, here
the very existence of the nation is menaced.

Isaiah brings this tragic condition immediately before our eyes
with the first verb which he uses, *"and they will fail."*[21] This
thought colors all that follows. What gives and sustains the life of
the country fails. First it is water from the sea. The statement is
general. Isaiah does not say "the water from the sea," but simply,
"water from the sea."

The sea to which the prophet refers is not the Mediterranean
nor the Red Sea but the Nile itself.[22] Even today the Arabs are
accustomed to speak of the Nile as the Sea.[23] Why, however,
should the Nile be designated a sea? It may be that at the
overflowing of its banks the Nile gave rise to this designation, and
it may be also that the prophet uses the word with conscious
reflection upon the "seas" in Genesis 1. The dry land and the seas

21 The form is probably a *Niphal* perf. of נשׁת; the root nšt has been attested
in Ugaritic. B reads καὶ πίονται, mistaking the verb for a form of שׁתה; Aq
αναποθησετα and S αφανισθησεται.

22 Cf. also 18:2; Nah. 3:8.

23 Some of the classical writers have given reasons why the Nile might be des-
ignated "sea." Cf. Pliny *Natural History* xxxv.11: *Nili aqua mari est similis;*
Herodotus ii.97; Diodorus Siculus i.12, 96; Seneca *Quaestiones naturales* iv.2.
Cf. also Koran, Sura 20:39, *yam* (cf. 28:6), and Ar. *baḥr* or *baḥr en'nil.*

are both necessary if man is to live upon this globe. Should water fail from the seas, the dry land will suffer. Likewise, the Nile is designated sea, a term which surpasses the thing designated. Just as the sea itself exceeds the Nile in greatness, so also will the actual dearth outdo Egypt's ordinary dearths in severity.

After this general statement, Isaiah mentions the river specifically. There can be no doubt but that he means the Nile, although he uses the noun anarthrously. Two verbs are employed to emphasize that this will be no ordinary dearth. The first merely suggests that the river will be dry. The second, however, reminds us of the *dry land* in the first chapter of Genesis. Indeed, it closes the second part of the verse, just as the word *sea* closes the first. Thus there appears a contrast between *sea* and *will be dry*, which calls to mind the distinction between *seas* and *dry land* in Genesis 1. The same word order also appears in Genesis 8:13, 14.

Egypt is dependent for her daily existence upon the Nile. The melting snows in the mountains of central Africa produce a steady supply of water. Combined with the torrential rains which fall in the land of Ethiopia, an inundation occurs twice each year. The first of these begins about the 15th of July and continues throughout the summer, and the second occurs in October. At its height the river reaches twenty-five to thirty feet. Should this water fail, the land would indeed suffer.[24]

6 As Isaiah had designated Egypt's life-giving river a "sea," so he now speaks of the canals or branches of the Nile as "rivers." When these arms of the main river are deprived of water, they become swampy and consequently give off a bad odor.[25] The water is practically gone; the rivers become low and finally dry. The choice of words, *rivers, brooks, reed,* and *rush* is designed to point to an

[24] For information concerning the Nile and its relation to Egypt cf. S. W. Baker, *The Albert Nyanza, Great Basin of the Nile and Exploration of the Nile Sources,* 2 vols., London, 1871; Emil Ludwig, *The Nile,* New York, 1937, is a popular work. The articles in various encyclopedias are valuable, particularly in the *Encyclopedia Italiana,* Vol. XXIV, 1949, pp. 823-826.

[25] והאזניחו — The root means *to be rancid.* The writing with *He* and *Aleph* is not necessarily incorrect, although 1Q omits *Aleph.* The form is probably denominative from אזנח , itself derived from זנח ; cf. אכזב and כזב. Actually the form אזנח does not occur. Dillmann states that *hiz-ni-ᵃḥ* appears elsewhere only in the figurative sense of *abhor* or *detest,* and suggests that it may be a mixture of Hebrew *Hiphil* and Aramaic *Aphel.* For the use of נהרות as referring to a canal, cf. Ps. 137:1 and Ezek. 1:1, 3; Ezra 8:31. Cf. Herodotus ii.108. Cf. also Ex. 7:19.

abundance of water, so that the severity of the calamity will stand out in greater contrast. The prophet characterizes these rivers as those of *Matzor*. Some take this word in the sense of defense, assuming that it refers to the banks of the rivers or canals which acted as a protection for the land. Others note that the word itself is really the singular of *mitzrayim* (*Egypt*) and interpret, *the rivers of Egypt*. If that is the case, however, we may ask why this particular word is here used, when elsewhere the common word for Egypt is employed? It may be that the usage is intentional and that the prophet deliberately intends to distinguish the place where the canals were, namely, lower Egypt, from Pathros, or upper Egypt.

When the water disappears from the canals the reeds and rushes that grow on the banks lose their strength, become sick, and die. In particular we may think of the papyrus reeds, which would be among the first to feel the effects of the drying up of the Nile.

7 The description is continued, the prophet now speaking of the *'aroth* which are upon the Nile.[26] This is a strong word and apparently refers to naked or bare places. These have often been assumed to be open meadows in contradistinction from the woodlands. This view has difficulty, for Egypt is not characterized by woodland. Probably the Hebrew word may reflect the Egyptian word *'r*, which means papyrus, and thus the reference would be to those places where the papyrus grows. Such spots would be at the Nile's mouth.[27]

Not only will the bare places dry up, but also those that are sown with grain.[28] To picture the suddenness with which such

[26] J. Reider ("Etymological Studies in Biblical Hebrew," *VT*, Vol. 2, 1952, pp. 115f.) thinks that a verbal form is needed. By a slight shift of consonants he obtains *w'ru t'ly y'wr*, "and the growths of the Nile will be laid bare." This forms a parallel to the following, but the word *t'ly* is not elsewhere attested, the form *t^e'ālāh* signifying *water-course* or *healing*. Nor is it necessary to connect *'ārôt* with the preceding verb (cf. T. W. Thacker in *JTS*, Vol. 34, 1933, pp. 163-165). For older interpretations of the word, see Gesenius, *in loc.*, and cf. Koran 37:145; 68:49. Note also B αχι. The word may be taken as an accusative of specification, the verbs following later.

[27] Dillmann insists that the reference must be to the mouth of the Nile and not its banks, which latter he believes should be designated by *sā-pāh;* cf. Gen. 41:3. As illustrations of the use of *peh*, he adduces Gen. 42:27; 29:2; and Josh. 10:18. Gray thinks that the mouth of the Nile is scarcely a place likely to be chosen to illustrate fruitfulness, but believes that the reference is to a mouth or opening.

[28] מזרע is *hapax legomenon*, and indicates not *seed* (Duhm) but the place where seed is sown. The reference could be to the alluvial deposit of the Nile,

places disappear, Isaiah employs two verbs which he had used together previously in 18:5. The first of these is an imperfect which expresses general action, but the second is a perfect.[29] It is a surprising difference in the usage of the tenses, but it beautifully and effectively portrays the suddenness with which the verdure of the land disappears. "It shall wither," and "it has been driven away." The final result is then succinctly stated: "it is not." A remarkable gradation thus appears in the description. First it is the Nile herself, then her canals, then the grass, and finally the meadows. Gradually the shadow of drought creeps over the entire land and the once greatly blessed country perishes.

8 It is not only the reeds growing by the river that wither, but those who must derive their livelihood from the river will also suffer. The Egyptians wail and mourn when the Nile deceives them. In Egypt fishing was an important industry, for when the Nile fills with water, it is also said to fill with a small fish, which forms a delicious diet.[30] Again Isaiah begins with a verb, *they shall mourn.* This mourning and lamentation is over the death of what once had brought life. In ancient times fishing appears to have been both by the hook[31] and the casting of nets. Isaiah's purpose in mentioning both methods of fishing is to show that all who derive

---

which would be rich soil for seed planting. The force of M may be brought out by the following literal rendering: *The bare places upon the Nile, at the mouth of the Nile, even every Nile seed plot, it will dry up and be driven away and is no more.* The combination of verbs refers to the complete destruction of plants. In speaking of *bare places* and *places of planting* the prophet has reference to these as places where something may grow, and, at least with the second verb, conceives of the land as producing seed, and so speaks of its being driven away.

29 The preterite expresses the unexpected rapidity of the action.

30 Cf. Gesenius, *Com. in loc.*; Num. 11:5; Herodotus ii.93; Diodorus i.36, 40; Strabo xvii.2.

31 Note that the direct object of the participle is preceded by a prepositional phrase. The participle is a construct, separated from the word *Nile* by a preposition; lit., *the casters of in the Nile the hook,* for *those who cast a hook in the Nile.* Cf. 5:11 for a similar construction. In the tomb of Khnumhotep at Beni Hasan, 19th century B.C., there is a wall painting depicting two Egyptians casting fish-hooks in the river. One is standing using a rod with line; the other is kneeling and has only a line and hook. Both have caught good-sized fish.

In the tomb of Mereuka at Sakkarah (6th dynasty), a relief depicts two groups or teams of fishermen hauling a net filled with fish from the river. The same relief also shows a single fisherman with a small net, and fish caught in fixed nets which are spread out under the water's surface.

their livelihood from the river will mourn. To them a tragedy has come. The rich river is dry, and haunting death faces them. The verse begins with the words, *they will mourn,* and closes with the utterance, *they languish.*[32]

9 Not only is the Nile dry and its fish dead, but the land also is no longer watered so that plants may grow.[33] Those who derive their livelihood from the growth of the land suffer as well as do the fishermen who depend directly upon the river. To express their reaction, Isaiah again begins with a verb, *they will be ashamed.* And there is indeed reason for their shame. Nothing grows any more, and they cannot produce as once they had done. These men are described by the word *'ovedey* (workers), which reminds of the modern word *fellahin* (workers).[34] They work in flax, which was prominent in Egypt. At the time of the exodus the flax and barley had been smitten (Ex. 9:31). The monuments illustrate the preparation of flax, which was either carded or combed so that it became fine.[35]

[32] אמללו is generally taken as a *Pual* from *'ā-mal.* It appears to be stative, denoting a physical condition.

[33] This verse goes back to v. 7, whereas v. 8 reflects upon vv. 5, 6.

[34] Dillmann thinks that the use of *'bd* in the sense of *bearbeiten* is surprising. What is more surprising is Dillmann's statement; cf. Ex. 20:9; Gen. 2:15; Deut. 28:39, etc.

[35] Cf. Ezek. 27:7; Prov. 7:16; Herodotus ii.37, 86, 182. On a wall painting from the tomb of Khnumhotep at Beni Hasan there is illustrated each stage of the work from the preparation of the raw material to the finished cloth. That Isaiah had an intimate knowledge of the processing of flax is shown by his mention of combed flax and white cotton. Large quantities of water were needed in the processing of flax, and Isaiah's description of the drying up of the Nile again shows his knowledge of the process and renders particularly vivid the statements of this verse. Cf. Pliny *Natural History* xix.1. After the flax has been thoroughly soaked, it is cut, dried in the sun, beaten out, and carded. This latter process is illustrated by a wall-painting (incidentally a fine work of art) from the tomb of Menua at Sheikh Abd el-Gurnah (18th dynasty, 14th cent. B.C.). A worker is shown holding a sheaf of flax, drawing it through the teeth of wooden (?) combs placed on an inclined board, thus separating the strands.

1Q reads a verb *hwrw,* so that some would find the caesura after *flax.* Penna, e.g., translates, ". . . *Saranno confusi i lavoratori del lino, scardatrici e tessitori 'impallidiramno.'*" This involves a division of labor between men and women which is not in accord with what is known from elsewhere. *piš-tim* is pl. of *pē-šet* (cf. Gezer Calendar), and is here f. At least I can see no reason for construing it as m. The f. adj. is a pl. of *šā-rīq* and denotes the flax as already combed or carded. The workers referred to would be those who prepared and carded the flax.

Together with the workers in flax the weavers of cotton cloth will suffer. Isaiah simply describes the material with which these weavers work as white stuff, but without doubt he has reference to goods of cotton, so common to Egypt. On his inscriptions the Assyrian king mentions byssus from Egypt, which may also be intended by this word of Isaiah's.[36]

10 This section of the prophecy closes with a general statement of the extent of the distress to come over Egypt, when the pillars of the land will be crushed.[37] What, however, does the prophet have in mind by the word *pillars*? The term is doubtless used in a metaphorical sense as in Psalm 11:3. Some think that it signifies the great and mighty as we today speak of "the pillars of society." It is likely, however, that Isaiah employs the word in a more general sense to denote all upon which the life of Egypt rests, her true foundations. When these are crushed, then life itself, which is supported by these pillars, must also fail. When the pillars give way, all the working men become grieved in their souls.[38] Here the reference is to the working class, and it is for this reason that some wish to refer the *pillars* mentioned in the first half of the verse to the upper class. The sorrow that characterizes the workers is deep, penetrating to the inmost part of their being. For them there is no hope, the whole foundation of the land has been destroyed.

11 Surely, fools are the princes of Zoan; the sages of the counsellors of Pharaoh, their counsel is brutish. How will ye say unto Pharaoh, I am the son of wise ones, the son of kings of old?

[36] Esarhaddon mentions byssus-linen *(sad-din bu-ú-ṣi)*, i.e., linen fabrics of good quality (cf. *ANET*, p. 2936), which he took together with much other spoil from Memphis. The word *ḥórāy* may be rendered *white material*. The form is pausal, and the *-āy* suffix is taken by Gesenius as an old pl. ending, by Drechsler as a denominative ending. B takes the word here as a synonym for *ḥúr*, Est. 1:6; 8:15.

[37] The thought of this verse is illustrated by the Egyptian inscription of Nefer-rohu (cf. *ANET*, pp. 444f.) . The suffix in *šā-ṭō-ṭey-hā* refers to Egypt, and the introductory words should be translated, *and all her pillars are broken down*. Cf. Jer. 14:3; 44:10. Attempts at textual emendation have been made, but the word may be used figuratively as *pin-naṭ* in v. 13; cf. also comments on 3:1. Eitan proposes to emend to *še-ṭi-ṭey-hā* and appeals to Coptic *štit, a weaver*. Cf. *HUCA*, Vol. 12-13, 1937-1938, p. 66; Talmon, "A Witness to Ancient Exegesis," *Annual of the Swedish Theological Institute*, Vol. 1, 1962, pp. 66, 67. 1Q reads: *whyw swṭṭyh mdk'ym* which may represent an ancient attempt at interpretation.

[38] The *nomen rectus* describes the part of the being that is affected by a mental or physical condition.

12 Where are they, then, thy wise men? that they may tell thee now, and that they may know what the LORD of hosts hath counselled against Egypt.
13 The princes of Zoan have become fools, deceived are the princes of Noph, and they have led Egypt astray, the corner of her tribes.
14 The LORD hath mingled in her midst a spirit of distorting, and they have led Egypt astray in all its work, as a drunken man leads astray in his vomit.
15 And there shall not be to Egypt a work which head and tail, branch and rush, may do.

11 Isaiah now reverts to the theme introduced in verse 3 in order to substantiate what he had said there. Turning from the suffering caused by material destruction in the land, he now looks to the intellectual life of Egypt. Those who should exhibit wisdom in seeking a way out of the difficulties were the princes of Zoan, but the princes are fools. This word Isaiah stresses, and we may render literally, *surely fools.* Zoan was an ancient city, built seven years after Hebron (Num. 13:22).[39] It was near the mouth of the Tanis branch of the Nile river, and is to be identified with Tanis the capital of the 21st and 23rd dynasties. The princes here mentioned were probably members of the court when it had existed at Tanis. Israelites who sought alliances with Egypt would probably have entered into negotiations with these princes, who perhaps for that reason are mentioned so emphatically.

The wise men who serve as the counsellors for Pharaoh give him stupid counsel.[40] It is probably not possible to identify this Pharaoh, although some think that he was Shabako (c. 715-700 B.C.?).[41] More likely Isaiah is speaking in general terms to show that those who advise the government prove to be useless in the time of crisis. Egypt's wisdom had been renowned. Moses, for example, was "learned in all the wisdom of the Egyptians" (Acts 7:22a).[42] The gift of finding wisdom, however, had been turned into something brutish.

[39] The modern San el-Hagar, about 2400 feet from the tell with the ancient ruins. Cf. Strabo xvi.1, 20.
[40] 1Q reads *ḥkmyh*, i.e., *her* (i.e., Zoan's) *wise men.* As M stands, the construct may serve as a superlative, *the wisest counsellors.*
[41] Penna thinks he could be a representative of the 24th dynasty, possibly Shabako or Tefnachte. The word Pharaoh is not a proper name, but represents the Egyptian *pr. 'o,* i.e. *great house.* Originally the words seem to have designated the palace and then its inhabitant. Cf. the older Turkish use of *Sublime Porte* in speaking of the sultan.
[42] Cf. also 1 Kings 9:5ff.; and Herodotus ii.77, 60.

In the latter part of the verse Isaiah introduces those who claim descent from wise men and kings. Kimchi believed that these were the words of the Pharaoh himself. In the light of the first part of the verse, however, it is more likely that the prophet is speaking of those who stand about the king and give him counsel. Some believe that two groups are included here, namely, the priestly caste and the warriors. Yet we should probably not make such a distinction. More likely the prophet is simply speaking of those who appeal both to wise men and to kings for their ancestry. No doubt the priestly class did boast of descent from wise men, but it doubtless also boasted of descent from kings. Hence, it appears that Isaiah is simply expressing incredulity that anyone could now boast of such descent. A time of crisis has come upon the nation, and those who should show themselves wise and useful are unable to do so. Whatever their ancestry may have been, it no longer is of help. A true son of wise men would show himself wise.[43] That the present counsellors of Egypt are unable to do.

12 With a Pauline triumph, Isaiah asks where the wise men of Egypt are.[44] To ask such a question is tantamount to saying that the wise men do not exist and that the only wisdom is that found in the Lord of hosts. To whom, however, is the prophet speaking? Penna thinks that he speaks directly to the Pharaoh to show him that he cannot trust at all in his counsellors. It could be, however, that, like Paul after him, Isaiah is simply uttering rhetorical questions, designed to cause the listener to provide the answer for himself.[45] Egypt may well ask where its counsellors are. "Where are they then, thy wise men?" In employing the singular *thy* the prophet speaks directly to the nation as though to say, "Thou, Egypt, hast boasted of thy many wise men; very well, where are they now? If thy wise men could be found they should make known to thee what the Lord intends to do, for they themselves should know what He will do."[46] As a matter of fact, however,

---

[43] For the form of the expression *son of wise-men am I* cf. Amos 7:14; Acts 23:6; Phil. 3:5. It is interesting to note that some of the Egyptian "instructions" in wisdom are written for the writer's son. Cf. *ANET*, pp. 414ff.

[44] For the form of the verse cf. Deut. 32:37f.; Isa. 47:12f.; Jer. 2:28.

[45] Kissane believes that the prophet is addressing the counsellor who speaks in v. 11, but on this Penna comments that the wise men in question would have known their ancestors.

[46] וְיֹדְעוּ — the jussive with *waw* may be used after questions which include a demand, to express the assurance of a contingent occurrence; "where are

these wise men cannot avert the calamities that will come upon Egypt; they did not even know the reason for these calamities.

There is a wisdom, namely, the divine purpose, and he who is wise will know this wisdom. In the nature of the case, inasmuch as they were steeped in polytheism and idolatry, the Egyptian "wise men" were no true wise men at all, for they had no knowledge of true wisdom. Isaiah's words are applicable to all times. The counsellors and statesmen who try to solve the problems of the world apart from the wisdom of God show themselves but fools, following a path that leads to destruction.

In this particular section the combination "the LORD of hosts" occurs frequently, yet never in vain. Here, for example, it stresses and emphasizes God's great power and the reason why He appears so terrible to His enemies. Marti apparently thinks it strange that the Egyptians were expected to know Jewish theology and especially Jehovah's eschatological plan concerning Egypt. But the God of truth dwelt in Zion; His ways and His works were known. He should have been worshipped by all the earth as the true God. The Egyptian wise men, instead of steeping themselves in their own superstitions, should have known the God of Israel. They should have known, not necessarily His "eschatological plans," but at least that He had all power and that when He brought punishment to Egypt, the only refuge would be to turn to Him. Had not the Exodus and its plagues left a mark upon Egypt that wise men would have noted?

Knobel remarks, and his comment is worthy of consideration, that the Egyptians at least should have suspected the Assyrian invasion.[47]

On the other hand, it would have been possible to have suspected the invasion of Assyria and still to have misinterpreted it. As Isaiah here stands in opposition to the Egyptian wise men, he reminds us of Joseph, yea, more even of Him of whom it was said, "Whence hath this *man* this wisdom?" (Matt. 6:54c) and "what wisdom is this which is given unto him?" (Mark 6:2b).

---

they? we would know, that they might declare" or "and let them declare." Note that the particle '$\bar{e}$-$p\hat{o}$ serves to lend vividness to the question. Isaiah uses the verb *counsel* perhaps with some irony as a contrast to the *their counsel is brutish* and *counsellors of Pharaoh* of v. 11.

[47] Knobel, *Com. in loc.,* "welche sie wenigstens ahnen könnten." Drechsler calls attention to the parallel passages 41:21-24, 25-29; 44:6ff.; 45:18ff.

13 Isaiah now gives the answer to the questions which he has just raised. The wise men are nowhere to be found because God has rendered them foolish. The thought of verse 11 is taken up, and it is shown that the assertion which was there made is fulfilled. Again Isaiah begins with a verb, *they have become fools*.[48] Thus the statement previously made is emphasized. The princes of Zoan have been rendered fools and so are of no help in the time of crisis. The princes of Noph also have been deceived. As the serpent beguiled Eve in the garden, so the princes of Noph, professing to be wise, have become fools. Inasmuch as they were not really wise, they were easily deceived. Previously Isaiah had mentioned only Zoan, but now he includes Noph or Memphis to show that the confusion was widespread.[49]

The disastrous consequences of this state of affairs appear in that these men will lead Egypt astray. Isaiah concludes his verse with an expression, "the corner of her tribes." The word *tribes*, so often applied to Israel, seems to designate not the nomes into which Egypt was divided, but rather the castes. The corner of Egypt's castes, according to a common usage of the word, would be the best or highest of her castes. The question then arises, are we to take this phrase as a subject or as an accusative of specification? Are we to render, "And the pinnacle of her castes will lead Egypt astray?" If we so render, there are difficulties, namely, the fact that the verb is plural and the subject singular. It may be, however, that the word *pinnacle* is so closely joined in thought to the following *her tribes* that it would account for a verb in the plural. We may, therefore, also take the phrase as an accusative and render, "And they will lead Egypt astray, even with respect to the pinnacle of her tribes." On this interpretation we are to understand that the princes of Zoan and Noph, themselves having become foolish, will lead even the best of Egypt's castes astray. If we adopt the first rendering, we are to understand that the best of Egypt's castes will lead Egypt astray. On the whole the rendering is preferable which takes *the pinnacle of her tribes* as an accusative of specification,

48 The first verb is *Niphal*, and means *to do* or *act foolishly*. B renders the second verb ὑψώθησαν, as though the root were *nāsā'*.

49 Noph, a designation of Memphis *(mn-nfr)*, the ruins of which are now found in the vicinity of Sakkarah — about 10 miles south of Cairo. During the 8th century it was superseded in importance by Thebes. In Heb. the word is also written Moph, e.g., Hos. 9:6.

but one cannot be dogmatic. The point of the verse is that the princes have led Egypt astray, and Egypt is the stay of her tribes.

14 Isaiah now goes back to ultimate causes. He does not begin this sentence with a verb but with a noun, *the Lord*. The word is placed first for emphasis, and immediately brings us to the cause of all that has been described. It is the LORD and no other; He whom the wise of this world despise. As once men were valiant to mix strong drink (5:22), so the LORD has mixed in Egypt a spirit that brings or produces dizziness.[50] The folly therefore which characterized Egypt did not come about in the "natural course of events," nor was it accidental, but resulted from a direct supernatural judicial action pronounced against the nation. As a result of this spirit Egypt will be led astray in all its work, namely, its economic procedure, daily business, and occupation.[51] What Egypt must do to live will suffer, because in the performance of this work the entire country will be led astray. This leading astray is of a most serious nature, and the prophet illustrates it by an unpleasant figure. As a drunken man stumbles about dizzily in his vomit, so Egypt will be led astray.[52] Isaiah's language is difficult to render literally, for, to make his thought more emphatic, he uses the passive form of the verb.

15 Reverting to the mention of Egypt's work in the preceding verse, Isaiah now asserts that there will be no work at all for

---

50 מסך — *to mix, to produce by mixing.* B ἐκέρασεν. The word may be used in its actual sense, or it may possibly be employed of infusing. The suffix *-ah* refers to Egypt and not to the princes. This latter reference is obtained by following B and rendering *within them,* an easier but unwarranted reading. Nor does the suffix refer to *corner* of v. 13. For *spirit of dizziness* or *distortion* cf. 29:10; Hos. 4:12. König thinks that the spirit is not a real being, but merely a personification of the distortion that will come upon the nation, as in 28:6; 29:10; Zech. 13:2. Drechsler, however, states that the spirit is not merely subjective and cites 1 Kings 22:19-23. Whether the spirit is a person or merely a supernatural influence may be difficult to decide. Delitzsch regards the spirit as a person, a "divine spirit of judgment" which uses the "wisdom" of the priestly caste and plunges the nation into "the giddiness of intoxication." The form *'iw'îm* is from *'iwwāh* and denotes a *warping* or *distortion.*

51 The plural verb may be impersonal, but it is more natural to refer it to the princes. It should be translated by the future and not the past (e.g., Delitzsch).

52 The *Niphal* suggests the thought of acting against one's will. Having lost all self-control the drunken man is constrained to act as he does. Cf. Job 15:31 and Isa. 28:7, 8.

Egypt.[53] Verse 14 had taken up the thought of verses 2 and 3 and shown the reason why the Egyptians were set one against the other; verse 15 now gives the consequences of the condition that prevails when a cruel lord is over the people. The work of Egypt, all that she as a united Egypt must do, will stop. Her daily life will cease, for she cannot perform the toil necessary to keep her in existence; nor will she be able to stand as a unit against any invading army. To show the universality in Egypt of this lack of work the prophet employs language that he had already used in 9:14.

16 In that day Egypt will be like women, and will fear and tremble from before the shaking of the hand of the LORD of hosts, which he is about to shake over it.

17 And the land of Judah shall become a terror unto Egypt; everyone that maketh mention thereof to it shall be afraid from before the counsel of the LORD of hosts which he is counselling against it.

18 In that day there will be five cities in the land of Egypt speaking the language of Canaan and swearing to the LORD of hosts; the city of destruction shall one be called.

19 In that day there will be an altar to the LORD in the midst of the land of Egypt, and a pillar near its border to the LORD.

20 And it shall become a sign and a witness to the LORD of hosts in the land of Egypt, for they will cry unto the LORD from before the oppressors that he send to them a savior and a mighty one that he should deliver them.

21 And the LORD will be known to Egypt, and Egypt will know the LORD in that day, and they shall serve with sacrifice and offering, and shall vow a vow to the LORD and shall fulfill it.

22 And the LORD will smite Egypt, smiting and healing, and they shall return unto the LORD, and he shall be entreated of them, and will heal them.

16 Isaiah now drops the parallelism which has characterized his discussion hitherto in this chapter and uses straightforward prose. The reason for this appears to be that he is now going to engage in

---

[53] Opinions differ as to the force of the preposition before *Egypt*. It may denote possession, or specification *(with respect to Egypt)*, or advantage *(for Egypt)* as well as source *(from Egypt)*. This latter use has found recent support in Ugarit, but it is to the credit of Gesenius that he had already noted it. He remarks that *Lamed* may designate the active cause not merely with an actual passive but also with passive concepts generally, and appeals to Gen. 38:25; Job 20:21; Ps. 12:5.

For Ugaritic cf. Cyrus H. Gordon, *Ugaritic Manual*, Rome, 1955.

a prophecy of blessing. To introduce the picture of judgment, he had used a figure (v. 1) which was a suitable introduction to a statement of the judgment given in poetry. For the sake of variety, he can now change his style somewhat and point out the blessing that will come with the judgment. He does not immediately proceed to that blessing, but introduces us to it somewhat gradually, first depicting the fearful condition of the Egyptians as they recognize the power of God's punishing hand.

The transition is made by the common phrase, "in that day," by which the prophet refers to the time of the judgment. At the time when God approaches Egypt in punishment, then the Egyptians will be as women.[54] Jeremiah later uses the same comparison of the Babylonians (50:37 and 51:30), and Nahum accuses the people of Nineveh of being like women (3:13). The point of the comparison is that the mighty men of Egypt will fear as women fear. In the two words employed to express fear (*harad* and *pahad*) there is a striking assonance. The first verb expresses the idea of trembling or being terrified, and it is this latter thought which seems to be present here (cf. 32:11). Egypt was terrified before the Lord. It is the concept of dread or awe which is connoted by the second verb. Thus, Egypt found herself in a terrifying awe before the Lord.

Some commentators claim that the text does not actually state what took place in Egypt to cause such dread. It is, of course, true that no detailed statement is made of precisely how God would visit Egypt in judgment; nevertheless, a general picture of such judgment has been given, and it is because of that judgment that Egypt now trembles. The verse before us does contain at least a clue as to the nature of the punishment. It is the shaking of the hand of the Lord that causes the terror. This shaking of the hand is preparatory to a smiting in anger. God's hand is outstretched over Egypt to strike her. She knows that the judgment is about to fall and God about to act.

Whence, however, does she derive such knowledge? Doubtless the Egyptians had already felt the first blows and experienced the first beginnings of punishment. Confusion was starting to enter the land,

---

[54] *women*—Herodotus viii.88 gives Xerxes' speech. "My men have become women, and the women men." As Antigonus II fell in flight, Sosius addressed him as Antigona (Josephus *Antiquities* xiv.16.2). In v. 13 *Egypt* is treated as f., and in v. 14 a f. suffix refers to her.

Hillers (*Treaty-Curses and the Old Testament Prophets*, Rome, 1964, p. 67) calls attention to treaty-curses that express the idea that warriors will become women.

and with it fear, which would develop into dread and terror. Yet
the text does not imply that the Egyptians know whence is the
source of their distress. Verses 16 and 17 are actually transition
verses, and cannot be separated too sharply either from what
precedes or from what follows. They present a picture of the climax
of the judgment depicted in the first verse of the chapter, and they
also contain the beginnings of an attitude of turning toward the
Lord.

17 A step in advance is taken in that this verse is more specific
than the preceding. In former times Egypt had had no hesitation
in carrying on battles in Palestine; now, however, the very mention of that land causes terror.[55] The wondrous power of the Lord
had been seen in the deliverance of His people. In times of need
God had been with His nation. Judah was the land which belonged to a God who could cause mighty deliverances (cf. 17:12-14
and 18:4-6).

Even to mention Judah causes fear among the Egyptians. Isaiah
uses a strangely constructed sentence which we may perhaps best
render, "Everyone who mentions it unto him."[56] What, however,
does this sentence mean? There are different interpretations, but
the suffix probably refers to Egypt. The sentence then has somewhat the force of the genitive absolute in Greek, "whenever anyone
mentions Judah to Egypt." In other words, Judah has become such
a terror to Egypt, that whenever anyone (the subject is indefinite)
speaks of or mentions Judah to Egypt (i.e., to the Egyptians) the
result is fear and dread. This whole sentence should be construed
with what precedes, so that we have the thought, "The land of
Judah will become a terror to Egypt whenever anyone makes
mention of it to Egypt." The Masoretes have not construed the
verse in this manner, but have left the second half without a
verb.

The second half should then be taken as an enlargement of the
first half. "He (i.e., Egypt) will fear from before the counsel of the
Lord of hosts which He is counselling against Egypt." What is here

---

55 *terror* — the word is to be pronounced *l^e-ḥog-gā'*, inasmuch as the ultima is
accented. The termination is Aramaic. The meaning *fear* or *terror* is given by
the ancient versions except Aq (γύρωσιν). But the root must be *ḥgg*, to make
a *pilgrimage* and also *to reel* (Ps. 107:27). Hence, König renders *eine Quelle
des Schwindligwerdens*, which I think is permissible.

56 Lit., *every one that mentions it* (Judah) *to it* (Egypt), *it* (Egypt) *is
afraid;* cf. GKC § 143 b. The f. suffix with the verb refers to the land of Judah.

stated is in reality a partial fulfillment of the promise of Deuteronomy 2:25, "This day will I begin to put the dread of thee and the fear of thee upon the nations *that are* under the whole heaven, who shall hear report of thee, and shall tremble, and be in anguish because of thee."

It should be noted that the conclusion of this verse parallels in form the conclusion of the preceding one, and its thought very clearly carries us back to the thought of verse 12. The object of Egypt's fear is the counsel of the Lord, although it does not follow that Egypt understood that counsel. That counsel was manifested in the plagues and strokes which were visited upon Egypt, and it was these, of course, which brought dread and terror to the nation. The fullness of the purpose of God, however, would not have been known to the Egyptians. In some sense, Egypt feared the Lord, and realized, even though imperfectly, that He was the cause of her suffering. Such fear of Him would lead to a turning to Him and a true repentance.

18 The tone changes. Judgment recedes, and blessing pours forth. The conversion of Egypt is taking place. Again Isaiah begins with his expression, *In that day,* a phrase which he often employs to introduce a new aspect of his subject or at least to emphasize a particular phase thereof. At the time when Egypt fears from before the judgment, blessing will pour out over the land. This blessing comes to light in that some of the cities of Egypt will speak the language of the true religion. Five cities, the prophet asserts, will be speaking the language of Canaan.[57] Why, however, is the number five employed? Is it to express the thought of a very few? Sometimes it seems to be so employed. Thus, we read, "And five of you shall chase an hundred" (Lev. 26:8a). Paul also used the word in this sense, "yet in the church I had rather speak five words with my understanding, etc." (1 Cor. 14:19a). It has been pointed out that the number of cities in ancient Egypt was very great, and that the number five would simply indicate that only a few of them were to speak the language of Canaan.

Others take the word simply as a round number and appeal to certain passages of Scripture such as Genesis 45:22; Exodus 22:1; Numbers 7:17,23; 1 Samuel 17:40; Matthew 25:20, etc. In this construction the word would merely suggest that a certain number

---

[57] The verb is not a mere future, *they will speak,* but rather expresses a condition, they will *be* (in the condition of) *speaking continually and swearing.*

of cities would speak the language of Canaan. Still others understand five specific cities to be intended, namely, Leontopolis, Heliopolis, Migdol, Daphne and Memphis.[58] Quite possibly, however, the numeral five is employed as the half of ten, the number of completeness, and so as an equivalent for many.[59]

These five cities are represented as speaking the lip (i.e., language) of Canaan. Here is reflection upon the book of Genesis, where we read that the whole earth was one lip (11:1). So also the words of the Lord, "Behold there is one people and one lip to all of them" (11:6a). The Lord expressed the intention of going down and confounding "their lip," and there, we are told, the Lord did confound the lip of all the earth (11:9). The lip of Canaan therefore is the language spoken in Canaan. This, however, does not refer to the Canaanitish language as such, spoken by the earlier Canaanites. The language is that in which the God of Canaan is worshipped; hence to speak Canaan's language is to speak the language in which the God of the Israelites is worshipped.[60] The Egyptians will no longer speak Egyptian, but the language which the Judahites speak, and thus they will be one with the Jews. They will speak this language for they will worship the God of the Jews. Hence to speak the language of Canaan is tantamount to saying that there will be a true conversion unto the Lord. In speaking the language of the promised land, the Egyptians will worship the God of truth.

In addition to speaking the language of Canaan, the Egyptian cities will also give their allegiance to the Lord, in that they will swear to Him. This action of the Egyptians in pledging their complete devotion and allegiance to God is a foreshadowing of what Isaiah later prophesied, "I have sworn by myself, the word is gone out of my mouth *in* righteousness, and shall not return, that unto me every knee shall bow, every tongue shall swear" (45:23). (Cf. also Zephaniah 1:5; 2 Chronicles 15:14.) It is not without point that Isaiah here designates God as the Lord of hosts, for it is necessary to emphasize His supreme sovereignty as over against the nothingness of Egypt's idols.

58 So Hitzig; cf. Jer. 44:1.
59 So some of the earlier writers, Cornelius a Lapide, Reincke, Hengstenberg.
60 Reincke, however, comments, *"Die Sprache Canaans ist hier offenbar die hebräische, worin die heil. Bücher des A.T. geschrieben sind."* He thinks that the spread of the religion of the Lord is represented as a spread of the Hebrew language. But Hengstenberg is correct when he remarks "that the language of Canaan is spoken by all who are converted to the true God."

The latter part of the verse is attended with great difficulty in interpretation. If we take the reading "one will be called the city of destruction," we may conclude that whereas five cities will speak Canaan's language, one will be destroyed. If this is correct, it would imply that there is a proportion of five to six cities that will believe in the Lord. One out of every six cities will perish, whereas five out of every six will believe. If this interpretation is correct, it will also give reason for the employment of the numeral five. It will simply assert that five sixths of the land will be converted, and the remaining one sixth will be ripe for destruction. The land as a whole, then, on this construction of the text, is not at this juncture represented as converted.

The principal reason why this interpretation is not universally accepted is that the designation "the city of destruction" is said to be out of harmony with the general context. This context, it is thought, has to do with blessing, not with its opposite. Another expedient therefore is often adopted. It is assumed, and the assumption may be correct, that the word rendered "destruction" (*heres*) should in reality be rendered "sun" (*heres*). The orthography is identical, with the exception of the first consonant. This reading is supported by, among other witnesses, the first Dead Sea Scroll of Isaiah. If it be correct, we are then faced with the question, what is the city of the sun? Immediately there comes to mind the city Heliopolis. Does Isaiah allude to this city in order to show that in the Messianic times, the city wherein the sun is now worshipped will become a city that worships the Lord? If so, the purpose of the prophet is to teach the complete overthrow of the contemporary Egyptian religion.

In recent times Penna has suggested another interpretation. He too would translate "the city of the sun," but he would take this in a Messianic sense. In favor of this Messianic interpretation, Penna points to the context, and to the phrase of Malachi, "the sun of righteousness," and also gives a stylistic reason. This text has often been compared with the accounts of the conquest of Canaan. Hence, on this interpretation, just as at one time the ark of the covenant was in the City of the Sun (Beth Shemesh), so in the Messianic age, Egypt will also have its city of the sun.

Each of these interpretations is worthy of consideration, and the reader will find a full discussion of them and of other proposed solutions in the note appended to this section (pp. 49f.). One cannot be dogmatic, and it is best not to decide positively in favor of one view as over against the others. The three that have been mentioned above have the most to commend them. Whatever be the precise significance of the latter part of the verse, we are fully warranted in holding that the passage teaches that there will come a time when Egypt in great part will worship the true God.

One point remains. We must note more carefully the comparison with the conquest of Palestine. This conquest started with small beginnings, and as it progressed, the five kings were taken. So it is to be in Egypt. The beginnings will be small, but finally five cities will speak the language of the true religion. The Gospel makes genuine conquests. The spread of the true religion, however, will occur only after the destruction of idolatry and severe divine judgments. In the state in which it is when Isaiah speaks these words, neither Egypt nor the Gentile world generally, can receive salvation. Punitive justice must prepare the way. Upbuilding is to be preceded by destruction; the evil must go that the good may come, for all that is set in opposition to God must be consumed by the fires of tribulation and suffering, that the kingdom of God may appear.

19 Again Isaiah begins with "in that day." A further characteristic of the glorious period to come is seen in that there will be an altar in Egypt dedicated to the Lord, and near the boundary of Egypt a pillar devoted to the Lord.[61] The language reflects the period of the patriarchs. As Abraham had gone through the land erecting altars to the Lord, so in Egypt there will be such an altar. This altar will not be memorial in nature, like that which the two and a half tribes built by the Jordan (Josh. 22:9ff.), although it does remind of that altar. Nevertheless, it will have religious significance, and upon it legitimate sacrifices to God will be offered. The prophecy does not conflict with Exodus 20:24, which permitted the building of altars in all places in which the Lord would record His Name. The altar upon which the sacrifices are offered simply stands as a representative for the entire cult as such. It is a case of *pars pro toto*. An altar dedicated to the Lord means that sacrifices offered to the Lord will be offered thereupon. In other words, the true religion will be found in Egypt; the true God will be worshipped there.

This altar is said to be in the midst of the land. Some have taken

---

61 The preposition of dedication, indicating that the altar is one dedicated to the Lord.

the phrase in a geographical sense, and have sought to find a reference to Memphis (cf. Jer. 44:1); but this is not necessary. To say that there will be an altar to the true God in the midst of the land simply means that the revealed religion will be found in the land.

The *matztzevah* is a stone memorial, which may possibly be suggested by its resemblance to the obelisk.[62] Originally the *matztzevah* was simply a single stone, such as Jacob erected at Bethel (Gen. 28:16-22). Here also there is a reflection upon the patriarchal period. There is reason for mentioning this standing stone as being on the boundary of Egypt, for as Jacob had erected the pillar because of God's presence, so the pillar in Egypt will indicate the presence of God. It would thus show that when one approaches Egypt and leaves Judah he comes into a land that is also the Lord's. He does not leave the Holy Land to enter a Profane Land, but simply continues in the land that is the Lord's and that worships Him.[63] Thus, in its entirety Egypt will be converted, a fact which is emphasized by the repeated phrase *to the Lord*. In verses 18-22 the word LORD occurs ten times. The blessings herein depicted come because of Him.

The *matztzevah* had often been condemned, inasmuch as it was connected with the Canaanitish religion. Yet here all heathenish significance is excluded. The obelisk that characterized Egypt is now to remind men of the Lord. When men are turned to God

---

[62] The word is derived from *nā-tzaḇ, to erect*. In Canaanitish places of worship it stood as a sacred pillar, and in Scripture is often mentioned in connection with the Asherim or other cult objects (Ex. 23:24; Lev. 26:1; Deut. 7:5; 1 Kings 14:23; 2 Kings 13:2; 2 Chron. 14:3; Hos. 3:4; Mic. 5:13). The erection of the pillar in Egypt shows that the land belongs to the Lord and indicates His lordship over the nation. Likewise, Jeremiah commands the destruction of the pillars of the sun god (43:13), for that sun god is no longer to be present in Egypt.

[63] It is true that in the Mosaic Law offerings are to be brought only to the national sanctuary (Lev. 17:8; Deut. 12:12; 13:12-17), and hence the Messianic age is usually pictured as a journey of the heathen to Jerusalem (Isa. 2:3, 4; 66:23; Mic. 4:2, 3); nevertheless, the picture herein presented is not in conflict with the idea of the centrality of Jerusalem. It rather brings to the fore another aspect of the Messianic times, namely, the conquest of the Gospel, and the lordship of Israel's God over heathen nations. I am at a loss to understand how Edelkoort can see nothing Messianic in this. Möller is correct in characterizing the passage, "es ist eine der Stellen, die den Universalismus in reinster Gestalt lehren" *(Die messianische Erwartung der vorexilischen Propheten,* Gütersloh, 1906).

they engage in acts of outward devotion, and this stone was to be a memorial of the fact that the land worshipped God.

20 Like the rainbow following the flood, so the altar and stone were to be signs, witnesses with binding force.[64] When the Lord sees these monuments, He will recognize His own and hear their prayer. He will look upon the stone and see in it a sign and witness that He is to hear and answer the Egyptians' cry for help. This is not to suggest that the Lord needs such reminders. The thought rather is that in Egypt[65] there will be God's own people to whom He will hearken, as He does to His own in Judah. It is, of course, the Egyptians who will be benefited by these stones. They are a testimony that the Lord will hear them when they cry.

The second part of the verse calls to mind the period of the Judges (cf. Judg. 1:34; 2:18, etc.); in the future there will also be oppressors of the Egyptians.[66] How strange that Isaiah should mention oppressors! The word emphasizes the fact that at one time the Egyptians themselves had been oppressors (the same Hebrew word is employed) of the Israelites. And herein is the wonder of God's grace. The Egyptians had been the oppressors of God's helpless people. Now, however, the Egyptians have turned to the Lord; and hence they themselves will know what all God's people know, that in this world they will have tribulation. The Egyptians will be no exception; they, too, will face oppression. Whenever there is a true conversion, there will in the nature of the case be oppressors, and from these God will send deliverance. We are not told who these oppressors are. Yet in the last analysis, the oppressors of Egypt will be Satan and his hosts, and in one way and another they will afflict the Egyptians as they afflict all of God's people.

As in the times of the Judges, so in the future God will send a deliverer.[67] Isaiah takes his phraseology from the book of the

---

[64] When any form of the verb *hā-yāh* is followed by the preposition *Lamed*, it is best translated *become;* hence, *and it will become a sign and a witness.* The subject is the thought of v. 19, the presence in Egypt of the altar and *matztzēḇāh.* Note that the second, third, and fourth words are introduced by *Lamed,* yielding a certain paronomasia.

[65] The words *in Egypt* are not superfluous, but call attention to the wonder of what is prophesied. Hitherto, such signs and witnesses to the LORD had been confined to Israel.

[66] כי may also be rendered *when.* It is difficult to decide, but possibly the clause is intended to explain why the signs will be in Egypt. Vulg., *clamabunt enim ad Dominum.*

[67] Weak *waw* with imperf., *that he may send.* The apodosis begins with *waw*

39

Judges, and thus signifies the greatness of God's deliverance. The Egyptians may know that from whatever oppression awaits them there will be deliverance so great that it may be compared with that given in the days of the Judges. When all is said and done, however, this Deliverer is Christ Himself.[68] The prophecy thus finds its fulfillment in the sending of many deliverers, but ultimately and supremely in Christ.

21 In the conversion of the Egyptians a gradation is expressed. First there is mention of an altar and standing stone, and of five cities. Now, in the present verse, it is Egypt without limitation or qualification which is said to know the Lord. The contrast between Egypt and the Lord is striking. Twice the names appear, "And there will be known the LORD to Egypt, and will know Egypt the LORD." In each instance, the verb "to know" appears before the two names.

The verse begins with the simple statement that the Lord will be known or will make Himself known to Egypt. This declaration implies more than that the Egyptians know the name by which God is called or invoked in Judah and also more than a practical recognition of their duties toward Him. The knowledge spoken of involves a recognition that Yahweh is the true God but it also includes a personal relationship to Him as one's own God. At the foundation of all true worship and religion there must be knowledge, and this knowledge is a divine gift. For our understanding of the verb *there shall be known,* we are reminded of Exodus 6:3, "by my name Yahweh was I not known unto them." In this latter verse, it is God Himself who reveals His Name to His people, and so also in the present verses it is God who makes Himself known to Egypt. At the same time such knowledge comes by faith, and we may ask with Paul, "how shall they believe in him of whom they have not heard? and how shall they hear without a preacher?" (Rom. 10:14b). The fact that Egypt believes implies that she has heard the message concerning God. Men have been sent; they have

---

cons. and the perf. *For they will cry unto the Lord that He send to them a deliverer and a mighty one, that he* (i.e., the deliverer) *should deliver them.* Note also that *wā-rāb* can be taken as a perf. with *waw* cons., *and he will strive.*

[68] Isaiah knows of only one Deliverer for the heathen nations, namely Christ. To this the whole Messianic tenor of the passage points.

40

carried the message; they have preached the truth. Egypt has heard the truth and believed. God has made Himself known to her.

As a correlative the prophet declares that in that day Egypt will know the Lord. This future knowledge is a result of God's having made Himself known to Egypt. It is a knowledge that expresses itself in true worship, and this worship Isaiah describes by using the symbols of the Old Testament dispensation.[69] He states that Egypt will offer sacrifices, and employs two words which denote both bloody and unbloody offerings, thus including the totality of sacrifice. Of course, inasmuch as he is speaking of the time of the Messianic salvation, sacrifices will in reality no longer be needed. Nevertheless, by means of this metaphorical usage of language, the prophet is enabled to express the truth that Egypt will worship God. In Old Testament times one who worshipped would offer sacrifices such as God commanded. In picturing Egypt as doing this, Isaiah, therefore, is simply asserting that in the future Egypt will worship God in an acceptable manner. He is not prophesying a time when the nation of Egypt will offer literal sacrifices upon actual altars.

The depth of Egypt's devotion is shown by the fact that she will also vow vows unto the Lord and will perform those vows.[70] The offering of vows was done on one's own accord as an expression of gratitude and thanksgiving (cf. Num. 30:1ff.). The Egyptians vow these vows only after they have come to know the Lord. Their vows, therefore, are not reckless and irreligious, but are taken in connection with the worship of God; and for this reason the Egyptians are zealous to fulfill them. This passage cannot be appealed to for support of any kind of vow. Vows of celibacy and perpetual poverty and the like which really have nothing to do with the knowledge of the Lord are not in view here. Calvin has gone to the heart of the matter when he remarks, "We never received permission to vow whatever we please, because we are too much disposed to go to excess, and to take every kind of liberty

[69] The verb '*ā-ḇaḏ* here denotes the performance of religious service, as in Ex. 13:5. Bultema believes that the reference is to actual sacrifices by which the Egyptians will symbolize the truth that Christ's blood has become precious to them. This interpretation, however, does not accord with the general tenor of biblical revelation.

[70] The *Piel* here has factitive significance. The *Qal* is stative, *to be whole, complete,* whereas the *Piel* denotes a bringing into realization of the state denoted by the stative, i.e., to make whole, complete. Cf. A. Goetze, "The So-Called Intensive of the Semitic Languages," *JAOS*, Vol. 62, No. 1, 1942, pp. 1-8.

with regard to God, and because we act more imprudently towards him than if we had to deal with men." The vows which the Egyptians take are not entered into lightly but seriously, and evidently out of deep concern for the knowledge of God, for the fact is emphasized that they will fulfill their vows. The true religion has thus fully conquered the land that once oppressed the people of God.

22 Egypt worships the Lord, and therefore is to be treated like a true child of God, for "whom the Lord loveth He chasteneth." As once the Lord had smitten Pharaoh with plagues, so in the Messianic time He will smite (in both instances the same verb is used) Egypt with blows, not to destroy Egypt, but that He may again heal.[71] Isaiah's expression is forceful, and we may render, "The Lord will smite smiting and healing." The smiting does not completely destroy the country, nor does the healing preclude further smiting. Basically, therefore, God's action is salutary for Egypt. It results in Egypt's turning to the Lord, and forsaking those things which had caused the smiting.

Isaiah's language reflects upon the smiting of the land at the time of the Exodus. When he says that the Lord will be entreated of the Egyptians, we are reminded of Pharaoh's command to Moses to entreat the Lord for him.[72] At that time, however, the favor of the Lord was not shown to Moses; now, when Egypt cries to Him, He will hear them. Once He had heard a cry which arose from Egypt; then Egypt held His own people in bondage and sought to preclude the promises from fulfillment. Now, however, Egypt herself will cry to God by reason of her afflictions, and He will truly be entreated of them. As a result, He will heal Egypt. The ancient enmity is gone and forgotten. They who once were stangers and aliens of the household of faith have now renounced their age-old superstitions and turned unto the living and true God. As a result, they receive the blessings which belong to all the people of God.

23 In that day there will be a highway from Egypt to Assyria, and

71 Two infinitives abs. (1Q, however, replaces the second by a finite verb) may be used co-ordinately; the latter then expresses an action which is antithetical to that expressed by the first; thus, *smiting, but also healing*.

72 In the *Niphal 'tr* is usually employed with *Lamed* referring to the worshipper; *He will be entreated with respect to them.* Cf. 2 Sam. 21:14.

Assyria will come into Egypt, and Egypt into Assyria, and Egypt
will serve with Assyria.

24 In that day Israel will be a third with respect to Egypt and Assyria,
a blessing in the midst of the earth,

25 Which the LORD of hosts hath blessed saying, Blessed is my people,
Egypt, and the work of my hands Assyria, and my heritage Israel.

23 With this verse we reach the culmination of unity in the
conversion to the Lord. The close connection between Egypt and
Assyria is expressed by means of the figure of a highway which
extends from Egypt to Assyria (cf. Vol. I, p. 400, note 29). Isaiah
merely uses a figure; he is not speaking of a literal or actual road
extending between the two countries. The two once hostile nations
will engage in friendly and brotherly intercourse, a fact which is
symbolized by their travelling over the road from one country to
the other. When men and nations come to know the Lord, their
mutual hostilities and animosities cease and they seek to act toward
one another as brothers. Both travel over the same highway,
delighting not only in the service of the Lord but also in mutual
help.

Assyria and Egypt had been two inveterate enemies of each
other and also of Israel. The God of Israel, however, was more
powerful than the gods of these countries and He brought it about
that they should know Him as their own God. The reference is not
to the Egypt and Assyria of Isaiah's day, but to the descendants of
those nations. In the time of the Messiah, what in Isaiah's day were
called Egypt and Assyria will serve the Lord. The conversion of
these two nations serves as a symbol of the conversion of all the
heathen. Standing as it were at the two opposite poles of enmity to
the Lord, these two nations represent the world power in all its
forms. It is the reversal of what occurred at Babel. At the tower of
Babel the world was dispersed, and individual nations arose. They
maintained their individuality, each characterized by this in common, that it did not know nor worship the Lord. Now, however, in
opposition to the false unity that Assyria was trying to introduce,
a unity which sought to bring men together not merely in one
great human empire, but also in heathenism and ignorance of the
Lord, the Lord Himself establishes a true unity. This He does in
the regathering at Pentecost and in the inclusion of the heathen
nations in the blessings of the Gospel of salvation.

The last clause of the verse may be rendered either, "and Egypt
will serve Assyria" or "and Egypt will serve with Assyria." If the
first rendering be adopted, it would express the willingness of one

nation to serve another in their devotion to God. In favor of this it may be argued that the highway is said to go from Egypt to Assyria, and that Assyria is first mentioned as coming to Egypt. If, on the other hand, the second rendering be accepted, we are to understand that the service of Egypt and Assyria together is one that finds its object in the Lord. Commentators rather generally have adopted this latter position, assuming at the same time that there is an intended allusion to the ordinary usage of *'eth* as the accusative particle, in order to direct attention to the wonder of the change. Egypt first serves Assyria, and then *with* Assyria. If these two hostile nations, which had been the leaders in opposition to the people of God, could be mollified and completely converted, then surely other nations less active in their hostility could also be converted. No enemy is too powerful for the God of Jacob to conquer.

The Mesopotamian power, however, particularly in Daniel, is a type of the opposition to God which culminates in the working of the man of sin. In his treatment of some foreign nations, Isaiah had pictured them as possessing a remnant, through which there will come deliverance. These powers therefore were not to be completely destroyed. Such was not the case with Babylon. In chapter fourteen Isaiah had severely condemned this nation. For the power of Mesopotamia as such, whether that power came to expression in Babylon or in its forerunner Assyria, there would seem to be no hope. But how is this to be reconciled with the statements of the present verse? In reality there is no contradiction. That spirit which at one time animated Assyria and Babylonia and continues to oppose the people of God and the Church of Christ will continue until it is destroyed by the coming of the Lord. In so far as that power manifested itself in Assyria and Babylonia there could be no deliverance for these nations. In other words, in Isaiah's day, the Mesopotamian power as such was the spirit of Antichrist, the forerunner of the Man of Sin. As such there could be no hope for it. Hence, Isaiah can represent the destruction of the king of Babylon in the strong terms that appear in chapter fourteen (cf. comments on that chapter). On the other hand, for the nations as such when considered apart from their being used by the spirit of Antichrist, there would be hope. Even those who have so strongly opposed the Lord as have these nations will find delight in His service at the time of the Messianic deliverance. At one time the spirit opposed to Christ had oppressed the people of God by means of Egypt and Assyria. Yet, even nations which had once been used of this spirit will find a deliverance when the Messiah comes. When then the prophet speaks of Egypt and Assyria as serving the Lord he is teaching that God has mercy even upon countries that have sinned as grievously as did these two.

24 Hitherto Israel had been the object of enmity, the point of division between Assyria and Egypt. Now, however, that status will change and she will become a blessing. As a third to the other two nations, she will complete the unity, and the three together will represent the entirety of the world in the worship of the Lord. It is a threefold or triple union of which Israel will be one member, a third part, equal with the other two. We may represent the force of the prophet's language as follows: "With respect to Egypt and with respect to Assyria Israel will be a third." In former times, Israel had indeed been a third, but a third which proved to be a bone of contention. In the Messianic age, however, she will be a third that will be a blessing. Not merely is this a blessing for the other two nations, but it is one to be found in the midst of the entire earth. Israel is the blessing in that the realization of the promises to Abraham is seen in her. Throughout her history she should have been a blessing, and in so far as she was true to the promises, she was a blessing. Yet Israel was not always true to the promises, and often became a source of stumbling. In the fullest and truest sense, however, Israel will become what she was destined to be, the land from which blessing flows to the entire earth.[73]

25 The chapter closes with a solemn benediction which God pronounces upon His three peoples. Israel has been a blessing, and so God will bless it.[74] The word translated "it" may be neutral and refer, not alone to Israel, but to all the three powers; for Yahweh is now the God of all nations, and not merely of Israel. The language of the blessing is such as could formerly have been used only of Israel; now, however, it may characterize the whole world. In this

---

[73] Cf. Gen. 12:1-3 and John 4:22. Note also Gen. 18:18; 22:18; 26:4; 28:14; 49:10; Zech. 8:13.

[74] The introductory word is often taken as a relative pronoun, e.g., B. Some take it as expressing purpose, but this is difficult in view of the following perfect. I would render, *in that the Lord will have blessed it*. The suffix may be taken in a neutral sense as including in itself the three nations just mentioned, or Israel. Dillmann would make *ᵃ-šer* refer to *blessing*, wherewith the LORD has blessed it. But in this case, we should normally expect a subsequent *bāh*.

chapter emphasis has been placed upon Egypt, and in verses 23 and 24 it was mentioned before Assyria; for that reason also it is here again mentioned first. Assyria is also mentioned, for it, too, belonged to the triumvirate of those who served the Lord. Isaiah takes three terms that hitherto had been exclusively used of Israel and now extends them to Egypt and Assyria, namely, "My people," "the work of My hands," and "My inheritance"; and these he uses to describe the united powers without discrimination. In the first place Egypt is identified as God's people. This is a strange designation, for it was from Egypt that God once brought forth the Israelites to form them into His people. So completely, therefore, is the oppression of the period of the exodus forgotten or pushed into the background that now Egypt herself can be designated, "My people." Assyria is the work of His hands, by which the prophet means that in a special and spiritual sense, Assyria is God's people. Israel had once been asked, "Hath he not made thee?" (Deut. 32:6b), and characterized with the words, "I have made thee" (Isa. 43:7b). The thought is clearly expressed in the New Testament with such terms as "his workmanship, created in Christ Jesus to good works" (Eph. 2:10); "Therefore if any man be in Christ, he is a new creature" (2 Cor. 5:17a). Could anything higher be said of Assyria? God's hand had formed her to be His own people. Lastly, Israel is described as "My inheritance." The term could equally well have been applied to the other two nations but it is probably given to Israel to call to mind the fact that Israel was chosen of old. In the mention of the three Israel is last, for in the introduction of the nations in relationship to Egypt (vv. 23, 24) Israel had also appeared last. The chapter thus closes with the word "Israel." Drechsler points out that if the nineteenth chapter belongs to the same general period as seventeen and eighteen there is a beautiful agreement among them. Ephraim had fallen in with Egypt, and so Egypt had a good reason for swallowing up Ephraim. Ephraim, however, turns out to be the suitable bridge between Egypt and Assyria over which the highway may pass.

When is this prophecy to be fulfilled? We may perhaps approach an answer by noting that the blessings herein depicted are entirely spiritual and are gifts of God. Isaiah is not picturing a time when there will be a truce among these three nations and when a literal highway will pass from Egypt through Israel to Assyria. He is rather portraying a time when those who once were enemies of God, Gentiles in the flesh, without Christ, aliens from the commonwealth of Israel and strangers from the covenants of promise, having no hope and without God in the world, will become one new man, and will be fellow citizens with the saints and of the household of God. Then the ancient enmity will have been abolished. The fulfillment of this promise, therefore, is Messianic. What Isaiah described in 2:2-4 will have come to pass; and they who were strangers and foreigners will be in that building, fitly framed together, which groweth unto an holy temple in the Lord.

SPECIAL NOTE

One of the earliest to deny the authenticity of parts of this chapter was Koppe, the German translator of Robert Lowth's commentary on Isaiah. He would separate vv. 18-25 from the earlier verses, for the picture of Egyptian misery given in the earlier verses was thought to be too different from the picture of bliss in which Egypt, together with Israel and the Assyrians, was to worship the LORD. Furthermore, he declared, neither Isaiah nor ony other Judean prophet would have designated Hebrew the language of Canaan. Finally, that the Assyrians whom Isaiah always considered the enemies of the Israelites should be called the work of Yahweh's hands, or the people of Yahweh, seemed to Koppe to argue that these verses were not from Isaiah.

Since the time of Koppe (and cf. also Eichhorn's *Einleitung*) there has really been little actual unanimity as to the authorship of the chapter. According to Duhm hardly a passage in the book is as non-genuine *(unecht)* as vv. 16ff., for if Isaiah had written these verses, he would have denied his other prophecies. Further, the desultory *(zerfahrene)* style, and the fragmentary piecing together of all kinds of small prophecies has its parallel only in the imitations and supplementations of the 2nd century. Marti denies the entirety of the chapter to Isaiah, and *IB*, while acknowledging that the language does have some affinities with Isaiah, thinks that vv. 5-10 may not belong to the poem in its original form. The first and third strophes, however, i.e., vv. 1-4 and 11-15, can apply to 714 B.C.

Let us begin with vv. 1-4. The representation of Yahweh riding upon a cloud, coming to Egypt, cannot be denied to Isaiah (Marti). It is true that in 9:7 the Lord sends forth a word that falls in Israel, but is Isaiah thereby precluded from ever modifying his thought? The whole situation here is different; the prophet's purpose is to show that the disturbances occurring in Egypt are due to God Himself, and not the result of a message sent forth from Him (see exposition).

Marti adduces the lack of any connection with some event that concerns Judah. But this prophecy is a "woe," beginning in a manner similar to the other "woes." Its connection with Judah is to be seen from its general position in the book (cf. Vol. I, pp. 409-415).

Note also vv. 17 and 23ff., which Marti denies to Isaiah. The repetition of Egypt or Egyptians (10 times in vv. 1-10) is said not to be Isaianic. But is not the burden of proof upon those who make such statements? Why may Isaiah not have used these words frequently in a small context? Why also is it unworthy of a writer such as Isaiah to mention the fishers and weavers (vv. 8, 9)?

The interior quarrels and wars of Egypt (v. 2) can very well fit the time of Isaiah. At that time there were internal disorders that culminated in the establishment of an Ethiopian dynasty. As to the "hard king," if one were to insist upon an actual ruler, and not refer the words to the Assyrian empire generally, as is done in the commentary, appeal could certainly be made to Sargon.

Marti further claims that the positing of monotheism and the comparison of Jewish religious doctrine with the wisdom of Egypt is not Isaianic. This argument of course would deny to Isaiah also the contrasts between God and the idols presented elsewhere in the book. It rests upon a failure to discern the true progress of thought in Isaiah.

Verses 16ff. are generally denied to Isaiah. They easily divide into five sections, each of which is introduced by the words "in that day." Furthermore, each of the sections deals with Egypt, and could easily be the work of one author. Can that author be Isaiah? The principal arguments against Isaianic authorship are the following: a) The prosaic style which gives the impression of being an addition. But Isaiah could well employ diversity of style. See the commentary on v. 16. Furthermore, the phrase "in that day" clearly refers to the judgment of vv. 1-15; and the thought of the judgment forms the basis for what follows in vv. 16ff. Fischer acknowledges that this section can go back essentially to Isaiah (". . . der aber im wesentlichen auf Isaias zurückgehen kann"). Verses 16ff. continue the argument introduced in vv. 1-15. b) The prophecy of the conversion of Assyria is said to have a parallel in the book of Jonah, which today is generally placed in postexilic times. In opposition to the postexilic dating of Jonah, however, note the arguments for an eighth century date which I have adduced elsewhere (An Introduction to the Old Testament, Grand Rapids, 1958, pp. 277-282). c) Certain phrases are said to call to mind passages such as Zech. 14:16 and Mal. 1:11. But it is just as possible that vv. 16ff. may form the basis for the passages of Zechariah and Malachi. d) The procedure of practically following the account of the conquest of the Holy Land does not favor attributing the account to an original author such as Isaiah. An argument such as this, however, is subjective. If the passage stood alone, such arguments might have some weight, but the passage is an integral portion of Holy Scripture (note also its similarity to 18:7; 23:15-18), and hence such arguments are of little value. We conclude then that there is no sufficient reason for denying this chapter or any of its parts to Isaiah.

NOTE ON ISAIAH 19:18

M must be rendered *city of destruction*, i.e., a city that is to be destroyed. This is supported by Aq and T אפֿנ and the Syro-hexaplaric (Aq could probably also support חרם). Objection has been made to this that it does not fit well into a prophecy of salvation.

Some scholars retain M but, appealing to Ar. *haris*, render *the city of the lion* (Duhm, Marti), with reference to Leontopolis. Josephus (*Antiquities* xiii.3.1-3) relates that Onias, son of the high priest Onias, was living in Alexandria, and seeing that the Macedonians were ravaging Judea, desired to build a temple in Egypt similar to the one in Jerusalem. In this he was encouraged by the prophet Isaiah who had lived six hundred years earlier and had foretold that a temple would be built in Egypt by a Jew (ὡς δεῖ πάντως ἐν Ἀιγύπτῳ οἰκοδομηθῆναι ναὸν τῷ μεγίστῳ θεῷ ὑπ' ἀνδρὸς Ἰουδαίου). Onias desired to build his temple in Bubastis, i.e., where there was a temple in ruins (Leontopolis is in the nome of Heliopolis). Onias sought this permission in a letter to Ptolemy and Cleopatra, who gave him his request. He proceeded to build a temple and altar, similar to that at Jerusalem, but smaller and poorer (μικρότερον δὲ καὶ πενιχρότερον).

The objection to this view is that Ar. *haris* is merely an epithet of the lion, and does not designate the lion itself. Duhm is not moved by this consideration, however, and thinks that similar half-revealing, half-concealing designations are characteristic of apocalyptic. The only way to get rid of Leontopolis, he thinks, is to do away with the sentence itself. The passage, however, is not apocalyptic, and the fact remains that we are not permitted to use חרם in the sense of the epithet *haris*. Whereas there is no philological difficulty in the equation, yet it would appear that in Arabic *haris* is really a modifier of the noun *asad* (lion), rather than a noun in its own right. Furthermore, if Isaiah had wished to speak of a lion, why did he not employ a word more suitable to his purpose?

In the Soncino Bible Dr. I. W. Slotki retains the reading of M but interprets figuratively. The phrase *city of destruction* he takes to indicate a city of idolatry. This cannot be supported linguistically, although Fischer adopts a somewhat similar position (Jer. 43:12ff.). Appeals have also been made to the Syr. *heres* to support a rendering *love, redemption*. Gesenius discusses these at some length (*Com. in loc.*).

Many modern commentators read ח in place of ה, thus obtaining *city of the sun*. This is now supported by 1Q, and is also attested by S, Vulg. (*civitas solis vocabitur una*), Ar., and several Heb. mss. If this reading be adopted (cf. Job 9:7) the reference would be to Heliopolis (cf. Jer. 43:13). If this is intended, however, why did not the writer merely designate the city as On (cf. Gen. 41:45, 50;

46:20; Ezek. 30:17). Penna thinks that there is a Messianic reference (see comments in exposition proper), and he may be correct. Jerome gave to this reading the translation *testa,* and supposed a reference to a city of Ostracine (city of potsherds). This might be taken as a reference to Tahpanhes (Jer. 43:9), whither Jeremiah was taken in Egypt. But why should such a name be given to one of the five cities?

The Targ. appears to combine the two readings: קרתא בית שמש דעתידא למחרב יתאמר היא הדא מנהון, i.e., "of the city, Bethshemesh, which is about to be wasted, it shall be said, It is one of them." This is an expansion, which supports the one reading as well as the other.

B reads πολις ασεδεκ (and Codex Sinaiticus ασεδ ηλιον which is clearly a conflate reading), and Gray thinks that this goes back to a Hebrew text. This name calls to mind the designation of Jerusalem in 1:26, and Gray believes that one of the Egyptian cities is to become an Egyptian Jerusalem, the city where legitimate and correct sacrifices will be offered. But, if five cities speak the language of Canaan, i.e., embrace the true religion, why should not legitimate sacrifices be offered in all five? Why should this particular designation be reserved only for one of the cities? Why should one be considered the ideal Jerusalem? Furthermore, it is not clear that B presupposes עיר הצדק. In an article in *Biblica* (Vol. 2, 1921, pp. 353ff.), Vaccari suggests that the reading of B is a false reading of עיר החרם, due to a transposition and substitution of a consonant *'ir hasedeh.* If B is original, how can we explain the origin of חרם? Possibly the origin of הרם could be due to a scribe who was opposed to the temple at Leontopolis.

4. EGYPT AND ETHIOPIA: A FALSE HOPE (20:1-6)

1 In the year of the coming of Tartan to Ashdod, when Sargon, king of Assyria, sent him, then he fought with Ashdod and took it.

2 At that time the LORD spake by the hand of Isaiah the son of Amoz saying, Go and thou shalt open the sackcloth from upon thy loins, and thou shalt put off from upon thy foot; and he did so, going naked and barefoot.

1 Isaiah now introduces us to a historical situation, one in which the judgment depicted in the previous chapter begins to manifest itself. Egypt was to be attacked, and those Judahites who desired to put their trust in her would see her confounded. The attack was to come through the hands of Assyria, on whose throne Sargon II was then reigning. It was in the year 711 that Assyria marched toward Egypt. Three years earlier, in 713, Ashdod had rebelled against Assyria. Its king Azuri had been removed and his brother Achimit placed upon the throne. This man was deposed by the people, however, and a man by the name of Jaman sat upon the throne in his place. Other cities of Philistia took part in the revolt, and Edom, Moab, and Judah were also invited to join. In addition the Egyptians also promised their help. As the present chapter shows, Isaiah was opposed to trusting in Egypt, and it may be that at this time some attention was paid to his words; for as far as we know, Judah was not attacked by Sargon, who was then at the height of his power. Jaman fled to Egypt for help, but was treacherously turned over to the Assyrians by the Ethiopian king then reigning in Egypt.

The older commentaries are at a loss as to the identification of Sargon. It is acknowledged by them that he is otherwise unknown, and Drechsler makes the useful suggestion that he is probably a co-regent with Shalmanezer.[1] Jerome seeks to explain the meaning

---

[1] *". . . sonst unbekannt. Man setzt ihn zwischen Salmanassar und Sanherib an."*
"Alle Schwierigkeit wäre gehoben, wenn man Sargon als mit Salmanassar

of his name,[2] and Kimchi identifies him with Sennacherib.[3] J. D. Michaelis identified him with Esarhaddon, and Vitringa with Shalmanezer. Lowth and Doederlein believed that he was Sennacherib. His inscriptions have now been discovered, and much is known about him.[4]

Why, however, did not Sargon himself come to Ashdod? Perhaps we cannot answer this question as we might wish. The fact simply remains that Sargon, as Scripture says, sent the Tartan.[5] His task was to quell the uprising at Ashdod. In the Scriptures the word Tartan occurs also in 2 Kings 18:17. It is now known that the Assyrian *turtanu* was one of three great officers of state, the other two being the *rab-BI.LUL* (the chief *BI.LUL* officer) and either the *nagir ekalli* or *abarakku*.[6] This officer of state represented the

---

gleichzeitig in der Eigenschaft eines Mitregenten sich denken wollte" (Com. in loc.).

[2] Jerome's comments are quite interesting. *"Sunt autem nomina* (i.e., Tartan and Sargon) *non Hebraea, sed Assyria, e quibus sonare cognovimus* Thartan, *turrem dedit, vel superfluus, sine* elongans. Sargon *autem* princeps horti." *"Et pulchre rex Assyriorum Sargon, princeps hortorum, dicitur voluptati et luxuriae deditus"* (PL, XXIV, 267).

[3] Kimchi states that this invasion was in the fourteenth year of Hezekiah. Kimchi definitely identifies Sargon with Sennacherib, and states that "our rabbis say that he had eight names."

[4] Sargon himself relates how he abolished the rule of Azuri and placed Ahimiti, Azuri's younger brother, over the people of his country. The Hittites, however (i.e., the inhabitants of the country), placed a Greek (Ia-ma-ni) over them. In rage, Sargon started out against Ashdod, and Ia-ma-ni fled to Musru, which, says Sargon, then belonged to Ethiopia. Hence, Sargon conquered Ashdod, Gath, and Asdudimmu, reorganized these cities and settled in them people from the East. The Ethiopian king put Ia-ma-ni in bonds and he was taken to Assyria. Cf. ANET, pp. 286-287. For the text cf. H. Winckler, *Die Keilschrifttexte Sargons*, Leipzig, 1889. During the year 712 Sargon himself undertook no major military campaigns, which would agree with Isaiah's representation that the *turtanu* fought against Ashdod. Cf. Tadmor, "The Campaigns of Sargon II of Assur," JCS, Vol. 12, 1958, pp. 22-40, 77-100.

[5] Tartan is not a proper name, but a title. He was the king's viceroy. The Akk. *tardinnu* means "second" (cf. 2 Kings 18:17). The form *tartanu* also occurs. Note 1Q *twrtn* which seems to reflect Akk. *turtanu*. A relief from Dur-Sharruken (i.e., Khorsabad) shows an Assyrian general standing with hand raised in greeting before Sennacherib.

[6] Cf. H. W. F. Saggs, "The Nimrud Letters," Iraq, Vol. 21, Part 2, Autumn 1959, p. 161. These letters also show that, in contrast to the poor conditions in Palestine, described in Isaiah 7, a favorable price level existed in Assyria. As a result of the administrative measures adopted by Tiglath-pileser III, the Assyrian government, as these letters reveal, was efficient in small details.

king and acted on his behalf. Tartan carried out his task, and in the very year of his coming to Ashdod, when Sargon sent him, set siege to the city and took it.[7] This capture of Ashdod was the prelude to entrance into Egypt, for the conquest of Ashdod was the key to the taking of Egypt itself. Ashdod was five kilometers from the sea, and about thirty south of Lydda, situated between Jamnia and Ashkelon. It is enough to state that Ashdod was taken, for with its capture the mission of the Assyrians was successful.[8]

2 The outcome of the Assyrian march is first stated, and then we are told of Isaiah's symbolical action. The prophet introduces the verse in a rather general manner, employing a favorite phrase, "at that time," by which he means merely to indicate that during this period God commanded him to act symbolically. If verse 1 refers to the actual outcome of the march, and if Isaiah was to go naked for three years, then it would follow that the command of God for the prophet to go about naked was issued three years before the actual conquest of Ashdod. When the rebellion of the Philistine states occurred, God had already given His command to the prophet.[9]

Isaiah recounts the revelation by saying that "The LORD spake through the hand of Isaiah." As in the seventh chapter so here the prophet objectifies himself. The expression "hand of Isaiah" simply indicates the person, or instrumentality, or power of Isaiah. God had once spoken to Pharaoh through the hand of Moses (Ex. 9:35b); the commandments were given through the hand of Moses (Lev. 10:11); in Numbers 17:5 (Hebrew) mention is made of a memorial, "even as the Lord spake through the hand of Moses to him." The phrase occurs again with respect to Moses in Joshua 20:2 and 1 Kings 8:53, 56, and in 1 Kings 12:15 the Lord is said to have spoken through the hand of Ahijah the Shilonite. The word "hand" thus designates the revelation of God as it is delivered by the prophet. It is not the reception of the message, therefore, but its deliverance that is in view. And this fits in well with the context. At the beginning of the revolt, Isaiah began to deliver this message;

7 *of the coming* — when the inf. const. is preceded by a noun in the const., the prep. *Lamed* is omitted. With the following inf. we have the order, infinitive, object, subject. The entire verse forms a protasis, the apodosis beginning with the second verse.

8 Cf. *ANET*, p. 286b; Hugo Winckler, *op. cit.*

9 In 1b Isaiah has anticipated the outcome of events. As in 7:1 so here he gives the final outcome.

or better, God spoke through the hand of the prophet to the people. What Isaiah proclaimed was his commission to perform the symbolic act. The deliverance of this message is essential for a proper understanding of the symbolic act, for the symbol must always be accompanied by the word; were that not the case, it could not properly be understood. It is Isaiah's commission which explains his action.

As with so many biblical commissions, this one also is introduced by the word "Go."[10] The prophet is to be an apostle, one sent of the Lord, and that for the performance of a particular act. In itself the word does not necessarily imply that he has received a commission which he is to discharge. He is first to unloosen the sack about his loins. But why was Isaiah wearing a sack about his loins? Was it a symbol of mourning? (cf. Isa. 3:24; 15:3).[11] It was the custom to wear sackcloth upon occasions of mourning, and the suggestion has been made that Isaiah was in mourning over the deportation of the ten tribes. Isaiah's primary mission, however, was to Judah; and there is no evidence that he wore sackcloth for such a purpose. Others have advanced the thought that the sack was an official dress worn by the prophets, and in support of this view they have appealed to the dress worn by Elijah (2 Kings 1:8) and John the Baptist (Matt. 3:4).[12] Appeal is also made to Zechariah 13:4 and 2 Kings 3:4, and there is the view that the reference is merely to the common dress of the humbler class of people. Each of these opinions is quite interesting; each is quite plausible; but the fact remains that we do not really know why at this time the prophet was wearing such a garment of rough, hairy cloth. Often this sack was worn over a tunic, although at times it may also have been worn next to the skin. We cannot tell, and it is best not to hazard a guess. When God spoke to him, Isaiah was wearing a sackcloth, and this he was commanded to remove.

Isaiah was also commanded to take the shoes from off his feet, and to this command he was obedient. The result was that he went about naked and barefoot. Like Hosea he yielded a blind obedience, not being told at first why he was to act as he did. If Isaiah, however, were to go about naked, would he not be conducting himself dishonorably? Would he not be doing something shameful that would cast despite upon his prophetical influence? In answer,

10 Cf. Isa. 6:9; 21:6; 22:15; 26:20.
11 Calvin, Delitzsch.
12 Cf. Alexander, Drechsler.

we can only say that acting in obedience to God can never be a thing of shame. As a matter of fact, however, the problem does not really arise in this connection, for Isaiah need not be thought of as having gone about completely naked. This is shown by the addition of the word "barefoot." Had he been completely naked, there would be no need for this additional description. In going about naked, he probably was simply wearing an undergarment, and so even in the eyes of the people, was not acting against what was honorable. He was merely going against custom in such a way that attention would be drawn to himself. Passages such as 2 Samuel 6:20 show that one in such a condition would be regarded as naked (cf. John 21:7).

In such a condition he was constantly to go about. Hence, we are to assume that Isaiah appeared naked in the discharge of his duty, not merely upon occasion, but that he went about this way constantly. Whenever he was seen upon the streets of Jerusalem, he was the object of attention and, indeed, humiliation, because of his lack of clothing. Through this humiliation Judah was to learn the lesson that God wished to teach. This is the only symbolical action recorded of the prophet, but it was not he alone who was humbled. Into this world there was to come one who could say, "I was naked, and ye clothed me not," who, "being rich, yet for our sakes became poor, that we through his poverty might become rich."

3 And the LORD said, Even as my servant Isaiah has gone naked and barefoot three years, a sign and a wonder concerning Egypt and concerning Ethiopia.
4 So shall the king of Assyria lead the captivity of Egypt and the exiles of Ethiopia young and old, naked and barefoot, with their buttocks uncovered, the nakedness of Egypt.
5 And they shall be afraid and ashamed of Ethiopia their expectation, and of Egypt their boast.
6 And the inhabitant of this isle will say in that day, Behold! thus is our expectation, whither we fled for help, to be delivered from the presence of the king of Assyria. And how shall we ourselves escape?

3 In this verse there begins the divine explanation of Isaiah's symbolical act. For a period of three years, as Isaiah went about his prophetic task, he was a living embodiment of the fact that the Egyptian kingdom would fall.[13] Cush or Ethiopia is now men-

___

13 The words *three years* are to be construed with *naked and barefoot*, and not with *sign and wonder*.

tioned, for Shabako reigned in Egypt from 714 to 700. In the prophecies which date from the reign of Hezekiah, Egypt and Ethiopia are frequently mentioned in close connection. Knobel and others have held that Isaiah appeared only once as he spoke the words of interpretation, and thus became simply a model to remind the nation of what he had said. But we do not know how often the prophet spoke of his commission and gave an explanation of his action. Penna feels that in verse 4 there is reference to a complete nakedness, and hence, that Isaiah is here carrying out the command only in vision. The language, however, implies that the action was actually performed, so that in the naked Isaiah the people would behold the naked and barren condition of that nation in which they had so wrongly placed their confidence. Moreover, inasmuch as three years is specifically mentioned, would it not be more likely that the reference was to an actual occurrence? During the course of this period of time, then, the prophet was to carry on his prophetic ministry, naked and barefoot. He may have spoken often of the commission which God had given him and which he was discharging, for he was a sign of the coming downfall of Egypt.[14] He was also to be a wonder, a word implying a mighty act of God, one which may be discerned in God's manifestation of His power in the carrying away captive of the Egyptians by Assyria.

4 With this verse the comparison is completed. As Isaiah, God's servant in faithfully discharging a symbolical action, had gone about naked and barefoot for three years, so the king of Assyria would carry off all the Egyptians naked and barefoot. Isaiah speaks of the king of Assyria as leading the Egyptians. The verb calls to mind Moses' leading his flock to the backside of the desert. It is a word also used of leading people into captivity. Just as sheep are completely subject to the shepherd and must be led, so the captive is subject to his captor. Egypt and Cush are to be taken captive, and this captivity is to be led away. Both Egypt and Cush are mentioned to show that the land on which Israel relied would be wholly taken captive.

The extent of the captivity is also expressed in that all classes of the inhabitants are said to be taken away, and these naked and barefoot. In 2 Chronicles 28:15 there is a statement that may cast

---

14 Gray thinks that this explanation was only given three years after Isaiah began to go about naked, and asks what had happened in the interval.

partial light upon the condition of captives: ". . . and with the spoil clothed all that were naked among them, and arrayed them, and shod them, and gave them to eat and to drink, etc."

Four words of some difficulty bring the verse to its conclusion, and these we may translate literally, "my uncovered ones as to the buttocks, the nakedness of Egypt." As the text stands it implies that these whose buttocks were exposed had been humiliated by God in this manner. Many expositors wish to emend the text in a minor way so that it may be rendered, "those whose buttocks are exposed."[15] This was a particular disgrace, which David's servants were once called upon to suffer. "Wherefore Hanun took David's servants, and shaved off the one half of their beards, and cut off their garments in their middle, *even* to their buttocks, and sent them away" (2 Sam. 10:4). The Egyptians, therefore, are to be carried away into captivity, and in a most humiliating condition. Egypt is now mentioned alone, inasmuch as it was the land in which the Judahites placed their confidence.

5 As a result of the disaster just mentioned the Judahites will be afraid of the countries which had been their expectation and boast. They will be confounded and filled with consternation at the fate of Cush, the object to which they looked for help, their expectation. Cush had been that object, and Egypt had been the glory in which they boasted.[16] Now, in place of expectation and boasting there is shuddering and shame. It is Isaiah, not the Assyrians, who announces this prediction. The verbs are indefinite and general, but there would seem to be no doubt that the people of Judah are to be taken as the subject.

6 In order to show how great was the chagrin of those who had trusted in Egypt, Isaiah employs the people's own words. At that time, when men will be disappointed in Egypt and Ethiopia, an inhabitant of the eastern coast and of the Mediterranean will give utterance to the belying of their trust in the words, "Thus is our expectation, whither we fled for help to be delivered from before the

15 I.e., h^a-$s\hat{u}$-$p\bar{e}y$ instead of h^a-$s\hat{u}$-$p\bar{a}y$. The present form is difficult to explain. The suffix may be that of the 1st person, but also a construct plural, the $\bar{e}y$ having been resolved into $\bar{a}y$. Duhm suggests that the word may be an absolute plural (cf. Judg. 5:15; Jer. 22:14). In *ANEP* there are illustrations of prisoners, pp. 296, 326, 332.

16 Compare Jer. 46:25. In the ancient power Egypt lay their vain boast; in the newly arisen kingdom of Cush, their trust.

king of Assyria, and how shall we ourselves escape?" Isaiah uses a strange designation for the speaker, identifying him as an "inhabitant of the coast." The word rendered *coast* may first of all indicate land in distinction from water, then the coast as opposed to inland, and then an island as over against the mainland. Here it indicates the coast of Palestine. It is *this* coast, says Isaiah, in order that thereby he may distinguish it from the coast of Egypt or any other coast. But why does he employ such a term? Why not merely speak of the inhabitants of the Holy Land? The answer appears to be that he gives a geographical designation to the people which characterizes them for what they really are and desired to be. Judah wanted to forget her heavenly calling, to turn from trust in God and, like a profane nation, place her trust in a human power. She was willing to act like an inhabitant of the coast where a profane people dwelt.[17] Well and good, so she shall be called. Paul similarly wrote to the Corinthians that he could not write to them but as unto carnal, "for ye are yet carnal" (1 Cor. 3:1, 3). Those who wanted to trust Egypt were no true people of God, no holy nation, but merely inhabitants of the coast.

When Sargon's army approached Egypt, the king Shabako handed over Jamani who had fled to him. It was not until later, however, at the time of Esarhaddon, that the prophecy received a greater fulfillment. Yet Sargon's approach did at least bring to light the weakness of the Egyptians. The chapter closes on a note of despair. "We had trusted in Egypt," so the argument runs, "and look what has become of her. How then can we possibly be delivered? What hope remains for us?" Those who trust in the arm of flesh can expect nothing but disillusionment.

[17] Actually the inhabitants of the coastal plain were the Philistines. Possibly to change or reject the word *midbar*, which agrees with other titles (vv. 11, 13), Isaiah's designation is intended to classify the Judahites with the Philistines.

5. BABYLON (21:1-10)

1 The oracle of the desert of the sea. As whirlwinds in the south, rushing on, from the wilderness it comes, from a terrible land.
2 A hard vision, it is made known to me; the deceiver deceiving and the spoiler spoiling. Go up, O Elam, besiege, O Media: all sighing have I made to cease.
3 Wherefore my loins are filled with pain, pangs have seized me, as the pangs of a woman in travail; I am bent from hearing, I am frightened from seeing.
4 My heart wanders; shuddering terrifies me; the twilight of my pleasure he has put for trembling for me.
5 Set the table, spread the cloth, eat, drink: arise, ye chiefs, anoint the shield.

1 Strange is the heading of this prophecy; a burden (cf. 13:1) which has to do with the sea. It appears to be a title without parallel in the Old Testament, although there is a somewhat similar phrase in Psalm 75:6b, "from the desert of mountains." As the word "mountains" is anarthrous in the Psalm, so in this heading the word "sea" is without the article.

Some commentators think that the heading consists of mere catchwords taken from the prophecy itself, which goes on to speak of "rushing from the desert." But the problem cannot be so easily solved. In the Dead Sea Scroll (1Q) we read, "the burden of the word of the sea," and in Codex Vaticanus the word *sea* is omitted. Inasmuch as the word *sea* is not found in the following prophecy, it is difficult to understand how it could have been taken from that prophecy and placed in the title.[1]

---

1 Some (e.g., *IB*) follow 1Q in omitting *desert*, and then take the consonants *ym* as a plural ending, combining with the preceding *dbr*, obtaining *dᵉbārim*, *words*. Thus, "words like storm winds, etc." Penna would reject all attempts to change or reject the word *midbar*, which agrees with other titles (vv. 11, 13; 22:1) and is taken up again in the second line. 1Q reads *dbr ym* and not *dbrym*, the two words being clearly separated by a space. Many follow B in omitting *ym*, but how then is its presence to be explained? M is the more difficult read-

There is an Akkadian phrase, *mat tamti* (land of the sea), which was applied to the region about the Persian Gulf.[2] This phrase, however, really does not explain the strange title of the present chapter. Marti has suggested that the title is somewhat similar to the phrase "in the bush" of Mark 2:26, and indeed the words do have an air of mystery about them. Certainly as they stand in the Masoretic text they constitute the more difficult reading. We shall seek therefore to interpret the language as it is. What has caused Isaiah to employ this strange terminology? Some think that he bases his thoughts upon the natural physical features of Babylon itself, for in 14:23 he had announced that city's desolation, and the natural features of the land are said to be used here as portents of this coming destruction. May it not be, however, that in speaking of Babylonia as the desert of the sea, Isaiah was simply thinking of Babylon as a great plain watered by a mighty river (cf. Gen. 11:2; Isa. 23:13; 27:1)?[3] We may compare his description of the Nile in 19:5. Babylon was a great plain, in which violent storms were to have free play.

Indeed, as soon as the prophet mentions the "desert of the sea," his mind turns to fierce storms. He begins with a preposition, "like storms from the Negeb,"[4] and immediately directs our thoughts not to the enemy, but to the fierce storms that come out of the southern district of Palestine (i.e., the Negeb).[5] These have their starting point in the southern or southeastern desert, and come with violent force (cf. Job 1:19; 37:9; Hos. 13:15). Their principal characteristic is that they "sweep through" from the desert. Indeed, we may better grasp the force of Isaiah's statement by

---

ing, and so to be preferred. Proposed emendations do not solve the difficulty. Kissane renders "by a grievous vision," omitting *ym* and substituting *m(hzwt)*. Barnes (*JTS*, Vol. 2, 1900, pp. 583-92) proposed to translate *ym* by "west." For 21:1-10 cf. R. B. Y. Scott, "Isaiah xxi:1-10; The Inside of a Prophet's Mind," *VT*, Vol. 2, 1952, pp. 278-282.

2 Cf. Dhorme in *RB*, Vol. 31, 1922, pp. 403-406, for a discussion of this term.

3 As Penna puts it, *"con riferimento all'Eufrate e alle sue ramificazioni, naturali o artificiali."*

4 It is possible that the prep. *Beth* should be rendered *from*, as is done in the Syriac. The prep. should not be emended to *min* (*BH*), for *Beth*, like Egy. *m* and Akk. *ina*, may mean *from*.

5 Negeb is a term used to denote the district between Hebron and Kadesh (Gen. 20:1) and later extended to include the southern parts of Palestine generally. The word means "to be dry," "parched." It occurs in Ug., *Ngb*. Negeb is dry, parched land, a fitting parallel to "terrible land" in v. 1b.

means of a literal translation, "like storms from the Negeb, in respect to sweeping through."[6] Such storms, arising in the Negeb, do not play out their force early, but, leaving the desert, sweep through the country that is to be affected. In their wake they leave desolation and destruction. An army like them is a destruction-bringing army.

More than a mere figure of speech is found here. There is truly such an army, one like these wild storms from the Negeb; and it will come from the desert, from a land that is terrible, and to be feared.[7] The reference is probably to Media and Persia from which the army came, for inasmuch as this land lay beyond the known civilized nations, it could be characterized as fearful. In saying that the army was to come from the desert, Isaiah probably had reference merely to the desert land east of Babylonia; or he may also have used this word figuratively to characterize the land of the Medes and Persians.

In our comments we have adopted the position that the army depicted is composed of Elamites and Medes, and that they come from Persia to attack Babylonia. In other words, the reference of this prophecy would be to the destruction of Babylon under Cyrus in 539 B.C. Can this interpretation be defended?

Several objections are raised against it, which we hope will disappear in the light of the subsequent discussion. It is claimed that if we take away the references to Babylon in verse 9 and the allusion to the Elamites and Medes in verse 2, there is nothing remaining to suggest Babylon. Most modern critics deny the possibility of reference to an attack upon Babylon anterior to that in 539 because no capitulation of the city to an army consisting of Medes and Elamites is known to have taken place before this time. The Assyrian army had assaulted Babylon at an earlier date; and it contained Medes, but not Elamites, for the Elamites always appeared as enemies of the Assyrians and were ready to unite themselves with any other nation, even Babylon, in order to attack the Assyrians.

It is further asserted that elsewhere in Isaiah the conquerors of Babylon are designated as sanctified ones, conscious of carrying out a divine plan. In this passage, however, little enthusiasm is said to be shown for these conquerors. Penna therefore refers verses 1-5 to

---

[6] The infinitive construct may have the force of the Latin gerund in -do, to express attendant circumstances. The root means, "to come by turns."

[7] Inasmuch as the subject of נב is indefinite, there is no need to emend to the feminine (BH).

a danger befalling Jerusalem or Judah because the Assyrian army is invading, although he acknowledges that verses 6-10 contain a dramatic account of the fall of Babylon. The Medes and Elamites, however, never invaded Palestine as this theory would demand. Penna further thinks that there was a military alliance and that there were several contingents of Elamite soldiers in the Assyrian army, possibly skilled archers (Jer. 49:35; Ezek. 32:24). He claims that the connection between verses 1-5 and verses 6-10 is easily explained. The prophecy concerning the fall of Babylon, he maintains, may be considered the prophet's answer to too much confidence in Merodach-baladan and any other alliance against the Assyrian power. There would then be several allusions to the beginning of the exile in 586, and the fall of Babylon could be any one of those under Sargon II or Sennacherib. The assault upon Jerusalem is thought to be that of Sennacherib in 701, a view which, according to Penna, offers fewer difficulties than any other; and in such a case he thinks the passage may be attributed to Isaiah.[8]

The second principal objection to interpreting this passage as referring to the downfall of Babylon is said to be found in the attitude of the prophet. Why, it is asked, would the prophet be moved with such great emotion over the downfall of the enemy of his people? A third objection is the statement that all of Babylon's idols had been dashed to the ground. It is claimed that Cyrus showed himself tolerant toward the idols of Babylon and did not destroy them. As the exposition proceeds we shall reflect upon these questions.

2 Having mentioned the oncoming army the prophet immediately speaks of his own reaction to the revelation. The vision in which he was permitted to see the message of God he describes as hard, because it had to do with matters which themselves were hard.[9] As Ahijah once had told the wife of Jeroboam that he was sent to her with a "hard" message (1 Kings 14:6), so

---

[8] Cf. Penna, *Com. in loc.* Note also Dhorme, *op. cit.*, who suggests that the reference is to the invasion of Sargon II, in 710. Dhorme's article may also be found in *Receuil Edouard Dhorme*, 1951, pp. 301-304. Winckler advocated 649, the year of Shamash-shum-ukin's death.

[9] The words *a hard vision* are not subj., but acc., the *nota acc.* being omitted. It may be, however, that instead of being the obj., the acc. is similar to the *ḥal* acc. of Ar., *in the state of* (i.e., *as*) *a hard vision, it was made known.*

the content of this vision to Isaiah was also hard. It was likewise hard for the prophet in the manner in which it came to him, for it apparently affected him not only spiritually but also physically. A message that in itself was grievous to be born would also bring heaviness to the one that received and must deliver it.

As to the origin of the vision, there can be no question. It is not the product of Isaiah's mind, nor did it originate in his mind; it was made known to him by God.[10] To describe the enemy that had caused the sighing which had come and would come to Israel, Isaiah uses four words, in each of which appear the two vowels, *o* and *e*.[11] The sound is striking, and we may translate, "the deceiver deceives and the spoiler spoils." These four words describe the powerful and oppressive rule of the Babylonians. In the first two we have a reflection upon the stratagem of war and in the second two upon the nature of the conqueror. It is this situation that calls for correction. Hence, a command must be given to the nation that is to overthrow Israel's oppressor. In Hebrew the words of the command to Elam form an alliteration, "go up, Elam." It may be noted that the command "go up" is also used of attack upon Jerusalem itself (cf. 7:1). Later writers spoke of Persia, but Isaiah mentions Elam, for in his day such a designation would be better understood by the Jews (cf. Gen. 10:22; 14:1, 9; Isa. 11:11; 22:6). Elam takes a place of precedence even over Media, which had already been mentioned in 13:17. Elam is to invade and the Medes to besiege. In vision, Isaiah lays a command upon these two foes who are to fulfill the purpose of God in attacking Babylon and bringing about her downfall. Almost imperceptibly the language changes to the first person, with the Lord as speaker. Far and wide Babylon and her oppressions had caused sighing. God, however, will bring these sighings of captive peoples to a close, for He will permit the Elamites and Medes to attack Babylon. With her downfall the earth again comes to rest, and the sighing which she had caused now ceases.

The reader should note the grandeur and majesty of this verse,

---

[10] Lindblom (*Prophecy in Ancient Israel*, Oxford, 1962, pp. 129ff., 198) labels this passage a dramatic vision and thinks that it offers an example of the phenomenon known to psychologists as the secondary or split personality.

[11] *habbógēd bógēd weḥaššōdēd šōdēd.* The perpendicular line after *bógēd* is *Paseq*, which separates two similar words. That after *šōdēd, however*, is the disjunctive accent *Legarmeh*. Note that the accent of *tzûrî* is *Milra;* usually, however, when the imper. of *Ayin-waw* verbs has an afformative, it is *Milel.*

as well as its strong dramatic effect. First there is a statement as to the character of the vision. Then in succinct form follows a description of the oppressor of God's people. Even the mention of this oppressor is apparently sufficient to cause the prophet to command Elam and Persia to set themselves against him. Lastly, the sovereign purposes of God are carried out, and the sighing which the enemy has caused ceases, for God acts.

3 The result which this vision produces upon the prophet is clearly stated. He begins with a connecting word, "wherefore," by which he refers not alone to the announcement of the downfall of Babylon, but to the entire contents of the preceding verse, the whole vision itself and all that it portended. This consideration is a sufficient answer to those who say that Isaiah would not be moved by the downfall of Babylon. Isaiah was moved, not merely by the announcement of that downfall, but by the entire "hard" nature of the vision. He was witnessing fearful things in the history of redemption, and these were sufficient to cause him to become agitated. The violent agitation which the impression of the vision produced upon him enables us to conclude how fearful the vision must have been. In the recording of the prophet's emotional response there is a didactic purpose, for the writing down of his emotions enables us to comprehend the severity of the vision. These emotions, in other words, give a heightening effect to the vision and the message. The loins were regarded as the seat of the intimate affections, and the heart that of the intellectual faculty. What filled Isaiah's loins was the pain of cramps. The word suggests turning and writhing.[12] A seizure had come upon the prophet, and the pangs such as a travailing woman has are his. The comparison is a strange one, characteristic of Isaiah, for the phrase occurs only in his prophecy.

From this it appears that the prophet experienced deep emotion not merely over his own people, but even over the enemy. He was a man of tender compassion, and the news that stark events were to overcome the world brings upon him painful anguish. The hearing of this message causes him to be bent over in pain,[13] and the

---

12 Cf. Nah. 2:11. The word may be rendered *anguish*.

13 Lit., *I am bent, bowed down, twisted.* Cf. Ps. 38:7. Dillmann takes the word in the sense, *I am dizzy, giddy, stagger (mir schwindelt;* cf. 19:14) . The context suggests that the prophet is deeply disconcerted. König, *bin ich wie verrückt;* Penna, *sono troppo sconvolto per udirlo.* B interpreted the root as meaning *do wrong.*

seeing of the vision leaves him terrified. The clue to such a reaction is found in the word "hard" of the second verse. This was a hard vision, for it had to do with the downfall of the power which had sought to destroy the kingdom of God by means of oppressing Judah. In His providence God permitted that nation to continue for a time. The time had come, however, for a change. Babylon must go that the kingdom of God may continue. Momentous issues are at stake which involve the people of God. The sighing which the oppressor had caused will cease. This was truly a vision that would affect anyone; how much more the one to whom it was given! Isaiah is taken up with feeling, as it were, into the message which he also has the responsibility to proclaim.

4 The description of the prophet's emotions continues. Like Joseph wandering in the field, not knowing where he was going, so the heart of the prophet wandered about (cf. Gen. 37:15). It was an erring heart, not that it strayed in the way of sin (Ps. 95:10), but in that it was not acting as a heart should. It was feverish and beating rapidly. Something of this nature seems to be the thought of the text, rather than the idea that Isaiah's heart was troubled because he could not understand the religious nature of the situation. As a result of the vision, shuddering,[14] by which the prophet means a general shaking and trembling of the body, has disturbed and terrified Isaiah.[15] The first clause of the verse is chiastically arranged: verb-subject-subject-verb. We may render, "There has wandered my heart-shudderings, they have terrified me."
The second main clause states that the time of evening had become a time of trembling. It was the twilight in which he ordinarily found pleasure,[16] with relaxation from the burdens of the

---

The preposition *Mem* is therefore causal: "I am bent over because of hearing," not "I am too bent over to hear." וילדה; in a near open syllable, when no distant open syllable with a short vowel precedes, a *u* or *i* vowel may drop to *Shᵉwa*. In pause, however, the vowel remains; hence the *Tzere* in the present form.

14 Cf. Job 21:6; Ps. 55:6; Ezra 7:18.

15 בעתתני —*has filled me with terror.* B βαπτίζει. The *Ḥireq* under *Beth* stands in a distant opened syllable. A syllable closing with *Ayin* which (inasmuch as *Ayin* will not take *Dagesh*) becomes opened, usually does not change its vowel. Inasmuch as a vowel now stands in a distant opened syllable (i.e., two places from the accent), a *Meteg* is inserted.

16 Driver (*Von Ugarit nach Qumran*, 1958, p. 44) appeals to Ar. *nasafa* and interprets *nešep* as "faintest suspicion, trace"; *my faintest wish has been turned into anxiety for me.* This is questionable.

day and time for meditation and rest. No longer, however, was the
evening a pleasure, for God had changed it to a time of shuddering
and dread. It may have been that in the evening the vision had
come to the prophet, and because of the vision, an evening could
no longer be regarded as a time of pleasure. Whether this be so or
not is difficult to say. Possibly Isaiah merely means that the evening
could no longer be for him a period of pleasure, because the terror
of the vision continued ever with him, thus changing the evening
time into one of shuddering terror.

5 In contrast to the agitated condition of Isaiah's own heart and
being is the carefree attitude of the Babylonians.[17] The historical
infinitives which the prophet employs lend brevity, rapidity, and
life to the description of the arrogant, worry-free enemy.[18] Isaiah
has already characterized Babylon as a city of luxury (14:11; and
cf. also 47:1, 8). Without actually naming them, the prophet describes those who had oppressed his people as arranging, or setting,
the table for the banquet, a phrase which brings to mind the
opposite expression, "arrange (or prepare) for war." The Babylonians were making preparations, but not the necessary preparations for war. They were preparing for a banquet. The thought of a
sumptuous feast is probably in mind, for Isaiah speaks in the same
language as that in which the Psalmist had addressed God, "Thou
preparest a table before me."

We would render the second phrase, "they set out (or lay over)
the carpet."[19] In Babylon these carpets were elaborately spread
out for feasts, and it is to that custom that Isaiah refers. In two

17 According to Dillmann, v. 5 is not a continuation of the vision, which
concluded in v. 2, but description of the working out of the vision begun in
v. 3. The connecting link between vv. 4 and 5 Dillmann finds in the mention
of the *evening*.

18 These infinitives may be taken as having the force of imperatives, as the
ancient versions do; but more probably they are narrative, and thus form a
striking contrast to the imperatives in 5b. The absence of the conjunction also
lends prominence to the staccato-like character of the description. *"Er schildert
sie uns (Hem. a.), er redet sie an (Hem. b.), ohne sie zu nennen, ohne irgendwie
den Übergang zu vermitteln, ganz angemessen der Kühnheit so mächtig
erregten Affekts"* (Drechsler). Cf. 59:13; Hos. 4:2; and Isa. 22:13; Hos. 10:4.

19 Lit., *they lay out the carpet;* not as Vulg. *speculare speculam.* So also
Targ., Syr., etc. In the *Piel tzph* means to overlay (with metal). Hence, the
rendering given above is probably to be preferred. Cf., however, J. Reider,
"Etymological Studies in Biblical Hebrew," *VT*, Vol. 2, 1952, p. 116, who, appealing to the Ar. *dfwt*, renders "Prepare the table, place an abundance of
goods, eat and drink."

words the heart of the banqueting is depicted, "they eat, they drink." This is to be the occupation of the Babylonians when the enemy is coming; and the description is true to fact, for on the night in which the city was taken, the Babylonians, as Daniel informs us, were engaged in banqueting.[20]

Suddenly the tone changes: "Arise," cries the prophet, for now the moment of crisis has come; "anoint the shield." The princes are addressed, for they were the ones responsible for the condition of the nation. That the princes were self-confident and unconcerned is shown in that they must be commanded to arise. Different suggestions are made as to why the shield should be anointed, but in all probability it is in order that the arrows that are shot against it or the blows that strike it in one way or another may be averted and may slide off more easily.[21] In the midst of the luxurious banquet comes the cry of alarm. There is effectiveness in Isaiah's manner of statement. In portraying the Babylonians as indulging in the feast he employs infinitives absolute. In arousing them because of the coming enemy, he uses the regular imperative. In the midst of the infinitives the imperative breaks in, just as in the midst of the feasting the cry of alarm intrudes. The prophetic message presents a strange picture, yet one which is consistent with the general scriptural truth that those who live carelessly will find themselves overtaken by the judgment unawares (cf. 5:13; and Jer. 51:39, 57). Isaiah is greatly agitated over the nature of the vision, yet at the same time he acts as a responsible being. To luxury-loving Babylon he attributes a continuance in luxury as though to say, "You have no concern; you believe that you are masters of the world; very well, continue in your feasting, but arise, the enemy is at the gate."

[20] Dan. 5; Jer. 51:39, 57; and cf. also Herodotus i.191 and Xenophon *Cyropaedia* vii.5, 15. The Nabonidus-Cyrus Chronicle does not mention the revelling (cf. *KB*, Vol. 2, pp. 134f.). Whether the prophet is depicting a literal banquet or whether he is merely using figurative language to portray the careless attitude of the Babylonians may be difficult to determine; probably he is prophesying the actual feasting and revelling of the Babylonians. In referring to Dan. 5 as a legendary account Gray is without warrant; cf. R. M. Dougherty, *Nabonidus and Belshazzar*, New Haven, 1929.

[21] Or, that the shields may not cut the flesh of their bearers (Gray); that the leather covering might be protected (Gesenius); to clean the shield from blood and rust (Thenius); to make the shields shine; to protect the shield against dampness (Dillmann). Cf. 2 Sam. 1:21.

6 For thus saith unto me the Sovereign One, Go! cause the watchman to stand: that which he sees let him tell.

7 And should he see cavalry, a pair of horsemen, those who ride the
asses, those who ride camels, then he shall hearken a great hearkening.

8 Then the seer would cry on the watchtower, O Sovereign One,
I am standing always by day, and on my place of watching I am
stationed all the nights.

9 And behold! here! there cometh a rider, a pair of horsemen. And
he answered and said, Fallen, fallen is Babylon, and all the idols
of her gods he has broken to the ground.

10 O my threshing, and the son of my threshing floor! What I have
heard from the Lord of hosts, the God of Israel, I have told you.

6 Isaiah now proceeds to substantiate what he has just said.[22]
Babylon will fall, he reasons, because he has been commanded to
station a watchman to report what he sees, and what he sees
concerns Babylon's downfall. The overthrow of Babylon lies in the
control of the One who possesses all power, and for that reason
Isaiah designates Him *the Sovereign One* (*ᵃdonay*).

Instead of merely predicting the future course· of events, the
prophet is commanded to station a watchman upon the lookout
point who will report what this future course of events is to be. In
so doing he is carrying out a regular prophetic commission, for he
is commanded to "go," and to "cause to stand" (i.e., to station) a
watchman.[23]

In what manner, however, is he to carry out this charge? It is
obvious that he cannot obey the command in a physical or literal
sense. He cannot take some actual spy and place him in a position
where he can see the approaching of the enemy army to attack Babylon. Inasmuch as Babylon is not to fall for many years after
Isaiah's day, it is clear that any watchman whom Isaiah might station could not see the event with physical eyes. The commission
has reference to the realm of vision. Since the publication of Hölscher's great study on prophecy, there has been a tendency to ex-

---

[22] Hence the introductory יכ, for v. 6 justifies what was commanded in 5b.
Dillmann believes that vv. 6ff. are the ground for the certainty of what was
said in vv. 1-5. Hence, they are not a continuation of the prophecy or a further prophecy concerning the end of the battle. But, whereas 6ff. is a ground
for what has previously been declared, it does also contain further prophecy
about the ultimate end of the battle.

[23] *cause a watcher to stand*, i.e., *station a watcher*. The article is used as in
2 Sam. 18:24 and 2 Kings 9:17, to express a single individual (one not yet
known) as present to the mind. Cf. GKC 126 q.

plain the various phenomena connected with the reception of the prophetic message as due to ecstasy.[24] According to this view the prophet was placed in a kind of frenzy in which he could perform different types of actions. In ecstasy then the prophet himself might carry out the commission of the Lord. His spirit was, as it were, divorced from his body and he was placed in a condition in which, to all intents and purposes, he was unconscious of what transpired in the actual world.

We may note, however, in opposition to such an interpretation, that throughout this vision Isaiah acts as a conscious, responsible individual. As he receives the message he is aware of its significance, so much so in fact, that he is deeply grieved for his own people. Nor will it suffice to say that this passage throws light upon the question of a split personality, as though the prophet somehow had the ability to become a second "I" other than his usual "I." Such a conception, if pressed, could bring us close to the realm of superstition and magic which characterized the ancient world.[25] Yet Marti in essence adopts this position when he says that the reference is to the visionary ability of the seer to become another than his usual "I" or heart. He is really a second "I." Zechariah, thinks Marti, also speaks of this second "I," when he mentions "The angel who speaks in me," which Marti interprets as the capability loaned to the prophet to receive God's revelation. This seer, continues Marti, is the eyes which the prophet has in addition to his own.[26]

It is, of course, true that the prophet actually receives a message from the seer; but we must remember that the whole episode actually is vision, and the very mention of a seer may simply be a visionary manner of speaking. Why may not the prophet in vision actually have stationed a second person to represent him as one who would see what was to transpire in Babylon? Inasmuch as the whole is vision, therefore, we are not to seek to identify some particular spot as the one in which the seer is placed. The placing of the seer is but a visionary way of stating that the prophet

24 Gustav Hölscher, *Die Profeten*, Leipzig, 1914.

25 Kissane thinks that this view attributes an extraordinary confusion of thought to the writer and that it goes against the plain meaning of the text. He would not identify the prophet with the watchman any more than Zechariah with the others mentioned in Zech. 1–2. Cf. Isa. 62:6.

26 Marti (*Com. in loc.*) adds, "*Der Prophet zerlegt sich in zwei Persönlichkeiten, die eine, die behähigt ist, Dinge zu schauen, welche der gewöhnliche Mensch nicht sieht, und die andre, die der gewöhnliche Mensch auch besitzt.*"

himself will be informed of what is to occur. In this manner Isaiah introduces an ideal watchman and has him report what he will see. We need not therefore maintain that the prophet actually divides himself into two persons, or that there is any suggestion of a split personality. The announcement which the visionary sentinel makes merely reveals how much Isaiah himself actually knows of the situation. Habakkuk was later to speak in somewhat similar vein: "I will stand upon my watch, and set me upon the tower, and will watch to see what he will say unto me, and what I shall answer when I am reproved" (Hab. 2:1).

7 Many take this verse as a mere recital of what the seer actually beheld. Possibly, however, we should render the first verb by the subjunctive, "and should he see."[27] The picture which the watchman will behold is that of the enemy advancing quietly, like a mighty caravan crossing the desert. In this caravan there are to be found battle wagons.[28] A yoke of horseback riders is also mentioned,[29] as well as a group of riders of asses and a group of camel riders. Penna thinks that the picture is merely that of an ordinary caravan crossing the desert, and not the picture of an army. The riders were simple travellers who would propagate the information concerning Babylon. In opposition to this, however, is the fact that the description given is too similar to that of the Persian army to apply merely to a band of travellers. The asses and camels, for example, were probably not used merely to carry the baggage and impedimenta of the army, but may also have been brought into the battle itself for the purpose of throwing the enemy into confusion. It is also quite possible that the picture here given is that of the army advancing two by two in the manner described by Xenophon.[30] There is an air of mystery about the scene. We are not told explicitly whence the army came or whither it is going. When the seer beholds this sight, he is to listen attentively, *with a great hearkening*, for the marching of this strange silent army across a great waste is an action filled with significance. The luxury-

27 The perf. with *waw* consecutive expresses a hypothetical occurrence in the future, *and should he see*. B is incorrect, καὶ εἶδον; Aq καὶ ὅσα ὄψεται is better. The apodosis is expressed by the last verb of the verse, lit., *he will attend an attentiveness, abundance of attentiveness.*

28 רכב is here collective. The word denotes a chariot, and in particular, *war chariots* (Isa. 43:17; Jer. 46:9).

29 *pā-rā-šîm.* Riders on horseback, cf. Ar. *fā-ris.*

30 *Cyropaedia* i.6, 10; iv.3ff.; vi.1, 28; vii.4, 17. Note also Strabo xv.2; Herodotus i.80; iv.129; Livy xxxvii.40.

loving city is about to be overthrown. If the seer will listen attentively, he will hear a message of tremendous importance.

8 In this and the next verse the fulfillment of the command is given. If the watcher should see such an army as that described in verse 7 (and, of course, he will see it), then he is to announce what he has seen. The Masoretic text should be translated, "and he cried, 'a lion.'" This rendering presents difficulties, and different explanations have been adopted.[31] It has been suggested, for example, that the mention of the lion shows the world-shaking significance of the events portrayed. It has also been held that the prophet now loses all patience and growls like a lion, or that the watchman merely announces that he sees a lion, with which word he describes the invader. With respect to this latter view Duhm remarks that the watchman sees not lions but donkeys. If the word is not taken as the object, it is generally understood in an adverbial sense and is somehow intended to indicate the manner of the watchman's seeing. Although some commentators feel that this last is not a possible construction, there is no grammatical objection to it.

The expression, however, is difficult; and none of the attempted explanations, valiant though they be, really satisfies. Since the discovery of the first Dead Sea manuscript of Isaiah another interpretation has found favor. That manuscript merely reads, "and the seer cried." This reading at once removes all difficulty, although it surely seems to be an easy solution. It may be the correct reading, and is adopted in the translation given above.

At any rate, what we have in this verse is the response of the watchman. He expresses in his cry the constancy with which he carries out his task. He addresses *my lord*. To whom, however, does he make reference? Is he speaking to Isaiah or to God Himself?

31 B και κάγεσον Ουριαν, Aq λεοντα, S λεαιναν, but T αφιηλ; Vulg. *et clamavit leo*. Gesenius takes the word adverbially, *like a lion* (cf. 51:12; 62:5), and points to Rev. 10:3. So also Ibn Ezra; Dillmann, "*mit Löwenstimme.*" König, "*Ein Löwe,*" regarding it as a cry from the language of the shepherd. Hence he rejects the "I see" of Guthe, Condanim, and Gray, the "see!" of Duhm and Feldmann, "the Seer" of Haller, "my ears" of Dillmann-Kittel, the "aha" of Ehrlich. The Targ. reads, "The Prophet said, etc." The reading of 1Q is simple, but it does not explain the presence of the difficult form *'aryēh*. It is possible that the word means, "man of Yahweh," the syllable *'ar* being the Hurrian *ari* (belonging to), or the Ug. *ari*. The whole might then be rendered "and the man of Yahweh cried." Cf. also F. Buhl, *ZAW*, Vol. 8, 1888, pp. 157-164, and Young, *My Servants the Prophets*, 1955, pp. 117-119.

The answer is perhaps difficult to discover. We may regard the watchman as giving a report to Isaiah himself. Should he see the army approaching, he would cry out to the one who had stationed him, namely, Isaiah. On the other hand, it may be that we are not to press the details, and we can simply regard the cry of the watchman as in effect the announcement of Isaiah himself calling out to God and announcing the approach of the enemy. The language is graphic, and emphasis is placed upon the watchman and his watchtower. "Upon the watchtower, O my lord, I (and the word is emphasized) am standing always by day." There is no doubt about the accuracy of the report, for it is a vigilant watchman who makes it. Even in the nighttime the watchman is vigilant, for he completes his sentence with the emphatic declaration, "and upon my place of watch I (again emphatic) am standing all the nights (i.e., every night)." The objection to the genuineness of this verse that if the seer were watching all the day and all the night he would have no time for rest, cannot be taken seriously. It is not an actual watchman of which the passage speaks, but merely a visionary experience; and the watchman is said to be always on the alert merely to emphasize the fact that the message he declares is a true one.

9 How are we to construe this verse in relation to what precedes? Is it a continuation of the watchman's report, or is it a declaration upon the part of God or of Isaiah? Perhaps one cannot be positive, although we may well regard it as a continuation of the speech of the watchman. Thus, after declaring that he has continually stood upon the place of watching, the watchman proclaims what he sees. That it is an important announcement appears from the introductory word "behold." A literal rendering of the language would be, "behold this, there is coming," i.e., "behold now, there is coming."[32] What first strikes the eyes of the watchman are wagons full of men. They are wagons used for journeying, not merely for transporting goods. A yoke or pair of horsemen is also seen. The procession here described is thought by many to be different from the larger one pictured in verse 7. That was a picture of the enemy army, bent upon the capture of Babylon, whereas this is probably a smaller army bringing back the tidings of victory. On the other hand, the possibility must be admitted that the watchman is describing the same army, but does not feel the

32 זה is an enclitic; cf. 1 Kings 19:5; Song of Sol. 2:8, 9.

need for repeating his description in every detail. On this latter view, which is probably correct, the watchman merely sees the army victorious after the fall of Babylon.

We need not assume that the actual announcement of Babylon's fall was made by a leader of the army. It may simply be that the watchman himself, answering to the circumstances about him, proclaimed the end of the great enemy of God's people. In a certain sense, what is announced is the basic theme of the entire book of Isaiah. It is the declaration that God has delivered His people from their great foe. It is the prelude to the triumphant messages of consolation found in chapters 40–66. In the days of Isaiah Babylon existed, but the Mesopotamian power was at that time principally manifested in Assyria. Later, however, Babylon's strength was to culminate in bringing about the exile, a calamity so great as to cause the theocracy to cease. From this calamity of the exile deliverance would come through Cyrus, whose army is here prefigured. Babylon, however, was merely the symbol of that greater oppressor of God's people, the spirit of Antichrist, who would do all possible to prevent Christ from coming into the world. In the fall of Babylon we see the triumph of Christ and the assurance that there will be victory and redemption for all His people.

It is well to note the construction of the announcement. Up to this verse there has been more or less a lingering over detail. Now however, everything is told in the quickest order. Stroke after stroke falls, for the victory is complete. Intervening and intermediate details are omitted for the purpose of bringing together the extremes, the beginning and the end. As Alexander remarks, "a masterly stroke which would never have occurred to an inferior writer."

In this description emphasis is placed upon the idols. Duhm claims that the writer has fallen into error in asserting that the idols were broken, inasmuch as Cyrus did not actually oppose the idols.[33] Indeed, Cyrus even issued a proclamation in the name of Marduk. Duhm's criticism, however, does not hold, for the text does not state that Cyrus broke the idols. The subject of the verb is not expressed, but it most likely is God, so that the reference is to the spiritual victory to be accomplished with the downfall of Babylon. Indeed, Delitzsch rightly suggests that the Old Testament here

---

[33] Note *Pataḥ* in *šib-bar*. The verb may be rendered impersonally, *one has broken;* i.e., *are broken*. ". . . so hat sich unser Verf. betreffs der Götterbilder geirrt, die von Cyrus nicht umgestürzt wurden . . ." (Duhm, *Com. in loc.*) .

expresses the spiritual inwardness of the matter in that it is the
Lord who dashes the idols to the ground. What is here predicted is
announced explicitly in Jeremiah 51:47, "Therefore, behold, the
days come, that I will do judgment upon the graven images of
Babylon: and her whole land shall be confounded, and all her
slain shall fall in the midst of her," and again,"Wherefore, behold,
the days come, saith the LORD, that I will do judgment upon her
graven images: and through all her land the wounded shall groan"
(Jer. 51:52). The idols are mentioned, therefore, not so much
because the Persians were averse to them, although such was the
case, but merely to emphasize the fact that with the fall of Babylon
the idols, representatives of the power of evil that opposed the
kingdom of God and its well-being, were completely destroyed. The
power of evil must now express itself in some manner other than
through Babylonian idols.

The report of the watchman is a prelude of the mighty revelations found in the latter chapters of the prophecy, and is intended
for the consolation of the nation. The people had hearkened to
Ahaz, and as a consequence the Mesopotamian power had been
brought upon them. Into its hands they were to be swept, and the
kingdom of God would all but be wiped from the face of the earth.
To those, however, who placed their trust in Immanuel, the
Mighty God, the rootshoot from Jesse's stump, there would come
the glorious news of deliverance: "And after these things I saw
another angel come down from heaven, having great power; and the
earth was lightened with his glory. And he cried mightily with a
strong voice, saying, Babylon the great is fallen, is fallen, and is
become the habitation of devils, and the hold of every foul spirit,
and a cage of every unclean and hateful bird" (Rev. 18:1, 2).

10 Speaking in the Name of the Lord, the prophet now goes to
the heart of the matter. All that had been said about Babylon had
been for Israel's benefit. Babylon had grown in strength and power, while oppressed Israel had suffered. In one word the prophet
gives utterance to his love and compassion for his nation. "My
threshing,"[34] he cries. The word represents crushing oppression,
and the suffix lends a tenderness to the cry. Oppression had come,

---

34 מדֻשָׁתִי—*that which is threshed.* As it stands the vowel in the distant open
syllable is defectively written; note the *Meteg.* Cf. Mic. 4:13; Hab. 3:12; Amos
1:3; Isa. 41:15; Jer. 51:33. The address with the suffix, as has often been noted,
gives to the whole a particular character of loving tenderness.

not at the hands of God, but at the hands of others. The nation had been threshed, yet was still God's people. The expression is laconic, yet, as Duhm comments, is more effective than whole pages of lamentation.

Parallel to the first cry is a second, "the son of my threshing floor." The floor belongs to the Lord, and the son of that floor is the grain which has been threshed thereupon. In God's providence He has permitted Babylon to thresh Israel, so that Israel, having been threshed completely, is now like the corn that has come from the floor. Babylon is thus seen to be the instrument of the threshing wrath of God. When, however, the storms of wrath are blackest and the clouds of judgment hang heaviest, the rays of deliverance appear. "What I have heard," declares the prophet, "that have I declared unto you." There is to come a deliverance. Babylon, the oppressing instrument of threshing, is to fall, and there will be a freedom for those that were threshed to grain.

SPECIAL NOTE

The first great Babylonian prophecy was that of 13:1—14:27. Like that prophecy this one also places us in the middle of the situation. Compare 13:2 with 21:1b. The significant thought of the passage is then stated. In 13:3 it is, "I have commanded my sanctified ones," and in 21:2 it is, "the deceiver deceives and the spoiler spoils." There are other comparisons between the two chapters which are worth making. A similarity of phraseology in the description of the coming of the enemy may be noted in 13:5 and 21:1b. The following comparisons should also be made: 13:2, 3, 17a with 21:2b; 13:6-8 with 21:3, 4; 13: 8 y*hilun with 21:3 halhalah; 13:7b with 21:4a; 13:11 with 21:2b; and 14:1, 2 with 21:10.

There is also a connection with following prophecies. 21:1b may be compared with 41:2, 3 and 45:1-3. The kernel of much that is developed later is found in chapter 21. 21:10, for example, contains the roots of the thoughts of comfort that are developed in 40:27-31; 41:8-13, 14-16. 21:10 is the first of the references to the Lord's destroying the idols of the enemy nation, Babylon; cf. 41:21-29. The words "Lord of hosts" found in 21:10 point forward to the exalted doctrine of God expressed in 40:12-16, 17-26, etc. It may be said that 21:1-10 carries us a step beyond ch. 13, developing the doctrine concerning Babylon, and is closer to the great prophecies of 40—66.

Later prophets reflect upon the language of 21:1-10. 21:3 may be compared with Nahum 2:11b; 21:6, 8 with Hab. 2:1; 21:9b with Jer. 51:8; 21:10 with Jer. 50:33, 34 and 51:33; 21:9b with 50:2, 38; 51:8, 47, 52.

75

6. EDOM (21:11-12)

11 The burden of Dumah. Unto me one is calling from Seir, Watchman, what of the night, watchman, what of the night?

12 The watchman saith: The morning cometh and also the night; if ye will inquire, inquire; return, come.

11 That the dawn of salvation will come is certain. Before the day breaks, however, there will be a long night of encroaching gloom. To show how all-embracing this gloom is, the prophet takes one example, and points out that even Edom will be affected. In the designation of his oracle he uses a more or less cryptic word, Dumah, by means of which he calls attention both to Edom (for the similarity in sound cannot be overlooked), and also to the stillness of death. A night like the night of death has come over the land; the name is symbolical, for Dumah means "stillness," and the allusion is to the deep utter silence of the dead. Edom, therefore, is the land of stillness, the land of the dead, the land where the stillness of death either has come or is about to come. By removing the *a* sound from the beginning of the word (*A-dom*) and placing it at the end (*dum-A*), Isaiah makes the very name Edom become a sign of Edom's future fate. The reference is thus seen to be cryptic, like the headings in verses 1 and 13, and 22:1.[35]

In vision, Isaiah hears voices which cry unto him from Seir.[36] He alone can give information concerning the outcome of the terrifying invasion; and in this call to him there is a tacit acknowledgment that he is a representative of the true God, who alone

[35] Hence, we need not assume that there is a reference to some Edomite town (Gray). Nor is *Dumah* a textual corruption of *Edom* (Feldmann); nor should we read with B, *Idumea*. Note that the word does appear in Gen. 25:14; 1 Chron. 1:30 as a personal name. Cf. Josh. 15:52. Four hundred kilometers east of Petra there is the oasis of Duma or Dumat al Gandal (cf. Alois Musil, *The Northern Hegaz*, 1926, p. 311). This was known to the ancients as Adumu, and is the oasis Al-Jowf. Gesenius says that Jakut in his dictionary of geographical synonyms mentions a Duma of Iraq and a Syrian Duman, and thinks that the latter, an important point on the boundary of Syria and Iraq, is here intended. Jerome mentions a Duma in Idumea, 20 miles from Eleutheropolis. It is possible, however, that these places may have been named from the present text. Cf. *Biblia e Oriente, Anno 2, fasc. 2*, 1960, p. 46.

[36] *crying*—the subject of the participle is not expressed, a factor which contributes to the aura of mystery surrounding the passage. The *unto me* is in the position of emphasis. "*Zu ihm, der vom Herrn bestellt ist, die Verwaltung der Geschicke der Völker in höherem Auftrage zu handhaben*" (Drechsler).

knows the actual state of world affairs. The voices cry from Seir, and this fact supports the view that in the name Dumah we have a reflection upon Edom.[37] As in a city that sleeps, the watcher of the night would be the only one awake and informed, so in the night of death that was creeping over the earth, Isaiah stood alone as a watchman.

The ordinary translation, "Watchman, what of the night?" does not bring out the full force of the original. We may more accurately render the question, "Watchman,[38] what part of the night is it?"[39] Underlying the question is the thought, "How much of the night has passed, how much more must we endure before the light of morning comes?" As a sick person lying awake through the long, agonizing hours of night cries out to know what the time is and how much of the night has passed, so Edom, feeling the oppression of Assyria, will call out to the prophet to ask him how much longer the oppression must endure. Only Isaiah can answer that question. It is an importunate question, and the importunateness is seen in that the question is repeated. It is the cry of a suffering people. How far spent is the night?

12 In the preceding verse Isaiah himself had been addressed as the watchman. In this verse, the watchman objectifies himself and speaks in the third person, for attention must not be drawn to the speaker but to the message itself, which is one of wondrous significance. The answer is crisp and direct and yet is shrouded with a certain veil of obscurity. "There comes morning and also night," cries the prophet. He puts the verb in the perfect in order to set forth the certainty with which the action it expresses will be accomplished.[40] Isaiah's language is also poetic, for he does not use the definite article either with the words *morning* or *night*.

What, however, is the meaning of the answer? As Isaiah spoke it would seem that darkness or night covered the earth. The shadow of the oppressing Mesopotamian power was spreading over the world, and that shadow shut out the light, bringing with it the

37 I.e., Mount Seir, the mountainous region southwest of the Dead Sea. Deut. 1:44; Gen. 36:20. The designation later applied (as here) to the hill country east of Arabah.

38 Cf. Isa. 52:8; 56:10; 62:6.

39 For the use of מָה cf. Job 5:1; Jer. 44:28; and for the figurative use of *night*, cf. 47:5; 5:30; 8:20ff.; Zeph. 1:15; Amos 5:18; Jer. 15:9.

40 The verb terminates in *Aleph* in place of *He*, so also in 1Q.

77

oppressing darkness of night.[41] Could there be relief from this night? Yes, there would be a morning coming and also a night. But a night is already with Edom. What then does Isaiah mean? Probably he means that there will be a morning with its saving light to those who have a refuge in the Lord, but that a night of destruction will fall upon all others. For them it will be an enduring, eternal night, from which there is no deliverance. There is nothing in this mysterious language to suggest that there will be morning and light for all men.

In support of the interpretation just given we must note the remainder of the verse. The Edomites are told what they are to do. If they wish to know the meaning of the message, they must seek earnestly.[42] In fact, they are actually commanded so to do. One is reminded of the passage in Deuteronomy 4:29, "But if from thence thou shalt seek the LORD thy God, thou shalt find *him,* if thou seek him with all thy heart and with all thy soul." God alone is a sure basis for deliverance, and the Edomites must look for such a sure basis. The last two words of the verse are abrupt: "Return, come." It is as simple as that. "Return," or simply, "turn." In their present condition there is no answer for the Edomites; they must come again in repentance to the Lord, and then they will be heard. At the present time they have no announcement of salvation. The time of deliverance has not yet come; Edom must again inquire and must come again. If she would receive the light of morning she must return, else for her there awaits only the coming of night. In reality the answer amounts to a rejection. For years the Edomites had been oppressors of Judah and hostile to her. If now at this time they come it will merely be to escape the might of Assyria and

---

[41] Tiglath-pileser III had marched against Arabia and made an Idumean king subject to tribute *(Kaus-malaka matu Udumuaa).* Cf. Rogers, *Cuneiform Parallels,* p. 322. Cf. also *ANET,* p. 282.

[42] בעיו —the original *yod* sometimes appears even before vocalic afformatives. Note the same phenomenon in *tib'āyûn* and *'ětāyû.* With respect to *'ětāyû,* note that a *Tzere* has replaced the compound *Shᵉwa,* a phenomenon which usually occurs before gutturals. Cf. also *'ē-pû* in Ex. 16:23. The verb concludes with an *Aleph,* as is sometimes the case with *Lamed-He* verbs. The three imperatives are asyndeta, thus giving greater distinctness to each individual particular. Note that they constitute the apodosis to a clause whose protasis consists of *'im* and the imperfect. Alexander Scheiber *(VT,* Vol. 11, 1961, pp. 455-456) proposes to take *gam* as the *Qal* perf. of a stem appearing in the Mishnah but not in the OT; *the morning came and the night is completed.*

the consequences of oppression; it will not be the coming with a pure heart. The prophecy of Zephaniah 3:9 was not ready to be fulfilled for Edom: "For then will I turn to the people a pure language, that they may all call upon the name of the LORD, to serve him with one consent." Possibly the very shortness of the prophecy is an indication of the rejection of Edom. Edom and Judah had been close, and hence, the shortness of the prophecy is surprising. Possibly for this reason also the superscription is cryptic. Roving bands marauded and finally destroyed Edom, and it became a perpetual Dumah.

7. THE ARABIANS (21:13-17)

13 The burden against Arabia. In the forest in Arabia ye shall lodge, O ye caravans of Dedanim.

14 To meet the thirsty they bring water, the inhabitants of the land of Teima, with his bread they go before the fugitive.

15 For from before the swords they fled, from before a drawn sword; and from before a bended bow and from before the weight of war.

16 For thus saith the Lord unto me, In yet a year like the years of an hireling, then will all the glory of Kedar cease.

17 And the remnant of the number of bows of the mighty man of the children of Kedar will become few, for the LORD the God of Israel hath spoken.

13 Here is an explanation of the answer given to Edom in verse 12. The land would be in such a state that caravans that were able to travel undisturbed in normal conditions and times would now have to leave the main road and lie in hiding among the bushes. The night would creep over Edom and extend even to Arabia. This present oracle is named by a word taken from the context itself (cf. 1 Sam. 1:18, 22).[43] The word *Arabia*, however, does not

43 Isaiah deviates from the principle hitherto employed in this section for forming titles, by naming the oracle after a word taken from the following context; yet this is done in such a way as to designate the object of the prophecy. Drechsler thinks that Isaiah does this here because not all of Arabia is intended, nor an individual tribe, nor the tribes that are named. The object of the following prophecy is not easily stated in a definite expression. In Hebrew the term '*ārab* is always the collective name of the Arabs. Penna would render *steppe*, dry land (33:9; 35:1, 6; 40:3; 41:19; 51:3), although he realizes that '*rābāh* would be more suitable. König, however, rightly remarks that "in the steppe" is not Hebrew (*unhebräisch;* also Duhm, Haller, Fischer).

refer to the entire land, but merely to a part of Arabia; and insofar as the title refers to Arabian tribes, it is a suitable one.

In the title and the following two words the combination of 'r occurs three times. It is strange that the prophet should describe the caravans as spending the night in a forest, for forests are rare in Arabia, if they occur at all. Possibly what the prophet makes reference to is simply the shrub and thicket.[44] In these it would be possible even for a caravan to make its camp and to remain unnoticed and hidden. Such a camp would not be near the main routes of travel, but far removed from them at a safe distance, so that any spies of the enemy, who would probably not know the land well, could not find the fugitives.

The caravans are said to belong to the Dedanim, who are mentioned elsewhere also in connection with Edom and Teima (Jer. 49:8 and Ezek. 25:13). Dedan was a region in Arabia, and its caravans were probably simply ordinary travelling caravans, such as characterized the Arabian desert.[45] The Assyrians first made an invasion into Arabia in 732 and then again under Sargon II in 725.[46] It is interesting to note that Sargon also brought Arabian troops into Samaria. When an invading army was occupying the land, it would be necessary for the caravans which belonged to the Dedanim to travel away from the regular routes, should they wish to proceed in safety. Armed merely with bows, the desert Arabians would be no match against the Assyrians with their long swords, javelins, shields, and composite bows. Nor would their fleet camels serve against well-armed Assyrian cavalry.[47]

[44] Gesenius discusses the etymology of the word, but I agree with Gray in questioning the suitability of rendering *stony ground*.

[45] Scripture speaks of Dedan in connection with Cush or Ethiopia (Gen. 10: 7; 1 Chron. 1:9), and Edom (Gen. 25:3; Jer. 49:8; Ezek. 25:13). Albright identifies it with *'el-'ulā* (*Geschichte und Altes Testament. A. Alt zum siebzigsten Geburtstag*, Tübingen, 1953, pp. 1-12).

[46] Tiglath-pileser III speaks of his depradations in Arabia, and of the queen Šamsi fleeing to the town of Bazu, a place of thirst. Sargon II speaks of crushing the Arabs who live far away in the desert (cf. *ANET*, pp. 284, 286).

[47] A relief from Ashurbanipal's palace at Nineveh (7th cent. B.C.) depicts the infantry and cavalry of Assyria pursuing Arabs fleeing on camelback. On each camel there are two men, one guiding the animal with a stick and the other, a warrior, shooting arrows with a simple bow. An illustration of the relief appears in *Views of the Biblical World*, Israel, 1960, pp. 46f. During the 7th century the Ammonites prospered under Assyrian protection and controlled the lucrative desert caravan trade. Cf. *BA*, Vol. 24, No. 3, 1961, p. 74.

14 There is a true protection in the desert, for the inhabitants of Teima bring water to the thirsty travellers. Teima is to be identified with the present oasis Teima, southeast of Maan. It was here that Nabonidus later spent much of his time while Belshazzar ruled over Babylon. Inasmuch as it was an oasis, Teima would be able to supply that most needed of blessings, namely, water. The language suggests that there was some kind of fixed arrangement, as though caravans travelling in the desert might count on help from the inhabitants of Teima. The subject of the first verb is probably general, and we may render, "To meet the thirsty one water is brought."[48] The mention of Teima shows how far into the desert the scourge of Assyria had reached.[49]

Not only is water brought, but also bread, even bread that belongs to the fugitive. In an unknown wild land the caravans might wander about in uncertainty. Yet the people of Teima will provide for them, bringing the food that they need.

15 These people who wandered about have actually fled, and are even in process of fleeing from before swords. War has come to the land of Arabia, and its black shadows are cast over the country. It is the hour of the powers of darkness, when men were trying to erect a universal kingdom, and the results of their efforts were to inflict misery and suffering. In Arabia, for example, men were dispersed and were fleeing for their lives. The enemy was ready to strike, and the inhabitants of the land to fear. It is a strong contrast. Those who once trusted only in their weapons now fear before swords. Four times in this verse the prophet introduces the phrase *from before*. There was much that the people had to fear. When man unites himself into a powerful organization in order to exist without God, there is good cause for fear. It is no mere imagining, but actual war and its dreadful consequences that inspire fear in the people's hearts. Nor is it merely warfare in general

[48] In 1Q the *Aleph* of the verb appears. The omission of *Aleph*, however, is not unusual. The perfect without כִּי gives the reason for what has just been stated. The subject is general; *tzā-mē'* is a collective.

[49] Teima, even today called Teima, is in the northern Hedjaz, a large oasis, with abundant water supply. Tiglath-pileser III also mentions it. Cf. *ANET*, pp. 283f., 306, 313.

Later Aramaic inscriptions (4th-5th century B.C.) may be noted, *CIS*, ii, 113f. Cooke, *NSI*, pp. 195ff. For a description of the modern oasis, cf. Musil, *The Northern Hegaz*, New York, 1926.

of which Isaiah speaks, but a sword[50] that is extended, given up, abandoned to itself, and allowed to do its worst. Together with the extended sword was a drawn bow, and the entire burden and heaviness that war brings.[51]

16 What is to be the outcome of this flight? Will the caravans escape the ravages of war? The Lord, who is the Sovereign One, has spoken to Isaiah; and what He has said Isaiah now relates.[52] A time has been fixed for the destruction of Arabia. This time is one year, a period exactly reckoned as laborers and employers reckon. The employer sets a definite time for the laborers to work and such a definite period of time will elapse before the military strength of Kedar is taken away. The word Kedar designates the people who are fleeing, for, as we learn from Genesis 25:13, Kedar was a tribe of Ishmaelite descent.[53] Some think that Isaiah now uses the name to represent all of the Arabian tribes generally. This may be; but it may also be that Isaiah simply mentions different tribes, first the Dedanim and now Kedar, for the purpose of showing that the catastrophe in Arabia would be widespread. The rabbis, on the other hand, applied the name Kedar to the Arabians generally. Jeremiah was later to prophesy in similar vein against Kedar. Delitzsch remarks, "When the period fixed by Isaiah for the fulfillment arrived, a second period grew out of it, and one still more remote, inasmuch as a second empire, viz., the Chaldean, grew out of the Assyrian, and inaugurated a second period of judgment for the nations. After a short glimmer of morning, the night set in a second time upon Edom, and a second time upon Arabia."

The reader should not overlook the paronomasia in *kalah kol k'vod*. Indeed, it would be well to read this verse aloud to note the striking and effective character of its sounds.

17 The message is one of sadness. For Kedar there is no hope. The night is to overshadow the land, and light will not appear.

50 The plural, *swords*, lends a certain emphasis.
51 *kōbed* is used of the flame (30:27) ; cf. also 1 Sam. 31:3.
52 כִּי introduces the justification of the previously announced (vv. 13-15) change, namely, that a catastrophe is soon to fall.
53 Some have thought that Kedar was the enemy of the Dedanites just mentioned. But a comparison with 16:13 would render this questionable. Kedar, as Penna states, represents a conquered people. Cf. also 17:3. 1Q reads *three years*, instead of *a year*.

Employing an unusually long row of genitives, Isaiah describes his subject. In contrast is the short verb, "they shall become few."[54] By means of this contrast and this glance at the strength of the weapons of the Arabs Isaiah places emphasis upon the contrast with verse 15.[55] In his forty-ninth chapter Jeremiah takes up the prophecy and applies it to his own time, mentioning both Dedanim and Kedar.

It is difficult to discover the precise fulfillment of this prophecy. It would seem, however, that with the events recorded in chapter twenty there was a step taken toward the fulfillment. More and more the power of Assyria grew, and more and more Edom and Arabia were eclipsed. With the downfall of Babylon, Edom and Arabia sank deeper into the background. Light came to Judah when the Son of God appeared upon earth. Then, indeed, there would have been a morning for Edom; but the morning was not recognized, for an Edomite (Herod the Idumean), rather than seeing the morning, sought to slay all the children of Bethlehem of two years old and under. Thus Edom and Arabia were cast aside, and finally the darkness of Islam covered the Arabian peninsula. It could not have turned out otherwise, for the God of Israel had spoken.

SPECIAL LITERATURE ON CHAPTER TWENTY-ONE

Eduard Sievers: *"Zu Jesajas 21:1-10"* in *Karl Marti Festschrift*, 1925, pp. 262-265.

Israel Eitan: "A Contribution to Isaiah Exegesis," *HUCA*, Vol. 12-13, 1937-1938, pp. 55-88.

Paul Lohmann: *"Das Wächterlied Jes. 21:11-12,"* *ZAW*, Vol. 33, 1913, pp. 20-29. This article seeks to show that originally Isa. 21:11, 12 was a humorous song of the watchers, which the prophet worked over for his purpose.

---

[54] Five members of a series are determined by a concluding gen.; lit., *and the remnant of the number of the bows of the mighty men of the sons of Kedar.* The pl. verb agrees not with *qē-dār* alone, but with the compound *bᵉnē-qē-dār.* Cf. also Gen. 26:12; Lev. 13:9; 1 Sam. 2:4; 1 Kings 1:41; 17:16; Isa. 2:11; Zech. 8:10; Job 15:20; 21:21; 29:10; 32:7; 38:21.

[55] The *Maqqeph* after *mispar* seems to be incorrect, for the emphasis is not *the number of the bows*, but *the bows of the heroes.* The word number is used in the sense of *all.* Compare 21:16, 17 with 16:13, 14; also 21:13-17 with Jer. 49:8, 28, 30.

A discussion of the "strophic" structure of 21:1-10 may be found in *ZAW*, Vol. 32, 1912, pp. 49-55, 190-198, and Vol. 33, 1913, pp. 262-264.

William Henry Cobb, *JBL*, Vol. 17, 1898, pp. 40-61.

8. Jerusalem as One of the Nations (22:1-14)

1 The burden of the valley of vision. What aileth thee now, that thou art wholly (all of thee) gone up on the roofs?
2 With shoutings full, O noisy city, a rejoicing village, thy slain, not are they slain with the sword and not dead in battle.
3 All thy princes have fled together, without the bow they were bound; all that were found of thee have been bound together; they have fled from afar.
4 Wherefore I said, Look away from me, I am bitter (or, let me be bitter) in weeping; do not be urgent in comforting me for the desolation of the daughter of my people.

1 In the preceding chapter Isaiah uttered three oracles dealing with Babylon, Edom, and Arabia. To these he now joins a fourth, which shares in common with the three preceding the thought of an oncoming storm. The storm is introduced in 21:1 as coming from a terrible land. In the oracle about Dumah, its effects are seen to have made themselves felt in Edom, and then again in Arabia. Now a storm bursts over the valley of vision. What, however, is intended by the phrase, "valley of vision?" Some wish to emend the text so as to read, "valley of Hinnom," which would not be satisfactory, for the subsequent verses suggest that all Jerusalem is in view. A similar type of heading also occurs in 29:1 where Jerusalem is designated "Ariel," the subsequent verses showing clearly that Jerusalem is intended. This would support the position that in the present instance the reference is to the city in its entirety rather than to one particular valley thereof.

If, however, the reference is to Jerusalem, why is the city designated a valley?[1] Jerusalem is herself surrounded by hills (Ps.

---

[1] 1Q omits *Aleph*, but the *Aleph* as a third radical often preserves the diphthong, which appears here in the construct. This is also attested by the conjunctive *Munaḥ*. The word is found in the abs. *gay'*, e.g., Num. 21:20, and in pause, 1 Chron. 4:39; without *Aleph*, Deut. 34:6. In Zech. 14:4 *gēy'* appears to be an abs., like *lēl* in 21:11 and 40:4, where the diphthong seems not to be preserved. The const. s. follows the regular rules for the diphthong, and

85

125:2) and is also set upon a hill; nevertheless, in contrast to the mountains round about, it may be regarded as a valley. Particularly is this true with respect to the Mount of Olives, from whose summit one may look down upon Jerusalem as it were into a valley (cf. Jer. 21:13). Implied in the designation may also be the thought that as the mountains surround a valley and exclude its inhabitants from the world round about, so the dwellers in Jerusalem were in a valley, shut off from the world, separated so that they might not look for help to the world around, but only upward to God.

We must not overlook the fact that there is a similarity between Isaiah's message to Jerusalem and that to Babylon in 21:1-10. In each case the designation in the title points to the actual condition of the nation in question in contrast to what that nation itself pretended to be. Babylon is called a "desert of the sea," whereas she claimed to be a rich and luxurious growth, revelling in her might. Jerusalem is but a valley, whereas she herself did not act like the inhabitants of a valley, but looked out beyond her horizon to the mighty arm of flesh that was appearing in the presence of the Assyrian king. In each instance, therefore, the title implies a contrast with the actual condition of the city or nation in question.

Jerusalem is the valley of vision, for it is the place where revelation is given. Although it is surrounded by mountains and shut apart from the world, nevertheless in this valley the light of heaven fell, and the words of God were made known. Here in the Temple was the dwelling place of God, and here the abode of His prophets, the men who proclaimed His words to the nation. There is no specific reference to Isaiah's house or even to that part of the city in which the prophet dwelt, but rather simply a general contrast with the thought that revelation usually comes from the height. Revelation does indeed come from on high (Isa. 32:15), but Isaiah's purpose at this particular point is simply to identify the valley as the place where revelation is to be found.

For what reason, however, is Jerusalem included in the tetralogy of oracles? Is it not incongruous to find a list of oracles dealing with Babylon, Dumah, Arabia, and then Jerusalem? Are not the

---

we have both *gēy'* and *gēy*. The gen., *vision*, denotes an attribute that characterizes the const.; *valley of vision* is the valley distinguished as the one where visions are received.

first three heathen lands, whereas the last is the dwelling place of God? The tetralogy begins with the city of worldly power, includes two districts which have felt the effects of that worldly power, and then concludes with the city of the living God. The inclusion of Jerusalem in such a list, however, is really not incongruous, for Jerusalem has looked to flesh; she has placed her confidence not in the living God whose prophets dwell within her walls, but in that mighty power of man which finally came to supreme expression in the empire whose name heads the tetralogy. For this reason Jerusalem has in effect become like the worldly powers; and she, too, must be included in the list of oracles. As an example of the manner in which Jerusalem has become occupied with the flesh Isaiah includes the case of one of her officials, Shebna (vv. 18ff.).

The message begins with a question of astonishment, "What. . .to thee?" which we must render in English, *What is the matter with thee?* or *What ails thee?* Drechsler would restrict the force of the question to surprise and astonishment. Probably, however, an implied rebuke is also found (cf. 3:15 and 22:16), as well as disapprobation. As Amos broke in at Bethel among the sinful inhabitants of the northern kingdom (cf. Amos 7), so Isaiah's sudden appearance may have seemed disconcerting to the revellers in Jerusalem.[2]

He speaks to the city as though it were a single individual. "Thou," he says, "all of thee,[3] hast gone up upon the roofs." To what, however, is the reference? Several answers have been given to this question. (*a*) Fischer suggests that after the fall of Samaria in 722 B.C., the Assyrian army may unexpectedly have come to Jerusalem to demand tribute and found Jerusalem unprepared. Sargon may have had to return to Nineveh, and the army therefore had quickly to be withdrawn. As a consequence the people ascended their roofs to rejoice. Fischer therefore would date the oracle in 722-721 B.C. All of this, however, is mere supposition. We know of no such invasion of Sargon. Furthermore, the content of the oracle implies a siege of far more serious nature.

(*b*) Penna and others find the reference in the later attack of Sennacherib (701 B.C.), and take the passage not as narrative

2 *then*—serves to lend vividness to the question. Sometimes *'ēpoh* is placed after the first interrogatory word, but here after the entire question.

3 *kullāk*—the Qametz may indicate a kind of secondary pause, giving an assonance with *lāk*.

THE BOOK OF ISAIAH

but as prophecy. In answer to this position, however, it should be noted that the prophet does not agree with the rejoicing of the people, whereas in actual fact he did support Hezekiah as over against Sennacherib. It should also be noted that the coming of Sennacherib was not unexpected, and that the city was well prepared for his arrival (cf. 2 Chron. 32:1-5).

(c) The interpretation herein adopted is that the reference is to the final destruction of Jerusalem under Babylon. In this tetralogy Jerusalem and Babylon have both been included. Jerusalem has in reality appealed to Babylon; unto Babylon she shall go. The time is desperate; Jerusalem can hold out no longer (2 Kings 25:4; Jer. 52:7). For a year and a half the city has been attacked. Possibly Zedekiah has fled, and there is a lull in the fighting. The people ascend the housetops to see more clearly what has happened; this action is what Isaiah does not approve. The entire passage, then, is to be taken as predictive prophecy and not the narrative of events that are already past, or that are in the near future. In a certain sense the prophet acts like an uncertain individual. What is the point, he asks, in the midst of such a trying time, to ascend the roofs in rejoicing, as though the danger were completely past? At the same time, with this question, he plunges us immediately into the heart of things.[4]

There are, however, objections to referring the events to the destruction under Nebuchadnezzar. If it applies to his time, so runs the objection, how are we to explain the later references to Shebna, and the measures described in verses 9-11 which seem to apply to Hezekiah?

In each of the suggested indentifications mentioned above there is difficulty. Indeed it appears practically impossible to adopt an interpretation that is free of difficulty. Nevertheless, the third view mentioned has the most to commend it. In this chapter it is true there are clear references to events that fall in the days of the approach of Sennacherib. The description given in verses 9-11, for example, seems to set forth just those measures that according to 2 Chronicles 32:3-5 Hezekiah adopted. At the same time there are difficulties in restricting the prophecy to the time of Sennacherib.

4 The astral cult was conducted on the roof (cf. 2 Kings 23:12a; Jer. 19:13; Zeph. 1:5a). The Babylonians designated the roof as the place of offering. Some have assumed that the people ascended the roofs to watch the country people flee to the city for safety, or in curiosity to watch the approach of the enemy.

It seems best to interpret the passage in a generic sense, as a description of the oncoming of an enemey and of the terrible worldliness and paganism found in the city of Jerusalem when that enemy comes. That enemy is really Babylon. In appealing to Tiglath-pileser, Ahaz had in reality appealed to the spirit of Babylon, for the Assyrian king was the first great representative of that human power represented in Daniel's head of gold and in the lion with eagles' wings (Dan. 2 and 7). In the present chapter we are given certain phases of the warfare which the Mesopotamian power brought against the city of God. It was a necessary warfare, for the city must be purged of its pagan elements. Such warfare may have led to temporary conversions and returns to the Lord, as in the case of Hezekiah. It did not, however, produce any lasting change in the city; and finally the Babylonian power came in the person of Nebuchadnezzar. When the city of God seeks help from the city of paganism, she will soon be controlled by the city of paganism. Verses 2 and 3 depict the final outcome of this struggle, whereas some of the succeeding verses picture certain previous phases thereof. In reality, however, it is a generic prophecy that we have before us; and it is this explanation that best accounts for references to various phases of the long struggle between the city of peace and light and the city of paganism and darkness, a struggle that saw the climax of its first great stage in the deportation of the inhabitants of Jerusalem to Babylonia.

2 Isaiah now gives a reason for the action depicted in the preceding verse. *In respect to shoutings full*—The word *shoutings* is emphatic, and is to be regarded as an accusative of specification.[5] It signifies blustering and crying noises which are powerful and strong. These may be sounds caused by the falling of the house walls, but more likely they are the excited cries of the populace, which filled the city with its shouts and noises: *a noisy city*. With these words the prophet may actually be addressing the city.[6] The force of the Hebrew word might best be expressed in English by *blustering*.[7] It is a word that pictures a multitude of blustering

---

[5] The verb of *copiae* is preceded by an acc., placed first for the sake of emphasis; lit., *with respect to shoutings she is full*.

[6] Some would take *city* as a vocative, the article being omitted, since the noun has already been defined by a preceding accusative. This is not certain, however.

[7] *hōmiyyāh* (cf. 17:6), omitted in B. The form is a part. f. s., although the

people who love life and want to keep their life. Isaiah had earlier characterized a multitude of people when he said that sheol had opened her mouth to receive them (5:14).

a city rejoicing—If the city is filled with noises and is blustering, how can it be called joyous? Possibly the description refers to the reckless indifference and gaiety that characterized the city even at the time that it was full of noise. Amid the blustering and shouting there is abandonment. People are gay, for they think that all danger is past. Zephaniah, in describing Nineveh, uses the same term; and his usage is enlightening. "This *is* the rejoicing city, that dwelt carelessly, that said in her heart, I *am,* and *there is* none beside me." It is a joyous city; but to rejoice at this time is to act foolishly, not knowing the true state of affairs.

After the threefold description, Isaiah deliberately addresses the city, and this he does by labelling the inhabitants *slain men.* The city possesses slain men, but they are not slain in battle by the sword.[8] Death comes to them by pestilence and hunger. Not to be slain by the sword would involve exposure to a more fearful death. *"They that* be slain with the sword are better than *they that* be slain with hunger; for these pine away, stricken through for *want* of the fruits of the field"* (Lam. 4:9). To be slain by the sword is to be slain in battle, and the prophet makes it expressly clear that the men of Jerusalem do not meet death in battle. At the same time the terrible death that overcomes them was due to war; it was one of war's fearful consequences. This description does actually apply to the last days of Jerusalem. "And on the ninth day of the fourth month the famine prevailed in the city, and there was no bread for the people of the land" (2 Kings 25:3; cf. also Jer. 52:6 and Lam. 1:19, 20; 2:12, 19; 4:3-5, 9, 10; 5:10). Such a tragic happening had early been prophesied, "I will send the pestilence among you; and ye shall be delivered into the hand of the enemy. *And* when I have broken the staff of your bread, etc." (Lev. 26:25; cf. also 26:29). The prediction is repeated in Deuteronomy (cf. 28:21, 48 and especially vv. 52ff.).

---

form *ho-mah* occurs in 1 Kings 1:41. Cf. Ar. *hamhama, to murmur* and Egy. *hmhm, to roar.*

8 *not—lô'* negatives a noun clause instead of *'ayin,* and is stronger; *not are they slain by the sword.* The gen. following the const. expresses the source from which the slaying comes.

3 The description continues with two more declarative sentences, each consisting of two parts. Having spoken of the dead generally, Isaiah now mentions the princes, by which he may have in mind the judges in particular[9] (1:10; 3:6ff.). "They do not fight bravely," he asserts, "but have fled together." The two parts of the verse are similarly constructed. Each begins with the word "all" followed by a noun with the feminine suffix (-ayik). Then comes a verb in the plural and an adverb. Two secondary sentences follow, each beginning with the letter Mem (i.e., m), and concluding with a verb in the perfect plural.

Although they should have been the first to defend the people, these rulers fled and were bound as prisoners, even though they had not been struck by the bow of war.[10] The verb that Isaiah here applies to the princes was later used of the "binding" of king Zedekiah (2 Kings 25:7).[11] Not only are the princes bound, but all who are found that belong to the city (lit., all thy found ones) suffer the same fate.[12] None is successful in escaping. Again Isaiah's language points to the statement made in 2 Kings 25:19, where the writer speaks of "the people of the land *that* were found in the city." It is a picture of gloom. The city is no longer glorious; her inhabitants die of famine, and her rulers, who should take measures to defend her and abide with her to the last, flee away, even to a distance; and yet all of them are captured and bound. Thus, the theocracy goes down in disgrace. The very members of the holy kingdom have betrayed that kingdom, and the people of the world take them captive and bind them. Yet the victory is still with the Lord; for from the destroyed theocracy, the first master stroke accomplished by the kingdom of this world, there is in time to arise the kingdom of God, when the dispersed of the theocracy will hear the preaching of the Gospel.

4 Inasmuch as this his own city is destroyed, Isaiah breaks out in

---

9 It is tempting to compare the Ar. *'al-qâ-dî*. Cf. Josh. 10:24; Judg. 11:6, 11.

10 Lit., *from the bow*—the prep. has the force, *without*, i.e. *(without one needing to bend a bow against them) they were made prisoners*. Torczyner (*Marti Festschrift*, p. 276) proposes to change the positions of *'srû* and *brḥû*, placing *they have fled* at the conclusion of 3a, and *they were bound* at the conclusion of 3b.

11 Actually אסר means *to be taken prisoner;* cf. Gen. 42:16; 40:3, 5.

12 The second *all* is a climax, *even all*. A certain gradation appears between *princes* and *all who are found*.

91

grief and lamentation. He had grieved over Moab (16:11) and even Babylon (21:3); hence, his sorrow over the fall of Jerusalem is the more to be expected. He acts as though some had tried to comfort him, and to these he responds.[13] The verb is in the past, *I said*, for the whole picture is vividly before the mind of the prophet. In reality, he is depicting the future, and employs this graphic means to express his own poignancy over the downfall that surely will come to Jerusalem. To so great an extent was Isaiah affected that apparently his weeping was not secret. His action showed that he had a true understanding of the theocracy. Grief came to him not because he thought the purposes of God were overthrown, but because the inhabitants of Jerusalem, who should have acted as a holy priesthood, had, by their sin and generally careless attitude, themselves been the cause of the city's downfall. When calamity comes to the Church every Christian must feel that calamity as though it were his own. The hymn writer has accurately stated the matter:

For her my tears shall fall,
For her my prayers ascend;
To her my cares and toils be given,
Till toils and cares shall end.

Such a public manifestation of grief would make clear that the situation was extremely serious and that the words of the prophet were not to be taken lightly. It was not a time for looking at the prophet. As Job in milder tones had asked, "How long wilt thou not look away from me?" so Isaiah, using the same verb, commands, "Look away from me."[14] No human comfort could avail, for Isaiah knew well the deep truth which he later penned, "In all their affliction he was afflicted" (Isa. 63:9). The blow by which Jerusalem fell was aimed at God; the grief felt by a devoted servant of God was a grief which God Himself shared. It was a time when the prophet must be bitter in weeping. Not to be bitter in weeping would be to ignore the import of what was happening. "Do not," says Isaiah, therefore, "be urgent in consoling me." This is not the time for consolation. He who later was to command that God's

13 König suggests that the prophet addresses those about him *(die Umgebung).*
14 Šā-'āh means to gaze steadily with interest. Cf. Job 7:19; 14:6. An interesting usage is found in Ex. 5:9. Note also the usage of *'ûtz* in the same context, Ex. 5:13.

people should be comforted (Isa. 40:1) himself now refuses to receive consolation. And he is right. At this time it would be wrong to give consolation. At this time all true servants of the king must break forth into weeping and cry out in lamentation. "For the daughter of my people," explains the prophet, uttering the words of the Lord, "is desolate."[15] In poetical picture language he depicts the nation as a woman to whom desolation has come. It is a tender description. She who is my people is destroyed. If then one should attempt to console the prophet and to turn him from weeping, would he not be performing an act that was not justifiable? How wrong for the women to weep over Christ on His way to the cross, and how wrong to console the prophet, now overcome with grief because Satan has appeared to triumph!

It is well to note the combination here of the concept *comfort* and *my people,* a preparation for the later declaration to give comfort when comfort is truly needed (Isa. 40:1).

> 5 For there is a day of confusion and trampling and perplexity to the Lord, the LORD of hosts in the valley of vision, breaking the wall and crying to the mountain.
> 6 And Elam bare a quiver, with riders, and horsemen, and Kir uncovered the shield.
> 7 And it came to pass that the choice ones of thy valleys were full of riders, and the horsemen, they have surely drawn up toward the gate.

5 Having mentioned his own poignant grief at the desolation of the city, the prophet now gives an explanation. Again, as in 2:11, he begins with the explanatory statement, "For a day..."; and again it is a day which belongs to the Lord, the God of hosts, a day that will bring confusion and trampling and perplexity.[16] It is a

---

15 Lit., *the devastation of the daughter of my people.* The phrase *daughter of my people* ·occurs only here in Isaiah (but cf. *daughter of Zion,* 1:8), and in no other prophet except Jeremiah and Lamentations, in which books it occurs frequently. The force of the phrase is, *the daughter who is my people,* i.e., *my people.*

16 The word *day* need not be repeated for each of the following constructs. By means of the threefold use of the similar sounding genitives, completeness is expressed. If any of these words is deleted, the force of the passage is weakened. The elipsis in the sentence may be filled in with *there will be,* or *it will be.* M. Weippert (*ZAW,* Vol. 73, 1961, pp. 97-99) relates קר to Ug. *qr,* and regards *qrqr* as the related verb. He renders,

> *Im 'Schautale' lärmte es,—*
> *Lärm und Geschrei gegen den Berg.*

day of confusion, such as had been prophesied originally by
Moses (Deut. 28:20). The word translated *confusion* may also
signify disorder and fear (cf. 1 Sam. 5:9,11; Amos 3:9). Trampling
also will characterize that day; but whether the word implies the
trampling of men marching in array or merely a general trampling
due to confusion, is difficult to determine. Lastly, it is a day of
perplexity. The word rendered *perplexity* is a practical synonym of
the first word, and indicates people who go about in uncertainty
without any fixed purpose, incapable of right decision. This had
been the case with Ahaz when he heard of the intention of the
two northern enemies. In itself the word would describe the confusion that might come upon any nation under dire threat of siege.
The three words, taken together, form a significant assonance;
mᵉhumah, mᵉvusah, mᵉvukah.

Such was the day that was to come over Jerusalem. In verses 1-4
the prophet seems to refer to the coming of Nebuchadnezzar and
the final destruction of the city. Does he continue to do so, however, in this and the following verses? Some say no, but it should be
remembered that this verse serves as an explanation of what has
gone before. The thought may be paraphrased as follows: "There
is good reason for the prophet to lament and refuse to be comforted, for a day of confusion is coming." In the light of this fact, it
would appear that Isaiah continues with the same subject. In
chapter two the day belonged to the Lord and had reference to
everything high and lifted up. Here the day also belongs to the
Lord, the God of hosts, and is to manifest itself in the valley of
vision. It is a day whose force will appear in Jerusalem itself, in the
breaking of walls and crying unto the mountains. The expression,
"breaking a wall," is striking. In the Hebrew there is a threefold
occurrence of the consonant combination *qr.* The reference seems
to be to the entrance of the enemy into the city; then the walls of
Jerusalem will be broken down.[17] The description in Kings is

---

[17] מקרקר, apparently a *Pilpel* part. occurring only here and in Num. 24:17,
chosen for the sake of the word play with *qir.* The Jewish grammarians and
commentators (Abulwalid Ibn Janah, Kimchi, and Ibn Ezra) explain the word
as meaning *destroy, demolish, tear down.* This is also attested by the Talmud
(*Bereshith Rabba,* 74), and the *Zohar* on Genesis (according to Gesenius).
Drechsler takes the word as indicating the action itself, *the dismantling,* which
really forms a better parallel with the following. If the form is a part. the
subject would probably be either *day,* or impersonal. Whether *qir* designates
the city walls or the walls of the houses is difficult to determine. Some (e.g.,

straight and direct: "And all the army of the Chaldees, that *were with* the captain of the guard, brake down the walls of Jerusalem round about" (2 Kings 25:10).

Lastly, the day is one in which people will cry to the mountain. Calvin thinks that this will be a call to the mount on which the Temple is situated. But at that time the people had forgotten God and would not likely look to the Temple mount for help. They were acting like Ahaz. Furthermore, many of them simply fled from the city. Penna suggests, although he thinks that the text may be corrupt, that the people are crying for help to Egypt, which lies beyond the mountains. This, however, would be a strange designation of Egypt. If an inhabitant of Jerusalem were to speak of a land beyond the mountains, he would probably have in mind a land east of the city. Furthermore, this view reads into the text, which says nothing more than that there will be a cry unto the mountain. Another view is that the cries of the people will reach unto the mountains and reverberate against them, and this is possibly what the prophet intended. In the city there is the sound of the walls being broken down and the people's cries reaching even unto the mountain.

6 Apparently Isaiah's purpose is now to show the magnitude of the invading army, and for that reason he mentions Elam and Kir, both of which were in the Assyrian army. Elam would have been known from Genesis 14; Isaiah also had mentioned it (11:11; 21:2), both as a district from which the people of God would be gathered and also as a besieger. Kir, too, is mentioned elsewhere in the Bible (Amos 1:5; 9:7; and 2 Kings 16:9), and is a land to which the Israelites were taken captive, and which may have lain in the same general region as Elam. Some have thought that the purpose of the verse is to mention the whole extent of the Assyrian empire, from south to north. It is difficult to demonstrate this, however, and more likely it may merely be that Isaiah wishes to mention two very distant places, each of which will have a part in the war. Possibly Kir simply stands for Media generally.

Elam has borne a quiver, for apparently it was celebrated for its archers (cf. Isa. 13:18).[18] Not merely on foot did the Elamites

---

Fischer) take *qir* and *šô'* as proper names (Qir demolishes and Šô' storms at the mountain).

18 *'ašpāh*, quiver; cf. Ug. *'špt*; Akk. *išpatu*; Egy. *'spzt*. Elam lay northeast of Babylon with its capital at Susa. Kir is the land to which the Assyrians de-

come, but that they might fight more effectively, with a wagon of men; i.e., with the wagons that bear men. The journey across the desert would be long and slow; hence, if Elam comes in wagons, she will be in better fighting condition. The following word is to be taken in apposition to the two preceding, and may simply be rendered "horsemen." It is therefore a completed army, embracing infantry, men in chariots, and cavalry. As for Kir, she too was ready for war for she had laid bare the shield in readiness for the attack. It is true enough that there were Elamite soldiers in the Assyrian army, but it seems that Isaiah's purpose in mentioning Elam and Kir is simply to point to the great distance from which the enemy who finally destroys Jerusalem will come.

7 In depicting the attack of the distant enemy Isaiah uses the past tense and writes in prose. Thus he turns our eyes from the approaching foe to the destruction that wasteth in Jerusalem. In so doing, he addresses the city itself. Jerusalem's choicest valleys are filled with wagons, he announces, and to express this thought he first uses the word "choice."[19] Immediately we see that the distruction is penetrating; not merely in some inconsequential way has the enemy struck, but the choicest of her valleys are filled. It is true that the word translated *valley* may refer to the open plain (1 Kings 20:28), but with reference to Jerusalem it would signify the valleys that filled the city or that surrounded it. These valleys have become filled[20] with wagons of war; and with respect to the cavalry, "setting they have set (i.e., they have assuredly taken their stand) toward the gate." What, however, is intended by the "gate"? Some say that the word does not designate the gate of a city, but merely the region of Judah. On the other hand, inasmuch as the prophet has been speaking of the city there is reason to

ported the Damascene Arameans; it was possibly in the same region as Elam. Some propose to emend the text and read, "and Aram will ride on horses." Gray gives good reasons for rejecting this proposal. Caesar describes the action attributed to Kir (*de bello Gallico* ii.21; cf. also Cicero *de natura deorum* ii.14).

19 *the choice of thy valleys,* i.e., thy choicest valleys. A noun in the const. before a partitive gen. may convey an attributive idea. Cf. Isa. 1:17; 17:4; 37: 24. Often such abstract nouns are themselves in the gen.; but *mib-har* usually is const., being emphasized because of the superlative character of its concept (cf. Drechsler).

20 As is usually the case, the verb agrees with the second noun in a const.-gen. combination, when the first is *all* or an abstract which expresses a quality of the genitive.

think that the "gate" here refers to the gates of the city itself. As a matter of fact the Assyrians did stand at the door of Jerusalem (2 Kings 25:1-4). The word, however, may possibly be intended in a figurative sense. To reach the gate of a city means to reach the city itself.

8 And he removed the covering of Judah, and thou didst look in that day to the armor of the house of the forest.

9 And the breaches of the city of David ye have seen, that they were many, and ye gathered the waters of the lower pool.

10 And the houses of Jerusalem ye have numbered, and ye have pulled down the houses to make inaccessible the wall.

11 And a reservoir ye have made between the two walls for the waters of the old pool, and ye did not look to the maker of it, nor did ye see its former.

8 Using verbs in the past tense as prophetic perfects, the prophet continues his description, which refers to something that has not yet taken place. The subject of the first verb may either be the Lord, or it may be indefinite. If the latter, which is preferable, we may render by the passive in English, *And the covering of Judah is removed.* Does this statement refer to the opening of the eyes of the Jews to their true plight? Paul spoke of the veil that is upon the heart of the Jews (2 Cor. 3:15,16), and some believe that in the present instance Isaiah is speaking of the removal of that which made the Jews insensible to the danger then about them. It is certainly true that there was a covering veil over the Jews of that time (cf. 25:7), but the following verses show clearly enough that the Jews did not really understand the danger that had come upon them. Instead of repentance they relied upon material means of defense. It is far better to understand this language as referring to the disgrace that had befallen the nation. In the Orient a woman uncovered is a woman dishonored (cf. 47:2; Nah. 3:5). As a commentary upon the situation one might note the lament, "Jerusalem hath grievously sinned; therefore she is removed: all that honored her despise her, because they have seen her nakedness: yea, she sigheth, and turneth backward" (Lam. 1:8). All that which protected the nation from shame and disgrace has been removed, so that Jerusalem now stands open to dishonor.[21]

21 *māsak* –the word is const., but the *Qametz* in the distant open syllable must be a long vowel. It should be accompanied by *Meteg.* Verse 8 may be taken as a protasis, *"when the covering,"* etc. Schultens (according to Gesenius)

What is the veil that is removed? Again opinions differ. Some refer it to the actual gate of the city, the capture of which is equivalent to the capture of the city itself; others think that it is the forts or fortresses wherein arms were stored and the soldiers quartered. It is perhaps difficult to say; what does appear sure is that when the veil is removed, the city is open to disgrace. The veil, therefore, in some sense, would be that which protects the city; and so the reference is to weapons of defense of some kind.[22]

The prophet now changes the gender of the verb, and personifies Judah as a woman. His language is abrupt, as though he said, "And the covering is removed, yet in that day Judah looked to the armory, etc." Hence, far from having her eyes opened to her own true condition, Judah, even in that day of disgrace, looked to material weapons for deliverance, weapons that were found in the house of the forest. This armory had been built by Solomon, and, inasmuch as it was constructed with cedars brought from Lebanon, and had great cedar pillars, became known as the house of the forest of Lebanon (cf. 1 Kings 7:2-6). Among other things it contained the golden shields which Solomon had made (1 Kings 10:17), and was one of the objects shown by Hezekiah to the envoys of Merodach-baladan (Isa. 39:2). Here then was no true conversion, no turning to the only One that could help; here was merely further reliance upon the arm of flesh which could not save.

9 Instead of commencing this verse with a verb, Isaiah places first, and so emphasizes, the object which he considers most promi-

---

claims that among the Arabs the phrase *to remove the covering (ghaṭṭān)* indicates that an enemy has given a people up to the deepest degradation. It is a picture taken from the realm of abuse and vituperation. Drechsler quotes Umbreit: *"Die entschleierte Frau ist im Morgenlande die Entehrte. Selbst Tänzerinnen entblössen den ganzen Körper, aber das Gesicht bleibt verschleiert."*

22 Fischer thinks that the covering is probably that of blinding (cf. Procksch). Some refer it to Jerusalem itself, but Judah had not yet been captured. In itself the word designates the curtain used in the Tabernacle, at the gate of the court (Ex. 27:16; 35:17, etc.), at the entrance of the tent (Ex. 26:36, 37), and to separate the most Holy Place (Ex. 35:12; 39:34, etc.). Cf. also 2 Sam. 17:19; Ps. 105:39. It is therefore that which would keep out the enemy and prevent its entering the city. More specific than this one cannot be. Even though *māsak* in itself does not denote clothing, it does not necessarily follow (Dillmann) that the phrase cannot be used idiomatically or figuratively as suggested by Schultens.

nent, namely, the breaches which former neglect and decay have brought about. Such neglect had been great, for these breaches were many. The picture is heartrending. The city of David, in which the presence of the Lord was found, was nevertheless a city whose walls had been allowed to go into decay. Isaiah uses the designation, *the city of David*, by which he means the section built upon the hill Ophel, the ancient site of the Jebusite town.[23] This might seem to be a last resort, the very city of David itself; but even here the walls had breaches. Even the city of David was allowed to go into disrepair. Here was a violation of the divine command, "Do good in thy good pleasure unto Zion; build thou the walls of Jerusalem" (Ps. 51:18). Can one now say that the "Lord loveth the gates of Zion more than all the dwellings of Jacob" or that "Glorious things are spoken of thee, O city of God" (Ps. 87:2, 3)? All those expressions in the Psalms which exalt the glory of Zion and her bulwarks have been neglected by the inhabitants. Here is not glory, but breaches. The walls of the city of God have been allowed to go into disrepair by those who dwell in Zion. Isaiah uses the verb in the plural, for he is addressing all the inhabitants of the city. Ye, everyone of you, he says, have seen these breaches, for they have become many.

Not only had the inhabitants seen the breaches, they had even done something to repair them. They had done the worst possible thing. Inhabitants of Zion, the city of the great King, had acted as though that King had nothing to do with their city. They had not turned to Him, but had adopted means of human devising for delivering themselves and repairing the sad condition in which the city found itself. First of all they had gathered the water of the lower pool, which is probably to be identified with the old pool mentioned in verse 11. It is quite possible that the modern representative is the Birket el-Hamra found at the exit of the Tyropoean valley.[24] At a time of siege, water was of extreme impor-

[23] The *city of David* lay south of the Temple area on the hill Ophel; cf. 2 Sam. 5:9.

[24] There is no other mention of the lower pool, but there is mention of an *upper pool* which presupposes also a lower one (cf. 7:3; 36:2; 2 Kings 18:17). Vincent (*Jérusalem de L'Ancien Testament*, Paris, 1954, Vol. I, p. 295) makes the following identifications: (1) *The upper pool* is the regulating basin, constructed at the natural mouth of the spring, before 'ain Oumm ed-Daradj, i.e., the spring Gihon. (2) *The lower pool* corresponds to the basin, known today as Birket el-Ḥamra, since (when) Ahaz had deflected the primitive outlet (*le déversoir primitif*) of canal II in the bottom of the Tyropoean, blocked by

tance; if the water supply of Jerusalem were cut off, the city could not last.

10 As far as form is concerned this verse is constructed similarly to verse 9. Again the object is placed first. Not only did the people gather water, but they also numbered the houses of Jerusalem. Why, however, did they do this? It has been suggested that they might then more easily defend the houses. More likely, however, the houses were numbered so that the people might know which could be spared and which were needed to provide materials for repairing the breaches in the walls of the city. It is possible that some of these houses were built either on the wall or so close to the wall that they made the defense of the city more difficult, and for that reason had to be destroyed. Primarily, however, the houses were destroyed in order to provide the necessary building material for repairing the breaches in the walls.[25]

The emphasis in this and the preceding verse has been on the water supply and the breaches in the walls. One is reminded of the actions of Hezekiah at the time of Sennacherib, when he took measures to protect the water supply; "Why should the kings of Assyria come, and find much water? Also, he strengthened himself, and built up all the wall that was broken, and raised it up to the towers, and another wall without, and repaired Millo in the city of David, and made darts and shields in abundance" (2 Chron. 32:4b, 5). Does not the similarity of thought, it might be asked, suggest that our prophecy has to do with the days of Hezekiah and Sennacherib? It is quite possible that the prophecy does speak of, or at least refer to, the actions of Hezekiah. It should be noted, however, that the Scriptures do not represent Hezekiah as acting apart from God. He was a man of faith, who combined faith and works in obedience to God. Here, on the other hand, the measures adopted were such as were done with no repentance. Hence, in all

---

the passage of the double rampart. (3) The pool between the two walls is the vast new reservoir created by Hezekiah at the emptying (*débouché*) of his tunnel-aqueduct, which became the Pool of Siloam. (4) The old pool is a simple parenthetical *(incidente)* designation of the upper pool in the text of Isaiah, which draws attention to its suppression by the fact that the spring itself was diverted to a wholly other point. *DOTT*, pp. 68, 209 applies these actions to the construction of the Siloam tunnel.

25 Note the omission of *Dagesh*, which brings about a change in the sound of the aspirate. For this reason *Dagesh* is usually not omitted in such letters.

probability, the description in the prophecy merely intends us to understand that such measures had often been taken, not only at the time of Sennacherib, but at other times also, and that reliance had been placed upon these alone. The mention of these defense measures does not provide a sure guide to the occasion about which the prophet speaks, for such measures might have been taken on several different occasions.

11 For preserving water the Jerusalemites had made a reservoir in which the water from the old pool was gathered, and this pool was placed between the two walls. But which two walls? Can they be identified? It is possible that between the old pool and the Kidron valley the walls formed a square into which the water was gathered. It may have been this to which the present prophecy refers.[26]

These measures Jerusalem had taken; yet she had not looked to the One who had brought about the crisis. This was strange, for she was the valley of vision. Here she should have seen, but here she did not even look. The words stand in contrast to the statement in verse 8, *Thou didst look* unto an armory, but *ye did not look* unto God. Jerusalem's inhabitants can see only what they can grasp with their hands.

In the second line of the verse there is a chiasm, giving the arrangement a-b b-a. Beginning with a verb, the verse likewise concludes with one. The two descriptions of God with respect to His people then occur side by side: its maker—its former.[27] By means of these two words the thought is expressed that the people of God are the object of His creative work. To the second word an adverbial clause is added which may be rendered "from afar." The reference is not spatial but temporal, and so those versions which translate "long ago" are not incorrect.

12 And the Sovereign One, the LORD of hosts, called in that day to

26 *miq-wāh*—Lit., collection, gathering, here used in the sense of reservoir. Cf. Ex. 7:19; Lev. 11:36; and Gen. 1:9. For its identification, cf. footnote 24. Note that the dual *hō-mō-ṯa-yim* is formed from the f. pl. Cf. 2 Kings 25:4; Jer. 39:4; 52:7. It is possible that the phrase may merely mean between the city walls, i.e., within the city wall, being used like the Latin *moenia urbis*.

27 *the one who made her*—the f. suffix stands for an indefinite obj., probably referring to the present crisis, although it could refer to the city. I regard the part. as s. despite the *yod*, for this is the normal writing of the *ay* diphthong in an open nonfinal accented syllable.

weeping and mourning and to baldness and to girding of sack-cloth.

13 And behold! rejoicing and gladness, killing oxen and slaying sheep, eating flesh and drinking wine; let us eat and drink, for tomorrow we die.

14 And there was revealed in my ears the LORD of hosts, Surely this iniquity shall not be expiated for you until ye die, saith the Sovereign One, the LORD of hosts.

12 The prophecy continues the description in the past (i.e., using prophetic perfects), now calling to what God Himself had directed. God is identified as *the Sovereign One,* for He has the power to decide what Israel must do and to control the movements even of the enemy nations. His power is also stressed by the designation, "LORD of hosts." At the time of the calamity God has called, in that through His prophets He has summoned the people to obedience.[28] His call, however, has gone unheeded. Of course, the very events of the calamity themselves also constituted a call from God to repentance, for everything that transpires should lead us to turn from our evil ways unto Him who is the Creator, so that, if we do not turn, we are without excuse. To Israel, however, He gave the additional blessing of special revelation, pleading with the nation through His prophets. That to which He called was a sincere and heart-felt repentance, which must express itself in outward signs such as weeping.

Coupled with this weeping there should have been mourning that the nation had departed so far from God. Had there been true mourning there would also have been the accompanying baldness and wearing of sackcloth, for both the shaving of the head as well as the wearing of sackcloth were signs of repentance and humiliation. One who thus attired himself might be considered a true mourner over the condition of the people. A mere outward expresssion of mourning in itself was not what God called for. Rather, "rend your hearts and not your garments" (Joel 2:13a). Nevertheless, if the heart was truly repentant it would also express that repentance by outward signs. It is this for which God called.

28 *in that day*—the reference is to v. 8b. The thought is: at that time more than at any other, and in a particular way. Kissane states that by repentance they might have obtained pardon. This is true, if we keep in mind that repentance is never the ground of pardon; the only ground of pardon is the grace of God manifested in the blood of Jesus Christ.

13 What God has called for is not granted. *Behold!* cries the prophet, and with this word he introduces what is strange and unexpected. Here is the opposite of that to which God had called. Here is rejoicing and gladness (note the alliteration and the predominant *s* sound), but not a rejoicing in God.[29] Rather, here is a carefree and careless rejoicing, one unconcerned with the stark and grim realities of the nation's condition. It is therefore a rejoicing that displeases God. Coupled with the rejoicing is the widespread indulgence in feasting, expressed in the descriptive terms, "the killing of oxen and the slaying of flocks." This was for the sake of indulgence, and that indulgence consisted of the "eating of flesh and drinking of wine." In themselves, eating flesh and drinking wine were no more sinful or abhorrent to Yahweh than was rejoicing. This, however, was the flesh of self-indulgence and the wine of luxury. It was not the fulfillment of one's necessity. It was that manifestation of self-confidence that characterizes those who give themselves over to the indulgence of flesh, unconcerned about the welfare of their nation. It was the precise opposite of the attitude for which God had called.

This attitude, so displeasing to Yahweh, might be summed up in the expression, "Let us eat and drink, for tomorrow we die." These words may not have been uttered by the revellers themselves; they are simply Isaiah's characterization of the revellers' attitude. They knew that danger would come and that they would soon perish. This did not matter. While there was time, they would enjoy themselves to the full.[30] The word "tomorrow" does not refer to the actual morrow, but merely signifies a short time. Here was an attitude of folly and also of desperation, for it was a preparation for death.

14 Passing from the word which describes the attitude of the

[29] This verse is very instructive as regards the use of the inf. abs. Note that it may take a direct obj.; two different forms from one root occur, *šā-ṭôṭ* and *šā-ṭô;* two of the inf. absolutes are employed for cohortatives. *Šā-ṭôṭ* may be intentional, to agree in sound with *šā-ḥōṭ,* forming a word play. All these infinitives are governed by *and behold!* and serve to express an exclamation. Possibly the *Paseq* merely calls attention to the inf. abs.

[30] Cf. Livy xxvi.13; Herodotus ii.193; Diodorus Siculus ii.23; the advice given to Gilgamesh, *ANET,* p. 90; A. Heidel, *The Gilgamesh Epic,* 1946; the proverb "soon he will die, I shall eat (all that I have) " *ANET,* p. 415; and "The Song of the Harper," *ANET,* p. 467; 1 Cor. 15:32. Eccl. 5:17 and 9:7ff. are not really parallel. The imp. *we shall die* denotes a specified action which is to occur in the future.

revellers, Isaiah asserts that in his ears the Lord of hosts has revealed Himself.[31] A word comes from the Lord, which will supersede and overpower the attitude of the people in their unconcern. This revelation is not merely a transitory act, but has a more or less continuing character. It is a word that has come and abides; its truth cannot be changed. The word of the Lord is expressed by means of a conditional sentence, or at least the protasis of such a sentence; and this lends to it the dignity and solemnity of an oath. "If this iniquity be expiated for you until you die," says the Lord, and the apodosis is omitted. According to the well-known Hebrew idiom, we may render, "Surely this iniquity will not be expiated for you until you die!"[32] The meaning is not that the people will atone for this iniquity through their death, for nowhere does the Scripture hold out any hope to men that their own death can atone for their sins.[33] Rather, it is a declaration (supported by the fact that it is an oath and that it is spoken by the Lord) that for this iniquity which the people have committed there will be no pardon. Death will come, and the people will die without having their iniquity expiated. The offense is treated like the unpardonable sin mentioned in the New Testament..[34] That there be no question about its sureness, Isaiah concludes his verse with the words, "saith the Sovereign One, the LORD of hosts."

A sure doom! a sinning, unconcerned, revelling people! a faithful prophet! This is the picture that the first fourteen verses of the chapter present. It is a Jerusalem that turns its back on its Maker. "O Jerusalem, Jerusalem—how often would I have gathered thy children together—and ye would not! Behold, your house is left unto you desolate" (Matt. 23:37, 38).

9. SHEBNA THE STEWARD (22:15-25)

15 Thus saith the Sovereign One, the LORD of hosts, Go, enter in unto this steward, unto Shebna, who is over the house.

---

31 The perf. with weak *waw* points not so much to one act as to a condition that continually reverberated in the prophet's ear. Cf. 5:9.

32 After עַד the imperfect may be used with a future sense. Cf. the usage of *šumma*, e.g., in Esarhaddon; D. J. Wiseman, *The Vassal Treaties of Esarhaddon*, London, 1958, lines 62ff., 73ff., etc.

33 ". . . sie werden tatsächlich durch ihren Tod diesen Frevel sühnen müssen" (Fischer, *Com. in loc.*).

34 Matt. 12:32; Mark 3:29; Luke 12:10.

16 What hast thou here, and whom hast thou here? for thou hast hewn for thyself here a grave; hewing on high his grave and carving in the rock a dwelling for himself.

17 Behold! the LORD is about to cast thee a casting of a man and to cover thee with a covering.

18 Rolling he will roll thee in a roll like a ball unto a spacious land, there thou wilt die and there will be the chariots of thy glory, the shame of thy master's house,

19 And I shall drive thee from thy post, and from thy station he shall throw thee down.

15 Hitherto the prophet has proclaimed the unconcerned and sinful condition of the nation in the face of approaching disaster. He now gives an example of the self-centeredness and luxury-loving attitude of the people as it is exemplified in a single individual, and that an individual of responsibility. This example is introduced by means of a command to the prophet himself. "Come now and enter"; with this command attention is directed to the man of high rank who was misusing his trust.[35] God is again described as the Sovereign One; for it is as the Sovereign One that He condemns the luxury of the nation when danger approaches, as well as the self-centeredness of Shebna. Instead of the usual preposition "unto" ('el), Isaiah uses the word 'al, which possibly contains a hint of unpleasantness, as though to say, "Go against this Shebna." Furthermore, the phrase "this steward" probably contains a shade of contempt. The office of soken was of great importance, probably one of the highest in the land.[36] A second title is also given Shebna, namely, "the one over the house." This office is attested at the time of Solomon (1 Kings 4:6), and could have been created by him. In Isaiah's day it had become a position of great significance, probably that of vizier. Later, however, it dwindled in

35 The force of the imperatives seems to be, *come now and enter;* cf. Gen. 45:17; Ezek. 3:4.

36 *hassōḵēn*—the steward, servitor. This form occurs only here, but cf. 1 Kings 1:2, 4. The root apparently means, "to be of service, benefit, use"; cf. Job 15:3; 22:2; 34:4; 35:3; Isa. 40:20 (and note *Hiphil,* Ps. 139:3; Num. 22:30; Job 22:21). In Amarna *sakânu,* to care for. The form is also attested in Ugaritic, *ᵃᵐᵉˡšakin māt Ugarit,* which occurs on a letter. A shorter form, *ᵃᵐᵉˡšak [in māti]* is found in a business contract. On the latter instance the office holder apparently had a Horite name, Enkite. The title is also attested in the alphabetic texts from Ugarit, *b'ly skn bn Ss,* and *dt bd skn.* Cf. Virolleaud, *Revue d'Assyrologie,* No. 37, pp. 132ff., No. 22, col. 3, line 9. Cf. also Akk. *Lu za-ki-ni.*

importance, and by Jeremiah's time was subordinate to that of scribe (cf. Jer. 36:12). Quite probably, David did not introduce this office when he established his kingdom, for it was an office that might detract from the glory of the king himself. Its introduction in the time of Solomon was likely a step in violation of the true nature of the theocracy, and its misuse is seen in the present prophecy. The office did continue until late in the history of the kingdom, as is shown by a late seal bearing the title, "Gedaliah who is over the house." Shebna's father's name is not given, which may indicate that Shebna was a foreigner. This fact is significant. Many commentators believe that Shebna was of Israelitish descent, but several factors oppose this.[37] (a) The name of Shebna's father is always omitted (see SPECIAL NOTE at the end of this section). (b) The name itself may be of Egyptian origin. (c) Isaiah makes a strong contrast between "here" in Jerusalem where Shebna is hewing out a tomb, and "there" where Shebna will be driven out. Possibly Shebna at this time was advocating an Egyptian alliance. Leaning upon Egypt instead of trusting Yahweh was no answer to the nation's great need. How great the contrast between Shebna and Isaiah! One unconcernedly builds himself a permanent tomb; the other weeps over the fate of his people.

Why, however, does Isaiah lay so much stress upon the position that the man held? Would it not have been sufficient merely to mention the name of this very well-known man? Had Isaiah merely mentioned the name, however, he would greatly have weakened his message. For a proper understanding of the situation we must briefly consider the nature of the theocracy. The kingdom of God was to be a nation in which God Himself ruled. His human representative was the king, who was to be a man after His own heart. In his entire life the king was to exemplify the justice and righteousness of the God for whom he acted. Indeed, he was a type of the great King to come, the Messiah. In the administration of the divine government, it was to be expected that the king would have helpers; but none would occupy his own central position. David, a man after God's own heart, did install certain government officials who performed functions that were to the advantage of the covenant nation. Among them we may mention the scribe and the speaker or recorder. These two offices were probably based upon

---

[37] שֶׁבְנָא—The name may be a short form of Shebanyahu. It may also be an Egyptian word, *šbnw* or *šbnw šrj*. Cf. H. Ranke, *Die aegyptischen Personennamen*, 1935, p. 330.

Egyptian models, the *sš* and the *whm.m.* Under David these were really officials of the covenant, the scribe writing down those things that were necessary and the speaker or recorder speaking for the king. One office, however, which was very prominent in Egypt is notable in the Israel of David's day for its absence. That is an office corresponding to the vizier. In the erection of such an office, there might very well be a threat to the true nature of the kingship and the theocracy. A king, such as David, who was determined to honor God in all his dealings, and who understood the nature of the theocracy, would see this danger. At the time of Solomon, on the other hand, when worldliness had entered in and the true charac-ter of the theocracy was no longer a concern, such an office might be created. We are probably not justified in asserting positively that Solomon created the office, although such may have been the case. In 1 Kings 4:6 we read almost casually that Ahishar was over the house. It may even be that at this point the position had not been officially created, for this description follows two others, namely, "over the host" (v. 4) and "over the princes" (v. 5). At this point the phrase may merely have a general significance to express a position of importance, and later may have come to be a technical designation for this position. In the fourth chapter of First Kings this expression is included with a list of officials. In Isaiah's day at any rate the position had grown in significance, so that it overshad-owed both that of scribe and recorder and probably other offices as well. What the precise duties of the man "who was over the house" were we cannot say. Probably the safest thing to say is that he was second to the king. His position then, if unwisely or wickedly employed, would be a threat to the theocracy. Inasmuch as Shebna occupied a position of such great significance and was misusing that position, Isaiah calls attention to the office as well as to the man.

16 However exalted the office of Shebna may have been, Isaiah had no difficulty of access to him just as he had no difficulty of access to the king. Nor does the prophet stand on ceremonial. He treats Shebna as Shebna deserves to be treated. Going to the heart of the matter at once, he boldly rebukes the steward. One word stands out in this rebuke; it is the word *here*. As the Danites had once asked Micah "Who brought thee hither? and what makest thou in this place? and what hast thou here?" (Judg. 18:3b), so Isaiah abruptly asks Shebna, "What to thee here and who to thee

107

THE BOOK OF ISAIAH

here?" (i.e., what hast thou here and whom hast thou here?). It is quite likely that the prophet was addressing Shebna at the grave itself, but the word *here* probably refers to Jerusalem rather than to the grave. Its threefold use in this verse forms a striking contrast to the twofold occurrence of *there* in verse 18. Isaiah appears to be asking, "What now is your relation to the city of Jerusalem? What are you doing in this time of Jerusalem's calamity? Here in Jerusalem you have taken an office that is no essential part of the theocracy, an office that can be misused, as you have misused it, even to obscure the central authority of the king, and to call attention to yourself. What right have you in Jerusalem? You have placed yourself upon an equality with those who do have a right here. You, Shebna, should be at the work of the theocracy, not engaged in satisfying your selfish desires. Instead, you have carved out a grave for yourself here. This is not the place for self-interestedness, but for concern over God's kingdom."

Isaiah does not condemn Shebna for exhibiting a rightful concern about his own future; but Shebna wants a luxurious sepulchre, and this personal desire overshadows his concern for the welfare of the nation.[38] At this point Isaiah's eyes pass, as it were, from the man Shebna himself to the sepulchre; and reflecting upon the grave and its preparation he describes the action: *hewing on high his grave and carving in the rock a dwelling for himself.*[39]

[38] Above the entrance to a rock-hewn tomb in the village of Shiloah, an inscription has been discovered, which may be translated, "This is the tomb of -yahu, who is over the house. There is no silver or gold here, but [. . . his bones] and the bones of his slave wife with him. Cursed be the man who opens this." The form of the letters applies to the time of Hezekiah, so this may very well be the tomb of which Isaiah was speaking. Shebna did not wish to be buried in an ordinary grave (2 Kings 23:6; Jer. 26:23). Cf. N. Avigad, "The Epitaph of a Royal Steward from Siloam Village," *Israel Exploration Journal*, Vol. 3, No. 3, 1953, pp. 137-152.

[39] Note that the language begins in the 2nd person, but passes over into the 3rd, the part. having the force of a vocative; cf. also Isa. 47:8; 48:1; 54:1, 11. The part. has the Ḥireq *compaginis*. This Ḥireq may possibly be an old construct ending, as in *'ᵃbi*. It is thought that this Ḥireq serves to give the part. more dignity. At least it does occur twice in this verse in impassioned speech. Cf. GKC § 90 *k-n*. *Mārôm* is a gen. after the part.; lit., *hewer of on high his grave*. The gen. indicates the realm in which that expressed by the part. occurs. Cf. Brockelmann, *op. cit.*, §§ 77f. Both the expressions *on high* and *in the rock* point to the haughty attitude of Shebna. A tomb carved in the rock would be one intended to last forever. Cf. Koran, Sura 41:28, *dār 'l-ḥald=the eternal house.* Interesting is the parallel *miš-kān*, dwelling, although the text speaks of his grave, not his dwellings. Shebna may

Like those who carve out their tombs in the rock so that they will endure perpetually, so Shebna hewed his tomb. Moreover, it was carved out high, apparently so that its occupant would be regarded as ranking among the kings and nobles. Of Hezekiah's death we read, "And Hezekiah lay with his fathers and they buried him in the ascent (apparently a prominent place) of tombs of the sons of David. . ." (2 Chron. 32:33). Interesting is the designation *dwelling*, for the tomb was conceived as a house (cf. 14:18).

In modern Jerusalem there are found today the "Tombs of the Kings" (*qubur essalatin*), access to which is by a 24-step staircase, carved out of the rock. These tombs are carved from the solid rock, some containing benches in the wall and shaft tombs, and some containing subsidiary tombs. According to Jewish tradition these tombs were known as the cavern of Zedekiah. In all probability, however, Helena of Adiabene was buried here. At least these tombs exemplify the care that could be expended in their preparation. Shebna was evidently seeking for the best and expending great labor upon it.[40]

17 Shebna may have planned one end for himself; Yahweh has planned another. Corresponding to the enormity of the guilt, Isaiah solemnizes his declaration with an introductory *behold!* The Lord whose kingdom Shebna had treated with unconcern will take action with respect to this unprofitable steward. As one hurls the spear and as Jonah was cast overboard, so the Lord is about to cast out or throw out Shebna. The cognate accusative lends force to the statement, *throw thee out a throwing*. He who had sought for the best of tombs that he might have a permanent resting place will not even have a common tomb in Jerusalem; rather he will be thrust out into a distant land so that he will die far from the land of promise.

In the King James version we read, *carry thee away with a mighty captivity*. The Hebrew word which is here rendered "mighty" is simply a common word often used to designate man in distinction from God. It could be taken as a vocative, in which case we should translate, *about to throw thee out a throwing, O man;* or else the word may be taken as an adverbial accusative, *as a man*.

---

have had many dwellings, but only one grave. The second line is not an inserted parenthesis in prophetical style, but simply a transfer of persons, which, as König claims, indicates a lack of sympathy.

[40] For a full description of the tombs cf. Vincent, *op. cit.*, Baedeker, *A Handbook of Palestine and Syria*, 1912, also gives a good description.

If this latter be adopted the thought is that although Shebna had sought the highest and best of tombs for himself in the city of God, he would be thrown out of that city as a mere man. In arrogating to himself certain prerogatives which did not belong to him, he was in effect placing himself above God. There is no place for presumption in the kingdom of God. Therefore, God would throw him forth from the land as a mere man. Corresponding to his own self-centeredness was to be his abasement in banishment. The casting out will be a violent one, and the last two words support this thought. *Grasping thee grasping*, we may render. In God's hands Shebna, like a ball, will be clutched, and thrown far from his own land. [41]

18 The threatening and announcement of Shebna's doom continues. Shebna's being cast out is now compared to the rolling of a ball into a broad and open space where nothing is present to hinder its rolling. As one winds a turban about the head, so Shebna will be wound; and this is expressed by a threefold repetition of the root idea, *winding up, he will wind thee a winding.*[42] Being wound up like cloth into a ball, Shebna will be hurled forth. The repetitions stress the elaborateness of the preparations for the steward's ejection. The land into which Shebna is to be ejected is described as *broad of hands*, i.e., it is spacious and wide, providing no obstacles to the free rolling of the ball.

Here, Isaiah had said to Shebna, thou art acting; but there, in that broad land, thou shalt die. This is prophecy that is certain of fulfillment, and the principle that it teaches is one of genuine application. He who is entrusted with authority in the Church of God and abuses that authority, making it subserve the ends of his own desires, will be banished from the people of God and die in a

---

41 *about to cast thee*—a Pilpel part. from *tûl*, to cast down, far away. The root is used of the casting of a spear, 1 Sam. 18:11; 20:33; of casting Jonah overboard, Jon. 1:5, 12, 15; of being cast out from one's fatherland, Jer. 16:13; 22:26. *gāḇer*=man, in pause. The word here points to man in distinction from God, i.e., a mere man. עטה probably means to wrap, envelop; cf. now Akk. *zṭū*, to be dark. The inf. abs. follows a part., thus intensifying the action expressed by the latter.

42 The finite verb, inf. abs., and cognate acc. are employed. Vulg. *coronans coronabit te. kaddûr*—in middle Hebrew the word means ball. Ar. *ka-di-ra*, to be thick. Akk. *kudûru*, circle, boundary. The meaning of the word here is not certain. It is to be construed with what follows, not with the three preceding cognate words. Apparently a verb is to be understood; *like a ball he will cast thee*, etc.

distant land, even apart from the people of God, an everlasting death. We who are HERE in the Church must ever watch and make our calling and election sure, lest we die THERE, far from God's presence.

The last clause is sometimes taken as though it might be rendered, *Thither thou shalt die and thither thy chariots of glory shall convey thee.* It is also possible, however, to translate, *thither will be thy chariots.*[43] All that in which Shebna gloried would go with him into banishment. The entire last clause may then either be rendered, *thither the chariots of thy glory will be the shame of the house of thy master,* or, *thither will be the chariots of thy glory, oh! shame of the house of thy master.* This latter rendering is perhaps preferable. Shebna was a spot in the household of Hezekiah, for Hezekiah sought to keep his household, i.e., his government, in line with true theocratic principles. Among our Lord's disciples there was one that betrayed Him; in Hezekiah's household there was one that, by his selfish actions, betrayed the king. Woe to us if in the household of our Lord we become a shame!

19 In order to prepare for a transition to the announcement concerning Eliakim Isaiah sums up in one short sentence the fate of Shebna.[44] The import of this is missed by Duhm, who says that once the steward is in exile Yahweh should not have to banish him any more. Such a conclusion is unnecessary. The *waw* consecutive which introduces this verse does not necessarily imply that the events recorded are temporally subsequent to those which have previously been mentioned; the *waw* consecutive here may have resumptive force. Hence, we may render, *and I shall drive thee from thy post.* That is the conclusion of the whole matter. Banishment is to come to Shebna, the direct result of the Lord's acting. He who occupied what was at that time probably the second highest position in the kingdom is to be driven from that post.

A change in person occurs with the last verb, "he will throw thee down from thy station." Such a change in person is sometimes

---

43 The wagons were a sign of luxury; cf. 2 Sam. 15:7; Isa. 2:7; Gen. 41:43; 45:19, 21, 27; Song of Sol. 1:9. Possibly they were evidence of Egyptian influence.

44 Note the chiastic structure of the verse: verb, prepositional phrase; prepositional phrase, verb. The word *ûmimmaʿᵃmāḏᵉḵā*, incorrectly written in *BH*, should have two *Metegs,* one for each distant open syllable. No emendation of the text is necessary; the change of persons is similar to 22:16, here after an implied vocative.

found after a vocative, and this would appear to support the position that there actually was a vocative in the preceding verse, *Oh! shame of the house of thy master*. At any rate, the change of person gives a livelier effect to the discourse; the latter verb may possibly be taken in an impersonal sense, *and from thy station one will cast thee down*. The two verbs are a strong confirmation of the fact that Shebna will be banished.

20 And it shall come to pass in that day that I shall call to my servant, to Eliakim the son of Hilkiah.
21 And I shall clothe him with thy tunic, and with thy girdle will I strengthen him, and thy power I shall give into his hand, and he shall become a father to the dweller in Jerusalem, and to the house of Judah.
22 And I shall put the key of the house of David upon his shoulder, and he will open, and there is none that shutteth, and he will shut, and there is none that openeth.
23 And I shall fasten him as a nail in a sure place, and he shall become a throne of honor to the house of his father.
24 And they shall hang upon him all the honor of his father's house, the offspring and the issue, all the vessels of small quantity, from vessels of bowls even to all the vessels of pitchers.
25 In that day, saith the LORD of hosts, the nail which is driven in a sure place will depart, and it will be cut down, and fall, and the burden which was on it shall be cut off, for the LORD hath spoken.

20 Shebna is to be banished, but the Lord will raise up one to take his place. The phrase *in that day* is characteristic of the language of prediction. At the time when Shebna is cast out, the Lord will call His servant Eliakim for the purpose of occupying the vacated post of Shebna. Eliakim is a servant of the Lord, both in his actual conduct and in the desires and purposes of his heart.[45]

45 Cf. 20:3. Eliakim means, God will establish, raise up; and Hilkiah, my portion is Yahweh. At least five different individuals bore the name Eliakim in Scripture. Two were ancestors of Christ (Matt. 1:13; Luke 3:30); one was a contemporary of Nehemiah and a priest (Neh. 12:41); one was a king of Judah (2 Kings 23:34; 2 Chron. 36:4), as well as the individual of whom Isaiah speaks. Three examplars of a seal impression, two found at Tell Beit Mirsim and one at 'Ain Shams, bear the inscription (on two lines), *l'lyqm n'r ywkn*, i.e., To Eliakim, the lad (i.e., servant) of Jokin. The word *n'r* evidently refers to a person of rank, and *ywkn* probably is an abbreviation of Jehoiakin. Cf. *DOTT*, p. 224.
The verb *call* is used of God. Cf. 42:5; 48:12; 49:1, where it is followed by the acc.; here, however, by the preposition.

When God designates a man *my servant,* He attributes high honor to that man; He asserts that that man is one who will serve Him. This designation was to be given to that One who above all others truly served God, even the "Servant of the Lord" of whom the prophet speaks later. An amount of recognition and possibly honor is attributed to Eliakim in that he is designated "son of Hilkiah." His father's name is mentioned, possibly to indicate that in every respect he may legitimately serve. It is to Shebna that God is now speaking, and the information conveyed must have brought with it a sense of utter despair. All that Shebna had labored for is taken from him and given to another.

21 The garments mentioned were evidently characteristic of the office from which Shebna was being deposed. By means of chiastic statement Isaiah announces that these garments will be given to Eliakim. The *kiton* was also a priest's garment (cf. Ex. 28:4), but here it may merely indicate the characteristic dress of Shebna.[46] It is possible that by the *kiton* and the girdle, Shebna had dressed himself as a priest. At any rate, whether this be so or not, what had been dear to Shebna will now be transferred to Eliakim. The whole is summed up in the phrase, *thy rule I shall give in his hands.* Here we see something of the power of the steward. He did rule, not as a king, but as a vizier. All this authority, power, and rule would be placed in the hands of a man that was more worthy to receive it.

Isaiah now points out the dignity to which Eliakim will be promoted with respect to the people themselves. Perhaps there is herein intended a rebuke to Shebna; those things which Eliakim was to do were the things that Shebna had not done. First of all he is to be a father to the inhabitant of Jerusalem and the house of David. Just as the Messiah is a father of eternity, so Eliakim is to be a father to the people. Implied in the word is all that tenderness and love that a father shows to his own children. "I was a father to the poor" (Job 29:16a). Perhaps the language points out what the steward should be, and does not merely serve as an actual prophecy

---

[46] כתנתך—the word is instructive in illustrating the use of a short *u* vowel in closed, unaccented syllables. Before *Dagesh forte* in a closed, unaccented syllable, short *u* generally appears as *Qibbutz,* otherwise as *Qametz Ḥᵃtuph.* אבנט does not designate any girdle generally, but that of the priests and nobles. *Tzere* is probably naturally long; cf. Lev. 16:4 where the *Tzere* is retained in the construct. Possibly the word is related to Egy. *bnd.* B has τὸν στέφανόν σου.

of what he in reality would be. Toward the inhabitants of Jerusalem, individually considered, he was to be a father. To each one of them he would exhibit the tender concern of a true father. Moreover, with respect to the government, the house of Judah, he was to show the same concern; for even the officialdom of the kingdom of God is in need of tender love. Luther expressed this attitude when he spoke of *"dein armes Christentum"*; his words show a true love and tender concern for the Church.

22 Not only would Eliakim occupy the position of Shebna, but he would also receive tremendous power and authority from God. In this statement, "I shall give to him," there may possibly be implied a rebuke to Shebna. The origin of the office, "over the house," is involved in some obscurity. During Isaiah's day at any rate, it seems to have grown in great significance; and this growth may well have been due to Shebna himself. There is no record in Scripture of the office's having been divinely established. Perhaps we are not going too far afield if we assume that without divine warrant and authorization Shebna had arrogated to himself authority and influence that did not rightfully belong to him. Eliakim, however, will possess a power divinely entrusted to him. He cannot be regarded as a usurper. Just as the master possesses the key to that house, and has complete authority with respect to permitting anyone to enter or to leave, and so entire authority over the house, so God will give to Eliakim a key to the house or dynasty of David. This key will be placed upon his shoulder, an expression which means that the responsibility of the Davidic government is to rest as a burden upon Eliakim's shoulder.[47] The importance of the position is seen in that this same description is applied to the risen Christ in Revelation 3:7. Eliakim's position was to manage well the great treasures of grace that were promised to David and to his house. Over this royal house he would have almost unlimited control. Were he to open the door, there would be no one at hand to shut it; and were he to shut it, no one would be present to open it. A man in such exalted position would yield an influence of great power over the king.

Why does God give to Eliakim such tremendous power? Is there not involved the danger that Eliakim's office may constitute a

47 In that the prophet says, *house of David,* and not merely *house of the king* or *house of Hezekiah,* he is referring not alone to the actual incumbent of the throne, but to its Messianic aspect.

threat to the king and so to the well-being of the theocracy? Has Eliakim entered into the place of Messianic type rather than the king himself? Perhaps these questions cannot be answered as fully as one might desire; the following line of thought, however, may at least point out the way to the correct answer. Although the king in Old Testament times was truly a type of the Christ, he was but a type, and not a complete equivalent of the antitype. Those duties which Christ Himself would exercise—for He alone is the Head and King of His Church—might, in the Old Testament dispensation, be delegated to ministers. We are then, first of all, to regard Eliakim as one who is a minister, a fact that is seen in the designation "My servant." The power of the keys was not actually placed in his hand but upon his shoulder, for final authority resided in the king as God's representative. As a servant or minister the power of the keys was entrusted to Eliakim, as in the New Testament age to Peter. It should be noted, however, that in the Gospels the figure of the keys is dropped and another, namely that of binding and loosing, is introduced. Here, however, as is the case in Revelation, the figure of the keys is carried through.

Eliakim was a minister, but he was more; he was a true administrator of the kingdom. Christ Himself had no need of such administrators, but Himself undertook the responsibilities for the absolute administration of the kingdom, a thought that Isaiah had earlier introduced (9:5). At this time in Judah's history there was particular need for an office such as that held by Eliakim. Shebna himself may have felt this need and out of wrong motives developed the power of the office. God gives to Eliakim, however, an authority in the office which will truly supply the need. Among the great nations of antiquity and in particular among the Assyrians, there was the "chief of drinking" (the Rabshakeh) who occupied a position of great authority. To counteract the position of an administrator of the kingdom of evil, there must be an administrator of the kingdom of God. Although the office itself may have been developed out of unworthy motives, God now invests the office-holder with power to use that office in a right way. When the Rabshakeh comes from Lachish with a great army to taunt the people of God, it is the government officials, headed by Eliakim the son of Hilkiah, who are described as being "over the house," who come forth to meet him. They hear the words of Rabshakeh, but in obedience to the king they do not answer him. The one "over the house," therefore, was still subject to the king.

Lastly, we may note that this office is not made hereditary. God promises the key to Eliakim but not to his descendants. The office continues, but soon loses its exalted character. It was Eliakim the son of Hilkiah who was exalted, and not the office in itself. Eliakim had all the power of a "Rabshakeh," and in him the Assyrian might recognize a man who could act for the theocracy.

23 The figure is now changed, and God asserts that He will fasten Eliakim as a peg in a sure place.[48] The place itself is sure, and hence the peg will be in a firm place from which it cannot easily be removed. The figure is that of a large nail or peg driven into the wall of the house for the purpose of suspending something upon it. Again Isaiah abruptly changes the figure, and states that Eliakim will become a throne of glory to the house of his father. The words reflect upon the latter part of the eighteenth verse. One who sits upon Eliakim, i.e., who rests upon him for support, will find glory and be honored.

24 Returning to the figure of a peg fixed in the wall, Isaiah declares that all men will seek to place their glory upon Eliakim. They will try to use him to obtain glory. By means of him they will seek to raise themselves to honor. To indicate how thoroughly members of his father's house will endeavor to procure glory through him, Isaiah goes into details. He speaks of the offspring (a masculine noun) and the issue or side shoots (a feminine noun).[49] Carrying out the figure of the house, he then speaks of all the vessels of a small king, lit, "of the small";[50] and these are further characterized as being "from the vessels of the bowls (such as were

48 Yā-ṭēḏ generally denotes the tent-peg and also a peg upon which something may be hung; cf. Ezra 9:8; Zech. 10:4; here the word is used figuratively. Gesenius adduces an example from the Vita Timuri, as the tent-pegs ('autād) of Mohammed ibn Mudaffir were driven in firm (thabitat), i.e., as his rule was made secure. Cf. also Koran 38:12, ḏū'lautād, referring to Pharaoh. The same idea of establishing permanent abodes appears in Jer. 24:6; 32:41; 42:10; 45:4. Yā-ṭēḏ is best taken as a circumstantial accusative: as a peg.

49 The pl. they comes from the collective force of house of his father in the preceding verse. The precise force of צֶפִעוֹת is not known. It is f., however, and stands parallel to the m. צֶאֱצָאִים, and thus denotes entirety; all the issue—whatever it may be, etc. Note the alliteration. Verse 24 constitutes a protasis, the apodosis following in v. 25.

50 Instead of agreeing with its noun, the adjective is treated as though it were an abstract noun; hence, not small vessels, but vessels of small (capacity or size). Note presence of the article.

employed by priests for mixing blood, cf. Ex. 24:6, and in the house for mixing wine, Song of Sol. 7:3)[51] unto all the vessels of the pitchers (i.e., jars, pitchers, or bottles made of skin)." In its entirety the house seeks to make use of Eliakim.

Did Eliakim, however, give way to the temptation of nepotism? It is almost universally held that he did, but there is no explicit statement to this effect in the text. Perhaps Drechsler is right in asserting that Isaiah in these words points to the downfall not of Eliakim but of his dependents. Perhaps, too, this episode is mentioned in order to make clear the great dangers that would attend the office. The very mention of the danger, however, may suggest that Eliakim had yielded to the temptation of, or at least had not opposed, the requests of his family. "His family makes a wrong use of him; and he is more yielding than he ought to be, and makes a wrong use of his office to favour them! He therefore falls and brings down with him all that hung upon the peg, i.e., all his relations who have brought him to ruin through the rapidity with which they have grasped at prosperity." These words of Delitzsch (*Com. in loc.*) may be correct, but we cannot prove them so. The text is clear at least in that it points out the danger of nepotism; and if nepotism be wrong in public life, how much more heinous when exercised in the Church of God!

25 Whether Eliakim actually was guilty of nepotism or not, we are expressly told that at the time ("in that day") when they hang all the glory of his father's house upon him he will be removed.[52] Apparently the usefulness of the office itself will have been exhausted. As to the historical fulfillment of this event, we can say nothing definite. When later the Rabshakeh came, Eliakim was still the one "over the house," and Shebna (probably the same as the Shebna of this chapter) was then the scribe. We are not told how this prophecy found its fulfillment, but we may be sure that it was fulfilled, and that its position in the prophecy would be no cause for shame on the part of Isaiah. The people would have known of the final issue of both Eliakim and Shebna.

Strange is the language that relates the removal of Eliakim. The man is not referred to by name; Isaiah merely says that the peg

---

51 '*aggānôṯ*—bowls; cf. Ug. '*gn;* Egy. '*ikn;* Akk. *agannu*.

52 According to Gesenius, Feldmann, and others the reference is to the removal of Shebna. This interpretation is as early as Ephraim Syrus and Theodoret. In 25b note the threefold alliteration, each verb beginning with a *Nun*.

which has been driven into a sure place will be removed. The statement is solemn and is characterized as an utterance of the LORD of hosts. Possibly there is reflection upon a violent removal, for it is said that the peg will be cut down and will fall. The burden which is upon the peg, hanging upon it, will be cut off, and so will fall to the ground. By means of this graphic figure the prophet points out the completed downfall of Eliakim. A fitting conclusion is given by the typical Isaianic phrase, "for the LORD hath spoken" (cf. 1:2). The usefulness of Eliakim's exalted position is at an end; were it to continue as it was under Eliakim it would not be for the welfare of the kingdom; its end therefore must come.

SPECIAL NOTE

אֲשֶׁר הבית על‎—1 Kings 4:6; 16:9; 18:3; 2 Kings 10:5 (הבית על‎); 18:18, 37; 19:2; Isa. 22:15; 36:3, 22; 37:2. The phrase may be rendered, "he who is over the house." In 1 Kings 16:9 it is used of an official in Tirzah, namely Artzah, when Elah was king. In 1 Kings 18:3, during Ahab's reign, Obadiah, a prophet and godly man, was "over the house." Here, no limiting city name is attached, and quite probably the office has now grown in importance in the northern kingdom. In 2 Kings 10:5 the office is mentioned in connection with "he who is over the city." Probably both the greater official and the city governor acted in concert.

An increase in the scope of duties appears in 2 Kings 15:5, where the crown prince Jotham who is "over the house" (the relative is here omitted) also performs the function of a judge, a function which belonged to the king. In 2 Kings 18:18 Eliakim is said to be "over the house," as Isaiah had predicted. Shebna is scribe and Joach the recorder. Here the three offices are mentioned together, with that of "over the house" being the more prominent. A similar mention is found in 2 Kings 19:2, save that instead of the recorder the elders of the priests appear. In the parallel passage Isa. 36:3, the three individuals are again mentioned, the name of Eliakim and Joach's father being stated, but that of Shebna being omitted. In verse 11 only the three names are found, whereas the usage in verse 22 parallels that in verse 3. In 37:2 the usage parallels 2 Kings 19:2.[53]

A three line epitaph from above the door of a rock-carved tomb in Silwan (Siloam) may be rendered:

[53] In 1935 S. H. Hooke (*Palestine Exploration Fund, Quarterly Statement for 1935*, pp. 195ff.) published a seal bearing the inscription, Gedaliah "who is over the house."

(1) This is (the sepulchre of—) yahu who is over the house. There is no silver and no gold here

(2) but (his bones) and the bones of his slave-wife with him. Cursed be the man

(3) who will open this!

On the basis of the calligraphy, this inscription is dated about 700 B.C. Cf. N. Avigad, "The Epitaph of a Royal Steward from Siloam Village," *Israel Exploration Journal*, Vol. 3, No. 3, 1953, pp. 137-152. Gevirtz, "West-Semitic Curses," *VT*, No. 11, 1961, p. 151.

An attempt in recent times has been made by R. de Vaux to show that on Egyptian papyri the name of the vezir precedes that of the scribe of Pharaoh and his herald. Hence he concludes that the office of Shebna was the Israelitic equivalent of the Egyptian vezir.[54] Each morning the vezir appeared before the king to report and to receive instructions. He then visited the chief of the treasury and had the "gates of the royal house" (i.e., the different offices of the palace) opened. All the affairs of the kingdom passed through his hands; he actually governed in the name of the king.

This was apparently the position that Joseph occupied. To him Pharaoh had said, "thou shalt be over my house" (Gen. 41:40; note Gen. 45:8, "a father to Pharaoh and a master to all his house"). It is well also to note that as Joseph was an administrator (*mōšēl*, Gen. 45: 8) of all Egypt and a father for Pharaoh, so Eliakim would have the administration and be a father for the people.

De Vaux remarks also that the common renderings of מזכיר as annalist or memorialist are incorrect, inasmuch as the *mazkîr* had a far greater function. Nor can one justify the translations *vizir* or *chancellor*. The exact equivalent is the Egyptian *whm.w*, "he who repeats, calls, announces"; the *whm nsw.t*, "herald of the king," is frequently attested. This official's duties may be found on a text in J. H. Breasted, *Ancient Records of Egypt*, II, §§ 763-771. Among other things he is to call particular matters to the Pharaoh's attention. This function is illustrated by Joseph's command to the cup bearer (*mašqeh;* cf. Akk. *rab shaqeh* and Hittite *GAL.GESTIN*), "and thou shalt remember me unto Pharaoh" (Gen. 40:14).[55] One text somewhat explicit about the functions of the *mazkîr* in Israel presents Joach, Hezekiah's *mazkîr*, as charged to parley with Sennacherib's officers at the gates of Jerusalem (2 Kings 18:18, 37; Isa. 36:3, 22).

The scribe also appears to have been an office copied from Egypt. De Vaux even believes that David's own scribe may have had a name comparable to the Egyptian *sš*, and argues that he was a foreigner

---

54 For one thing, there is an almost identical Egyptian equivalent of the title, namely, *ḥrj pr*, "head of the house."

55 Begrich would render this, *"bringe mich zur Anzeige,"* i.e., bring me as a witness against.

inasmuch as his father's name was not given (2 Sam. 8:17; 20:25; 1 Kings 4:3; 1 Chron. 18:16) .[56]

LITERATURE

R. de Vaux: *"Titres et Fonctionnaires Égyptiens a la cour de David et de Salomon,"* RB, Vol. 48, 1939, pp. 394-405.

J. H. Breasted: *Ancient Records of Egypt.*

Joachim Begrich: *"Sôfer und Mazkīr,"* ZAW, Vol. 58, pp. 1-29.

Henning Graf Reventlow: *"Das Amt des Mazkir,"* Theologische Zeitschrift, Vol. 15, 1959, pp. 161-175.

[56] This threefold organization perhaps sustains some relation to the fact that David grouped his "mighty men" in threes (cf. 2 Sam. 23:9ff.) . The Heb. word *shalish* is derived from the root *š-l-š* (three). In the Mediterranean world military commanders were grouped in threes.

"Together with them I was third ($\tau\rho\acute{\iota}\tau\sigma$)" (*Odyssey* xiv.470-71) .

"And with them Cebriones followed as the third" (*Iliad* xii.85-107) . In the fifth triad Sarpedon is the leader ("And he stood forth beyond all"—lines 101-104) . Likewise Abishai was "chief among three" (2 Sam. 23:18a) . Cf. Cyrus H. Gordon, "Homer and the Bible," HUCA, Vol. 26, 1955, p. 83.

Lastly, attention must again be directed to the three Assyrian officials, *turtanu, rab BI-LUL* and *nagir ekalli* or *abarakku.* Perhaps it is safe to say that a military triad was common both to the Aegean and Semitic world, and that this gave rise to the system of Triumvirs, found in Assyria, Palestine, and Egypt. David was not only influenced by the military triad system, but to an extent by the governmental triad system. Solomon, however, perhaps because he had been influenced by Egyptian officials, permitted the system to be more completely established.

10. TYRE, THE SEA POWER (23:1-18)

1 The burden of Tyre: Howl, ships of Tarshish; for it is laid waste, without a house, without an entrance; from the land of Kittim it is revealed to them.

2 Be silent! O inhabitants of the isle; the merchants of Sidon crossing the sea have filled thee.

3 And in great waters was the seed of Sihor, the harvest of the Nile was her revenue, and she was a traffic of nations.

4 Be ashamed, O Sidon! for the sea saith, the strength of the sea, saying, I have not travailed, and I have not borne, and I have not brought up young men nor have I reared virgins.

5 Even as the report concerning Egypt, they are pained at the report of Tyre.

1 It is fitting that the oracles directed against the nontheocratic nations conclude with one against Tyre; for as Babylon was at the heart of the kingdom of man, so Tyre was the central city of human commerce. Babylon was the center of land power, and Tyre of power on the sea. There was a contrast between them, however; for Babylon, as center of the kingdom of man, had extended her sway by warlike means, conquering other peoples and incorporating them into her intended worldwide kingdom; whereas Tyre has extended her sway and influence through peaceful means, such as trade and commerce and the planting of colonies.

All that today remains of Tyre is an insignificant little village known as Sur. The Tyre of antiquity, however, had a distinguished history (see SPECIAL NOTE). The oldest part of the town, known as Palaetyrus, lay on the mainland; but the seaport town was located on two rocky islands off the coast. King Hiram had connected the two islands by means of an embankment, and had also brought water to the larger island. This larger island was the pride of Tyre, as Ezekiel points out, "Because thine heart is lifted up, and thou hast said, I am a God, I sit in the seat of God, in the midst of the seas . . ." (Ezek. 28:2). Alexander the Great is said to have destroyed Palaetyrus completely, and to have employed the building materi-

121

als taken from it for the construction of his renowned embankment, which made possible an approach to the island city. The modern town and the mainland are now connected, the modern town lying at the north end of what was formerly the large island.

Instead of directly announcing the downfall of Tyre and the cessation of all her commerce, Isaiah begins with an imperative, thus lending vividness to his dramatic speech. In fact, each section of this chapter commences with an imperative (cf. vv. 1, 2, 4, 6, 10, 14; this is repeated again in the second main section of the chapter, v. 16). Plunging into the midst of the situation, as it were, the prophet commands the Tarshish ships to howl; they are to break out in piercing lamentation and wailing. People would have understood the reference easily, for these were the ships that plied Tyre's trade. Isaiah lends vividness to his words by personifying them. Similar dramatic beginnings are also found in 13:2; 14:29; 21:13; and 22:1. The command to howl is masculine, but the ships are feminine. There is no real difficulty, however, for it is a *constructio ad sensum*, the great stress being placed upon the imperative.[1] What is uppermost in the prophet's mind is the necessity for wailing; the subjects, namely the Tarshish ships, are almost mentioned in an afterbreath. These were the merchantmen that carried Tyre's prosperous trade to all parts of the then known world; they were successful ships, but their days of service to Tyre were at an end.

Isaiah gives a reason for his command; namely, destruction has been accomplished.[2] The verb is one often used with the names of cities, although in this particular instance the name of the city, apart from its mention in the title, is not introduced until the fifth verse. From this very fact we may see how essential the title is. If the title be removed, the latter part of the first verse does not yield

1 *Howl!*—the 2 m. pl. is employed in addressing a f. subj.; cf. 32:11. That the form is intentional is shown by its repetition in v. 14, where the f. suffix is found, *mā-'uz-zᵉ-ḵen*. The f. pl. form is not attested, but the m. pl. appears 3 times within the compass of vv. 1-14. The f. suffix in v. 14 is to be expected, but the m. imper. has a striking sound, and probably for that reason it is chosen.

2 The perfect, here used impersonally, often appears after כי to express the reason for a previous command, even though the fact expressed by the perf. may not yet actually have occurred. In the mind of the writer, it is so certain of occurrence that he employs the perfect.

a good sense. It then merely asserts that something is devastated without saying what.

The result of the devastation is that there is no house left in Tyre which one may enter.[3] The devastation is complete and utter. Ships coming from Kittim had been told of this destruction. Hence, they cannot continue on to Tyre and land there, for the city is destroyed. Where is this Kittim from which the ships had set sail? In the Scriptures the word refers in a general sense to the islands of the Aegean sea as well as the coast of Greece and possibly also to that of southern Italy. On the island of Cyprus itself there had been a Phoenician settlement known as Kition. Isaiah possibly means that as the Tarshish ships approached the islands of the northern Mediterranean, they learned of Tyre's devastation from other ships that had sailed from these islands.[4] Some commentators think that the ships had actually stopped at Cyprus, and there been informed of the destruction. At any rate, the information about Tyre originated in the northern Mediterranean and was conveyed in some manner to the returning Tarshish ships.

2 Isaiah now issues a second imperative, addressing it to those who were at home on the Phoenician coastland. The Phoenician inhabitants are commanded to be silent, for a tragedy has occurred, and the great mourning that followed this tragedy should produce silence (cf. Lam. 2:10).[5] Tyre is here designated *the island*, although possibly the reference may include the coastland generally. A reminder of the former greatness of Tyre renders more vivid the command to be silent. Now, a new condition is present. Merchants of Sidon, by which Isaiah probably means to designate Phoenicia generally, have filled the city.[6]

---

[3] Lit., *for it is devastated (away) from a house*, i.e., it is without a house. The second נמ is dependent upon the previous phrase, hence, *so that there is no entrance;* cf. 24:10.

[4] For Kittim and Tarshish, see SPECIAL NOTE. The use of *nig-lāh* is surprising, for it generally refers to the revelation of secret and mysterious matters, whereas *hug-gad* applies to communication of ordinary events that have taken place. Here the verb refers to the wholly new and unexpected, surpassing all thought.

[5] *dommû—be silent!* In some mss. *Dagesh* is surprisingly omitted from *Mem.* Kissane would connect with Akk. *damânu, to mourn*, but this is questionable. The verb *have filled thee* is pl., resolving the collective *sô-ḥēr, merchants*. Some would emend to read *his messenger*, thus avoiding a change of person. Nevertheless, such a change is not necessary. *'i—island*, is related to Egy. *'w*. Drechsler believes that the inhabitants of the islands here and in v. 6 are Tyrians, as this view alone, he thinks, maintains the gradation between vv. 2-5.

[6] *Sidon—*cf. *Iliad* vi.290ff.; *Odyssey* iv.618; Ovid *Fasti* iii.108, and biblical ref-

3 The description of Tyre's former glory and importance is continued in this verse. At the same time there is a change from the second to the third person. Turning from direct address to the city, Isaiah now speaks of her in the third person in a more or less impersonal manner. He mentions the sea over which the merchant vessels travelled as "great waters." Ezekiel later speaks of the rowers of Tyre, which have "brought thee into great waters: the east wind hath broken thee in the midst of the seas" (Ezek. 27:26). Isaiah designates what was carried over these great waters as the seed of Sihor, by which he means the seed produced in or by Sihor. What however does he intend by the word Sihor?[7] Some derive the word from a root meaning "to be black," and then refer it to the Black River, which takes its name from the black slime that made Egypt fertile. This is a doubtful explanation; the word probably is used merely as a designation of a river on the eastern border of Egypt, perhaps an eastern branch of the Nile. Isaiah in this passage is probably employing the term as a synonym for the Nile itself. This seems to be supported by the parallel phrase, *the harvest of the Nile*. The two expressions then denote what the Nile produces or brings into existence. Thus we may discover the force of the verse by rendering, "And in great waters is the seed of the Nile, the harvest of the Nile is her (i.e., Tyre's) produce." The Phoenician merchants carried the produce of the Nile in their great merchant ships over the mighty waters of the sea, and this became the revenue of Tyre from which she acquired her wealth. Perhaps the reference is primarily to grain, which was apparently scarce in Phoenicia, and yet grew profusely in the rich soil of the well-watered Egyptian land. Isaiah thus hints that the Nile is the source of Egypt's wealth and produce. Apart from the river Egypt would be able to bring forth little.

In a concluding clause the prophet summarizes what he has previously stated. Tyre's revenue became the gain or traffic of nations. The produce that Tyre received from Egypt she used in trade with other nations; indeed, it was largely this which enabled her to carry on such traffic. She was at the center of this traffic, and thus she prospered and flourished.

---

erences Gen. 10:15; Judg. 1:31; Ezek. 27:8; Acts 27:3. Sidon, modern Saida, is located on the Phoenician coast about 25 miles north of Tyre.

7 *Sihor*, in the prophets, occurs only here and in Jer. 2:18; cf. Josh. 13:3.

4 As Isaiah had previously enjoined the trading ships to howl and the inhabitants of the island to be silent, so now he commands Sidon to be ashamed. Apparently he introduces Sidon by way of contrast. Tyre, the center of the country's commerce and the source of its wealth, has been destroyed; should not what remains mourn? Sidon therefore represents what remains after the downfall of Tyre. Does Sidon, however, merely designate the remainder of the country, or is the word used to express a polarity between the two great cities? Does it stand in contrast to Tyre? This question is difficult if not impossible to answer. Without Tyre, Sidon's welfare will not be secure, and possibly it is this latter thought that Isaiah would emphasize; if one of the great cities goes, the other will also.

Isaiah commands Sidon to be ashamed, for she hears Tyre mention her own destruction. Isaiah speaks of Tyre as "the sea," although he uses this strange word anarthrously, as he did when in verse 2 he designated Tyre "island." When Kissane asks how the fall of Tyre could have made the sea childless, his question misses the mark.[8] Isaiah does not state that the fall of Tyre made the sea childless. He simply gives to Tyre the poetic name "sea," which he qualifies by identifying Tyre as the fortress of the sea. In this language there is gradation. Not only has the sea spoken, but even the fortress of the sea. The designation does, as a matter of fact, correspond accurately with the actual situation of Tyre. It is not the "old Tyre" upon the mainland of which the prophet speaks, but the island city; and it is this island city that now speaks out in complaint.[9]

In the complaint the island city personifies itself as a woman who has borne no children, as one who has not travailed. The language is strange, for actually Tyre had done all she could to become great and prosperous. And she had succeeded! Now, however, all was gone; and Tyre speaks as though she had never had any fortune. What has befallen others has not happened to her. Others, she laments, have toiled and brought forth, but not Tyre. To continue the personification, we may say that other women have labored and have brought forth children, but Tyre has not

---

8 Cf. *Com. in loc.*

9 Cf. 17:9, 10; 25:4; 27:5. Note retention of the *Qametz* in a distant open syllable; the word is in construct. This is strange if the *Qametz* represents a short vowel, and the corresponding Arabic word has a short vowel, *ma-'â-ḍun*, a *refuge*. *Qametz* is treated like a naturally long vowel and should be accompanied by *Meteg.* חלתי —cf. Ug. ḥl; Akk. ḥâlu, *to have the pains of labor.*

THE BOOK OF ISAIAH

even labored, and consequently, has brought forth no children.

The last clause of the verse, with its purely Isaianic language (cf. 1:3), fits well into what is often called a *qinah* (lamentation) metre. It contains two verbs but only one negative; this negative, however, does duty for both verbs, so that we may render, *and I have not brought up young men nor have I reared virgins.* Tyre has borne no children, at all; in such an expressive manner is she made to state the full destruction that has come to her.

5 Even Egypt is affected by news of the downfall of Tyre. In these five verses there has been a certain progression of thought. First, the fact of Tyre's devastation is stated (v. 1b). The silence of mourning comes over the Tyrian inhabitants, and then all Phoenicia listens to Tyre's grief and lament. Finally, even Egypt is shaken. In short, terse, effective sentences Isaiah shows how the report affects Egypt. "Even as," he begins; and we should expect him to continue with a verb. This he does not do, but introduces immediately the noun, "a report." This report (lit., *something heard*) goes to Egypt, for rumor travels fast.[10]

When the report reaches Egypt the country travails. Fallen Tyre had lamented that she had not travailed, but Egypt, hearing of Tyre, does travail. Tyre's destruction thus brings Egypt into the line of the extending and expanding world power of Mesopotamia, for Egypt knows that with the downfall of Tyre, she herself will be next in line to feel the effects of the outreaching empire of Assyria; the outstretching arms of the growing world power have now even conquered Tyre. Egypt herself, therefore, must face the oncoming foe. Egypt knew that her own material prosperity and welfare had been in large measure dependent upon Tyre. Tyre's removal from the scene, however, now made clear to Egypt that she too stood in the line of conquest.

6 Pass over to Tarshish, howl, ye inhabitants of the isle!

7 Is this to you a joyous one? from the days of old is her antiquity; her feet used to carry her afar off to sojourn.

8 Who hath counselled this against Tyre, the one who bestows the crown, whose merchants are princes, her traders the honorable ones of the earth.

9 The Lord of hosts hath counselled it, to profane the elevation of all beauty, to degrade the honored of all the earth.

---

[10] The abrupt language is effective; cf. 26:9. We might understand a verb, *as a report is told to Egypt. Tzor* is an objective genitive.

6 Isaiah now proceeds a step farther. Having described the tragic and sad desolation of the city itself, he appeals to its inhabitants to find a refuge in their colonies. Again he commences with an imperative, using the plural form, for he has in mind the inhabitants as individuals. During the siege of Alexander the Great the Tyrians sent their children and old people to Carthage for safety, for at that time Carthage was probably a Tyrian colony.[11] One is reminded of the beautiful language of Vergil:

> *Urbs antiqua fuit, Tyrii tenuere coloni,*
> *Karthago, Italiam contra Tiberinaque longe*
> *ostia, dives opum studiisque asperrima belli. . . .*

The prophet mentions Tarshish, for it may have been the principal colony. Inasmuch as the leading city can no longer provide a safe refuge and haven for its inhabitants, they must find that haven elsewhere. The mention of Tarshish here and also in verse 10 points to the unity of the section, connecting it with the early verses (cf. v. 1).

A few inhabitants, however, do remain.[12] They are to howl over the city, and their lament is justifiable. Even the necessity of taking refuge in the colonies is but a further bitter result of the calamity that has come upon Tyre. What is left to the inhabitants of Tyre but to break forth in piercing wailing?

7 What has become of this city whose rejoicing had been mingled with haughtiness?[13] Now there is in her only a band of poor refugees, and it is difficult to recognize in them the once rejoicing city of trade. Isaiah still addresses these refugees, and possibly

---

[11] Cf. Diodorus Siculus xvii.41, and Quintus Curtius iv.3.15.

[12] Those addressed, according to Dillmann, are not the Tyrians, but the Phoenicians. Gray finds the subject in the Phoenicians of the Palestinian coast, which would be supported by Gesenius' identification of *'i* with the Phoenician coast; cf. 20:5. Kissane thinks that those addressed are the merchants and sailors returning to Phoenicia from their voyage. Gesenius calls attention to the decision of the richest merchants in Holland in the year 1672 to remove to Batavia, if Holland could not be delivered.

[13] עליזה —note omission of the article, which may be for the sake of euphony; 1Q, however, has the article. Lit., *is this then to you (the) rejoicing one?* The word contains a secondary connotation of haughtiness; cf. 22:2 and 5:12. לכם is an ethical dative. Delitzsch renders, *is this your fate, thou full of rejoicing?* But the change in number involved is difficult to understand. The "rejoicing" has reference "to the bustle of commercial enterprise and also to the luxury and pride of Tyre" (Alexander).

includes in his address all who at one time had had pleasure in the supremacy of Tyre. "You have praised and rejoiced in Tyre," so his thought runs; "where is she now? Is this the city that produces rejoicing?" To contrast her former glory with the present condition Isaiah remarks that her antiquity is from days of old. He uses a play upon words (*qedem* and *qadmatha*), but he is not employing mere redundant expressions. Some think that he intends to mention both the origin and the antiquity of the city; more likely, however, he is merely expressing the idea that the generic or general expression of belief in the antiquity of the city (*her antiquity*) is based upon the fact that she is indeed so old (*from days of old*).[14]

The verse concludes with a further description of Tyre's widespreading reach. Isaiah speaks of her feet as those that never rested nor remained still, but were in constant motion, always carrying Tyre somewhere. He does not use the perfect but the imperfect, to suggest that, although the actions had taken place in the past, there was continuation and a lasting quality to them.[15] "Thy feet carried thee about," he says, "and did not cease." Both expressions, *thy feet,* and *carry thee about,* suggest the idea of spontaneity. Tyre acted entirely upon her own. By means of this vivid language the prophet presents the idea that Tyre's feet had carried her so that she might colonize in distant places. It is a succinct manner of summing up Tyre's colonizing activity.

8 It is time to ask a question. If such a great catastrophe has come over Tyre, it surely cannot have been accidental. There must have been planning behind it. Who, however, had planned such a thing? Who would dare devise a means to bring it about? What has happened is clearly the result of planned foresight; but who, asks the prophet, was responsible for it? Isaiah intends to answer the

[14] According to Herodotus (ii.44), the priests of Hercules boasted that their temple was 2300 years old; and Arrian (ii.16) calls it the oldest temple known to history. Josephus states that it was built 240 years before that of Solomon (*Archaeology* viii.3.1) and Justinus (xviii.3) that it was founded by the Sidonians in the year of Troy's destruction. In Josh. 19:29, the first mention in the OT, it is designated *the city, the fortress of Tyre,* i.e., *the fortified city of Tyre.* Cf. SPECIAL NOTE.

[15] *They used to carry her.* Alexander, however, translates by the future. It has been objected that the reference is not to flight to the colonies, for the flight is in ships. But the prophet is employing figurative language. He has actually personified Tyre as a woman, and merely points out how her feet have carried her about.

question, but waits until the following verse to give his answer. First, he must reflect once more on the former greatness of Tyre.

The planning was undertaken specifically against Tyre, and it was Tyre who crowned other kings.[16] The prerogative of crowning others had belonged to Tyre, had it not? Who then has dared to devise a plan whereby the king of Tyre would be deprived of a crown and Tyre herself of a king? Apparently Isaiah has in mind the activity of Tyre in crowning the kings who reigned in her colonies.[17] This is not to deny that Sidon also at times may have crowned kings in Cyprus. The emphasis, however, is upon the city that gave prominence to Phoenicia, and she is the chief one who bestows crowns.

Not only did Tyre bestow crowns, but her regal character also appeared in other respects. Her very merchants were princes and her traders the honored ones of the earth.[18] By this forceful language Isaiah does not mean that the merchants were actual princes, but merely that among merchants they might be so regarded. They were the princes of merchants, traders to whom were due the highest of honors. In this language the prophet pictures the great dignity, power, authority, and prestige of Tyre. Who could possibly devise the destruction of such a significant city? Does not the very question suggest that only a superhuman power could do so?

9 That such was the case is clearly seen from the answer. The Lord of hosts who is also the God of Israel devised this plan.[19] As He had planned and purposed with respect to Babylon (14:27) and Egypt (19:23), so also has He purposed concerning Tyre. This purpose is first expressed by the phrase, "to profane the pride of all glory." The verb employed is one that is used of profaning

---

16 Vulg. really weakens the effect by rendering *quondam coronatam, who had been crowned*. So also Syr., Targ. 1Q omits the *yod* and hence may read a passive participle. The city would then be regarded as crowned queen.

17 Cf. Herodotus i.136; iv.152; Strabo xvi.

18 Gesenius recalls that an envoy of Pyrrhus spoke of the Roman *senata, vidi civitatem regum. traders*—lit., Canaanites. Cf. *JNES*, Vol. 20, No. 4, Oct. 1961. Cf. Job 40:25; Prov. 31:21; Hos. 12:7; Zech. 14:21. The commercial activity of the Canaanites apparently led to the application of their name to merchants generally. Gesenius illustrates similar semantic developments, e.g., Chaldean for astrologer; and *"wie wir mit Italiäner, Schweizer, Savoyard, Jude, fast immer die Vorstellung des Geschäfts verbinden, welches diese Landsleute in unsern Gegenden betreiben."*

19 The suffix in *has purposed it* refers to *this* in the question of v. 8.

what is holy and so rendering it common and accessible to all, taking away from it its peculiar character of holiness. Here, then, the verb suggests the rendering common and profane of what has been dedicated to glory. The pride and boast of Tyre is to be removed, so that she will be humbled and lose all her former glory. Ezekiel spells out the thought in even greater detail, "they shall draw their swords against the beauty of thy wisdom, and they shall defile thy brightness" (Ezek. 28:8). Tyre had said, "I am of perfect beauty" (Ezek. 27:3b), and Ezekiel had addressed Tyre: "Thus saith the Lord GOD; Thou sealest up the sum, full of wisdom, and perfect in beauty" (Ezek. 28:12b).

Included in the counsel of God was also the purpose of bringing into disrepute the Tyrian merchants. God had degraded (lit., *made light*) the land of Zebulon and Naphtali (8:23), and now He would make light (i.e., degrade) the heavy ones (i.e., the honored) among traders. Their condition was to be completely reversed. Isaiah implies that the honor would be entirely removed, and nothing would be left. This verse as an answer to the preceding agrees with it in both its beginning and conclusion. Thus:

> v. 8 Who has purposed this?
> . . . . .
> the honored ones of the earth.
> v. 9 The Lord of hosts has purposed it.
> . . . . .
> the honored ones of the earth.

At the same time, the twofold use of "all" in the latter half of the verse appears to give the passage a wider application. Not only does it include reference to verse 8, but probably to all the threatenings that have gone before, threatenings which involve the entire world empire set in opposition to God. A full end is to be made, so the thought runs; all pride of glory and all the honored of the earth are to be brought to naught, for the Lord has purposed.

This verse makes clear the fact that God governs the world, and that He carries out His purposes as He will. These purposes have to do with the salvation of His own and the destruction of His and their enemies. In His own good providence He permits evil nations

130

and men to continue for a time, but at His appointed moment, the moment that is in agreement with His purpose, He acts and brings to destruction all that stands in the way of His eternal purposes. His purposes will not fail, for He is sovereign.

10 Pass over thy land like the Nile; daughter of Tarshish, there is no longer any girdle.

11 His hand he stretched upon the sea, He caused kingdoms to shake: the LORD hath commanded respecting Canaan to destroy her strongholds.

12 And he said, Thou shalt no more rejoice, O thou oppressed one, virgin of the daughter of Sidon; to Kittim arise, pass over, even there there will not be rest to thee.

13 Behold! the land of the Chaldeans; this is the people which was not; Assyria founded it for dwellers in the wilderness; they have set up his towers; they have laid bare her palaces; he has set it for a ruin.

14 Howl! ye ships of Tarshish, for your strength is laid waste.

10 Isaiah now addresses Tarshish by means of the phrase, *daughter of Tarshish*. In like manner he had spoken of the *daughter of my people* (22:4). It is a tender mode of address, designed to single out Tarshish as a representative of all the colonies of Tyre. To illustrate the freedom which the colonies now have, Tyre being destroyed, Isaiah commands them to pass freely over their land like the Nile. The point of the comparison seems to be that just as the Nile overflows her banks, and freely crosses Egypt, so the colonies are now without the restraining hand of Tyre. Isaiah had first presented his charge against Tyre, announcing her destruction. He had then commanded the remaining Tyrians to take refuge in their colonies. Now he addresses the colonies, and by means of a command shows them their complete freedom from Tyre's restraining hand.

As a reason for the command, the prophet remarks that there is no longer any girdle. The phrase is a strange one, and it is difficult to understand its precise significance. In the light of the context, however, it would seem that the girdle is mentioned to symbolize the restraining force of Tyre. The girdle has been removed, so the argument runs; and as a consequence, the colonies may move about freely as they wish.[20] Some have held that Tyre will be so

[20] *Girdle* (cf. Egy. *moh;* cf. Lambin, *op. cit.,* p. 152) is used figuratively for bonds. The reference would not be to a girdle such as worn by the nobility,

completely plundered that she will not even have a girdle left. Were this the case, however, why would the prophet single out the girdle for particular notice? Calvin believes that the reference is to the location of the city, which had been protected on all sides. But the context seems to support the view herein adopted.

11 In verse 1 Isaiah had announced the devastation of Tyre; he now introduces several details of that devastation including the manner in which it was carried out. Again he speaks of the sea, but this time uses the definite article. Up until this point the prophet has directed his threatenings against the powers of the land; now he is considering a power that depended upon the sea. By mentioning the sea, therefore, he is not referring to Tyre, as he did in verse 4, but rather to the sea as the source of Tyre's livelihood and the scope of her rule. On the sea Tyre was sure of safety, for she believed herself to be the master thereof. There was One, however, whom alone the winds and the waves obeyed. As the Syrians had had to learn that the God of Israel was no local god of the mountains (1 Kings 20:23), so Tyre must learn that the God of Israel has power over the sea and that the sea will feel the punishing power of His outstretched hand. Isaiah speaks with vigor and emphasis. *His hand,* he begins, forming a *casus pendens;* and the words, being placed in an emphatic position, are the symbol of punishment (cf. 5:25; 9:11, 16, 20; 10:4; 14:26, 27). God has Himself stretched out His hand, for the time has come when He desires to bring to desolation the haughty city on the Phoenician seacoast.

In stretching out His hand, He has also shaken kingdoms that formerly had not been shaken. These included the Phoenician coastland, and the countries dependent upon Tyre. Egypt also is probably to be included (v. 5), as well as the lands beyond the sea (v. 12). But the chief object of the Lord's punitive hand is Canaan.[21] It is against (*'el*) her that He has issued a command, and

---

but possibly to a cord or loin cloth of the slave; cf. 3:4. Cf. Herodotus i.163; iv.52; Diodorus v.38; Josephus *Archaeology* ix.14.2; Ezek. 26:17.

21 כנען —here used in the restricted sense of Canaan. Cf. also Josh. 5:1, and *NSI*, p. 350. מעוזניה —In the inf. the *He* is sometimes elided; cf. Isa. 3:8; 29:15; 33:1. Note also the omission of *yod* in an inf. const. *Hiphil,* which is not common. 1Q, however, exhibits both *He* and *yod.* 1Q reads *m'wzyh.* It appears that *Dagesh forte* is resolved by the insertion of a *Nun.* 1Q would really seem to support this. Delitzsch, however, maintains that there is a transposition of

this command is for the purpose of destroying her fortresses. The verb *command* is not a mere synonym of *stretched out his hand*, but rather indicates that the providence of God is an unfolding of what He has decreed. No mere purposeless chain of events, therefore, is occurring; but rather a plan is being carried out, which is the result of God's own commands.

12 The verse begins with the words *And he said*, which are to be taken as resumptive. They simply point to a further carrying out or expression of the message of the Lord. It is as though the prophet had said, "Furthermore, in addition to what has just been related, the Lord also said. . . ." With this introductory statement, *And he said*, we are prepared for the further revelation given in this verse. Isaiah now speaks to the daughter of Sidon, for Sidon evidently represents what remains after the downfall of Tyre. "Do not proceed to rejoice again," says the prophet, "for there will be no ground for rejoicing. The country is conquered and the virgin daughter of Sidon is overcome."[22] Isaiah's expression may be literally rendered, *virgin of the daughter of Sidon*, by which he merely intends to compare Sidon with a virgin. This virgin, he adds, is one that is conquered. The verb may be used of maltreatment both in the sexual as well as in the social and juridical sphere. Sidon is oppressed, overcome, conquered, but nevertheless she is the virgin of the daughter of Sidon. We may best understand the prophet as addressing her first as the *overcome one*, and then as the *virgin of the daughter of Sidon*.

Sidon must not rejoice, so the argument continues, but must flee. She has been lethargic. She must now arise, and flee to Cyprus (Kittim). To do so, however, will not bring her the rest that she desires.[23]

---

letters and that we should read *mā-'un-zey-hā*, and compares *tām-nú*, Lam. 3: 22, and *qoḇ-nó*, Num. 23:13.

22 הַמְעֻשָּׁקָה—Note omission of *Dagesh* in *Mem*, which is unusual, for *Dagesh* is generally retained in the liquids. For exceptions cf. GKC § 35 b. The word stands first for the sake of emphasis. *virgin—bᵉ-ṯû-laṯ* is construct, *the virgin of the daughter of Sidon;* each gen. is epexegetical, hence, *virgin daughter of Sidon*. The reference is not specifically to Tyre as the daughter city of Sidon, nor even to Canaan, i.e., Phoenicia, but actually is an address to Sidon herself; for Sidon represents Phoenicia. *Kittim*—expresses the acc. of place, and precedes the verb to give emphasis.

23 The construction is impersonal. Cf. Job 3:12; Neh. 9:28.

13 Just as verses 8 and 9 within the compass of verses 6-9 called attention to the One who accomplished Tyre's destruction, so within the compass of verses 10-13 this verse points to the land from which comes God's instrument in performing His work. One might expect the prophet to direct attention to the Chaldeans themselves; but, strangely, he would have his hearers look to their land instead. It has been objected, for example by Dillmann, that the author would not have written *land of the Chaldeans* instead of *Chaldeans*. But why would not Isaiah have written this way? His purpose was to direct men's attention to the east, from whence Tyre's conquerors came. It is the desert land from which the invader comes, and to this desert land one must look if he would understand the calamity that has befallen Tyre.[24]

Isaiah follows these introductory words with a parenthesis that bristles with difficulties. We may translate: *This is the people,*[25] *it was not; Assyria founded it to be desert dwellers.* The prophet's purpose, it would seem, is to point out that the people who are now dwellers in the Chaldean desert are those whose power came into significance by means of Assyria. The sentence *this is the people it is not* means, *this is the people which was not.* Such a strong statement is not a denial of the previous existence of the Chaldeans, but merely means that the nation had not previously possessed a significant existence. It did not have the great, powerful, organized form that characterized it when it came to the Mediterranean coast and wrought Tyre's destruction.[26]

What brought the Chaldean people to power and significance? It was Assyria, as exemplified by Tiglath-pileser III, which caused the Mesopotamian power to come to great life and to extend its territory by conquering other nations. This process came to its great culminating point under Chaldea, whose king was the head of gold of Nebuchadnezzar's colossus.

Thus, we would render the verb *yasad* by *establish* or *found*, and interpret it in the figurative sense given above. This interpretation finds support in Habakkuk 1:12b, "O LORD, thou hast or-

[24] Jeremiah follows Isaiah's practice; Jer. 25:12; 50:1, 45; Ezek. 12:13; and *land of Babylon*, Jer. 50:28; 51:29.
[25] Some hold that the pronoun is attributive but in an emphatic position, *this people*; cf. Ex. 32:1; Josh. 9:12; Green, *Hebrew Grammar*, § 252:2a. On the other hand, the usage is probably normal; *this is the people.* The force is either *this people which was not* or *this is the people which was not.*
[26] Cf. Deut. 32:21 for a similar usage.

dained them for judgment; and, O mighty God, thou hast established them for correction," and in Psalm 104:8.

The phrase has been taken to mean that the land of the Chaldeans had been colonized by the Assyrians.[27] But this goes counter to the known facts of history, and it may well be questioned whether such is the meaning of the verse. In the light of the entire emphasis of this particular section of Isaiah (i.e., chapters 13–27) we think that it is not. The prophet, in other words, is not speaking of the physical origin of the Chaldean nation.[28]

It is God who brings nations to power and prestige. Assyria, however, has taken unto herself the prerogatives that are God's alone, and has brought into motion the great force that culminated in the Chaldean power; and in this sense she has established that nation.

The latter half of the verse consists of three short, unconnected sentences. *they have set up his towers*—One cannot be certain, but it would seem that these three short sentences relate what Tyre herself had done. The first sentence asserts that the inhabitants of Tyre have set up protective fortresses or towers to protect the city from the oncoming enemy.[29] It is also possible, however, to refer the language to the Chaldeans and to their manner of warfare. If so, the thought would be that the Chaldeans had set up towers which they used in besieging the city. It is a question, however, whether the Chaldeans actually used such towers as instruments of besieging.

they have laid bare her palaces—The meaning of this verb is apparent from Isa. 32:11.[30] The reference is to a stripping of the palaces of all their ornament and contents. Again, the question arises, Who is the subject?

he has set it for a ruin—Here the subject is singular, and it

---

[27] Thus Rosenmüller, "*ab Assyriis congregati, et in urbes collecti sunt.*"

[28] Kissane would substitute *Assyria* for *land of the Chaldeans*, and holds that the words *this was the people, it was not Assyria* were added later. Others propose to substitute *Kittim* (Duhm) or *Canaan* (Driver) for Chaldeans. Duhm labels the passage "*eine böse crux interpretum.*"

[29] בחין—cf. Egy. *bhn* ($Q^e re$) . בחן designates a tower; cf. 32:14. The plural suffix with a singular noun probably refers to the collective concept *people;* cf. Jer. 13:20; $K^e tiv$ Mic. 1:11. *They* (the people) *have erected their watchtower.*

[30] The root is probably *'arar, to lay bare*. Cf. Jer. 51:58 and Ps. 137:7; Hab. 3:13. The suffix in *her palaces* refers to Tyre.

would seem to refer to the invading army.[31] The Chaldean has set Tyre for a ruin. The three short sentences at least indicate the rapidity by which the work, stroke by stroke, is carried out. Even though there are difficulties in the interpretation, the central emphasis is clear. The work of destroying Tyre will be carried out successfully and completely.

Thus, majestic Tyre, praised for her stand against Assyria, falls by an offshoot from Assyria. Desert dwellers bring about the downfall of the great city of culture. The fortress of the sea, supposedly impregnable, falls at the hands of inhabitants of the steppes, using the weapons of land armies.

14 Again Isaiah commands the ships of Tarshish to howl. This closing verse of the first section is similar to the opening one, and thus forms a fitting ending, rounding off the whole. The unity of the section is apparent. Twice the prophet has asked questions, and in thirteen verses has employed nine imperatives. One advance, however, is noticeable. In verse 1 a general statement was made, "it is devastated." The subject was not mentioned; here, however, a subject is mentioned, namely, "your strength." It is the strength of the Tarshish ships to which Isaiah refers, and that strength was Tyre. The root that appears in this noun had been employed before, for Tyre had been described as the fortress (*ma-'oz*) of the sea, and the Lord had given a command to destroy fortresses (*ma 'uzneha*). Because of her policies and vigor in executing them, the ships of Tarshish could ply their trade. With their strength gone, however, they could but howl.

15 And it shall come to pass in that day that Tyre shall be forgotten seventy years, according to the days of one king; after the end of seventy years it will be to Tyre as the song of a harlot.

16 Take a harp, go about the city, O forgotten harlot; play well, sing much, that thou mayest be remembered.

17 And it shall come to pass at the end of seventy years that the LORD will visit Tyre, and she shall return to her hire, and shall play the harlot with all the kingdoms of the earth upon the face of the ground.

18 And her gain and her hire will be holiness to the LORD; it shall not be stored and it shall not be hoarded; for her gain will be to those who sit before the LORD, to eat to satiety, and for choice clothing.

---

[31] Drechsler takes the singular suffix as a bringing together of the previous plurals.

15 The following four verses are written in prose and form a contrast to the preceding fourteen verses in poetic style. The reason for this is to make more prominent the conclusion of the preceding. What is now stated gives the result of the destruction of Tyre. In characteristic manner Isaiah introduces this section with, *And it shall come to pass in that day.* It is the language of prophetic prediction, and is similar to that found in the latter part of chapter nineteen. "At that time," the prophet declares, "when Tyre will be devastated, she will be forgotten for seventy years. She will be erased from the minds of men and they will not think of her, a condition which will continue for seventy years. Formerly her name had been upon the lips of all; for seventy years it will be on the lips of none. For the lifetime of a man (threescore and ten years—Ps. 90:10) this forgetting will continue."[32] The period of time is further specified as "according to the days of one king," a phrase that is subject to various interpretations. Some hold that the reference is simply to the ordinary life span, and that the reason why Isaiah speaks of "one king" rather than "one man" is that he is dealing with kings. This can hardly be regarded as convincing. The phrase is exceedingly difficult, but the following observations may be in place. It refers not to the lifetime of a king but to the length of his reign. This is shown by Isaiah's use of the phrase elsewhere (cf. 1:1; 7:1, etc.). Passages such as 16:14 and 21:16 give a clue to understanding the words. They show that the phrase means "according to human reckoning," or "as men would reckon the days of a king." Hence we might paraphrase: "seventy years as men reckon the reign of one king." Seventy years, however, is a long time for a king to reign. Possibly the point is that it is wiser to make the reckoning too high than too low, in order to show that for a very long time Tyre will be forgotten. This interpretation is obviously not entirely satisfactory, but it has fewer difficulties than other views.

---

32 וְנִשְׁכַּחַת—1Q omits this word and everything following to כְּשִׁירַת. 1Q would therefore be translated: "And it shall be in that day to Tyre like the song of a harlot." Dillmann and König regard the form as a part., although a part. after *waw* cons. is not normal (but cf. Gen. 20:16); one would also expect an auxiliary to follow the participle. Dillmann claims that even as a perf. 3 f. for *niš-kᵉ-ḥaṭ* there is difficulty, inasmuch as only in the *Lamed-He* and *Lamed-yod* verbs does *-aṭ* serve for *-ah*. Dillmann takes it as an Aramaism, like Ezek. 46:17.
The form, however, is not a part. (59:15), but a pret., possibly dialectical, preserving the original *t;* cf. Deut. 32:36. To avoid the occurrence of two accented syllables, the accent is retarded; cf. 1 Chron. 14:2.

137

The latter part of the verse is fairly clear. At the end of the seventy years, i.e., when the period of seventy years has expired, then the fortune of Tyre will be like that which is depicted in the well-known song sung by forgotten harlots. It seems best to take the word *harlots* in a generic sense, i.e., the song is one that harlots sing, and not the song of any one particular harlot. Why, however, is such a comparison made? Apparently because the trade of Phoenicia could suitably be compared with prostitution. For the satisfaction of fleshly desire men were seeking as much gain as possible. It was an apt comparison, similar to that which Nahum made of Nineveh: "Because of the multitude of the whoredoms of the well-favored harlot, the mistress of witchcrafts, that selleth nations through her whoredoms, and families through her witchcrafts" (3:4). Note also: "For all nations have drunk of the wine of the wrath of her fornication, and the kings of the earth have committed fornication with her, and the merchants of the earth are waxed rich through the abundance of her delicacies" (Rev. 18:3). For the sake of material gain men may sell their souls, as well as for the gratification of fleshly appetites and desires.

16 This verse gives the words of the song. It is probably the remains of some profane, popular song that Isaiah incorporates into his prophecy. The song is evidently sung by a harlot who has become old and forgotten and is addressing herself, singing in self-pity in the hope of attracting attention.

Take the harp—This instrument was used in the feasts of the luxurious inhabitants of Judah which Isaiah had earlier condemned; see 5:12. It was a stringed instrument that could be carried in the hand and played in accompaniment to the song as the harlot went about seeking to draw attention to herself. This is the first step she must perform in order to accomplish her purpose.

go about the city—Men will not come to her; she must go in search of them. In Proverbs 7:10ff. there is an illustration of what is intended. The classical writers contain allusions and illustrations of the same thing.[33] The picture is that of an oriental bagadere, who went about the streets of the city singing in the hope of gaining notice.

---

[33] Horace *Epistolae* i.14, 251: *"nec meretrix tibicina; cuius Ad strepitum salias."*

O forgotten harlot—In these words the singer addresses herself, expressing a tone of self-pity. Her own charms are no longer sufficient; she must rely upon song and music to come to her aid. The designation *forgotten* ties in with the same word applied to Tyre in the previous verse.

play well—lit., *do well in respect to playing*. The emphasis falls upon the adverbial concept. In playing the harp she must do well, else she will not be noticed.

multiply song—One song will not be sufficient; she is so completely forgotten that she must give all possible effort to her task. She knows that to regain her former status is a well-nigh hopeless task. She must, therefore, if she is to succeed, sing song after song.

that thou mayest be remembered—These words come as a concluding climax. All works up to this; all this effort and striving is in order that she may be remembered. To be forgotten is the greatest calamity. Horace mocks at a harlot who is old and forgotten. But here is no mocking at the harlot; here rather is the setting forth of her tragic condition in such a way as to arouse pity over the hardness of her lot. The poem is beautifully constructed, each line corresponding perfectly as to the number of words, and each line furthermore consisting of three pairs of words with the climactic thought appearing last.

17 Leaving the song of the harlot, Isaiah returns to his prose predictions. *And it shall be*, he says, and so resumes the prophecy. At the end of seventy years the Lord will visit Tyre, this time not to punish her, but to help and to restore her. The result of the Lord's action is that Tyre will return to her hire. In the song the harlot had made every effort to draw to herself the notice of men. Tyre will do likewise. She will have to bend every effort to regain her strength. This, however, she cannot do. She can only recover her former position when the Lord permits her to do so. Sometimes God visits a nation to punish it; sometimes for its advantage. God takes special action; and because He does, Tyre may once again ply her trade and obtain the hire that comes therefrom.[34]

Once again she will begin her former lucrative gain; and this action is described in the words, *she will play the harlot with all*

---

34 Jer. 27:22. אתננה—note the absence of *Mappiq in the suffix* (and the Masoretic note, "*lô' mappîq hē'—non est producens literam He*"). I do not understand why *Mappiq* should be omitted. The word is explained by *saḥ-rāh* in v. 18.

the kingdoms of the earth. As before, so now her trade will be universal. This last aspect is emphasized by the addition of the phrase, *upon the faces of the ground.* These words are difficult to interpret. In Genesis 2:6 they refer to a definite locality that is watered by the "mist" arising from the earth. Here too there appears to be a contrast between "earth" (*'eretz*) and "ground" (*ᵃdamah*). One cannot press the language unduly, but possibly Isaiah means to say that Tyre's traffic will be universal: it will be present wherever a nation is found upon earth. Why, however, is the trade still designated by the term *commit fornication?* The answer would seem to be that the purpose of Tyre still was self-gratification, the making of money. She was not concerned at this point with the welfare of the kingdom of God, but only with what she could obtain. She would, therefore, sell her goods for what she could receive in exhange. Despite her downfall, she still would act as a harlot.

18 Again Isaiah begins with *And it shall be,* and with this phrase points out that, whereas Tyre may have purposed one thing with her trade, the result would be different from what she had intended. She had planned that her trade and hire be gain for herself; such, however, was not to be the result. Instead they will be holiness to the Lord. Deuteronomy 23:18 forbade using the hire of a harlot for a vow, for such was an abomination to the Lord. What is described here, however, is metaphorical and is not a violation of the Mosaic commandment.[35]

These gains of Tyre will become "holiness," i.e., dedicated gifts, to the Lord, set apart for Him, gifts which partake of the nature of holiness. It is nevertheless a startling and perhaps even shocking picture. We can best understand it on the presupposition that Tyre has truly become converted.[36] She has fully returned to her former prestige in trade, but the ends of that trade are now different. We should probably think of a gradual and not a sudden change. Tyre began as before, seeking only her own ends; and so her traffic might still be called "playing the harlot." A change does come, however; and those ends which she first sought are now abandoned, and Tyre gives her gifts unto the Lord.

[35] Dillmann thinks that putting together a literal and figurative expression is not Isaianic.

[36] Some scholars, however, e.g. Dillmann, think that the conversion of Tyre is not in view, but that the emphasis is rather upon the treasure of the Tyrians returning to Jerusalem.

it shall not be stored and it shall not be hoarded—This is the opposite of what formerly was the case. "And Tyre did build herself a stronghold, and heaped up silver as the dust, and fine gold as the mire of the streets" (Zech. 9:3). Formerly she had stored up her gain for herself; now she dedicates it to the Lord. This she does not of compulsion, but freely. Gladly she gives what she has acquired to the Lord. One mark of the truly converted person is the willingness with which he gives to the Lord and recognizes that all that he has belongs to the Lord.

This gain will not be for herself but will be given to the servants of God. These are described as *those who sit*. Possibly there is intended by these words an allusion to the relationship between the disciple who sits listening to his master and the master who instructs (cf. 2 Kings 4:38). Perhaps the word also has a wider meaning and may contain a reflection upon the chambers occupied by priests and Levites when they were serving in the Temple. Whatever the precise force of the words may be, the reference is to those who serve as master. They are therefore true and devoted servants of the Lord.

In line with the Masoretic accentuation the words should be rendered, "for (it is) to those who are sitting; before the Lord will be its reward." This division emphasizes the fact that Tyre's hire will be given before the Lord, and so will truly become holy. The purpose of giving these consecrated gifts is then stated: *to eat to satiety and for choice clothing.* At first sight this language is startling; and some, such as Marti, have completely missed its true significance. It is well to note Marti's words: "*qodesh* means only a 'dedicated gift', Judaism is partly returning to the old heathenism; ethics no longer speaks out as with the prophets (cf. the Corban of the New Testament, Mark 7:11), if only the gain of Tyre's world trade redounds to the good of the Jews, that they can eat enough and be elegantly clothed. . . ." By means of these figures, "eating to satiety" and "being well clothed," the prophet, however, simply means that the people who serve God will be blessed in rich measure. Tyre's gains will contribute to this end. As Tyre's own colonies had once stood in relationship to herself and to the sanctuary that was in her midst, so now she will stand in relation to the Temple of the true God. She will be dependent upon that God and will devote her gains to His service. The result will be blessing for those who serve at His Temple. It is the same thought that we find, expressed elsewhere in Scripture: "The kings of Tarshish and of

141

the isles shall bring presents: the kings of Sheba and Seba shall
offer gifts" (Ps. 72:10). Such gifts were really brought to the Lord
Himself, and we may see a true fulfillment of the prophecy, although not an exhaustive one, in the action of the wise men bringing gifts to Jesus. Furthermore, the blessings of the age to come are
sometimes pictured under the figures used here. "The king's
daughter is all glorious within: her clothing is of wrought gold"
(Ps. 45:13).

SPECIAL NOTE ON ISAIAH 23:13

According to Marti, if we follow Meier in reading *Kittim* for *Kasdim*
everything becomes clear. While the transition is not easy, nevertheless, Marti holds that if we assume the presence of *hiš-mîd* preceded by
an abbreviated form *K"*, we may understand how *Kasdim* arose. Thus
we may render, *See! he has devastated the land of the Kittim.* The rest
is a gloss, for *zeh* often introduces glosses. After the gloss was accepted into the text, it itself served enlargements and changes. Originally it read, *this is the people, which is a colony of mariners (See-
fahrer), which established its towers, cities and palaces.* Marti takes
tzî-yîm in the sense of *Schiffer,* appealing to Num. 24:24; Dan. 11:30.
The *'ōr*rû,* he thinks, is a corruption of *'ārāw, his cities.* The purpose
of this remark was to designate the Cypriotes as one of the Sidonian
colonies, but it was misunderstood. The *'ᵃ-šer yᵉ-sō-dāh* was read
'aš-šûr yᵉ-sā-dāh; and finally, *it was formerly not* came into the text.

Delitzsch thinks Ewald's conjecture may be right, namely to substitute *Canaaneans* for *Chaldeans.* Thus, he translates, "Behold the
land of the Canaaneans: this people has come to nothing; Asshur has
prepared it for the beasts of the desert." Delitzsch thinks that *lō'* may
have substantive force (Jer. 33:25). Delitzsch realizes, however, that
the mention of seventy years in the following is decisive proof that
Isaiah had the Chaldeans and not Asshur in view as the destroyers of
Tyre.

Penna thinks the text affirms that Tyre was destroyed by the Chaldeans, and that this is to be taken in connection with Nebuchadnezzar's siege. A natural reading of the text, however (*the land of the
Chaldeans, this is the people, it was not Assyria, etc.*), shows a polemi-
cal note that wanted to exclude any reference to an Assyrian invasion
or occupation. Such a text, thinks Penna, lends itself to corrections
and manipulation: *"Naturalmente un testo come questo, con un ritmo
poetico difficilmente riconoscibile, si prestava bene ad essere rimanipo-
lato e corretto."* Penna then mentions some of the proposed corrections.
Among these is the hypothesis that omits the words, *the land of the
Chaldeans* and *it was not.* This makes the Assyrians responsible for the
destruction of Tyre. This explanation, however, Penna points out,

requires a meaning for *yā-sad* not attested elsewhere. Penna thinks that a gloss is present and that the verse affirms that the Chaldeans (13:19) have brought about the destruction. The plural verb is a *constructio ad sensum* agreeing with *Chaldeans*.

Bruno is quite radical in his emendations. In place of *behold! the land,* he would read *han-na-ʿᵉrātz;* Ps. 89:8, *the fearful.* This would be the subject of *yā-nûᵉh* (v. 12). He renders: "12b *Zu den Kitthaern, auf! zieh hinüber—auch dort wird dir keine Ruhe gönnen* 13 *der Fürchterliche. Nachdem er ihren Hafen zerstört hat', gibt es kein Volk, dass ihn zum Weichen bringen könnte.*" This is without textual support.

Bentzen follows Procksch in assuming that Assyria was the original subject, and Sidon the object. He takes the order, *Behold! Assyria founded it, they* (i.e., Assyria) *erected its towers.*

Dillmann believes that the literal interpretation does not yield a good sense, at least not one that Isaiah would have intended. Why the mention of *the land of the Chaldeans* and not merely *Chaldeans?* After discussing the various proposals and pointing out their weaknesses, Dillmann, assuming the presence of glosses, renders, *Siehe das Hand der Ch. . . . er hat es den Wüstentieren bestimmt . . . hat es zum Trümmerhaufen gemacht.* This sentence comes from the Persian times, refers to the fall of Babylon, and was transformed by a glossator (*c.* the time of Alexander the Great?) into its present form. Possibly *Kasdim* is a later insertion. "*Was D u. sonst aus dem V. herausbraut ist Schaum.*"

It will be instructive to note how an older interpreter deals with this text. After the prophet has shown how Jehovah is the supreme cause of Tyre's overthrow, declares Rosenmüller, he calls attention to the instruments which God had decided to use in this work. He translates: *En terram Chaldaeorum! hic populus non fuit: Assur fundavit eum deserticolis.* By the land of the Chaldeans the prophet refers to that region which extends from Babylon and the Chaldean mountains to the Persian boundaries. זה העם stands for, "this people was not a people," i.e., great, illustrious, as in Deut. 32:21. Hence, *en!—non ita pridem in desertis vagatos, nullum habentes nomen, nullam rempublicam,* like the type of life depicted in Job 1:17.

Cf. Wilhelm Rudolph, *"Jesaja 23, 1-14," Festschrift Friedrich Baumgärtel,* Erlangen, 1959, pp. 166-174.

SPECIAL NOTE: TYRE - TARSHISH - KITTIM
Tyre

Phoenician צר; Ug. *Sr-m;* Amarna and Akk. *surru;* B τύρος.
The origin of Tyre is lost in obscurity. Herodotus claims that it was founded in the 28th century. In the 14th century B.C., it was an established city, for the Amarna texts speak of it. Abimilki (Abimelek), its king, remained faithful to the Egyptian Pharaohs, although several

were turning to the Amorites. Likewise, in Keret, we read of the "shrine of Asherah of Tyre."

Egyptian power and influence in Syria, however, was on the decline, a fact that appears from the Wen-Amon text. More and more Tyre, losing its position of dependency on Egypt, grew in stature, becoming noted for its trades and shipping.

2 Sam. 24:7 shows that the border of the Israelite kingdom extended to Tyre; and David's palace was constructed with the help of Hiram, king of Tyre (2 Sam. 5:11; 1 Chron. 14:1). Hiram also furnished Solomon with cedar and cypress wood in exchange for wheat and oil (1 Kings 5; 1 Chron. 22:4; 2 Chron. 2:3-18). At the time of Solomon there were interesting relationships between Judah and Tyre (cf. 1 Kings 7:13-45; 9:11-14; 9:26-28). The harbor of Tyre, probably on the south side of the island, was protected by a breakwater, 820 yards in length and about 9 in width, built by Hiram.

Later, Jezebel, daughter of Ethbaal, king of Tyre and priest of Astarte, married Ahab, king of Israel (1 Kings 16:31), and sought to introduce the Baal worship into Israel. Tyre grew in wealth and power, becoming noted in particular for its production of purple. About 850 B.C., Tyrian colonists founded Carthage in north Africa, and Tyrians worked the gold mines of Thrace (Strabo).

In 876 Tyre began to pay tribute to Ashurnasirpal of Assyria, and it also suffered in the battle of Qarqar, 853. Nevertheless, despite the tribute which it was forced to pay, it continued to assert its independence. Tiglath-pileser III besieged it, as did also Shalmanezer. Siege was laid to the city for 5 years, but in 722 it made a treaty with the Assyrians. Finally, the Tyrian King Elu-eli was expelled by Sennacherib and replaced by Ethbaal of Sidon. Sidon was destroyed in 677 and Baal of Tyre then paid tribute to Esarhaddon.

Later Nebuchadnezzar besieged Tyre for 13 years before being able to conquer it, in 572. With the advent of Persian power Sidon became more prominent than Tyre, and in 520 Carthage became independent. In 351 Sidon was destroyed by Artaxerxes III Ochus; and after the defeat of the Persians by Alexander, Sidon surrendered. Tyre, however, resisted the Greeks, depending upon its location to save it. Tyre stood alone, for the other Phoenician cities did not come to its aid. Alexander built a mole, about half a mile long and 200 feet wide, extending out from the coast. With the aid of this mole he was able to attack Tyre for 7 months and then conquer it. Alexander's revenge on the defeated city was cruel, for 2000 of its leaders were hanged and about 30,000 of the inhabitants sold into slavery.

The city never again attained its former glory, although in 126 B.C it became independent, remaining a center of commerce and industry throughout the Roman period. In A.D. 636 the Arabs conquered the city; and today it is but a small coastal town, the modern Sur, having about 6000 inhabitants.

See: P. K. Hitti, *History of Syria*, 1951; A. Poidebard, *Un grand port disparu: Tyr*, 1939; G. Contenau, *La civilisation phénicienne*, 1928; W. B. Fleming, *The History of Tyre*, 1915.

Tarshish

In the Bible Tarshish appears as the name of a place, far distant from Palestine, difficult to locate. In Isa. 23 the ships of Tarshish are connected with Kittim, i.e., Cyprus and the Aegean. Gen. 10:4 and Isa. 66:19 also tie the word in with the Greek world.

On the other hand, passages such as 1 Kings 10:22; 2 Chron. 9:21 (cf. Ps. 72:10) ; 1 Kings 22:49 point in a different direction, as also 2 Chron. 20:36; namely, Eziongeber and India. Tarsus in Asia Minor has also been proposed, and Tartessus in Spain at the mouth of the Guadalquivir river has been supported by many. At present there is a tendency to locate Tarshish in north Africa.

Kittim

According to Josephus (*Antiquities* i.vi.1), the word Kittim comes from the name of the city-state Kition (Latin, Citium, today Larnaka) on the southern coast of the island of Cyprus. In Phoenician inscriptions the city is designated כתי. By the time of Isaiah the island's population was largely Greek. (Cf. also Gen. 10:4; 1 Chron. 1:7.)

Under Sargon, Cyprus became subject to Assyria, and could no longer be a haven for Tyrian ships or for Phoenicians who sought to escape Assyria. Esarhaddon claimed that his power extended from Cyprus as far as Tarshish.

Whereas generally in the Old Testament the word stands for Cyprus, the book of Daniel refers it to the Romans (Dan. 11:30) .

Cf. G. Hill, *A History of Cyprus*, I, 1940.

B. GOD'S SOVEREIGNTY MANIFESTED IN SALVATION AND JUDGMENT; CONCLUSION TO CHAPTERS 13–23 (24:1–27:13)

INTRODUCTION TO CHAPTERS TWENTY-FOUR–TWENTY-SEVEN

With these chapters we come to one of the most remarkable sections of the entire prophecy. It is obvious that they form a close connection with the preceding prophecies against the nations. Indeed, they are a fitting conclusion to those prophecies. On the other hand, if chapters 24–27 are simply an isolated unit, they are practically impossible to understand. That this is the case is shown by the different interpretations which have been advanced on the part of those who deny these chapters to Isaiah and also deny their integral relationship to what has gone before.

As the exposition proceeds, we shall endeavor to point out the close relationship which actually does exist between these chapters and those which have gone before. The reader may at this point be interested in a few obvious relationships. Let him compare

24:13	with	17:5, 6
24:16	with	21:2
27:9	with	17:8
25:3	with	1:8; 23:18

It is not merely by comparison of individual verses or phrases, however, that one sees this relationship. Here we find mention of a land and of a city or cities, and these are not designated by name. Here is mention of cities, towers, high walls; and again no identification or designation of them is given. Yet they are to be cast down and made equal to the surface of the land (cf. 25:2; 26:5, 6; 27:10, 11). We read of powerful rulers or tyrants whose downfall is celebrated (24:16; 25:2, 4, 5; 26:10, 11; 27:1, 4, 5, 7, 11). The mention of these matters raises questions. What is the prophet talking about? Why does he not identify more clearly his themes?

These questions really receive an answer when we perceive that he is now uniting into one, as it were, all those enemies of God's people which he had previously (chapters 13–23) discussed individually. Consequently, when he now predicts judgment it is not local but universal,

146

one which will cover the entire covenant-breaking earth; and in this judgment the theocratic nation Judah will also be included (24:1-13, 15, 16, 18-23).

After this widespread judgment (and essentially the same picture is found in 2:12ff.) there will come a world-embracing salvation (25:6-8; 26:9, 21; 27:1, 6), with the result that the remnant saved from the four corners of the earth will praise the glory and majesty of God, and the prisoners who have been delivered from Assyria and Egypt will worship the Lord in Jerusalem (24:15-16; 27:13). As Hävernick well sums up the relation of this section to the preceding: "The connection with chapters 13—23 is not merely external: our prophecy is the inner fruit, the result of the perceptions granted to the prophet, whereby these first find their true conclusion and explanation and are raised to their highest unity."

1 Behold! the LORD is about to pour out the land and make it empty, and he will turn down its face, and will disperse its inhabitants.

2 And it shall be, as with the people, so with the priest; as with the servant, so with the master; as with the maid, so with her mistress; as with the buyer, so with the seller; as with the lender, so with the borrower; as with the creditor, so with the debtor.

3 The land shall utterly be emptied and utterly spoiled, for the LORD hath spoken this word.

1 In characteristic manner Isaiah begins with a tremendous "behold!" and thus strengthens the significance of what he is about to say.[1] With both feet, as it were, we are plunged into the midst of catastrophe and judgment. These are events of great moment, and they deserve to be thus introduced. In a few short bold sentences, Isaiah compactly sets forth the heart of the judgment which is pictured in the following sections. This is a characteristic procedure of his. Although the word "behold!" does refer to something that will take place in the future, it does not necessarily indicate the immediate or even near future. In fact, from these words alone, it is impossible to tell precisely when the events described will occur. That must be determined on the basis of other considerations. Isaiah had used this same word, for example, in announcing the birth of the Messiah in 7:14; and we meet with it twice more in these

1 *Behold!*—a characteristic Isaianic opening (cf. 3:1; 7:14; 17:1; 19:1, etc.), pointing to the future, and usually to the near future. It may upon occasion refer to the past. B, however, translates the verbs as future. Procksch thinks that the introductory *hinneh* characterizes the prophecy as a vision.

147

chapters, namely 25:9 and 26:21. Certainly, the prophet does not refer to what is past, as Gesenius suggests in his commentary. The real theme of the prophecy, however, is not the catastrophe but the Lord. Immediately following the ejaculation are the words, *the Lord.* As in 2:12ff. emphasis had been placed upon the Lord of hosts, for He is the One who would act, and then upon the judgment to follow when the Lord had been exalted, so here, before we hear about judgment, we are brought face to face with the Lord.[2] Two participles are then used and these are followed by two finite verbs, each being introduced by *waw* consecutive. The two participles present a striking sound, *boqeq, boleqah.*[3] We may probably render the first, "will empty," in the sense of laying waste. It is difficult to tell precisely what figure is intended, although some, by reason of an appeal to the Arabic, believe that it is the figure of a bottle being turned upside down and emptied of its contents, the verb alluding to the sound as the vessel is being emptied.[4] This cannot be pressed, however; and possibly we do better to appeal to Jeremiah 19:7, "And I will make void the counsel of Judah and Jerusalem in this place; and I will cause them to fall by the sword before their enemies, and by the hands of them that seek their lives: and their carcases will I give to be meat for the fowls of the heaven, and for the beasts of the earth." We may render the second participle, "make it empty," and note that the root of this word is also found in Nahum 2:11, a passage which speaks of the devastation of Nineveh.

At this point the prophet merely states in a general manner that the Lord will empty the earth. How the Lord will do this is later given in greater detail (cf. v. 16b), where mention is made of the

---

[2] The introductory particle is not immediately followed by participles, but, as in 7:14, by the subject upon whom attention is to be focused, here, the LORD.

[3] The assonances and other rhythmical effects in these chapters are striking and effective. Duhm, however, who here tries to imitate the assonance (*leert und verheert die Erde*), remarks, ". . . doch übertreibt der Verf. ein wenig in dieser Beziehung."* Let the reader read aloud several times the Hebrew of these chapters and he will realize how forceful Isaiah's method is. The root *bqq* is found again in 19:3; 24:3; Jer. 19:7; and 51:2, which may reflect upon the present passage. The root *blq* appears in Nah. 2:11, and *bqq* in Nah. 2:3.

[4] E.g. Penna, ". . . *etmologicamente sembra indicare lo svuotamento di una brocca, di un'anfora ecc., alludendo al rumore caratteristico (ebr. baqaq) prodotto in tale operazione.*" So also Alexander: Ar. *baqbaqa*, which is used of the humming caused by water being poured out through the narrow mouth of a jar.

plunderers, and of the natural phenomena that accompany the world judgment. What, however, is meant by the word "earth"? Some would limit its reference to Judah alone, which might seem to be satisfactory as far as the context of verses 1-3 is concerned. In verse 4, however, the word is employed as a parallel to *tebel*, which means the inhabited earth.[5] Hence, the word must here have a wider significance. Calvin may be right in limiting the concept simply to those countries which were known by the Jews, namely, the "Egyptians, Assyrians, Moabites, Tyrians and such like." This practically amounts to referring the word to the inhabited earth.

Employing now the perfect with *waw* consecutive the prophet says, "and he will distort its faces," i.e., its surface. It is generally thought that underlying this verb is the idea of twisting or distorting something so that it becomes unrecognizable.[6] Possibly the reference is to the ravages that war brings, and that so upset and displace everything that it no longer looks as formerly. As a result of the distorting, the prophet continues, the Lord will scatter abroad the earth's inhabitants. We are reminded of Babel, when the Lord did "scatter them abroad upon the face of all the earth" (Gen. 11:9b). As at that time God scattered men over the face of the earth, so again would He scatter them over an earth which had become distorted through judgment. This verse does not state how God is to carry out the judgment; it speaks merely in general and universal terms, and presents the coming catastrophe as something all-embracing.

2 As a result of this judgment, all distinctions in class will be obliterated, and a complete reversal of the regular order of daily life will be effected. All differences between classes of people, and in particular, all subordination, will cease, for all men will be equal and no one will be ahead of another. What is here pictured is actually a form of socialism; it is a punishment that will come upon the earth as a result of God's punitive judgment. But the verse has a deeper sense. Not only will class distinctions be wiped

---

[5] So B τὴν οἰκουμένον. Some mss. add ολην; cf. Ziegler. 1Q on the other hand renders האדמה. Conceivably this is Samaritan influence, for Hempel points out that in Deut. 31:21 the Samaritan substitutes '*dmh* for '*rtz* (*ZAW*, 1934, p. 287).

[6] The root is used also in 21:3, but the *Piel* in the sense of "overturn" appears only in Lam. 3:9.

out, but in particular, before God there are to be no distinctions. In His sight all men will be treated equally. Looked at from still another standpoint, we may say that all, irrespective of position, will feel the effects of the judgment. As in 3:1ff., so here, we are given a picture of anarchy. When all the distinctions of class are completely obliterated, then anarchy follows. As long as there is actually present a true form of government, then in the nature of the case distinctions among men must exist. Political philosophies which seek to break down all distinctions among men and to make people equal, if followed through consistently, would lead to lawlessness. When the distinctions among men are wiped out, individual initiative is destroyed, and, inasmuch as chaos then replaces government, life is no longer safe. Only one obliteration of distinction among classes is really a blessing, but that is an obliteration wrought by Christ through the gift of the Gospel: "Where there is neither Greek nor Jew, circumcision nor uncircumcision, Barbarian, Scythian, bond nor free: But Christ is all, and in all" (Col. 3:11).

In order to emphasize his point Isaiah introduces six pairs of opposites of a most diverse kind, and in each term includes a double comparison. "And it shall be," he says, "like the people like the priest."[7] We may first note the presence of the definite article with each noun in the comparison. Probably it denotes the genus, an emphasis which in some instances might have been lost, had the word in question been anarthrous.[8] It may be also, as Duhm suggests, that the article before each of the eleven words makes it possible for those words to begin with the syllable ka, and thus to lend a certain emphasis to the whole.[9] Some commentators think that, had Isaiah written this passage or had it even been written by some pre exilic author, the contrast would have been between

7 והיה followed by כ–כ; cf. Hos. 4:9. Note also Gen. 44:18; Josh. 14:11; 1 Sam. 30:24; Ezek. 18:4; Dan. 11:29. The idiom serves to indicate that in a certain sense two terms are identical. The force is not "A is like B" or "B is like A" but rather "A is like B and B is like A." The Greek, ὁ λαὸς ὡς ὁ ἱερεύς κτλ. does not really bring out the full force of the Hebrew. Here, as far as the calamity is concerned, the people and priest are the same.

8 The article does not lose its force, but serves to indicate the genus, the whole class of objects, "like the people, like the priests." כגברתה—Quite possibly the article is prefixed to this noun, despite its suffix, in order to preserve an assonance with the other nouns. Cf. Jouon § 140 c; GKC § 127 i.

9 ". . . dass jedes Wort nur einmal determiniert werden darf, mit dem Artikel versehen, um das Wort wie alle anderen elf mit der Silbe ka beginnen zu lassen, des Klangspiels wegen" (op. cit., p. 173).

people and king.[10] That the priests are mentioned is thought by some scholars to point to a period of composition after the exile, when the priests would have been regarded as the ruling class (cf. Ezra 10:5). For this reason, it is argued, the passage makes a contrast between the priests on the one hand and the common people on the other.

In the first place, however, we must note that the contrasts are not between an individual and a group, but between different classes of people. Were there reference to the king we should expect the text to read, "like kings, like people," and not "like king, like people." The distinction between king and people is later implied in a general manner when Isaiah makes a contrast between master and servant.[11] In Hosea 4:9 we read, "And there shall be like people, like priest: and I will punish them for their ways, and reward them for their doings." Hosea apparently places his principal emphasis upon the priests' failure to impart the knowledge of Yahweh, whereas in the present passage the emphasis is not restricted to the religious sphere. What Malachi says, however, is also pertinent: "For the priest's lips should keep knowledge, and they should seek the law at his mouth: for he is the messenger of the Lord of hosts" (Mal. 2:7). As a representative of God the priest did occupy an exalted position and one of authority. Hence, as a result of the judgment the priest would become just like the laity; no longer would he be a fit representative of God. All distinction between priest and laity would be obliterated. Henceforth, the priests were to be no more holy or sacred than ordinary people. A nation wherein such a distinction is broken down is one whose members have all fallen away from the Lord. That the priest is mentioned in place of the king is not therefore necessarily an indication of postexilic age. To the common man the contrast between priest and himself—for he had much to do with the priest —would seem far stronger than a contrast with the king. The contrast between priest and people is one that would have force at any

---

[10] Gray simply assumes that the writer was postexilic. So also Marti, etc. Mulder sums up the argument: "*Hier word nie koning en volk teenoormekaar gestel nie, maar wel priester en volk. Van die monargie is hier nie meer sprake nie en die priesterschap staan aan die spits.*"

[11] "*Der Gegensatz van König und Unterthan erscheint nachher in viel allgemeinerer Gestalt, in Form des allgemein menschlichen Gegensatzes von Herr und Diener*" (Dreschsler). Penna also makes the pertinent remark, "*ed e possible che all' uomo comune apparisse molto più accentuata la distinzione fra sacerdoti e laici che non fra re e sudditi.*"

time, and Isaiah's purpose is to employ opposites or contrasts of a general nature such as might have validity at any period, and would not be bound to any particular place or time.

With his second contrast Isaiah enters the realm of the relationship between those who serve and those who are in authority. This is a sacred relationship and without it government cannot continue. A true mastership should be a blessing to true servanthood, and the relationship between master and servant should be a sanctified one. Even this relationship, however, is to be broken down by the judgment; and at the same time distinctions in gender will be forgotten. In any well-ordered state there must exist the distinction of master and servant or employer and employee. It is the prerogative of the master to command and of the servant to obey; and when this ceases to be the case, there is no longer a well-ordered society. The attempts of men to abolish this distinction can only lead to harm and to ultimate dissolution of sound government.

Commerce also is necessary in a well-ordered government, and with its cessation chaos enters in. With this comparison, however, the order of expression changes. In the first two comparisons there was an ascending grade of contrast—people, slave, servant girl; here, however, it is a descending order—buyer, lender, creditor. At the same time Isaiah also introduces another type of contrast. In the first two comparisons he had contrasted what was common and what was noble; here, however, there is a contrast between those who possess and those who do not possess, and also the expression of a form of authority which one exercises over another: "The rich ruleth over the poor and the borrower *is* servant to the lender" (Prov. 22:7).

The last comparison introduces a gradation. Not only is the distinction between borrower and lender to be obliterated, but also between the one who is a usurer and the one against whom there is a creditor. Thus, in the first comparison the one who borrows the money is mentioned first, whereas in the second it is the one who lends money at interest.[12] Contrasts of the most drastic nature are introduced; as a result of the judgment, the world will be completely turned upside down.

3 In a short sentence Isaiah sums up what the condition of the world will be as a result of God's judgment. Harking back to the

---

[12] Kimchi distinguishes *lāwāh,* "*usurpetur de pecunia mutuum data,*" and *nāšā',* "*de frumento, vino, oleo caet.*"

root which he had used in verse 1, the prophet now gives a word-play of vigorous force. We may render, *emptied there will be emptied the earth, and spoiled it will be spoiled*.[13] In the first two verses there had been no allusion to any human agent in this destruction; the Lord alone had been mentioned as the One who would bring it about. Now, however, in this Hebrew word which we have translated *will be spoiled*, there is probably an allusion to a human enemy, for the root is sometimes used of the effects of an invasion. By means of the heaping up of alliteration and similar-sounding words the prophet is able to convey the idea of utter completeness.

The certainty of the judgment cannot be in doubt, for in typical fashion Isaiah announces that God has spoken this word.[14] This is the basis—and there can be no better—on which the certainty is founded. *God has spoken*—It is indeed a favorite formula with Isaiah, and it explains the triumphant and majestic character of his prophecies. It reminds us of the beginning of his prophecy (1:2), but it is found frequently elsewhere in his writings as well. Were we to seek for the source of Isaiah's confidence which enabled him so boldly and assuredly to proclaim his message, we should find that source in the fact that Isaiah believed in a verbal revelation—God had spoken.

4 The earth mourneth, fadeth; the world languisheth, fadeth: the highest of the people of the earth languish.

5 And the earth has become profane under its inhabitants, because they have transgressed the laws, violated the statute, frustrated the everlasting covenant.

6 Wherefore a curse hath devoured the earth, and the inhabitants of it were reckoned guilty; wherefore the inhabitants of the earth are scorched, and there are few men left.

7 The new wine mourneth; the vine languisheth, all those who rejoice in heart do sigh.

8 Ceased is the mirth of drums; there has come to an end the noise of exulters, the mirth of the harp has ceased.

9 With the song they shall not drink wine; bitter will strong drink be to them that drink it.

---

[13] The root *bzz* appears in Isaiah more frequently than in any other OT book. The verbs have Ḥolem instead of Patah, probably to establish assonance with the inf. absolute.

[14] Cf. 1:20; 40:5; 58:14. Lindblom suggests that this is the Isaianic counterpart to Ezekiel's "I the LORD have spoken."

10 The city of desolation is broken down; every house is shut up from entering.

11 A cry for wine in the streets; all gladness had become darkened; departed is the mirth of the earth.

12 In the city is left desolation, and with ruin is the gate crushed.

4 Isaiah continues his description of judgment, pointing out in addition to what he has already said that the earth is in mourning. In the first three verses of the chapter he had described actions or events; now, however, he proceeds to set forth a condition. Up to this point he has placed the description in the future, using either the perfect with *waw* consecutive or else participles or even simple futures. Beginning with this verse, however, he employs perfects; and these are possibly to be understood as prophetic.[15] The events described have not yet occurred, but they are so vivid to the prophet's eyes that he pictures them as though they had already transpired.

The paronomasia is most striking and is to be found primarily in the presence of the labial letters, *l, m,* and *b*. The prominence of the *a* sound is also significant. As appears from the next verse, *the earth* probably designates the land itself in distinction from its inhabitants. At the same time, since in these verses the word *tebel* (inhabitable earth) is employed interchangeably, we are to understand the reference to the entire earth and should not restrict it to the land of Palestine alone.[16]

Emphasis, however, does not fall so much upon the earth as upon what the earth does; and in order to bring out this emphasis we may render, *Mourned, faded is the earth; languished, faded the world: languished are the high ones of the people of the earth.* The verbs are perfects, but we may use the English present; for the prophet looks out upon the desolate world, as it were, to describe it as he sees it.

The first verb personifies the land. The curse which had fallen upon the earth because of Adam's sin, has, as it were, now come to

<hr/>

15 "*Diese Praet. sind lauter sogenannte Praeterita prophetica, der Übergang vom Fut. ins Praet. lediglich dadurch bedingt, dass, während es der Prophet in vv. 1-3 mit Handlungen und Ereignissen zu tun hatte, von v. 4 an Schilderung von Zuständen eintritt*" (Drechsler) .

16 Kittel asserts that תבל is never used of the land of Judah but always of the inhabited world (ἡ οἰκουμένη) , as in 26:9; 27:6. Hence, he takes עם הארץ in the sense, "inhabitant of the earth."

full expression, and destroys the earth, so that the earth mourns.[17] Earlier Isaiah had spoken of the gates of the city as mourning, and Amos characterizes the pastures as mourning.[18] Now the entire earth, as though grieving over one that is dead, engages in mourning. She is in mourning apparel and wears the necessary signs of such mourning. Accompanying this first verb is a second, used of the drying up and withering away of plants, and thus fittingly serving to express the exhausted condition of the earth.

With the second member of the first line a different pair of verbs is employed. The first of these (*languisheth*) suggests that the strength of the earth is gone or exhausted, and that the earth itself is lying without power. It is used of a woman without children, and also of vegetation. Isaiah had earlier employed it to describe the fields of Heshbon (16:8) and the Nile fishermen (19:8). Here it is strengthened by the repetition of *faded*. "Just as plants without cultivation and proper care may fade away and die," we may paraphrase the thought, "so the earth, now suffering under the curse that has come upon her through the punishment of judgment, languishes, mourning and fading away."

Not only the earth itself, but also the highest of its inhabitants feel the judgment. There is question as to the proper force of the last words of the verse,[19] but we would take the text as it stands, regarding the word *height* as an abstract used for the concrete. It is the highest part, i.e., the high ones of the people of the earth. The highest among men will feel the judgment, and so the verse introduces a contrast between the earth itself and the men who live upon it. Even the highest among earth's inhabitants waste away, we learn; for as a result of oppression from without, the lack of normal trade and business and the breaking of the bands of society within, everyday life can no longer continue.

5 The prophet now points out clearly that the judgment which has overtaken the world is a result of the faithless dealing of earth's

---

17 The verbs are characteristically Isaianic. Cf. *'bl,* 3:26; 19:8; 33:9; 57:18; 60:20; 61:2, 3; 66:10; *nbl,* 1:30; 28:1, 4; 34:4; 40:7, 8; 64:5; *'mll,* 16:8; 19:8; 39:9. Cf. also 33:9 and 34:3.

18 Amos 1:2.

19 By emending *'am* to *'im* we obtain, "the height (i.e., heaven) together with the earth." But, as Gray points out, had the writer wished to picture the heaven here as affected by judgment, it is not likely that he would have devoted two and a half lines to earth and only half a line to heaven. In what follows, heaven is out of the picture.

inhabitants. It is necessary, however, to say a word about the syntax. The perfects are not prophetic perfects, but form a unit by themselves. The first word, *earth*, is a *casus pendens;* and the following sentence completes or supplements that *casus pendens*.[20]

Hence, we must render:

AS FOR THE EARTH—*it has become profane under its inhabitants,*

> (explanation of this statement)
> *for they have transgressed laws;*
> *they have changed the statute;*
> *they have made void the covenant of eternity.*

What receives the emphasis here is *the earth*, and what is of supreme importance is that the earth has become profane.[21] Just as Palestine itself, the Holy Land, had become profane through the sin of its inhabitants (Num. 35:33; Deut. 21:19; Jer. 3:9; and Ps. 106:38), so also the entire earth became profane when the ordinances given to it were violated.[22] The world was created for the glory of God, and man was placed upon it to serve God and to develop the earth for Him. When man transgressed, the earth, for man's sake, fell under a curse (Gen. 3:17). As a result of man's sin, the whole creation groaneth and travaileth in pain, for it partakes of the curse that man's sin has brought (Rom. 8:19ff.). Transgression is against the law of God, and this is expressed by the terms *law, statute, everlasting covenant*. The laws which God has revealed to His people bind all mankind; and hence, the work of the Law of God written on the human heart, for example, may be described under such terms.[23]

---

20 Marti takes "the earth" as a nominal sentence, introduced by the conjunction, and renders, *"Da die Erde entweiht ist."* It is the earth conceived as bearing inhabitants.

21 *ḥānᵉp̄āh—has become polluted*, B ἠνόμησε, but S renders ἐφονοκτονήθη. Syr. *'eṭdamyaṯ*, sprinkled with blood. Vulg. *similis fiat*. The preterite is not prophetic, but sets forth the past in relation to the content of the preceding verses. It is emphasized by some commentators (e.g., Drechsler, Kittel) that there is a stress here upon the sin of murder; cf. 26:21. The root *ḥnp* is frequent in Isaiah; cf. 9:16; 10:6; 32:6; 33:14.

22 *under*—The thought is that due to the sins of the inhabitants who lived upon it, the earth has become profane. The versions, however, are really interpreting when they render *on account of*.

23 What laws are referred to? Vitringa takes the reference to the natural and popular law, rather than to the positive Law (*ad describendum ius naturae et gentium*). This opinion, asserts Gesenius, really goes back to Ibn Ezra, but is contrary to the Hebrew spirit, which knows no other than the revealed Law.

The Law was not specifically revealed to the Gentiles as it was to the Jews at Sinai. Nevertheless, according to Paul, the Gentiles do by natural instinct those things which are prescribed by the Law. In so doing, they show that, by reason of what is actually implanted in their nature, they reveal the Law of God unto themselves; and this fact shows that the work of the Law is written on their own hearts.[24] In transgressing those things prescribed in the Law, however, it may be said that the Gentiles were actually transgressing the Law itself. Here, the plural is used to show that the Gentiles had transgressed divine commands and ordinances, and also that their sins were many and varied. We may say that the Gentiles transgressed specific items of the Law, a thought which the plural form of the noun would also support. It was a transgression of the divine will generally, or as Calvin puts it, "all the instruction contained in the Law."

The mention of "statute" is perhaps intended for the sake of specificity, for inasmuch as both commandment and promise are included in the Law, this word stresses the commandment. Men have so changed the commandment by their transgression, that it is no longer what it was. It has been transgressed and regarded as though it were not in existence.[25]

Lastly, we are told that men frustrated or made void the everlasting covenant. The language appears to have originated in or at least to have been prominent in the regal terminology of antiquity. The reference seems to be to the covenant made with Noah after the flood. This covenant was universal, for it was said to be made not only with Noah and his seed but also with every living creature (Gen. 9:9, 10). It was also an eternal covenant. "Neither shall all flesh be cut off any more by the waters of a flood; neither shall there any more be a flood to destroy the earth" (Gen. 9:11). At the same time it was an unconditional covenant. It involved no commandment whose fulfillment or obedience was required for the promise to be fulfilled. How, therefore, could one break or violate the Noahic covenant?[26]

---

[24] Paul does not actually speak of the law written on the heart, but "the work of the law written in their hearts." See John Murray, *Romans, NICNT*, Grand Rapids, 1959, Vol. I, p. 74.

[25] *they have altered, violated*—The Qal may be used in a transitive sense; cf. Judg. 5:26; Job 20:24. Cf. Cheyne in Smend, *ZAW*, Vol. 4, 1884, p. 165.

[26] Jenni ("*Das Wort 'ōlām im Alten Testament," ZAW*, Vol. 65, 1953, pp. 18ff.) holds that the term derives originally from the regal language. The phrase occurs

Calvin would restrict the reference to the covenant of grace
made with the fathers. The language is permissive of this interpretation, and Calvin is correct when he interprets the word "eternal"
by saying that the covenant ought to be in force in every age. "It
was to be transmitted, in uninterrupted succession, from father to
son, that it might never be effaced from the memory of man, but
might be kept pure and entire." It must be noticed, however, that
those who have frustrated the eternal covenant are not merely the
Jews but the world generally. The frustrating of the covenant is
something universal. For this reason we may adopt the position
that the eternal covenant here spoken of designates the fact that
God has given His Law and ordinances to Adam, and in Adam to
all mankind. These ordinances involve a positive glorying in God
in all one's ways. The heathen, however, have not glorified God;
they have acted as though He did not exist; they have made unto
themselves idols. In so doing, they have departed from Him and
from all the benefits that He grants to those who follow Him. They
have turned from His ways, and gone unto their own way. It would
seem, therefore, that insofar as they have perverted the meaning of
life, they have frustrated the covenant that God made with man in
order to set forth this truth.

Isaiah uses the language which is characteristic of the Mosaic
legislation, and thus describes the universal transgressions of mankind. "The wicked shall be turned into hell, and all the nations
which forget God" (Ps. 9:18) .

6 As a result of the universal transgression, the curse will devour
the entire earth. The alliterations used are remarkable. In the
clause *curse hath eaten earth—'alah 'ak^elah 'aretz*—each word begins with an *Aleph,* which is also the initial consonant of the root
of the following word. As in the preceding verse, despite the use of
Mosaic terminology, the reference was to a universal transgression
and had to do with all men, so here also, the language continues
to be Mosaic, and the reference is still universal. For an understanding of the language, therefore, we must consider its usage in
the Mosaic cult.

To apprehend the nature of the curse we may compare

---

16 times in the OT. Many commentators refer it to the Noahic covenant, but
Schmidt applies it to the Sinaitic covenant (*Der Ewigkeitsbegriff im Alten
Testament,* 1940, p. 69) .

Deuteronomy 28:15ff.; 29:19ff.; and Leviticus 26:14ff. It is a curse
that comes from God, for it is the consequence of the transgression
of His laws. It is not, however, limited to the Israelites, but,
inasmuch as the inhabitants of the entire earth have transgressed,
affects the whole world. It is the same curse that lies over fallen
mankind in the picture given by the Apostle (Rom. 1:18–3:20).

Like fire this curse "eats" the earth, so consuming it that it is no
more. "It is the curse that goeth forth over the face of the whole
earth" (Zech. 5:3). It is a fire that burns and devours completely.
(Cf. also Isa. 1:31; 5:24; 9:18; 10:16, 17; 29:6; 30:27ff.) As a result
of this devouring curse, the inhabitants of the earth are reckoned
to be guilty; and being reckoned guilty, they must suffer. Following the view of some of the fathers, Calvin refers the words to the
desolation of those who transgress, and renders, "are made desolate" (*desolati sunt incolae eius*). Appealing to Joel 1:18 Gesenius
translates, "Its inhabitants made atonement" (*es bussten seine
Bewohner*).[27] If such a meaning is possible, however, it must be
reserved for the *Niphal* stem, which is found in Joel 1:18. The
force of the verb in the present context may be illustrated by
Jeremiah 2:3, which we may render, "Holiness is Israel to the
Lord, the beginning of His produce; all who devour him shall be
reckoned guilty, evil shall come upon them, saith the Lord." The
thought is that if anyone devours Israel (note the similarity of
language to our present verse), he will be looked upon as one who
is guilty of a crime and liable to punishment. It is that thought
which Isaiah also expresses. Inasmuch as the inhabitants of the
earth have transgressed, they too are to be regarded as violators of
the law, and consequently deserving of the punishment that must
come to those who transgress.

To introduce the statement of the punishment, the prophet
repeats his "therefore." He connects this word with the description
of the transgression of the preceding verse, and prepares for the
statement of the punishment. The first verb, in the light of the first
Qumran Scroll, is probably to be translated *they have diminished,*[28]

---

[27] Bentzen renders, "*de maa bøde for deras skyld,*" and compares Hos. 14:1;
Joel 1:18; Ps. 5:11; 34:22; Jer. 2:3.

[28] חרו; Procksch derives the word from חור and reads *hāwerû—bleek wees;*
cf. Isa. 29:22. 1Q reads *hwrw.* Lindblom suggests that it arose through error
of hearing from *hlw,* and compares the change of sound in Job 6:25 *nmrtzu*
and *nmltzu.* It has also been suggested that the word is an error for *hrbw.* B
reads πτωχοὶ ἔσονται, which would seem to represent *dlw.* S however has

159

a rendering that fits in well with what follows. Hence there is no need for emending the text.

Mankind is almost totally wiped off the face of the earth. At this point Isaiah does not state how this will be accomplished, whether by sword or by famine. His language, however, shows that there is to be a remnant; not all of mankind will be destroyed. Penna suggests that with this mention of the remnant no thought of a future mission is found; and this, he says, is characteristic of Isaiah.[29] But the answer is not far to seek. Isaiah is here speaking of the whole world in the same terms that he elsewhere uses to describe the people of God. He has taken the language of the theocracy, terms such as *laws, statute, eternal covenant, they are reckoned guilty,* etc., designations which belong to Israel; and he has applied these to the whole world. Now, to show the severity of the judgment, he states that in consequence of man's sin only a few men will be left.[30] The language is characteristically Isaianic.[31] Naturally, Isaiah does not go farther and mention a mission of this remnant, for the remnant as such has no mission. The remnant of Israel would of course ultimately carry out the will of God in becoming the holy seed through which salvation was finally to come to the world. Not so, however, with the remnant of the world. It has no mission. Its existence is merely mentioned. The judgment is complete; the world is judged. There is no more to say.

7 When judgment comes upon the world all the sources of joy

ἐκτρυχωθήσονται, and Vulg. *insanient.* Drechsler derives the word, in common with many, from *ḥrr,* but remarks, "Doch hat man den Sinn des Propheten nicht gerade (Vitr.) auf innere Gluth zu beschränken." The accent is *Milel;* there should be two *Pashtas,* the first to indicate the position of the accent, as in תהו (Gen. 1:2), the second a postpositive. Cf. A. Guillaume, "The Dead Sea Scroll of Isaiah," *JBL,* Vol. 76, 1957, pp. 42f.

29 *Mz'r* occurs only in Isaiah 10:25; 16:14; 24:6; 29:17. Penna comments, "Nell'ultimo distico si accenna alla pochezza degli nomini scampati (13, 12), ma non vi e nessuna allusione a una loro missione futura, quale e connessa con l'idea del 'resto' in Isaia."

30 This picture is based on the earlier description of the curse given in Deut. 28:16-44, 53-57, 62-68; and Lev. 26.

31 Lindblom remarks, "Unser Dichter zeigt also eine deutliche Neigung dazu, sich in der sprachlichen Welt Jesaias zu bewegen" (op. cit., p. 17). Would not a better statement be that Isaiah himself was the author? S. B. Frost (Old Testament Apocalyptic, 1952, pp. 143ff.) maintains that these chapters were written by one who deliberately posed as Isaiah.

and gladness are destroyed.[32] Using the same verbs employed in verse 4 of the entire earth, the prophet now applies these verbs to the new wine and the vine, employing figures that, as has often been pointed out, remind of the description in Joel 1:10-12. Isaiah does not mean, as Rosenmüller suggested, that the wine mourns because there is none to drink it, or because foreigners and not natives drink it, but because it partakes in the sorrow of the land. The word "new wine" or "must" is used by way of metonymy for the grapes that contain the must.[33] Thus there is a beautiful parallelism with the "vine" mentioned in the second clause. The grapes mourn in that they present a withered, sorrowing appearance; the vine which bears the grapes combines with them, as it were, in giving this appearance. All nature, in other words, shares in the sorrow of the land; the picture is the opposite of that given earlier in 14:7, 8.

Those who enjoy the wine of the vines also groan;[34] they who usually are *rejoicers of heart* are now mourners and groaners; the life which they must now face without the fruit of the vine is one that causes only sighing and anguish. Lovers of luxury are now haters of plainness. The *rejoicers of heart* are all too often those who forget God; when He deprives them of their luxury, they do not turn to Him, but sigh at their own supposed misfortune.

8 Isaiah continues his description of the languishing earth with three short sentences, each consisting of three words, and each beginning with a verb followed by a complex subject, the first member of which is in the construct state. The first and last lines begin with the verb *shavath* (*there has ceased*) and the second with *hadal* (*there has come to an end*).[35] These words bring out emphatically the thought of the verse, namely, the ceasing of

---

32 Bentzen, however, comments, *"Her er tale, ikke om fjendtlig haergens resultater, men om en naturbegivenhed"* (*op. cit.*, *in loc.*). Lindblom thinks that the words, "the new wine mourneth, the vine languisheth" look like a gloss, for in the following we are not told that the wine has disappeared, but only that it has become bitter to the carousers. But there is no objective textual evidence to support this supposition, and the words do lend themselves to a satisfactory interpretation.

33 In Aqht ii.6.7, *trt* is found as a synonym for *yn*.

34 It is generally claimed that *'nh* is late Hebrew; it occurs however in Isa. 21: 2; 35:10; and 51:11; Ps. 31:11 (Davidic); Job 3:24; 23:2; Ps. 6:7 (Davidic). The noun *anh* (sighing) is found in Aqht ii.1.18, *anh. gzr* (the sighing of the hero).

35 Cf. 5:12, 14; Amos 6:4; Job 21:12; 1 Macc. 3:45.

161

mirth.[36] What Isaiah depicts is the opposite of what is set forth in
Jeremiah 33:10, 11. The rejoicing of the timbrels, i.e., the rejoicing
caused by the timbrels, has ceased (cf. 5:12); and with its ceasing
there has disappeared the luxurious festivals to which the music of
the timbrel or tambourine was an accompaniment. There has also
come to an end the noise made by those who are revelling or
exulting. How readily the carefree exulting of light-hearted people
comes to an end when the reality of judgment appears! The
rejoicing produced by the lyre also ceases.[37] Isaiah mentions the
people between the two instruments; they are, as it were, hemmed
in by the music; and when the music ceases, the exulting of the
people comes to an end. It is a light-hearted and not a deep-seated,
profound rejoicing, for it is a rejoicing divorced from God and
devoted only to enjoyment. Isaiah is not condemning music as
such, for music in itself is one of God's most wondrous gifts; he is
pointing out rather that revellers, whose delight comes only from
drunken festivals, sigh and groan when there is taken from them
that in which they find their only pleasure.

9 In addition to the musical instruments there was the accompaniment of human voices in song, although it is not stated whether public singing is intended or merely the general singing that
accompanied drinking bouts. Whatever its nature, however, it is a
song that gives pleasure; and hence the word is placed first in the
verse to emphasize it.[38] It may be that this description, in which a
contrast with the present situation is pointed up, merely means
that the time will come when drinking accompanied with song will
cease. On the other hand, Isaiah may intend to stress the lack of
song which gave so much pleasure, and to suggest that men would
drink, but unaccompanied by song. They would drink merely out
of need, and not in the pleasurable conditions that had formerly
been the case.

Isaiah is not condemning the drinking of wine as such; but this
drinking was possibly accompanied by songs of a lascivious nature,
and hence, the whole procedure, supposed to give pleasure to the

36 The typically Isaianic character of the language should be noted. *Mśwś* is
found in 8:6; 32:13, 14; 60:15; 62:5; 65:18; 66:10; and only 7 times outside of
Isaiah; *š'wn* occurs in Isa. 5:14; 13:4; 17:12 (twice), 13; 66:6; and *'lyz* in Isa. 13:
3; 22:2; 23:7; 32:13 (otherwise only twice, in Zephaniah, in passages that are
based on Isaiah). The double occurrence of *šbṭ* calls to mind Isa. 14:4b-21.
37 *Tóp* is a timbrel or tambourine, and *kinnôr* a zither or possibly a lyre.
38 Cf. 30:32 for the use of *Beth*.

participant, became little more than a drunken orgy. If men were to drink wine without this song, it would be that they might thereby blot out reality; and such wine would not give them the pleasure which they formerly had had (cf. Amos 6:5, 6).

Corresponding to the absence of song is the fact that the strong drink, now divorced from song, becomes bitter to those who drink it. Isaiah obtains a certain emphasis by means of the chiastic arrangement of his language. In the second half of the verse he places the verb first (*it is bitter*), and then mentions the strong drink. Such drinking feasts therefore were not confined to wine, but were feasts at which strong, intoxicating drink also flowed freely. This present verse forms somewhat of a climax. In verse 7 the failure of the wine is stated; in verse 8 that of the song and rejoicing; in this one both are mentioned together.

10 A new facet is here introduced. What has been stated previously has had reference to men and their enjoyment; to the world generally. Now the prophet speaks of a city of desolation which is broken. Again, he places the verb first, so that our thought will dwell not so much upon the city as upon the concept expressed by the verb, *she is broken.* A broken city is one that is defeated and destroyed. To express the desolate condition of the city Isaiah even uses the word *tohu* (*desolation*), which in Genesis 1:2 described the unformed condition of the earth.[39] It is an apt word to characterize a city that has suffered the ravages of war, and consequently lies desolate. In the following century, Jeremiah found it suitable to use of Palestine after the armies of Nebuchadnezzar had laid that land waste (cf. Jer. 4:23).

To what, however, does the prophet have reference by his phrase, *city of desolation?* Many have applied the terms to Jerusalem, others to Babylon, and others have taken them in a general sense. One point at least should be noted. The judgment hitherto described has affected the entire world and not merely the land of Judah. Nevertheless, the terminology employed has to a large extent been that revealed in the Sinaitic legislation. Hence, we simply conclude that the universal sin and judgment are also to be understood in such terms. It would seem to follow, therefore, that the city of destruction must in some sense be representative of the universality of the sin and judgment. Consequently, the phrase

---

39 *Tôhû* appears in Isa. 24:10; 34:11; 44:9; 45:18, 19; 59:4; 40:17; 41:29; 29:21; 40:23; 49:4; and only 9 times in the remainder of the OT.

either signifies the city, which represents world power generally, or else the phrase is to be understood as indefinite. This does not mean that there is a definite reference to Babylon, although it is quite possible that there may be reflection upon Babylon. What seems to be clear is that this city is the city of the world, and represents the world that has sinned and has felt God's judgment.

Although the city has been broken, nevertheless, some of its houses are still standing. These have been shut, however, so that no one may enter them. They are closed to the traffic of the city and so shut off from it. It is a city of closed, inaccessible houses, and so not a city at all. Isaiah employs a figurative method of describing the completeness of the desolation. As in Genesis 1:2 the earth was desolation and so not a place for man to dwell, so now the city is desolation and its houses no longer places of normal dwelling.

What precisely is intended by the statement that the houses are closed so that no one can enter? Does the prophet mean to say by this figure that the houses are destroyed so that in the fullest sense the city is one of desolation, or does he mean rather that the inhabitants are so terrified and filled with fear that they bolt themselves in their houses in order that no one may enter? The latter view is probably correct, although one cannot be dogmatic. The verb *suggar* (closed) suggests that there was an actual closing of the doors of the houses, rather than that the doors were merely blockaded by the debris of the fallen city.[40]

In this picture the city becomes in actual fact what it already was in nature. Through their sins its inhabitants had introduced desolation and confusion into the world, and so the place of their dwelling becomes a desolation like the beginning. The nature of the city was desolation; the destiny and final end of the city will also be desolation.

[40] Kissane thinks that the houses are shut up because there are no inhabitants left. But how would this make it impossible to enter the houses? Alexander finds a reference to the obstruction of the houses' entrance caused by the ruins. Dillmann, Gray, Procksch, Lindblom, Bentzen, etc., think that out of fear of the enemy people have locked their houses so that no one can enter, and also because the streets and markets had nothing more to offer. Mulder agrees with Rudolph that the inhabitants have destroyed their own houses; cf. 25:12; 27:10. Duhm gives a number of reasons; "*sind die Stadttore beseitigt, so sind die Hausturen verschlossen, weil die Bewohner teils tot oder flüchtig sind, teils sich nicht hinauswagen und sich vor ungebetenen Gasten furchten. . . .*" *from entering*—cf. 23:1.

It is not entirely clear why the prophet designates the city with the word *qiryah* rather than *'ir*. Reichel thinks that this is to refer merely to a portion of the city, but there is no evidence to support this supposition; nor is it clear that the word designates a city as composed of men. *Qiryah* seems to be a mere synonym of *'ir*. May it not be that it simply serves to stress the indefiniteness of the reference?

11 The train of thought is claimed by many to be broken by the first part of verse eleven. Gesenius, believing that the verse was probably taken from Joel 1:5 and that it is out of place here, remarked that in a city destroyed by barbaric enemies the people would have something more important to complain about than the lack of wine. Many agree that the verse is out of place and try to fit it in elsewhere. On the other hand, it is found in all the manuscripts and versions, including 1Q; and there is no objective evidence for denying the correctness of its position. We shall, therefore, seek to interpret the verse as it stands.[41]

A word about the form of the immediate context may not be out

---

[41] *"Wahrscheinlich aus Joel 1:5, aber wie unpassend steht es hier! In einer von einem barbarischen Feinde zerstörten Stadt, wo Tausende umgekommen waren, gab es doch, sollte man denken, Wichtigeres zu beklagen, als dass kein Wein da sey: wenn dieser auch, wie die Ausleger bemerken, einen Theil des Reichtums des Bewohner ausgemacht hatte."* Gesenius has perhaps stated the objection as cogently as anyone. Kissane holds that the verse forms a natural sequel to vv. 8, 9. Even Penna comments, *"L'autenticita del primo stico del v. 11 e per lo meno molto discutibile."*
On the other hand the verse seems to fit into a particular scheme of verses alternating with a beginning verb or noun. V. 8 verb, 9 noun, 10 verb, 11 noun, 12 verb. Furthermore, a contradiction between this and the preceding verse is not necessarily involved. If the inhabitants are in their houses, the city is not deserted even though it may be described as broken. If we assume that the inhabitants have shut themselves in their houses, this must be taken in a general sense. It does not mean that there would be no one at all in the streets. If there really were a glaring contradiction between 11a and 10, surely the learned "disciple of Isaiah" who inserted v. 11 at this point might have noticed it. Isaiah's purpose is to contrast the once mirthful city with its present desolation. Once the sound of mirth—now a cry even for wine; in other words, the former condition has passed. But not only is wine missed, even all mirth and rejoicing have disappeared. Cf. 16:7-10.
Drechsler calls attention to the threefold structure of this section: Introduction, vv. 1-3; Conclusion, vv. 13-15 (three verses) ; Body, consisting of three subsections of three verses each, vv. 4-6, vv. 7-9 and vv. 10-12. Likewise, within the individual verses the expression of parallelism is usually threefold, e.g., vv. 4, 7, 8, 11. *tzwḥh*—a plaintive cry; Jer. 14:2; 46:12.

of order. Verses 8, 10, and 12 each begin with a verb, whereas verses 9 and 11 begin with a noun. The first word of the verse is a noun meaning "outcry." It is not the outcry of drunkards for more wine, but that of the ordinary inhabitants for refreshment. As the people needed bread for sustenance, so they needed wine for refreshment, and for quenching their thirst. It was bread and wine that Melchizedek brought out to Abram after the battle with the eastern kings. The cry has to do with wine, and it is an outcry of anguish that is heard in the streets.[42]

Over the joy of the city the sun has set, and joy has entered into evening; darkness has come. Indeed, the rejoicing of the whole earth has been carried into captivity.[43] Thus, with these striking figures, the prophet continues his description of the desolation that has fallen upon the earth.

12 As verse eleven shows, there has been a great departure. Joy is gone; rejoicing and gladness are no more. There is, however, something left behind,[44] namely, desolation,[45] and with it the crushing[46] of the city's gate. The *shammah* (waste, appallment) is a word that calls to mind the exile. Earlier, Isaiah had used it (5:9) to describe the desolation of the land's houses. The prophecy paints a grim picture. The one-time mirth and rejoicing that accompanied the revellings of the people have gone, and in their

[42] In Lam. 4:4 bread alone is mentioned, but in Lam. 2:12 both bread and wine.

[43] Lindblom does not refer *mśwś* in 11c to the joy of all the earth, but renders it, "*Gegenstand der Freude des Landes*," and compares 13:19; he interprets it to mean that the noblest of the people of the city have been carried into captivity. To support his view, Lindblom appeals to Isa. 32:14; 60:15; 65:18; Ezek. 24:25; Lam. 2:15; Ps. 48:3. But one cannot be certain. In keeping with the universalistic language so frequent in this section, Isaiah may intend a universalistic reference here also. In a certain sense it is true that in the exile joy departed from the earth and went into captivity.

[44] נשאר forms an effective antithesis to גלה. The form is a perf. 3 m. s., although several manuscripts read a participle (i.e., with *Qametz*). The subject, however, is feminine. Either the verb is to be taken in a neutral sense, or else שמה is best construed as a *Hal* accusative, "it has been left in the city as desolation." I prefer this latter.

[45] desolation—*hapax legomenon*, an acc. of the product.

[46] *yukkat*—Hophal imp. of *kātat*. The form is taken to stand for *yûkat*, but I question this. It appears to be after an Aram. analogy, and represents original *yuk-kat*, whereas *yûkat* represents *yû-kat*. The statement in GKC (§ 67) that "the vowel before Dages, is, of course, short," really says nothing. The question is, why is the *Dagesh* present?

place waste and desolation remain. Accompanying this waste is the fact that the gate, the most important part of the city, will itself be smitten so as to become nothing but ruins. The first part of the verse shows that there is a desolation within the city; the second part that the outer section or gate is also in ruins. The destruction is truly complete.

13 For thus it will be in the midst of the land, in the midst of the peoples, as the shaking of the olive tree, as the gleanings, when the vintage is ended.

14 They will lift up their voice, they will sing, for the majesty of the LORD, they will cry from the sea.

15 Wherefore in the east glorify the LORD, in the isles of the sea the name of the LORD, the God of Israel.

13 In characteristic fashion—for only Isaiah among the prophets uses the expression, *and thus it shall be in the midst of the land*—the prophet now sums up and describes more clearly what he has previously been stating. The introductory word "for" need not be understood as introducing a logical conclusion; it often has merely connective force.[47] Here such seems to be the case, and so we may paraphrase the thought, "What has just been described is sure to occur. For indeed, in the midst of the people it will be as a shaking." The English version, "when," is not correct. The second word, "thus," points forward to the comparison with the shaking of the olive tree.[48]

What is to take place occurs not only in the midst of the land but also in the midst of the peoples.[49] Thus it is implied that not

---

[47] כִּי appears, however, to reflect upon the immediately preceding verse, insofar as this latter contains elements that presuppose a complete destruction of the people. For an interesting discussion of the force of this particle cf. Johannes Pedersen, *Israel*, I – II, 1926, pp. 117ff.

[48] König comments that it *"zeigt darauf hin, dass V. 13 nicht mit Dim.-Ki., v. Or., Gray, Feldm. Zum Vorhergehenden zu ziehen ist."* The question does not rest entirely upon the force of כֹּה. What is stated in footnote [47] is also pertinent. B reads ταῦτα πάντα.

[49] Kissane calls attention to the "futures," affirming that they are here employed to give a summary of the final result. Lindblom, however, thinks that יִהְיֶה refers to a present situation. I can see no reason for departing from the normal force of the verb at this point. Isaiah seems clearly to be speaking of something that is to take place in the future. *in the midst of the land*—Isaiah alone of all the prophets employs this expression; cf. 5:8; 6:12; 7:22; 10:23; 19: 24. Otherwise it is found only in the Pentateuch and in Ps. 74:12. The exegetical question is whether Isaiah is speaking only of the downfall of Judah

all peoples will be destroyed but only some. In 17:5, 6 the same figure had been applied to Israel; here it refers to the nations. But, as here used, it is not a mere imitation of chapter seventeen. One is tempted to sympathize with the comment of Alexander with reference to those who think that at this point a later writer has imitated chapter seventeen: "The Prophet is thus reduced to a dilemma; if he does not repeat his own expressions, he is a stranger to himself and his own writings; if he does, he is an imitator of a later age." After the olive tree has been shaken, there still remain olives upon the tree. After the first harvest, the gleanings, i.e., what remains after the harvest, are still on hand. So it will be with the judgment. After it has fallen, a remnant will still be present.[50]

14 The opening words of this verse are impressive. Isaiah declares that "they" will lift up their voice. To whom, however, does he refer? What is the antecedent of "they"? Apparently the antecedent is to be found in the remnant whose existence is implied in the previous verse. What remains after most of the olives have been shaken from the tree and the gleaning after the first plucking of grapes at the completion of harvest, symbolizes the remnant who will survive the judgment. They will raise their voice. Perhaps in order to make the word emphatic, and perhaps also to avoid taking the verbs impersonally, the prophet uses the personal pronoun, "they."[51] Isaiah does not explicitly state why the remnant praises

---

(Rudolph) , or whether it is Judah considered as the center of the world. On this last view the phrase, *in the midst of the peoples* would emphasize the dark character of the judgment. As Drechsler comments, *"Einöde inmitten wogenden Völkergetummels, Wüstenei mitten in der ringsum bewohnten Welt."*

Passages that show that Jerusalem is the center of the earth are 2:2ff.; 19:24; Mic. 4:1; Lam. 3:45; Ezek. 5:5; 38:12. Jerusalem is also said to be the sanctuary of the Lord of hosts; and Zion is the throne of Yahweh, the King of the world (Lindblom) .

50 The remnant probably is not to be equated with the few left in Judah when Jerusalem has been destroyed (cf. Kissane) . עֹלֵלוֹת—what remains over from the first gleaning for a second gleaning, i.e., the actual harvest.

51 Marti thinks that the pronoun also forms a contrast with the first person of v. 16 (cf. Jer. 17:18; Ps. 120:7). Kissane refers *hēm-māh* to the remnant left "among the peoples" (v. 13) ; Lindblom applies it to the Jews of Palestine regarded as a gleaning; Marti takes it of Jews of the diaspora in the West, whether of the Asiatic coast and islands or of Egypt itself. Gray regards the text as corrupt, but thinks that if v. 14 is the proper continuation of v. 13, then the pronoun must be explained by what precedes. Gray rejects the idea that there is a contrast with v. 16. If, however, he argues, we explain the pronoun by what precedes, it can only refer to those who escape the judgment.

God, but quite possibly the reason lies in the very fact that it is preserved alive and has escaped the ravages and destroying power of the judgment.

The cry is loud, for the criers lift up their voice to be heard. The second verb may be rendered, *they gave a ringing cry,* or *they cry aloud,* as though desirous that all should hear them,[52] as they set forth their subject, the majesty of the Lord. Lastly, it is stated that they neigh or give a shrill cry from the sea. These words would teach that even distant nations, those living on the coastlands, will also praise God. On the other hand, in the light of previous references to the noise of the sea (cf. 5:30 and 17:12), it may be that Isaiah means to suggest that the remnant cries out more shrilly than does the sea itself.[53] If this is the case, he is saying that, although the sea (by which he would have in mind the turbulent nations) had once cried out, now those who remain after the judgment cry out more strongly than did the sea. On this latter point we cannot be dogmatic. One thing is clear. The deliverance places a song of rejoicing in the hearts and on the lips of those who remain. Judgment often gives way to rejoicing.

15 Isaiah now directly addresses those who had been praising God, and commands them to continue doing so.[54] His language is

---

Does this remnant, however, consist of Jews or Gentiles? Gray does not wish to be dogmatic, but suggests that the reference may be to the Gentiles. Smend, on the other hand (*ZAW*, Vol. 4, 1884, pp. 168f.), holds that vv. 14, 15 can only be explained according to the first words of v. 16.

52 ירנו—the word stands asyndetically. Procksch and Mulder propose to place the *Atnaḥ* with the preceding word. This is unnecessary, for the *Tiphḥa* shows that the two words are to be separated. There are three units to 14a, "they—will lift up their voice—they will sing."

53 Gesenius is decisive in rejecting this interpretation. צהלו—to *neigh, cry shrilly,* here, in joy and praise. The form may be a prophetic perf. (cf. 12:6; 54:1), construed with *Beth.* Sperber, however (*JBL*, Vol. 62, 1943, p. 195), takes it as merely continuing the imp., "they sing—they shout." Gray translates by the past, and Lindblom would read in an imperative. The verse has several characteristically Isaianic words.

54 The introductory '*al-kēn* is said to cause difficulty. Kissane thinks that there is no apparent reason for the particle, and he proposes to read '*el-kᵉnap,* whereas Procksch and *IB* propose '*lzw.* Neither of these can claim textual support; however, Gray thinks that no satisfactory interpretation of the verses in their present position is possible, but suggests that the relation between vv. 14 and 15 may be that, inasmuch as the heathen are praising God, so also should the scattered Jews. Mulder correctly brings out the force of the particle, "*op grond van sulke toestande.*" We may paraphrase, "they will praise God;

difficult. His second word may be rendered literally, *in the lights;* but what is meant by such an expression?[55] Possibly it refers to the east, from whence light comes, and if so, forms a contrast with the sea, which stands for the west or the coastlands of the Mediterranean.[56] Thus, the two parts of the verse may be said to refer to all places, both east and west. The entire world is thus called upon to praise the Lord. It will honor the Lord in that it will ascribe to Him the weight of glory that is His due. There is but one true God, and that One is Israel's God. All men are to praise Him and Him alone. The result of judgment will be the universal praise of the true God.

16 From the wing of the earth songs we have heard, beauty to the righteous; and I said, Leanness to me, leanness to me, alas, for me! plunderers plunder, even with plunder do plunderers plunder.

17 Fear and pit and snare are upon thee, O inhabitant of the land.

18 And it shall come to pass that he who flees from the voice of the fear will fall into the pit, and he who comes up from the midst of

---

wherefore, ye who have been described as praising Him, continue to do so." M is supported by B διὰ τοῦτο, and by all the ancient versions.

55 אורים—omitted in B. Generally it is taken to designate the east, the place where the sun rises. Perles (in the *Analekten*, 1922, p. 56) applied it to Beirut, hence, the inhabitants of Beirut. Apart from the questionable etymology, such a specialized reference would hardly serve here as a contrast to the isles. The Targum renders *light* ("when the light comes to the righteous, they shall give glory before the Lord"), Vulg. *in doctrinis*, Saadia "at the time of the appearance of his light." Kimchi takes it of cities in the valleys and not in the mountains; he connects it with אור כשדים. Ibn Janah, as given by Gesenius, applies the word to "distant islands." Gesenius himself agrees that the context here demands reference to a district which would either be the East, the realm of light, or the North, a suitable contrast to the isles of the West. He also appeals to Ar. *'al-'awr* (North) as forming a contrast with West; cf. Ps. 107:3; Isa. 49:12; note also West and South, Deut. 33:23; North and East, Amos 8:12. Commentators might well take to heart Gesenius' words: "*Unnöthig aber sind die zahlreichen zum Theil geschmacklosen Conjecturen, die hier versucht worden.*" As the word stands it must form a contrast to "isles of the sea." Its precise philological explanation, however, is difficult to determine. Lindblom thinks that the word with the meaning "regions of light" is here used as a *hapax legomenon*.

56 *islands*—i.e., in the West. Cf. 11:11 and the comments at that point. The const. pl. is found in Isa. 11:11 and 24:15, and in both instances is followed by "the sea." The abs. pl. occurs 12 times in Isa. 40–66 (9 in chapters 40–55 and 3 in 56–66). Apart from Isaiah the pl. abs. is found 10 times. The s. occurs 3 times in Isaiah (20:6; 23:2, 6) and twice in Jeremiah.

the pit will be taken in the snare; for the windows from on high have been opened, and the foundations of the earth are shaken.

19 Utterly broken down is the earth; utterly cracked through the earth; utterly shaken is the earth.

20 Reeling there will surely reel the earth, like a drunken man, and it shall totter like a booth, and heavy upon it will its transgression be, and it shall fall and not rise again.

21 And it shall come to pass in that day the LORD will visit upon the host of the high place in the high place, and upon the kings of the earth upon the earth.

22 And they shall be gathered with a gathering as prisoners in a pit, and shall be shut up in a dungeon, and after an abundance of days they shall be visited.

23 And the moon will be confounded, and the sun ashamed, for the LORD of hosts reigneth in mount Zion, and in Jerusalem, and before his elders there is glory.

16 Verse 16 constitutes an introduction to the section that follows, and verse 23 a conclusion. Separating these two verses are three groups each consisting of two verses. The first part of verse 16 takes up the thought with which verse 15 concluded, namely, praise sung to God. To show the universality of this praise, Isaiah begins with the words, *from the wing of the earth,* by which he means earth's farthest extremities.[57] The word is singular, but may be understood generally, "We have heard songs which have come even from the extremity of the earth." There is no need, nor indeed is it possible, to define the sense more closely. By means of these songs[58] the praise to God of verses 14 and 15 is made known to all the earth. The phrase *we have heard* is probably intended in an indefinite or general sense, i.e., "songs have been heard." If the literal force be retained, the "we" would include the prophet, who speaks out his own feelings.[59]

By means of the phrase "beauty to the righteous" the prophet apparently intends to set forth in very brief compass the content

---

[57] *K⁰nap* in combination with *hā'āretz* has collective force; cf. 11:12; Job 37: 3; 28:13; and Ezek. 7:2. Penna, however, thinks the reference is to a definite location, *"molto lontana dalla Palestina,"* but suggests that it may stand in place of the plural to describe the entire earth. In translating by the plural, B is simply bringing out the sense; it does not presuppose an original Heb. plural.

[58] Cf. 25:5, and Job 35:10.

[59] Drechsler thinks that Isaiah sees himself transported in the spirit into the midst of that blessed time in the future. Penna says that the prophet and his companions (v. 13) hear the song raised from a land that until then was pagan.

of the song that is sung.[60] Different views of the relationship of these words are held, but we may interpret them as stating that a beauty of glory belongs to the righteous. In the light of 4:2 that beauty is seen to be the Branch of the Lord, and that Branch is the Messiah. The beauty of the redeemed is Christ. For those who have escaped the ravages of the judgment and have been delivered therefrom there is truly a glory and a beauty, namely, their Deliverer.

Calvin and others think that the word "righteous" is here applied to God, so that the song of the delivered ones becomes a paean of praise to God Himself. It is of course perfectly true that He alone is the Righteous One, but it is possible that the ones delivered from the punishing judgment may also bear this name.[61] The name is not given to them for any intrinsic righteousness, but as Isaiah elsewhere makes clear, because they have received from God a righteousness upon the basis of which they may themselves legitimately be designated "righteous."[62] Up until this time, it had not been known that there was a beauty for the righteous; when the judgment comes, however, this fact will be published abroad by means of song. It will then be universally known that for the righteous there is beauty.

The prophet next draws attention to himself, indicating his own reaction to the song of praise. He uses the past tense, because his

[60] Cf. 4:2; 28:1-4; 13:19; Ezek. 20:6, 15; Dan. 11:16, 41. "Righteous" is here employed collectively of the servants of God. Hitherto their beauty had been either partially or completely hidden, but now it will be manifest for all the world to see. This view is in part supported by the contrast with Isaiah's own condition, "Woe to me," and by 26:2ff.

[61] Marti applies the term "righteous" to the righteous people of the law (26:2; Hab. 1:4, 13; 2:4). Penna comments, "*Ora si tende a vedervi la nazione o Israele redento da tanta catastrofe (Gray, Kissane, Fischer, Rudolph).*" Drechsler applies the term to God's servants completely, which is essentially the position herein adopted. Hitzig took it as the conqueror, and Knobel and Bredenkamp applied it to God; but God is never thus named in Isaiah. Kittel therefore refers the term to the pious members of the community. Gesenius takes it of the righteous among mankind.

[62] It cannot be stressed sufficiently that Isaiah does not employ such terms lightly. That the term applies to those who are righteous is supported by 26:2 ("righteous nation"); 26:7 ("a way for the righteous"); 26:9 ("the inhabitants of the earth have learned righteousness"); 26:10 ("let him, i.e., the wicked, not learn righteousness"). These passages show that the righteous are to be distinguished from the wicked, as in Ps. 1, and that righteousness must be learned; i.e., that men are not by nature righteous, but need to receive their righteousness from. Another.

actual speaking had already taken place in the vision. As Delitzsch points out, the situation was similar to John's response to the angel in Revelation 7:14. It was in the vision that Isaiah spoke; now, looking back upon what he had seen and recording what had happened, he employs the past. His speaking is as it were a response or reaction to the songs of praise that he hears.

Isaiah's cry is one of sorrow and grief. The first word, *razi*, is probably to be rendered *leanness*.[63] Between it and *tzᵉvi* there appears to be an intentional contrast of meaning as well as a paronomasia. "To the righteous there is *tzᵉvi*," we may picture Isaiah as saying; "to me there is *razi*." As the one word suggests all that is beautiful and to be gloried in, so the other points to what devours and consumes, a weakening or sickness that eats away the strength of the body. For the sake of emphasis Isaiah repeats the phrase, and follows it with an "alas is me." Even though there is beauty for the righteous, there nevertheless exists that which consumes the forces of the prophet. Elsewhere he had expressed himself in similar vein, "I will weep bitterly, labour not to comfort me, because of the spoiling of the daughter of my people" (Isa. 22:4). It was a cry of bitter sorrow, because the people were being destroyed. No one understood better the sorrow of Isaiah than Paul, who himself cried out, "I have great heaviness and continual sorrow in my heart. For I could wish that myself were accursed from Christ for my brethren, my kinsmen according to the flesh" (Rom. 9:2, 3).

The reason for the prophet's grief is expressed in five words in the last line of the verse. Each of these words is based upon the same root, twice appearing as a participle, twice as finite verbs in the perfect, and once in a noun form.[64] All this we may render

---

[63] *my leanness*—the double occurrence, followed by "woe is me," is of significance. The form may be derived from *rā-zāh*, to be lean; cf. 17:4 and 10:16; Ps. 106:15; Zeph. 2:11. Gray thinks then that it should be pointed *rᵉ-zi*. In combination with *li*, the word loses its accent, so that the *a* appears in a distant open syllable and is accompanied by *Meteg*. The vowel, therefore, appears to be naturally long. Drechsler compares *'ᵃ-ni* and *na-qi*, but I question the validity of this comparison. The versions (not M as Gray states) apparently understand the word as an Aram. loan word from Persian (cf. Sir. 8:18), *my secret*. In this context, however, the word must stand in opposition to *tzᵉbi*.

[64] Cf. 21:2; 22:18; and Jer. 12:1. The versions, as well as a number of modern scholars, understand the root *bdg* in the sense of "deceive" or "deal faithlessly." Others, however (e.g. Kissane, Lindblom, Rudolph), take it as "to spoil," "to rob." Mulder thus translates, "*rowers roof, roof roof die rowers.*" This view has much to commend it, particularly in so far as the context seems

literally, *plunderers plunder* (the perfect may express present action); *even with plunder do plunderers plunder*.

One cannot be dogmatic as to the exact meaning of this root, for that is difficult to ascertain; and it is possible that it may also be rendered in English by *deceive*. Isaiah, therefore, is either speaking of those who by means of deceit are leading the people to destruction or of outside enemies who are plundering the nation. The five-fold appearance of the root, however, and even the two pausal forms, seem to indicate the highest degree of emphasis. His own people are the objects of attack, and it is this which affects the prophet. He can have no joy while the people of Zion suffer.

17 The consequence of the plundering is set forth in this verse. The plunderers plunder, and as a result all that remains for the land's inhabitants is fear, the pit and snare.[65] Whether Isaiah is actually taking up a popular proverb and applying it to a specific situation, is difficult if not impossible to determine. The assonances of the verse lend force to its meaning and also tie it up closely with the last part of the preceding verse. Attempts to retain the alliteration in translation are interesting; thus, *Grauen, Grube und Garn* (Marti) ; *terrore, trabocchetto e tranello* (Penna). It is possible that the imagery here used is taken from the language of hunting. The wild animal fears its pursuers, then finds the pit; if it avoids the pit, it is taken by the snare. It finds no escape.

18 Isaiah now carries out and explains the figures which he has just used. The voice of the fear from which one flees[66] is the voice produced by the one who causes the fear. The reference is to what produces fear in the hunted, whether it be the hunter himself, his weapon, or something else. The judgment, therefore, is inescapable, for it presses in on all sides. Should, however, the fleer escape the fear, he will fall into the pit;[67] and if he is able to climb out of the pit, he will be taken by the snare. Capture is sure; there is no escape.

---

to require it; and it is apparently supported by the usage of the verb in 21:2; 33:1; Hab. 1:13; and cf. Prov. 23:28.

[65] The same words appear in Jer. 48:43, 44 in the oracle about Moab. Gesenius gives Augusti's rendering, *Entsetzen, Verletzen in Netzen*. Cf. also Amos 5:19 for the same thought expressed in different words.

[66] *voice*—i.e., the sound of whatever causes the fear. To flee from the sound of what causes fear is to flee from the object of fear itself.

[67] *npl* + *'el*—"to fall into"; cf. 2 Kings 6:5.

When, however, the judgment does come it will be as universal and of similar conclusive significance as the flood in Noah's days. Just as that deluge was all-destroying, so will this judgment be also. The similarity of the language to that employed of the flood in Genesis 7:11 shows that Isaiah is alluding to that flood.[68] At the same time, although there is an obvious allusion to the flood, Isaiah does not teach that there will be a repetition of that flood, for it was expressly revealed (Gen. 8:21) that such a means of universal destruction would never be repeated. The words teach that when the power of heaven acts the very foundation of the earth is affected. This truth is expressed poetically. The "windows from on high" are the windows through which the power from on high will flood. When the windows are opened, the tremendous cataracts originating on high pour through. In Genesis 7:11 and 8:2 there was also mention of subterranean water; but Isaiah makes no mention of it here, for he is not giving a slavish description of the Noahic flood. The consequence of this tremendous downpour is that the foundations of the earth shake.

It is sometimes held that the prophet here takes up the ancient mythological ideas and transfers them to the realm of eschatology. Lying in the background, we are told, there is the ancient myth of the god who subdues rebellious powers, and is subsequently enthroned as king. The only real evidence that can be cited in support of such a position is found in the Ugaritic texts. We would render as follows:

> And there answered Aliyn
> Baal . . . I shall place Kethir son of
> the sea, Kethir, son of the assembly.
> Let him open a window in the house,
> a window ('rbt) in the midst of the palace,
> and let there be opened a cleft in the clouds.
> (Baal 7, lines 14-19)

This is a difficult text, however, and there are many questions involved in its interpretation. The only real resemblance with the

---

68 Here the force of the Hebrew is particularly significant. It is not "the windows of on high," but "the windows which are from on high"; i.e., "windows will be opened, even windows which are from on high." Penna thinks that the text presupposes the Hebrew cosmological conception which spoke of immense reservoirs of water above the firmament and of columns which sustain the globe. Does this language, however, really set forth ancient Hebrew cosmology, or is it not rather merely forceful poetry?

Isaiah passage is the occurrence of the word *'rbt*. Certainly, the evidence is too slender to use for establishing the theory that the prophet took old mythological material and transformed it into eschatology.[69]

19 In one of the most striking and tragic utterances of the entire prophecy Isaiah proclaims earth's destruction. Even the arrange-ment of the words presents a truly plastic effect. The threefold occurrence of *'eretz* (*earth*) is striking, thus: *'aretz—'eretz—'aretz*. In each of its three appearances this word is preceded by two others, the word immediately preceding being in each case a *Hitpolel* perfect, before which stands an infinitive absolute. We may thus translate so as to bring out the full force of the arrangement of the verse:

> broken—there is broken down the earth;
> cracked through—there is cracked through earth;
> shaken—there is shaken earth.

Thus, the three infinitives absolute stand almost in each case as a *casus pendens*, stressing the thought to be emphasized; and in each instance a statement is made which connects this basic thought with the earth.[70]

In the description there appears to be an ascending gradation of thought. The first verb implies a breaking or shattering, as though pieces of the earth were broken off; it is probably onomatopoeic. The word is suitable for describing an earthquake or some great convulsion that breaks the earth in pieces. The second verb is probably stronger, and suggests that the earth is actually divided by being split through; while the last verb denotes a violent or great

[69] The text may be transliterated: *ktr. bn ym. ktr. bnm. 'dt. ypth. hln. bbhtm urbt. bqrb (.) hklm. w.y(p)th. bdqt. 'rpt.* Driver (*op. cit.*, p. 101) takes *ym* in the sense of "day," *ktr* as "cunning man," *rbt* as "lattice." *foundations*—in the nature of the case these would be the strongest.

[70] *rô'āh*—GKC § 67 regards the *He* as due to dittography. The form is ab-normal, for we should expect *rô^{a'}*. Drechsler construes the word as nom. act. substituting for an inf. abs. (cf. Prov. 25:19). The accent is *Milel*, possibly to show that the f. ending is not of prime importance when the word serves as an inf. absolute. Possibly the two following infinitives have also exerted an in-fluence. Green regards the form as contracted and with a paragogic ending. Note that the infinitives are *Qal*, whereas the cognate form is a derived stem. Drechsler thinks that the repetition gives a particular effect, for everything is concerned with what happens to the earth. Note that even in the repetition a certain variety is achieved by employing the definite article only once.

shaking of the earth. Quite possibly the imagery or figure of the earthquake lies at the basis of the portrayal, but Isaiah's purpose is not to describe an earthquake; rather he is pointing to a tremendous shaking of the earth that will come when the punitive judgment of God strikes.

20 Continuing his description the prophet again speaks of the earth, portraying it as shaking or tottering, swaying to and fro like a drunken man.[71] In further picturing this swaying of the earth, Isaiah compares it to a *mᵉlunah,* a word which he had used earlier in 1:8 to refer to the hut in the vegetable garden. This structure was light and frail, and evidently swayed with the wind. Some interpret the word of a hammock,[72] but there is question as to whether it can have such a meaning. If, as is probably the case, the word does designate a shelter, such a shelter would be temporary, possibly hastily thrown together, and not able to stand against the strong blowing of the wind.

Isaiah gives the reason why the earth is so shaken; it is that her transgression now weighs heavily upon her. Using similar imagery David had said that God's hand was heavy upon him (Ps. 32:4), by which he meant that his sins were ever before him. As though bearing a heavy burden, the earth now staggers under the load of her own transgression. Marti suggests that the earth will disclose her blood (26:21) when the Lord comes to punish her. This blood, which she gives forth to be cleansed with, works as a poison, he claims, so that the earth is again shaken with sickness.[73] It is questionable, however, whether Isaiah is referring at this juncture

---

71 Both the first two roots are used with gradation. With the first this is accomplished by the inf. abs. and the imperfect. In the second it is produced by the derived form. Between the two roots there is alliteration.

72 *mᵉlûnāh*—cf. 1:8, where the word apparently refers to a hut in which watchmen spend the night. There the point of comparison was that of aloneness; here it is that of shaking or swaying. In what sense can this concept be applied to a hut? Some, therefore, give the word a different connotation, applying it to a hammock. Gesenius quotes Carsten Niebuhr's description of such hammocks in Yemen.

The Syr. and Targ. translate by "hammock," as does Saadia also (*'irzal*) ; and Gesenius appeals to the Qamûs for a definition of the *'irzal* as "a place which garden watchers take in the branches of the palm trees, out of fear of lions." Kimchi, however, takes the word as designating a booth.

73 Marti: "*das auf ihr vergossene Blut, das sie 26 ²¹ wieder herausgiebt, um dann gereinigt zu sein, wirkt wie ein Gift für sie, so dass sie wie von giftiger Krankheit geschüttelt wird.*"

to anything more than the fact that the transgressions which the inhabitants of earth have committed now weigh heavily upon the earth.

The earth falls and will not add to rise (i.e., will not rise again) .[74] The language is taken almost word for word from Amos 5:2. The judgment is final. "One cannot deny to this representation of the blowing of the judgment in vv. 18b-20 a poetical effect; the constant repetition of the word *eretz;* the unyielding hithpolels and hithpolals paint strikingly the gigantic convulsions of Nature and the assonances show the breaking forth, thrusting out and the staggering of the mighty surfaces."[75]

21 Coming at the theme from a slightly different angle Isaiah now announces that at the time of the judgment, when the earth has fallen and will no more arise, God will visit in punishment both upon the hosts of the high ones on high (i.e., heaven) and on the kings of the earth. The host comprises not merely the stars but also angels. It is thus the host that belongs to the height in distinction from those who are upon earth. It is true that in verse 4 the word *marom* had reference to inhabitants of this earth. The present context, however, makes clear that it here refers to something that is not on earth. The phrase really is equivalent to "the army or host of heaven."[76] They are to be visited on high where they are. We thus learn that there are forces, not residing upon this earth but on high (*marom*), who have influenced the rulers on this earth to turn against God and to transgress His laws. The judgment, therefore, will also be visited upon them, for they are partakers of earth's transgression. Paul's comment is entirely apposite: "For we wrestle not against flesh and blood, but against principalities, against powers, against the rulers of the darkness of this world, against spiritual wickedness in high places" (Eph. 6:12) . Of this judgment our Lord spoke, "Now is the judgment of this world; now shall the prince of this world be cast out" (John 12:31) . And Paul also speaks of this judgment, "and having

---

74 Cf. Rev. 20:11.

75 Only the last stichos of verse 20, according to Duhm, is an unfortunate literal citation from Amos 5:2.

76 The phrase designates the stars, 34:4; 40:26; 45:12; and the angels, 1 Kings 22:19; 2 Chron. 18:18. Cf. the excellent treatment in A. H. van Zyl, "Isaiah 24-27; Their Date of Origin" in *New Light on Some Old Testament Problems (Papers read at 5th meeting of Die O.T. Werkgemeenskap in Suid-Afrika)*, 1962.

spoiled principalities and powers, he made a shew of them openly, triumphing over them in it" (Col. 2:15).[77]

In addition to the host on high the kings upon the ground are to feel the judgment. The word "height" had suggested a contrast with "earth," but it also presents the concept of totality. All, whether on high or on earth, the highest in both spheres, will be subjects of the judging God. By mention of the kings, the prophet shows that the highest on earth are those who are responsible (cf. also Isa. 34:4; 65:17; and Hag. 2:6).

The kings of the earth have waged war against the Lord (Acts 4:26, 27) and against the Lamb (Rev. 17:14). There thus appears a history of heavenly powers, paralleling that of earth. Heavenly powers have rebelled against their Creator and have stirred up earthly rulers to make war against the Lord and against His anointed. They fail, for the Lord is King of Kings and He judges them.

22 Isaiah continues his theme, pointing out that the armies of heaven and the kings of the ground will be imprisoned, and then, after many days, will be visited by God in punishment. To describe the imprisonment, the prophet says, "and they shall be gathered a gathering."[78] The root is used of one's being gathered unto his fathers in death (e.g., 2 Kings 22:20), but it is also employed of imprisonment. Thus, "And he (i.e., Joseph) gathered them unto the prison three days" (Gen. 42:17). The gathering which will come upon them is like that of a prisoner (lit., a bound one) being taken unto the pit.[79] Just as a prisoner is taken to a pit and cast therein, so will the host on high and the kings of the earth be put in a pit. Even the preposition (in) probably exhibits a certain

---

[77] Calvin takes the phrase "arm on high" as a metaphor by which Isaiah denotes kings and princes "who shine and sparkle in the world like stars."

[78] אסיר is adverbial, "and they shall be gathered a gathering in the state of being a prisoner." Cf. 22:18. The word is omitted in 1Q. It expresses a subordinate thought, a circumstantial thought, and may be regarded as an acc. of state (Ḥal). אספה, following the verb, serves as an inner or cognate accusative. The threefold alliteration should be noted.

Bentzen takes 'assîr as a collective concept, prisoners, in apposition to 'asēpāh, which is a hapax legomenon. The word 'assîr is difficult. Jerome translates, et congregabuntur in congregatione unius fascis in lacum. B omits the word. Lindblom gives a useful discussion of the textual problems. The translation herein adopted is legitimate, however, and the text does yield a good sense.

[79] The choice of the prep. seems deliberate; cf. 2 Kings 4:4; Job 6:16; Nah. 3:12.

nuance, namely, the idea of going downwards into the pit. In itself, the word "pit" refers merely to a prison, or dungeon. Isaiah uses it in 14:17 of Sheol, and here it would seem to be used figuratively to designate the place of eternal torment which is reserved for the fallen angels and for those who know not the Lord. The same thought appears in 2 Peter 2:4, "For if God spared not the angels that sinned, but cast them down to hell, and delivered them into chains of darkness, to be reserved unto judgment"; and Jude 6, "And the angels which kept not their first estate, but left their own habitation, he hath reserved in everlasting chains under darkness unto the judgment of the great day."[80] Whether or not Isaiah actually intends Sheol by this language is not entirely clear. What is clear is that he is describing the fate of the army on high and the kings of earth as that of being bound in such a manner as is a prisoner who is cast down into a pit. It is a place from which there is no escape.

To stress the idea that there is no possibility of escape it is stated that the prisoners will be shut up in (again note the preposition 'al) a prison (a place that is shut up). After an abundance of days, they will be visited, and the nature of the visitation, as the context shows, is one of punishment. The visitation, however, is not to occur immediately upon the arrest of the prisoners, but only after a long time. Isaiah does not state how long a time, nor does he say why it is to be after a long time. Calvin and others assume that this is to teach the saints patience, and in this assumption they may very well be correct. It is well to ask when the "many days" begin, for the proper answer to this question will enable us to ascertain the purpose of the phrase. There are two principal views. On the one hand it is held that the beginning of the "many days" is coincidental with the raging of the enemies of God. On this interpretation the enemies are conceived as storming against God for many days, and then they will be visited in judgment. Thus, Hengstenberg, for example, interprets: "after the beginning of their raging, which was to continue for a series of centuries, until Christ at length spoke: 'Be of good cheer, I have overcome the world.'" He thus interprets the visitation of the nations being gathered together.

A second view, and one which seems to have more in its favor, is to take the beginning of the "many days" as coinciding with the

80 Cf. also Enoch 10:12; 91:12ff.; John 12:31; 1 Pet. 3:19; Rev. 9:1, 2.

imprisonment of the enemies of God. On this view their imprisonment lasts for "many days" until finally the last judgment reaches them. It is this interpretation that is supported by the New Testament (2 Pet. 2:4; Jude 6).[81] Revelation 20:1-6 also presents the same theme from a different aspect. And we may remember the words of the demons to our Lord, "What have we to do with thee, Jesus, thou Son of God? art thou come hither to torment us before the time?" (Matt. 8:29). In what the Scripture teaches concerning the final doom of the evil one and his hosts there is much of mystery. His doom is sure, yet, during the "many days" our only hope and consolation is to fly for refuge to the wounds of our Lord, where alone one may be safe from the fiery darts of the wicked one who goes about as a roaring lion, seeking whom he may devour.

23 The prophet now sets forth the end result of the judgment. All powers of this world will be removed, and the eternal kingdom of God will be established in Jerusalem. This truth is taught by means of symbolical language. The moon was created to rule the earth by night (Gen. 1:16), but the moon will be abashed or ashamed in that day, for "the city has no need of the moon or of the sun, that they should shine in it" (Rev. 21:23). The verb implies that the moon will be too shy or reticent to shine, for it will realize that it is not needed. Isaiah uses a poetic word for "moon," a word that really means "white." The glory of the moon is her whiteness, but this whiteness will disappear in confusion. Isaiah also personifies the sun, which is said to be ashamed, as though its shining were now something to be ashamed of. Indeed, such is actually the case, for the glory of God will shine there, and its light is the Lamb (cf. Rev. 21:23b). The sun was to rule the earth by day, and in so doing, would bring blessing to the earth in fulfilling the divine command. On the new Jerusalem, however, there will no longer be need of the light of the sun, for the very glory of God will give light. Should then the sun try to shine, it ought indeed to be ashamed. To designate the sun Isaiah employs a word meaning "hot" (*hammah*).[82] The glory of the sun is her heat, but this heat will disappear in shame. In comparison with the light of the glory of God, the light of the sun would cause the sun to be ashamed. In

---

[81] According to Robert Culver, *Daniel and the Latter Days*, Westwood, N. J., 1954, pp. 32, 50ff., these verses must refer to the Millennium.

[82] In Ps. 19:7 the term *hammāh* is employed of the heat or glow of the sun.

thus personifying the sun, Isaiah shows that the sun is really an obedient creature. A certain emphasis is procured by placing the two verbs first; "Abashed is the moon; ashamed the sun."[83]

There is a reason for this reaction upon the part of moon and sun, namely, that the Lord will reign in mount Zion and in Jerusalem. The thought is that at that day the Lord will take over the kingdom and reign in splendor. In 1 Kings 16:29; 22:41, e.g., the force of the verb "to rule" is seen. "And Ahab the son of Omri reigned over Israel (i.e., began his reign over Israel) in the thirty-eighth year of Asa king of Judah, etc." The verb does not mean that after the judgment the Lord will become king and begin his reign. Rather, at that time, when His foes have all been put under foot and cast into the pit of everlasting punishment, then the reign of God will be seen in all its fullness and wondrous power and glory. When the kingdom of evil is fully put down, the kingdom of God will be manifest as truly all-embracing. He who reigns is the Lord of hosts; and we may perhaps note that in the light of verses 21, 22, this designation is particularly chosen. The hosts from on high that opposed God will be destroyed; but the true Lord of hosts will reign forever.

The seat of the reign is Zion and Jerusalem. As an Old Testament prophet, Isaiah uses the figures that were known to him to depict the spiritual salvation of the New Testament and the eternal age. His meaning is not that the reign will be held on the actual physical Zion that was known to him; both Zion and Jerusalem are rather figures of the seat of the eternal kingdom.

In this reign the Church will be glorified, a truth which is expressed by the words, "before his elders is glory." The elders are his, i.e., God's, and they represent the government of His people, the Church. In Israel they thus served, and they also serve in His Church. The thought then is that the assembled people of God, in its official capacity, is before Him, and before them is glory. In the revealed majesty of the Lord there is opened for them an abyss of glory. At Sinai the Lord had once manifested His glory (Ex. 24:9ff.) ; so now, in the eternal kingdom that glory will ever be before His elders. Of this same scene John speaks: "And round about the throne were four and twenty seats; and upon the seats

---

83 Drechsler interprets, *rex factus est, regnum adeptus est.* In view of recent emphases upon a festival of the ascension of the throne (*Thronbesteigungsfest*), however, such an interpretation must be guarded. Mulder remarks correctly, *"Maar dit hou nie in dat Jahwe voor die tyd nie koning is nie."*

I saw four and twenty elders sitting, clothed in white raiment; and they had on their heads crowns of gold" (Rev. 4:4).

It is true that the Messiah is not mentioned in this verse, but that is not sufficient reason for the assumption that no room is here found for the Messiah or for any king other than Yahweh.[84] As a conclusion to the prophecies of the foreign nations, it must be shown that Yahweh is truly God and in control of the outcome of the nations' future. The nations had boastfully asserted that Yahweh was no different from other gods; they had captured other gods, the same was to be the fate of Yahweh. It is necessary therefore that the prophet make clear that Yahweh alone is to be exalted; it is He alone who reigns. To say that this emphasis excludes the Messianic work is without warrant. The prophet mentions the Messiah when it is necessary to show that the Messiah is the One whom God employs to accomplish the work of redemption and to establish His kingdom. That Isaiah does not mention the Messiah whenever he speaks of the kingdom is no evidence that at that particular point there is no room for a Messiah. In Revelation 21:4 John says that "God shall wipe away all tears from their eyes; and there shall be no more death, neither sorrow, nor crying, neither shall there be any more pain: for the former things are passed away." Does John intend by this language to rule out entirely the work of Christ and to assert that God will bless His people apart from Christ? To ask that question is to show its absurdity. Likewise, in the case of the present passage, the fact that Isaiah does not here mention the Messiah merely shows that it was not his purpose so to do. That such lack of mention excludes the work of the Messiah is a conclusion that has no warrant.

The passage reaches its climax in the word, "glory." ". . . Then only does God receive his just rights, and the honour due to him, when all creatures are placed in subjection, and he alone shines before our eyes" (Calvin).

---

[84] So, e.g., Gray. Mulder expresses similar thoughts and quotes Gemser ("*De testamentische heilsverwachting toch ligt niet in den Messias maar in die paroesie van Jahwe*").

CHAPTER TWENTY-FIVE

As a song of praise followed the description of the fall of the world power and the establishment of God's kingdom given in chapters ten and eleven, so also after the prophecy of God's great judgment in chapter twenty-four, Isaiah inserts another song of praise.

1   O LORD, my God art thou; I will exalt thee, I will praise thy name for thou hast done a wondrous thing, counsels from afar off are faithfulness, certainty.

2   For thou hast made it from a city to a heap, a fortified city to a ruin, a palace of strangers from being a city, it shall never be built.

3   Wherefore a powerful people will honor thee, a city of awe-inspiring nations will fear thee.

4   For thou hast been a refuge to the poor, a refuge to the needy in his affliction, a refuge from the storm, a shadow from the heat, for the breath of the awe-inspiring ones is as the storm against a wall.

5   Like heat in a dry place, the noise of strangers thou wilt bring down; like heat in the shadow of a cloud, the song of the awe-inspiring ones will he bring low.

1 Isaiah now reverts to the thought of 24:14, where he had depicted the people as singing God's praises. In 24:16-23 he gave the reason why the people sang, namely, the fact that God had triumphed over His enemies and that He reigns eternally. Isaiah himself now joins in glorifying the Name of his God.

In what role, however, are we to conceive him? Is he transported in vision to the end of the days, or as the representative of the redeemed; or simply as a prophet does he praise God? Possibly a dogmatic answer cannot be given, but it may be that merely in his capacity as a prophet, upon learning of the wonder of God's deliverance, Isaiah exalts God in his song. Isaiah has the benefit of special revelation; having received the word from God he knows

184

judgment will surely fall upon the nations and that the Lord will triumph. Hence, as a prophet, he breaks out into the praise of his God. At the same time he also engages in a further explanation of some of the matters which he has already mentioned.

He begins in a common lyric style, not employing any particular formula, such as "in that day," but immediately directing attention to the One who is the object of his praise, the Lord. It is the Lord who has chosen Israel to be His people and who has redeemed the nation. When Weber asserts that Christ is meant we can agree with him, for it is in Christ that the blessings of redemption have come. Isaiah acknowledges that the Lord alone is his God. He recognizes no other, and thus is really speaking out against idolatry. He makes a solemn profession of monotheism.[1] The God whom the prophet worships, Yahweh, is his God, and He alone is the one whom Isaiah confesses as God. None other is deserving of his adoration and worship. The personal element in this ascription should not be overlooked. The LORD who has executed the judgment depicted in the closing verses of the preceding chapter, and has wrought deliverance for His people, is also the prophet's own God, to whom the prophet may come in confidence. God, who must judge the nations, nevertheless hears the prayers of His people individually. Surely such a God is deserving of all praise.

As once God had stated (1:2) that He had raised (*romamti*) sons, now the prophet declares that he will exalt (*'ªromimᵉka*) God.[2] This he does in his song, extolling the glories and attributes of his Redeemer. What is expressed in the song, however, is also to appear in the thoughts and deeds of Isaiah, who with his whole being determines to exalt the LORD, and to praise Yahweh's Name, i.e., Yahweh himself.[3] Emphasis falls upon the word *Yahweh*. It is God as covenant God, as God of Israel, as the Deliverer, who is to receive the praises that the prophet utters. This is borne out by

---

[1] The common rendering is, "thou art my God" (Duhm, Guthe, Feldmann, Penna). König, however, prefers, *"der du mein Gott bist,"* regarding the other as too flat. Furthermore, he thinks that the common rendering leads to the conclusion that vv. 1-5 are intended as words of the delivered Israel and not of the prophet. Others render, "Jehovah, thou my God!"

[2] As is obvious, this is Isaianic language. The remainder of the song is in the form of a doxology, in which use is made of frequently occurring formulas. Cf. Ps. 54:8; 118:28; 145:1. Drechsler points out a rhyme in *'ªrômimᵉkā* and *šimᵉkā*. Note the Ḥireq in *'ªrômimᵉkā* in place of a *Tzere*. Normally we should expect *Sᵉgol*.

[3] Cf. Ps. 54:8; 138:2.

the explanation given, for what brings forth the prophet's praises is the judgment and deliverance accomplished by Yahweh.

The two words *pele'* and *'etzoth* belong together and call to mind the same combination of roots in 9:5, a reminder which may indicate that even there the Messiah is really not out of the picture.[4] As the text is accented, we should render, *Thou hast done a wondrous thing, namely, counsels, etc.* What God has done is a wondrous thing, something that only God could do, a wonder like the miracles in connection with the deliverance from Egypt (cf. notes on 9:5). His counsels have been from afar, i.e., devised long ago. The utter destruction of the enemy nations is something that men do not grasp, for the nations had seemed to be all-powerful; yet they have been cut off. This is a wonder, but it is what God had long ago devised.[5] What He does is not precipitate nor rash, but is the outworking of His eternal purpose and decrees. It is faithfulness and certainty, i.e., a perfect faithfulness. The combination of the two words lends force to the statement.[6]

2 This verse gives a reason why God is to be praised. One of the wonderful counsels that has been fulfilled is the destruction of the world city. It is, however, only one of these counsels, an illustration of what they were. The wondrous counsels are not exhausted in the downfall of the world city.

Whatever be the precise force of the words "city" and "village" in this verse, we may be sure that Isaiah is not speaking of

4 Cf. Ex. 15:11; Ps. 77:15; 78:12; 88:11. König thinks that *'ētzāh* is joined by zeugma also to what follows. Duhm likewise, who renders, *Wunderbeschlüsse.* König believes that Feldmann's rendering, *Wunderpläne,* is false. Both words are nouns, exhibiting the relationship of appositional gen.; i.e., a wonder of counsels, wonderful counsels. I cannot understand the basis of König's objection. Mulder and Lindblom also adopt this construction. The combination of roots is found only in Isaiah; cf. 9:5; 28:29. Cf. H. S. Nyberg, *Studien zum Hoseabuche,* p. 24.

5 Cf. 22:11. The word *rāḥôq* occurs 14 times in the prophecy: 6 in chapters 1—39 and 8 in chapters 40—66.

6 The two words combined probably exhibit a certain gradation. Cf. J. C. van Dorssen, *De Derivata van de stam 'mn in het Hebreeuwsch van het Oude Testament,* Amsterdam, 1951. There is no warrant for regarding the second word merely as a liturgical addition.

Some take the two words as predicates, "counsels from afar are faithfulness and truth." If, however, the construction of the sentence herein adopted be allowed, the words may be taken either as an adverbial acc., *in respect to faithfulness and truth,* or else as a pred. complement, *even faithfulness and truth.* A conjunction is probably to be understood as in Job 30:3, 14; 38:27.

Jerusalem. It is unlikely that he would praise God for the destruction of his own city, the city in which God's dwelling was located. Isaiah's concern was for the welfare of that city. It is also unlikely that he could speak of a palace of strangers with respect to Jerusalem, although he had indeed stated that strangers were devouring the land (Isa. 1:7). The word "strangers," however, would seem to indicate some place other than Jerusalem.

A literal translation of the words is: *for thou hast placed from a city to the heap.*[7] The word "city" is indefinite, inasmuch as it is anarthrous.[8] Although the construction is somewhat cumbersome, the meaning appears to be, "thou hast changed a city into a heap." It is perfectly possible that the reference may be to one particular city, such as Babylon; but it is by no means necessary to adopt such a reference. It may also be that the prophet is simply enunciating a general truth, namely, that God's wondrous counsels have been carried out in that He has completely overthrown the order of things. A city is a place of organization and order, but God has changed it to a heap.[9] On this construction the word would simply refer to cities generally.

This interpretation is supported by the phrase, "a village fortified to a place of ruin." Here again indefiniteness is maintained, but there is the additional information that the city is fortified. The gradation continues in that the city is designated a place of strangers.[10] By mentioning the place Isaiah designates the city, which is evidently conceived in its unity and stateliness as centering in a beautiful building. A castle or castles would be the distinguishing feature of the city. Penna aptly calls attention to the *Hofburg* of the German cities. To destroy such a place was really to make the place no more a city. God had acted in such a manner

---

[7] No definite object for שמת is given, and thus the concept of generality is maintained, an incidental evidence that the prophet is not speaking of one particular city. There is really an ellipsis of the inf. *hᵉyōṭ;* cf. also Isa. 7: 8; 17:1. Smend identifies the city with a Moabite city (cf. vv. 10-12).

[8] This is similar to 24:10-12. Kissane and others would supply the definite article; some would simply drop the prep. and leave the word indefinite (Lindblom, König, Rudolph, etc.).

[9] מפלה occurs elsewhere only in Isaiah 17:1; 23:13. The language reminds of the boasts on the Assyrian inscriptions, e.g., *a-na tilli ú kar-me u-tir, to a ruined mound and ploughland I turned (it),* Sennacherib's sixth campaign.

[10] Cf. 1:7; 29:5; and Ps. 54:5; Jer. 30:8; 51:51. Gesenius refers the language to the destruction of Babylon's palaces, Duhm to John Hyrcanus (cf. Josephus *Antiquities* xiii.10-3).

that the place ceased to be a city, and so thorough was His work that it would never be built again.

3 As a result of the catastrophic changes wrought by the Lord, the carrying out of His wondrous counsels, a strong people will honor Him and a city of awe-inspiring nations will fear Him. Different identifications of the "strong people" have been proposed, but the context seems to require that they be those who belong to the nations of the world, the peoples who had sought to destroy the theocracy, and not to the theocratic nation itself. They are a "strong" people, for thus they had described themselves. When the world cities are overthrown, they see the power and wondrous counsels of the Lord, and honor Him in a religious sense.[11]

We must not overlook the profound theological teaching that if the Gentiles are to worship God their own united power must first be destroyed. As long as the Gentile nations, represented in Isaiah's day by the Assyrians and Babylonians, sought to control the world and to incorporate the theocracy within their own kingdom, there could be no hope for their salvation. Babylon and all that it represented must first be destroyed. The ecumenical power of man must be broken, that the nations may learn that the Lord is the God of all the earth, and may praise Him. The destruction of world cities has brought about this result. Now the strong people no longer seek the destruction of God's city and kingdom; now they honor Him as the true God. They come to Him in obeisance. Now too, there exists a village consisting of awe-inspiring nations which fear God. It is a strange phrase: *a village of nations.* Perhaps Isaiah means to show that the powerful cities of the world are passed away, and the habitation of nations can only be called *qiryah* (village). The word *village* is taken in a collective sense, and the verb is plural to refer to the actual individual inhabitants of the city.

The conversion of the heathen is thus brought about in a twofold manner. First, the world cities must be removed; and secondly, there must be a true spiritual turning unto God, such as is represented by the verbs "honor" and "fear." To honor God is to ascribe unto Him and to acknowledge as belonging unto Him the honor that is His. To fear Him is to approach Him in reveren-

11 Cf. 24:15. B has ὁ λαὸς ὁ πτωχός, but it is clear that Isaiah begins to speak of Israel only in the following verse. The two epithets '*az* and '*āritz* produce a similar effect, as in 18:2, 7; '*āritz* is an Isaianic word; cf. 13:11; 29:5, 20; 49:25.

tial awe. This latter is a spiritual work, and is accomplished only by spiritual means, namely, the working of God in the human heart as a result of the effective preaching of the Gospel. How wondrous are the counsels of God! He can change a city into a heap; but greater than that, He can change a powerful people and awe-inspiring nations into those that honor and fear Him. Such a God is truly deserving of praise!

4 Not only has God destroyed the cities, but He has also shown Himself a refuge for His own people. This is another reason why He is to be praised. Isaiah begins this verse with *ki* (for), the third time in a series of four that he has used the word.[12] God is to be praised, because He has been a place of refuge. As in Psalm 31:5; 52:9, etc., the word "refuge" is used figuratively. Those who have found the Lord a place of refuge are the poor, a designation which stands in obvious contrast to the "strong people" who have been the oppressors. These characterizations have a particular reference to the catastrophe that has come upon the earth. They also make clear that Yahweh is a God who does delight in helping those that are in need of help.[13]

In the ancient world, gods were sometimes praised in prayers because they showed mercy to the needy. For example, a Hittite prayer to the sun contains the following thoughts:

> Thou, Istanu, art father and mother of the oppressed, the lonely and the bereaved. Of the lonely and oppressed thou, Istanu, dost restore the claims.

This particular prayer goes on to say, "The cause of the dog and the pig thou decidest."

---

12 Drechsler points out the remarkable symmetry that is found in these verses. Vv. 2, 3 (the offensive) follow naturally from v. 1, and so do vv. 4, 5 (the defensive). 1b *ki*, 2 *ki*, 3 *'al-kēn*, 4 *ki*, 4b *ki*.

The *ki* of v. 4 is parallel to that of v. 2 and gives the reason for the song of praise in v. 1. As Lindblom suggests, the work of God is described from a new standpoint; Yahweh has shown Himself to be a refuge for the needy.

13 There is a strong contrast between the *dāl* and *'ebyón* of this verse, and the *'am-'āz* and *góyim 'āritzím* of the preceding. The contrast is further heightened by the addition of *batztzar-lô*. Isaiah does not employ a suffix, *in their affliction*, but a circumlocution, *in affliction to him*, which has the force of *when they were afflicted*. Several would identify the *dāl* and *'ebyón* as common terms designating the national misfortune of the Israelites in exile. Gesenius, however, acknowledges that at times the expressions may be used of the pious among the Israelites. Kissane applies the words simply to the people of Israel.

Here, however, the prophet is not merely uttering vain generalities. He is praising God, because in this crisis God has shown Himself in very truth to be a place in which the poor, namely, God's own afflicted people, might find refuge. The thought is not merely that the poor find God a place of refuge, but that, when they are afflicted, God is a refuge to them. It is one thing to utter generalities about a god helping the needy; it is something entirely different when the needy, at the time of crisis, find a true hiding place in their God. Such is the God whom the prophet now praises. When His people are in need, then He is present with His aid.

The latter part of the verse calls to mind the thought of 4:6. Isaiah combines two figures, representing opposite conditions, to express the idea of oppression. When the storm comes and pelts down hard with driving rain, washing away all before it, the Lord is a shelter. When the burning heat would destroy, He is a shadow. Isaiah then gives a partial explanation of these figures: "The breath of the awe-inspiring ones is as the storm against a wall." The breath is the violent spirit which characterizes those who fight against the poor. It is like a storm which beats heavily against a wall. It does not blow the wall over, but is itself forced to change course. It is an ineffectual storm, as are all storms which are directed against God's purposes and His kingdom. A storm beating against a wall does not accomplish its purpose.[14]

5 In the phrase, "a refuge from the storm, a shadow from the heat" (4b), Isaiah had introduced two metaphors. In 4c he took up the first of these, the storm, and now he mentions the second, i.e., the heat. At the same time he also brings to mind the phrase, "breath of the awe-inspiring ones," but now characterizes it as *the noise of strangers*.[15] In direct address to God, the prophet declares that God will subdue the noise of the awe-inspiring ones. What he alludes to is the noise and tumult which they make as they turn against God's people. The comparison is interesting. Isaiah employs

[14] The Isaianic character of the language of this verse should be noted. *Zerem* is found 7 times in Isaiah, and elsewhere only twice. The proposal to read *qôr* (*cold*, i.e., winter) for *qîr* (*wall*) is not recent, and it is without textual support. *Lectio difficilior praestat!*

[15] שׁאון; cf. 24:8; 13:4; 17:12, 13. There is no objective textual warrant to support an emendation of the text. As Gray points out, *noise* forms a better parallel to *song* than does *pride* (Duhm). It should be noted that B's rendering of this verse can only be regarded as an interpretation.

a gradation in his thought. Not only is there heat, but it is the heat of a dry land, a land burning under the sun and suffering from lack of moisture in the atmosphere. What, however, is the point of the comparison? We are not immediately told how it is that the heat of the dry land—burning, intense heat—is removed. The answer is retained for the second part of the verse. Just as a passing cloud can obscure the heat of the sun and so protect the land therefrom, so easily will the Lord bring to silence the boasting noise of the tumultuous armies.[16]

6 And the LORD of hosts will make for all the people in this mountain a feast of fat things, a feast of wines on the lees, of fat things full of marrow, of wines on the lees, well refined.

7 And he will swallow up in this mountain the face of the covering which covereth upon all peoples, and the web, which is woven over all the nations.

8 He has swallowed up death for ever, and the Lord GOD will wipe away tears from upon all faces, and the reproach of his people he will turn aside from upon all the earth, for the LORD hath spoken.

6 Isaiah now returns to the description of chapter twenty-four, which description he had interrupted in order to utter a hymn of praise to the God who could perform the work of judgment and of salvation. As in ancient times (1 Sam. 11:15; 1 Kings 1:9, 19, 25) it was customary after a coronation to sacrifice and to celebrate a sacrificial meal, so also after the Lord takes up His reign in Jerusalem, there is to be a festal meal. It is the Lord, however, who provides the banquet, for all is of His grace. He who makes the feast is designated the LORD of hosts, a phrase which recalls 24:23, where it was stated that the LORD of hosts reigned.[17]

16 Cf. 24:16. Some interpret the verb as *Qal*: "the song of the tyrants is brought low." The *Hiphil*, however, supports the parallelism better. The change in persons is usual.

17 Dillmann regards the feast as a sign of homage to the king for his subjects when he takes over the rule (1 Kings 1:9, 25; 1 Sam. 11:15). Gray thinks that after His accession to universal sovereignty Yahweh gives the feast to all His subjects. Cf. *HTC*, p. 147.

As Penna points out, many exegetes speak of this passage as eschatological; but it is difficult to prove that the reference is to the events that conclude human history. The universalism herein pictured, however, is not in conflict with later emphases in Isaiah (contra Duhm).

Gray ("Kingship of God in Prophets and Psalms," *VT*, Vol. 11, 1961, p. 23) thinks that this section of Scripture makes abundant use of the mythology of Baal as king. God's feast on Zion reminds him of Baal's "housewarming" when,

Isaiah does not immediately give the object of the verb. He does not straightway tell us what it is that God will do. He does declare, however, that God's action will be for the benefit of all people. The nations cannot find blessing in themselves, nor can they discover it in Israel until God first establishes His eternal kingdom in Zion. There must be judgment and the establishment of the kingdom in order that there may be a feast for all nations. The language is all-inclusive. No nation as such is to be excluded from the blessings which the Lord brings. The Assyrian kingdom (and all the kingdoms later represented in Daniel's colossus) had sought to be universal. None of these, however, was truly ecumenical, for all were of human origination. Only the kingdom which God establishes is universal and in the true sense of the word ecumenical. The good things that God provides are for all nations.

Isaiah mentions the seat of the kingdom before he states what it is that the Lord will do. The kingdom is to be erected "in this mountain," i.e., Zion,[18] a designation which takes us back to 24:23 where the same words are found. Hitherto Zion had been insignificant and despised; now it is to be the seat of God's reign, the center from which blessing is to flow to the entire world. The thought is basically the same as that expressed earlier in chapter 2:1-4. As Zion here is to be taken in a figurative sense, referring to the Church of God, so also is the banquet to be understood figuratively, as signifying the spiritual blessings that God brings to mankind through His kingdom.[19] The thought is also expressed in Psalm 22:27: "Let the humble eat and be satisfied; let them praise the LORD that seek after Him; may your heart live for ever."

What God does for all nations is to make a feast consisting of the

---

risen from the dead, he is King triumphant. The victory over death is thought to be a reflection upon Mot's discomfiture. The feast is also thought to be evidence of apocalyptic. *Enuma Elish* mentions a feast at which the gods acknowledge Marduk as King (iii.131–iv.32). But in these feasts only the gods partake of the meal. Cf. the excellent discussion in A. H. van Zyl, *op. cit.,* pp. 44-57.

[18] The concept of *the mountain of the Lord* is typically Isaianic; cf. 2:2ff.; 4:5; 8:18; 10:32; 11:9; 16:1; 18:7; 29:8; 30:29; 31:4; 37:32; 56:7; 57:13; 65:11; 66:20.

[19] Bultema interprets these verses as teaching what Jesus will do for all people when He returns. He believes that he can bring no strong objection against a simple, literal interpretation, but thinks that believers with their new bodies can certainly partake of this feast!

best and most choice things that food and drink can offer. It consists of "fat things," the plural indicating the choiceness of the food, and its right preparation with all that should accompany it (cf. Gen. 49:20; Isa. 55:2; Jer. 31:14; Ps. 63:6; Job 36:16; Neh. 8:10).[20] By means of gradation Isaiah now characterizes the banquet as one of wine that is matured by resting undisturbed on the lees. A play upon words as well as a gradation appears between sh^emanim (fat things) and sh^emarim (lees). This latter word originally signified holders or preservers, and then came to designate the wines that had rested a long time on sediment or dregs, and so had become more valuable. The wine lay on the lees to increase its strength and color. Allusions to this practice are found in Jeremiah 48:11; see also Zephaniah 1:14.

In the latter part of the verse Isaiah proceeds to emphasize both of the two similar-sounding words, and to each he adds a *Pual* participle in the plural, which serves to describe the words more fully. Thus, the fat things are said to be full of marrow and the wines are well refined.[21] These were the best of the fat things, and were most acceptable in the banquets, as well as in the sacrifices. The wines on the lees would be well filtered and refined. In this feast the best is offered to the nations.

When God establishes His kingdom and reign from Zion, all the world will be blessed. What the world will receive from Him is not the paltry, disappointing philosophy of men, but the precious truth of the everlasting Gospel. To a world covered with the darkness of sin, there will break forth the rays of true light, for in His light the world will see light. What he offers will truly satisfy, bless, and enrich mankind. The good things of His house are those which alone quench the thirst and still the hunger of needy men. Whenever in Old Testament times a sacrifice was celebrated, there was a prefiguration of this great feast.[22] Of interest is the prominence of

---

[20] Fat was considered the most desirable part of the animal. It was a symbol of abundance (Ps. 26:8). In the peace offerings the fat parts were burned on the altar for the Lord (Lev. 3:3-16; 7:25). Cf. also Gen. 49:20 and Isa. 55:2; Jer. 31:14; Ps. 63:6; Job 36:16; Neh. 8:10. The word literally means *oils;* cf. 5:1 and 10:27.

[21] ממחים—*Pual* participle: note retention of *yod* in the diphthong *āy* before the pl. ending. The verb is a denominative of *mō^ah, marrow,* occurring only in the *Pual.* The word is *hapax legomenon.* The *yod* of the *Lamed-yod* stem remains; *m^emuḥeh (m^emuḥāy).*

[22] Mowinckel, *Ps. Stud.,* Vol. II, p. 296.

the sound *im*, which lends a poetical character, as though the humming of musical instruments were heard.

7 If the feast of the Lord is to be enjoyed, there must be a removal of those things which prevent men from enjoying it. The darkness, both of ignorance and sorrow, which now covers the earth, must first be removed. The purpose of the present verse is to state that this darkness is taken away. To stress the disappearance of the darkness of ignorance and sorrow Isaiah uses a word which he has already employed elsewhere. He had stated that God would swallow up the counsel of Egypt and so destroy it (19:3), and now declares that God will swallow the faces of the covering.[23] This strong expression gives assurance of the complete disappearance and destruction of the enemy. Its emphasis falls upon the rapidity and completeness of the disappearance rather than upon the manner.

On this very mountain whence God reigns He is said to swallow the covering. We are not necessarily to understand the swallowing up as taking place subsequent to the making of the feast. Rather, two statements are made that show forth the fullness of the deliverance that the Lord will provide for His people. On the one hand, He will make a feast; on the other He will swallow up the covering.

Isaiah uses a strange characterization; God is said to swallow the face of the covering,[24] which evidently refers to that part of the covering that is turned toward the one who beholds it. The language is evidently taken from the custom of wearing a veil in mourning or sorrow (cf. 2 Sam. 15:30; 19:5; Jer. 14:3ff.).[25] It is a veil that covers the peoples, and when this veil is removed, the cause of sorrow is also removed. There will then no longer be need or reason for wearing the veil.

Over all the nations there is also a web, which is woven as a covering.[26] The word "web" is a parallel to the preceding "cover-

23 בלע occurs often in Isaiah; cf. 3:12; 9:15; 19:3; 28:4, 7; 49:19. Penna thinks that the verb accentuates the idea of greedy rapidity rather than that of the elimination of an object. Cf. 2 Sam. 20:19ff.; Lam. 2:5.

24 Note *Paseq*, which here separates two words similar in orthography but not in meaning. The first is a noun, the second a *Qal* participle, whose usual form would be *lāṭ*. The noun is *hapax legomenon*, although the verb occurs about three times (2 Kings 16:7; Ezek. 32:30; Zech. 10:5).

25 Cf. also *Odyssey* viii.92.

26 *The web*, woven as a covering. In this sense the word also occurs in Isa.

ing." What, however, is the reason why such a veil is over the heads of peoples, and why are they mourning? Two basic answers are given to these questions. On the one hand it is said that the covering represents the spiritual blindness and ignorance that cover and characterize all peoples who are without the Lord. The veil, it is sometimes claimed, points to the spiritual dullness and hardness of heart that are found in those who know not the Lord. A second view, and one that we think to be correct, maintains that the covering represents mourning for suffering. The suffering may be caused by the judgment which is meted out to the earth, but more likely it is due to calamities that have come upon the nation. These calamities are not those brought by the judgment previously described, for those upon whom that judgment comes will find no escape; they will be destroyed in everlasting punishment. Here, however, the very wearing of the covering is a sign of mourning for calamity: it is a covering caused by sorrow.

What begets the sorrow and mourning is stated in the next verse, namely, death. Death has reigned over the nations, and has brought calamity with it. All the sufferings that have come to the world eventuate in this greatest calamity. From the hard, fierce bondage of this ruler, there appears to be no hope. Therefore, the peoples wear a covering that they may mourn their miserable condition. God, however, will remove this covering, for there will no longer be need for it. When the Lord holds His feast on Zion, the nations may come and partake, freed of all causes for mourning and sorrow. That they may thus come is due to God's grace and not to their own merit. The hope of the nations is thus to be found in God and His redemptive work, and not in the nations themselves. These are words of the utmost practicality, and of universal applicability. Even today the nations are busily engaging in trying to remove the covering by their own efforts. But it is God alone who swallows up that covering. Deliverance from death is a work of grace.

8 Here triumphant grace shines through. Isaiah does not con-

28:20. The verb נסך in the sense of "weave" is found only here. Drechsler thinks it is incorrect to understand a reference to the removal of mourning. Rather, he thinks, it is similar to the smearing over of the eyes, and the overgrowth of the heart, here designating obtuseness and dullness for spirituality. The connection with v. 8, argues Lindblom, proves that the reference is to mourning.

nect this verse with the preceding by means of the conjunction, but in a far more effective manner announces in an independent statement the truth that God has swallowed up death forever.[27] At the same time, there is a connection with what precedes, at least in thought, even if not grammatically. Having declared that God would swallow up the covering, the prophet now takes the same verb and uses it to express a general truth, namely, that God has swallowed up the cause of sorrowing and mourning, indeed of all misery, namely death.

Isaiah uses the definite article with *death*, to stress the fact that it is well known that death has been a terror to mankind. Hitherto, death itself had swallowed up all else. As in Genesis 2:17 so here, the word "death" includes all the evils which attend it. When death is swallowed up, so also are all the miseries that it brings. Furthermore, death is to be swallowed up forever; it will never again reappear. Paul's interpretation is entirely true to the Old Testament: "death is swallowed up in victory" (1 Cor. 15:54b). The book of Revelation brings out the meaning clearly: "there shall be no more death" (Rev. 21:4b).[28]

When God begins to reign on Zion, He will provide a feast of rich things for the nations, and He will at that time also swallow up death, so that there will no longer be any cause for mourning and sorrow. This is the entire picture in compact form. From the New Testament, moreover, we learn that with the establishment of the kingdom on Zion, the Church, the blessings herein predicted were indeed fulfilled. By His death Christ did swallow up death in victory. At the same time, we also learn from the New Testament that the effects of sin remain, and that only with the second advent of Christ will we see the promised blessings realized to their fullest extent. Isaiah is speaking of the fundamental victory of the Lord; he does not bring into the picture all the characteristics of this present age. In its highest sense, Alexander rightly points out, this

[27] The perf. without *waw* here occurs in a description of the future, and thus serves asyndetically to stress one aspect of the description. Paul's usage, 1 Cor. 15:54, agrees with Theodotion's text. B reads κατέπιεν ὁ θάνατος ἰσχύσας —death, having become strong, swallowed (them) up.

[28] *lānetzaḥ*—lit., *for perpetuity, endurance, everlastingness*. With the prep. it may best be rendered *for ever*. B ἰσχύσας; Aq T εἰς νἰκος; S εἰς τελος. In Aram. the root has the significance, *pa'al, to conquer*; and *nitzhānā'* is *victory, triumph*, Syr. *n^etzaḥ, to conquer*. What a cause for thanksgiving, that the inspired apostle did not follow B at this point!

blessing may never be realized by any individual until after death.

Isaiah's purpose is to comfort his people with the assurance that God will triumph, and that when He begins to reign in Zion, then blessing such as the world has never known will accompany that reign. Following the declaration that God will swallow up death, Isaiah introduces a figure of tender beauty. Choosing a word that stresses God's sovereign power, the prophet declares that the Lord (*ªdonay*) will wipe away tears from all eyes.[29] As a parent comforts and soothes the child, so the God of all power wipes away the tears from the eyes of His people. Outwardly, evil culminates in death; subjectively, it leads to tears.[30] For a parent to wipe away the child's tears is not difficult; but for God to wipe away the tears from His people's eyes, there must first be removed the evil which had caused the tears; and to remove evil, there must be a conquering of him who had the power of death. No longer, however, will the faces of His own be covered with tears, for God has removed the cause of those tears. The New Testament makes clear how He has done this. He has done it in the Person of His Son, who offered Himself a sacrifice to put away sin. Behind the beauty and glory of the blessings herein depicted there stands the Cross of Calvary.

The reproach of His people is that which lies upon them because of their sins.[31] Isaiah is not referring necessarily to the exile, although that may be encompassed in his thought. Rather, he is simply pointing to the fact that the people of God were resting under a reproach which their own sin had brought upon them. This was not necessarily a physical calamity, but could also include all suffering and sorrow, shame and disgrace. It may be also that through its sin Israel had become a reproach, and brought not blessing but shame to the world. This reproach, which because of Israel, therefore, lay also upon the world, is to be removed by God. Finally, as though to assure us of the certainty of what he has announced, Isaiah adds the comforting words, "For the LORD hath

29 וּמָחָה is a regular perfect with *waw* consecutive, and is to be translated by the future.
30 Gesenius acknowledges that the language will permit the renderings, *misfortune* and *good fortune*, instead of *death* and *life*, but rightly prefers the latter translations.
31 The concept of removing the reproach of the people occurs again in Isa. 54:4; 61:7.

spoken." The prophecy must therefore with certainty be fulfilled.

Barnes comments that the poet Robert Burns once remarked that he could not read this verse without being affected to tears, and Barnes rightly points out that nothing but the Gospel will produce such a result. Alexander comments that this is "a sufficient proof that he [Burns] was not aware of the German discovery, that this prediction is an extremely lame and flat composition, quite unworthy of the Prophet to whom it has from time immemorial been erroneously ascribed." One can sympathize with these strong remarks when he notes the manner in which this verse is handled, not only by German critics, but by others also. Only the revealed religion of the Bible can give true comfort to man and can evoke from him tears of loving joy and gratitude, for only the revealed religion of the Bible presents a God of true love and compassion who paid the price necessary to swallow up death and to wipe away tears. Despite the blindness of some critics and their failure to understand this verse, the Christian heart will ever stand in awe at the unspeakably wondrous truth that is here revealed.

9 And one will say in that day, Behold! this one is our God, we have waited for him, that he might save us; this is the LORD, we have waited for him; let us rejoice and be glad in his salvation.

10 For the hand of the LORD will rest upon this mountain, and Moab shall be trodden down in its place, as straw is trodden in the water of the dunghill.

11 And he shall spread forth his hands in its midst, even as the swimmer spreads forth his hands to swim; and he will humble his pride, together with the spoils of his hands.

12 And the fortress of the high fort of thy walls, he hath cast down, humbled, brought to the ground, to the very dust.

9 In this and the following verses the prophet proceeds to unfold more fully what he had just presented. When the salvation comes, then people will boast in their God. Then they will see that they did right in trusting the promises of God, and they will not be ashamed of their confidence. Their hopes will be fulfilled, and they can boast and rejoice therein.

In that day when God wipes away all tears, people will speak His praises. The verb is impersonal, and probably indicates the redeemed generally.[32] Not only will Israelites praise Him, but all who have received His blessings. They will call attention to the God who has done such things for them and who is their own God. For Him, they say, they have waited, i.e., they have waited for Him to fulfill His promises in order that He might save them.[33] They have believed that what He promised would be fulfilled in their own deliverance, and now they have seen that their hope was not in vain. Indeed, this God is none other than the covenant God of Israel, the LORD, in whom the people have placed their trust.

Therefore, the people encourage and exhort one another to rejoice and to exult in the salvation which they have received from Him. They may truly say that it is "His salvation," for it comes from Him, and He is its author. The emphases in the verse are important. Note the suffix, His, and the word *this*. It is as though the nation had said, "This is the God of whom we have so often spoken. Look now, as we have trusted in Him, so He has brought to pass what He promised."

10 With this verse the picture changes and a contrast is introduced. On mount Zion all is peace and blessedness, for there is the kingdom of God. Across the Jordan, however, there is another mountain, that of Moab. The singular *mountain* stands for Moab's mountains generally. Between these mountains and Zion there is a great gulf fixed, like that between the rich man and Lazarus. One who stands on the hills between Jerusalem and Bethlehem and looks across the Jordan valley to Moab will be impressed by the depth of the valley which separates Judah from Moab. Upon mount Zion God has descended in mercy and grace, but upon the mountain land of Moab His hand rests heavily and will press down Moab underneath Him.

Why does Isaiah introduce such a contrast at this particular point? The answer is that Moab had been an inveterate enemy of Israel, and is here mentioned by way of example to show that the haughty enemies of God's people will be destroyed.[34] For God's

---

32 Cf. French *on dira.* 1Q *w'mrt* is not necessary. B ἐροῦσι may merely be an attempt to give the sense.
33 Driver translates, *that he might save us.* In 9b the people are represented as already saved, hence, the verb is here better translated by the subjunctive than as a simple future. The word ישועה is frequent in Isaiah.
34 Dillmann thinks that the manner in which these words about Moab are introduced shows that the climax of the passage is not found in vengeance

people there will be a salvation in which men may boast; for those who have despised God and turned against Him there will be only punishment and destruction. Israel had been despised and looked down upon; now she will be exalted: Moab had been haughty and proud; now she will be abased and brought to shame.

The language is striking. The hand rests,[35] and Moab is threshed or tread upon, trampled down. There is really a change of figure. It is not the hand resting upon Moab which tramples it down; rather, the trampling down is a consequence of the hand resting upon the land.[36] But the trampling itself is accomplished by other agents than the hand. Isaiah employs the idiom, *under him*, or *under itself* (i.e., *in its place*), which was used also by other prophets; cf. Amos 2:13; note also Isaiah 46:7; Job 40:12; 1 Samuel 14:9; 2 Samuel 2:23. The idiom does not refer to the hand but rather to Moab itself, as though Isaiah were saying that Moab would be trodden down under himself. It is a strange way of speaking, but shows clearly that Moab is to be completely subjugated. No longer, therefore, need Israel fear any invasion or even harassment from this enemy, for it will be wholly subdued.

To show how thoroughly Moab will be trodden down, the prophet introduces a comparison which points out the great degradation as well as the destruction that is to come upon Moab. Translated literally, the words read, *as there is threshed the straw heap in the waters of the place of dung.* Between the words *mathben (straw heap)* and *madmenah (place of dung)*, there is both alliteration and assonance; and the word *madmenah*, by its form, reminds of the Moabitish city Madmena.[37] If this translation be correct, it indicates that just as straw has been tramped on and

---

against Moab, but that it is merely an episode in the picture of the future (similar to 63:1ff.). Some (Guthe, Kissane, etc.) seek to emend to *'ōyēḇ*.

35 יד יהוה is a common Isaianic expression; cf. 1:25; 11:11, 15; 19:16; 31:3; 34: 17; 40:2; 41:20; 43:13; 48:13; 49:2, 22; 50:2, 11; 51:16, 17; 59:1; 62:3; 64:7; 66:2, 14. In 11:2 the Spirit of the Lord rests *upon*.

36 *nāḏōš*—cf. Job 39:15; 2 Kings 13:7, *there will be trampled down;* cf. Akk. *dašu, to tread down upon.* *Hiddûš* is evidently intended for an inf. const., the normal form being *hiddōš.* Possibly the orthography is intentional to distinguish from the inf. abs. Gesenius takes this as a shorter form, because of the const. state.

37 Cf. Jer. 48:2 for a similar word play. Dillmann questions whether there is an intended word play on the Moabite city. The *Kᵉtiv* is probably to be read. Gesenius comments on the *Kᵉtiv*, ". . . *es ist das allein Passende, da im folgenden Verse das Bild eines im Wasser Versinkenden fortgesetzt ist. . . .*"

left in a pool to putrefy, so Moab also will be trodden down. Some commentators think the language exhibits the hatred of the writer against Moab. May it not be, however, that Isaiah simply uses a forceful manner of describing the severe punishment that is to come to this supreme enemy of God's people? When our Lord said, "it is better for thee to enter halt into life, than having two feet to be cast into hell, into the fire that never shall be quenched: where their worm dieth not, and the fire is not quenched" (Mark 9:45b, 46), are we to see in these words a hatred toward those who are lost? No more is there any hatred in the present passage.[38]

11 The defeat will be ignominious, and Moab will try to save itself. The straw has been tramped upon and left to putrefy in the place of dung, but Moab, having been so tramped upon, will spread out its hands to swim.[39] Moab is said to spread out its hands in its midst. To what, however, do the words, *in its midst*, refer? Possibly to the place of dung, the pool in which Moab is now conceived as attempting to swim. Of this, however, we cannot be certain. The thought seems to be that even as the swimmer is spread out (Isaiah uses the passive) ready to swim, so Moab in its difficult condition attempts to spread itself out that it may swim and not sink.[40]

Moab's attempts fail, for instead of keeping itself afloat and so saving itself, it will cause to bring low its pride, together with the spoils that its hands have acquired; i.e., it will sink.

12 Leaving the figure of Moab swimming in order to save its life, the prophet now turns directly to Moab and addresses it, that Moab may know her destruction was brought upon her by one in whose hands her destiny lies. The language is somewhat general, and Isaiah is not referring to any particular Moabitish city. By *the fortress of the high fort of thy walls*,[41] he means to call attention

38 Marti and Duhm. Duhm's statement is particularly strong. *"Das von Moab gebrauchte Bild zeugt von dem tiefen Hass und Widerwillen der Juden gegen dies Jes 16 Jer 48 und Zph 2* ₈ ₁₀ *als prahlerisch, verlogen und schadenfroh gekennzeichnete Volk. . . ."*

39 Apparently the Targum takes "Lord" as subject, and in this is followed by Ibn Ezra, Kimchi, Mulder. But the struggle of the swimmer better suggests Moab's lack of power. Note *Patah* in place of *Tzere* in the accented syllable of the perfect.

40 The m. suffix, as Gray points out, would not naturally refer either to "waters" or to "dunghill." Probably therefore it is to be taken generally as referring to the place designated by the two words.

41 The language forms a more elegant expression for, "thy walls the high

to the strength that resided in the fortified and highly walled cities of Moab. These were thought to be a sure stronghold, capable of protecting Moab from the enemy. Even these strongholds will be brought low.

Three verbs are employed to emphasize the downfall and humiliation of Moab. The subject of the verbs is not mentioned, but in all probability it is God to whom the prophet refers. The three verbs stand together and give a striking emphasis to the verse; *he hath brought down, he hath humbled, he hath brought to the ground.* Three perfects stress the fact that the destruction is complete, and therefore, the kingdom of God on Zion need no longer fear the haughtiness of the kingdom of Moab on the eastern hills. The prophet's language is general, not pointing to a specific conquest, but summing up what has been said about Moab, and stressing the fact that, just as the kingdom of God will be established on Zion and will certainly endure, so the kingdom of Moab will surely be brought low and perish. This is strengthened by the final words, *to the very dust.* Moab is laid low; she will rise no more.

---

and the fortified" (cf. 2:15 and 30:13). The use of the substantives serves to emphasize the concepts more strikingly. Cf. also Jer. 48:1 and Isa. 33:16.

CHAPTER TWENTY-SIX

1 In that day this song will be sung in the land of Judah: We have a strong city; salvation does he place as walls and ramparts.

2 Open the gates that there may enter a righteous nation, keeping faithfulness.

1 Moab and her high-walled fortresses have been laid low, but in contrast there is a city in whose existence the redeemed may rejoice. As men look to the future outcome of events, possessing the assurance that God will accomplish His mighty purposes, they break out into song and praise. The song of praise agrees with 25:9 and goes back to 24:23. At the same time it forms a contrast to what was said about Moab and its destruction in what immediately preceded. *In that day* refers to the time when Moab will be destroyed, as well as to the time of Israel's exaltation in the kingdom of Zion. The verb is passive and impersonal, *there will be sung*.[1] No subject is named, but the thought is that this is the song that will be sung by those who are in Zion. It is a song that will fill Judah, for Zion will then be the boast and glory of the entire land. *A city, strong, there is to us*.[2] Zion is the subject of the song, and is mentioned first. Moab's cities were to be overthrown, but Zion stands firm. There had been cities which had been falsely and undeservedly praised (25:2, 12); but in contrast to these is the one city that is truly strong, and that city belongs to those who sing. The song also indicates a contrast between the people of Moab and

---

[1] וּשַׁר—only occurrence of the *Hophal.* 1Q reads a *Qal* active, *yšyr.* Possibly the present form is really a *Qal* passive.

[2] *a city strong*—in contrast to the previous situation, 24:10-12. There is also a contrast with the false strength of 25:2, 12. This city is truly strong, for the Lord is her bulwark (cf. 25:4). Lindblom thinks that there was a partial reconstruction of Jerusalem's walls in 485 B.C. Penna believes that the passage may be taken as a prophetic vision of what would happen in the future and as a contrast with the unnamed city doomed to destruction.

The words are to be rendered, "we have a strong city" (cf. Ps. 18:10; 61:4), "a city is strength to us."

those of Zion. The Moabites had been brought into shameful disgrace, like straw left in the pond to putrefy; the people of Zion had been delivered, and could sing the Lord's praise; they were without spot or wrinkle or any such thing.

In the last clause there is a certain amount of alliteration; namely, the *ysh* in the first two words and the two *h*'s of the last two words. The object is placed first and so given the position of prominence and stress. Salvation characterizes this strong city and constitutes its defense.[3] This salvation has been placed by God; for although the subject of the verb is not expressed, it is to be found in the word "Yahweh" understood. Salvation is placed as walls and strength for the city. A city whose fortifications are salvation is truly a city of strength, both in opposition to the falsely praised fortifications of Moab (25:12) and also because the Lord is the strength (*ma'oz*) of the city (25:4).

The two final words of the verse imply a complete defense. The first word simply designates the walls which surround the city, and the last suggests a rampart. David Kimchi referred it to the little wall that belonged to the outer fortification, as 2 Samuel 20:15. It is also thought by some to designate the space between the outer and inner walls. We may safely assume that it refers to a rampart, without endeavoring to specify its precise significance. This city, walled and girded with salvation, would be utterly impregnable, for God was her sure defense.

2 The city is not yet inhabited, for, like the garden in Eden, it was first made by God for those whom He loved and wished to be its inhabitants. The singers, therefore, continue with their song, addressing the ones who have charge over the gates. In mentioning the singers, Isaiah may merely be employing a poetic device to show that the city was now ready to receive those who had the

---

[3] The construction is, "he (i.e., Yahweh) places salvation (as) its walls and ramparts" (cf. Ps. 110:1; 91:9; Jer. 17:5). This city does not need ordinary fortifications; its strength is its very nature of victory and salvation (cf. Ps. 125:2; Zech. 2:9). For the combination walls and ramparts, cf. 60:18. The conjunction with *ḥēl* is pointed with *Qametz* (cf. 5:30), which is normal in a near open syllable. Actually, however, the normal usage becomes abnormal, and the *Qametz* is principally used to connect word-pairs. In *ḥēl* the *ay* diphthong is present, although the corresponding Arabic word *ḥawl* contains the *aw* dipthong. The word seems to denote something that is round about.

Dillmann and Duhm prefer to render, *zu Heil setzt er Mauern u. Zwinger.*

right to enter.[4] The picture seems to be that of pilgrims who have come a long way to enter the city. Having finally arrived they cry out, as they have the right to do, that the gates of the city be opened for them to enter. Those who have come on this pilgrimage also describe themselves as a righteous nation. They are a nation that stands in right relationship to justice and the law, and so are truly righteous. Inasmuch, however, as the walls and ramparts of this city are salvation, it is clear that this righteous nation, composed of those who have come from all over the earth (see 24:16, e.g.), is a nation that possesses no inherent righteousness.[5] It is rather one that has received righteousness from the King who reigns in Zion and who has prepared the city for His people. It is a people that has not been rejected in the judgment, whose rebuke has been taken away (25:8), who has been saved by the LORD (25:9). This nation, therefore, is righteous, because it has received its righteousness from the Lord, Yahweh of hosts.[6] Into the holy city of God there will not enter anything that defileth; the people that was defiled, however, will enter in; for their defilement has been removed and they have received the Lord's righteousness. Truly, it is a righteous nation that will enter. That they thus designate themselves is not a mark of pride but of deepest humility. Their boast is in the righteousness that comes from God.

keeping faithfulness—A nation that is righteous will also be the guardian, preserver, and custodian of faithfulness.[7] This is a faithfulness in the covenant and toward the provisions of the covenant. The nation, therefore, will act as a covenant nation should. The concepts of righteousness and faithfulness are often associated in

---

[4] The subject of the verb is not actually mentioned, and it is not of particular importance what the identity is of those addressed. Mulder speaks of them as *"die poortwagters"* (cf. Ps. 118:19). This is really saying little, but perhaps it is better than Jerome's view that angels are addressed.

[5] In the deepest sense Jerome is correct when he asserts, *"Urbs fortitudinis nostrae Salvator est, id est Jesus. Et ponetur in ea murus et antemurale."* His following comment, however, is not justified, *"Murus bonorum operum, et antemurale rectae fidei, ut duplici septa sit munimento."*

[6] It *keeps faith* with Yahweh and observes the law, not to obtain righteousness, but because it is righteous (cf. 1:26; 33:14; 35:8-10; Ps. 15; 24:3-6). None of these passages teaches that righteousness comes by good works.

[7] One who keeps faithfulness is one who himself has a faithfulness to keep. He is himself steadfast and unmoveable, not because his inherent character is such, but because God has made him such. אמנים is best rendered *faithfulness*. It denotes a quality of steadfastness, immobility, unanswerableness (cf. 1:26; Rev. 22:14; Ps. 118:19, 20).

205

the Old Testament. Earlier, for example, Isaiah had characterized the redeemed and renewed Jerusalem as a city in which righteousness and faithfulness were to dwell (1:26). This faithfulness is preserved by means of a life of faith, a believing in and trusting in the promises that were given to the people. It is this faith that overcomes the world and in the end will be victorious (Acts 2:10, 13), and one who exhibits such a faith is one who keeps faithfulness. There is no room here for human merit, for it is the Lord who gives us faith and preserves us faithful. As Calvin remarks, "out of wolves He makes sheep"; and again, "As soon as he begins to check and reform our hypocrisy, he at once calls us true and upright."

In the Jerusalem of Isaiah's day, the disparity was greatest between the idea and the actuality—a city from which the constant threat of an oppression and capture by the heathen would be taken away (26:1); a community that, in the stand of complete holiness, would avoid all nuisance (26:2). This is the song, verses 1, 2; for they are a unit, whereas verse 3 introduces a new thought. Beginning with verse 3 the language introduces a tendency to reflection, which reaches a high point in verses 9, 10. The analogy of other songs supports this: 1 Samuel 18:7; Isaiah 12:1, 2 and 4, 5; 24:16 and 25:9; 25:1-5; 27:2-6.

3 The mind stayed, thou wilt preserve in peace, because in thee it confides.

4 Trust ye in the LORD even to eternity, for in JAH the LORD is an everlasting rock.

5 For he bringeth down those who dwell on high; the lofty city, he layeth it low, he layeth it low unto the ground; he bringeth it unto the dust.

6 The foot shall tread it down, the foot of the needy, the steps of the poor.

3 Verses 3-6 set forth the certain ground of the people's hope, and this ground is introduced in the present verse by means of a general truth, which the speakers declare to be the result of their own experience of God's goodness. There are, however, difficulties in the interpretation. In the first place, is the word *yetzer* to be taken in the sense of thought or mind? As far as the word itself goes, its basic meaning is *form*. It may then come to designate that which is formed, namely "purpose," "plan," "device." We speak of a frame of mind, and such also may be the force of this word. Does

the word then in this particular context refer to the thought itself
or to the mind that frames that thought? Is Isaiah teaching that the
idea of justice and faithfulness among the people is a firm one or
that the framer of such a thought is firm?[8] The latter is probably
correct. The word thus has reference primarily not to the thought
itself, but to the mind that frames the thought. This conclusion is
supported by the verb and the repetition of the word *peace*. It is a
mind or disposition that is well stayed, or steady.[9] The disposition
is stayed on God, and hence the rendering of King James is not
incorrect, "whose mind is stayed on thee." Ibn Ezra renders, *he
whose mind is stayed on thee, thou, O God, dost preserve him in
peace*. This well brings out the sense. The thought of the passive
participle, *samuk*, appears in the New Testament, "established in
the faith" (1 Pet. 5:9), "grounded and rooted in the faith" (Col.
2:7), and "the steadfastness of your faith" (Col. 2:5). Thus, the
phrase "a mind stayed" means, "a man whose mind is stayed."

Just as the righteous nation is a keeper of faithfulness, so God,
whom the speakers now address, will keep in perfect peace those
whose minds are stayed.[10] To give the proper emphasis Isaiah
repeats the word *peace*. Wholeness and fullness of well-being, true
repose in the sunshine of God's favor, belong to those whom God
keeps. Inasmuch as the Masoretic accents oppose the construction,
yetzer is not to be taken as the verb's object, but is to be construed
as an accusative of specification. Hence, we may render, *As for the
mind that is stayed, thou wilt keep (it) in perfect peace*. The
outcome of events will be peace, and it is this peace which the
mind fixed upon the promises of God will receive.[11] For a long

---

8 *Yētzer* is actually *form* (cf. 29:16), used with and without *heart* (Gen. 6:5;
8:21; Deut. 31:21). Not hope (Ewald), nor view (Hitzig), but "form of the
heart."

9 *sāmûk*—supported, steady, well stayed; cf. Ps. 112:8. It expresses the
thought that Isaiah utters in 7:4 and 30:15, the opposite of the human mind,
swaying in fear, buffeted about and carried by every wind of doctrine.

10 The change of persons is not uncommon. The first two words are taken as
an independent clause by Procksch, Hylmö, Lindblom, Feldmann, and this is
supported by the accentuation. To paraphrase, "As for a mind that is well
stayed, thou wilt keep (it), etc." Many simply take the words as accusatives of
the verb (Dillmann, Gesenius, Delitzsch, Duhm, etc.). The verb derived from
htzr (not *ytzr*) forms a word play with *yētzer*.

11 The emphatic doubling occurs also in 24:16; 27:5; and, with the same
words, in 57:19 (cf. Jer. 6:14; 8:11). The doubling is also found in 1Q and
gives a superlative idea. It is lacking in B, and Syr., but not in the Hexapla
transcription (cf. Ziegler, *Isaias*, 1939, p. 210); and hence the double writing is

time it may have seemed that the people of God had no real peace. Nevertheless, God has concluded a covenant of peace with His people, and the peace of this covenant He will keep for them. They will know the peace that He alone is able to give.

Lastly the prophet gives a reason for the statement just made. *Baṭuᵃh* is a passive participle, as in Psalm 112:7, but is to be translated in an active sense, *trusting*.[12] The last clause is a description of the actual condition of things and not a setting forth of the reason why God keeps such a mind in peace. The emphasis upon steadfastness in this verse is striking, and possibly calls to mind the fact that the human heart by nature is not stable. It is a mind that wavers and changes with every shifting wind of doctrine, for it has no firm foundation upon which to rest. When it reposes upon the Lord, however, it abides firm and constant, preserved in His perfect peace, for it rests, not upon the changing sands of human opinion, but upon God, the Rock eternal and unchangeable.

4 Truth makes men evangelistic; indeed, only the truth can incite a man to evangelism. The fact that God is the One who keeps in perfect peace the mind that is stayed upon him leads the singers, i.e., the righteous nation, about to enter Zion, to command all men to place their trust in Him.[13] The command is addressed, not by one group of singers to another, but by those who sing of Zion unto all who will listen. It is the cry of the redeemed to all men to place their trust in the One whom the redeemed have found to be a true Rock. The command to trust involves a renouncing of all confidence in oneself or in any other man, and a sole reliance upon the confidence in Yahweh alone. Why, however, should one trust in Yahweh? The answer may be framed as follows. The prophets tell men that they are sinners, that they have broken the law of God and disobeyed His commandments. Therefore, a certain judgment is coming upon them which will result in their punishment. If they would escape the judgment, have hope in this

---

not to be explained as dittography. That its presence disturbs the metre (*"Den Beweis wird die metrische Analyse liefern"* [Lindblom]) is not a cogent argument. Textual emendations *metri causa* are to be rejected.

12 *bāṭûᵃh—confisus*, but may be rendered in English by the active. Omitted in 1Q.

13 The imperative reflects upon the passive participle of the preceding verse. This is correctly seen by Dillmann, *"Mit Wiederaufnahme von* בטוח *ermahnen sie sich gegenseitig, solches feste Vertrauen auf immer festzuhalten."* König speaks of it as a kind of anadiplosis to 3b.

life and the true peace that God alone can give them, they must place all their confidence in God. They cannot obtain peace for themselves, for their own minds are unstable and rest upon nothing solid. They must trust in the Lord, for He alone is able to give them peace. Furthermore, the confidence demanded is not temporal and fleeting, but one that will endure forever. Obviously, therefore, it must be a gift from God Himself. If the mind of man is unstable, it clearly cannot become eternally stable through its own powers. When the mind becomes the opposite of what it is by nature, the reason is that God has changed it.

The singers give a reason why men should place their confidence in the Lord. It is that He, *Yah*, the covenant God of Israel, is a rock of ages (i.e., of eternity).[14] We may interpret the last clause either, *for Yah the Lord is a rock of ages* or *for in Yah the Lord is a rock of ages*. In either case, the meaning is the same. The Lord, i.e., Yahweh, the God of Israel, is a rock who endures forever. All the storms and vicissitudes of time cannot change Him, for He stands sure and eternal. The mind, therefore, which rests upon Him, likewise cannot be moved. In speaking of God as a rock, the prophet is thinking primarily of the fact that He is a firm and sure foundation, upon which the mind of man may rest. At the same time, there need not necessarily be excluded the thought that as a rock God is also a hiding-place.[15]

5 Isaiah displays a beautiful progression of thought. Trust in the Lord had been the cry of those who would enter the city. Now, the prophet proceeds to show that there is also a reason for this latter assertion. The Lord is a rock of ages for He has brought low the dwellers on high and the high city. The verb is perfect,[16] but may

---

14 *ᵃdēy-ʿaḏ*—Isaianic expressions; cf. 65:18. *Yāh* is not to be omitted. The prep. should probably be rendered *in,* and not taken as *Beth essentiae* (so also König). But Dillmann, following Ewald and Gesenius, takes it as such, noting that it here stands before the subject. Gesenius thinks that the phrase may either be rendered "for Jah is God, a Rock of eternity," or "for Jah Jehovah is a Rock of eternity."

15 Cf. 17:10; 30:29. When Dillmann says of *ʿōlāmîm,* "nie bei Jes.," we cannot agree. The word is found in 26:4; 45:17; 51:9; and the const. in 45:17. It appears in none of the other prophets except Dan. 9:24. Apparently what Dillmann means is that it appears in none of the passages he attributes to Isaiah. *Tzûr* as used of God is found among the prophets almost exclusively in Isaiah.

16 A prophetic perf.; cf. 25:12. König, however, renders, "*er hat sie sinken lassen.*" These verbs are common to Isaiah.

express a contemporary event. It may also be translated by the past, and in this case would represent the standpoint of the singers of verse 1.

To identify the city is probably impossible. Various suggestions have been offered; but most likely the prophet is simply expressing the general truth, so common to the Bible, that the Lord abases the haughty and exalts the humble[17] (cf., e.g., Ps. 75:5-10). At the same time this general scriptural principle has here come to expression, in that God has brought low those who have set themselves up on high in opposition to His kingdom and in one way or another have vexed the kingdom of Judah. In the phrase, *high city*, the thought of inaccessibility is implied. The adjectives are to be taken in a figurative sense; the dwellers on high are those who are haughty, who act as though they were above others; indeed, princes and rulers may be in mind particularly. The high city has in its own estimation set itself on high. It is proud and haughty.[18]

In the latter part of the verse there are three verbs, each a Hebrew imperfect, which may be rendered, *he layeth it low, he layeth it low unto the ground, he bringeth it unto the dust*.[19] The first two verbs are spelled almost alike, and give emphasis to the thought of humiliation which is now to become prominent. They thus bring to the fore the true condition of the city and people. The people had regarded themselves as high; as a matter of fact they are to be brought so low that the dust will be their final resting place.

---

17 For a discussion of the identity of the city see SPECIAL NOTE on Isaiah 24-27.

18 The phrase "dwellers of (the) height" is explained by the following words, "high city." The concept "height" emphasizes the idea of inaccessibility. Cf. Ps. 18:49; 9:14.

19 V. 5b should be divided into three members.

> 1. *yaš-pi-len-nāh.*
> 2. *yaš-pi-lāh 'ad̠-'e-retz.*
> 3. *yag-gi-'en-nāh 'ad̠-'ā-p̄ār.*

The first form should be separated from the following; it contains in itself the thought of abasement. This form, with the -en-nāh suffix, gives better stress than the following form with the simple suffix.

The second form (omitted in 1Q) takes up the verb again, and with the modifying words adds the thought that abasement will even reach to the earth. (Note the connecting vowel *a* with the imperfect.)

The third form (also with an *a* connecting vowel) emphasizes and enlarges the thought expressed by the second verb. The divergence of the second verb from the first speaks for its genuineness, despite the fact that it is omitted both in 1Q and B. Its presence is more difficult to explain than its absence. There is no warrant for Lindblom's suggestion that the imperfects be changed to perfects.

In the word *dust* there may possibly be an allusion to the grave.

6 The description continues, declaring that those whom the dwellers on high had oppressed now trample the fallen city under foot,[20] and thus assure its full subjection. It is first stated that a foot tramples them.[21] For the dwellers on high to be trampled under foot is indeed humiliation. The humiliation is seen to be even greater when we read that the feet that do the trampling are those of the ones who themselves had been oppressed. They are the needy and poor, who formerly had suffered from those who dwelt in the high city. Isaiah's figure shows the complete defeat of the enemies of God's kingdom and the full exaltation of those who in the eyes of the world were regarded as insignificant and poor, and who had suffered at the hands of unjust oppressors. The figure is a strong one, but it is necessary to show the complete reversal of position which will take place.

7 The way for the righteous is straight, straight wilt thou level the path of the righteous.

8 Also in the way of thy judgments, O LORD, we have waited for thee; to thy name and thy remembrance (was our) soul's desire.

9 With my soul have I desired thee in the night, surely with my spirit within me do I early seek thee, for when thy judgments come to the earth, the inhabitants of the world learn righteousness.

10 Let compassion be shown to the wicked, he does not learn righteousness; in the land of right he will do wrong, and will not see the exaltation of the LORD.

7 The prophet now introduces a prayer to God in which he expresses the hope of the righteous, and in which several moral and ethical maxims are incorporated. The first words may be rendered literally, *the path for the righteous is straight,* i.e., "straight is the path of the righteous." The emphasis falls not upon the path but upon "straight,"[22] for Isaiah does not wish to place

---

[20] The first verb of v. 6 continues the rhyme in *-ennāh*. Together with the imperfects of 5b, it expresses the consequences of the principal action of 5a.

[21] רגל, omitted in 1Q, is emphatic, *even a foot will trample.* It also forms an alliteration with the following word. *P'm,* foot, occurs in Ugaritic as *p'n.*

[22] This is the reason for the prophet's circumlocution. The "way" is not a picture of the virtuous course of the pious, but of his blessed course of life (not merely *seines Gluckes*). Cf. Prov. 3:6; 11:6. The opposite (as Gesenius points out) is that on a rough, stony way men would stumble (Isa. 8:14). *Mēy-šā-rîm* is plural, and signifies a way that is free from difficulties.

attention upon the path on which the righteous must travel but rather upon the blessedness that comes to the righteous who travel this path. The course of life is here presented under the common figure of a way. The way of the wicked is crooked and there are many obstacles therein; on the other hand, the way that is prepared for the benefit of the righteous is straight. It does not follow that the righteous will always be prosperous in a material sense, but it is true that the righteous man has a lamp to his feet and a light to his path to guide him, and that he walks through life with the Spirit of God indwelling him, so that he is protected from many of the snares and pitfalls that await the wicked (cf. Ps. 91).

There are two possibilities in construing the latter part of the verse. We may either render, *straight—the path of the righteous thou dost level*, or *O thou straight one* (i.e., *upright*), *the path of the righteous dost thou level*. On the first construction the word "straight" is taken as an accusative of specification; on the second it is regarded as a vocative. It is difficult to decide between the two, but possibly the first is to be preferred. The verb contains the concept of levelling or smoothing out something and adds to what was stated in the first half of the verse. The way of the righteous is straight, because God smoothes it out, removing from it whatever obstacles may stand in the way of travel.

Herein is taught a principle of divine providence, namely, that the way of the righteous is in the hands of the Lord. Even though at times it appears that only the wicked benefit in this life and that the righteous are forsaken, nevertheless, it is God who evens out and smoothes the way that the righteous must journey; He has truly removed from them obstacles that would keep them from reaching their goal. "But for this," as Calvin so beautifully remarks, "they would easily fall or give way through exhaustion, and would hardly ever make way amidst so many thorns and briars, steep roads, intricate windings, and rough places, did not the Lord lead out and deliver them."

8 The prophet begins this verse with somewhat of a gradation. By means of the word *'aph* (*surely*) he takes up the thought of a way, and now adds the information that it is a way of God's judgments.[23] Isaiah uses the word as an adverbial accusative, which we may render, *in the way*. The thought is that we were in the way or path in which God's judgments would be meted out.

---

23 Dillmann, for example, renders, "*und wirklich, ja*"; Lindblom, "*fürwahr.*"

Drechsler refers this to the past, when there was yet the possibility of temptation for the people to turn aside from the way at Sennacherib's approach. For this view he finds a support in the double use of the *way*. This argument is not convincing. It seems rather that the reference is to the judgments of God, not as manifested in His law and statutes, but in His punishment of the wicked and in His establishment of the eternal kingdom of Zion. The act of waiting for the judgments of God was one of faith, and of belief that these judgments would actually be carried out. In the company of those who wait, Isaiah includes himself, for he too is among the ones who will sing the song of redemption. ". . . Though our eyes are not gratified," says Calvin, "by an easy and delightful path, and though the road is not made smooth under our feet, but we must toil through many hard passages, still there is room for hope and patience." The present order of things has not yet experienced God's punitive judgments in their fullest extent, yet the righteous wait with patience until God is ready to manifest His judgments.

In the second half of the verse the same thought is expressed in different words. The longing of the soul (for the soul is conceived as the seat of the affections) is for the Name of God, i.e., God in the manifestation or expression of Himself in His works. The prophet is referring to more than the mere appellation by which the God of Israel is designated; he is rather using a synonym for God Himself. The expressions "name" and "memorial" are synonymous.[24] "This is my name for ever, and this is my memorial unto all generations" (Ex. 3:15b; note also Ps. 30:4). This Name has been remembered and become a memorial because of a manifestation of God's power and majesty such as the exodus from Egypt. The soul's longing is for the Name of God and for the memorial of that Name, insofar as there is a recollection of the mighty acts in Egypt, deeds that are a pledge or earnest of even greater acts of God which again would cause His Name to be remembered.

The last two words are to be taken generally. "Desire of soul" is the desire or longing that is found in human souls.

9 Here the language takes on a more personalized nature, and uses the first person. From this it does not follow that it is the

<hr>

24 Cf. Hos. 12:6; 14:8.

prophet himself, in distinction from others, who is praying. Sometimes the prophet proclaimed his messages in the first person, but not always. It is really the redeemed nation that is in the foreground. We may note how often the prophet has engaged in *concatenatio,* i.e., the taking up again of a word that had just been used in the preceding verse. Note 3b and 4a *(baṭuᵃḥ* and *biṭḥu)* , 7a and 8a *('oraḥ),* 8b and 9a *(naphesh* and *naphshi).*

I myself have awaited thee—The words "my soul" are probably a circumlocution for the personal pronoun of the first person.[25] Parallel to this is the phrase, "my spirit," which also is construed with the verb in the first person. Here, too, we should render, *also my spirit,* i.e., *I, within me, do I early seek thee.* The words "within me" constitute gradation in the parallelism. Not only my soul, the prophet would say, but also my spirit within me, forms the longing subject.

The second verb means, *to look early, to desire,* and stands in contrast to *in the night.* By some the word "night" is taken to refer to the long period of affliction which preceded the execution of God's judgments. But there appears to be a contrast intended between "night" and "look early." The prophet thus expresses the thought of a longing for God at all times. Even during the night this longing continues, and the morning finds the soul still looking for God.

There is a reason for this longing, for "when thy (i.e., God's) judgments are to the earth, then the inhabitants of the world learn righteousness." Isaiah is saying that when the judgments of God are exercised upon earth, at that time, those who dwell upon the earth learn what justice and righteousness are.[26] When His judgments are withheld and men seem to prosper, they tend to forget God. On the other hand, when times of adversity come and the judgments of God are felt, at that time men do learn God's righteousness. Thus, the punishing hand of God may serve a benefi-

25 Actually, *my soul* would seem to be a circumstantial *(Ḥal)* acc. *In my soul, I*—cf. 10:30. It could also be construed as a *casus pendens; As for my soul, I, etc.* We may render freely, *I myself.* With the exception of Ps. 132: 13, 14 *'iw-wāh* is used with *nepesh* as subject. Note the perf. and imp. in 9a, the first denoting past, the second future time. "I have waited and will continue to look eagerly."

26 כאשר may be rendered *when.* It is also possible that it may mean *even as,* or *according as.* If so, the verse would teach that in the measure that God's judgments are exercised upon earth, men learn righteousness. Cf. S. Talmon, *Annual of the Swedish Theological Institute,* Vol. I, 1962, pp. 67, 68.

cent purpose, in that it leads a sinner to repentance. It is of import to note that men must learn righteousness, for they are not righteous by nature. Their heart and its inclinations turn away from true righteousness. When, however, the chastising hand of God is felt, at such a time men may learn what they hitherto have not known. God is the teacher, and the instrument which He often employs to teach righteousness is His judgment.

10 Not all men turn to the Lord and learn righteousness when His punishing judgments are felt; the judgments bring only His own people to repentance. Hence, in times of calamity and misfortune we should not expect to see all men repent of their evil ways and turn to the Lord. On the other hand, even if favor is shown to the wicked, he will not abandon his wickedness nor will he learn righteousness.[27] What, however, is meant by the phrase, "to be shown compassion?" Possibly it is the opposite of judgment. When good times come upon man, should he not then learn righteousness? The reference is probably to the blessings of the earth, sunshine, rain, and harvest; the material benisons of life, the absence of war, and a satisfactory enjoyment of life. Even when these tokens of compassion are showered upon the wicked, they will not teach him righteousness. And favor is indeed shown to the wicked! How rich and full are the daily compassions with which God visits the earth. Men, however, are not thankful; they do not acknowledge the true source of these blessings, but continue on in a way of blindness, seeking to explain life in terms of man, denying the Creator and living in that manner which most pleases themselves. Even the mercies of life will not teach righteousness. That is the work of the Spirit of God alone.

Furthermore, it may be that in the very preserving of the life of the wicked, and the postponing of the judgment, favor is shown. In holding back the outpouring of judgment, God is showing compassion; for when the judgment falls, then mercy ceases. Should this truth not cause us to cry out in thankfulness to God for His mercies and favors, to see His hand in all things, to hate our sins and to turn unto Him in humble love? Yet God's goodness is despised, and the wicked do not learn righteousness from it.

Not only do they not learn righteousness, argues the prophet,

[27] *Let compassion be shown*, possibly a *Qal* passive; cf. Ug. *ḥnn*. This imperfect in a protasis states a possibility which is strongly denied by the apodosis. No conditional particle is used.

but even in a land of right they act wrong. A land of right (lit., *right things*) is a land in which things are done in accordance with righteousness, where there would be no compelling force to make men do wrong. Of their own free will (and the will of fallen man is free only to do evil), wicked men turn to wrong. Even a land where right abounds will see the wicked do the opposite of right.

What is saddest of all is that even in a land of right the wicked will not see the exaltation of the LORD. But why not? The answer can only be that the blindness of the eyes of the wicked is a tragic reality, and the hardness of his heart and dullness of his understanding so great that in himself he does not have ability to turn from his wicked ways and live. If the wicked is to turn, there is only one power that can cause him to do so, and that is God Himself. Even a land of righteousness is not sufficient. Salvation is of grace, sovereign grace, the grace of God alone.

> 11 O LORD, thy hand is high, they will not see; they will see and be ashamed at thy zeal for thy people; yea, the fire of thine enemies will devour them.
>
> 12 LORD, thou wilt set peace for us, for also our works thou hast wrought for us.
>
> 13 LORD, our God, there have ruled us lords beside thee, but only in thee will we cause to remember thy name.

11 Having uttered the profound thoughts of the preceding verses the prophet now addresses God directly. His contemplations about the divine government cause him to look to the LORD, Israel's God; and so each of the three following verses (11, 12 and 13) begins with the word *Lord*. And it is the power of the Lord in action that Isaiah wishes to emphasize. Hence, he remarks, *thy hand is high*. The raised hand is not necessarily a symbol of threat but merely an indication of the exercise of power. When the hand is lowered, it is a sign of inactivity, but when raised, it shows that the person is about to act or is acting, giving expression in action to his power. That the judgments of God should bring the righteous to repentance and that His favors should be dispensed while the wicked remain in their wickedness, is an evidence that God is displaying His power in the carrying out of His purposes. "Thou hast a mighty arm: strong is thy hand, and high is thy right hand" (Ps. 89:13; cf. also Deut. 32:27).

Wicked men, however, do not see that God's hand is high.[28] They do not perceive, for they are blind; and they grope about as blind men, searching for some meaning in life. They come into contact with reality but do not know what it is. In this respect they are like the Judahites, "this people" of chapter 6, of whom it was said, "see ye indeed (*ra'ah* is here used) but know not" (cf. also 5:12).

Yet *they will see*—Isaiah does not contradict himself, but uses the verb with a slightly different connotation. The wicked do not see, i.e., perceive or understand, the working of God in history; but they will see, i.e., experience, His uplifted hand. When they do experience His power, they will realize how great is His zeal on behalf of His people. Then, however, it will be too late; experiencing God's power at that time will bring only shame. God's zeal for His people is His determination to carry out His purposes of salvation and to procure for Himself a redeemed people. That this may be accomplished, however, the wicked must be punished; and this punishment or judgment itself is an evidence of God's zeal on behalf of His own.

Lastly, Isaiah states that fire will devour the enemies of God. The zeal of God is like a flame, which will consume those who throughout their lives have been God's adversaries. It seems better to refer the fire to God's zeal, rather than to war or to the fire of eternal punishment. Thus it is the fire of God's zeal that will consume His adversaries. A clear-cut passage such as this refutes the notion of some theologians, that the grace of God will ultimately become victorious in the sense that it will finally save all men.

12 Again the Lord is addressed. The prophet now looks to the future, and the tenses of the verbs change. In thus praying to God, Isaiah expresses a strong hope and assurance which is based upon what has already been experienced. He employs a strange verb, one that is used of setting something on the pot, and of setting or placing a person in the dust. In this particular context, however, it evidently is used in the sense of *ordain* or *establish*. God, there-

---

[28] *zeal of the people*—objective gen., the zeal that is felt for the people. In the verb ye-ḥᵉ-zāy-wûn, note both the epenthetic *Nun*, and the retention of the *yod* in a pausal form. The usage of the verbs in this verse is instructive; rā-māh is perf. with present force; ye-ḥᵉ-zāy-wûn is fut. in a dependent sentence (without seeing), but ye-ḥe-zû is imp. (they will see). We may bring out the force of wᵉ-yē-ḇō-šû by rendering, "being ashamed they shall see."

fore, Isaiah is saying, is the One who establishes the peace which is for our benefit.[29] That this is the work of God and not of man is stressed by the fact that the divine Name is placed first. The peace is for the benefit and help of man, a peace that comes when the work of judgment has been completed. As so often in the prophecy, Isaiah again attributes the work of peace to God, for a heart filled with enmity cannot establish peace. Peace that is pure and perfect comes from the Source of true peace, even the LORD.

A further action of God is now mentioned which shows that He will truly establish peace, namely, that all the works which are for our benefit, He has done for us.[30] There is not even one work that He has not done for us. The language, "all our works," does not refer to works that we have done, nor indeed to our spiritual tasks or exercises, but rather to those works that are for our blessing and profit.[31] All these works that are for us, and so truly ours, God Himself has done for us, and through us. He has done all that is essential and necessary for our perfect peace and well-being. Herein is a triumphant statement of the wonder of salvation. In the LORD man finds all that he needs for true peace.

13 For the third time in succession Isaiah begins a verse with LORD, in this verse identifying the LORD as "our God." What the prophet wishes to establish is the truth that the Israelites have a God and that Yahweh alone is their God.[32] Yahweh it is who formed them into a nation at Sinai, who delivered them from the bondage of Egypt, brought them through the hardships of the wilderness into the land of promise, and established the Davidic kingdom. Yahweh, and He alone, is the God whom they profess. More than that, He is their God, for He has wrought marvelous works of judgment and established a true and everlasting peace.

29 1Q has erroneously written *tšpṭ. šā-ḥat* is generally regarded as a denominative. For its usage cf. 2 Kings 4:38; Ezek. 24:3; Ps. 22:16. Cf. Ug., *spd.* In Old South Arabic the root means "to give," and this appears also in B Sos.

30 כי—justifies the confidence expressed in 12a from the experiences of the past.

31 מעשינו—omitted in B, which has πάντα γὰρ ἀπέδωκας ἡμῖν; also Syr., the thought being that God has requited us for all our evil deeds. Dillmann refers the word to all that we have done (Ps. 90:17) and what has happened to us (Eccl. 1:13; 8:9, 11ff.) ; "our entire history" is God's work. The word is used of human deeds (1 Sam. 19:4) but also of God's great deeds for His people (Ps. 106:13; 66:3) .

32 our god—cf. 25:9; in these events the honor of God as the protector of His people and their owner is at stake.

There have been masters apart from Yahweh, and these had been the sovereigns of the people. Isaiah employs a word that calls to mind the *baals* of Canaan. It may be, however, that the prophet merely wishes to institute a comparison without particular reflection upon the *baals*. Just as the *baal* is the husband of the lawful wife, so also Israel during the course of her existence has had husbands or *baals* who had been sovereigns or rulers for her. God is the true protector and possessor of Israel, but there have been others apart from him whom the nation has recognized and acknowledged. First there was Egypt; then came the peoples of Canaan, and then those of the lands round about. Each became a sovereign lord, in that its will ruled over the Israelites.

Nevertheless, in Yahweh alone do the Israelites make mention of His Name. The thought is clear, and there is no need at this point of following the Septuagint or of emending the text.[33] Other sovereigns were not truly sovereign and have done nothing for the help and deliverance of Israel. Through Yahweh alone true help has come, and for that reason, the Israelites will remember and make mention of His Name in praise.[34]

> 14 Dead, they shall not live: ghosts they shall not rise: therefore, thou hast visited and destroyed them, and made to perish all memory of them.
>
> 15 Thou hast added to the nation, O LORD, thou hast added to the nation, thou art glorified; thou hast moved far all the ends of the land.

14 Isaiah now turns to those who had acted as tyrants over God's people. These can no longer harm Israel, for they are dead; and inasmuch as they are dead, the people can enjoy undisturbed the blessings of God's goodness. "As for the dead," so we may para-

---

33 Lindblom would delete *'elōhēynú* because it makes the verse rhythmically unreadable (*unlesbar*). He would then render the following, "Have other lords besides thee ruled over us?" and this question is to expect a negative answer. The reason for this is that *zulāti* is always used with a negative. The answer then is, "No, through thee alone do we praise thy Name." Mulder agrees with this rendering.

We should expect the order בְּךָ לְבַדְּךָ (Ps. 51:6; Prov. 5:17). In Eccl. 7:29 לְבַד appears as an adverb. I cannot see any reason why בְּךָ cannot be rendered *through thee*. The one real difficulty is the presence of זוּלָתְךָ without a negative.

34 It is characteristic of Isaiah to designate God as *'ādón;* cf. 1:24; 3:1; 6:1; 7: 14; 10:16, 33; 19:4.

phrase, "they will live no more.[35] They have passed from the scene of this earth and are departed. Men will see them no more alive on the earth." These dead ones are really shadows,[36] and for that reason cannot arise again to trouble the people of God. The same thought is expressed by Isaiah when he speaks of the Babylonian oppressor: "For I will rise up against them, saith the LORD of hosts, and cut off from Babylon the name, and remnant, and son, and nephew, saith the LORD" (Isa. 14:22).

It is a mistake to use this verse to support the position that no general resurrection of the dead is taught here, but only a resurrection of the just. What Isaiah is speaking of is not so much a resurrection, as the fact that those who had once acted as lords over Israel are now dead, and cannot return to life again to afflict the Israelites. He is not denying that in the general resurrection they too shall arise unto everlasting punishment. On that particular subject he is not now speaking. What he is saying, however, is of comfort to the Israelites, for it teaches them that in the kingdom founded on Zion, they shall be free from those who formerly had oppressed them.

The prophet introduces the second part of the verse with a "therefore," a word difficult to interpret. Possibly the thought is: "Therefore, in order that they may be dead and not live and be shadows and not rise, thou hast visited and thou hast destroyed them. . . ." On the other hand, it is possible to refer the "therefore," as does Marti, for example, to the thought of verse 14a, serving as a parenthesis. We may then paraphrase as follows: "Only through thee do we make mention of thy name—the dead will not live, etc.,—therefore, inasmuch as only through thee do we make mention of thy name, thou hast visited, etc."

God has visited the wicked in punishment and He has also destroyed them and made all remembrance of them to perish. There is a contrast between the making mention of God's name, in verse 13, and the obliteration of all remembrance of the name of the enemies. The destruction of the enemy is a work of God, and to Him alone the credit for this work is assigned. If the righteous are to enjoy the blessings of the kingdom of Zion, the wicked must be destroyed.

---

[35] Cf. 1 Kings 17:22; Job 14:14; Ezek. 37:5, 10.

[36] B ἰατροί, which represents a different pointing, rō-p̄ᵉ-'îm; Aq ραφαιν. The word means *shades, ghosts*, a sense which it also has in Ug., e.g., 124:8. The word is also used of people; cf. Gen. 14:15; 1 Aqht 20:36-37, 47.

GOD'S SOVEREIGNTY IN SALVATION AND JUDGMENT, 24:1 — 27:13

15 In the destruction of the enemy and the establishment of the kingdom, God has added to the people. This thought is important, and Isaiah mentions it twice to give it proper emphasis. In so doing he employs the perfect, "Thou hast added to the nation." The reference is the same as that found in 9:3. If, however, the perfects be stressed, and translated by the past, they would seem to refer to some past event, which would obviously conflict with what is stated in verses 17-19, wherein a complaint is made that the land is not yet filled with inhabitants. Furthermore, it is difficult to see what the reference might be, if the verbs look back to some event in the past. It is best, therefore, to take the verbs either as optatives or as prophetic perfects.[37] If they are optatives, they express a wish of the prophet, "Mayest thou add to the nation"; and this could very well be the meaning. On the other hand, if the verbs be construed as prophetic perfects, they then fit in well with the whole picture and describe something that has not yet occurred but which will take place in the future. Adding to the nation would be an action of blessing, in that the nation would become increased through the inclusion of more members. This would redound to God's honor.

As far as the interpretation is concerned, we would say that in the light of the previous verses, with their emphasis upon the kingdom of Zion, the reference of the present passage is to the inclusion into the chosen people of the Gentiles. This, of course, is not explicitly stated; but a characteristic of Messianic prophecy is the trait that the work of the Messiah will bring blessing to the Gentiles and that the truth will be made known to them.

---

[37] Lindblom interprets that God has given to the people more than they possessed before. The ל is to be distinguished from 'al or 'el in that it designates the ordinary dative; cf. Lev. 19:25; Prov. 9:11 (elsewhere 'al and 'el are used). If the verb is taken as an actual pret., it seems to teach what is contradicted by vv. 17 and 19, where the complaint is that the land is not full of people. Dillmann thinks that the reference is to the period of David and Solomon.

After the perfects of v. 13, thinks Dillmann, it is not possible to take these as prophetic perfects, nor can they be precatives unless a lû precede them. In answer to the last it is sufficient to note the Arabic usage, e.g., la-'a-na-hu 'l-la-hu, may God curse him, ra-ḥim ma-hu 'l-la-hu, may God show mercy to him. The context makes clear that the reference is to the future, a fact that is not precluded by the pret. of v. 13. Indeed, a transition between the past (lords have ruled) and the future is made by the imp. (naz-kîr). Furthermore, even according to Dillmann, the perfects in these verses refer to different periods.

Lastly, the idea of the increase of the nation is expressed under the figure of enlarging the boundaries of the land.[38] God is said to have made far the ends of the land, so that they are at a greater distance the one from the other. The land must be larger in order that it may contain those who have been added to the nation.

16 O LORD, in affliction they visited thee, they uttered a whisper, thy chastisement was upon them.

17 As a pregnant woman draws near to bear, she writhes, she cries out in her pangs, so have we been from before thee, O LORD.

18 We have been pregnant, we have writhed, as it were we brought forth wind; deliverances we do not make for the land, and the inhabitants of the world will not fall.

19 Thy dead ones will live, my dead bodies shall arise. Awake and sing, ye that dwell in the dust: for thy dew is as the dew of herbs, and on the earth on the dead ones thou dost cause it to fall.

16 Looking back to the dark period before the redemption had actually arrived, the people objectify themselves and remember how often they had sought God. Not only after the deliverance did they turn away from idols, but even before, they had come to the true God in humble and quiet prayer. In contrast with the deliverance they refer to the previous period as one of affliction, a period which had been introduced when Ahaz turned against the promises of God and sought the aid of the Assyrian king. "Wherefore the wrath of the Lord was upon Judah and Jerusalem, and he hath delivered them to trouble, to astonishment, and to hissing, as ye see with your eyes" (2 Chron. 29:8).

During this period of affliction, nevertheless, the Israelites visited God in their prayers and supplications. Isaiah here uses the word *visit* in an unusual, yet perfectly legitimate manner.[39] He simply wishes to say that they had sought the Lord with interest and desire. They looked to Him for they were in need of His help. It was not a vain seeking, but one that their distress compelled them to engage in. For times of distress and suffering do cause

---

[38] That the reference is to the people of Judah is shown by passages such as Deut. 4:6; Isa. 10:6; Jer. 7:28; Hag. 2:14; Zeph. 2:9; Ps. 33:12; 106:5 (the land in which Israel dwells). Cf. 11:14; 27:12; Obad. 18ff.

[39] For uses of the root *pqd* cf. Isa. 23:17; 24:21; Judg. 15:1; 1 Sam. 17:18. Drechsler comments that it "*ist hier von denen, die sich bekehren, gesagt, sofern sie sich umsahen nach dem Herrn, Hulfe bei ihm aufsuchten.*" The people as an indefinite majority (*Vielheit*) is subject. On the basis of Gk. ἐμνήσθην Gray, Lindblom, etc., prefer to read the 1st pl., an easier reading.

God's people to look unto Him and to express their longings for deliverance. During prosperity it is easy to forget the Lord and to live a life of practical atheism. Affliction, however, often drives a person to God, for it makes him understand that his life is truly in God's hand. Therefore, in such a time the people had visited God with their earnest supplications.

Their manner of prayer and supplication, however, had been strange. In times of need and affliction, one usually cries aloud to God for help. In this instance the people merely uttered a whisper. The language is quite striking; if rendered literally, it is: *They poured out a whisper,* and it is probably to be understood in the sense of Vergil's *fundebant preces* (*Aeneid* vi.55). The force of the verb may be seen from the action of Hannah, who, according to her own words, "poured out my soul before the LORD" (1 Sam. 1:15b). The idea of pouring out the prayer would suggest that the soul of the praying one is filled with the thoughts which he wishes to utter to God, and that he pours these out in great abundance. And indeed prayer should not be a burden, but a spiritual exercise in which one, out of the abundance of the heart, speaks unto God.

This outpouring, however, had taken place only in whispers.[40] When Hannah prayed, her lips moved, but her voice was not heard. It was, therefore, a scarcely audible prayer, merely a whisper. Those who thus prayed were characterized by great fervency of spirit. The intensity of their being was so great that they truly spoke to God from the heart, with the result that their prayer appeared to be only a whisper.

In the last clause Isaiah's purpose is not so much to give the reason for the whispered prayer as it is to state the length of time that the prayer lasted. As long as God's chastisement was upon the people, so long did they pour out their whispered prayers. The chastisement was grievous to bear, and yet it was serving its

---

[40] *they poured out*—attested also by 1Q; the final *Nun* is unusual, but there is no reason to assume that the text is in error. This paragogic *Nun* is also found in Deut. 8:3, 16 where it draws the tone to the ultima as though the forms were imperfect. The root צוק here has the force of יצק (cf. Job 28:2; 29:6). In this sense שפך is also used; cf. Ps. 102:1. Lindblom, however, explains the word as a nominal form, synonymous with צוקה and מצוק, meaning oppression, affliction (*Bedrängnis*). Gray and Duhm would point *tzā-qôn*, cn the basis of B θλίψις; but how explain a shift from *u* to *o* (=*a*)? Cf. GKC § 441, TT § 6, Obs. n. lḥš; cf. 3:3, *Beschwörung* (adjuration, solemn appeal). Cf. Talmon, *op. cit.,* p. 71.

purpose in that while it was present the people prayed earnestly to God.

17 Isaiah now introduces a comparison, the purpose of which is to show not merely that the Israelites in their affliction suffered in an extreme manner, but rather to point out that they themselves had engaged in strenuous efforts of their own to free themselves from their afflictions, and that these efforts had been in vain. This present verse, therefore, brings in a comparison which explains verse 18.

By means of the phrase, "like a pregnant woman," Isaiah vividly introduces his comparison. This pregnant woman draws near to bear; her time of bearing is about at hand. Hence she writhes and cries out in her writhing, for her pain is great.[41] The prophet then argues that his own people, including himself, have acted similarly. We too, he asserts, as the affliction grew stronger, have writhed and cried out in pain. And we are thy people. The comparison thus concludes in a prayer.

What was the relation of this writhing to God? To express the relation, the prophet employs a phrase that may be rendered, *from before thee,* which might imply that the writhing actually led to a separation from God. It is also possible to translate *on account of thee.* Yet the first interpretation probably has the most to commend it, namely, that the writhings of the nation were its own efforts to free itself from its distress, and that these efforts with their attendant cries were of such a nature that they did not bring the nation any closer to God, but in effect tended to lead it away from Him.

18 Isaiah now proceeds to explain the comparison. "We have been pregnant," he says, "but our outcome has been different from that of an ordinary pregnant woman. The period of pregnancy should be a prelude to that of the bliss and joy that obtain when

---

[41] Cf. Isa. 13:8; 21:3; 37:3. Also Hos. 13:13; Mic. 4:10. Note the asyndetic construction, *she writhes she cries out;* i.e., *she cries out as she writhes,* or *in her writhing.* Some of the older interpreters (e.g., Gesenius) took the writhing as a figure of the exile. But this is not warrantable (see SPECIAL NOTE). Later the phrase *writhing pains of the Messiah* became a fixed designation in Jewish theology of the period of woe before Messiah's advent.

Of particular interest is the reading of B $\tau\hat{\omega}$ $\dot{\alpha}\gamma\alpha\pi\eta\tau\hat{\omega}$ $\sigma\sigma\upsilon$ which Seeligmann (*The Septuagint Version of Isaiah,* Leiden, 1948, pp. 25f.) regards as a Christological gloss. Cf. Matt. 3:17; Mark 1:11; Luke 3:22.

the child is born into the world. In our case, however," so the prophet's argument continues, "the outcome was not similar. We were not only pregnant, and writhed in the throes of our pregnancy, but we did not bring forth a child that would cause rejoicing. For us there was no such period of rejoicing, for we merely brought forth wind." "We had believed," so we may paraphrase the underlying thought, "that we should truly bring forth a deliverance for ourselves, a deliverance that would free us from our afflictions. As a matter of actual fact, however, we brought forth nothing whatever that could be a cause of rejoicing."

As a figure of nothingness "wind" is most fitting.[42] Isaiah later finds it suitable to describe the idols. "Behold! they are all vanity, their works are nothing; their molten images are wind and confusion" (41:29).

"Inasmuch as our labors at deliverance have been fruitless," the prophet's argument continues, "we do not accomplish any salvations with respect to the land." The plural, "salvations," expresses the concept in all its fullness; all its component parts, as it were, are included. "All our efforts," Isaiah reasons, "are in vain, for they have wrought nothing. Our land was in need of deliverance, and we confidently believed that we of ourselves could produce such a deliverance. In this we have fully failed." To what, however, does the prophet refer? It would seem that these remarks go back to the initial apostasy on the part of Ahaz, when he rejected the promises of the Messiah offered by Isaiah and turned instead for help to Tiglath-pileser. This action brought a train of consequences in its wake which continued to harrass and to plague Judah. The reference, however, is not merely to outward suppression and affliction, but also to the spiritual condition of the nation, a condition which soon came to expression in its outward acts.

Not only did the nation not bring salvation to itself, but also the nations of the world, who were the great oppressors of Judah, had not fallen. Human efforts apart from God had not brought about the downfall of the enemy oppressor.

19 Nothing more clearly shows the ineffectiveness of human

---

[42] The rendering *as we bore, it was wind* is not supported by the Masoretic accents, which would yield, *as though we had born wind*. This does not require the insertion of היה, *it was as though*, etc., as Dillmann argues. At the same time, the first rendering yields a good sense.

efforts to accomplish deliverance than the fact that God brings
to pass the salvation that man cannot attain. Through the attempts of the nation no deliverances came, and the inhabitants
of the world, the oppressors of Israel, had not fallen. Nevertheless,
as a matter of actual fact, those of the people who had died will
live again. It is a positive declaration on the part of Isaiah, not
merely the expression of a wish. What man has lost, God can
restore. His purposes will be carried out, irrespective of what man
may say or do. The verse thus constitutes a glorious declaration of
triumph; more than that, it is also a prayer directed to God, for
the possessive pronoun, *Thy,* has reference to God Himself. Those
who have died are His; for that reason they shall live.

In thus addressing God the prophet sets an example for all to
follow. It is a time of crisis, judgment, and death, when the
struggles of men are shown to be unavailing, and hence, a time of
despair. Then it is that Isaiah looks to God and addresses Him.
Before God he carries His thoughts and finds his comfort and assurance in the truth that what is not possible with man is possible with
God.

The language is not to be taken figuratively, for God's dead are
those who in His Name have actually died physically. "Yea, for thy
sake are we killed all the day long; we are counted as sheep for the
slaughter" (Ps. 44:22). The thought is made more vivid and is
even strengthened by the additional phrase, *my dead bodies shall
arise.* Here the noun is singular, *my corpse,* and the verb is plural;
for while the noun refers to the nation as a unit, the plural of the
verb points to the individuals who compose the body entire.[43]
Certain contrasts must be noted. First there is the contrast in the
possessive pronouns: *thy* dead ones, but *my* corpse. In thus speaking the prophet identifies himself with the Lord's purposes. The
dead ones are those who belong to the Lord, but the nation is
Isaiah's. He is concerned over its downfall as is the Lord, for he
speaks as a prophet of the Lord. To be noted also is the chiastic
arrangement of the words, an arrangement which lends strength to
the description; thus, *there will live* (A) *thy dead ones* (B), *and
my corpse* (B) *they will arise* (A).

By means of this additional statement, *my corpse they will arise,*

43 *my corpse*—the feminine noun is construed with a masculine verb and is
used collectively, *my dead bodies.* The pointing is strange; we should expect,
nib̲-lā-ti. As it stands, the form is abs., and the *yod* is not paragogic, nor
did it arise by dittography from the following *yod.* It is attested in 1Q.

the prophet clearly introduces the doctrine of the resurrection of the body. This is acknowledged even by Gesenius, who says, "That this passage actually contains the doctrine of *the resurrection of the body*, appears without doubt from the words." Gesenius then goes on to say that this should cause no difficulty if we place the composition of the passage in the exile, when the Jews received this as well as other doctrines from the Zoroastrian theology, and applied them to their Messianic conceptions. It is not necessary, however, to resort to such an explanation. There is no essential difference between *thy dead ones* and *my corpse*, for both expressions refer to men who are dead. At the same time, the latter phrase does emphasize the fact that the dead are bodies or corpses, and that these will arise.

We need not assume that this doctrine would be too advanced for the day of Isaiah, and that it was only received by the Jews from the Persians during the time of the exile or later. The true doctrine of the resurrection of the body is a revelation received from God, and not a doctrine to be discovered by unaided human reason. Furthermore, it must be noted how Isaiah himself has prepared for this doctrine. This he has done in setting forth the eternity of the Messianic kingdom (e.g., 9:6, 7), the abiding character of the day of the Lord (2:12ff.), and the hope of the redeemed to everlasting glory (chapter 12).

To exclude any possibility of thinking that the resurrection of the body is not intended, Isaiah speaks of the dead ones as awaking. In itself the language shows that the state of death is not one of annihilation, but rather one that may be compared to a sleep from which there is to be an awaking, either to the life of God or to eternal punishment.[44]

With the following verbs we have a hendiadys, namely, *awake giving out a ringing cry*, lit., *they shall awake and they shall cry out*. The verbs are imperatives, addressed to the dwellers in the dust, i.e., the dead ones.[45] But who can command the dead to live? The question of the Lord is pertinent, "Son of man, can these bones live?" (Ezek. 37:3a). And the only answer that can be given to

---

44 For the picture of death as a sleep, cf. also Ps. 13:4; Job 3:13; Jer. 51:39, 57; Dan. 12:2; and note also John 11:11.

45 *dust*—Note Ps. 7:6 where *dwell* and *dust* are combined, and also Job 7:21; 20:11; 21:26; and cf. Dan. 12:2. In Ps. 22:16 occurs the phrase, *the dust of death*. In modern Arabic *turab* (dust) is a designation of the cemetery. *awake*—taken as a perf. by B Aq S T Syr. Targ.

these questions is that of the prophet Ezekiel, "O Lord God thou knowest" (Ezek. 37:3b). "For in death there is no remembrance of thee, in Sheol who will give thee thanks?" (Ps. 6:6). Isaiah's command, however, is not in vain. As a serious, devoted servant of the Lord, he well knows that no mere command which he can utter can perform the wonder (for such it is) of bringing the dead to life shouting the praises of God. The work of resurrection from the dead is a supernatural one, which only God Himself can perform. "Behold, I will cause breath to enter into you, and ye shall live: and I will lay sinews upon you, and will bring flesh upon you, and cover you with skin, and put breath in you, and ye shall live, and ye shall know that I am the Lord" (Ezek. 37:5, 6). It is really in the name of the Lord, therefore, that Isaiah commands; and this he does with the confidence that God Himself will raise the dead. Either this interpretation is correct or we are left to the supposition that the language is meaningless, representing nothing more than a pious wish on the part of the prophet. Against such a supposition, however, there lies the whole thrust of the prophecy. It is not the command of the prophet in itself, however, that causes the dead to arise shouting for joy; it is the almighty power of the one ever true and living God.

A reason is given why the dead should hear the prophet's voice and awake singing; and in the giving of this reason, the prophet, in the high animation that moves his speech, addresses the Lord. To render his words in English is difficult, for the meaning of one of these words is not clear. Either Isaiah is saying to God, *for the dew of lights is thy dew,* or else he is declaring, *for the dew of plants is thy dew.*[46] If he is speaking of the dew of lights, probably he means the dew of heaven or a dew which gives life. The thought would then be that a dew which brings refreshment is the dew which is of the Lord. It is not entirely clear that this is the prophet's meaning, however. In 2 Kings 4:39 the word is rendered *plants,* and if this be correct, the prophet is asserting that the dew of God is like that which refreshes the plants. For an illustration we may note Psalm 72:6, "He shall come down like rain upon the mown grass." Whichever of these two renderings be adopted, we are to understand the dew as referring to the refreshing grace of God

---

46 *'ōrōt*—In Ps. 138:12 the singular form occurs in the sense of *light,* and cf. Esther 8:16. The Targ. may be rendered, "for a dew of light is thy dew to the doers of thy laws." Those who take the word in the sense of *light* interpret of a life-giving dew; Hos. 14:6; Isa. 45:8. Cf. Mulder's discussion, *op. cit.,* p. 51.

which causes the dead to come to life. For this reason the prophet may command the dead. They are to come to life, for God sends a refreshing dew to them to give them newness of life and vigor.

In yet another manner Isaiah describes the resurrection of the dead. As for the earth, he concludes, it causes the shades to fall, i.e., to fall away from it and to grow. The shades are in the earth, in Sheol; and the earth, conceived, as it were, as a great mother body, which usually gives back nothing, now gives up its shades, causing them to fall from it. This causative usage of the verb with *earth* as subject is reminiscent of the first chapter of Genesis, "and the earth caused to go forth. . . ." At a word from the Lord, the earth gives forth to growth what He commands.

> 20 Go, my people, enter into thy chambers, and shut thy doors after thee, hide thyself for a little moment, till the wrath be past.
>
> 21 For behold! the LORD is going out from his place, to visit the iniquity of the inhabitant of the earth upon him, and the earth shall disclose her blood, and shall no more cover her slain.

20 Turning from contemplation of the complete deliverance and resurrection to come upon the people of God, the prophet in a practical manner addresses that people. The period of oppression and suffering has not yet ended; the future glory which he has just described is not yet actually a reality. It is not to be brought about, however, by means of human might and power, but only through quiet waiting and expectation as God works out His wondrous purposes of redemption. To bring to his people this truth, namely, that the redemption is not immediately to appear, Isaiah utters the comforting and consoling command, *Go, my people.* The language is reminiscent of the command to Moses in Exodus 12:22, and the designation of the nation as *my people* is a characteristic tender trait. They are a people who belong to the Lord, a people whom He loves, and whose future salvation He will indeed accomplish.

Thus He addresses them as a Father would speak to his child. "This painful postponement of the promised resurrection," writes Alexander, "could not be more tenderly or beautifully intimated than in this fine apostrophe." As in the book of Deuteronomy so here, the nation is addressed as an individual. It is to go into its chamber, there to await in silence and prayer the coming redemption. Calvin in effect takes the language as figurative when he asserts that the chamber is simply calmness and composure of mind. Indeed, this thought is involved, but the latter half of the verse

makes clear that the action here commanded is for the sake of
safety as well, and hence the language is more than figurative. The
period of indignation is still present, and Isaiah employs the word
indignation as a designation of the wrath of God poured out upon
the nation on account of its rejection of Him. It is a figure that
describes the exile and all its attendant consequences. If the people remain in their chambers and bolt the doors,[47] they will be
protected from the wrath and punishment that is to be poured out
upon their pagan captors and oppressors. As long as the indignation remains they are to remain in their chambers and there
await salvation. Thus, by means of this command the lesson is
taught that deliverance is to be accomplished by the Lord alone.
His people are to wait for Him to act.

21 Continuing, Isaiah adduces a further reason why the people
are to remain in their chambers with locked doors. It is a reason of
great significance, and hence, is introduced with the word *behold!*
The LORD, Yahweh, the God of Israel, the God of those who are
hidden in their closets, is about to go forth from His place. He is
conceived as having been in a particular place, and from this place
He is now to go forth to accomplish His purposes. This place of
the Lord is heaven. "Behold, the LORD is about to go forth from
His place, and He will come down and will tread upon the high
places of the earth" (Mic. 1:3).[48]

The Lord's purpose is "to visit the iniquity of the inhabitant of
the earth upon it, i.e., the inhabitant." It may be noted that
inhabitant is singular, thus designating all who dwell upon the
earth. Possibly the Israelites are excluded here, but that they are is
by no means clear. It would seem that all who dwell upon earth

---

[47] The locking of the doors suggests the determination completely to shut
oneself in from the outside world and to turn alone to God. דלתיך—a dual,
changed by Qᵉre to the singular, but the singular dā-lāh is not attested, only
de-let.
   In favor of the Kᵉtiv is the agreement in form with hᵃ-dā-rey-kā. The dual,
however, may also express the plural; cf. 45:1. hᵃbi—Qal imper. 2 m., possibly
exhibiting Aramaic influence; cf. Hos. 6:9. There would be no need to change
to the feminine. *a little moment*—cf. Ezra 9:8; cf. 54:7. *be past*—lit., *until
(there) will pass over wrath.* The Kᵉtiv would omit Maqqeph, which is preferable to the Qᵉre, for the *waw* indicates that a naturally long vowel is intended. Note absence of article with zā-'am. The word is decisive; it is *wrath*, the
determined wrath of Yahweh, that lies upon the people; cf. 10:25 and Dan.
8:19; 11:36.
[48] Cf. Hos. 5:15 and bi-mᵉ-ḵó-ni in 18:4.

will have their iniquity visited upon them; only for those who in obedience to God await within their locked chambers will there be a deliverance or escape. In forceful language Isaiah teaches that the iniquity which men have committed will be caused to be visited upon them again. Thus, the punishment which that iniquity deserves will be meted out to men. The thought is that the inhabitants of earth have done iniquitously; such actions render men guilty before God and therefore liable to punishment, and hence God now comes to mete out that punishment.

Indeed, punishment must be meted out. The blood of those who had been slain lay in the earth, crying out as it were for vengeance, just as had Abel's blood (Gen. 4:10, 11). Likewise Job had called out, "O earth, cover not thou my blood and let my cry have no place" (Job 16:18). And Ezekiel, "For her blood is in the midst of her; she set it upon the top of a rock; she poured it not upon the ground, to cover it with dust; that it might cause fury to come up to take vengeance; I have set her blood upon the top of a rock, that it should not be covered" (24:7, 8).[49] As long as the blood was not actually swallowed up or covered it would cry aloud for vengeance. The earth, however, will now reveal the blood of those that have been slain, and no longer cover them, so that their blood may call aloud for vengeance. Then a perfect justice will be administered, and the inhabitant of earth will feel the guilt of his own iniquity visited upon himself.

---

[49] Gesenius calls attention to a similar concept in Aeschylus, *Choëphor* 66, 67, and to the beliefs of the Arabs as expressed in the Hamasa that there will be no dew or rain on such a place.

CHAPTER TWENTY-SEVEN

1 In that day the LORD with his hard and great and strong sword will punish Leviathan the fleeing serpent, Leviathan the tortuous serpent, and he will slay the monster that is in the sea.

1 In 26:21 there was mention of the Lord's visiting the iniquity of the inhabitant of the earth upon him; in the present verse there is mention of the Lord's visiting with His sword upon His enemies. Furthermore, this visiting with the sword is said to be "in that day," a phrase which here ties in with what had been stated in 26:21 and goes back to the catastrophe of 24:17-23. The first point, therefore, that must be stressed is the close and intimate connection with the preceding. "That day" is the day of punishment, the day when Yahweh will visit His punishment upon all His enemies. The phrase, therefore, is eschatological.[1]

This visitation is said to be with the sword, and the sword is described as hard and great and strong. Moses had already spoken of this sword: "If I whet my glittering sword, and mine hand take hold on judgment; I will render vengeance to mine enemies, and will reward them that hate me. I will make mine arrows drunk with blood, and my sword shall devour flesh; *and that* with the blood of the slain and of the captives, from the beginning of revenges upon the enemy" (Deut. 32:41, 42). And again Isaiah speaks of that sword: "For my sword shall be bathed in heaven; behold, it shall come down upon Idumea, and upon the people of my curse, to judgment. The sword of the LORD is filled with blood, it is made fat with fatness, and with the blood of lambs and goats, with the fat of the kidneys of rams: for the LORD hath a sacrifice in Bozrah, and a great slaughter in the land of Idumea" (Isa. 34:5, 6; cf. also Isa. 66:16; Zech. 13:7, where the reference is to the death of the Messiah; Rev. 1:16 and 2:12).

1 *will visit*—an obvious reflection upon 26:21, which described Yahweh as going *out to visit.*

Three epithets are given, and Duhm has suggested that they correspond to the three enemies to be slain. This may well be. The sword is said to be *hard*, which would suggest that it cannot easily be broken; it endures while it smites the foe; it does not become dull or lose its sharpness. Possibly also it is to be thought of as relentless. The sword is described as *great*, for it is mighty and powerful and sufficient to slay all the enemies of the Lord. Lastly, it is a *strong* sword; not one that will fail, but one which will be fit to be wielded by the arm of the Lord. The punishment which the Lord metes out will be sure and unfailing. The power of destruction resides not in the sword itself, but in the Lord who wields it; and to say that the sword is strong is but another way of saying that God Himself will effectively carry out His punishment.[2]

What, however, are the enemies that will be the object of God's punishment? The first object of punishment is said to be Leviathan.[3] In Psalm 74:14 the word may refer to an imaginary creature, for we read of the "heads of leviathan." It is probable that Isaiah here employs the word in the same sense. On the texts from Ugarit we find the following language (note its similarity to the language of the present passage):

> *ktmhs. ltn. btn. brh*
> *tkly. btn. 'qltn*
> *šlyt. d. šb't. ršm*[4]

We may render:

> When thou dost smite Lotan the fleeing serpent
> (And) shall put an end to the tortuous serpent
> Shalyat of the seven heads. . . .

---

[2] *sword*—cf. Deut. 32:41, 42; Ps. 7:13; 17:13; Isa. 34:5; all these passages speak of the sword as representing God's punitive power.

[3] *Leviathan*—mentioned in Scripture as a sea monster, Ps. 74:14; 104:26; Job 3:8. In Job 40:25 it seems to be identified with the crocodile. *Tannin* appears in Isa. 51:9; Ps. 74:13; 91:13; 148:7; Jer. 51:34; Lam. 4:3; and in a different sense in Gen. 1:21. B renders τὸν δράκοντα; the word never has the article, nor does it occur in the plural. The etymology is not sure; possibly it is from *liw-yāh, winding*, with a suffix. An eighth-century B.C. relief from Malatya depicts two Hittite gods, equipped with spears, clubs, etc., fighting against the coiling (winding) dragon Illuyankas. Cf. *ANET*, pp. 125, 126 for the text, and *ANEP*, pp. 218-229 for illustration and description.

[4] Cf. *Ugaritic Manual*, 1955, p. 148 and *ANET*, pp. 137b, 138d.

fleeing—cf. Gordon, *Orientalia*, Vol. 22, 1953, pp. 243f. Whereas the Bible uses the term *nā-ḥāš* for serpent, Ugaritic has a term related to *pā-ṭen*. Cf. also *Anat* 3; 37-38, *ištbm tnn išbm(n)h mḫšt bṯn 'qltn*, "I muzzled the Tannin, I surely muzzled him, I smote the writhing '*qlṯn*."

Here Leviathan appears to be a mythical serpent-like creature with seven heads. Testimonies to belief in the existence of such a mythical creature are also found in the cuneiform documents of ancient Mesopotamia.[5]

The similarity of language between Ugarit and Isaiah's text shows a very definite relationship, but how is this relationship to be explained? As in Ugarit so also here, Leviathan is an imaginary being; but it does not follow here that in Isaiah God is represented as fighting against a mythical monster. Isaiah rather is merely employing these terms as descriptive figures of speech to refer to certain nations which are the enemies of the Lord. As we today might speak of an enemy nation as a monster, or of some hostile ruler as a demon, so Isaiah is speaking of the enemy nations under similar terms.[6] The ancient mythology has furnished him in other words with certain figures of speech, and that is all. He is not asserting that Yahweh will actually contend with mythical monsters, nor does he show himself in any sense influenced by the mythology of antiquity. Rather, just as we today may employ terms taken from mythology for the purposes of illustration, so did Isaiah.

He is not then influenced by Babylonian tradition nor even by the conceptions held in ancient Ugarit. Quite probably the people to whom the prophet addressed himself would have understood his allusions, for they were likely well known in his day. Were this not the case, he would have no reason for employing them. Inasmuch as they were current terms, he finds them suitable for his own usage. They serve as ample descriptive terms to show that complete victory will belong to God Himself. The outcome of the battle is assured; Yahweh will be victorious.

It is not without purpose that the prophet indicates that the serpent is in the sea, for the mention of the sea adds to the aura of mystery that adheres to the declaration. The sea is a region far removed from man's rule and power and even from his knowledge.

---

[5] Cf. Heidel, *The Babylonian Genesis,* 1951, pp. 107f. for references, and for a full discussion of the relation between Scripture and the ancient near eastern cosmogonies.

[6] Penna remarks: *"Non si puo negare una relazione di dipendenza del nostro testo dalla leggenda ugaritica; ma e possibilissimo che, come altrove e come capita anche in autori cristiani rispetto a espressioni mitologiche pagane, essa sia limitata solo al vocabolario."* Penna refers to the instructive article of Augustine Bea, in *Biblica,* Vol. 19, 1938, *"Ras Samra und das Alte Testament,"* particularly pp. 444ff.

In this mysterious region is the sea monster, yet even the denizen of this unknown domain will be slain by the sword of Yahweh.

That Isaiah is employing figurative language is unquestionable. In what sense, however, are his figures to be understood? Those who seek to find an identification for each of the symbols are unable to reach an agreement as to that identification. This, of course, does not prove that it is wrong to seek such identification, but it is significant that unanimity has not been found. Some seek to find three kingdoms, usually Assyria, Babylonia, and Egypt. Others have held that only two kingdoms are represented, and still others that the reference is to but one.[7]

It seems more likely, however, that the prophet is teaching that enemies of all kinds, those who belong to the heights and those that belong to the depths as well as those that live in the most inaccessible places, will suffer the punitive judgment of God. Wherever the spirit of opposition to God has appeared, in whatever kingdom it may be, there God will show Himself victorious.[8]

2 In that day, as a vineyard of wine, afflict her.
3 I the Lord do keep her, every moment I shall water her; lest any hurt her, night and day do I keep her.

---

[7] Cf. Penna, Gesenius, etc. Penna thinks that the immediate context (26:21), and the fact that elsewhere mythological names are used to indicate countries (e.g., Ezek. 29:3; 32:2; Ps. 74:14, etc.), suggests the reference to pagan nations. Some of the older commentators, Kimchi, Ibn Ezra, Jarchi, Vitringa, Lowth, and Rosenmüller, and more recently Procksch, think that the reference is to three beasts and so to many powers, whereas Eichhorn and Gesenius believed that several epithets were used to designate one beast. This one power, says Gesenius, is not Egypt, but Babylon. Although only Leviathan and Tannin are mentioned, nevertheless, the repetition of Leviathan with diverse appositions is thought to support the view that three creatures are intended.

[8] This is not modified by the fact that later prophets use this basic prophecy in an individualizing sense, and even with different application; compare Ezek. 29:3; 32:2 with Jer. 51:34. Cf. also Isa. 51:9 and Rev. 12:3ff.; 13:1ff. בים—in this region which in so high a measure was removed from the rule and even the knowledge of men. Hence, monsters of all kinds and all places, great monsters above (Hem. a.) and below (Hem. b.), the monstrous inhabitants of the most inaccessible realms, of the heights of heaven and the depths of the sea, suffer the judgment. The verse is obviously to be understood symbolically. The thought is: the powers of every sphere and of every kind that are opposed to God, powers on high that have not kept their principalities, kings and kingdoms on earth in which the natural power against God had acquired form, have fallen to the punishing judgment. The thought of the verse is identical with 24:21.

4 Fury is not in me, who would set briers and thorns against me in battle? I would go through them, I would burn them together.

5 Unless he lay hold of my strength and make peace with me; peace let him make with me.

6 He shall cause them that come of Jacob to take root: Israel shall blossom and bud, and fill the face of the world with fruit.

2 Beginning with this verse and continuing through the sixth verse, the Lord Himself speaks. The language is somewhat broken, to show the excitement of the prophet in setting forth the Lord's message, a message that reflects upon the parable of the vineyard in 5:1-7.[9] In that passage the prophet sought to show that the Lord had planted a vineyard, but, inasmuch as the vineyard had failed Him, He would destroy it. Here, the purpose is the opposite. Here, the Lord uses the figure of the vineyard in order to show that He will regather His people. Both passages have this in common, that the Lord is the speaker, and the Lord's speech is set forth by the prophet.

The introductory *in that day* has reference to the time of visitation, as in 27:1. It is eschatological. At the time when Yahweh will visit His enemies in punishment, there will be a vineyard. The word vineyard is emphatic. It calls to mind at once the parable of 5:1 and places in proper focus the central theme of the passage. With this word we are immediately brought face to face with Israel. To mention a vineyard is to be reminded of Israel, the people of God.

What kind of vineyard is this? According to the Masoretic text it is a vineyard of wine, i.e., a vineyard that produces wine. This word would show at once that the vineyard was successfully fulfilling the function for which vineyards exist. It is quite unlike the picture given in 5:1ff. This picture, however, is thought by many to be unsuitable; and on the basis of some of the ancient versions they would make slight emendation of the text, in order to obtain the reading, *vineyard of pleasantness*. In particular, appeal is made to

9 After the words *in that day* we are perhaps to understand, *it will be said;* however, this is not necessary. The verse may be literally translated, *on that day, with respect to the vineyard,* etc. Drechsler, however, believes that it is wrong to connect the two parts of the verse in this way and to regard the second part as the words of the prophet. Penna acknowledges that there is no textual warrant for inserting *it will be said* or anything similar, but thinks that this is better than some of the proposed emendations. Lindblom, e.g., would translate, "A pleasant vineyard is the Lord's, I the Lord keep it."

Amos 5:11.[10] At the same time, it should be noted that the Qumran Isaiah manuscript clearly reads *ḥwmr (wine)*, and hence, we may retain that meaning. If we do, then the phrase presents a striking antithesis to 5:1ff. In that parable, the Lord intended to destroy the vineyard, because it did not produce wine as it should. Here, however, the entire picture is changed.

The imperative in the latter part of the verse is generally translated, *sing to her*, although this rendering is acknowledged to involve difficulties.[11] Alexander renders *afflict her*. In the first place he does not refer the *to her* to the vineyard, inasmuch as this latter word is masculine, but to Jerusalem or the daughter of Zion, the people of God considered as His spouse. Alexander adduces the following arguments for his rendering. (*a*) No one has been able conclusively to point out precisely where the supposed song concludes. This raises the presumption, at least in this instance, that a song whose ending cannot be discovered may also not have had a beginning. (*b*) In the next few verses there is nothing in particular to distinguish them as song. (*c*) It is incongruous to make a song which the people are supposed to sing begin with the words, "I Jehovah keep it, etc." (*d*) In 5:1ff. the verb "sing" and its cognate noun "song" appear, whereas here there is no cognate noun. (*e*) Of the 56 cases in which the *Piel* of *'anah* occurs, there are but three "in which the sense of *singing* is conceivable." (*f*) The usual meaning of the verb in the *Piel* stem is here quite appropriate, namely, "to afflict." The thought then is that the enemies of the Church are addressed and commanded to do their worst to God's people. They cannot succeed for God still protects His own. In favor of this interpretation is the allusion to affliction

---

10 *wine*—cf. Ar. *ḥamr* and Ug. *ḥmr;* Deut. 32:14. This is supported by Vulg. *vinea meri*, and Syr. B reads καλὸς ἐπιθύμημα, presupposing *ḥmd*, which is possibly supported by the Targ., *kkrm nśb*, i.e., *like a choice vineyard*. 1Q supports M. The phrase is then similar to the *kerem zayiṯ* in Judg. 15:5; the connection indicates the further meaning of vineyard. *Kerem* is usually m., but in this combination is regarded as f.; cf. 2 Kings 4:39, *ge-p̄en*. It is possible that B and Targ. reflect the parallel passages Amos 5:11 and Isa. 27:2.

11 Gray acknowledges that neither the rendering *sing ye to it* (Num. 21:17) nor *sing ye of it* (5:1) is very probable and hence thinks the text may be suspect. The *Piel* has the sense of singing in Ex. 32:18 and possibly in Ps. 88:1. Even in Ex. 32:18 the *Piel* may be questioned, and each form may be a *Qal* inf. construct. If this is so, it is questionable whether the *Piel* is ever employed in Scripture in the sense of *sing*. On the other hand the *Piel* is commonly used in the sense of *afflict*. We may note other occurrences in Isaiah, 60:14; 64:11; 58:3, 5.

in verses 4, 7, 8, and 9. Alexander acknowledges that the weight of tradition is against him, but remarks that his proposed rendering removes a number of difficulties by returning to the correct meaning of the verb, and also that no one seems to have noted the facts which he has adduced concerning the usage of the verb. Furthermore, while acknowledging the difficulties in this interpretation, Alexander declares that they are not nearly as great as those involved in the usual view. He consequently renders, *In that day, as a vineyard of wine, afflict her,* or *in that day afflict for her the vineyard of wine.* The thought is that through the prophet God commands those who are hostile to His people to afflict Jerusalem. They may do their worst, but because God is with His people, He will triumph.

3 Inasmuch as the verse begins with *I the Lord,* commentators find a difficulty, and wish to assume *saith the Lord,* as understood. If, however, these are not the words of a song, this difficulty vanishes. Enemies may afflict God's people, but He keeps watch over her. In 5:2 He had stated that He had erected a tower in the vineyard, and now He Himself is watching over the vineyard from that tower. The feminine suffixes here have the same reference as in verse 2; namely, Jerusalem regarded under the figure of a vineyard. The picture here given is the opposite of that in chapter five. Here, God will do everything for His vineyard; there He had already done all that was necessary and hence had decided to destroy the vineyard.

Indeed, He will water it without interruption. The expressive phrase, *all moments,* indicates that God will continually watch over His vineyard.[12] In chapter five He would command the clouds not to rain upon it; now He will cause it to drink without ceasing.[13] Streams of grace flow without ceasing to His own. It is necessary that God do this, lest one visit punishment upon the people. In Isaiah 5:5 God would break down the vineyard's walls, so that the animals enter and trample it; here He will protect it, that not even one (the singular is to be noted) may bring any kind of destruction to His vineyard. There are many enemies ready to destroy Jerusalem, were that possible. They cannot succeed, for there is One who watches vigilantly. "He that keepeth Israel shall

---

12 Cf. Job 7:18; Isa. 33:2.
13 *I shall cause it to drink*—the imp. asserts a fact of definite occurrence within a certain period.

neither slumber nor sleep" (Ps. 121:4). Night and day, God will protect His own. The night is mentioned first, for that is the time when protection from without is most needed.[14] It is a watch that knows no break nor interruption.[15] What was taken away from the vineyard in chapter five is now restored; more than that, a better condition is given. Formerly, God had protected His vineyard through certain delegated arrangements, now He Himself is its watcher. The Lord watches over the Church in such a manner that destruction can never come to her.

4 In chapter five the Lord declared that it was His purpose to punish the vineyard. Now He will not punish but protect. This thought is introduced by the assertion, *I have no wrath.*[16] This wrath is gone; it is spent. Whatever anger there may once have been against the vineyard is passed. The word *wrath* is first in the sentence, and so emphasized. It calls to mind what was once the situation. That situation, however, is no longer present. Most peoples would indeed like to believe that there is no wrath on God's part toward them. It is deceptive, however, so to believe, unless one has the assurance from God Himself that such is the case. With God's people, this is no vain boast. Toward them there is no wrath. "WRATH"—that which once had hung over the heads of the elect—has been removed.

The next clause is difficult, but the rendering that is best supported grammatically is, *Oh! that I might meet the thorns and briers in war.*[17] In chapter five the thorns and briers would come up in the vineyard after the Lord had laid it waste. They would be the last step in its destruction. No longer could it produce, for it

---

14 Cf. 1 Kings 8:29; Jer. 14:17 and Isa. 34:10.

15 *'etz-tzⁿ-ren-nāh*—In a near open syllable, the short *u* or *i* may drop to *Shᵉwa*. Here, before *Resh* the *Ḥateph-Qametz* appears in a principal pause. Sometimes, *Ḥateph-Qametz* appears when the original vowel was *Ḥolem;* cf. examples in Num. 23:25; Job 2:7; Ezek. 41:4; Jer. 31:33, etc.

16 Cf. 26:20. The thought is the opposite of 5:5-7; cf. 5:25. Some would read *ḥô-māh*, wall, e.g., Lowth, Procksch. In support of this latter, appeal might be made to 26:1. But in 5:5 there is mention of a protection, which God will tear down; hence reference here to a wall seems to be without point. The word can also be read, *ḥam-māh*, sun, but this does not fit in well with the context.

17 Lit., *who will give me.* After a modification of the original meaning of the verb, the remoter object (here it would be לי) is appended to the verb in the form of an acc. suffix; i.e., instead of *who gives to me*, simply *who gives me*, i.e., *Oh! that I had!*

would be but a field of thorns and briars. Now the attitude of the
Lord has changed. Now, He would meet those thorns and briers in
war as enemies.[18] If He declares war upon them they will be
conquered and destroyed. These are the true enemies of the
vineyard, and serve as a figure for the godless and dangerous enemies of the nation (cf. 9:17; 10:17).

Changing the figure, the Lord then announces that He will step
in her, i.e., either the people of Jerusalem conceived as the
vineyard, or the suffix may be taken as neutral referring to the
thorn and brier.[19] The announcement is that God will step forward against them as in battle. By disregarding the accents we may
also obtain the rendering, *In battle I shall step forward against
them.* Final destruction will come in that the Lord will burn the
thorn and thistle, the enemies of His people. This is the fire of
which mention had been made in 26:11. Throughout this verse
there is the note of ringing challenge. No enemy is too great for
Israel's God. He is truly the sovereign Ruler over all things, and
He disposes of His enemies as He will. How wondrous to know
that such a God through grace is on one's side!

5 Even for the enemies there is a hope, however; but that hope
can only be found in a turning to the Lord. The first word is
probably to be rendered, *except,* and thus we obtain the rendering, *except he seize or lay hold upon my place of refuge.*[20] The
allusion seems to be to the seizing of the altar as a place of refuge.
"If anyone (for the verbs are indefinite) should take hold of
that place of refuge or asylum which is Mine, then he will make
peace with Me."[21] The thought is that there must be a complete
seeking of the asylum or refuge which God provides, if one is to be
delivered. It is illustrated by the action of Adonijah: "And Ado-

18 Note the asyndeton; cf. 32:13. These two words, *šāmîr, šayit,* are definitely Isaianic.

19 *'ep-śʰ-'āh*—in *BH* with a simple Shᵉwa, but the compound Shᵉwa serves to
preserve the *u* vowel, and may also be present because of the guttural. Cf. note
15.

20 Lit., *or else let him take hold of my stronghold,* i.e., *unless he take hold,*
etc. Cf. Ar. *'āw yus-li-ma, unless he become a Moslem* (subjunctive), *TT,*
p. 217; Lev. 26:41.

21 Cf. 25:4. The form appears to be *mā-'ôz,* with long *a,* yet the corresponding Ar. form is *ma-'āḍ,* with short *a.* The subj. of the verb is the enemies of
God's people, represented in the previous verse under the figure of thorns
and thistles.

nijah feared because of Solomon, and arose and went, and caught hold on the horns of the altar" (1 Kings 1:50).

The following phrase calls to mind the action of Joshua, who "made peace with them" (Josh. 9:15), although its emphasis here is different. In detail this passage is difficult, but it does show the tender concern that God has for sinners.[22] Inasmuch as He offers so many rays of hope, how shall we escape if we neglect His salvation, when the final word has come, the final opportunity to believe? "Now is the day of salvation."

6 The thought of the preceding is continued, but the figure of the vine is abandoned and that of a tree substituted, together with a straightforward explanation. It is difficult to discover whether these words are spoken directly by God or whether they are the prophet's words.[23] The verse has its difficulties, and it is not always possible to solve them. As to the first phrase, we may render, "he shall cause the coming ones to take root," or, "in the coming ones (i.e., the coming days) he shall cause to take root." It is difficult to make a choice, but probably the latter construction is to be preferred.[24] The thought then is that in the future time God will cause His people to take root. It is not a blessing to be accomplished during the life of the prophet, not contemporary with him, but one which is to be fulfilled in the coming days. Here the vine is really identified as Israel and Jacob. This vine is to be planted in the future so that it can bear fruit.

Emphasis is now placed upon the growth of what has taken root. Jacob will flower, for this is the significant point. Not only will it take root but it will grow to fullness and produce flower.[25] In

22 Note the transition from the *Hiphil* jussive to the ordinary imperfect. The two imperfects express circumstantial clauses, so that the whole may be rendered, *unless he lay hold of my strength, making peace with me*, etc. The repetition provides emphasis, which is further heightened by placing the object first in the second circumstantial clause.

23 Luther, followed by Delitzsch and others, maintains that the Church is here speaking.

24 Alexander translates: *(In) coming (days) shall Jacob take root.* Cf. Eccl. 2: 16. הבאים is an acc. of time, in which the action occurs; cf. Jer. 28:16. *take root*—37:31; Ps. 80:9ff.; Hos. 14:6ff.; Ezek. 19:10ff.

25 יציץ—an imperfect which probably has the force of a jussive, *may it blossom*. The two verbs indicate that growth has taken place in the fullest sense. Cf. Ps. 92:8 for the reverse order. As Drechsler points out, elsewhere, *pā-raḥ* may include the bursting of the buds (Gen. 40:10), but here this action is regarded as the culmination. Growth therefore has developed to its completion.

every respect it will fulfill its function as plant. The term *Jacob* is often used, particularly in the second part of the prophecy, to denote the entire people of Israel. Israel will break forth in growth, and the consequence is that the entire surface of the world will be filled with her produce.[26] All over the surface of the inhabited world, the fruit of Jacob and Israel will fill the land. This is a beautiful way of expressing the truth that Israel will influence the entire earth. The truth of God, given to Israel, will fill all the earth. In the missionary proclamation of the Gospel this truth finds its fulfillment. The picture is that of 24:1, 13; 26:18; and also of 2:2-4.

> 7 Like the smiting of his smiter did he smite him, or like the slaying of his slain was he slain?
>
> 8 In measure, by sending her away, thou dost contend with her. He removes her by his hard wind in the day of the east wind.
>
> 9 Therefore by this will Jacob's iniquity be expiated, and this is all its fruit to take away his sin in his placing all the stones of the altar like limestones pulverized, so that groves and incense stands will arise no more.
>
> 10 For a fortified city shall be desolate, a dwelling broken up and forsaken like the wilderness. There the calf will feed, and there it will lie and consume her branches.
>
> 11 When its boughs are withered, they shall be broken; women come, lighting it; for it is not a people of understanding, wherefore its maker will not have pity upon it, and its maker will not have mercy upon it.

7 The purpose of this verse is to answer by means of a negative question the complaint that Israel had been smitten as had her oppressors. Did God smite Israel as He smote those who smote Israel? Such negations are sometimes expressed by means of a question; cf. 2 Samuel 7:5 and cf. 1 Chronicles 17:4. Gesenius refers to a custom of the Indians who answer their letters with, "What more is there?" i.e., to say. Everything that should be said has been said. We may bring out the force of the entire verse as follows: "Is it that like God's smiting of Assyria, He has smitten

---

26 The picture is the opposite of 5:24. With this verse there is a change in the tone, and a transition to prophetic discourse occurs. *they will fill*—the subject is Jacob and Israel. *t^e-nû-ḇāh*—fruit, produce. Cf. Judg. 9:11; Deut. 32: 13. The word must be taken in a figurative sense, as indicating the blessings which Jacob and Israel, at peace with God and prosperous, will produce.

Judah? or like the slaughter of those slain of the enemy has Judah been slain?"[27]

There is a distinction in the chastisements of God. The enemy, whom God had used as His instrument in the punishment of Judah, would be completely destroyed by punishment. ". . . Thou hast visited and destroyed them, and made all their memory to perish" (Isa. 26:14b). On the other hand, the punishment extended to Judah was for the purpose of purification, in order that a remnant might be preserved, from which in time the Redeemer would come—and it was the presence of the remnant which constituted the difference. "O LORD, correct me, but with judgment; not in thine anger, lest thou bring me to nothing" (Jer. 10:24). Thus, even in the chastisement—for such this visitation upon Israel really was—there was mercy and goodness. It was a chastisement visited upon "Israel, my son, my first born," and hence, quite different from that which came upon "thy son, thy first born." It is well that we be able to interpret the visitations of God. Upon the "vessels of wrath, fitted for destruction," they bring destruction; upon "my son, my first born," they show the faithfulness of God to His promise, and His mercy in not destroying men for their sins.

8 The general sense of verse 7 is clear, but the eighth verse is one of the most disputed in this section. As this verse is translated in the King James Version it does not yield a good sense, and some of the other translations are no better. In this verse and in the ninth Isaiah's purpose is to emphasize with respect to Israel certain points that are necessary for the understanding of the whole picture, namely, that where a terrible burden of judgment has fallen upon the whole earth, Judah suffers but mildly. We would therefore translate, *In measure, in the sending her away, thou dost contend with her. By his hard wind he removes her in the day of the east wind.* The thought may then be paraphrased as follows: "By sending Judah away into exile in moderation, thou art trying to contend or reason with her. In a day when the east wind blows, thou dost remove Judah by thine own hard wind." It will be best to consider this verse word by word. *In measure*—The Hebrew word is

---

27 *makkēhû*—an objective gen., lit., *is it like the smiting of the one (the world power) who smote him (Israel) did he (God) smite him (Israel)?* Emphasis falls upon the general concept of smiting. Cf. 16:9.

7b may be rendered, *or like the slaying of his* (i.e., *the enemy's) slain ones was he (Israel) slain?* The suffix in *his slain ones* refers to the suffix in *his smiter* in 7a.

very difficult, but there is good reason for adopting this translation.[28] The basic thought seems to be that God has punished
Judah according to measure, determining precisely this measure
so that Judah will not perish by a punishment that exceeds this
measure. At the same time, inasmuch as the word is probably a
reduplicated form, the thought may also be present that this
measure is one of moderation, of gradualness. The visitation will
not be fatal, but will be one of moderation.

by sending her away—i.e., in the Lord's sending Judah away.
Why, however, is the feminine suffix used? In Isaiah 50:1 this word
is employed of divorcement. It may be, therefore, that here the
picture is that of the sending away, in the sense of renouncing
Judah as one renounces a wife. If this be the meaning, then this
strong verb refers not to the exile necessarily, but rather to the fact
that the nation is no longer to be considered as the theocracy. The
figure of the people as the wife of the Lord is often used in
the prophets. Hence, just as a man sends away the wife whom he
divorces, so the Lord sends away the faithless nation which had
once constituted the theocracy.

thou didst contend with her—i.e., by means of punishment thou
dost bring judgment upon her.[29] Isaiah now addresses God direct-

28 Traditionally this word has been regarded as a contraction of *bi-sᵉ-'āh*
sᵉ-'āh with an inserted *Dagesh;* cf. Green, *Hebrew Grammar,* § 24 a. Aq and S
both render ἐν σάτῳ σάτον, and T ἐν μέτρῳ μέτρον; Vulg. *in mensura contra
mensuram.* Targ. and Syr. *with the measure;* Saadia, *according to its measure,*
thus, *measure for measure,* i.e., with moderation. The doubling is thought to
express the concept of a steady progress from one to many. Hence, "gradually,
not all at once." Gesenius interpreted, *according to the measure,* i.e., the right,
but with the secondary concept of moderation. He appeals to Jer. 10:24; 30:11;
46:28. Gesenius condemns appeals to the Arabic as due to a failure to understand the force of *sᵉ-āh,* a *definite measure.* He thinks that such appeals are
not compelling *(erweislich)* or suitable *(passend).* In particular he regards
as unsuitable the appeal to *sa'-sa',* which designated the shepherd's sound sa-sa.
B μαχόμενος. Despite his objection, however, many consider the form a *Pilpel*
or reduplicated infinitive. Cf. G. Driver, *JTS,* Vol. 30, pp. 371ff. I can see, therefore, no real reason for departing from the traditional rendering. Yet what is
surprising, since Isaiah's purpose is to speak of the moderation of the judgment
which Israel must experience, is that he lays so much stress upon the fearful
weight of the judgment. At the time when such a dreadful storm will break
over the world, Israel will receive a punishment which will not completely
destroy her, but out of which a remnant will return. Cf. also J. Herrmann in
ZAW, Vol. 36, 1916, p. 243.

29 The imp. indicates continuation in past time: *thou hast constantly con-
tended with her;* the verb is usually employed with a prep., but cf. Job 10:2.

ly, changing from the description in the third person to direct address in the second. In 25:5 he changed from the second to the third person. The sending away of Judah is a means of contending with Judah, pointing out to her through punishment that her iniquity has brought this sad train of events upon her. God uses chastisement as a means of bringing His own people to their senses.

He removes her by his hard wind—King James renders, *He stayeth his rough wind.* The verb, however, simply means *to remove.*[30] It is a thought that has appeared in Isaiah from time to time, the removing of the people from their land, for here it is the exile that is in view. Although the definite object of the verb is not expressed, it is clear that the prophet is thinking of Judah. Here as elsewhere the means of the divine judgment is expressed under the figure of a strong wind or storm. "I will scatter them as with an east wind before the enemy; . . ." (Jer. 18:17a, cf. also Job 27:20, 21). Isaiah uses a significant adjective. The wind that will carry the nation away is a hard wind. The exile is not to be an easy thing for Judah. The theocracy will pass, and the nation in humiliation will be carried captive by another power hostile to it.

in the day of the east wind—The thought is that on a day when the east wind is blowing, God will carry the nation away. As is well known, this east wind, or sirocco, is a strong, powerful, vehement wind (cf. Job 27:21; Ps. 48:8; Jer. 18:17; Ezek. 27:26; Gen. 41:6; Hos. 13:15). Perhaps in the language itself there is a suggestion that the powerful east wind will nevertheless be of temporary, passing nature. It is not a constantly blowing wind, but one that happens to blow on a certain day; and on this day when it is blowing, the Lord punishes His people.

Without doubt it is difficult to connect this verse with the preceding in any necessarily logical sense. Isaiah does not develop his argument logically, but simply emphasizes in this verse the fact that the punishment to come upon Judah will be a mitigated one. That the prophet proceeds in this way, rather than by means of presenting a logically developed argument, is not sufficient warrant for denying to him the authorship of the present verse.

9 With this verse Isaiah draws a conclusion from what he had just stated. "Therefore," he argues, "inasmuch as the punishment

---

[30] Cf. Ar. *wa-ga-'a, to thrust;* Prov. 25:4; 2 Sam. 20:13.

will be temporary and will not completely destroy the nation, by means of this punishment the iniquity of Jacob will be purged away." Together with this purification of the sin of Jacob, all the implements of idolatry will be destroyed as well as Jerusalem herself.

be expiated—As may be seen by a comparison with Isaiah 6:7, this word really means *expiated* or *atoned*. At the same time, the present context shows that it is here employed by metonomy for the effect, namely, purification or purgation. The thought is found also in Proverbs 16:6, "By mercy and truth iniquity is purged: and by the fear of the LORD *men* depart from evil." In other words, the prophet is not stating that the exile provided an atonement for the iniquity of Israel, but merely that by means of the exile, there was purification.[31] The exile was a purifying or purging experience, and as a result of it, Judah emerged with her iniquity purified. Here is an anticipation of what Isaiah later declared, "She hath received at the Lord's hand double for all her sin" (Isa. 40:2).

this is all its fruit—These words should stand as a unit by themselves, and the word *all* may even be taken adverbially, *entirely, wholly*. At any rate a disjunctive accent accompanies *pᵉri, fruit*, and thus separates it from what follows. In the light of this arrangement of the verse, the word *fruit* would really signify *use* or *intended purpose*.[32]

to take away his sin—lit., the taking away (removing) of its sin. These words are the subject of which the preceding phrase is the predicate. The whole may therefore be set forth as follows: *The removal of his sin is the whole fruit or purpose*. Here again is a removal; this time, however, it is not the removal of Judah but of Judah's sins. Judah herself must be taken from her land if her sin is to be taken away. All is the work of God. He removes her that He may remove her sin. The destruction of Jerusalem thus becomes the occasion and cause of blessing.

in his placing all the stones, etc.—In these words we are told how God takes away the sin of Judah.[33] This He does, in that He

---

31 וכפר—cf. 22:14. The exile may have been the means, but it was not the ground of purification.

32 *Fruit* had already been used in a metaphorical sense, 3:10; 10:12; it is the purpose of the removal of the nation's sin. Penna emends the text to read *kō-fer lᵉ*, "*prezzo per*." *Kōl* may be taken adverbially, *this is wholly the fruit.*

33 *By this* and *this* have reference to what follows. Their thought is taken up with *in his placing.*

places all the stones of the heathen altars like limestones which have been ground to powder. In these words Isaiah describes the destruction of heathen altars, and shows that these altars were the occasions of Judah's sin.[34] In her worship she had allowed this mixture of heathenism, and in so far, was faithless to the Lord.

will arise no more—For a discussion of the nature of these images, cf. the comments on 17:8. Isaiah speaks in the active voice, as though the images might arise in their own strength. Their day, however, had passed. There is an element of sadness in the description. God had formed His people into a theocracy, but it became a nation ruled by idols. Therefore, it must go into banishment, and in this banishment be freed from its idols. These will perish, never to rise again.[35] In exile, however, there would be a nation whose very life was filled with idolatry. Hence, while the exile would purge from the idols of Palestine, it would bring Judah into contact with other idols and with foreign gods. Were not God carrying out His purposes of redemption, there would be no hope for Judah or for the world. What stands out with crystal clarity is that Judah does not have within herself the power of true repentance or amelioration. Her heart inclines not after the Lord but after idols.

10 Thus, after stating that the visitation to come upon Judah will be one of moderation, Isaiah goes on to point out that nevertheless, the visitation will indeed come, and Jerusalem will be destroyed. At this point, it would seem, the "fortified city" is Jerusalem. Alexander refers it to Babylon, and Drechsler takes it generally.

If the reference be to Jerusalem, the introductory *ki* must be rendered *yet,* or *for.* This, however, is the principal difficulty if we take the city mentioned as Jerusalem. The thought then may be paraphrased, "The punishment meted out to Judah will not be total; it will be mingled with mercy. Yet Jerusalem will become desolate." At the same time this difficulty also obtains on any other identification of the city.[36] Why does the prophet introduce his thought with the word "for"?

---

34 מזבח—the singular serves to include all items of the same species, i.e., *all altars.* מנפצות—shattered, i.e., pulverized.

35 The imp. expresses a consequence, and the clause is conditional, *so that they do not rise,* etc.

36 עיר—a *casus pendens,* lit., *for a fortified city, it shall be desolate.* Note that the noun is indefinite.

The language is indefinite, a point not to be overlooked. "The visitation will be mitigated, for a fortified city will become desolate." The language is reminiscent of Lamentations 1:1 and 3:28. If the fortifications of the city feel the force of destruction, surely the remainder of the city will perish.

a pasturage broken up and forsaken—The thought is that the once fortified and hence enclosed city has now become an open pasturage which is accessible to all who wish to enter it. This pasturage is described as *driven away, banished,* which evidently means that it is a pasturage whose inhabitants have been banished or driven away. It is thus forsaken, and like a wilderness.

Earlier (7:25), Isaiah had described the desolation that would come upon Judah. He takes up this description again, pointing out that cattle would graze and lie down there and consume the branches. These are the branches that belong to the city. When the city itself is destroyed, the cattle enter and devour whatever remains of its ruins.[37]

11 Isaiah continues the description, building upon the figure introduced by mention of the branches, now speaking of the boughs.[38] Thus, he subtly introduces the figure of a tree to represent the fallen city. When the branches become dry, they are broken by women who come out to gather wood. Thus, even the ruined city now produces something. In contrast to what it at one time brought forth, it now can produce only branches fit for firewood. This alone is its harvest. In a land where there are few forests, firewood would be difficult to procure. "And when he came to the gate of the city, behold, the widow woman was there gathering of sticks. . ." (1 Kings 17:10; cf. also Num. 15:32, 33). The prophet himself had already (17:19) alluded to this.[39]

Isaiah now begins an explanation, and the connection of this thought may be expressed as follows. "A tragic fate will come over

---

37 *and consume*—the perfect with *waw* consecutive may be used after an imperfect, which has frequentative force; thus, *it lies* (i.e., *is wont to lie*) *and will consume her branches.* נעזב in the sense, *being abandoned,* is Isaianic; and מׁשלח occurs only here and in Isa. 16:2 (f. 50:1) among the prophets. סעיף appears in Isa. 2:21; 17:6; 57:5 and nowhere else among the prophets.

38 *in the being dry of her harvest*—here the word has collective force, *boughs, branches.* The verb is f. pl., and we need not assume that it is used for a f. singular. The subject is collective, or it may even be *its branches* of the preceding verse. Thus, *when its boughs dry, its branches are broken.*

39 אותה—the f. suffix refers to the *boughs, qā-tzír,* that have become dry, lit., *causing it to take fire.*

Jerusalem, for the inhabitants thereof are a people devoid of understanding, and hence, they shall be punished." No matter how much insight this people might seem to possess in certain respects, in that which was of supreme importance it was deficient. The description agrees with what Isaiah had earlier stated (cf. 1:3).[40]

Inasmuch as the people is thus devoid of understanding, the One who made and formed it will not show mercy nor pity to it. God is the maker and the former of all men, but these descriptions seem to apply with particular force to Judah. In 43:1 God identifies Himself as the One who formed Jacob, and in 44:2 He is said to be the One who made and formed Jacob. Hence, there is peculiar appropriateness in applying the reference to the people of God. Inasmuch as this nation has received special blessing of God by being formed into the theocracy, it can expect no mercy, but the theocracy will be fully destroyed. This does not conflict with what had earlier been stated. The thought is that the city of Jerusalem, the representative of the theocracy, must be destroyed without mercy or pity. Nevertheless, the people themselves will not utterly perish from off the earth, for God is yet mindful of His promises of salvation. Judah, however, did not recognize that God was its Maker and Former. Instead, it made and formed the idols which were its undoing.

12 And it shall come to pass in that day that the LORD will thresh out from the channel of the river unto the stream of Egypt, and ye shall be gathered one by one, O ye children of Israel.

13 And it shall come to pass in that day, that a great trumpet will be blown and those who are lost in the land of Assyria will come and those cast out in the land of Egypt, and shall bow down to the LORD, in the holy mountain, in Jerusalem.

Idolatry has led to the downfall of the theocratic nation. In bringing about that downfall God shows no mercy nor pity, for the city of Jerusalem must fall completely. Nevertheless, the judgment is but the prelude to blessing, for in that day when the calamities come upon the nation, the work of regathering will begin. It is

[40] Note the negative character of the expression and the prominence given to the negative in contrast with 1:4. *For NOT a people of discernment is it.* Apart from Jer. 23:20 *bi-nāh* is found only in Isaiah. The plural expresses intensity. The pronoun *hû'* also receives a certain amount of emphasis. Most naturally it would refer to Jacob and Israel.

difficult to ascertain precisely the reference to the phrase, *in that day*. Either it refers to the downfall of Jerusalem just mentioned, or else in a more general sense to the coming of the judgment that has been set forth throughout these chapters. It is difficult to decide, although, despite the difficulties that it involves, it possibly refers to the events related in the immediately preceding verses.

Continuing the figure of a tree, the prophet describes the purification by means of the figure of one striking the tree and so shaking the fruit from off its branches.

Isaiah describes the regathering by means of the figure of threshing grain.[41] His language, however, is quite difficult. The verb employed may be used of the beating off or knocking off of olives from the olive tree. If that is the correct figure, then the prophet pictures the regathering under the figure of a tree, the berries of which are beaten or knocked off. But the verb may also refer to the beating out of the grain from the ears. If this is the figure, and probably it is, then the land of Palestine would seem to be the threshing floor on which the beaten-out grains fall.

Difficulty, however, is caused by the following word, *shibboleth*, which is open to two interpretations. On the one hand, if it refers to the ear of grain, it is tempting to take it with the preceding verb and to understand the reference in the second sense mentioned above, namely, the beating out of corn from the grain. The word may refer, however, to the flowing or course of a stream; and in connection with the following *river* this is quite a natural interpretation here. It seems best to take it in this latter sense.

On the whole, the figure is probably to be understood as follows. The Lord will beat so that the fruit or grain falls, and the regathering may then be compared to such a falling. This will be done so as to regather men so that they will occupy the once promised land in its widest extent. The prophet now proceeds to describe that extent.

41 Among the prophets *ḥbṭ* occurs only here and in Isa. 28:27. For the figure generally, cf. Isa. 17:5 and note the similarities in vocabulary. In Deut. 24:20 the root is used of the beating of an olive tree so that the olives will fall off; in Judg. 6:11 and Ruth 2:17, however, it refers to the beating out of grains of corn. The latter seems to be in view, for in speaking of the beating of an olive tree Isaiah used *nā-qap*, e.g., 17:6; 24:13. The prep. *min* indicates the sphere in which the beating is to occur. It is to be in the district from the flowing of the river unto the brook of Egypt, and not in the lands of the exile. Hence, the emphasis here is not upon a return from exile, but upon an ingathering which results from a judgment occurring within the realm of Israelitish dominion in its widest extent (cf. Gen. 15:18; 1 Kings 8:65).

channel of the river unto the stream of Egypt—The stream or river of Egypt is without doubt the Wadi el-Arish, and the river is the Euphrates. These terms do not describe the land into which the people are to be regathered, but rather the places from which they will be brought. Assyria and Egypt are the two great representatives of the powers that took Judah captive. From Assyria and from Egypt, therefore, the people will again be regathered.

Isaiah closes the verse with a tender address to the sons of Israel.[42] The gathering will not be a mighty influx, but one by one. The Hebrew may be rendered, *with respect to one, one.*[43] That is, in the return of the people the greatest exactness and care will be shown. Each one is of importance, and the work of regathering will not cease until each one comes to Jerusalem.

13 By means of a different figure Isaiah now sets forth the same truth as that contained in the previous verse. Thus, he closes this section with a note of hope. Here he places the emphasis upon the regathering of God's dispersed people; the sign for this regathering will be the blowing of a trumpet. The verb is impersonal, *in that day there shall be blown (one will blow) on a great trumpet.*[44] Such figurative language symbolizes the call for return. We are not to conceive of a literal trumpet being blown. If, therefore, the blowing of the trumpet is a figurative expression, may we not consistently assume that the description of the regathering is also figurative, intended to describe a coming together unto God in Christ, and not an actual return to the mount of holiness in Jerusalem?

As a result of the trumpet's being blown, those who are lost will be regathered. The description is interesting. Earlier, Moses had taught the Israelite to say when he appeared at the sanctuary, "An Aramaean ready to perish *was* my father" (Deut. 26:5a). Now,

---

42 *and ye*—emphatic, in contrast to those who will perish in the beating or will have been carried away by the storm (v. 8).

43 Cf. Eccl. 7:27. The form *'a-ḥad* is not always const., and often stands in close connection with a following word; cf. Gen. 48:22; 2 Sam. 17:22; Zech. 11: 7. The form *'e-ḥād* stands for original *'aḥ-ḥad*. The combined forms are to be regarded as one word.

44 Dillmann remarks that the reference is to be taken literally *(eigentlich)*, and not merely as a picture *(blosses Bild)*, and appeals to the article and adjective *(wegen des Artikels u, des Beisatzes g r o s s)*. But the word *trumpet* is anarthrous, and the adjective simply indicates that the trumpet's sound is to be heard far and wide; cf. Isa. 5:26; Zech. 10:8; Hos. 11:10; Isa. 11:12; Zech. 9:14.

there must, as it were, be a new beginning for the nation.[45]
Through the punishment of the exile, the nation has ceased to be
the theocracy. It now is a perishing nation, but this perishing
nation will be regathered. Gesenius thinks that the term *the lost
ones* is equivalent to exile, and calls attention to the old German
usage of *Elend* for *Verbannung*. In itself, however, the term need
not have that connotation. Are we to think of the words "An
Aramaean ready to perish" as describing someone in exile or even
about to go into exile? The word refers here to one who is
without God, who had been separated from Him, and in that sense
banished. At the same time, those here described as lost are those
who will be cast into exile.

Isaiah mentions the places of banishment, namely, Egypt and
Assyria. It is well to note that he speaks of Assyria, for she was the
power that in his day constituted the severe threat to the theocracy.[46] The two words that describe the dispersed, namely, *lost* and
scattered, are used elsewhere of cattle, thus, "Woe be unto the
pastors that destroy and scatter the sheep of my pasture! saith the
LORD" (Jer. 23:1; cf. also 50:6; Ezek. 34:12-16). Egypt and Assyria
are mentioned inasmuch as they were the two great powers that
had held the people of God captive and away from the land of
promise. As long as the people were under the domination of
Assyria and Egypt they could not see the realization of the promise.

It is necessary to state the purpose of the regathering. It is that
the dispersed ones may worship the Lord; it is for the purpose of
accomplishing something spiritual, not that the Jews may establish
a political state in Palestine. This worship is to be conducted in
the mount of holiness in Jerusalem. Isaiah reflects upon his earlier
usages, in 24:23, and 25:6, 7, and 10. This is the great and central
purpose of the return. The first thing to be accomplished, indeed,
the purpose of the entire ingathering, is that the dispersed ones
may worship the Lord in Jerusalem. In the light of this description
it would seem that the verse refers, not primarily to the exile, but
to the return of sinners in Jesus Christ. It is in Him that God has

[45] *they that are lost*—the word is used of lost sheep, Jer. 23:1; 50:6; Ezek. 34:
4ff.; Ps. 119:176; 1 Sam. 9:3, 20.

[46] Those who deny this passage to Isaiah point out that the term *Assyria*
may be used of Babylonia and Persia (Ezra 6:26). This is true, but need not be
assumed here. Certainly the designations Assyria and Egypt admirably fit
Isaiah's day. *the dispersed ones*—cf. 11:12; 16:3ff. Merodach-baladan II is
proclaimed by Marduk, "This is the shepherd that brings the scattered together" (*mupaḫḫiru sepḫati*).

gathered into one His people scattered throughout the earth. "That in the dispensation of the fulness of times he might gather together in one all things in Christ, both which are in heaven, and which are on earth; even in him" (Eph. 1:10).

SPECIAL LITERATURE ON ISAIAH 24—27

Rudolf Smend, *"Anmerkungen zu Jes. 24–27," ZAW*, Vol. 4, 1884, pp. 161-224. Smend holds that these chapters come from between 500-300 B.C. and probably from the fourth century. The hostile power is that of Alexander, and the city is neither Babylon nor Nineveh but a city of Moab.

Ernst Liebmann, *"Der Text zu Jesaia 24–27," ZAW*, Vol. 22, 1902, pp. 1-56, 285-304; Vol. 23, 1903, pp. 209-286; Vol. 24, 1904, pp. 51-104; Vol. 25, 1905, pp. 145-171. A thorough study of the versions.

A. H. van Zyl, "Isaiah 24–27; Their Date of Origin," in *New Light on Some Old Testament Problems (Papers read at 5th Meeting of Die O.T Werkgemeenskap in Suid-Afrika)*, 1962. A defense of the Isaianic authorship of these chapters.

Edward Robertson, "Isaiah xxvii 2-6," *ZAW*, Vol. 47, 1929, pp. 197-206. Holds that this passage has an Arabic basis.

P. Lohmann, *"Die selbständigen lyrischen Abschnitte in Jes. 24—27," ZAW*, Vol. 37, 1917-18, pp. 1-58.

M. J. Lagrange, *"Apocalypse d'Isaie (xxiv-xxvii)," RB*, Vol. 3, No. 2, 1894, pp. 200-231. Holds to the Isaianic authorship of these chapters.

W. Rudolph, *"Jesaja 24–27"* in *Beiträge zur Wissenschaft vom Alten Testament*, Leipzig, 1908.

SPECIAL NOTE ON ISAIAH 24—27

"Let it be once established that no human critics can determine *a priori* the measure of divine revelation granted to any prophet, and all possible grounds combine to vindicate Isaiah's authorship of ch. xxiv-xxvii, as demanded by its place in the book of Isaiah."

"The particular judgments predicted in the oracle against the nations (i.e., ch. xiii-xxiii), all flow into the last judgment as into a sea; and all the salvation which formed the shining edge of the oracles against the nations, is here concentrated in the glory of a mid-day sun" (Franz Delitzsch).

I. Unity of the Section

For the most part scholars adhere to the view that chapters 24—27 form a unit. As Maurer put it, *carmen efficiunt continuum*. Since the time of Duhm, however, doubts as to the unity of the section have more frequently been expressed.

Duhm made a distinction between oracle and later poetry, classifying as oracle 24:1-23; 25:6-8; 26:20–27:1, 12, 13, and as later poetry, 25:1-5, 9-11; 26:1-19, plus 25:12; 27:2-5.

According to Lindblom, apart from a few later insertions (*Zutaten*) we have to do with two parallel rows of poems. In one of these emphasis falls upon the end time, world judgment, and the kingdom of God, in the other upon contemporary historical events, the destruction of a heathen world city, and the present condition of the community in Judea. Lindblom thus aligns himself with those who have divided the "apocalypse" into apocalyptic oracles and noneschatological songs.[47] In the "apocalypse" we have, he thinks, a series of eschatological poems, a series of songs of praise or rejoicing, three smaller glosses, and a popular lamentation (26:15-19).

In distinction to this R. H. Pfeiffer thinks that there is no proof that the hymns were not an integral and original part of the "apocalypse." His argument is that most of the later apocalypses are characterized by chaotic arrangement.[48]

In 26:1 there is explicit mention of song (*this song*). Possibly 25:1ff. may also be designated a song, for it involves a change of person and contains the thought of praise, *I shall praise thy name*. This section may not be a formal song, but it is at least a lyrical section.[49] In the exposition proper it has been pointed out that the verb עַנּוֹת in 27:2 is to be taken in the sense "afflict" rather than in the sense "sing."

It thus becomes difficult to distinguish sharply between the "songs" and the narrative. Says Umenhofer: "The relation of the songs to the narrative is one of naturalness and not abruptness. The songs are not to be conceived of as interpolations that haphazardly interrupt the progress of thought, but rather as reflections upon the narrative, expressive of great feeling and hope. There is no need to disjoin the two classes of passages and then invent a theory as to how they were combined. The best explanation of the entire section is to accept it as originally being a whole, since there is no evidence to the contrary as respects its historical transmission" (*op. cit.*, pp. 3, 4). With this conclusion we find ourselves in agreement.[50]

II. Authorship of the Section

Modern scholarship is nearly unanimous in denying this section to

---

[47] *Op. cit.*, p. 62.
[48] *Op. cit.*, p. 443.
[49] Cf. the excellent discussion of the unity of this section in the unpublished thesis of Kenneth Howard Umenhofer, *An Interpretation of Isaiah 24–27*, May 1961.
[50] Gray, who regards the so-called songs as separate from the narratives, nevertheless asserts that they are not far from the narratives in point of time, which, he thinks, was the postexilic period.

Isaiah, and in ascribing it to a postexilic period. Gray has stated the case for this position as well as any, and we may profitably consider his arguments.

A. The general condition of the people points to a postexilic date. Gray acknowledges that definite and particular references are elusive, but asserts that general conditions are clear and significant. Among these he appeals to (1) the helpless condition of the Jews awaiting deliverance; (2) political dependence; (3) no king, but the priesthood as highest rank; (4) the people an object of reproach, scattered throughout the earth. Even the passage in which reference is made to Assyria is characterized by lateness of circumstances, language, and ideas (27:13).

B. The ideas expressed in these chapters also point to the postexilic period, and probably to a very late part of it. Indeed, Gray thinks that these ideas are so advanced that he wonders how any part of the prophetic canon can be late enough to contain them. Among these ideas are (1) the well-established belief in the resurrection of individual Israelites (26:19); (2) the prediction of the abolition of death (25:8); (3) the idea of the imprisonment of the heavenly host (24:22); (4) Yahweh's visible enthronement in Zion (24:23); (5) the picture of the nations as violators of the eternal covenant, and certain other conceptions supposed to appear in "Deutero"-Isaiah.

C. The style and language of the section are said to be certainly postexilic. Gray describes this style as that of apocalypse. There are also peculiarities of vocabulary and one or two of syntax. The constant use of paronomasia and even of rhyme is said also to indicate non-Isaianic authorship.

It will be necessary to subject these assertions and claims to examination. In the first place there is the assertion that the general condition of the people as portrayed in these chapters points to a postexilic date. Gray appeals to 25:1-4, 9; 26:5-12, 16-18; 27:7 as showing that the Jews were in need, waiting for Yahweh's marvelous deliverance.

Drechsler believes that the prophecy finds a fulfillment at the time of Hezekiah and the deliverance from Sennacherib. The long reign of Ahaz, with its attendant disasters, is over, and a good king is on the throne. It is a time of thanksgiving and of praising God. For our part, however, we are unable to accept such a local and restricted application of the prophecy. It must be remembered that the section begins with *hinneh* followed by a participle, and so is probably to be understood as pointing to the future. We would interpret as follows. In chapters 24—27 the prophet sums up the prophecies concerning the nations which appeared in 13—23. Not only does he sum them up, but provides, as it were, a capstone to them, revealing what their ultimate issue is to be. A judgment is to come, by which judgment the prophet has in mind the calamity of the exile and postexilic periods; and this judgment is to be followed by the salvation of the Messianic age. The chapters thus agree well with the general tenor of prophecy.

With this brief statement before us we may now examine its defense, and this can best be done by considering first the arguments for a postexilic date which Gray has adduced. With respect to the claim that the general conditions depicted are those of the exilic and postexilic periods, we may note that to a certain extent this is true. It is not consistently true, however. Furthermore, thanksgiving is given to God not for return from the exile but for spiritual salvation.[51]

25:1-4 is a beautiful prayer of the prophet in which with remarkably Isaianic language, he exalts God for His wondrous deliverance. There is not a word in the passage to support Gray's view that the speaker is the Jewish community, now oppressed by some undefined power. The speaker speaks as though the deliverance has already been accomplished. It is an ideal situation, similar to that in chapter 12, in which the prophet describes God's wondrous deeds as already having been accomplished. The heart of the prophet's cause for rejoicing lies in the fact that the city, representative of the oppressing kingdom of man, has been destroyed. Either this, in which case the unnamed city is to be regarded as Babylon, or else the city is mentioned to show that the general order of events has been changed. Likewise, in verse 9, there is an appeal for rejoicing and being glad in the salvation which Yahweh has accomplished. As in general in prophetic teaching, "return" or "deliverance" from bondage has reference to the Messianic salvation, so also here.

In 26:5-12 the reasons for rejoicing are given in greater detail, and the additional factor of the righteousness of God's judgments is stressed. In vv. 16-18 the desperate plight of the nation is brought to the fore. All of this shows that the exile is indeed the heart of the judgment, but it does not follow that the passage could only have been written after the exile.

It would be difficult to prove, however, that 26:13 showed that the people were actually politically dependent. Included in the Ba'alim of the verse we are probably to understand Egypt, and then the peoples

51 24:17, 18 occurs again in Jer. 48:43f. with minor variations. At first sight it might be argued that the editor of 24—27 inserted these verses from Jeremiah. This falls to the ground, however, for it is not characteristic of Isaiah to quote other prophets. Jeremiah, however, is noted for just this trait. Thus, Jer. 48: 16ff. appears to have been formed after Isa. 13:22 and 14:4-6, and Jer. 48:18 after Isa. 47:1. (". . . eine solche Art und Weise der Entlehnung" says Delitzsch, "ist in der jes. Sammlung ohne Beispiel.") Compare also Jer. 49:7-22 with Obad. 1-9.

of Canaan. This verse (see exposition) has no particular reference to the exile.

In the exposition on 24:2 we have pointed out that this verse does not imply a time such as the exile when there was no king. And 25: 8, which speaks of the reproach of God's people that lay upon all the world, may include the exile, but in a deeper sense, refers to the reproach that Israel's sin has brought upon it.

Before considering the contents of 24—27 more fully, it is necessary to note more carefully the relationship that it sustains to the earlier prophecies. It would seem that in 24:1-3 Isaiah is taking up again the thought of 7:18-20, and that these two passages, presenting different aspects of the same subject, complement one another. 24:1-13 says nothing about the origin of this catastrophe, and the calamity with which it closes; for knowledge of this we turn to chapter 7. On the other hand, from chapter 7 we do not learn of the end of this punishment, but chapter 24 speaks abundantly of this. Also 7:18 shows that the beginning of the punishment is with God's summoning Egypt and Assyria; but according to 27:13 it concludes with His calling home the dispersed from Egypt and Assyria.[52]

24—27 also sustain a relationship to chapters closer at hand as well as to chapter 7 and the preceding. In 22:1-14 Isaiah complains about Jerusalem's luxurious life; the judgment of 24:1-13 comes partly because of this sin (cf. 24:8; 22:2). In 22:1-14 Isaiah also condemned seeking deliverance through material means; in 24—27 Isaiah stresses the only hope of deliverance. (Compare 27:11b with 22:11b.) In 22: 14 the power of death is shown, but in 25:8 death is swallowed up. 22:4, 12 proclaims a time of crying, but 25:8 declares its end.[53]

Note also the relationship between chapter 19 and 24—27. There is first a mention of the events through which the judgment comes (compare 19:1-4 with 24:1-3), then a description of the situation as it will be in consequence of those events (19:5-15 with 24:4-13). Linguistically,

---

[52] 24:1-3 corresponds with 7:18-20, reasons Drechsler; the events are the same, but the direction in which they lead us is different. The same may be said of 7:19, 20 in comparison with 27:12. The condition of desolation, intended in 7:21-25 for Judah, in 27:10, 11 is taken up again, and 27:2-6 shows that Israel's condition will be quite different. In 24:4-13 as in 7:21-25, wine plays a principal role. Compare also 27:4 with 7:23-25, and 27:10 with 7:21-25.

It will be well to continue Drechsler's argument. Through 7:17-25, he claims, we see the connection with earlier prophecies. Thus 24:1-13 takes up 6:11-13. The conditions presupposed in 24:1-13 are those anticipated in 5:5ff. Compare in particular 24:7-9 with 5:10-14. 24—27 also form the opposite to chap. 5 in that they picture the restoration from depravity to former glory. In this respect compare 27:2-6 with 5:1-7. Comparison may also be made between 24:1-13 and 3:1—4:1, and compare 24:4, 5 with 4:5, 6.

[53] Compare also 26:19-21 with 22:1-14.

compare 19:3 with 24:1 (the root *bqq*), *the enumeration* in 24:2 and 19:2, 3b, and the description in 19:5-15 with 24:4-13; and also note נאנח, אמלל, אבל, נבל in 24:3-13 and אמלל, קמל, in 19:5-10. עצות of 25:1 takes up 19:12, and compare פחד in 24:17 with 19:16, 17. The first half of 19 is taken up in 24:17-23, and the second half in 25:3 and 25:6-8.

The prophecy of Moab (chapters 15, 16) is also taken up in 25:10-12, and these two should be carefully compared.[54]

With respect to Gray's contention that the ideas of this section betray a postexilic date, the following may be said. This section is characterized by certain ideas which do not appear explicitly elsewhere in Isaiah, namely the thought of death and its conquest in 25:8 and the resurrection, 26:19 (cf. v. 14). "In this category we may also place the insight into the world of spirits, 24:21, 22." But death, as mentioned in 25:8, is simply the bringing together in one of the entire content of all the preceding announcements of judgment. The same is true of the mention of resurrection. (See Gray, *Com. in loc.*) These thoughts fit in well as the climax or capstone of Isaiah's teaching up to this point. To trace the history of an idea is a very difficult thing. How can anyone prove that the idea of the resurrection of individuals was not known in Isaiah's day? Penna rightly asks whether it is logical to affirm that the idea of the resurrection of the body is not found in the Old Testament because the Sadducees of our Lord's day denied it? Gray's argumentation is based upon the particular theory of the development of Israel's religion that was dominant in his day.[55] He wonders how any of the prophetic canon can be late enough to contain these ideas, for he thinks they belong to the time of Daniel, which he dates at about 165 B.C. or later. Daniel, however, as we have shown elsewhere, comes from the 6th century B.C.[56]

Lastly, as to the style of chapters 24–27, there is no reason why it cannot be that of Isaiah. In many respects it resembles that of the second part of Isaiah and differs from passages which certain critics are willing to attribute to the "genuine" Isaiah. There is a plethora of paronomasia, rhyme, antithesis, repetition of words, and some

---

[54] Without seeking to develop Drechsler's argument further we simply present here a few more comparisons with preceding passages: 17:6 with 24:13; 21:2b with 24:16b; 13:10 with 24:23; 9:5, 6 and 16:5 with 24:23b; 4:2, 5 and 11:10 with 24:23b; 9:5; 11:2, 5; 23:8, 9; 19:12, 17 and 14:24-27 with 25:1; 17:1 and 23:13 with 25:2; 13:11 and 19:4 with 25:3.

[55] Robert Dick Wilson, *Studies in the Book of Daniel*, Second Series, New York, 1938, pp. 124-127.

[56] Cf. *The Prophecy of Daniel*, 1949, and in particular the excellent works of Robert Dick Wilson, *Studies in the Book of Daniel*, First Series, New York, 1917; Second Series, New York, 1938.

words which only occur later; but the style is certainly purer than the Hebrew of the postexilic period. Penna, for example, points out that Aramaisms are few, and that, with the possible exception of *raza* (24: 16), Persian words are missing. Lindblom even speaks of a conscious imitation of Isaiah (*Nachbildung*) and S. B. Frost (*Old Testament Apocalyptic,* 1952, pp. 143ff.) holds that these chapters were written by a man who deliberately posed as Isaiah. Hence, he labels them Pseudo-Isaiah. In the notes we have called attention to the presence of a specific Isaianic vocabulary in these chapters. The presence of these words is a strong support for Isaianic authorship. Let it be noted also that Isaiah did delight in paronomasia, and in these chapters he engages in it more than elsewhere, because these chapters form the climax of all that has preceded. Remove these chapters from their preceding context and they hang in the air without meaning. At the same time what has gone before is then without conclusion. In the deepest sense, these chapters belong to Isaiah, who goes on, as Delitzsch says, "from glory to glory." The whole cycle, as Delitzsch further remarks, "is so thoroughly Isaiah's in its deepest foundation, and in a hundred points of detail, that it is most uncritical to pronounce the whole to be certainly not Isaiah's simply because of these peculiarities."[57]

III. The Nature of the Section

According to many modern scholars chapters 24—27 are to be regarded as an apocalypse. Whether this is the case or not depends upon our definition of apocalyptic. It will not do to appeal merely

---

[57] In the fourth edition of his work Delitzsch unfortunately modified this position, asserting that the contents of these chapters must be referred to post-Isaianic times. Their author was a disciple of Isaiah's who here surpasses his master. But it is strange, thinks Delitzsch, that tradition has been so careless as to let this prophet's name sink into oblivion. We would agree that it certainly is strange. But is the memory of the prophets due to mere tradition, or are the prophetical writings the Word of God? Delitzsch has here fallen far from the high position that characterized the earlier edition of his commentary. At the same time he still holds that the words of this section contain nothing later than the Assyrian period, the prophecy nowhere passes beyond the political horizon of Isaiah's own time, and these chapters are the finale to chapters 13—23 in the strictest sense of the word.

Penna thinks that the section was the work of a prophet who could be called an enthusiast of Isaiah, and who admired his style and vocabulary, and that it probably came from Jerusalem about 539 B.C. He does not make out a vigorous case for this, but merely remarks that the historical background is different (*risulta assai diverso*) from that presupposed by the true Isaiah. Likewise his vague and yet so emphatic manner is different from the great prophet. An editor placed it where it is as a fitting conclusion of the oracles against the nations. The linguistic similarities led him to do this.

to the etymology of the word.[58] On the other hand agreement as to what actually constitutes apocalyptic is difficult to obtain. We may distinguish between the literary and religious traits which are often said to constitute apocalyptic.[59] Among the literary traits are pseudonymity, symbolism, rewritten history, written visions. It is, of course, not possible to separate these literary traits entirely from the religious ones. The religious traits include vision as a mode of revelation, esoterism, abundance of symbolism.[60]

If we read 24—27 however, we note that pseudonymity is entirely lacking.[61] The writer does not take some figure of old and make him the recipient of angelic revelations. Nor do these chapters present themselves as revelations to a select group of initiates, nor as containing hidden secrets preserved by angels. For that matter there is nothing in these chapters that can specifically be identified as visionary, such as is true of portions of Daniel, Ezekiel, and Zechariah. Some symbols are present, it is true, but a comparison with Enoch or the Apocalypse of Baruch or some similar work shows how completely diverse they are. There is symbolism, but historical names also appear. Nor are the other supposed elements of apocalyptic present. Isaiah 24—27 is true prophecy, sustaining an integral relationship to the prophecies that preceded it. Only understood thus can it be interpreted properly.

The City of Isaiah 24—27

Within the compass of these chapters there is mention of a city that is destroyed, but it is not named. What city is intended? Is it Babylon, Jerusalem, Nineveh, Tyre, Sidon, Samaria, Carthage? All these have been proposed as well as others also, including Rome. Some have interpreted the city symbolically, as the city of evil or a personification of Satan.

The city is designated both 'ir and qiryah. It is an exalted city (26:5), inhabited by rejoicers who love wine (24:7-9). The inhabitants are haughty (25:2). It is a brave city (25:2; 27:10). It has a robust people (25:3) which considered it impregnable. It is razed to the ground (26:5) and left desolate (27:10). It is the city of chaos (24:10),

---

58 Cf. the discussion in Umenhofer, *op. cit.*, pp. 13ff.

59 Cf. George E. Ladd, "Apocalypse, Apocalyptic," Baker's *Dictionary of Theology*, 1960, pp. 51-2.

60 Lindblom lists transcendentalism, mythology, cosmological orientation, pessimistic treatment of history, dualism, division of time periods, the doctrine of two ages, playing with numbers, pseudo-ecstasy, artificial claims to inspiration, pseudonymity, mysteriousness. Cf. also H. H. Rowley, *The Relevance of Apocalyptic*, London, 1944, p. 23.

61 Umenhofer remarks that "it stands in the context of a work whose author is identified as Isaiah the prophet" (*op. cit.*, p. 18).

where animals pasture (27:10). God is to be praised for its destruction (24:14ff.) In accomplishing its overthrow God has manifested His justice (26:7ff.; 27:11), His faithfulness to His promises (25:1), and His zeal for His people (26:11).

More than this, one is not warranted in saying. The prophecy is vague in its references to the city. In the overthrow of the city, probably a representative of the power of man in opposition to God, God has triumphed gloriously.

III. True Deliverance Is Found Not in Egypt But in the Lord (28:1 — 35:10)

A. THE LORD'S PURPOSE (28, 29)

1. Samaria Ripe for Judgment (28:1-29)

1 Alas! the crown of the pride of the drunkards of Ephraim, and the fading flower, the ornament of his beauty, which is on the head of the valley of fatness, those smitten down with wine.

2 Behold! there is to the Lord a strong and mighty one, like a storm of hail, a destroying tempest, like a storm of mighty rushing waters, he brings it to the ground with the hand.

3 With the feet will be trodden the crown of the pride of the drunkards of Ephraim.

4 And there shall be the fading flower the glory of his beauty, which is upon the head of the fat valley, like the first ripe fruit, before it is summer, which he that sees it sees, and while it is yet in his hand he swallows it.

1 In preparing for the first of the great historical points about which his prophecies cluster, Isaiah had spoken of peace and blessing, for this point (chapter seven, with the promise of the Messiah over against the dark background of the rise of Assyria) was essentially one that would result in blessing. In preparing for the second great historical point (the invasion of Sennacherib and the reign of Hezekiah), Isaiah speaks of woe and desolation. The first point centered about the reign of Ahaz and the blessing of the Messiah. A wicked king was upon the throne, and against the clouds of gloom the promise of hope was uttered. Exactly the reverse obtained when Hezekiah was king. A good king was on the throne, but there was no promise, only the oncoming of the Assyrian king, and the portent of doom. Hence the prophet's emphasis upon woe and desolation.

This prophecy, therefore, together with the following five chapters begins with the word "woe." As is known (cf. 4:1) the word may possess slightly different nuances; but here what is most prominent is the thought of impending disaster. Even in this verse the nuance in the word "alas" is not lacking, but what the prophet above all else wishes to do with this mournful-sounding word is to call attention to the tragedy that is about to come upon God's people. With this chapter we pass to the second part of the second great section of the prophecy. Until this point, the prophecies, for the most part, had clustered about events of the lifetime of Ahaz. Judah was in the center of Isaiah's thought, for the great threat posed by the presence of Tiglath-pileser III was one which in time would bring about the downfall of the theocracy.

Now, however, we have come to the time of Hezekiah. The fatal appeal to Tiglath-pileser has already been made, and Judah has begun to suffer the effects of that appeal. Israel also had suffered and Samaria alone remained, rejoicing in her independence and boasting in the excellence of her position. A different atmosphere prevails. May there not now be the possibility of escape from Assyria by way of appeal to Egypt? It is that question which dominates Hezekiah's period until the oncoming Assyrian will destroy the possibility of such an appeal. In Egypt there is no hope; indeed the only hope remaining is the Lord, and in so far as Judah turns from the Lord, she will certainly perish. There was indeed somewhat of a revival of the true religion during Hezekiah's reign, but it was a revival coupled with the desire to enlist the aid of Egypt. In order that the nation may learn the true nature of the condition in which it finds itself, it must be made aware of the fact that woe hangs over it. First of all, Judah must learn that she is like Samaria and that she too must be humbled. Micah, who prophesied during this period, also began his prophecies with reference to Samaria.

Samaria, therefore, has not yet fallen. She remains as *the crown of the pride of the drunkards of Ephraim*. Here is a heaping up of genitives that is quite significant.[1] Samaria is a crown of pride and also a crown of the drunkards of Ephraim. Some of the older expositors thought that there was an allusion to the custom of wearing garlands and crowns at feasts, and that for that reason the people are called drunkards. It is far more likely, however, that the

---

1 *Crown of pride*, i.e., proud crown. Gesenius asserts that the Hebrews knew the custom, also prevalent among the Greeks and Romans, of wearing crowns at banquets (Wisdom 2:7, 8).

epithet "crown" has a topological reference, for Samaria was situated on a hill, which is thought to have suggested a crown. Possibly the designation may have been a favorite one of the inhabitants themselves. The Ephraimites were proud of their city and boasted in the beauty of its location. Modern excavations have confirmed the biblical description of the luxury and elegance which characterized the city (cf. Amos 3:1ff.; 4:1; 6:1).

Why, however, are the inhabitants designated drunkards? Among expositors Drechsler stands almost alone in asserting that the prophet is not speaking of actual drunkenness but of something far worse, namely, a pride that delights in the flesh and finds pleasure in trifles rather than in love to the Lord. Isaiah, thinks Drechsler, is not condemning licentiousness here or in verses 7 and 8. On the other hand, most expositors believe that Isaiah is speaking of actual drunkenness, for when we compare passages such as Amos 4:1; 6:1, 6 it seems clear that actual drunkenness was one of the more prevalent and prominent sins of Samaria.

the fading flower, the ornament of his beauty—Isaiah changes the figure, and now speaks of Samaria as a flower; it is, however, as his prophetical eye discerns, a flower that is about to fade or fall. Thus he alludes to the imminency of the disaster to come upon Samaria. Samaria, like a beautiful flower, nevertheless has within itself the seeds of death and is ready to fade. This flower, Samaria, about to fade, is the ornament of Ephraim's beauty, i.e., the ornament that makes Ephraim beautiful. We may bring out the force of the entire clause by rendering, *the flower of its beautiful ornament is a fading one.* The alliteration between *tzitz* and *tzevi* is striking.

The second half of the verse connects with the first in that the relative pronoun goes back to "crown" and "flower." We may translate, *the crown of pride and the flower which are upon the head of the valley, etc.* Isaiah calls the hill upon which Samaria was situated a head, a fitting description of the hill rising above the surrounding valleys, a hill which bore a crown, even the city itself. The valley is one of *fatnesses*, i.e., a fat valley, one that produced luxuriously.[2]

2 גיא—the following pl. is intensive, *fatnesses*, i.e., the *very fat* valley. Note that a gen. here follows the absolute. So also 1Q. Delitzsch points out that the logical relation overrules syntactical usage, and adduces Isaiah 32:13 and 1 Chron. 9:13. But we cannot rule out the possibility that in Biblical Hebrew a gen. might follow a noun in the abs. state. Cf. Ezek. 6:11; 45:16; 46:19; 2 Chron. 15:8; Josh. 8:11. Note also the Egy. *tph.t wr.t iwnw, the great holes of Heliopolis.* Cf. Gordon, *Ugaritic Handbook,* I, p. 44.

those smitten down with wine—In the translation this phrase does not connect with the preceding. It may be, however, that the phrase is really preceded by a noun in the genitive, so that we should render, *the valleys of the fatnesses of those smitten down with wine.*[3] The syntax is difficult, but if this is the meaning, then Isaiah is declaring that Samaria was on the top of valleys that produced luxuriously, and that the produce of these valleys went to those who were smitten down by wine. Isaiah's language is vivid, and contains a warning against the excessive use of wine. Just as a man hammers an anvil, so wine hammers a man till he falls down. Alexander quotes Gill: "smitten, beaten, knocked down with it as with a hammer, and laid prostrate on the ground, where they lie fixed to it, not able to get up."

Although the prophet does not specifically mention Samaria by name, it is clear that he has that city in mind. The luxurious situation and the ease with which the fat valleys produced resulted in a materialistic attitude, a love of ease and luxury, so that in reality Samaria was but a flower about to fade.

2 Having set forth its true condition and character, the prophet now proceeds to state what will happen to Samaria. By means of the arresting word *Behold!* he directs attention to the fact that the Sovereign One is in control even of this situation and that He possesses a strong and mighty one who will carry out His purposes with respect to Samaria. Luther and others have preferred to translate the first clause, *a strong and mighty one is from the Lord,* and there can be no objection to this upon grammatical grounds. It does seem better, however, to take the preposition in its usual meaning, and to regard the clause as asserting that the Sovereign Lord possesses a strong and mighty one who will do His bidding.

Most commentators find here a reference to Assyria, either in the person of its king, or as represented by its armies. In either case, the thought is essentially the same. Whatever be the precise signifi-

---

[3] Drechsler describes Samaria as the beautiful (Amos 3:15), the rich (Hos. 9:6; 12:9; 13:15), the finely civilized (Amos 3:12, 15; 6:4-6), the strong city (17:3). For classical parallels cf. Plautus *Cas.* 3, 5, 16; Tibullus i.2.3; Martial iii.68.

As it stands *hᵃ-lú-mēy* is a gen. depending upon the abs. *šᵉ-mā-nim.* Possibly this word is abs., because it contains a secondary concept and circumscribes the adj. *fat; upon the head of the fat valley of those struck with wine.* Brockelmann, following Duhm, states that the relative is missing, § 82 e, but this is not necessary.

cance of the words "strong and mighty" they refer to an instrument which the Lord intends to use in the visitation upon Samaria. For the sake of emphasis Isaiah speaks of God as the Sovereign One (*ᵃdonay*). This is significant, for it makes clear that the God of Israel is the One who has at His disposal the armies of men. He is sovereign to protect His people, but He is also sovereign to punish them at His will.

like a storm of hail, a destroying tempest—By means of this comparison Isaiah seeks to represent the severity of the judgment. In this figure there is pictured the strength of the strong one and the might of the mighty one. The destroying power of a hailstorm is well known, and it is the element of destruction which characterizes this tempest. Isaiah had earlier spoken of the need of refuge from such storms (cf. 4:6 and 25:4).

like a storm of waters, mighty, rushing—Isaiah now employs a further comparison to emphasize the severity of what the Sovereign Lord will do to Samaria. The construction of the phrase is interesting—*like a storm, even waters, mighty, rushing*—and calls to mind Genesis 6:17, "Behold! I am about to bring the flood, even waters, etc." The allusion may perhaps serve to bring to the fore the catastrophic nature of the storm that God would send against Samaria. At the same time, by placing the word *waters* immediately after *storm,* Isaiah is enabled to stress the two adjectives, *mighty* and *rushing.*[4] In describing the tumult of the nation Isaiah had earlier spoken of *mighty waters* (17:12). Perhaps, therefore, he wishes to suggest that in the flood which is to overwhelm Samaria and bring about its destruction, there will be involved tumultuous nations.

he brings it to the ground with a hand—Although the verb is in the perfect, it is to be translated by the present, as in Amos 5:7.[5] The verb suggests the idea of casting to the ground, but the object is not stated, nor has it been mentioned earlier in the verse. At the same time, in the light of verse 1, it is clear that Samaria is intended. In this verse, however, the stress must fall upon the judgment itself, for that is the central theme.

The last phrase, *with a hand,* is difficult. Does it merely suggest the ease with which the city is overthrown? Or is *hand* a synonym of power? This latter interpretation would fit in well with the

4 Cf. Akk. *šatapu,* to overflow.
5 The pret. is used of the certain and inevitable future, for Isaiah sees Samaria already brought low to the ground.

mention of mighty waters. Perhaps it is not possible to decide dogmatically between the two. Certainly the destruction of Samaria manifested power; at the same time, its destruction was accomplished merely by a hand. The length of the Assyrian attack against Samaria does not really constitute an objection to this latter interpretation.[6]

SPECIAL NOTE

Of interest is the contrast between verses 1 and 2 as far as arrangement is concerned. In the first verse in Hebrew there are three groups of four words each:

> *crown of the pride of the drunkards of Ephraim*
> *a flower fading is the ornament of his beauty*
> *valley of fatnesses, those smitten down of wine.*

Every member of these phrases is a noun or participle, and each of these complexes consists of two pairs of words, the second pair in the genitive relationship in dependence upon the first pair in such a way that the second group is really dependent upon the first word of the clause. Thus, the words *crown, flower,* and *valley* are the three words upon which the second member or group really depends in genitive relationship. At the same time, whereas in clause 1 there is a true construct relationship between the first and second group, in clause 2 the second group is really predicative to group one, and in clause 3 we apparently have an example of an absolute used in the genitive relationship. In verse 2 on the other hand, there is an assertion followed by a comparison, then a comparison followed by a principal sentence, thus giving a chiastic order to the arrangement of the sentence.

3 In continuing the description the prophet states that feet will destroy the city. This mention of feet seems to support the view that the preceding verse referred to the actual hand. A casting down was not sufficient. On the city that had been cast down the feet of the victorious soldiers will trample. This latter is a continuous act, whereas the casting down of the city was regarded as momentary.[7]

---

6 B has βίᾳ and this is followed by Saadia. König even translates *mit Gewalt,* and this is apparently the view of most. But Dillmann renders, *so gewaltige Kraft hat er, dass er durch einen Streich seiner Hand sie niederwirft.* Vitringa connects the words with the rain, *which he brings down with power.* The construction adopted in the translation is, however, more natural.

7 It is not necessary to assume that the 3 f. pl. is used for the singular. Rather it is employed in a collective sense. Note the *Patah* of the accented syllable, which is usual, and not due merely to pause. עטרת is not normally a

4 Isaiah now sums up his thought concerning Samaria, and in so doing employs expressions already used. "This flower which is about to fade." We may paraphrase his thought, "the ornament of Ephraim's beauty, which is upon the head of the valley of fatnesses is like a fig before the summer time comes. When one sees such a fig, while it is yet in his hand, he swallows it."[8] The fig harvest is in August. Sometimes, however, the figs ripen early. Should anyone see one of these ripened figs before the time of harvest had come, he would eagerly pick and immediately devour it. The point of the comparison lies in the rapidity with which Samaria is destroyed. Nahum employed a similar comparison to express rapidity, namely, that of the figs being shaken and falling into the mouth of the eater (Nah. 3:12). Here, however, the hand seems to hold and at the same time to cast into the mouth.

Thus, the announcement of Samaria's doom leaves no hope for the Ephraimites. Those who have received earth's luxurious produce, and who enjoy the gifts of God, but despise the Giver, may expect such gifts to be soon cut off.

5 In that day the LORD of hosts will become a crown of beauty and a diadem of beauty for the remainder of his people.

6 And for a spirit of judgment to him that sitteth over the judgment and for strength to them that turn war to the gate.

7 And also these through wine have gone astray and through strong drink have wandered, priest and prophet have gone astray through strong drink, they have been swallowed up from the wine; they have wandered from the strong drink; they have erred in vision; they have wavered in judgment.

8 For all the tables are filled with vomit, filth, there is no place.

---

collective, but is so construed here, hence the plural verb. Cf. also Ex. 1:10; Judg. 7:7; 1 Sam. 12:21, etc. It is the compound construction, which gives to the word its collective force. To change this word to the plural, as *BH* suggests, is not necessary.

8 *the flower of that which fails.* The adj. stands in the gen. after a noun in the const.; but cf. v. 1. *the first ripe fruit*—the *He* contains a *Mappiq* which should not be omitted. It is euphonic *Mappiq*, for the *He* is probably not a suffix.

סרחב—the verb usually follows this negative, but here there is an ellipsis of the verb; lit., *in the not yet (being) of summer.* הראה—cf. the common Ar. expression, *qa-la qâ-'i-lun.* The indefinite subj. is expressed by means of paronomasia between subj. and pred., lit., *which the seer sees it,* i.e., *which a person would see.*

5 When Samaria has fallen, then God's people will see what their true ornament and beauty is. The thought of this verse closely parallels that of 4:2ff., and the verse itself forms a contrast to verse 1. When the false object of pride has been removed through the sovereign work of the God of Israel, then it will appear that the LORD Himself, the Lord of hosts, will be the crown of glory. Unless the true glory can conquer and displace false glory, it is not actually true glory.

Isaiah slightly modifies the language of verse 1 in that he substitutes the word *tzevi* (beauty) for *ge'uth* (pride), for this latter word may possess an unfavorable connotation. Furthermore, by using *tzevi* he forms a striking alliteration with *tzephirath* (diadem). The use of alliteration and the prominence of the *tzu* and *tzf* sounds in the first part of this verse is striking.

We perhaps have warrant for rendering *diadem of beauty*.[9] There are thus two expressions, each consisting of two words, and each containing a construct relation, namely, "crown of beauty" and "diadem of beauty." Both are introduced by a preposition in Hebrew and so we should render, *the Lord will become a crown of beauty and a diadem of beauty.* Furthermore, both of these predicates refer to one subject, the Lord. In 4:2, on the other hand, with which this verse should be contrasted, there are two subjects, the "Sprout of the Lord" and the "fruit of the land." To each of these subjects there are two predicates, consisting of a single noun each. Both in 4:2 and here the difference in the manner of statement is due to what has preceded. Thus, verse 1 sets the form for the present verse, whereas in 4:2 it was set by 2:12-16 and by 3:18-22.

the remnant of his people—Here this phrase seems to have particular reference to those who remained after Samaria had fallen. The remnant therefore would be principally Judah, although it might also include any of Ephraim and the north who remained after Samaria's downfall. A passage such as 10:20-22 would seem to be applicable at this point.

6 Isaiah now proceeds to point out in some detail the manner in which the Lord will be the true beauty of His people. *and for a*

---

9 צפירת probably means *plait, chaplet, coronet,* a meaning attested by the ancient versions. The etymology, however, is still questionable. Cf. Judg. 7:3; Ezek. 7:7. Gesenius agrees with the "old Arabic rabbis" (*die alten arabischen Rabbinen*), who give the root meaning as *go about, surround,* hence, *turn about.*

spirit of judgment—The Masoretes have correctly placed an *Atnah* with the word *mishpat* (judgment), for the thought is complete in itself, and must be stressed by being set apart.[10] Not only does the Lord become a crown of beauty but He also becomes a spirit of judgment, and in so becoming reveals how He is also the crown and diadem of beauty. The language does not mean that God fills the judges with a spirit of judgment, but rather that He Himself becomes that Spirit of judgment. There is clear reflection upon 11:2. He who places upon the Messiah the sevenfold Spirit, will place Himself upon judges as the Spirit who brings forth true judgment. He thus gives to the judges both the power and the zeal to judge justly.

to him that sitteth over the judgment—A minor exegetical question arises as to whether the verse teaches an actual sitting on the judgment seat or simply a sitting for the purpose of judgment. In support of the latter, appeal is made to the usage of the words, "to sit upon," which seem to indicate purpose (cf. 1 Sam. 20:24; 30:24). The thought would then be that one is seated for the purpose of pronouncing judgment. On the other hand, there is the emphasis of Psalm 9:5, "Thou didst sit upon the throne as the righteous judge." It is difficult and perhaps not possible to decide decisively between these two. Indeed, they are not really to be divorced, for the one who sits upon the tribunal is the one who is there for the purpose of pronouncing judgment; and the one who sits to pronounce judgment is the one who is upon the tribunal. The reference is of course to the judge, for he could pronounce those decrees which affected the welfare of the people. Lack of justice in the court is a sign of a decadent condition, yet true judgment can only be pronounced by one who has received of God the Spirit of judgment.

and of power—The Lord who is the Mighty God (10:21) and who gives the spirit of power (11:2) now shows Himself as the true power to those that turn war at the gate.[11] The reference is to those who go forth against the adversaries and drive them out of

10 Dillmann, however, thinks that this is incorrect, and that *Atnah* should be with *ham-miš-pāṭ; BH* likewise.

11 מֹשִׁיבֵי—the first preposition may also govern this word.

שָׁעְרָה—The word is in pause, and the *He*, missing in 1Q, may be *He* locative. The *Qameṭz* appears in an accented syllable, followed by silent *Shᵉwa* under a guttural. T took the word in a partitive sense, ἀπὸ πύλης, as did also Syr. and Saadia, but the language does not permit this.

the field of battle, pursuing them back to the gate of the city from which they have gone forth. It is the gate of the enemy stronghold, and hence, the warriors who receive their strength from the Lord are such as are fighting defensive battles. They do not themselves go forth in battle to attack, but simply are enabled through God's power to resist and to turn back the approaches of the enemy. The false beauty had vanished in time of crisis; the true beauty, however, remains. In Judah there will be a true and righteous government, one thoroughly supported and strengthened by the Lord.

7 Isaiah now seeks to introduce a contrast between Judah and Samaria. The remnant of His people, to whom He would be a crown of beauty, had themselves gone astray through wine. The words, *and also these,* serve to point out the unity of this verse with what has preceded. The thought is that whereas Samaria, the pride of the Ephraimites, must perish, nevertheless the Lord will be a crown of beauty to the remnant of His people; and yet even the remnant is as drunken with wine as was Samaria. These are words of sadness; even those surviving the judgment are naught but drunkards.

through wine have gone astray—Wine is mentioned first and so emphasized as the cause for the people's staggering. Of interest is the use of the definite article, as though to point out the well-known object, wine. Yet in writing as he does, Isaiah is not condemning the use of wine as such. Wine in itself, the fruit of the vine, is a gift of God, to cheer the heart of man and God (cf. Judg. 9:13). God's gifts, however, can easily be perverted, and it is a perversion of which Isaiah is here speaking. In mentioning wine the prophet really intends us to understand drunkenness. Men have drunk wine to the point where they stagger, and it is this that the prophet condemns. The verb suggests reeling, or rolling and meandering to and fro in drunkenness.[12]

Isaiah then engages in a gradation. Through wine they stagger, through strong drink they wander. The sounds are exceedingly

---

[12] Accent *Milra,* whereas the normal accent should be *Milel.* This same peculiarity characterizes all the *Lamed-He* verbs of this verse and gives a strange emphasis to them. Alexander thinks the point of the verse is to indicate sensual indulgence "and the spiritual evils which it generates." Calvin takes the words "wine and strong drink" metaphorically, although literally in v. 1. His argument is that the people were like drunken men, and he would supply *as* before *through* wine. But linguistically this is not permissible.

expressive. "Isaiah's indignation is manifested in the fact, that in the words which he uses he imitates the staggering and stumbling of the topers; like the well-known passage, *Sta pes sta mi pes stas pes ne labere mi pes.* Observe, for example the threefold repetition of *shagu-taghu, shagu-taghu, shagu-paqu.*"[13] All these verbs the prophet places in the preterite, thus implying that drunkenness was a habit long entrenched in the office holders.

Earlier there had been a distinction between the entire nation and the "remnant of my people." Now, there is even to be a breaking down of the members of the remnant. Isaiah speaks first of the priest and the prophet as the two spiritual leaders, the priest representing the nation before God, and the prophet the official spokesman of God to the people. These two groups were intended to be the mediators between the nation and Jehovah. In the most sacred act of worship, the approach to God in the Temple, the priest was to officiate and present before God the claims and conditions of the people. On the other hand, when speaking officially, the prophet was the spokesman of God, in whose mouth God's very words had been placed (Deut. 18:18). When the prophet spoke, it was the actual words of God that he pronounced. Of all men, the priest and the prophet with their high responsibilities should have been humble and devoted before the Lord and have set an example of godliness to the nation. They, however, had stumbled through strong drink, and through wine they had been swallowed up. It is a vivid expression, the wine swallowing them up so that they are completely devoured thereby. In other words, they have become completely drunken, wholly the slaves of wine.

To make sure that there is no misunderstanding of his words, Isaiah goes on to say that they go astray on account of the strong drink. Even in the vision they stumble. In the very act of seeing or performing the work of a seer, the prophet does not give the people the message of God, but, due to his drunkenness, staggers. When the decisions of judgment are to be pronounced, he wavers. It is a sad picture. Both these entrusted officers of the theocracy fail. They have allowed wine and strong drink so to master them that they cannot give to the nation the messages that it needs. And

---

13 Delitzsch, *com. in loc.* The usage of the prepositions in this verse is interesting; *b* indicates means, *through* wine; i.e., because of wine, by means of wine, they became drunk; and *min* points to the consequence or effect, and may be rendered *as a result of.* Speiser (*JBL,* Vol. 82, Part 3, 1963, p. 304) renders *p⁰liliyāh* as reasoning.

if these spiritual leaders are of such a character, can we expect the people of the land to be better? The high task of proclaiming the Word of God was degraded, because the prophets loved wine rather than God. And the priests, honored in that they could pronounce those decisions which would be for the weal of the nation, wavered, for they were overcome with strong drink. It was a people ripe for judgment, a judgment pronounced by the Word of God, which lives and abides forever.

Drechsler calls attention to the structure of the verse, and we may translate his words as follows: "In Hemistich a the principal matter is that wine goes to their head; it is drunkenness that beclouds them. In Hemistich b on the other hand emphasis falls upon the degree of drunkennesses, 'staggering, going astray.' " Note that in the first part of the verse, the expressions "through wine," "through strong drink," precede the verbs; in the second half of the verse the verbs precede. The repetition of the verbs suggests that the drunkenness is constant, ever continuing.

8 In language of the strongest realism Isaiah now makes vivid the truth which he has just expressed. Although there have been many attempts to interpret the language of this verse in a figurative manner, such attempts do not satisfy. The language is strong and almost repulsive, but it makes clear the depraved condition of those who would be the spiritual leaders of the nation. As in 32:13, the introductory *ki* may be rendered *indeed,* somewhat like the *und zwar* of German. Thus, it singles out an instance of what the prophet has been saying. The tables upon which one should eat have become tables covered with the filth of the drunkards.[14]

To show that it is not merely an occasional instance of such filth that one must meet, Isaiah speaks of the tables being filled with vomit. We should probably take this word as a construct and render, *the vomit of filth,* i.e., filthy vomit. It is a sickening picture, and as though to give it a final emphasis Isaiah adds that there is no place remaining where cleanness may be found. This thought is expressed by the two short words, "without place." When such

---

14 Note omission of the definite article in the poetical, prophetical style, even though the noun may be regarded as definite. There is no warrant to refer this to tables connected with the temple worship. Some of the older interpretations were purely fanciful, thus, the tables are tribunals, covered with the filth and vomit of injustice (Grotius) ; schools in which false doctrine is taught (Vitringa) ; the filth of corrupt conversation (Cocceius) .

disgusting drunkenness is found, it speaks volumes as to the true
spiritual condition of the nation.

9 Whom shall he teach knowledge? and whom will he cause to perceive report? Those weaned from milk and those removed from
the breasts.

10 For rule upon rule, rule upon rule, line upon line, line upon line,
a little here, a little there.

11 For with stammering lips and with another tongue will he speak
to this people.

12 Unto whom he saith, this is the rest, give rest to the weary, and
this is quiet, but they were not willing to hear.

13 And the word of the LORD shall be to them, rule upon rule, rule
upon rule, line upon line, line upon line, a little here, a little
there, to the end they may walk and stumble backwards, and be
broken and be snared and be taken.

9 To stress the utter depravity of those to whom he speaks,
Isaiah introduces them as mocking him. Far from being a nation
devoted to God, Judah was a wicked nation, whose wickedness was
even willing to express itself in mockery of the prophet. These
words are difficult, but we would paraphrase the thought as follows:
"Whom does he think he is teaching; to whom does he think he is
explaining God's revelation? Let him search as widely as he wishes,
he will not find any who is in need of such teaching. Is it to those
who are weaned from milk and who are old and no longer need
their mother's breasts?" This question would then demand an
answer such as, "We know what we are doing, and we do not need
wisdom such as this prophet is seeking to give us."

A closer analysis of the language will be helpful. *Whom*—In the
Hebrew the interrogative is preceded by the accusative particle, as
in 6:8. The position of the word gives it emphasis, "let man look
where he will throughout the land, he will find no one who should
be the object of such teaching."[15] *knowledge*—Here is clear evidence that the ministry of Isaiah was regarded as teaching. In
declaring the word of God the prophet was instructing the nation
as to God's will. This was done by preaching, by the public
declaration of the words of God. At the same time the verb is made
as impersonal as possible. It places stress upon the act of teaching
rather than upon the one who does the teaching. To this teaching
there was a definite content, namely, the knowledge of the divine

15 אֵת appears before *mi*, but apparently never before *mah*.

274

will. In 11:2 the Spirit is described as the Spirit of knowledge. Here the word signifies information concerning the works and ways of God and the corresponding requirements which God makes of men. A true knowledge thus consists not merely in the understanding of what God's will is but also involves obedience to that will.

report—Lit., *that which has been heard* by divine revelation. As in 53:1, however, the word comes to signify what is proclaimed; it is thus the word of God, first heard by the prophet and declared by him to the nation.[16] Such a report, however must be understood, and to understand it one must be instructed. Hence, in his act of proclaiming the word of God, Isaiah was endeavoring to cause the nation to perceive the true meaning of what had been heard. Even the nation, in its mocking of him, recognized this as his true function.

weaned from milk—Those who had just been weaned from the milk of their mother's breasts would not be fit recipients for the preaching of divine wrath and judgment.[17] Why then does Isaiah preach to Judah? Does he think he is instructing those who have just been weaned? Does he regard us as children, mere babes, so the people reason, who need the simplest of instruction?

removed from the breasts—In effect, these words constitute a synonym to the preceding, and serve to strengthen the idea. The instruction which Isaiah is giving is for those who have just been weaned. For the Judahites, however, something else, we may assume, was needed. Marti may be entirely right when he suggests that other measures were regarded by them as necessary, for example, wise political actions. For these men of Judah, as Marti suggests, had no idea of the power of the "knowledge of God" in the prophetical sense (Hos. 4:1, 6; 5:4; 6:6).

10 Now the mockery of the despisers comes to clear expression, as they utter their drunken stammering, seeking to imitate and caricature the message of Isaiah. The introductory *For* serves to give a reason for what the prophet has just said in that it introduces an example of the attitude of the nation.

rule upon rule—In the light of Hosea 5:11 we must take this

---

16 Cf. the usage of the root in v. 22 and Jer. 49:14.

17 The passsive part. const., employed as a connective in the narrative and followed by a prep. which separates it from the *nomen rectus*. The same is true of the following const., which is a parallel to this one. Cf. also 9:2; 5:11; 30:18.

word *tzaw* as a genuine Hebrew word meaning, "rule" or "commandment." Possibly it is a shortened form of *mitzwah*.[18]
Drechsler cleverly renders it *"Bot"* instead of *"Gebot."* Probably,
considering the usage in Hosea, we are justified in saying that in
itself the word contains a slight tone of depreciation, for in Hosea
the word refers to the arbitrary commands of men as over against
the divine law. By using this shortened form, the people cast ridicule upon the teaching of the prophet. His laws are like little petty
annoyances, one command after another, or one joined to another,
coming constantly.

line upon line—Lit., plumbline. The use is figurative, for the
word is the practical equivalent of the preceding, *rule upon rule.*
These words form a striking assonance, and it is a characteristic
device of Isaiah to employ sounds for the purpose of producing a
particular artistic effect (cf. also 18:2, 7). Here the prophet wishes
to bring to the fore individual laws, and yet to show that these
individual laws form an unbearable whole, a deluge, as it were,
of irritating precepts. This he does by the use of monosyllabic
words, by the repetition of the same word, and by a suitable paronomasia.

a little here, a little there—Such was the impression which Isaiah's teaching made. The nation received no coherent picture, did
not understand his proclamation in its fullness, but merely regarded it as incoherent, disparate bits of instruction cast here and
there. Wherever one turned he encountered the prophet's instruction, but he had no clear idea of the meaning and force of that
instruction. What he heard seemed to him to be only broken bits.
Some have thought that actually only bits of words were heard.

[18] The Syriac, however, rendered *tibtô 'al tibtô wtibô 'al tibô,* thus deriving
tzaw from *tzô'āh* and *qaw* from *qî'* of the eighth verse. B gives a strange
rendering: θλίψων επὶ θλίψων προσδέχου, ἐλπίδα ἐπ' ἐλπίδι. Theodoret relates that
the Nicolaitans and followers of Basilius applied this *qaw* to the aeon which
came upon the world in Christ, or to the world in which the Redeemer dwelt.
Apparently these phrases had a part in the Gnostic system (Irenaeus; Epiphanius *Haereses* 24).

There have been interesting attempts to render these words in translation;
Vulg. *manda remanda, manda remanda, exspecta reexspecta, exspecta reexspecta,
modicum ibi modicum ibi.* Jerome: *praecipe, praecipe, impera quae facere
debeamus; exspecta paulisper, exspecta modicum.*

More recent scholarship refers these forms to letters of the alphabet. Cf. R.
H. Kennett, *Ancient Hebrew Social Life and Custom as Indicated in Law, Nar-
rative and Metaphor,* 1933, p. 12; G. R. Driver, *Semitic Writing,* pp. 89f., and
Hallo, *JBL,* Vol. 77, Part 4, 1958, pp. 337f.

Thus, Eichhorn seeks to imitate this in German, *Ges..ges..gel..gel,* for *Gesetz, Gesetz, Regel, Regel.* It is questionable, however, whether that is what Isaiah intends. Rather it seems as though he is stressing the fact that it was impossible to escape from the force of the teaching which everywhere confronted men, yet did not make a unified impact upon them, because they encountered only bits thereof.

11 The relation of this verse to the preceding is difficult to determine, and several variant views have been proposed. On the whole, the view which is set forth here seems to be most free of difficulty. In the two preceding verses the people have been presented as speaking in a caricaturing tone, deriding the teaching of Isaiah. Now, in the present verse, Isaiah declares how God will speak to this people. His introductory word *ki* may thus be rendered, *but, as a matter of fact.* The *ki* forms a parallel to the introductory *ki* of the preceding verse. At the same time it introduces a contrast, as far as the content is concerned. In verse 10 the people mock the words of the prophet; in the present verse, Isaiah states how God will as it were mock the people.

with stammering lips—Lit., with stammerings lip. These appear to be mere unintelligible mutterings, so that those who hear will hear gibberish. The following phrase, however shows that the reference here is to another language. Hence God will speak to the nation in a language that it does not know. They had regarded His speaking through the prophet as so much nonsense; as a matter of fact, He would now speak to them in such a way that they would not understand, but would only hear sounds which would seem to them as vain babblings. It is probably correct to see here a reference to the coming of the Assyrians, whose language, naturally, the Judahites would not understand. From this time on the Assyrians, whom Ahaz had called upon the scene, would command the affairs of Judah, and the Jews would have to deal with those who spoke this Assyrian language.

Perhaps there is a slight difference of nuance between "lip" and "tongue." In Genesis 11:1, 6, 9 the two words are employed in close connection. *Saphah* refers to the outward organ, the lip, whereas *lashon* (tongue) perhaps includes both the outward organ and the inward thought. Cf. also Isaiah 29:13 and 33:19. The *tongue* here probably refers to a people, as Isaiah later says, "I will gather all nations and tongues" (66:18). The thought then is that God will speak to Judah by means of people who speak a language different from that of the Jews. This will not be a speech in words primarily, but will be discerned in the mighty deeds of destruction which this nation, a tool in the hands of the Lord, will work against Judah and the theocracy. It will be a message directed to "this people." In this designation we are brought again in memory to the commission which God had given to the prophet. When he speaks to "this people," they will not hear. They mock his words, confident in their own wisdom, and for that reason God will speak to "this people" by means of a language or tongue that they will not understand. From this point on Judah is to come under the domination of foreign peoples.[19]

12 In speaking to the people in a tongue which they do not understand, the Lord is not acting capriciously, for He had already spoken in clear tones to them, pointing out the true way to peace and rest.[20] Isaiah inserts the present verse in order to lend a contrast to the preceding and to make its message more forceful. Thus, he introduces Yahweh as one who had already spoken unto them, i.e., "this people." This speaking had been carried out over the course of the years through the prophets. Whenever they spoke, denouncing sin, pleading for repentance, pointing to coming destruction, it was God who spoke through them.

In two short words the entirety of the prophetic message is couched. "This is rest." Micah apparently throws some light on the force of the word when, in speaking of the sinful actions of the people, he exclaims, "This *is* not *your* rest" (Mic. 2:10). Micah has just been decrying the condition of the nation. That condition does not express their true rest. Their true rest, it would seem, is to be found in the opposite, in obedience to the commands of the Lord.

---

[19] This verse is referred to by Paul in 1 Corinthians 14:21, in order to show the purpose of tongues as a sign for unbelievers. Paul's language generally agrees with Aq.

[20] אֲשֶׁר—note the *L*ᵉ*garmeh;* either *who says unto them,* or *which, he saith unto them,* i.e., *unto whom he saith. Whom* refers to the people of v. 11. *rest*—the word may also mean *resting place,* and may be employed figuratively for *security,* cf. 2 Sam. 14:17. אבוא—the final *Aleph* is omitted in 1Q, and Penna suggests that it should be so read. Cf. also Josh. 10:24. Ps. 139:20 and Jer. 10:5 should really not be appealed to in this connection, as in both these instances the *Aleph* is really the final consonant. I question whether it is the work of an Arab copyist. It may be an archaic form, which comes down in the common Ar. pl., e.g., *fa-ʿa-lû'. hearing*—without the prep. the inf. is stronger. Whether it is a direct obj. or a circumstantial acc. is difficult to tell.

In other words, it is a spiritual rest of which Isaiah is speaking, a rest that is to be found in God alone. In its broadest sense the word is thus a practical equivalent of salvation, including particular emphasis upon the blessings that salvation brings.

give rest to the weary—These words do not express the manner in which rest is given, but really constitute somewhat of a parenthesis. Alexander paraphrases, "This is the true rest, let the weary enjoy it." The imperative is directed to the people of Judah. Not only does God through His prophets point out the true rest, but He also wishes the weary to find that rest. The thought is akin to the "Comfort ye" of 40:1. It was a weary people, worn out by sin and rebellion; to cause this people to have rest was a command to walk in the way of true rest, namely, to obey the commands of the Lord; to do the very opposite of what the people were actually doing.

and this is the quiet—cf. 34:14. In thus repeating the thought of repose, Isaiah emphasizes how forcefully and vividly God has spoken to the people. The second word, however, is built on a causative stem, and possibly may stress the fact that the repose obtained is received from someone other than the recipient.

but they were not willing to hear—This is the tragic conclusion, reminding us of our Lord's "but ye would not" (Matt. 23:37). The quiet and repose which the Lord offered to them they did not want; instead they wished to adopt their own measures to combat the foe and to meet whatever problems might come their way. The message of Yahweh did not seem to them to be quiet and repose but instead an annoying babbling (cf. also Acts 17:18). Hence, rejecting the words of God which bring repose, they are willing to obey the words of those who speak another tongue, and whose yoke is not easy nor their burden light. Thus, the unbelieving, ungrateful nation hastens on to the destruction which by its own apostasy it has invited.

13 Isaiah now continues the thought of verse 11.[21] When the message of God had come to them bringing quiet and repose, they had mocked it; God's Word to them was but a babbling. Now, His Word would indeed be a babbling, for He would speak to them by means of a people whose language they could not understand. Isaiah repeats the language of verse 10, save that here that language

---

21 *and it shall be*—as a result of the judgment of v. 11. The words continue the thought of *he will speak* in v. 11. Despite Alexander, the *waw* is consecutive.

279

is the predicate in an entire sentence. God's Word will be to the nation just what the nation had regarded it, but God's Word will bring destruction to that nation which had so mocked the sacred words of the Holy One of Israel.

There is a reason given why God's Word will take this form, and Isaiah expresses this reason by means of five verbs which in the fullest measure set forth the doom of Judah. *they may walk*—Lit., "go." As many commentators have rightly pointed out, this verb does not merely modify those that follow, but in itself expresses a distinct act. The hearing of the Word of God causes the people to set out in motion so that they go to their destruction. Instead of arresting the people and causing them to remain, the message of God compels them to walk. They proceed, spurred on as it were, until destruction meets them. *and they will stumble backwards*— The way of the transgressor is hard, for the people not only will stumble but they will stumble backwards. They are not their own masters, but are overcome by the obstacles that meet them in the way. Note that the thought of this verse is based upon 8:15. *and they will be broken*—A strong figure to express the complete downfall of the sinner. *and be snared and be taken*—Herein forms the climax. In these two expressions taken from 8:15, there is possibly an allusion to the captivity. The people are like an animal that has been caught, stopped in its course and taken captive in a snare. They had thought themselves free, but the Word of the Lord which they had caricatured now in fact impels them upon the course that leads to their captivity.

14 Therefore hear the word of the LORD, O men of scorn, rulers of this people, who *are* in Jerusalem.

15 Because ye say, We have made a covenant with death, and with hell have we made a vision, the overflowing scourge when it has passed through, will not come upon us, for we have made false-hood our refuge, and in fraud we have hid ourselves.

16 Therefore, thus saith the Lord GOD, Behold! I lay in Zion a stone, a tested stone, a corner stone of value, of a firm foundation; he who believes will not be in haste.

17 And I shall place judgment for a line, and righteousness for a level, and hail will sweep away the refuge of lies, and waters shall over-flow the hiding place.

18 And there shall be covered over your covenant with death, and your vision with hell shall not stand, the overflowing scourge, for it passeth through, and ye shall become a trampling for it.

19 As often as it passes over, it shall take you; for in the morning, in the morning, it shall pass through, in the day and in the night, and only trembling is the understanding of the thing heard.

20 For the couch is too short to stretch oneself, and the covering too narrow to wrap oneself.

21 For like mount Perazim the LORD will rise up, like the valley in Gibeon will he rage, to do his work; strange is his work; and to perform his task; foreign is his task.

22 And now scoff not, lest your bands be strong, for an end and that determined I have heard from the Lord GOD of hosts upon all the earth.

14 Enough has been said of the mockery of the people. They must again hear the message of judgment. With an introductory *therefore,* Isaiah sums up what has just been said.[22] "Inasmuch," we may paraphrase, "as this people is a mocking one, wholly corrupt, and unresponsive to the Word of God, they are to have their attention directed to the judgment which God will bring." As earlier (1:10) the prophet had commanded the "men of Sodom" to hear the word of the Lord, so now he enjoins the "men of scorn" to do the same. The men of Sodom were the inhabitants of Judah and Jerusalem whose characteristics were those of the Sodomites, so also the "men of scorn" are those whose chief characteristic is scorning God's Word. The noun translated *scorn* (*latzon*) is found in Proverbs 29:8; "Scornful men bring a city into a snare; but wise *men* turn away wrath."

God speaks to His despisers. These men mocked His Word, spoken through the prophet. Following the desire of their own hearts, and despising the Law of the Lord, they, as rulers of the nation, were on the course of bringing the nation into destruction. To them the command is given, and with this command, grace— one last opportunity, as it were. "You mockers," the prophet cries out, "cease from the folly of your way, and now, hear the Word of the Lord, the Word in which alone the way of salvation is to be found."

Isaiah becomes more specific in his identity, designating the scoffers, *rulers of this people.* Earlier (v. 7) he had emphasized the teachers, spiritual leaders of the people; now attention is directed to the governmental rulers. The phrase "this people" is usually

---

22 *Therefore—"all das Vorangegangene zusammen fassend"* (Drechsler). *Lā-tzón,* in place of the ordinary *lē-tzim* (e.g. Ps. 1:1) involves a special emphasis.

found in an atmosphere of judgment and threat, such as characterizes the present passage. In their mockery of God's Word both the spiritual and secular leaders were one. The entire nation was in deep need of repentance.

The verse closes on a note of sadness. Whether the relative *who* is to be construed with "rulers" or "people" may be difficult to determine. At any rate, both rulers and people are in the city which belongs to the Holy One of Israel. The sin of deriding God's Word is unusually heinous when it is committed by those who live near the Temple of the Holy God. Not ignorant barbarians, but the rulers of Judah have derided the truth of God. There is good reason for the earnestness of Isaiah's words.

15 In this verse Isaiah gives a reason why the men of scorn should hear the Word of the Lord and also why it is necessary for God to lay in Zion a corner stone.[23] What is given is not the actual language of the scorners but an evaluation of their actions. Were these actions translated into words, they would be words such as these. To state it otherwise, here is an expression of the carnally devised thoughts and purposes of the scorners; and inasmuch as thoughts such as these have motivated their actions, God Himself will intervene and erect in Zion a stone.

Isaiah addresses the rulers of "this people." *ye have said*—Not in so many words, but this is what they had purposed in their hearts. *We have made a covenant*—The thought is similar to that expressed in Job 5:23, "For with the stones of the field is thy covenant, and the beast of the field is at peace with thee." If one has made a covenant with death, death will not harm him, for he and death are at peace. "You are acting," so the prophet's thought would seem to be, "as though death and the grave will not overcome you nor claim you. They come to others, but you are exempt. Round about you you have beheld others fall, and even seen the ten tribes go into captivity, but you think that death will pass you by." *Sheol*—In this context the word is little more than a synonym for death (cf. Job 10:21ff.; 38:17; Jer. 9:21). *we have made a league*—Although there is a textual difficulty at this point, the thought

23 In v. 14 the Lord through His prophet addresses the scorners, and declares that because they were in such a position that they regarded His words as mockery, He must act in judgment. In v. 15 He grounds His description of the Judahites as *scornful men*. "Ye are men of scorn, and must receive judgment." We may paraphrase, "for ye yourselves have said, etc." Cf. Ludwig Köhler, *ZAW*, Vol. 48, 1930, pp. 227f.

appears to be that an agreement with Sheol has been made.[24] The people speak as though they had done this of their own volition. It is a brazen confidence in human ability to solve all problems in its own strength.[25]

the overflowing scourge—Here in the description of the punishment is a mixture of figures. How can a scourge or whip be said to overflow? Isaiah takes the figure of a scourge from 10:26 where he had already used it to describe the cruel coming of the Assyrian. He had also already employed the figure of overflowing waters (8:8; 10:22). The two words form a striking assonance (*shoṭ shoṭeph*) and unquestionably belong together.[26] Delitzsch points out that a whip when cracked moves in wavy lines, and he appeals to Jeremiah 8:6. Gesenius adduces an interesting example from the Koran 89:13, "Thy lord pours over them the scourge (*sauṭa*) of punishment."

The Judahites recognize that an overflowing scourge will pass over them, but they are not afraid, for they think that it will pass

---

24 חזה, lit., *seer*. The form is actually a part. used for the abstract *hā-zūṭ* (v. 18). In 29:11 *hā-zūṭ* stands for *law, revelation*. In 5:7 the part. *rō-'eh* appeared for the abstract. At the same time, it is not really clear how the meaning *league* comes to adhere to *hō-zeh*. B supports this meaning, διαθήκην, and Vulg. *pactum*, Targ. *shᵉlama'*, but S has *hez-wo'*, which is not clear. BDB suggests that there had been a vision with Sheol by means of necromancy, as a result of which the people felt secure.

25 Jennings holds that the covenant was made with a human representative of death and Sheol. The prophecy will be fulfilled in the future, thinks Jennings, when there will be a Jewish state so organized that it can make an alliance. In the Ugaritic texts *Mot* is the personification of the spirit of destruction and hostility. But it is very questionable whether there is any reflection upon that fact here.

26 There is actually a mixture of two figures. One is derived from the "great waters"; cf. 8:8 and 10:22, and for the other cf. 10:26. 1Q reads *swṭ*, which is also *Qᵉre*. To emphasize the subj. it is placed first and as a result the position of *ki* is not the normal one. The *Kᵉtiv 'ā-bar* is to be preferred to the *Qᵉre*, for vv. 15 and 18 are evidently not intended to be identical.

For a discussion of the interpretation of *swṭ* as flood, cf. Barth, *ZAW*, Vol. 33, 1913, p. 306; Vol. 34, 1914, p. 69; and Poznanski, *ZAW*, Vol. 36, 1916, pp. 119f. Barth thinks that the figure of an overflowing scourge is not suitable and appeals to Koran 89:13 and to the Ethiopic in support of the translation, *an overwhelming flood*. But the Koran does not necessarily lend support, for the Ar. word *sauṭ* may also mean *portion*. It is strange that Barth does not appeal to B καταιγίς, nor to T κατακλυσμός, although Aq and S support *whip*, as does Vulg. also, *flagellum*. Poznanski thinks that the *Kᵉtiv* also supports Barth's rendering and he appeals to the Targ., Ibn Ezra, Eliezer of Beaugency and Ibn Ganah.

them by. Of this they feel confident, for they have a refuge, which they themselves have made, in falsehood and lies. What Isaiah means is that the Judahites employ politics of devious nature so that they can adapt themselves to every situation. They are governed by expediency; if a lie will suit their purpose, they will tell it; if dissembling is to their advantage, they employ it; the choice of means brings no embarrassment. Doubtless, there is a tone of irony in Isaiah's words. The people would not themselves so characterize their refuge. Probably, when they told their lies and employed their political expediency, they did what people have always done in such circumstances: they proclaimed their ways as ways of truth and right. As Jennings remarks, men "always attach fairest words to foulest deeds."

They were skillful in deceit and treachery of all sorts, the art of dissimulation and secret intrigue and anything else that belonged to the methods of false diplomacy and common politics. 30:1ff. and 31:1ff. give examples of how active these people were at their work. When Isaiah calls these deeds by their right names, the contrast between their true nature and the people's own estimate of them leaps into sharper focus. Their policy probably came to expresssion in their desire to turn to Egypt for help against the oncoming of Assyria, for this may have been one manifestation of the political policy prevailing in Judah.

Isaiah's words bring to the fore the confidence which Judah placed in itself. Judah herself had done everything that she thought necessary in order to be safe. Her confidence was in the work of her own hands and the thoughts of her own mind. She does not need the Lord; she has herself. In the verse the prophet paints a picture of self-confident man, yet in the background looms destruction.

16 Against the background of the nation's vain and misplaced confidence in its false security Isaiah utters one of the grandest Messianic prophecies in his entire work. This prophecy in some respects calls to mind the situation present in chapter seven. As the unbelieving Ahaz had rejected the sign proffered of the Lord, and consequently the Lord Himself had given a sign, so here, the Lord again takes action, setting in contrast to the weak foundation upon which Judah trusted, the true and tried Stone which alone is a foundation upon which one may rest.

As in 7:14 so here the prophet introduces his message with *therefore*. Inasmuch as the situation is what it is, namely, that the people of Judah are overconfident and have placed their reliance in what can only bring destruction, the Lord must act. The word is not a mere resumption of the *therefore* of verse 14, for here it serves to set forth the Lord's action in contrast to the nation's folly. As in 7:14 it was the Sovereign One (*'ᵃdonay*) who gave the sign, so here it is the Sovereign One (*'ᵃdonay*) who speaks. In the laying of a stone in Zion the power and might of God are displayed, and the word *'ᵃdonay* is most suitable to express the thought of God's power. Again, included in the word is the suggestion that the Lord alone is powerful and able to carry out what will truly benefit the nation.

As in 7:14 the prophecy was introduced with the word *behold!* so also here. In that prophecy, however, attention was directed to the mother of the Messiah, whereas here it is turned to God Himself. Thus God is made prominent, for the work of founding the Stone is one of sovereign grace. God's initiative stands out. Man's power could not erect the Touchstone; such a work is God's. To place God in the foreground Isaiah employs a strange grammatical construction, the thought of which we may express as follows: "Behold! it is I who have founded, etc." The suffix is in the first person, but the verb is the third person perfect. Involved here is a change of person such as is frequent in the prophetical writings.[27]

What is this foundation stone of which the prophet speaks? Isaiah had earlier employed the word of the founding of Zion (14:32). Here, however, the thought is that God has implanted firmly and deeply in the earth a stone which cannot be easily moved, and upon which one may build a house with perfect safety. Of importance is the past tense, for the stone has already been laid in the ground; and inasmuch as there is laid a firm foundation, it is mere folly to place one's confidence in a foundation not firmly laid.

Emphasis falls upon the fact that God has placed the stone in

---

[27] The change in person is natural, and *BH*, Penna, etc., are wrong in proposing an emendation to the participle. There is an ellipsis, which Rashi correctly explains, "Behold! I am he who founds." Thus, the subj. of the relative sentence refers to the suffix in הנני. Furthermore, the part. would place the transaction in the future, whereas in itself the pret. raises the question whether the action is in the historical past or ideal future. The context demands the past, as far as the laying of the stone itself is concerned, but what is built upon the stone is future. As analogies of the change of person Gesenius adduces *c'est moi, qui a fondé*, and Ar. *'innama' qâ-ma 'ana'*, only *I arose*. 1Q, however, has a participle.

285

Zion, for only in Zion is a true foundation.[28] To turn to Egypt or, for that matter, to any other human source for aid was to turn from the one foundation that was secure. Zion herself is not the foundation, for Isaiah expressly states that God has laid the stone *in* Zion.

The basic passage upon which the conception of the Stone is founded is Genesis 49:24, in which the "mighty one of Jacob" is said to be the "stone of Israel." In Deuteronomy 32:4 God had been called a *rock* (*tzur*) and in Isaiah 8:14, 15 God is identified both as a stone and a rock. In 9:6, however, we were told that the Messiah is God, and so are prepared for the statement of the present verse, so replete with Messianic characteristics, namely, that God Himself has laid in Zion a stone.

Isaiah first presents the picture generally, as it had been earlier given of the Lord Himself (cf. 8:14, 15) to represent Him as immoveable and unchangeable, the firm foundation and unshakeable rock upon which one can rely when all about gives way. Hence, the stone is first mentioned as such, that our attention may be concentrated upon it alone. What stands out is the Stone—firm, strong, immoveable, in contrast to the shaky refuge of lies.[29]

How striking the contrast! In place of lies, a stone. Judah relied upon lies and falsehood; God has laid in Zion a stone. Perhaps it is well to note that God's action is already accomplished. Yet if that be the case, how can the stone be Jesus Christ, who would not come to earth for many years subsequent to Isaiah's time? The answer is that the decree of God goes back to eternity; the plan of salvation has been determined, and is to be accomplished in time. The foundation stone has been laid by God, and what He has decreed is as good as accomplished. The verb in reality corresponds to the thought of Micah, who also prophesied at this time of the Messiah as "of old, even from everlasting." "What is historically realized," says Delitzsch, "has had an eternal existence, and indeed an ideal pre-existence even in the heart of history itself (ch. xxii.11, xxv.1, xxxvii.26). Ever since there had been a Davidic government at all, this stone had lain in Zion. The Davidic monarchy not only had

28 *in Zion*—some regard the prep. as *Beth essentiae, I make Zion a foundation;* cf. GKC § 119 i. Grammatically this is possible, but contrary to the thought of the context.

29 For this reason we are not to delete the word as proposed in *BH*. In his use of the passage Peter did not need this particular emphasis and hence quotes freely (1 Pet. 2:6).

in this its culminating point, but the ground of its continuance also. It was not only the Omega, but also the Alpha. Whatever escaped from wrath, even under the Old Testament, stood upon this stone."

Isaiah immediately goes on, however, to characterize the stone. It is a stone of testing, i.e., one that can be relied upon, a touchstone.[30] In other words, by means of this stone men will be tested. To some it will be an occasion of offense; to others, a foundation for their souls and lives. It is Jesus Christ who divides men; they are known by their attitude toward Him. *a corner stone*—The words may be rendered literally, *a corner (stone) of the preciousness of a fixed foundation*. The stone is described as a *corner*, and hence, a stone that is distinguished, binding the two sides of a building. It was thus a stone with an essential position in the entire structure. It is not merely one stone among others, but one large corner stone which supports the entire building. We may note Psalm 118:22, "The stone which the builders rejected, is become the chief corner stone."

The two nouns are to be taken together, so as to give the sense, a "precious corner (stone)," to show that in itself the stone is of value. Such valuable stones were used in foundations (1 Kings 5:17; 7:9-11). *fixed foundation*—The language emphasizes the unshakeable character of the stone. This foundation has been fixed, firmly laid, so that it cannot be moved.[31] *he who believes*—The reference is to the one who believes that this stone is truly laid by God. Such a one believes that God has founded this stone, and

---

30 בחן—*testing*, a stone that has been tested and is approved for use. *BK* describes it as a grey, greenish schist gneiss. Sethe (*Die Bau- und Denkmalsteine der alten Ägypter und ihre Namen*, pp. 864-912) identifies *bō-ḥan* with Egy. *bḥn-w*, which can be used of a number of stones from the Wadi Hammamat, related to granite and diorite. Upon the basis of Egyptian practice Sethe translates *touchstone*. Lambdin (*JAOS*, Vol. 73, No. 3, p. 148) raises linguistic difficulties: Egy. *bāhan* would become Heb. *bōhan*, whereas this is a *Quṭl* (segolate) form.

The idea of a touchstone need not completely be rejected, however. *Bahan* is used of the testing of metals and metaphorically of the testing of men's hearts; cf. Ps. 17:3; Prov. 17:3; Job 23:10. Köhler (*Theologische Zeitschrift*, Vol. 3, 1947, pp. 390-393) maintains the text practically unchanged, and renders, "the corner where a foundation meets the other foundation," "*die Ecke, wo eine Grundmauer (ein Fundament) die andre (das andre Fundament) trifft.*"

31 מוסד—*a founded foundation*, i.e., a firm foundation. The second word is a part., but note *Dagesh* in the sibilant.

herefore looks to it as the foundation upon which to rely.[32] In ɔther words, he has faith in the stone. This does not mean that he places confidence in a literal stone, but in what is symbolized by the Stone, namely, the Immanuel whom God had promised to be the deliverer of His people.

will not be in haste—This is spoken in contrast to those who do ɔot believe. In the way of the Lord there is quietness and repose (cf. v. 12). Those who rejected this way, however, chose for themselves a way of life that involved lack of repose and rest. Theirs was an agitated, excited, wearisome way. Yet one who believes the promises of God, need not haste, for he possesses repose and quiet. Very beautifully and true to the thought of the Old Testament, the New Testament renders this verse, "will not be ashamed."[33] Isaiah speaks deeply on the helter-skelter, meaningless life that characterizes men outside of Christ. In Him there is not only salvation; there are also the quiet and peace that are essential for a truly well-ordered life.

17 The prophet now continues the figure of a building. Reverting to the first person, the Lord says that He will set judgment for a line. As the builder measures the stones which he has placed together by means of a measuring line, so the Lord will measure the spiritual stones of the building by means of justice. If the stones cannot meet the measurement of justice they will be discarded. Again, Isaiah takes up the word *line* (*qaw*), but this time uses it of a line for measuring. God also employs a line, by means of which He determines the level and smoothness of the stones, and this "level" is righteousness. If then the Judahites are to be measured by justice and righteousness, what hope is there for them?

The result of God's activity is that divine judgment sweeps away the refuge of lies in which the nation thought to find safe-

---

32 Blank (*Prophetic Faith in Isaiah*, 1958, p. 38) rejects *the one who believes* as a translation of *ma'ᵃmin*, and would substitute *a people that keeps faith*, and regards the foundation as the formula, "A people that keeps faith has no cause for panic." The definite article with the part. refers more naturally, however, to an individual. Furthermore, the *Hiphil* of *'mn* means *to trust* or *believe*, not *to keep faith* with someone.

33 שׁיחי—also in 1Q. Many interpret this to mean a fleeing in haste from the coming storm (e.g. Dillmann). But the word best serves to show the hurriedness that stands in opposition to the quiet of the one who trusts. B reads οὐ μὴ καταισχυνθῇ and this is adopted in the New Testament. Vulg. *non festinet*. There is no objective evidence to support the emendation to שׁימי. Cf. also Luke 2:34.

ty.[34] "Hail" is a figure used for divine judgment (cf. v. 2), and the manner in which this divine judgment works is figuratively expressed by the words, "sweep away." Before the driving storm of hail, the refuge made of lies blows away and is found no more. The refuge is not Egypt itself, but the act of placing one's trust in that which was no true refuge. All the devious devices and alliances which had been made with Egypt and other nations will be blown away before the storm of God's judgment which will overtake the nation. It is interesting to note how Isaiah takes up the language of verse 15, "lies our refuge," and here inverts it.

the hiding place—Again the prophet employs the language of verse 15 and also goes back to verse 2.[35] Judah had become like Samaria as far as guilt was concerned; hence, Judah might expect that just as judgment would overtake Samaria so would it also come over herself. Wherever one may seek to hide himself, the waters of judgment will overflow and submerge that place of refuge.

18 Isaiah now addresses the nation directly, beginning with a verb in which he expresses what will become of the nation's covenant with death. This covenant will be covered, i.e., obliterated, so that one cannot read it. Possibly the prophet is thinking of a tablet with writing which has been rubbed out so that it can no longer be read.[36] It may be, however, that he is doing nothing more than using a figurative expression to show that the cove-

---

34 יעה, hapax legomenon. mšqlṭ is a level, leveling instrument. The form is in pause. וסתר—note word order; object, subject, verb. Hail and floods also serve as pictures of divine judgment in 30:30 and 32:19. As in 9:6 mišpāṭ and tzᵉdāqāh are used together, for they characterize God's reign.

35 This reflection upon v. 2 appears in the use of hail, waters and will overflow. If, as far as guilt is concerned, the Judahites are equal to Samaria (vv. 7, 8; cf. vv. 1, 3) the same will be true as to punishment. Those whom God reproves wished to be accounted pillars in the Church, yet they were doing their best to raze it to the foundation.

36 and there shall be covered over—a m. verb with following subj. f. singular. Such a variation from the normal rule may occur when the pred. precedes the subject.
Note the chiastic arrangement of 18a. כפר elsewhere is used in the Pual of blotting out in respect to guilt; cf. 6:7; 22:14; 27:9. Here it is employed in the sense covered, obliterabitur foedus vestrum. Houbigant was probably the first to propose the emendation wᵉtupar, and will be broken; cf. Jer. 33:21. But the change is not necessary. Gesenius thinks that the reference is to striking out the letters with a stylus, and compares Aram. and Syr., where the root means to wipe away.

nantal terms have been completely annulled and are no longer binding.[37] Death then is no longer bound, so that death may now reign over Judah.

Likewise the agreement which the people thought they had with Sheol will not hold up.[38] Isaiah simply takes up the boast of the people and shows how they have no refuge whatever in which to find a hiding place. He considers their boast step by step and exposes it completely. And as for the overflowing scourge, when it does pass over, the nation will simply become a trampling for it. In verse 15 Isaiah had used the perfect, for there the idea of the flood passing over was simply one suggested as a possibility by the people; here, however, the imperfect is employed, for the language here is that of prophecy and the overflowing of the scourge is a certainty.[39]

A third figure now appears. How, we may ask, can a scourge overflow and trample? Perhaps Alexander has commented as wisely as any on this point: "The attempt to reconcile the language with the artificial rules of composition is in this case rendered hopeless by the combination of expressions which cannot be strictly applied to the same subject. An army might trample, but it could not literally overflow; a stream might overflow, but it could not literally trample down. The time perhaps is coming when, even as a matter of taste, the strength and vividness of such mixed metaphors will be considered as overweighing their inaccuracy in relation to an arbitrary standard of correctness or propriety." With the word "trample," however, the thought is brought to the fore that an army is coming, and Judah will be trodden under foot (cf. 5:5; 7:25; 10:6).

19 Taking up the thought with which he had concluded the previous verse, Isaiah now directs attention to the enemy and its destroying power. "As often as he passes over," he asserts, going

---

37 In ancient times treaties were not to be broken. Esarhaddon requires of his subjects: that they are not to alter the words of the treaty, nor consign it to the fire, nor throw it into the water, nor bury it in the ground, nor in any way destroy it or cause it to disappear or sweep it away (*ta-sa-pan-a-ni*) ; cf. lines 410-413 of the Vassal Treaties. Cf. also the curses on the Sefire Inscriptions; cf. *JAOS*, Vol. 81, No. 3, 1961, pp. 178-222.

38 In place of *ḥôzeh* of v. 15, the abstract *ḥā-zūṯ-ḵem* is used.

39 *it passeth*—imp. instead of the pret. of v. 15. In v. 15 we have the nation's boast wherein the scourge is merely conceived as something that might come; here, however, the fut. is intended to emphasize that the scourge will pass over.

back to the concept of the scourge, "he will take you." The people had acknowledged that the overflowing scourge would pass over but they thought that it would not come unto them (v. 15). Isaiah then declared that it certainly would pass over and they would become a trampling (v. 18). Now he goes a step further to point out that the scourge will pass over not merely once but many, many times, and whenever it should pass over (or, as often as), it would take the people.[40] Wave after wave will pass over, and there is no escape. Each succeeding wave will take the people away. The word does not necessarily refer to the exile, but to their being taken away from the presence of God, as seen from Jeremiah 15:15, "take me not away from thy long-suffering."

Isaiah now proceeds to give a reason for his statement. The scourge will pass over every morning; every morning it will make as it were a new beginning, and will continue throughout the day and night, and then begin again the next morning. In other words, it will be a steady, continual overflow from which there is to be no delivery or avenue of escape. The nation was confident that the scourge would never reach it; as a matter of fact, the nation will never be able to escape from the scourge's reach.

Again the prophet goes back to the people's derision of his preaching. There is a revelation, a thing heard, and the people will have an understanding of it. What, however, is their understanding to be? This Isaiah answers in two words: *only trembling*. These words he puts in a position of emphasis by placing them first, and we may translate, *and only trembling is the understanding of the thing heard*.[41] The meaning is not that to perceive the message itself is a fearful thing, but rather that the result of such perceptive hearing will be to tremble. Thus, the language stands in sharp contrast to what the people themselves have said of Isaiah's preaching. On hearing him preach, they had mocked; now they will have learned better; now they will hear the word of God, and trembling will arise in their hearts.

20 To support the truthfulness of what he has just said, Isaiah

---

40 Lit., *from the sufficiency of, as often as.* זְוָעָה, *trembling,* cf. Jer. 15:4, Hab. 2:7. כִּי introduces the reason for the statement of 19a.

41 I cannot agree with Gesenius in his translation, *nur das Gerücht zu vernehmen, ist Schrecken.* Rather, as the Masoretes have indicated, *only* is to be construed with *trembling.* The thought is that the perceiving of the report brings only trembling.

adopts a proverbial manner of speaking.[42] The situation of the people, he remarks, is like that of a bed too short to stretch oneself on. Just as a bed that is too short does not give to a man the necessary rest, so the condition of the people is such that it will not provide for them in the straits in which they find themselves. The bed upon which they lie is not such a one as will provide for them the rest that they need; in other words, they are in such a condition that they cannot escape the wrath that is to come.

In the second half of the verse thought is expressed by means of the figure of a cover too narrow to wrap oneself in. The condition does not meet the necessities of the people. The figures are vivid, and well adapted to express the truth that the prophet has in mind.

21 Again Isaiah begins a verse with "for," this time to illustrate the nature of God's punitive judgment. This he does by comparison with two events taken from the history of the nation. In the first place he makes a comparison with Mount Perazim.[43] Apparently the reference is to Baal-Perazim (2 Sam. 5:20), where David smote the Philistines. David himself gives an explanation of the name which he gave to the place, "The LORD hath broken forth upon mine enemies before me, as the breach of waters." We may note the emphasis upon "breaking forth" in this comment, and also the reference to waters (cf. in the present chapter verses 2, 15, 17, 18). With this comparison, therefore, Isaiah indicates the manner in which the Lord will arise for judgment. The verb "will arise" points out that the Lord is ready to take action against His people (cf. 2:19).

A second comparison is with the valley in Gibeon, in which Joshua had fought against the five Canaanitish kings (Josh. 10:8-14). Here the Canaanites were destroyed by hail. "...The LORD cast down great stones from heaven upon them unto Azekah, and they died: *they were* more which died with hailstones than *they* whom the children of Israel slew with the sword" (Josh. 10:11). This fits in well with the emphasis upon the hail sweeping away the refuge of lies in which the people of Isaiah's day placed their

---

42 Thus, *ki* gives the reason why the people can no longer laugh. Lit., *for there has become short the couch from*, i.e., *is too short for.*

43 *Perazim*—cf. 2 Sam. 5:20; 1 Chron. 14:11, the hills between Jerusalem and Bethlehem. *Gibeon*—2 Sam. 5:25; 1 Chron. 14:16, generally identified with El-Jib, a few miles (about 7) north of Jerusalem. In both places David confounded the Philistines.

confidence. In an outbreak of rage, such as had been shown in the valley in Gibeon, the Lord will come upon the nation. His visitation will be the result of His anger, directed toward sinful men.

The purpose of His rising and His raging is to accomplish His work (cf. 5:12), even the work of judgment. Yet Isaiah describes this as a strange work, and the performing of his task as something foreign.[44] This does not mean that in His work God will act as a stranger or foreigner would act. Nor does it mean that retributive justice is something foreign or alien to God's nature. God is love; but God is also a consuming fire, and the work of punishment is right and just. An essential attribute of His nature is His vindicatory justice. Apparently what Isaiah means (although the language is difficult and one must not be dogmatic), is that what is to take place is something unusual, foreign from the ordinary course of providence. The punishment of the theocracy is an event of such strangeness that it causes one to pause and meditate. God appears to be destroying His own work. He had promised that salvation would come through the theocracy. Yet now He is about to destroy that theocracy. Is not that going against His own purposes? Surely this would appear to be a strange work, one foreign to what God usually does!

22 An appeal to the nation is now in order, and in this appeal the tender concern of the prophet and ultimately of the Lord Himself stands out. *And now*—These words are well fitted to introduce the conclusion to what has just been said. Inasmuch as the judgment is a sure event, it is well now to take heed and act accordingly. *scoff not*—An imperative is what the people need.[45] Isaiah of course takes up the designation of verse 14, as though to say, "You men of scorn, scorn no longer. If you continue scoffing, you will find that your bands are firm and do not remove." These bands were devious methods of deliverance relied on by the people, such as alliances with Egypt. They were the bonds by which the nation was tied or bound to its false hopes and confidences. If the people continued scoffing, these bonds would be strengthened, not in that they would become tighter, for they were not loose

---

[44] Green (*op. cit.*, p. 273) takes the adjectives *strange* and *foreign* as possibly attributive, placed first for emphasis. But in such a case, should not the adjective have the article? It is better and more forceful to construe the adjectives as predicates.

[45] תתלוצצו—*act as a scorner, a lētz. bands*—in 1Q the more common pl. appears; cf. also Jer. 2:20; 5:5; 27:2; 30:8.

bonds, but in the sense that they could not be loosed or broken. The nation would be so tightly bound with them that it would perish because of them. Such is the end that will come if the people persist in their foolish course of scoffing at the Word of God.

Taking up a thought which he had already introduced (cf. 10:23), Isaiah speaks of the judgment as an "end and that determined." By means of this language, later employed by Daniel in his remarkable prophecy of the seventy sevens, the prophet has in view the end of the theocracy which has been determined in the counsels of God. Judah must learn the truth that an end is coming to the theocratic nation. Moreover, this end does not represent a change of mind upon God's part, but rather is something that has been determined. It is an end, but more than that, it is a determined end, and hence, there can be no talk of its being averted. Reflecting upon the word $sh^emu'ah$ (the thing heard, v. 9), Isaiah declares that he has heard (shama'ti) from the Lord. As he had introduced the prophecy with reference to God as the Sovereign One, so he brings the message to its conclusion with a similar reference. Inasmuch as the Sovereign One has revealed to him this truth, it is to be accepted as something sure.

Not lacking is the idea of universalism expressed by the words over (against) all the earth—An easy way out of the difficulty caused by the presence of these words is to regard them as a gloss. For that procedure, however, there is no warrant. Inasmuch as Isaiah in this chapter has not been talking about a universal judgment, but has placed his stress upon the devastation which the Assyrian would cause to the theocracy, we must understand this phrase in the light of the context. The destruction of the theocracy, therefore, would appear to be an event which in a certain sense represents a judgment of God against the entire earth. Israel was designed to be a light to lighten the Gentiles, a blessing to the world; and with her removal from the scene, the earth would suffer. As long as the Temple stood in Zion, so long could the blessing of truth be found in a world filled with idolatry and superstition. When that Temple is destroyed, however, then the earth itself will immeasurably suffer. In this sense, it would seem, the final words of the prophecy are to be understood.

23 Give ear and hear my voice, hearken and hear my word.

24 Does the plowman plow every day to sow? Does he open and harrow his ground?

25 Does he not when he has levelled its surface, cast abroad black cummin and scatter cummin, and set apart wheat in rows, and barley
   in a determined place, and spelt in his border?

26 And he teaches him aright, his God instructs him.

27 For not with a threshing instrument is the black cummin to be
   threshed, or the cart wheel turned upon the cummin; but with a
   rod is the black cummin to be beaten, and the cummin with a
   staff.

28 Bread corn is bruised, but not for ever will he certainly thresh it;
   and he sets going the wheel of his cart, and his horsemen will not
   bruise it.

29 Also this has gone forth from the LORD of hosts; he is wonderful
   in counsel, great in wisdom.

23 By means of four imperatives Isaiah commands the people
to hear what he has to say. Although his principal message is concluded, he would add to it a parable by way of explanation and
illustration. His first two imperatives call to mind his first address
to heaven and earth (1:2). The words "voice" and "words" show
that the message was one which he was about to deliver orally.
After the tremendous message which has just been delivered, it
might easily be that these following words setting forth the message in parables would sink somewhat into obscurity; and the
imperatives are designed to prevent that. What follows is important; it is to be heard and obeyed.

24 By means of a pertinent question (which expects a negative
answer), the prophet focuses attention upon what he is saying.
every day—I.e., all the time, not the whole day. The usage is similar to that in Genesis 6:5 (cf. also Isa. 65:5). The thought is not
that the plowman plows all day long and does nothing else,
but that he is constantly, daily plowing. Although Isaiah speaks
of the worker as a plowman, he has in mind the peasant, a
farmer who must perform all the chores necessary to keep the
farm in operation. Perhaps plowing was one of the most arduous
and time consuming of these tasks, and for that reason is singled
out for mention.

Not much is known today about the plow used in biblical times.
It seems to have consisted merely of a wooden stick with metal tip
drawn by oxen (cf. 1 Kings 19:19). Before the introduction of
iron, the plow points were made of copper or bronze; but these
metals were not hard, and, to judge from the excavations, were

295

easily bent and dented. Iron was harder, and made possible larger and evidently more serviceable points.

to sow—These words are added in order to state the purpose of the farmer's work. If he is to sow, must he be engaged in constant, unending plowing? The answer to this question is negative; there is also other work that he must do. *he will open*—This is the first of these other works, but what exactly is this work? Some have thought that it is a second ploughing, and this is possible. Others believe that the word is in effect a repetition of the thought expressed in the question. On this interpretation the force would be, "Does the plowman always plow in order to sow; does he plow and harrow?" In the light of Exodus 28:9, 36, it has been suggested that the action was that of making furrows in the field. This is probably correct. Either the action represented by the verb *he opens* is synonymous with that of harrowing, or it refers to a making of furrows by means of a hoe or possibly by a second plowing. Perhaps it is an action which has to do in particular with the breaking up of clods of earth. In ancient Israel the iron points of the plow could not penetrate very deeply, possibly three or four inches, and so were not really able to make furrows suitable for sowing.

harrow his ground—Involved in the root idea of this verb is the thought of dragging.[46] Indeed, the work of harrowing may simply have been the dragging of branches to smooth over the ground that had been ploughed. The harrowing of the ground, terrace by terrace, was particularly important in sloping terrain like that in the Jerusalem hills, to check the run-off of rainwater and thus prevent soil erosion. We are not necessarily to take these two verbs in chronological order. Isaiah does not mean that the work of opening must precede that of harrowing. All he is saying is that in addition to plowing the land, the farmer must also perform the work of opening and harrowing.

his ground—The words lend a certain important effect to the thought, for they show that the ground belonged to the farmer and was the object of his concern and care. So the theocracy, which would feel God's punishing hand, yet which in the last analysis would see accomplished His purposes of salvation, was the object of God's special love and tender care.

---

46 Cf. Akk. *šadâdu*, to draw, drag; *"aratione per transversum iterata, occatio sequitur, crate vel rastro, et sato semine iteratio"* (Pliny *Historia Naturalis* xviii.20) .

What, it may now be asked, is the point of Isaiah's illustration? Some have suggested that it merely illustrated differences in the manner of God's providential working. Such an explanation is too general and does not really go to the heart of the matter. In the earlier verses of this chapter the prophet presented both promise and judgment. The promise (vv. 5, 6) cannot fall to the ground nor can it be annulled. How then are we to reconcile the promise with God's sure work of judgment (vv. 14-22)? The answer is that these two are not mutually exclusive, but both are necessary for the accomplishment of God's purposes with His chosen people. His purpose is the ultimate salvation of His own and thus the glorification of His Name. He is to be seen as the "crown of beauty and the diadem of beauty" of His redeemed. At the same time, if His people are truly to be redeemed, all enemies, including those who only outwardly are members of the theocracy, must be visited in judgment. For the full accomplishment of His plan, therefore, there must be both the work of salvation and that of redemption. Both are essential in order that the ultimate end of the deliverance of His people be accomplished.

It is this that Isaiah's illustration seeks to point out. To bring about the sowing, the farmer must do more than one thing. He must of course plow, but that is not all. In addition he must also open the ground and harrow. So with God. In order that His land be fully prepared for sowing, He gives both the promise and the threat. It is this message that the prophet commands the people of Judah to hear.

25 Isaiah continues his questions. The work of the farmer is not all one of breaking up; it is also one of sowing so that the ground will bring forth.[47] The farmer has broken up the soil; he will also show care and concern over it. We are not told how he levels the ground, but this expression may be simply a synonym for har-

---

[47] The preterites may suggest that the acts are often repeated. It is also possible to render, "Is it not when he has levelled, that he scatters and sprinkles?" König translates, "*Ist nicht vielmehr das der Fall? Wenn er ihre Oberfläche eben gemacht hat, so streut er Schwarzkümmel aus und streut andern Kümmel.*" קצח is black cummin, B μελάνθιον. Vulg. *gith*, a word of Semitic origin. Penna suggests that it may have come into Latin through Punic and compares the Hebrew *gad*—coriander. שׂורה—possibly *in rows*, attested in 1Q. I would take it as an adverbial accusative. נסמן—*in an appointed place*, lacking in B. The form is a *Niphal* part., and Gesenius takes it as *designatum*, i.e. in designated (*bezeichneten*) places; so Targ.

rowing, and the action may also consist of the dragging of branches over the face of the ground. *black cummin*—The chiastic order of the language should be noted. "He casts abroad black cummin, and cummin he scatters." The *qetzaḥ* is black cummin, the *nigella sativa,* used for seasoning, having small black acrid seeds. *cummin* —*Cuminum sativum,* a plant grown as a condiment.

The description continues, the other activities being the setting of wheat in rows. The word used is not clearly understood, but seems to indicate the furrows in the ground in which the seed is planted.

barley in a determined place—The sowing is done not in a haphazard manner, but in definite, appointed or determined pla- ces. *and spelt in his border*—The suffix may refer to the field generally, so that we are to understand the spelt (if that be the significance of the Hebrew) as planted along the border of the field. Why this is so is not clear. It is also possible to refer the suffix to the farmer himself. In either case the meaning is about the same; the spelt is planted on the edge of the field, forming the border or rim of the barley field. The farmer does his work carefully and according to plan, with proper regard to place and method and the different crops to be grown.

26 That the farmer acts in this wise manner is due to a gift of God who instructs him. God instructs him correctly and teaches him. This seems to be the natural reading of the verse, namely, to make "God" the subject of both verbs. On the other hand, we must note the view of Drechsler, who would apply the first verb to the farmer and the second to God. We might, on this interpretation, render, *and prepares it according to the rule that God teaches him.* This interpretation is possible and does not materially affect the sense.

What the farmer does God teaches him.[48] This is not to say that the instruction comes to the farmer through special revelation. Rather, it is a general statement that man's knowledge of agricul- ture is a gift given to him of God. Man does not proceed in his work on his own, for unaided he would not know what to do.

The farmer knows what he is doing; he is not groping in

48 *and he teaches*—Lit., *corrects;* the perfect with weak *waw* seems to express frequentative action. This idea is supported by the parallel verb and the general context. Note the chiastic order of the verbs. Vergil Georgics i.147, and Lucretius v.14 attribute horticulture to the gods Bacchus and Ceres; and Diod. i.14, 15, 17 says that Isis and Osiris taught it to the Egyptians.

ignorance, hoping vainly that the procedure he follows will result in a good crop. He is one who knows from God what he should do, and therefore acts accordingly. One who saw the farmer at work and did not understand what he was doing might ridicule and question the wisdom of his procedures. Such a person, however, would merely be exhibiting his own ignorance and lack of understanding. Likewise, scoffers might think that there was no rhyme or reason to what the God of Jacob was doing. They would be far wiser if, instead of questioning the wisdom of His mighty acts, they were to acknowledge their own ignorance of His ways and would submit to His just judgments, acknowledging them to be ways of righteousness and judgment.

27 There is indeed a right way of carrying on farming operations, and the prophet now states what that right way is. Hence, he begins by giving a proof that the farmer follows the instruction of the Lord when he carries out his agricultural work. The form of Isaiah's statement is striking, for he places the negative first to show how the farmer does not perform his work. "Not with a threshing instrument," he says, "is the black cummin to be threshed." The threshing instrument probably consisted of boards with sharp, pointed, iron nails which would be drawn over the grain spread on a floor in the open air. Such a threshing instrument would be too heavy to thresh the black cummin properly.

As fas as the cummin is concerned, says the prophet, the cart wheel is not to be turned upon it.[49] Another form of threshing instrument is evidently intended here, one which ran on small wheels or rollers. Possibly these wheels had teeth like a saw, and so could crush the grain. At any rate, whatever the precise nature of these instruments may have been, it is clear that they were not suitable for threshing the grains mentioned. They were too heavy for so delicate a work, and for that reason the farmer would not use them to carry out his purposes.

A good way for accomplishing these ends is at hand, however. With respect to the black cummin, a rod will suffice to beat it, and

---

[49] 'ôpan, wheel—the force of the negative extends also to the second clause. In yûs-sāḇ note Dagesh Forte in the sibilant. In יחבם the conjunctive accent appears with Qametz, having been removed from the ultima because of the immediately following disjunctive; this is the phenomenon of Nasog Ahor. The Tzere of the ultima is now changed to Sᵉgol, because, with the removal of the accent the ultima has become a closed, unaccented syllable.

a staff will be sufficient for the cummin itself. The arrangement of the words is interesting, for as in verse 25 there is here also a chiastic presentation of the thought. Furthermore, corresponding to the introductory emphatic negative of the present verse is the introductory armative of the second half of the verse.

28 Even the bread corn must be crushed, but not by means of heavy threshing instruments.[50] In the preparation of flour, it will be crushed by grinding. We may render the opening words of the verse, *As for bread, it shall be crushed*. This crushing is evidently to be accomplished by means of threshing, although this is not necessarily implied in the verb. The following clause justifies such an interpretation. Threshing, however, is not to be continued for ever, for it would destroy the corn as well as the chaff. In other words the farmer must be careful to crush not the corns but only the straw.[51]

What the farmer does do is set forth in the second half of the verse. He sets in motion the wheel of his cart. Apparently the wheel is sufficient to crush the grain, but on the other hand he will not thresh it with his horses. If the animals walked over the grain, they

---

[50] In 1Q *lhm* is omitted. The syntax of 28a is extremely difficult, but the following explanation seems to be as free of difficulty as any. *Lehem* is an obj., not subj., and the verb may be taken impersonally. The first phrase is best taken as a question, but there is no need to insert the interrogative particle *(BH)*. *Does one crush bread?* or lit., *as for bread shall it be crushed?* i.e., so that it is destroyed. The answer is negative, but the negative particle must be understood. The answer may then be rendered, "No, for not forever does one thresh it." The Vulg. reads, *panis autem comminuetur. Verum non in perpetuum triturans triturabit illum.* This takes *ki* in the sense of *ki 'im*, and I am not convinced that this is permissible. Drechsler's translation may also be possible. *Zu Brot wird's zermalmt, denn nicht ewig dreschen thut man's.* Here the thought is that corn is crushed to bread, and then the crushing ceases, for one does not thresh forever. So Luther, *Man mahlet es, dass es Brod werde.* Here the difficulty is to take *lehem* in the sense of the finished product, for in the construction *lehem* seems to refer to what receives the action of crushing, not what is a product after the crushing has ceased.

S. C. Thexton, on the basis of emendations, renders, "Corn for bread has to be ground. For he does not go on threshing it indefinitely—clattering his wagon wheel (over it) and winnowing it; no—he has to crush it" *(VT*, Vol. 2, 1952, pp. 81-83, 116).

[51] אדוש—an inf. abs., but the root אדש does not appear elsewhere in the OT. 1Q reads הדש, which could be read *hid-dûš*. Drechsler suggests that it was an incorrect form, used for emphasis' sake, and compares the stems *'āsap̄* and *sûp̄* in Zeph. 1:2; Jer. 8:13 and 48:9. Possibly the root is *dûš* with a prefixed *Aleph* for the infinitive.

would crush it with their hooves. For the corn of bread this was too severe a treatment, and the farmer will not use it. In like manner God measures the instruments of His purpose to the condition of His people; He employs what will best carry out His holy will.

29 In the treatment of the grains the farmers act with prudence and wisdom. Such behavior on their part is a gift from God (v. 25). But there is also something else that is from God, namely the divine dispensations in God's dealings with men. This (i.e., the contents of vv. 14ff.) also comes from God. Indeed, it has gone out from the Lord of hosts, and in so speaking Isaiah is asserting that it has found its origin in Him. The dispensations are difficult to understand, comprising as they do both promise and threat; but they are divine, and hence exhibit omnipotent wisdom.

Employing language which he had earlier used of the Messiah (cf. 9:5), the prophet makes two remarkable statements concerning the working of the Lord of hosts. In the first place "He causes counsel to be wonderful." The plan and purpose of God is one that is seen to be truly divine, devised of God alone. Likewise wisdom is magnified by God. His wisdom is not that of a mere man but is magnified far above the wisdom of man; it is wisdom that exemplifies the thoughts of God Himself. Before the strange counsel of His holy will as applied to the tottering theocracy one could only cry, "O the depth of the riches both of the wisdom and knowledge of God! how unsearchable *are* his judgments, and his ways past finding out!" (Rom. 11:33).

SPECIAL NOTE ON THE STONE

The primary exegetical question of 28:16 has to do with the identity of the stone.

A. Knobel (also Hitzig) identifies the stone with Jerusalem. It alone is to remain unconquered. He appeals to Zech. 12:3. To answer the objection that the stone is founded *in* Zion, he construes the preposition as a *Beth essentiae,* and cites 26:4; Ps. 124:8. But there are serious objections to this view. It is questionable whether the *Beth essentiae* appears here. Dillmann categorically denies it. It may also be asked why Jerusalem should be compared, not merely with a stone, but with a corner stone, for the corner stone is significant in holding the building together. Furthermore, Zech. 12:3 offers a different comparison entirely. Jerusalem is a heavy stone which will hurt those who lift it. Lastly, even the wicked in Jerusalem (cf. vv. 14-18) will be beaten down by their refuge. Even Jerusalem itself will not be an escape for them.

B. Maurer (Gesenius, etc.) says that the corner stone seems to be Hezekiah (Lapide *angulari et fundamento significari videtur Hizkia,* cf. 32, 1. 33, 17). But nowhere does Isaiah teach that the nation's hope rests in man. In fact, his teaching is the contrary; cf. 2:22. Theodoret, consequently, remarked that this interpretation was utterly foolish. It should also be noted that the stone is founded in opposition to the refuge of the people, namely, falsehood. The antithesis of falsehood is not a man, but truth.

C. Some refer the stone to the remnant (e.g., Skinner, who interprets "the foundation already laid of a spiritual community to be built by God after the judgment" [*Com.* p. LXVIII]). This does not fit in well with the language. The stone guarantees truth and right in opposition to the refuge of falsehood, so that the one who has confidence in the stone will not be in haste. Can this be said of the remnant, when even the remnant itself must be subject to further purgation (6:13)? What is said in (B.) about confidence in man is also applicable here.

D. Kissane expresses a view which from time to time has made its appearance, namely that the stone is confidence in the Lord. On this interpretation the stone and the one who believes are to be identified. At least three objections to this view may be made. (1) The stone has already been laid when Isaiah speaks, whereas the words *he who believes* express the reaction of a person to the announcement of the prophet and to the stone itself. The act of believing has reference to God's act of founding the stone. To this act all men will respond, either by way of faith or by way of unbelief. Those who respond by way of faith will not hasten. (2) This view would require that we hold that God has set up in Zion confidence in Himself as a touchstone. But has not that always been the touchstone by which men are judged? Was that not the touchstone by which Ahaz, for example, was condemned? (3) The stone was erected in opposition to the false refuge of the nation. Does confidence in Yahweh form a sufficient contrast or is it not rather Yahweh Himself or some Object in which confidence may be reposed that forms a genuine contrast?

E. That which God has founded in Zion is His dwelling among men in the Person of His Son, Jesus Christ. The Stone is an Object in which men may place their trust or confidence. This view is also supported by the following considerations.

(1) The Messianic interpretation is expressly adopted in the New Testament. Referring to Christ, Paul employs the words of this passage, "Every one who believes on him will not be put to shame" (Rom. 10:11). Earlier (9:33) Paul had again employed this passage,

blending it with Isa. 8:14, "Behold, I place in Zion a stone of stumbling and a rock of offense, and he who believes in him will not be put to shame." This is used to show that the Israelites had stumbled upon the stone of stumbling (Rom. 9:32), for, not having sought it by faith, they did not attain to the law of righteousness.

In 1 Pet. 2:6, 7 we again find reference to these two passages and, in addition, to Ps. 118:22, "Wherefore it is contained in the Scripture. Behold! I place in Zion a chosen stone, a precious cornerstone, and he who believes in him will not be put to shame. To you who believe (he) is precious, but to those who disbelieve, the very stone which the builders rejected, has become the head of the corner, and a stone of stumbling and a rock of offense." In Matt. 21:42-44 the reference is to Ps. 118 and Isa. 8:14, 15, whereas in Acts 4 it is to Ps. 118.

(2) According to Hengstenberg the stone is the kingdom of God, the Church; cf. Zech. 3:9. What is said of the kingdom of God, however, refers first to its head and center. This truth is illustrated by Isa. 14:32. Here, however, a distinction must be made between Zion and the stone. Whereas, in a certain sense, the Davidic dynasty may be included in the reference, what is primary is that in which trust may be reposed, namely the Davidic ruler *par excellence,* Christ.

2. The Iniquity of Jerusalem and the Announcement of Deliverance (29:1-24)

1 Alas, Ariel, Ariel, the city where David camped. Add year to year, let the feasts revolve.

2 And I shall distress Ariel, and there will be sadness and sorrow, and it shall be to me as Ariel.

3 And I shall camp like a circle upon thee, and I shall shut in upon thee with an entrenchment and I shall raise against thee ramparts.

4 And thou shalt come down, out of the ground shalt thou speak, and thy speech shall be low out of the dust, and thy voice shall be like a ghost, out of the ground, and out of the dust shall thy speech mutter.

1 Having spoken of the destruction of Samaria, the crown of the pride of Ephraim, Isaiah now turns to the south and addresses his remarks to Jerusalem, the capital of the southern kingdom. His introductory word, by the poignancy of its very sound, would seem to point out his concern for the city of David. He addresses the city by the term Ariel, and whereas there is no doubt that he thereby has Jerusalem in mind, there is question as to the precise significance of this unusual designation.[1] Apparently Isaiah does not

---

1 אֲרִיאֵל—a much disputed term. B πόλις Αριηλ, transliterated in Aq, S, T. From vv. 7, 8 it is clear that the reference is to Jerusalem. Theodotion, possibly misled by B (and followed by Theodoret, Eusebius, and Epiphanius), applied the term to 'Αρεόπολις, a "*Moabitarum urbe celebri*" (Rosenmüller). 1Q reads '*rw'l*, which might have been pronounced '*a-rû-'ēl*. (Penna also suggests Uruel. This would have to be 'û-rû-'ēl, i.e., a naturally long vowel in the distant open syllable. Penna thinks that we have here the first part of the name Jerusalem and the word for God. Philologically, this is questionable; we should expect '*ᵃ-rû-'ēl*.) It has been suggested that there is an intentional substitution of '*ēl* for *šālēm*, to avoid any reference to a Canaanitish deity (cf. *Syria*, Vol. 14, 1933, pp. 133, 137f., 147f.). Vulg. reads *Ariel, Ariel civitas*, but Jerome explains *leo dei*, deriving the word from '*ᵃrî, lion* and '*ēl, god*, ". . . *quondam fortissima vocatur Jerusalem*." This view has been widely adopted but interpreters differ as to its precise significance. Dillmann, for example, says that Zion is strong as a lion in God, queen among cities (Mic. 5:7), a lioness for her

304

employ the term in a restricted sense to apply merely to the hill known in David's time as the "city of David," but includes by the designation all of the Jerusalem of his own day. From the following clause we are safe in asserting that the reference is to David's own city, and this reference is expressed by a symbolical name, the exact significance of which we cannot with certainty determine. It should be noted, however, that this symbolical name of Jerusalem stands in relation to the reference to Samaria in 28:1 just as 22:1 stands in relation to 21:1.

Ariel was the city in which David had encamped, once so loved of God and now ripe for destruction.[2] The allusion appears to be to David's siege and conquest of Zion (2 Sam. 5:7-9). Quite possibly we are to understand the "camping" as an encamping against Zion, rather than of an actual pitching of tents there. On the other hand, the thought may simply be that David did make Zion his dwelling place.

Add year upon year—Isaiah appears to speak in irony, as though to say, "The destruction will indeed come, and there is no averting it. Keep on as you now do with your regular sacrifices. Let one

---

oppressors, an invincible royal city. But one may seriously question the suitability of such a designation for Jerusalem. The Targ. has *altar of God*, and in this is followed by Saadia. (Cf. 2 Sam. 23:20; 1 Chron. 11:22.) Rosenmüller says that it bears this designation by metonymy from the altar of burnt offering. Appeal is sometimes also made to Ezek. 43:15ff. It is very questionable whether the word *hā'ᵃ-rî-'ēl* is the same, because of the definite article; and the element *'ᵃrî-* is probably from *'ā-rāh*. It is possible, however, that the form may have become stereotyped, and hence the presence of the article may not be an insuperable objection to identifying the word with that in Isa. 29:1. On the other hand, the form *ha-har-'ēl*, which supports the word, is not a compound with *'ēl*, but a form like *kar-mel* from Kerem. In Ezekiel the word indicates the part of the altar where the victims were burned. We may also note the Mesha stele, *'r'l*, which Galling interprets as *Bronzeaufsatz des Altars*. (Cf. Albright, *The Religion of Israel*, p. 244, and *JBL*, Vol. 39, 1920, p. 138.) Mention may also be made of the view that the word signifies "mountain of God," *har-'ēl*, but the philological objections to this are strong. Appeal has been made to Babylonian *'arallu*, but again both philological and religious reasons rule this out. The rendering "sign (*segno*) of God" is obtained by assuming that the element *'ᵃrî* is from *yā-rāh* (Akk. *arû*).

Perhaps appeal should be made to Ug. *ary*, kinsman, dependent, Egy. *r.*, Hurrian *'ari*, man of. The word would then mean "belonging to God, possession of." This suggestion is put forth tentatively.

2 *the city*—The const. is followed by a finite verb, as Hos. 1:2 (not Gen. 1:1), Akk. *awat iqbi, the city where David camped.*

year follow another; you cannot escape the judgment." The command suggests that the people should allow one year to succeed another in the course of life that they are pursuing; this would not preclude the certainty of the judgment.

let the feasts revolve[3]— This phrase is to be taken in conjunction with the preceding. "Even though more than one year should pass, even though it should appear that the peace that you are now enjoying is one that will never be interrupted, even though you should think that the present order of events will continue forever and that you will die in peace as your fathers did, nevertheless, suddenly, what you have not expected will break in upon your lives, and the visitation of God will have reached you." Isaiah is addressing those same people who boasted that they had made a covenant with death and an agreement with hell. Carnal security would be no true foundation for them to rest upon.

We may sum up the thought of the entire verse. "Ariel, you are the very city in which David once had made his dwelling, but you, Ariel, are in a precarious position. Woe unto you! You refuse to realize your true condition, but you will soon discover that your present security is no security at all. Go on therefore, as you have been doing. Add year to year, for you think that your present condition will continue indefinitely. Celebrate your feasts regularly, year by year as you have been doing. It will be of no avail."

2 Taking up the thought of verse 1, Isaiah points out that there will be an interruption to the regular course of celebrations in that God will plague Ariel. This verse falls naturally into three parts, and each of these represents the order of the three following verses.[4] *I shall distress Ariel*—The Lord Himself here takes up the word of threat.[5] He announces that He will act, and thus removes any question as to the certainty of the visitation. As David at one time had besieged Jerusalem, so the Lord will now oppress her. He will confine her, place her in straits, as it were, so that she will be crushed by the pressing of judgment upon her. The announcement is general (I shall oppress), but becomes specific by means of a preposition, so that we may render, *I shall oppress with respect to Ariel.*

and it will be sadness and sorrow—The subject is the city itself.

---

3 ונצקתי—note that *Nun* is not assimilated.

4 Thus 2a sums up v. 3, 2b v. 4, and 2c v. 5.

5 *And I shall distress*—note *Meteg* with the antepenult, and the *Milra.*

306

As a result of God's distressing her, Ariel will be sadness and sorrow. This is a forceful way of saying that the city will be full of sadness and sorrow. Isaiah employs two similar sounding words, difficult to reproduce in translation, words which again occur in Lamentations 2:5. Interesting attempts have been made to reproduce the reading of the Masoretic Text in translations, such as Vitringa's *moeror ac moestitia;* Penna's *lamenta e lamentela,* and several German commentators' *Gestohne und Stohnen.*

and it will be to me as Ariel—This phrase is difficult to understand. Is it to be taken as in some sense indicating that the city will be destroyed? Or, on the other hand, is the last clause to be understood in a favorable sense, as indicating that the city will truly be an Ariel afterwards, and so will be what it once was intended to be? In the light of verse 8 the latter position is probably to be preferred. Yet we should not make any deductions from the name Ariel, for, as has been pointed out in footnote 1, the precise force of that name is not known. The sense seems to be, "Even though I shall oppress Ariel, nevertheless she will be with respect to Me as an Ariel should be." Thus, when the oppression comes and it would seem that Ariel will indeed perish, nevertheless, Ariel will resist the oppression, and prove herself to be a true Ariel. "As Jacob once wrestled with the angel," the thought seems to be, "so his descendants will again wrestle with Me and My overtures of grace. They will point to the promises of salvation and plead for their fulfillment. Hence, I shall remember My ancient promises to My people, and will redeem them. The earthly Jerusalem may fall, and its inhabitants go into captivity, but My promises will not fail, and My people will contend with Me to remember My promises." On this construction the words *to me* seem to have the force, *against me.* Hence, we may translate this last clause, *and with respect to me shall be an Ariel.*

In these verses there is a strong emphasis upon the working of God. Although Assyria was His instrument in the destruction of the theocracy, yet Isaiah does not mention the Assyrian at this point.

3 The Lord now describes the manner in which He will oppress the city; and the language in which the description is couched makes clear that the Lord is speaking of a spiritual, not a literal, oppression. His camp will be pitched against the city for the

307

purpose of destroying it, and it will be about the city like a circle
through which there is to be no escape.[6]

and I shall besiege thee—In itself the verb means merely "to
besiege." A good example of its usage is Daniel 1:1, which speaks
of Nebuchadnezzar's coming to Jerusalem and besieging it. At the
same time the general concept is modified here by the word "en-
trenchments." The reference is to some kind of palisade or siege
works. It is the Lord Himself who besieges; whether in the mention
of the palisades there is a secondary allusion to the Assyrians, the
instruments of His siege, is difficult to say.

ramparts—Another stage or phase of the siege.[7] The reference is
to siege works or ramparts, but one can only conjecture how they
are to be used in the siege. In order that the siege be successfully
carried out, however, they must be erected; and it is the Lord who
does this. The Lord attacks the city as though it were not in reality
an Ariel. Once David had attacked the Canaanitish city of
Jebus; now the Lord again lays siege to what is in reality a
Canaanitish city. David had conquered it so that the true
Jerusalem might be established, and Yahweh now conquers it for
the same purpose.

4 Continuing his address to the city, the Lord now declares that
from her condition of defeat she will yet speak.[8] The relationship
of the first two verbs is interesting, and we may render, *and thou
shalt be brought low; from the earth thou shalt speak*. These two
verbs are coordinate, standing in an asyndetic relationship to one
another. At the same time the first verb expresses the state or
circumstances under which the action of the second takes place.
Hence, we may render the first verb by an adverb. *Low—thou shalt
speak from the earth*. When the city speaks, she has already been
brought low, and her voice, which has been abased, comes from the
dust. In this dust she is a mourner, perhaps also as one who is
ready to plead that even now there may be a pardon and an
averting of the ultimate destruction.

6 *like a circle round about.* Cf. Akk. *dûra, an enclosing wall,* also *perpetuity.*
Ar. *dâra,* to circle, also used of besieging a city. B reads ως Δαυιδ, and this is
accepted by Penna, *Io mi accampero 'come David' contro di te,* but Aq, T
σφαιραν, and Vulg. *quasi sphaeram,* as though the Hebrew word were *kaddûr,*
ball (so also some of the Rabbis). Drechsler, *ring;* cf. Lk. 19:43; 21:20.

7 *mᵉ-tzû-rót—ramparts, siege works;* the long *u* is defectively written. Cf.
Ezek. 4:2.

8 V. 4 takes up v. 2b again.

To emphasize how completely the people will fall the prophet states that when the city speaks, its voice will be like that of a departed spirit and its words as mutterings that come from the earth. The departed spirit is really one that does not belong to this earth; for it does not speak with a clear voice, but only with mutterings. Such will be the voice of Judah. Once Judah was filled with the voice of scorn and mocking; now its voice will be like the whispering of shades (cf. 8:19). A spirit without flesh or bones cannot speak with a loud voice; nor will Judah when she is fallen. Gone is the voice of arrogance; in its place, the voice of the one in humiliation.

5 And the multitude of thy strangers will be like fine dust, and like chaff passing over the multitude of the terrible ones, and it shall be in a moment suddenly.

6 From the presence of the LORD of hosts it shall be visited with thunder and earthquake, and great noise, tempest and storm, and flame of devouring fire.

7 And it shall be as a dream, as a vision of the night, the multitude of all the nations fighting against Ariel, even all that fight against her and her stronghold, and distress her.

8 And it shall be as when the hungry dreams, and lo! he eats, and he awakes, and his soul is empty; and as when the thirsty dreams, and lo! he drinks, and he awakes, and lo! he is faint, and his soul craving; so shall be the multitude of all the nations that fight against mount Zion.

5 Abruptly Isaiah turns to a statement of what will happen to the enemies of Judah; yet he is still addressing Judah. His introductory words, "and it shall be" correspond to the "and it shall be" of the preceding verse; and the prophet first mentions the object of comparison before the object which is to be compared. Dust (*'avaq*) is to be distinguished from *'aphar* by its fineness. The enemies will be like light, fine dust, not merely like dust as such. And this thought is even strengthened by the addition of the word *fine* (*daq*). After this the object to be compared is itself introduced, namely, *the multitude of thy strangers*. Isaiah uses a word that he has already employed, namely, *hᵃmon* (the groaning, moaning multitude). It is this multitude of strangers that has oppressed and will oppress the theocracy, and whose destruction is sure. They are characterized as strangers; but the word is also used to indicate enemies (cf. 25:2 and Ps. 54:9), and hence there is no reason for emending the text (cf. 2 Chron. 32:7).

309

Verses 5 and 4 form a strong contrast, particularly in that no connective particle is employed. This merely serves to heighten the contrast.

A second comparison that serves to indicate the completeness of punishment and the ease with which the enemy is carried away is that of the chaff that passes over; Lowth poetically renders *flitting chaff*. With great ease and lightly the wind carries away the chaff so that it disappears and is found no longer.[9] So will the multitude of the terrible ones who afflict the theocracy be dispersed (cf. 13:11; 25:3-5).

By means of a striking alliteration Isaiah expresses the suddenness with which the enemy will be dispersed (*petha' pith'om*).[10] Inasmuch, however, as the Babylonians did conquer Jerusalem and took the people captive, it is well to ask how this fits in with what Isaiah is here saying. The answer would seem to be that in this discourse, directed against Ariel, Isaiah is not speaking of any specific attack upon Jerusalem such as that of Nebuchadnezzar, but rather is simply giving "a metaphorical description of the evils which Jerusalem should suffer at the hands of enemies, but without exclusive reference to any one siege, or to sieges in the literal sense at all" (Alexander). This is supported by the fact that the evils mentioned in the latter part of this present chapter are of a spiritual nature.

6 Isaiah now returns to the use of the third person which he had already employed in verse 2. In verses 3-5, however, the second person appears, and the third person continues in verses 7 and 8. Jerusalem, therefore, is not directly addressed in this verse, but is referred to objectively. The visitation comes from the Lord of hosts, and that fact is emphasized by being mentioned first in the verse. Whether the visitation is one of blessing or of punishment is a question upon which scholars differ. Penna, for example, thinks that it is a visitation of benevolence and protection, for he claims that the context demands this. On the other hand, many of the commentators believe that the visitation is one of punishment. Delitzsch claims that the verb should be taken in a neuter sense,

---

9 וכמץ—Note the omission of the article, which may occur when the object compared is defined by means of an attribute.

10 *piṭ'ōm*—contains an adverbial *u* ending, which is characteristic of some Semitic languages. Cf. "Adverbial *u* in Semitic," *WThJ*, Vol. 13, No. 2, 1951, pp. 151-154.

punishment is inflicted. This question is difficult, if not impossible to decide. It should be noted that the infliction or visitation upon Jerusalem follows the dispersing of the enemies (the tyrants) who had distressed God's people, and for that reason we may say that the reference is not restricted to the Babylonian conquest of Jerusalem. Jerusalem will be visited by the Lord of hosts; the precise nature of this visitation we cannot positively determine.[11]

Certain phrases, however, do describe the visitation. It will be with thunder, earthquake, and a great voice (i.e., noise), expressions that point to the power and majesty of God but which are here not intended in a literal sense. Isaiah presents the two words as a paronomasia and also with a threefold alliteration (*be ra'am uve ra'ash*). The language is elsewhere employed to denote a theophany.

The picture is one of great grandeur, for even elements of nature are involved and move at the coming of the Lord. Tempest and storm are present as well as the flame of devouring fire. The visitation is a terrible one, inspiring awe in the beholder. At His coming the world of nature cannot be at ease for His coming is majestic, accompanied by the voice of thunder and the noise of the elements in agitated motion. Before Him nothing can stand, for a fiery flame, devouring all, is with Him. As once He came down upon Sinai's mount, so now Jerusalem will be visited with His presence.

7 Again Isaiah introduces a verse with *And it shall be.* The comparison with the dream is intended to show that just as a dream quickly vanishes away, so will the one who threatens the destruction of Ariel. As things are in a dream, so is the enemy of God's people. The reference is not to a dreamer, but to the vanity of the dream itself, which soon passes.[12] The dream is further characterized as a vision which belongs to the night (cf. Job 20:8; 33:15; 4:13). Isaiah's purpose is not to identify the two, but merely to show that just as a dream and a night vision quickly disappear and vanish away, so will the enemy of God's people.

---

11 תפקד—the f. is to be taken in a neutral sense. א־וכלה—normally, an *i* vowel (here *Tzere*) in a near open syllable not preceded by a distant open syllable with short vowel should change to *Sh⁰wa*. Possibly the influence of pause here retains the *Tzere*.

12 It is, however, possible to construe *as in a dream*, taking *h⁰lôm* as an acc. of state.

311

The enemy is identified as the "multitude of all nations who fight against Ariel." Again the word "multitude" is used, and the enemy is further described as "even all that fight against her and her stronghold and distress her."[13] A certain amount of success, therefore, is attributed to the work of this enemy. The fortress mentioned is evidently the hill Zion (cf. 2 Sam. 5:7). The enemy concentrates not merely upon Jerusalem but particularly upon her fortress, Zion, the city in which David had lived. Figuratively, the reference would be to the Temple as the dwelling place of God. In attacking the heart of the city, the dwelling place of God, the enemy was seeking to destroy the city completely.

8 Having compared the enemy to a dream that quickly vanished, the prophet now compares him to the dreamer himself. As so often in this immediate context, the present verse also begins with *And it shall be.* Here the phrase serves to connect the verse with the preceding, and to introduce a further thought on the same subject. For, while here the enemy is compared to a dreamer, in reality this merely emphasizes what already had been said, namely, that a dream itself is fleeting, and soon vanishes away. The dreamer is a hungry man who dreams that he is eating. Perhaps the word includes the thought of eager desire for food, so that our English word hungry is possibly not quite strong enough to represent the full force of the Hebrew. The implication is that the enemy is eager to devour the theocracy, but that before he can accomplish his desire he is thwarted. The words "and behold!" are often used in dream narratives (cf., e.g., Gen. 40:9), and serve to focus attention upon what is the heart of the dream. Here it is the desire of the enemy, namely, eating, i.e., conquering Jerusalem and Judah. Such a dream, however, will not continue indefinitely, for the dreamer awakes, and then his soul is empty. This thought is given emphasis by the order of the words, *empty is his soul.*

A second comparison is then introduced. The enemy is compared to a thirsty man who in his dream is drinking. When he awakes he is tired, and his soul is craving. Here there is a gradation in the description. What in the previous comparison had been expressed in one clause, namely, "empty is his soul," is here presented in two clauses, namely, "and behold! he is tired," and

---

13 *and all of the fighters against her and her stronghold*—the genitives of nearer definition appear in the form of suffixes.

"his soul is craving." The first comparison confined itself to a negative statement, whereas here there is a positive declaration. Furthermore, the sentence is introduced by "behold!" which reflects upon the "behold!" of the dream. It is as though the prophet were saying, "In his dream he is drinking as he desired to do. Yet, in reality, it is but a dream; behold! what really is the truth, namely, that he, instead of drinking, is wearied out." The second occurrence of "behold!" removes us from the fantasy of the dream to the reality of the situation. The enemy dreams that he is conquering; in truth, he is worn out. More than that, while he is tired, his soul is craving.[14] The term employed suggests that the soul is rushing or running about, longing for water. Isaiah pictures a defeated and disillusioned enemy. Apparently the dream of conquest simply whets the desire of the enemy to conquer. Worn out, however, he is unable to do more than long for conquest. The enemy had counted on being able to devour Ariel; in actual fact, the enemy himself is the defeated one (cf. 9:11; 28:4; Num. 14:9).

Commentators have noted parallels to the thought expressed in this verse. Homer (*Iliad* xxii.199ff.) states:

> *As in a dream one is not able to pursue one fleeing before him,*
> *Neither is one able to flee nor the other to pursue . . .*

Vergil (*Aeneid* xii.908):

> *And as when slumber seals the closing sight,*
> *The sick wild fancy labours in the night,*
> *Some dreadful visionary foe we shun,*
> *With airy strides, but strive in vain to run;*
> *In vain our baffled limbs their powers essay,*
> *We faint, we struggle, sink, and fall away;*
> *Drained of our strength we neither fight nor fly,*
> *And on the tongue the struggling accents die.*

(Translation by Pitt)

---

[14] Penna renders *con lo stomaco vuoto*; Fischer, *seine Gier*; Steinmann, *l'estomac creux*. *Nepeš* does seem to be used here as the seat of the appetites; cf. 5:14; 56:11; 58:10. שׁוֹקֵקָה—note the retention of *Tzere*, and cf. footnote 11. The root means *to rush about, to run*, here figuratively describing the soul that is longing or craving for water.

Lucretius (iv.1091ff.):

And as when one who is thirsty in sleep, seeks
and liquid is not given, which can quench the
burning in the members: But he seeks the
likeness of liquids, and toils in vain,
He thirsts, drinking in the midst of a rushing
river.

9 Delay ye and wonder! blind yourselves and be blind! They are drunk, but not with wine; they reel, but not with strong drink.

10 For the LORD hath poured out upon you a spirit of deep sleep, and hath shut your eyes; the prophets and your heads the seers he hath covered.

11 And the vision of all has become to you like the words of the sealed book, which they give to one who is learned, saying, Pray read this, and he says, I cannot, for it is sealed.

12 And the book is given to one who is not learned, saying, Pray read this, and he says, I cannot, for I am not learned.

13 And the Lord saith, Because this people draws nigh with its mouth, and with its lips it honoreth me, and its heart is far from me, and their fearing me is a precept of men, which hath been taught.

14 Therefore, behold! I will add to treat this people strangely, very strangely, and with strangeness, and the wisdom of its wise ones shall be lost, and the prudence of its prudent ones shall hide itself.

9 Isaiah now proceeds to give the reasons why the judgment will come upon the people. What had been prophesied at the time of his call, namely, the blindness and hardness of heart of "this people," has now become a reality. Under Ahaz there was a general apostasy and turning from God, at least as far as the king himself was concerned. Under Hezekiah, there seemed to be a true repentance. Hezekiah himself sought the Lord, but the people were only true to God in an outward sense. In reality, there had been no genuine conversion. Isaiah therefore deals with such a people in the manner in which it deserves; ironically, he commands them to continue in their present condition.

Delay ye and wonder—The verbs are cognates, and the assonance is noticeable. The first verb expresses the idea of hesitation or delay, and is not a precise synonym of the second.[15] It is the

---

[15] The root *mhh* means to *linger, tarry, delay.* Cf. Ar. *mahat, delay;* Vulg. *obstupescite.* The form also appears in 1Q; to emend to *hit-tam-mᵉ-hú,* as in Hab. 1:5, would destroy the symmetrical parallel of v. 9a.

hesitation of one who is in wonder and hence unable to speak or to act. Isaiah is saying to such a one: "Don't act, don't speak, continue in your state of wonder and hesitation." Continuing with assonances, the prophet gives two further verbs.[16] Here in the choice of the verbal root, there seems to be an allusion to 6:10. The people are commanded to smear something over their eyes in order that they may be blind and not see. In the two pairs of verbs we have in each instance a *Hitpael* followed by a *Qal*, which would seem to point up the thought that the action mentioned was one which the people themselves chose. They chose to be blind; they chose to hesitate, and Isaiah is simply commanding them to continue in such a condition as long as they wished.

Turning from this direct address the prophet now describes the people in the third person. There is thus shown the reason why he ironically commands them to continue in the condition in which they wished to be. He might have continued his address in the second person, "you who are drunk, etc.," but in employing the third person he can speak with a certain disdain of the people. It is a drunken people, but its drunkenness is more serious than that of wine. As a drunken man cannot reason clearly, so this people, drunken in a spiritual sense, cannot think clearly concerning those matters which are its greatest concern.

As a consequence of its drunkenness it wanders or reels about. Something other than strong drink has intoxicated this people and caused it to act as a drunkard. The two phrases "but not with wine," and "but not with strong drink," seem to indicate the strongest kind of drunkenness. These are the members of the theocracy, those to whom the promises had been made, those who were to hear the deliverance of the Lord. Having just announced the full destruction of the enemy of God's people, the prophet, speaking as the mouthpiece of God, must now turn to the people themselves and find them utterly insensate to the wondrous message of deliverance which he had proclaimed. Drechsler compares the situation with the spiritual blindness of the disciples when Christ announced to them the message of His death and resurrec-

---

16 יְשַׁע—*to sport, take delight in.* 1Q reads *hts's'w* with *t* written over the second *s*. In 6:10 the root is used of smearing over the eyes; cf. Zeph. 2:1. בְּעוּ is accented *Milra*, whereas *Milel* is normal. *wine*—acc. expressing cause; cf. 51:21 and 28:1, 4, 7. Gesenius adduces an interesting parallel from Motanabbi, *ša-did 'ls-sakr min ghair la-mi-dâm,* "intoxicated and not from wine."

tion. They were "fools and slow of heart to believe," but the people of Judah are wicked as well.

10 Returning to a direct address to the people Isaiah gives the ultimate cause for the nation's spiritual lethargy. Penna remarks on the Semitic tendency to pass over second causes (*"non si dimentichi mai la tendenza a sorvolare le cause seconde in uno scrittore semita. . ."*). The reference to God here, however, is not to be dismissed in such fashion. It is true that men are responsible for their actions, and it is true that in sinning they brought blindness upon themselves; but it is also true that the ultimate cause was God Himself, who in His sovereign good pleasure had decreed that the nation should persist in blindness and spiritual drunkenness. Calvin is at his best in discussing matters such as this, and his words are worth consideration, for they go to the very heart of the matter: "As it belongs to him to give eyes to see, and to enlighten minds by the spirit of judgment and understanding, so he alone deprives us of all light, when he sees that by a wicked and depraved hatred of the truth we of our own accord wish for darkness. Accordingly, when men are blind, and especially in things so plain and obvious, we perceive his righteous judgment."

As He pours out the Spirit from on high (cf. 32:15) so also He has poured out a spirit of deep sleep. This deep sleep is not necessarily a consequence of the spiritual drunkenness but rather is a description of the same condition. The people are drunk, so we may paraphrase the thought, for God has poured out upon them a deep sleep. Their condition of stupor is described in verse 9 as that of drunkenness, in the present verse as that of a deep sleep. This is not a natural but a divinely imposed sleep, such as that which fell upon Adam, so that the one upon whom it comes is unaware of what goes on about him.

In the second part of the verse the prophet is no longer addressing the people in its entirety, but merely a part thereof, in which the guilt and sin culminates. Such a distinction is really presupposed by what follows in verses 11 and 12. In verse 11 the one who is learned stands for the leaders or educated part of the nation, whereas in verse 12 the unlearned one represents the mass of people. Some have sought to obtain a symmetrical arrangement of the verse by rendering, *and he has shut your eyes, even the prophets; and your heads the seers he has covered.* This is not necessary, however; and it is better to render, *and he has shut your eyes; the prophets and your heads the seers he has covered.* The eyes of the people have been shut, so that they of themselves cannot see. More than that the prophets, who had spiritual insight into God's will and who spoke forth that will, God had covered, with the result that they were as blind men, and indeed became blind leaders of the blind. The leaders (heads) are described either as those who see or simply as "the seers," and they too, like the prophets, have been covered. The blindness which has come upon the nation, therefore, is one that God Himself has imposed. In His inscrutable wisdom, He willed that the nation which should have been a light to lighten the Gentiles should itself be blind and stupefied.

11 "God has placed upon all the nation a deep sleep with the result that the vision of all that I have prophesied unto you has become like the words of a sealed writing." The word *all* is not to be restricted to what has just preceded, but includes the entire course of messages which have to do with the fortunes of the nation. All God's purposes with His people are to the people as a closed book. The revelation was known to the nation, but the nation had no understanding of and consequently no belief in the verity of that message. From the time of his call Isaiah had carefully set before the people both the nature of the danger that threatened to destroy Judah and also the will of the Lord with respect to the deliverance which he purposed to accomplish. All of this, so earnestly and boldly proclaimed by the prophet, might as well have been a closed writing, inaccessible to anyone. The people, walking about in the darkness of a deep sleep, paid no attention to it.

The mention of a sealed writing goes back to 8:16, but from this language we are not necessarily to conclude that the prophecy at this time was at hand in written form. The point is not that the prophecy was present in writing, but rather that the delivered revelations of the prophet are compared to a book that was sealed. A sealed writing is one rolled up and sealed. In order to read it one would first have to break the seal and to unroll the writing. As long as the writing was sealed, there would be no possibility of reading it, and there would be no point in asking a learned person to read such writing. Weber, however, takes the reference to sealing in a figurative sense. It is the writing itself, he thinks, that is mysterious. Even a learned person, who knows the art of reading and writing, is unable to understand the writing; for although he may be able to make out the letters and to pronounce the words,

317

nevertheless, the meaning is sealed to him so that he does not understand what he is reading. The reply of the learned one, however, "I cannot (i.e., read it) for it is sealed," seems to imply not a lack of ability to read but simply that one cannot read for he does not know what to read. The thing to be read is sealed.

12 Not merely the learned ones cannot read, but also the ignorant. The writing is given over to one who does not know writing, and a similar command is placed upon him.[17] His reply is that he does not know writing. Whether he actually sees the words of the book or not he does not attempt to read, for he is ignorant. The learned man could not read, for the book was sealed; the ignorant cannot read, for he does not know how to read. All among the people, therefore, are unable to read. Before them the revelation of God had been presented in clear words. To the learned and wise of this world it was meaningless, for it was to them as a sealed writing; to the ignorant it came as without meaning for they did not even have the ability to understand a revelation. All, therefore, without exception, were spiritually obtuse. Before them all the revelation of God, proclaimed through His faithful prophets, shone forth in the majesty and glory of the powerful Word; but over the entire people a deep sleep had fallen. It was a nation drunken and tottering about, groping, but never able to find the truth.

This is perhaps as sad a picture as is to be found anywhere in the Old Testament. When one considers all the manifold and rich gifts that the gracious God had given to this people; when one reflects that it was His design to make of this people a "kingdom of priests and a holy nation," and then reads of the rebellion and apostasy that characterized the nation, one can but wonder at the goodness and patience of God. Yet, God's purposes were not frustrated. Although in its entirety the nation turned its back upon Him, in His gracious wisdom God preserved alive in even this nation those that feared His Name, and in the fullness of time sent forth His Son, about whom there would be gathered those who loved His appearing and who would be truly a "kingdom of priests and a holy nation," even more, "a chosen generation, a royal priesthood, an holy nation, a peculiar people; that ye should shew forth the praises of him who hath called you out of darkness into his marvellous light" (1 Pet. 2:9).

17 *unto him who*—the prep. belongs to the antecedent understood.

13 This verse constitutes a protasis, the apodosis following in verse 14. The words are uttered by the Lord, and the term used to designate Him is one that calls to mind His almighty power. It is God the all-powerful who now speaks in characterization of His people. As is frequently the case He designates the nation with the depreciatory "this people," as though to say, "This people upon which a spirit of deep sleep has been poured out, and which, drunken, totters about, etc." Isaiah employs a chiastic arrangement in the first part of his protasis, namely, "Inasmuch as there has approached this people with its mouth, and with its lips it honors me." The people have come near in order to perform a religious service, but it is one that is done alone with the mouth; it is purely external. In the following expressions there is a remarkable change of persons, "and with its lips they honor me." Such change of persons is fairly common, the singular here pointing to the nation conceived as an individual, and the plural emphasizing the body of the nation itself, comprising all its members. The lips of this individual speak, and thus the people honor God; but by this language its hypocrisy is shown.

By means of a circumstantial clause, Isaiah shows that the worship of the mouth and lips was one in which the heart, the organ of true worship, was far from the Lord (cf. Jer. 4:3, 4; 24:7; 31:31ff).[18] If the true organ of worship had distanced itself, or made itself far away from the Lord, then any coming near to Him would be in pretense only. Although Hezekiah himself was a devout king and earnestly sought to bring about a reform, yet the idols were not completely abolished, and the heart of the people inclined after the old ways. There had been at best but a superfi-

---

[18] *and its heart*—the conjunction introduces a new subject in express antithesis to *its lips;* the clause is circumstantial, and the subject is placed first for emphasis. ויראתם—the verbal noun (inf. const.) takes a pronominal subject suffix and governs an objective pronoun; cf. *qutluhu 'iyyáhu, his killing him. command*—i.e., a commandment of men which has been taught, lit., a command . . . a taught one. *mlmdh*—a pred., modifying *command* (const.) and so also imparting a certain definiteness to it.

The proximate reference of Isaiah's language is of course to his own contemporaries. Nevertheless, through the Spirit of Prophecy he spoke also concerning the Pharisees of Christ's day, for Christ expressly states that such was the case. "Well did Isaiah prophesy concerning you" (Matt. 15:8; Mark 7:6). His quotation follows essentially the Septuagint (Codex B), and His accusation is that the Pharisees teach the commandments of men as though they were doctrines from God.

cial, not a genuine conversion. Religion was on all hands, but the heart of the people sought not the Lord.

In a certain sense the people did fear God. Their fearing of Him, however, was simply a command of men, a thing that was learned. The fear of which the prophet speaks is to be understood in an outward sense alone; it is really a synonym for the religious service or worship. It was not a fear proceeding from the heart. The fear of the Lord is the beginning of wisdom, but such fear proceeds from the heart and is characterized by a devotion of the whole being to God. This fear which Isaiah now mentions was external and so no true fear at all. It consisted merely in commandments that had originated from men, rather than in divine revelation. It was something that had to be learned from other men. Those who thus worshipped were taught of men and not of God. Human authority was sufficient for their worship; but human authority is not sufficient for God.

In reproaching the Pharisees (Matt. 15:9) our Lord had in mind specifically the requirements which they had imposed upon the law. There was growing up a great body of oral tradition which finally came to written expression in the Mishnah and the Gemara; and this, according to Christ, made vain the Word of God. In Isaiah's day there was of course no such body of oral tradition. To what then did the prophet refer? The answer would seem to be that the people "worshipped" God in the way that pleased them, but not in the way that was prescribed. This they did in that they regarded the outward form of worship as sufficient, irrespective of the attitude of heart. The priests evidently encouraged this, exhibiting a concern only that the worshipper bring the requisite sacrifices, but not that he come to the Lord in humble artd true devotion.

14 This verse is the apodosis to the preceding. "Inasmuch as the hypocritical worship of the nation is a fact, God will act." God calls attention to Himself with a forceful "behold!" for He is the one who is again about to perform a wonder.[19] The verb desig-

---

[19] יוסף, also 1Q. The Masora evidently intends the 3 m.s. *Hiphil* (cf. Isa. 38:5); hence, *Behold! me (it is I) who will add.*

lhply'—the verbal idea is intensified by the inf. abs. of the same stem and by a noun; thus, *to do wonderfully in doing wonderfully and* (i.e., even) *a wonder.* The inf. abs. is adverbial, modifying the inf. const., and the noun is an accusative. The root idea of *pā-lā'* is *to be separate, distinct,* but the noun means

nates God's marvelous actions often displayed in the deliverance of His people. Here it does not refer to a work of judgment or punishment in particular, but to what surprises or sets in astonishment. Alexander's translation "strange" is, if anything, too weak. Perhaps it is not possible to bring out in English the precise force of the word. What Isaiah says is that God will treat this people, or perform a work with respect to this people, such as only God can do. By means of paronomasia this thought is strengthened, *doing wondrously and a wonder.*

This work of God which he will perform with respect to "this people" brings about the perishing of its wisdom. God will so act that the people's wisdom will perish; it will disappear and vanish completely from the scene (cf. 19:1, 9-15 and 1 Cor. 1:19). This is not a new working of God, but a continuation of His previous working. Under Ahaz' reign also, human wisdom had sought to exalt itself above divine revelation. It appeared at that time to be the course of prudence and wisdom, in spite of divine warnings to the contrary, to call in the help of the Assyrian. Nothing but ruin came as a result of that plan, however. Now, the people thought themselves hidden, so that Assyria could not come to them; and they falsely believed that Egypt would be an ally and refuge. Once more their wisdom must be shown to be folly. And the thought that the Lord would not give up His own possession must also be shown to be false. The wondrous work of the Lord was to bring the people into such a condition that all confidence in human wisdom would be demonstrated as foolish. No one, not even the wisest of men, would know a way out of the difficulty; none would have an answer, for in man there is no light, no knowledge, no understanding.

Strong indeed is the prophet's language. He states not merely that wisdom itself will perish, but specifically that the wisdom of the nation's wise ones will be lost. When the wise ones, who should know what to do in time of crisis, have no wisdom, then truly the condition of the nation is precarious. Or is it? Then the nation may turn to the Lord, the only source of true wisdom and perception. By means of a parallel construction, Isaiah emphasizes the thought. The prudence or perception of the nation's prudent or perceptive ones will hide itself. Thus it appears that in the time of need

---

a wonder. The verb seems to be a denominative. 1Q spells the root in each instance with final *h*.

there will be no wisdom; all perception will completely have disappeared. Man is without wisdom, for God has acted in a wondrous way.

15 Alas! those who go deep from the LORD to hide counsel, and their works are in the dark, and they say, Who sees us, and who knows us?

16 Your perversion! Is the potter to be reckoned as the clay, that the thing made should say of its maker, He made me not, and the thing formed say of its former, He does not understand?

17 Is it not yet a very little while, and Lebanon shall turn to the fruitful field, and the fruitful field be reckoned to the forest?

18 And in that day shall the deaf hear the words of a book, and from obscurity and from darkness the eyes of the blind shall see.

19 And the humble shall add joy in the LORD, and the poor among men shall rejoice in the Holy One of Israel.

20 For the violent is at an end, and the scoffer is consumed, and all who watch for injustice are cut off.

21 Making a man a sinner for a word, and for him disputing in the gate they laid a snare, and turned aside the righteous through deceit.

15 That God should completely remove all human wisdom in a time of crisis is truly a wondrous thing. Those who are thus bereft of wisdom are to be pitied, for in reality they themselves through their wickedness and their hypocritical worship have removed wisdom far from themselves. In this verse the responsibility of the people is brought to the fore, and their pitiable condition called to attention. To show that the people try to hide their counsel deep from the Lord, Isaiah employs an interesting mode of speech. "They make deep from the Lord," he says, "to hide counsel."[20] The thought apparently is that if they go deep enough they can escape the seeing eye of God. Hence, emphasis falls upon the act of going deep, as though this might truly bring one away from the Lord.

The counsels of the nation manifest themselves in plans of

---

[20] *go deep from*—either in the sense of going deeper than the Lord, and so being more hidden than He, or else going where He cannot reach.

והיה—after a part. the perf. with *waw* consecutive expresses a present action as the consequence of a continuous or repeated action in the present; *who make deep and therefore (it is)* (their works) *in darkness,* i.e., their works are in darkness.

action. When these works are in the dark, supposedly hidden from the Lord, then the people are confident that all is well. Then they think that none can see them and know what they have done. Perhaps at no point does the folly of human wisdom manifest itself more than here, in that those who form mere human plans think it is possible both to devise and to carry out these plans apart from the Lord.

16 Such conduct upon the part of man deserves a rebuke from the prophet, and hence he cries out, "Oh! your perverseness."[21] Since the time of Luther, who saw the true force of these introductory words (*wie seyd ihr so verkehrt*), many, perhaps most, expositors have rightly considered the opening words of the verse an ejaculation. The first word may be rendered "perversity" or "absurdity." "Contrariness" also brings out the thought. What Isaiah has reference to is the attitude that would attempt to hide anything from God. One who would do this obviously does not think that God is all-knowing. From lesser gods or from tribal deities things can certainly be hidden. From gods created in the image of man it is easy to hide anything. The people of Judah are not dealing with such gods, however; they are rebelling against the one ever living and sovereign Jehovah, who controls all things, and who knows all things. To endeavor to hide anything from him is pure contrariness. It is a perversion, an overturning of the true relationship between God and man. God is the Creator and man the creature. To attempt to hide anything from Him is to act as though He were ignorant and hence not truly the Creator. In truth it is but a denial of the fact that He is creator. More than that it is in effect an elevation of man above the Creator; for man thinks that he can fool the one who made him. Thus, in the deepest and most profound sense, all sin, all error, all philosophy grounded merely upon human wisdom, all idolatry—these things are perversions.

We might expect Isaiah to complete his poignant cry with words such as, *how great it is!* Possibly because of his intensity or excitement, however, a portion of the exclamation is suppressed. As the words now stand their force is, *how great is your perversion!* Could

---

21 One of the few instances where '*m* introduces a question, which stands in a disjunctive relation to what precedes. Cf. 1 Kings 1:27; 2 Kings 20:9; Prov. 27:24; Jer. 48:27. Robinson, *ZAW*, Vol. 49, 1932, p. 322, upon the basis of emendation renders, "Shall the potter be accounted as the finished vessel, or as the clay?"

Isaiah, however, have spoken in such a vein? Marti maintains that Isaiah did not engage in theological discussion with his opponents but simply regarded them as rebellious (30:1). The concepts of potter and vessel and creator and creature, he thinks, appear only in "Deutero"-Isaiah. In answer, we would say that only in the broadest sense can this language be termed theological discussion. It is the perverseness (and surely that is rebellion) of the people which is at the heart of these words. But, on the other hand, why may not Isaiah have reasoned with the nation? Did he not utter the words of 1:18? Did he not reason with Ahaz before the coming of the Assyrian (7:1ff.)? And surely there is no ground for denying to him the figures of the potter and the clay nor of the creator and the creature. Passages such as the present one simply form the basis upon which the later passages in Isaiah build.[22]

By placing the analogue first, the language of the first comparison is made quite emphatic. "Is it that like the clay, the potter is to be reckoned?" The comparison thus teaches that to reckon the potter as the clay would be to degrade the potter, for between the clay and the potter there is a profound abyss, just as also between the Creator and the creature, between God and man. To imagine clay revolting against its potter is impossible. The thought is frivolous; man rebels against his Creator, because his will is depraved. His action, however, is as foolish as would be the clay turning against the potter. The potter has power over the clay, not the other way round; the Creator has power over His creature, not the creature over the Creator.

As the Hebrew text is accented, it must be translated, *Is it as the clay of the potter he is to be reckoned?* The following comparison between the former and the one formed, however, seems to support the interpretation that we have adopted, namely, the contrast between the clay on the one hand and the potter on the other.

Man is like the clay. He was made; he did not make himself. Elementary as this truth is, its denial lies at the basis of much modern thought and action. God is ruled out of the thoughts of man, and man is regarded, at least to all intents and purposes, as existing in his own right. He thinks that he has no need of God.

22 Cf. Isa. 45:9ff.; 64:7; Jer. 18:6. Penna remarks *"Esso* (i.e., the comparison between God and the potter) *è implicito in tutti i testi* (Gen. *2, 7s; Ger. 1, 5; Am. 7, 1 ecc.), nei quali l'azione creativa di Dio è descritta col verbo jāṣar—plasmare (jōṣēr—vasaio)."* Cf. also Rom. 9:20-23.

Hence, he says of God, "He did not make me." Words more wrong, more foolish, more soul-destroying have never been uttered by human lips! How great was Augustine's delight, when, as he tells us in his *Confessions*, he asked the stars to tell him about their God, and they replied with a loud voice, "He himself made us." Here is the heart and the beginning of all wisdom, and it is this which the men of Judah by their perverseness were denying.

Equally foolish would it be for the thing that was formed to say that the one who formed it had not perception or understanding. If the One who forms has no perception, then certainly the one formed in the very nature of the case has no perception. The Christian Church suffers greatly whenever a wave of devotion to Irrationalism comes over it, for Irrationalism says that God has no perception.

17 By means of a proverbial expression Isaiah announces a complete and deep-seated change. The language is poetic, and we are not to endeavor to determine precisely how much time is to elapse before the promised changes will take place. In a little while Lebanon will turn aside from what it now is and become a paradise.[23] It will be turned into a Carmel, i.e., its opposite. The word *karmel* indicates a fertile ground in which plants and trees can grow in abundance. Lebanon of course designates the mountainous wild country. In a little while the mountainous country will be turned into a fruitful field that brings forth abundantly for the benefit of man. On the other hand, the fruitful field will be reckoned as the forest itself. There will be no distinction made between forest and garden. It may be, as some commentators assume, that the interpretation of these comparisons is that Judah will be cultivated and made like the fruitful garden, whereas Assyria will be turned into the wild forest land.

18 Having set forth under the figure of Lebanon and the fruitful field the great change to come, Isaiah now emphasizes that change by another description. At the time when Lebanon and the fruitful field will become one, then the deaf will hear the words of a book. The deaf are not those who are physically deaf, but spiritually so, who do not hear the promises, for they had become to them as the words of a sealed book.[24] There is an obvious allusion to what the

---

23 wšb—the perf. with *waw* cons. after a determination of time.
24 Penna, however, applies the words to those who are physically deaf and

prophet had earlier said in verses 13 and 14. A spirit of deep sleep had been poured out upon this nation so that it could not hear. Their hearing will not be a mere physical act, but a physical act that results in deep-seated obedience. Of course the Jews heard the words of Isaiah with their physical ears, but they were to them but idle words. There was no response of obedience.

What is the book to which reference is made? It is not the book of the Law, but simply the writing in which the promises of God were found, which had hitherto been sealed to the nation.[25] This interpretation is clearly supported by the reflection upon the sealing of the writing which had earlier been made. The book which no one, not even the literate, could read, will at that time be understood by all, even the deaf.

In the second part of the verse the language constitutes a contrast, at least as far as form is concerned, to that of the first part. No direct object is given, but instead the former condition of the blind is stated. The blind had been in obscurity and darkness. This condition will be removed, and the eyes, now freed from their blindness, will see. Like the first part of the verse, this one also is to be taken generally as denoting a complete reversal of conditions. It does not specifically refer to the Gentiles alone, but to all, primarily those of the preceding verses, who had walked in darkness and blindness. By means of these figures we see the completely radical nature of the change to come.

19 As the preceding verse set forth a change in the intellectual views of those who were to experience salvation, so this verse reveals that there will also be a change in their welfare. Just as the preceding verse did not single out those who were physically handicapped among the nation and so emphasize that only a part of the

---

blind ("*si trata di veri ciechi e sordi*") . In the period of blessing, he thinks, even bodily infirmities will be healed.

Although Isaiah intends spiritual blindness, it is possible that his thought is based upon the fact that in ancient times reading was performed aloud (cf. e.g. Acts 8:30) . Deaf people, therefore, could not hear such reading. Cf. Alfred Tacke, *ZAW*, Vol. 31, 1911, pp. 311-313.

25 Maurer, however, says, *de libro legis dicitur, ut apud Arabes 'al-ki-tâb de Corano.* Gesenius appeals to Ps. 40:8; Dan. 9:2; and Koran 2:53, "We gave Moses the Book and the Discrimination *(furqân).*" But were the reference to the Mosaic Law we might expect an additional designation as in 34:16. Also, there is an obvious reflection upon v. 11. The omission of the definite article is probably poetic.

nation would experience blessing, so also this verse does not single out the humble as a particular part of the nation. The "humble" and "poor" of this verse are the same as the "deaf" and "blind" of the former.[26] What the prophet is teaching is that salvation is so great that it accomplishes a radical change in the nature of things. Those who once were deaf and blind now hear and see; those who were humble increase in joy, and the poor rejoice.

In construction the verse is arranged chiastically, beginning and concluding with a verb. Who are the oppressed or humbled ones of whom Isaiah speaks? The prophet is probably not singling out those who necessarily were afflicted and humbled in a physical sense. He rather is designating those who are now believers. In the eyes of the world they would be regarded as humbled. The sense seems to be the same as that used by our Lord, "Blessed are the meek" (Matt. 5:3). Perhaps the thought may be paraphrased as follows: "Those whom the Lord regards as deaf will now hear, and those whom men regard as humbled will now add joy." These add joy in the Lord in that they themselves rejoice, and so add to the joy already present. This joy is "in the Lord," and so is a holy rejoicing, exhibited by those and only by those who have experienced the Lord's salvation.

The second designation has peculiar force, in that it signifies the poor, and none else, from among men. The words possibly contain a secondary connotation of piety. Those whom men regard as poor are the ones who will rejoice. Isaiah chooses a general word, 'adam, which heightens the concept of lowliness. We may bring out the force of the two words by rendering *poor men*. The thought has often been used in the Old Testament to designate those who are afflicted by men but who will be blessed of God (cf. Ps. 5:12; 32:28-32). These will rejoice in the Holy One of Israel, i.e., in His wondrous work of salvation. He will be the cause of their rejoicing. When men experience the deliverance from God they rejoice in God their Maker and Redeemer.

20 There is good reason for such rejoicing, for salvation consists in a deliverance from the oppressors under whom the people had formerly suffered.[27] The tyrant will come to an end, and the

---

26 *the poor of men*, i.e., *poor men*—In all probability the const. and following gen. give to the phrase the force of a superlative, *the poorest men*.
27 כי—followed by the simple perfect sets forth the reason for what was expressed in the preceding verse. *wklh*—The perf. with weak *waw* expresses an act which is coordinate with the one just mentioned.

scorner will cease. These words describe those who hitherto had afflicted God's people. The verb expresses the past with relation to the preceding verse. The people will rejoice, for the tyrant has disappeared. At the same time, from the standpoint of the prophet the verb expresses the future. The promise herein set forth has not yet occurred when he speaks. It is a blessing that will take place in the future.

With the words "tyrant" and "scorner" no definite article is used, and for this reason and also in keeping with the general tenor of the thought, it would seem that the reference is not to any specific tyrant or scoffer. We are not, therefore, to identify the tyrant with Sennacherib nor even with tyrants among the people. The word suggests rather all that can be classified as tyrannical. No more will tyrants—whoever or whatever they may be—oppress God's people. With them all who scoff will also come to an end (cf. 28:14, 22).

By means of a third verb the prophet states that those who watch for iniquity will be cut off. With diligence and industry they watch for the opportunity to do harm and evil.[28] Isaiah has mentioned three types or classes of evil. One expresses itself in the violent doing of wrong, another in contempt of the truth, and the third in that deceitfulness which looks for an opportunity of wrong-doing. As Alexander has emphasized, wherever the truth of God is proclaimed, these three forms of evil make themselves manifest. From such evil God has wrought deliverance.

21 With this verse Isaiah proceeds to show how it is that those who wait for evil go about their business. What they do is mislead men into sin.[29] The participle is in the construct, so that the rendering must be, *the causers to sin of a man*, i.e., *those who cause a man to sin*. The noun *'adam* designates the lower class of mankind, as opposed to *'ish*. The word of which the prophet speaks is the judicial process, as shown by Exodus 18:16; and the preposition is best rendered, *by means of*.[30] Hence, we would

28 Gesenius applies this expression to those who watch over the right and should cultivate it, but instead maintain wrong. But usage supports the interpretation adopted in the text; cf. Jer. 31:28; 44:27; Dan. 9:14. Maurer is correct, *qui omne studium in hoc contulerunt, ut non aequum fieret, sed iniquum.*

29 In the *Hiphil* the root means to cause to mislead into sin, e.g. 1 Kings 14:16; 15:26ff.; Jer. 32:35; etc.

30 *word*—may also refer to the word of those who are led into sin, thus: causing men in their words to sin, i.e., in what they say are made to sin.

translate the first clause, *those who cause a man to sin by means of a word.* Precisely how this is done is difficult to say. Through their word (which possibly is a deceitful and misleading one) they cause others to sin. From the following parallel phrase, however, it is often assumed that this takes place in a judicial proceeding.

The parallel clause confirms what has just been stated. The one who argues his cause or pleads his dispute in the gate, where the court session was held, is one for whom the evil ones lay a snare.[31] The picture is that of a man who is seeking to show the justice of his cause (the noun has the sense of arguing, disputing, pleading) in the court before the judges, and of evil men laying a snare so as to catch him or trip him up in his argument. It is another way of endeavoring to show that he is guilty and that the cause which he pleads is not just. These evil ones wish by their deceitful tactics to make the just man appear guilty.

and turned aside the righteous through deceit—Lit., *and they stretched out through desolation the righteous.* The verb refers to an act of turning aside the righteous so that he will not receive justice (cf. 10:2). This is accomplished by means of "desolation." Isaiah uses a noun which he had already employed (24:10) and which is found in Genesis 1:2. Here the word probably signifies lies and falsehoods, anything that is vanity and not based upon truth. By such dishonest means do these evil ones seek to defraud the righteous. He whose claim in law is just is the object of trickery and deceit; and by these means his claim is "stretched," so that it is regarded as false and worthless (cf. Amos 5:12). It is quite possible that these evil deeds are done by judges themselves. In 21a they act as accusers; in 21b they are apparently the accused. In 21a the righteous are the accused, and in 21b they are the accusers.

> 22 Therefore, thus saith the LORD unto the house of Jacob, he who redeemed Abraham, Not now will Jacob be ashamed, and not now will his face turn pale.

---

[31] *they lay bait, lure*—Green explains this form as 3 pl. preterite of קוֹשׁ *(yā-qōsh).* The addition of the *-un* ending, seen also in *yā-ḏe-'ûn,* Deut. 8:3, 16 and *tzā-qûn,* Isa. 26:16, would take the accent and place the *Qametz* in a distant open syllable where it would be replaced by *Sheᵉwa.* BDB takes the form as an imp. of *qwš,* which root does not appear elsewhere in Biblical Hebrew. If the form were from *qûš,* we should expect *yᵉ-qō-šûn,* for *yᵉ-qō-šûn* would be a jussive, and its presence here would not suit the thought. Cf. also Dillmann, "*Die im Part. begonnene Beschreibung wird im Impf. fortgesetzt (5, 11.23 u.o.)."*

23 For when he seeth his children, the work of my hands in his midst,
they shall sanctify my Name, and they shall sanctify the Holy One
of Jacob, and the God of Israel they shall fear.

24 And those who wander in spirit shall know perception, and the
murmurers shall learn doctrine.

22 The introductory word, *therefore*, reflects upon what has
immediately preceded. Inasmuch, so the argument runs, as there is
such a glorious future for the people of God in their deliverance
from the wicked, the Lord speaks. The coming time of blessing will
make all clear. Hence God addresses the house of Jacob, a phrase
that includes all the descendants of Jacob. It is the entire body of
descendants in itself which is here in view, the redeemed who are
heirs of the promises that God had made to Jacob.

The Lord is described as the One who has redeemed Abraham.
Between the relative pronoun *who* and its antecedent *the Lord,*
the phrase *unto the house of Jacob* is inserted. It is clear, however,
that the antecedent is the LORD, otherwise the reference would
be to Jacob as having redeemed Abraham, which clearly does not
make good sense.[32] Here is introduced a thought that will reappear and be developed in the latter part of the prophecy. We hear
in this sentence, as Drechsler points out, the sound of Isaiah
40–66.

There is difference of opinion as to what is intended by the
redemption of Abraham. Marti feels that there must be reflection
upon the later Jewish legend according to which Abraham had been
persecuted in Ur of the Chaldees and was delivered therefrom by
God,[33] whereas others apply it to Abraham's removal from a land
of idolatry. It may be, however, that the word is a general term for
deliverance, including the whole calling of Abraham with his
separation from the pagan world, and his being chosen as a bearer
of the promises of God. The word is used also of the deliverance of
the Israelites from the bondage of Egypt.

God has redeemed Abraham, and so Jacob will not now, nor
ever, be ashamed.[34] Nor will his face pale, as though blanched
from shame. God had once brought Abraham out of Ur of the

[32] Gesenius calls attention to Hensler's interpretation: Jacob, "whom He had
freed with Abraham." But the phrase *house of Jacob* seems to refer to the
descendants of Jacob rather than to the ancestor as an individual.

[33] Marti, *Com. in loc.*

[34] *now*—refers to the time when Jacob will see his sons. The word is used
as in 9:6; Mic. 5:3, and not in the sense of *therefore; demnach, also.*

Chaldees and separated him from the heathendom of the day in order that he might be the ancestor of a multitude which should belong to the Lord. Likewise, from the great body of the physical nation, steeped in superstition and unbelief, God would also separate the house of Jacob as the basis of the true people of God.

23 The words of this verse give a reason why Jacob will not be ashamed. He will see his offspring, whom God has given to him, and they will be in the midst of his natural descendants. They will sanctify God's Name and glorify Him as the one who has brought about so great a work of deliverance. Such is the general meaning of this verse, but there are difficulties in the details of interpretation. Again Isaiah begins a verse with *ki,* his purpose being to ground the truth of what has just been stated. "There is a reason," we may paraphrase, "why Jacob will not be ashamed, and that reason is that when he sees his seed, they will glorify God." So strong and powerful were the oppressors of God's people, that it would seem that they would actually destroy the covenant promises. In reality, however, the outcome was to be something quite different; the promises of God would be fulfilled, and Jacob would see his seed.

when he seeth his children—To many expositors the presence of the words "his children" is a source of difficulty. Some, therefore, would render, *when he (i.e., his children) sees.* This, however, does not resolve the difficulty, for it makes the phrase unnecessary. Others omit the suffix entirely, and in this they have textual warrant. The verse could then be translated, *when his children see the work of my hands.* Still other expositors simply omit the words "his children." Others omit both the suffix and the words "his children" and render, *in seeing the work of my hands, they will sanctify, etc.*[35] If, however, the text be retained as it is, there are two possibilities. On the one hand we may take the suffix of the infinitive construct in a pleonastic sense, and render, *and when his children see it, i.e., the work of my hands;* or else we may translate, *and when he (i.e., Jacob) sees his children, the work of my hands.*

Either one of the last two suggestions is permissible, although I incline toward the latter rendering. By the term "his children"

35 Dillmann: *wann er* d.i. *seine Kinder;* B, S, T, and Syr. omit the suffix; *BH* proposes to omit *yldyw,* but the words are found in 1Q; Gesenius: *When my children see it, the work of my hands;* Penna: *poiche vedendo 'l'opera delle mie mani fra loro.*

Isaiah does not refer to the natural descendants of Jacob, the Jews, but rather to those whom he has already mentioned in verse 18, the deaf and the blind. These, it would seem, by their very nature could not be heirs of the promises. There would, however, be a complete revolution, such as that described in verse 17, and then they would be recognized as the heirs of salvation. They are the work of God's own hand, in that, through His sovereign grace, He chose them to be His own and wrought in their hearts the work of regeneration. They are a spiritual seed of Jacob in that they were born, not of the flesh, nor of the will of man, but of God. Of them the prophet was later to speak: "Thy people also shall be all righteous: they shall inherit the land for ever, the branch of my planting, the work of my hands, that I may be glorified" (60:21).

We must, however, seek to identify more precisely the ones that are intended by this phrase, "the work of My hands." Included is the remnant that remains among the people of God after the judgment. The first judgment to affect the nation was the exile, and from this exile there would be a remnant. In the deepest sense, however, the remnant would be those who ultimately are saved. Included among them are devout Jews (as to the flesh), but also the Gentiles. We may very well think of the Church as the work of God's hands. The Gentiles are referred to in the New Testament as Abraham's seed; and if they are Abraham's seed, they are certainly Jacob's also. In its broadest sense, then, the phrase simply includes all the redeemed.

in his midst—This phrase is difficult, and one cannot positively assert precisely what it is that the prophet intends to express. In its most natural sense, it would seem to suggest that the spiritual seed will be in the midst of the physical descendants of Jacob, the Jews. Possibly then the meaning is simply that among the physical children of Jacob there will be found His true children, who are the work of God's hands.

That a spiritual seed is referred to is demonstrated by the description, *they shall sanctify my Name.* To sanctify God's Name is to regard that Name as holy and to act accordingly. It is to acknowledge Him as the Holy One of Israel, the One who is indeed the God of gods, utterly distinct from His creatures and separate from all evil, and to submit oneself to Him and His ways in all things. The mark of a true victory on God's part is that men will sanctify His Name.

In the second half of the verse there is a general statement that men will sanctify the Holy One of Jacob. Although the verbs are here to be taken in an indefinite sense, it does not necessarily follow that the subjects are different from that of the first part of the verse. Rather, the second half of the verse is an emphatic statement that the redeemed will sanctify the Lord. In English, therefore, we may render the introductory *waw* by *yea*, or *indeed*. The Holy One of Jacob is the One whom Isaiah saw in his inaugural vision. Here, the Name of Jacob is employed because of its presence in this context. This interchange in the use of Israel and Jacob is anticipatory of the prophet's practice in the latter chapters of the book. As Delitzsch well comments, "And in fact, throughout this undisputedly genuine prophecy of Isaiah, we can detect the language of ch. xl.-lxvi. Through the whole of the first part, indeed we may trace the gradual development of the thoughts and forms which predominate there."

At the same time the word Jacob is also employed to indicate that men will one day worship as God that same God that the ancestor Jacob worshipped. He alone is to be recognized as deserving of reverence, just as Jacob acknowledged Him and no other. In the presence of the God of Israel men will feel dread and fear. There can no longer be room for derision of His work, for the work of His hands in trembling fear will sanctify His Name.

24 In a remarkable manner Isaiah connects sanctifying the Name of God with the learning of understanding and perception. The subject of the verbs of this verse, it would seem, is the same as the subjects of the verbs in 23b. This is true, even though the subject is here described as *those who wander in spirit* (lit., the wanderers of spirit). These are identical with the deaf and blind of verse 18. They wander in spirit, for they have succumbed to false teachings and they know not where to turn. Furthermore, they are murmurers, for they resist the truth. All this, however, will be changed, for they will know, i.e., possess insight (cf. Job 38:4), and they will learn doctrine (cf. Prov. 4:1). It is God's work that will accomplish this. What is clearly taught in this passage is that knowledge of understanding is something that men must learn, and this they learn from God their Teacher. Nor do men understand doctrine until they are taught it of God.[36] Those who will glorify

36 *leqaḥ—learning, teaching*, in the sense of receiving *(lqḥ)* teaching; cf. Prov. 4:10. Gesenius aptly compares Aram. *qabbalah*, and Samaritan *nśib*

Him are those that are taught of Him. They alone possess knowledge and learning.

(Deut. 32:2), and B λημμα, *oracle,* from λαμβάνω, and *accipere* (Cicero *de natura deorum* iii.1) in the sense of having insight, understanding.

B. THE JUDEAN ALLIANCE WITH EGYPT (30, 31)

1. To Trust in Egypt Is to Be Deceived (30:1-33)

> 1 Alas! rebellious children, saith the LORD, to execute counsel, but not from me, and to pour out a libation, but not my spirit, for the sake of adding sin upon sin.
>
> 2 Who walk to go down to Egypt, and my mouth they have not asked, to take refuge in the protection of Pharaoh, and to trust in the shadow of Egypt.
>
> 3 And the protection of Pharaoh will become to you a shame, and trust in the shadow of Egypt confusion.
>
> 4 For his princes are in Zoan, and his messengers arrive at Hanes.
>
> 5 All are ashamed of a people who do not profit them, who are not for help and not for profit, but for shame and also for reproach.

1 Sin is cumulative; one sin leads to another. Having turned to Assyria for help instead of relying upon God's promises the nation finds a great enemy hovering over it. To avoid the bondage of this enemy, the people now look to another human source of deliverance, namely Egypt. Indeed, there may actually have been a pro-Egyptian party in Hezekiah's court. The present prophecy, however, relates not so much to one particular act as to an attitude of mind, which in the face of danger turns to man rather than God; it is this attitude wherever manifested that the prophet condemns.

Isaiah had already spoken of those who "seek deep to hide their counsel from the Lord. . ." (29:15), which may very well be a reference to seeking aid from Egypt. The folly and sin of Ahaz are to be repeated. Evangelist that he is, the prophet cries out "Alas!" for it is a situation that calls forth concern and compassion. People who acted in this manner are to be pitied, for they err in their counsel. To them also belongs the fearful designation, *rebellious children,* language which reflects upon the *rebellious son* of

335

Deuteronomy 21:18-21. Such a son would not hear the voice of his parents; he was gluttonous and a drunkard, deserving the penalty of death by stoning. Israel and Judah are like that rebellious son (for probably the prophet has the entirety of the people in mind); they will not hear the word of the Lord, but rather are satisfied with their own desires. They too are deserving of death.

At the same time the people are still designated *sons*. God has not abandoned them, but in punishing them acts as a father must act toward his own rebellious son. Earlier Isaiah had characterized the nation's princes as rebellious, but now he applies the epithet to all the people (cf. 1:23).[1] The root idea of the adjective is "turning aside." The people turned aside from Yahweh; they did not wish to hear His Word. Instead they turned unto their own desires and devices, and in so doing revealed their rebelliousness.

It is not merely Isaiah who thus characterizes the people, but the Lord Himself, for the characterization is expressly stated to be an oracle of the Lord. This rebelliousness manifests itself in the performing of counsel that is not from God and also in pouring out a libation. We are probably to render, *because they execute counsel,* for a causal concept apparently underlies this usage of the preposition and the infinitive construct (cf. also 1 Sam. 14:33; 19:5). The action attributed to the people is not merely initiating or taking of counsel, but the actual carrying out of the counsel which they had devised (cf. 2 Sam. 17:23). The counsel, however, neither comes from God, nor is it carried out by Him. It is entirely of human origin and execution. In the devising and carrying out of such counsel the nation is characterized as rebellious.

A second action is attributed to the nation, namely, the concluding of a covenant.[2] Actually, the action is described in the terms, *a pouring out of libations;* but inasmuch as such an action took place at the ratifying of a covenant, we may probably conclude that what the people are accused of is the actual entering into a covenant. This evidently was an agreement with another power (Egypt) by which Judah sought protection against Assyria. The prophets had been endued with the Spirit who spoke through them. The nation, however, did not inquire of the Spirit, i.e., they did

---

1 Cf. also Isa. 1:2, 4, 23; 65:2; Jer. 3:22; 5:23; Hos. 9:15.

2 *mskh*—Possibly the word may have the sense of *a libation,* evidently used in the making of a covenant. Cf. σπένδεσθαι σπονδήν; Vulg., however, *ordiremini tela,* lit., *to weave a web,* perhaps in the sense of a plot, i.e., the negotiations with Egypt.

not consult the prophet, but went ahead on their own.[3] For this
reason they were willingly adding sin to sin.[4]

2 Isaiah now points out, or better, the Lord through him, what
these rebellious sons do. They go down to Egypt for help.[5] In the
Scriptures travel to Egypt is spoken of as downward, for Egypt lay
lower than Jerusalem. The Judahites go down to Egypt, without
consulting the mouth of the Lord Himself.[6] Such action exhibits
the outworking of a counsel that was not of divine origin. To ask
at the mouth of the Lord is to consult His prophets; hence, in
disobeying Him the nation ignored His prophets. Ahaz was a
classic example of such disobedience, and his example was now
being widely followed.

The purpose in turning to Egypt was to become strong by means
of Pharaoh's strength and to take refuge in Egypt's shadow.[7] That
there was danger before them, the people recognized full well.
Pharaoh, however, was thought to be a mighty king, able to protect
those who took refuge with him. Would not his shadow, it was
asked, give protection to all who came under his wing? Yet this was
strange counsel. At one time Israel had been under the shadow of
Egypt and Egypt had been her oppressor. From this dreadful
oppression and bondage the Lord had delivered Israel and had
warned her against returning to Egypt. "Ye shall henceforth return
no more that way" (Deut. 17:16c). How soon Israel forgot the
ancient deliverance of her God! She was now willing to abandon
her true king and to turn to the nation which formerly had been
her great oppressor.

3 *my spirit*—dependent upon the prep. *min;* cf. Isa. 28:6. Penna, however,
renders *nel mio spirito.*

4 *sfwt*—also in 1Q; not to be emended to *sepet.* This is a *Pe waw* verb,
which, when the first radical is dropped in the *Qal,* has tendencies to follow
the pattern of *Lamed He* verbs; cf. Isa. 29:1; Num. 32:14; Deut. 29:18; and the
Mesha inscription (line 21 should be read *lis-pōt*).

5 *walk*—i.e., they set out; their walking is for the purpose of going down.

6 *my mouth*—the position of the words renders them emphatic; cf. Gen. 24:57.

7 לעוז—we should normally expect *la-'ûz,* but the abnormal writing also occurs. Cf. Josh. 2:15; Ezek. 10:17. The root is *'ōz* or *'ûz;* cf. Ar. *'â-ḍa, 'wḍ.*
refuge—The *Qametz* is evidently a naturally long vowel and hence, in the construct, is not replaced by *Shᵉwa.* The *Holem,* however, remains, even though
the syllable is closed and unaccented. With the suffix a pure short *u* vowel
appears, save that usually with the 1 s. suffix, a *Shureq* is written. *laḥ-sōt*—after
Lamed with the inf. const. a closed syllable is normal.

3 It goes without saying that such conduct and such plans would fail. The third verse consists of two parts which correspond to the two members of verse 2b. Isaiah clearly states that the stronghold of Pharaoh, as far as the people were concerned, would become an object of shame. And as for protection under the shadow of Egypt, that would become a source of confusion. Why this was so is not stated, whether it was that Egypt went back on her agreement, or whether she was simply unable to provide the trust and protection that Judah needed. Reliance upon human resources instead of divine help, however, is always a cause of shame.

4 The prophet gives a reason why trust in the shadow of Egypt is a shame, but the verse is difficult to interpret. The first difficulty appears in the presence of the suffixes. If these refer to the rebellious sons of verse 1, there is a resumption of the third person, the usage of which had been interrupted by the introduction of the second person in verse 3. The change in person is abrupt but possible, and the references would be to the princes and messengers of Judah.[8] These princes as ambassadors together with the messengers of Judah had penetrated the extent from north to south of the Egypt of that day. Apparently Zoan and Hanes are considered as small seats of dynasties, and their mention shows that the ambassadors of Judah have penetrated the land. "Even to Hanes" we may paraphrase, "have these ambassadors penetrated, so determined are they to receive Egyptian aid and protection." Zoan is to be identified as Tanis (cf. 19:11). Strabo referred to it as even in his day a great city (xvi.1.20). It is near the modern San el Hagar about 800 meters from the ancient ruins on one of the eastern branches of the Nile. The twenty-first and twenty-second dynasties originated in Zoan. The name Hanes occurs only here in the Bible; it has been identified with the *Heracleopolis magna* of the Roman period and is probably the modern Henassijeh el madina about 18 kilometers west of Beni Sueif.[9]

5 Repeating the thought of verse 3, Isaiah now points out that

---

[8] Duhm, however, following Hitzig, refers the suffixes to Egypt, suggesting that the proper names demonstrate the north-to-south extent of the Egypt of that time, and also because in the battles with Shabako they had often been named in Palestine. Cf. A. Kuschke, *ZAW*, Vol. 64, 1952, pp. 194f.

[9] Hanes—Ashurbanipal, in his first Egyptian campaign, mentions Ḫi-ni-in-ši, whose king was Na-aḫ-ki-e. Cf. Egy. *ḥn-n-stnj*, "the king's mansion"?

all who seek Egypt, whether they be the princes in Zoan or the
messengers that have reached Hanes, will be ashamed.[10] They
have come to the Egyptians, a people that cannot profit them. The
Egyptians are not for help or profit, and hence it is foolish to go to
them to seek what they cannot give. All that God's people can
receive from such a nation is shame and reproach. This appears
strange, for Egypt was a powerful nation; Egypt, however, could
not provide the deliverance from Assyrian threat that Judah needed; only God could be her true refuge and protection.

> 6 The burden of the beasts of the south, in a land of suffering and
> distress, from them come the lioness and the lion, the adder and
> the fiery flying serpent; they carry on the shoulder of young asses
> their wealth and on the hump of camels their treasures, to a
> people who do not profit them.
>
> 7 And Egypt, in vain and to no purpose do they help. Therefore I
> cry concerning this, their strength is to sit still.
>
> 8 Now, come, write it upon a tablet with them, and upon a book in-
> scribe it, and let it be for the last day for a witness for ever.

6 Most commentators regard the opening words of this verse as a
title supplied by a redactor, and therefore, in reality, a gloss. If
this is the case, a problem arises. If we omit these words there is
nothing in the context to suggest a change of subject or the
beginning of a new section of the prophecy. Why, then, would a
redactor have inserted a title at this particular point? Realizing the
cogency of these questions Alexander denies that there is a title
here at all, and simply renders the words as an exclamation, *Oh!
the burden of the beasts*, or else *As to the burden of the beasts*. On
this interpretation the verse is merely a continuation of what has
preceded.

No strong objection can be raised against this procedure; yet, at
the same time, the word *massa'* (burden) is often employed in the
book as a title. Why may not Isaiah himself have inserted a title at
this point? In verses 1-5 the prophet has presented in bold strokes
the theme with which he is concerned. This, as it were, is his text,
which he desires to develop and expand. From now on he sets
forth the considerations and conclusions that he wishes to develop
from this text, and the first of these is the great deception which is

---

[10] Read *hib-'iš*, from *bā'aš*, which could have the metaphorical sense of dishonored; cf. 1 Sam. 27:12. The form *hô-bi'š* is ungrammatical; cf. Zech. 10:6
for a similar case.

to come to Judah for her vain confidence in another nation. Judah had expended tremendous toil for nothing. God, the spring of life, was abandoned for vanity and nothingness.

That he may bring this thought out into the open and turn the spotlight of Judah's attention upon it, Isaiah begins as it were anew. He sets apart the thought of deception and frustration as though they formed a separate and unique oracle, that men may see clearly the significance of what he is saying.

Isaiah therefore heads the section, "The oracle concerning the beasts of burden." These are described as "beasts of the south," for their destination lies to the south.[11] Isaiah is not referring to the adders and the flying serpent, but to the asses and camels mentioned in the latter part of the verse. These animals were laden with goods from Judah, sent down to Egypt in order to obtain the favor of the Egyptian power.[12] The ambassadors and princes have already been mentioned; it is really only for the sake of variety of expression that the prophet now speaks of the beasts of burden. The suggestion of Hahn and Delitzsch that the magnates of Judah who had less understanding than the ox and the ass should be grouped with these beasts, is interesting, but it is questionable whether it is correct.

It is not to the beasts as such that the prophet directs attention but to the beasts as they trudge through a land of sorrow and distress. This land is not Egypt nor is it Judah, but the wasted desert that lies between them.[13] Just as apostate Judah spared no means to obtain the help of Egypt, so the prophet inserts phrase after phrase depicting the dangers that lay in an approach to Egypt. A row of three subordinate phrases introduces the action of the Judahites. Here is one of the saddest pictures in all Scripture. Once God had led the ancestors of the nation through this

---

11 *bhmwt—BH* suggests pointing *bᵉ-hē-mót*, but the form is normal for a const. plural. At the same time, as in the various cases within chaps. 13-23, the word is an objective gen. after *maśśā'; the burden about the beasts of the south.* For the construction of the superscription cf. 21:13 and 22:1.

12 This seems to be the only OT reference to asses as beasts of burden, rather than as riding animals (Judg. 10:4; 12:14; Zech. 9:9).

13 Procksch suggests that the embassy was to Arabia. This would be to take the word *negeḇ* in a restricted and technical sense. Isaiah is speaking generally, to indicate the desert region that lay between Palestine and Egypt. Quite possibly the actual route lay along the coast. As Penna suggests, the prophet speaks of the more inland zone to impress more clearly the dangers that it contained.

very desert when He brought them from the country of their bondage. He it was "Who led thee through that great and terrible wilderness, wherein were fiery serpents, and scorpions, and drought, where there was no water: who brought thee forth water out of the rock of flint" (Deut. 8:15; cf. Jer. 2:6). Now, utterly unmindful of what God had once done for the nation, the people traverse this same wilderness for the purpose of seeking protection from the nation that in ancient times had been the home of their bondage. Isaiah uses a number of subordinate phrases as though thus to emphasize the great difficulty that lay in the way of Judah's foolish action. He also achieves a striking effect by employing the two similar-sounding words *tzarah* and *tzuqah* (*suffering* and *distress*), words which in the Hebrew both begin and end alike. This suffering and distress would be the lot of travellers through that desert. Even in Isaiah's day the journey would not be free of such difficulties.

In this desert land there were lions which attacked the travellers and his animals and made the desert journey difficult.[14] There were also dangerous serpents, the viper and the flying fiery serpent.[15] Isaiah names all the animals and serpents with collective nouns, thus suggesting the presence of many of each kind.[16] Travel through desert regions is dangerous because of the presence of the serpents. Through such a land God had brought His people in safety, but now voluntarily they chose to travel through this land for the purpose of finding aid from the people who could not help them. The action speaks for itself.

On the shoulders of the asses, the beasts already grown and ready for service,[17] and on the humps of the camels, the people laid their burdens, so that these animals might march on through the desert carrying their goods to a people who would be of no profit.

7 This verse corresponds to verse 5 as verse 6 corresponded to verse 4. It sets forth the reason why Egypt is a land that will not profit. *And Egypt*—Thus the prophet introduces his subject, fo-

---

14 Cf. 5:29. ‫ליש‬—*lion*, cf. Ar. *layth*, and Bochert, *Hierozoicon*, 3.125-137.

15 There is no warrant for the assertion that the "Seraphs" are demonic beings in the form of winged serpents (Cf. Martin Noth, *Überlieferungsgeschichte des Pentateuch*, 1960, p. 134). Cf. Herodotus ii.75; iii.109; Ammianus Marcellinus xxii.15.

16 *among them*—i.e., the suffering and distress.

17 *'yr*—male ass; the young animal ready for work; Judg. 10:4; 12:14; cf. Ar. *'ayr. dbšt*—camel's hump; cf. Ug. *gbtt;* Akk. *gupšu.*

cusing the attention directly upon that land to which Judah wished to turn for aid.[18] *in vain and to no purpose do they help*—With these words Isaiah characterizes the country to which Judah looked for help. Egypt may try to help, but her efforts amount to nothingness and vanity; they are no help at all; they bring Judah no profit. It is for this reason that the prophet, speaking in God's Name, calls the land *rahav*. Elsewhere this term is used as a poetic name for Egypt (cf. Ps. 87:4; 89:10; Isa. 51:9). In itself the word merely means *arrogance, storm*. It is apparently used, however, in some biblical passages, to designate the serpent or crocodile, and thus refers to Egypt conceived as a great serpent or crocodile lying along the sea. As applied to Egypt the word suggests that the land was a storm let loose upon the Israelites, a storm that would devour them if it could. The nation itself as a powerful entity together with its gods would rise as a storm against Israel. It was truly a Rahab. The construction of the final words is difficult. The object of the verb appears to be given in the words, "A Rahab are they— a resting." In other words the object is expressed in a sentence. As the Masoretic accents suggest, the words "Rahab are they" belong together. These words set forth the common opinion or designation of Egypt. In the eyes of the Egyptians and possibly of men generally, they were regarded as a Rahab, a powerful monster that could devour and destroy. In reality, however, they were but a *sheveth* (a resting). This latter word designates a ceasing of activity, a period of resting, and thus forms a suitable contrast to Rahab. Thus Egypt is to be known not as Rahab, but as a ceasing, or resting, and so as a power that can be of no help to God's people. God has spoken; His mark as it were is upon Egypt. She is no Rahab, but only a resting.[19] "Lo, thou trustest in the staff of this broken reed, on Egypt; whereon if a man lean, it will go into his hand, and pierce it: so is Pharaoh king of Egypt to all that trust in him" (Isa. 36:6). Thus Egypt receives a new name, "A Rahab are

18 *And Egypt*—the words form a *casus pendens*. *As for Egypt (it is in respect to) nothingness and vanity they help*.

19 The accents in 7b are correct; cf. Ex. 14:3; Lev. 11:8, 10; Isa. 9:20; Prov. 4: 22. *Therefore I have called this* (i.e., Egypt) *A Rahab are they? No, a resting*. A common emendation, at least as old as Michaelis, is to combine the consonants and read *ham-maš-biṯ*, lit., *who causes to cease*. Other proposed emendations are *ham-mᵉ-šab-bēṯ, who is inactive; ham-moš-bāṯ, the reproved trust*. RSV renders, "Rahab who sits still." But Gesenius correctly remarks that these emendations "*wird man bei einer richtigen Auffassung leicht entbehren.*"

they? No, rather a resting." Egypt's mighty power is gone; the nation is not what it once was.

8 A declaration such as Isaiah has just made should convince anyone that Egypt had lost her Rahab character and had become a mere *sheveth* (resting). At the same time the truth expressed by this declaration must be written down so that, after Israel herself had learned by experience that Egypt could not help, the words might stand as a corroboration of what had been prophesied. Thus, verse 8 is a command addressed to the prophet himself, and the introductory words *Now, come* draw his attention to the command. Having expressed so severe a characterization of Egypt the prophet is now to hearken to what God says and obey God's command to write.[20] He is not commanded to write down only the last three words of the preceding verse, as some have suggested, but the content of the message that has just been delivered concerning trust in Egypt. As in 8:1, 16 this message was to be written in order that it might be preserved. The writing is to be done upon a tablet (see comments on 8:1) where it might be kept so that it would always be before the people's eyes, that they might be warned and admonished thereby. Possibly what the prophet means is that the writing is to be done before the eyes of the people; it is difficult to ascertain the precise force of the prepositional phrase *'ittam* (*with them*).

Some commentators have sought for a distinction between *tablet* and *book*. Thus, Maurer, to take an example, holds that the prophet was commissioned first to prepare a tablet and then to inscribe his message in a book. This involves a double task. The word *sepher* (book) may also mean *writing*, and the two parallel expressions are really commands to do the same thing.[21] In writing on a tablet, Isaiah is also inscribing his words in a writing. The purpose for this action is also expressed as a command, *and let it be*. The words constitute a divine fiat, similar to those uttered at the creation, that the writing is to exist for a latter day. This is a message to be taken with deadly seriousness. Judah is embarking upon a course almost as disastrous as that of Ahaz, who turned to

---

[20] *ktbh*—the form seems to presuppose *ku-t͜e-bi;* cf. Akk. *purus* and Ar. *'uktub.* The f. suffix refers generally to the verbal idea expressed in the preceding sentence, i.e., the fact that Egypt is to help in vain and their strength is to sit still.

[21] Some would give to *sēper* the meaning *bronze;* cf. Akk. *siparru,* Job 19: 23; Hab. 2:2; J. Friedländer, in *JQR*, Vol. 15, 1902, pp. 102ff.

Assyria for help. Now, to avoid the consequences of that fateful move, the people of Judah are ready to commit a similar folly, to turn to Egypt for aid against Assyria. Egypt cannot help them; in great crises only God can be their stay. They must learn that Egypt is a weak reed, and the words of this truth are to stand as a monument in their midst that they may ever be reminded of the folly of trust in man. In the deeper sense, the words would also be a testimony to the fact that the ancient promises of God are sure and true, and that, despite the folly and sin of the people, in His own good time, God will bring those promises to fulfillment. Trust is to be placed not in Egypt but in God. Salvation, in the deep sense of the word, will come to the world through God and not through man.

9 For it is a people of rebellion, lying sons, sons *that* will not hear the law of the LORD.

10 Which say to the seers, See not! and to the prophets, Prophesy not for us right things, speak to us smooth things, see deceits.

11 Turn aside from the way, incline from the path, cause to cease from before us the Holy One of Israel.

9 Had Israel been an obedient people there probably would have been no need to preserve the prophetic message in writing, for then the mere word of the prophet would have been sufficient.[22] But Israel was not obedient, and for that reason the message must be preserved that the justice of God's judgment and the truthfulness of His words may be known by posterity, and that the Israelites themselves may have a constant reminder before their own eyes. Using language which he had employed in the first chapter (cf. 1:4, *people, sons*) Isaiah identifies the nation as a people, but of rebellion. It is a nation of sons, to be sure, but of sons who are lying.[23] There is question as to the precise significance of the epithet. Some think that the emphasis falls upon a habitual denying of God the Father; others that it is found in a deceiving of the hopes and expectations of the One who had been so gracious. Perhaps one cannot decide positively between these two views, although the context points to a relation between children and the One who has blessed them. They are children who disappoint this One.

Isaiah goes to the heart of the matter when he states that they do

22 *ki*—for, expresses the reason why the message must be written down.
23 *kehāšîm*—lying, mendacious; the underlying form is *kah-ha-šîm*.

344

not want to hear the Lord's Law. It is expected of children that
they delight to hear what their father taught them; these sons,
however, are rebellious. They have no real love for their heavenly
Father, for when He speaks, they do not wish to hear. If they were
willing and hearkened, they would eat the good of the land (cf.
1:19). They, however, even though they are sons, are disobedient.
The law which they do not wish to hear is the message that Isaiah
is proclaiming to them concerning the folly of placing trust in
Egypt.

10 In this verse the prophet gives proof of the rebellious character of the nation. Not merely did they refuse to hear the Law of
God, but they also sought to instruct the prophet what to say. It
was not enough that they would not hear; they must themselves
tell the messengers of God what they are to preach. Human wisdom is more palatable to them than divine truth.

Isaiah is not giving an actual quotation of the words of the
people. They did not use these precise words in addressing the
prophets. Rather, what Isaiah here is doing is setting forth the
nation's attitude. These people did not want the prophets to speak
forth the Law of God; they preferred that the messengers of God
should speak the things that they themselves desired to hear. At the
same time Isaiah had rightly gone to the heart of the matter. As
Marti points out, in the deepest sense these were the words of the
people. This is a true expression of what the people desired.

In describing the messengers of God Isaiah does not employ the
term *prophet*. He speaks rather of seers and beholders.[24] These
two words are practically synonyms, and in both of them the
emphasis rests upon the "seeing" of a revelation. But the function
of both is also similar; they are men who declare the Word of God.
To the seers the people say, "ye shall not see," by which they mean,
"ye shall not continue seeing in the manner in which ye have been,
and as a result of having seen, ye shall not speak forth the message." In other words, the seers were no longer to act as genuine
seers. There is really no warrant for the assumption that those

[24] For a discussion of the significance of these terms cf. *My Servants the
Prophets,* 1952, pp. 56-75. Note also 1 Kings 22:8; Jer. 38:4. Those who preach
contrary to the people's wishes are disliked. Cf. *Iliad* i. 106:
"Prophets of evils, you have never spoken to me what is good (τὸ κρήγυον).
Always to thy heart is it dear to prophesy evil. But a good word thou hast
neither spoken nor brought to pass."

addressed are necessarily false prophets. True enough, there would have been men who were perfectly willing to speak forth flattering messages; but here the idea is that the people go to those who had been receiving messages from the Lord and command them to cease acting as they had been. In the parallel expression the word *hozeh* is employed. Between this and *ro'eh* there is no essential difference. Both were men who had received their messages from God by means of visionary experiences. When the *hozeh* had received his message he delivered that message and it proved to be right and profitable.

The command is first stated negatively and then positively or affirmatively. It expresses a conscious, deliberate rejection of what was right and a positive desire for what was wrong. What the people desired to hear were smooth things and deceits. Luther brought out the basic thought by his translation, *Preach soft to us.* Smooth things were flattering things which did not point out the sinfulness and unworthiness of the nation but rather commended it. Unbelief always desires to hear "smooth things."[25] In fact these "smooth things" were deceitful, for they did not set forth the truth. The nation itself did not label the messages deceitful, but deceitful they were. As the nation consisted of deceitful sons, who deceived their Father, so it wanted to hear messages that were in accord with its own character.

The command of the people does not suggest that the prophets cease their function of speaking. Speaking prophets were necessary for the presence of religion, and these people wished to be religious. There was no objection to the prophets' carrying on their activities, provided those activities did not point up the true condition of the nation. Religion is always welcomed by the unbelieving world; it is the preaching of the Gospel that causes controversy.

11 Isaiah now continues the command that the people addressed to the prophets. In commanding the seers to turn aside, the people desire that these messengers of God deflect from the way in which they had been walking. They are to cease acting as true prophets of Yahweh, and instead, to act as false prophets. The way in which they had been walking was that of proclaiming fearlessly the Law of God. It is this way that the nation wishes them to forsake. From this road they are to turn aside in order that their ministry may

---

25 *h⁰-lā-qôṯ—smooth* and hence *welcome things*, the opposite of *n⁰ḵôḥôṯ*. *ma-h⁰-ṯal-lôṯ—deceits, illusions.*

take a direction that leads not to truth but to the satisfaction of wicked men.[26] A culmination is reached in the command "to cause to cease from before us the Holy One of Israel." Quite possibly, as many have pointed out, there is reflection upon the fact that Isaiah in his preaching often employed the designation of God, "the Holy One of Israel." Without a doubt the people were tired of hearing that beautiful designation, for it pointed up the contrast between the exalted character of God and their own worthless condition. More than that, however, seems to be in view. If the prophets would cease preaching the message of God and would turn to a message of their own understanding, which would flatter the nation and cause it to be content with its lot, what the prophets in actual fact would be doing would be to cause the Holy One of Israel to cease from the minds of the nation. When the truth is no longer proclaimed, the God of truth disappears from the hearts of men. This it was that the people desired.

12 Therefore, thus saith the Holy One of Israel, Because of your despising this word, and ye have trusted in oppression and perverseness, and have relied thereon,

13 Therefore, this iniquity will be to you like a breach falling, swelling out in a high wall, whose breaking may come suddenly, at an instant.

14 And its breaking is like the breaking of a potter's vessel, broken without mercy, so that there is not found in its structure a sherd to take up fire from a hearth, and to skim water from a pool.

12 It is time to state the consequences of the nation's rebellious attitude. The people apparently thought that they could control the prophets and so banish from their minds any thought of Yahweh, the Holy One of Israel. For this reason the Holy One of Israel speaks. The One whom the nation would cause to cease is the One who will cause the nation to cease. He speaks, and His words are an announcement of destruction to come. Yet He gives a reason why this is so, and that reason is found in the people's despising the word that Isaiah has spoken.[27] At the same time the

---

[26] *min-nē*—only here. The *Hiphil* appears to be used intransitively in the sense of *turning aside,* and so there is an elipsis of the proper object.

[27] *because ye despise*—lit., *because of your despising.* This construction of the prep. and inf. is usually continued by a finite verb rather than by a second, coordinating inf. *mo-'os-ḳem—your despising.* Underlying the normal inf. *me-ōs,* there is a second form, *Qutul.* With the suffix of the 1st person we would get

people had exhibited trust, not in God's promises but in oppression and perverseness. This term *oppression* is to be taken generally. It refers not to one particular act of oppression but to the general attitude of the nation as exemplified in its leaders. Probably it points out the attitude of the leaders to the prophets, in that attempts were made to stifle the preaching of these messengers of God. This was done so that nothing could stand in the way of their own desires. Oppression was the key to accomplishing their will. Coupled with it was perverseness. Isaiah's word is an infinitive form of a root that means *to turn aside.*[28] It signifies what is devious or crooked, and is exemplified in the actions described in 29:15. They themselves had desired such a refuge (28:15); their own words therefore prove the truthfulness of what Isaiah is charging.

These are the stays upon which the people lean. There is a gradation in the prophet's description. Not merely do they trust in these things, but they also lean upon them for support. Those who look upon trust in God and His promises as impractical would do well to consider the nature of the substitutes that man offers.

13 Verse 12 gives the ground for punishment; verse 13 announces the punishment; verse 12 is a protasis and verse 13 the apodosis. The connection may be paraphrased, "Inasmuch as what has just been related is true, therefore a punishment will come." Both this and the preceding verse begin with the word *laken* (therefore). Isaiah goes to the heart of the matter immediately and characterizes the attitude of the people as an iniquity, indeed, as an iniquity that will affect the people. "This iniquity will be to you," he says, and his meaning is that with respect to the people their iniquity will become like a breach. The language of the comparison is difficult and we must consider it phrase by phrase.

like a breach falling[29]—These words have occasioned difficulty, for

---

mo-'sî. With the heavy suffixes, however, *mo'-sᵉ-ḵem.* The guttural takes compound *Shᵉwa, mo-'ᵒs-ḵem,* which is not possible, since there must be a full vowel in a closed, unaccented syllable, *'os.* The *Shᵉwa,* therefore, is lengthened, giving the present form, the *Meteg* being inserted since there is now a full vowel in a distant open syllable.

28 *nlwz—what is devious, crooked, Niphal* part. of *lwz;* cf. J. Van der Ploeg, *OS,* Vol. 5, 1948, p. 145.

29 *about to fall*—The thought is not of a forest stream that rushes against a wall, nor of a broken wall (BDB), but probably of a crack or breach, about to descend in the wall.

it may be asked how a breach in a wall could be about to fall. Possibly what is intended is a breach that is sinking and so will lead to the collapse of the entire wall.

swelling out—As the breach sinks it widens and grows larger in size. This occurs in a high wall so that when the fall occurs it will be that much greater and more fearful. In all probability the picture is that of a high wall of clay or mud. The dampness or moisture causes it to weaken and a fissure begins to form. The rent begins as it were within the wall itself, and as it descends grows larger and larger, until finally the wall topples over. So the sin of the people within the nation itself increases in magnitude, until finally it causes the nation's destruction. The downfall of the theocracy, in other words, is not really to be attributed to the Mesopotamian power; that was but an instrument in God's hands to carry out His purposes of punishment. What actually caused the downfall of the theocracy was the sin within. It was a falling sin, a sin swelling out, found in the high wall of Judah. Thus the punishment of judgment comes, not merely through sin but from sin itself. While the breach or rent may slowly descend, it finally reaches the point where the wall can no longer stand, and the breaking of the wall thus occurs instantly.

14 Isaiah continues the description of the broken wall. The first verb is probably to be taken either impersonally or as a passive.[30] It is possible that the antecedent is the breach itself, and that the breach is that which breaks the wall. Isaiah's comparison is very vivid, for the earthenware vessel of the potter breaks easily. This is emphasized by the word "broken," which expresses the result. Without mercy or pity the vessel has been broken.[31]

Furthermore, among all the fragments of the broken vessel there is not found even one sherd that is sufficient for any useful purpose. Fire and water are mentioned as opposites supplementing one another. The sherd is good neither for the one nor the other. If it cannot be used to take up fire from the hearth or even to skim water from a pool or well then it has no use at all; it is good for nothing. What a picture of the end of Judah!—a number of scattered, broken sherds, good for nothing.[32]

---

[30] Delitzsch takes Jehovah as subject, whereas Drechsler finds the subject in the breach, which, continually sinking, brings about the collapse of the wall.

[31] *one does not spare*—The phrase is used adverbially, *unsparingly*.

[32] *mᵉ-ḵit-tā-ṭô*—hapax legomenon; *its crushed fragments*. *yā-qûḏ*—passive

15   For thus saith the Lord GOD, the Holy One of Israel, In returning and rest ye shall be saved, in remaining quiet and in confidence shall be your strength; and ye were not willing.

16   And ye said, No, for we shall flee upon horses; therefore shall ye flee; and upon the swift will we ride; therefore will your pursuers be swift.

17   One thousand from before the rebuke of one, from before the rebuke of five ye shall flee, until ye are kept like a pole upon the top of the mountain, and like the signal upon the hill.

18   And therefore the LORD waits to be gracious to you, and therefore He is high to show you mercy, for a God of judgment is the LORD; blessed are all who wait for Him.

15 The introductory word "for" justifies the description of the nation given in verses 9-11. It is asseverative, strengthening the claim of the prophet. This precise force is difficult to bring out in English, but we may perhaps paraphrase as follows: "Ye have trusted in Egypt, but your trust is in vain. It is the Lord who is in control of all things and who will bring judgment upon you. For your salvation is to be found in returning and rest." Thus, the present verse really forms a contrast to verse 6 and to every expression of what the nation was actually doing for its own deliverance.[33]

To strengthen what he says, Isaiah mentions the Lord. Just as the Holy One of Israel had pronounced the certainty of coming judgment (vv. 12-14), so also does this same Holy One of Israel announce wherein true salvation is to be found. The repeated designation of God as "the Holy One of Israel" is a rebuke to the self-centered and truly godless "theocracy." At the same time God is here also designated "the Sovereign One," for He is the God of power who alone can accomplish the nation's deliverance. The deliverance is a work of might and power and cannot be obtained by trusting in Egypt; it can be wrought only by One who is all-powerful, the Sovereign One, the GOD, the Holy One of Israel.

---

part., *what is kindled.* For the root *ḥśp* cf. Moshe Held in *Studies and Essays in honor of Abraham A. Neuman*, 1962, p. 284.

[33] The purpose of v. 15 is to state wherein salvation consists, not the ground of salvation. Hence, Penna's rendering, *dalla concessione e dalla calma dipende la vostra salvezza*, is to be rejected. The salvation does not depend upon these things; it consists of them. The salvation depends upon the grace of God alone. The strange reading of B, στενάξης, gives to the Hebrew verb *na-ḥat*, a sense attested by Ugaritic *(nwḥ)*, *to moan;* cf. also Hab. 3:16.

The means by which salvation is to be obtained are simply returning and rest. The first word is general, and suggests a turning unto God, a true conversion. Then follows a specific example of how this turning is to be accomplished. The word that Isaiah chooses forms a striking contrast to the actual conduct of the nation. They were busy sending messengers and beasts of burden laden with goods to procure the favor of Egypt. They were active, busily occupied in the task of trying to save themselves. Such, however, was not the way of deliverance, but only in rest, in a ceasing from human activity and a resting upon the grace of God.

Salvation, however, is not merely negative; it also consists in victory over evil. It involves power to act as sons of God. Israel was to have a power, a true strength that would manifest itself over her enemies; but that power was to be found in quietness and in confidence, not in the frenzied activities which at present characterized her. Isaiah had commanded Ahaz to be still (7:4), but Ahaz would not do so. Rather he set an example for his people in the matter of disobedience.

A sad climax brings the verse to its conclusion, "But ye would not." It is the same sad refrain that our Lord uttered concerning Jerusalem. "If ye be willing," God had promised through the prophet; but the nation was not willing. It was carrying out what had been proclaimed concerning it. Its heart was fat, its eyes smeared over, and its ears shut; it would not.

16 Rejecting the true way of deliverance, the people themselves state how they intend to seek that deliverance. They would appeal to Egypt for horses, and with the help of horses would flee. In times of antiquity the horse may have become a symbol of pride. It is related of Plato, for example, that he dismounted from his horse lest he be filled with pride because of him. In the Scriptures the multiplying of horses is often condemned, for they would signalize a strong army in which men would trust (cf. Gen. 50:9; Ex. 14:6ff.; 15:1; 2 Chron. 12:3; Jer. 46:4, 9; Song of Sol. 1:9; 2 Kings 18:24; Deut. 17:16).

The verb forms an interesting paronomasia with the noun, "upon horses we shall flee" (*sus nanus*). Some wish to translate *to hasten*, but the verb has its ordinary meaning, *to flee*.[34] The

34 E.g., Maurer, *celeri cursu vehemur*, like the Latin *fugere* in Vergil's *Georgics* iii.462: *cum fugit in Rhodopen atque in deserta Getarum*. But it is questionable whether *fugere* need here bear such a connotation. Rosenmüller renders, *super*

nation desires not to hasten but to flee the danger. It recognizes the presence of that danger, and wishes to flee from it, using horses to accomplish its desire. If this is what the people want, says Isaiah, this is what they shall have. "Therefore, ye shall flee." Their desire is granted, but the prophet does not state what is really involved in flight. It remains for the second half of the verse to make that clear.

Isaiah now continues the words of the unbelieving nation, words that indicate a gradation in the thought. Not only did the people desire to flee upon horses, but, more than that, they also wished to ride upon swift horses. The gradation appears alone in the noun. Not mere horses would serve, but horses that were fleet of foot. Upon these they would ride, believing that these could carry them to safety. In the first verb, "we shall flee," there was combined the double thought of fleeing unto that which was desireable, namely, deliverance, and fleeing from the threat of the punishment that would overtake them. Here, however, the verb "to ride" is sufficient. If the people can ride upon swift horses, their end, complete deliverance, will, they think, be attained.

In the last clause Isaiah takes up the root (to be light—*qll*), but now applies it to the pursuers of the people. It is as though he said, "Ye would be upon something swift. There will indeed be something swift; not the horses upon which you ride, but the men who pursue after you." Thus, the counsel of the people is brought to naught; they would flee, but they will be overtaken. There is no help in flight in Egypt (cf. Hos. 14:3; Amos 2:14, 15; Ps. 20:8).

17 Just as confidence in swift horses was a vain illusion, so also is trust in a multitude. God has determined to punish His rebellious sons, and so there is no possibility of escape from Him. A thousand will flee before the rebuke of one.[35] Even before the rebuke of five the people will flee. Here is really a reversal of the conditions prevailing when the nation was on its way to Canaan. "And five of you shall chase an hundred, and an hundred of you shall put ten thousand to flight: and your enemies shall fall before you by the sword" (Lev. 26:8). "How should one chase a thousand,

---

equis emicabimus, taking the verb as cognate with *nütz*. Rosenmüller follows N. Schroeder and gives references to classical authors to support his interpretation.

35 *'hd* follows *'lp* immediately (also in 1Q) in order to emphasize the contrast, *even a thousand.*

and two put ten thousand to flight, except their Rock had sold them, and the LORD had shut them up?" (Deut. 32:30). The mere rebuke on the part of one is sufficient to put to flight even a thousand. Certainly mere numbers will be of no avail in the day of punishment. Some expositors would emend the text to read, *and a multitude before the rebuke of five.* This is unnecessary, however, for the emphasis here is on the small group that rebukes. Furthermore, to introduce an extra word really breaks the clear connection with what follows. Isaiah is saying that "ye will flee until ye are left." It is that thought which would be obscured by the addition of an extra word in the second half of the first line of the verse.

The result of the fleeing is that the people will be reduced to a mere remnant, remaining alone in place of the once vast host. Possibly the prophet has in mind the comparison which he had once (1:8) made of Jerusalem. Here, however, he likens the remnant to a mastpole. The word *toren* means a mast, but it is difficult to conceive of a mast upon a high hill; and so it would seem that what Isaiah has in mind is a tall pole such as might serve as a mast upon a ship. That tall pole now stands at the top of the mountains. What the prophet wishes to stress is the solitariness of these poles. They stand alone, no tall trees about them; and all may see them, for they are the only tall objects upon the hills and mountains. This is what will come upon those who place their trust in Egypt. Human help leads to loneliness as well as to destruction.

18 The introductory word, *therefore,* has occasioned difficulty; but it is best to take it in its ordinary sense.[36] The meaning of the prophet is then: "Ye will pursue your foolish way of trust in Egypt, and a judgment will surely overtake you. For that reason the Lord will wait to show mercy to you." He must first complete His work of judgment before He can manifest that of compassion. The introductory "and" is not without purpose, for it connects the thought with what has preceded. The verb "to wait" simply means, as it is elsewhere employed, "to wait with an earnest expectation and longing, with a desire for something."[37] God's

---

36 The *waw* before *lāķēn* is not superfluous, for the prophet is introducing an entirely new thought and with this *waw* compresses the whole content of vv. 15-17.

37 *lhnnkm*—before the heavy suffix a *Patah* appears, which I cannot explain. Note, however, the strange pointing, *lᵉ-ḥe-nᵉ-nāh,* in Ps. 102:14. Possibly the *Patah* is due to Aramaic influence.

purpose is to show mercy, to be gracious; but until the judgment is past He will not do this. He longs, however, to be gracious, and earnestly awaits the time when He may. Akin to this thought is the description of the Lord as long-suffering.

The clause is strengthened by the parallel expression, "and he will be high to show mercy."[38] The idea is that of exalting Himself, so that He may manifest mercy to the people. In showing mercy God is exalted and high. In explanation of this it is stated that the Lord is a God of judgment. This statement has caused difficulty, however, for it seems to ground God's mercy in His justice. Does Isaiah mean to say that inasmuch as the Lord is a God of judgment, for that reason He will exhibit mercy? Different attempts have been made to avoid the difficulty. Thus, it has been proposed to translate by words such as *rectitude,* or to hold that the clause does not relate to righteousness or justice in the strict sense. Again, some would render the particle *ki* by *although.* All of these expedients are interesting, but it may be well questioned whether they are justifiable. Why may not the words be interpreted just as they stand? If they are so interpreted, we are to understand the prophet as saying that God will wait to show mercy, for God is a God of justice who will not show mercy until it is time for Him so to do, and who will pronounce a blessing upon all those who wait upon Him. In other words, the fact that God waits to show mercy is due to His being a God of justice.

Whereas He waits to exhibit mercy, He also pronounces a blessing upon those who wait for Him. Isaiah has said much about those who do not wait for the Lord, and so he will close the verse with a statement concerning those who do abide Him. They are willing to abide in faith, trusting the Lord to act in His own time; they look forward to and long for the fulfillment of what He has promised (cf. Zeph. 3:8 and Dan. 12:12). The Lord is waiting to show His favor, and those who wait in expectation are blessed (cf. Ps. 2:12; 25:3; Isa. 49:23; Lam. 3:25).

19 For the people in Zion shall dwell in Jerusalem, thou shalt weep no more, he will surely be gracious unto thee at the voice of thy cry; as he hears it he will answer thee.

20 And the Lord will give you the bread of affliction and water of op-

---

38 *le-rah-hem-kem*—the presence of the *Segol* is natural in place of *Tzere,* for the syllable is closed and unaccented.

pression, and thy teachers will no more hide themselves, and thine eyes will see thy teachers.

21 And thine ears shall hear a word from behind thee, saying, This is the way, walk ye in it, when ye turn to the right, and when ye turn to the left.

22 And ye shall regard as unclean the covering of thy idols of silver and the sheathing of thy image of gold, thou shalt scatter them as an abominable thing. Away! thou shalt say to it.

23 And he shall give the rain of thy seed, with which thou shalt sow the ground, and bread, the produce of the ground, and it shall be fat and rich; thy cattle shall feed that day in an enlarged pasture.

24 And the oxen and the asses working the ground shall eat mash fodder, which one winnows with the sieve and fan.

25 And it shall come to pass upon every high mountain, and on every hill lifted up, streams, channels of water, in the day of great slaughter, in the falling of towers.

26 And the light of the moon shall be as the light of the sun, and the light of the sun shall be sevenfold, as the light of seven days, in the day of the Lord's binding up the breach of his people, and the stroke of his wound he will heal.

19 To exhibit the truthfulness of what has just been stated in verse 18b, Isaiah continues with the thoughts of this verse. In what manner, however, are we to construe the first verb of the sentence? It is possible to translate, *For those who are in Zion shall dwell in Jerusalem,* or, *For the people will dwell in Zion, even in Jerusalem.* The King James Version renders, *For the people shall dwell in Zion at Jerusalem.* Others translate with the vocative, *O people in Zion, who dwell in Jerusalem.* This last rendering, however, does not do justice to the introductory *ki (for),* and so glosses over the entire connection between this and the preceding verse. Furthermore, as Delitzsch points out, were this a vocative, we should certainly expect to find the personal pronoun "thou." We might also very well expect a relative pronoun before the participle; and in addition, this long description of the people seems quite strange in a vocative construction.

Either, therefore, we should render, following the natural order of the words, *For the people in Zion shall dwell in Jerusalem,* or following the Masoretic accentuation, *For the people shall dwell in Zion, (even) in Jerusalem.* In either case the prophet's purpose is to assure the people that the hopes which they entertain of salvation will not be deceptive. They dwell in Zion, David's city; they

355

are in Jerusalem where God has His dwelling. They dwell in the tents of the Lord Himself. This is to be their future portion.

For this reason the prophet turns to the people, addressing it in tender fashion in the singular as though speaking to one individual. "There is no need to weep for ever, for when thou dost cry to God He will be very gracious to thee."[39] Emphasis falls upon God's graciousness, for Isaiah uses an infinitive absolute, *being gracious, he will be gracious to thee.* The blessing is sure and firm. As soon as He hears, He answers the cry of need. The verb is in the perfect, whereas the preceding verb was imperfect. The use of the tenses is not without purpose. According to God's hearing, He has answered the cry.[40]

20 The first verb is to be taken as a simple future with *waw* consecutive, *and he will give.* If a condition is present it is implied and not expressed. He who gives these rations is the Sovereign One, who has at His disposal the welfare of men. The following phrases are generally taken as being in the construct relation, namely, "bread of affliction and water of oppression." This is not correct, however, for the words are in apposition; and we should render, *bread which is affliction,* and *water which is oppression.*[41] The language refers to food that is given to prisoners (cf. 1 Kings 22:27), and hence the phrases may be construed as appositional genitives, *bread of affliction* and *water of oppression.* It is not necessary to assume a construct relationship, nor assume that Isaiah is teaching that the people actually shall be made prisoners and so eat the fare of prisoners. What he is saying is that a period of affliction will surely come, a period in which the life of the people will be characterized by affliction and oppression.

If a condition or concession was implied in the first verb, the apodosis is now stated in that the teachers will no more hide themselves as they had been wont to do. These teachers were the

<hr/>

39 *yhnk*—for *y^e-hon-ḵâ*, i.e., *yā-ḥōn* (pointing in accordance with Barth's law), *yā-ḥōn-ḵā* > *y^e-hon-ḵā.* The *u* vowel is then thrown back to the preformative, giving *yoh-n^e-ḵā* (cf. Gen. 43:29).

40 *'ā-nāḵ*—note pausal form of the m. suffix, occurring frequently with *Lamed-Aleph* and *Lamed-He* verbs. *As soon as he heareth, he hath answered thee.* This usage of the perf. corresponds to that of the imp. of vivid description, and lays particular emphasis upon an individual aspect of the description.

41 *Leḥem* and *mayim* are not constructs but absolutes, and the following words have appositional force; some mss. have the s., and Vulg. reads *ultra doctorem tua.* The pl. may serve to express majesty.

prophets, who by hiding were keeping the people from the true Word of God. That they hid was due to the hardheartedness of the people themselves, for since the time of Ahaz, when it had been prophesied that "this people" would not hear the Word of the Lord (cf. Isa. 6), the prophets, it would seem, had kept themselves from sight. Now, however, they will again undertake their open ministry; and the eyes of the people will see them.[42] A theocracy without the public ministry of the Word of God was in a dangerous condition; particularly dangerous was that condition when the people themselves desired it.

21 The description is continued by the statement that the people's ears would hear a voice from behind. The language is difficult; if the people's eyes see the teachers, why do their ears hear a voice from behind? It is generally assumed that the figure is that of the shepherd who follows his sheep calling out to them. Possibly also it is that the people, having turned aside, have now left their teachers behind them. We must not press the figures too closely. The eyes of the people will see their teachers, and their ears will hear. The voice is the word of admonition and instruction proclaimed to the people. This they will hear calling them to repentance and to a returning to the Lord.

The message is clear and direct. The people have turned aside from the way and must have the true way pointed out to them. This is the task of faithful teachers. It is not enough, however, that one know the truth. He must also do the truth. "Be ye not hearers of the Word only, but doers also." When the way is shown to the people they must also hear the command to walk therein (cf. Deut. 28:14).

The last words of the verse are difficult. Either they state a truth, "for ye will go to the right and ye will go to the left," or they are temporal, "when ye go to the right and when ye go to the left."[43] Whereas the details are difficult, nevertheless, the thought seems to be that instruction is necessary, for this is an erring people which will go astray, and which must have the true way of life pointed out

---

42 *and they shall be beholding*—A finite verb is here employed in order to stress and define more exactly (here with respect to time) the idea of duration which the part. expresses. Note also that although the part. is f. pl. its subj. is a dual.

43 תאמינו—for *tēy-mi-nû*, an inaccuracy in orthography. Verbs *Pe-Aleph* and *Pe-yod* alternate often.

to it. That way had been set forth earlier in verse 15 as a way of rest and returning. To forget this way would be easy, for the right and the left were ever present to beckon the people. Hence, the need for constant instruction.

22 Even following the spiritual reforms of Hezekiah, idolatry continued in the land. One result of the visitation of God's grace would be the putting away of all idolatry. The first verb may be rendered, as shown by 2 Kings 23:8ff., *and ye shall make unclean.* By not using the idols, the people would defile them, i.e., regard them as unclean. Apparently these graven images were covered with gold and silver, as depicted in Deuteronomy 7:25: "The graven images of their gods shall ye burn with fire: thou shalt not desire the silver or gold *that is* on them, nor take *it* unto thee, lest thou be snared therein: for it *is* an abomination to the LORD thy God." The coverings were of gold and silver, not the idols themselves, although grammatically the words may be construed either with *tzippuy* (coverings) or with *p^esilley* (idols).[44] Probably we can bring out the true force of the words if we render, *the silver coverings of your idols.* The idols themselves were probably constructed of wood; cf. Isaiah 2:20 and Jeremiah 10:3, 4. The verb is plural but the noun suffixes are singular. There is no need for textual emendation, for this variation is apparently intentional. The plural presents the picture of entirety; the people as such will remove the idols, all of them. At the same time the singular points to the action as that of individuals. The nation would declare the idols unclean only as individuals did so. In the individuals' acting, the nation would act.

By means of a parallel expression the prophet is enabled to point out how completely the idols will be done away. "The sheathing (or case) of the molten image of thy gold," i.e., "the golden case of thy molten image," stands in parallel construction to the words "the covering of the idols of thy silver." Together the two phrases suggest completeness; all idols of whatsoever kind will be regarded as unclean. Again, the image itself was made of molten metal (cf. Isa. 40:19), but the covering in this instance of gold. The people would take the pieces of these images and scatter them. First, however, they would crush and break them. To show the

___

44 *^apuddāh*—the sheathing of the idol images. *dāwāh*—unwell, menstruous. There is a m. s. suffix in *lô*, although the antecedent is plural. It is probably a distributive use of the singular.

complete contempt with which the idols will be regarded, Isaiah employs a strong expression that indicates something that has been rendered unclean through being touched by a menstruous woman. The word is feminine but is apparently to be understood in a neuter sense. As one in disgust casts away something that is thus unclean, so will men cast away the destroyed idols. It is difficult to conceive a picture of greater contempt than this. In the light of the beauty of the grace of God the idols of this world become objects of contempt and disgust. The action of rejection will be accompanied by a cry, as though to say, "Good riddance." "Go!" men will call to these idols. It is the end; the nation has turned from idols to serve the living and true God.

23 In place of the suffering caused by the judgment, the people of God will experience the rich and luxurious blessings of a prosperous land. Penna remarks that the passage begins with the principle that virtue and material well-being constitute a constant binomial. But the material blessings herein depicted (if they are such) are gifts of God which are given of His free grace and mercy to the remnant which through no merit or virtue of its own is preserved. This verse is a presentation of grace, rich, full, and free. It begins with an activity of God. "And he will give," we read; and the verb refers to gifts, not to something merited or earned. This gift is that of the "rain of thy seed," by which Isaiah means "the rain that causes thy seed to grow." After the long months of summer heat, the early rain, falling toward the close of November, is most welcome. This seed which the rain causes to sprout forth is that with which the Palestinian sows his lands.[45] The ground produces richly, for God has sent the rain and man plants the seed. It is man's land for he works it and seeds it, but the source of power which causes the land to produce is God Himself. The address is tender, spoken out of a heart of love to the one who loves the soil and its produce.

Corresponding to the rain is the "bread, the produce of the ground," which is also a gift of God. These words are to be construed as the object of the verb, "he will give." With the description, "and it shall be fat and rich," the prophet makes a

---

[45] *which*—the instrument by which the action is performed is regarded as a secondary or remote object. *lehem—bread*, depends upon *and he will give*. The following clause constitutes a dependent gen., *bread of the produce*, etc. I am not convinced that *lehem* should here be rendered *bread-corn*.

general reference to the bread that is God's gift (cf. Gen. 49:20). What God gives is the best. This bread is rich in nourishment and meal. The abundantly producing pasture will be a blessing at that time for the herd, which will feed in an extended pasture where they will find nourishment in abundance.[46] If the pasture is an extended one, that would imply that at one time it had been narrower and was now enlarged.[47] God has prepared all for the enjoyment of His people.

24 Isaiah has been speaking of the blessings that would come to man. Now he turns to those domestic animals, the oxen and the asses, that serve man. Even for them a time of richness is in store. The oxen were beasts of burden used primarily in the work of plowing; the asses, on the other hand, served for riding. This distribution of work was not always observed, for Deuteronomy 22:10 forbade the using of an ox and an ass together for plowing. In the Near East one can even today see interesting combinations of beasts engaged in plowing. For agriculture these were the two indispensable animals, mentioned already by the prophet (1:3). For these beasts of labor there would be the diet of a mash sorrel fodder. The first word, *b⁰lil* indicates a forage which has been fermented by means of soaking, and the second word, *hamitz* denotes seasoned fodder.[48] This was evidently a diet preferred by these beasts. As men were accustomed to winnow that grain which would be for man's own food, so now will they also winnow the grain that is to be the food of the beasts. Thus it is prepared free from anything foreign and is suited to the nourishment of the animals. In this process of winnowing, both the sieve and fan were employed; in other words every means was used to prepare the food as well as possible for the beasts. When the nation was in its sinful, rebellious state, hard conditions prevailed for the beasts of burden; when the blessing of salvation will have come, then there will be a luxuriant living even for these beasts.

25 With this verse Isaiah continues to describe the great change

---

46 *thy cattle*—the form is s. with collective force.

47 Hengstenberg had denied that *kar* could mean *pasture*, but we may now appeal to Assyrian *kirū, grove*. Here the context demands such a rendering.

48 *blyl*—a mixed fodder, possibly a mash; cf. Akk. *ballu* and *bulilu. hmytz*—seasoned (with salt?). This was possibly a delicacy reserved for cattle that were being fattened for human consumption. *zôreh—one is sifting.* The part. is indefinite and the subj. not expressed.

for the better that will be wrought, and this he does by showing that there will even be abundance of water where it had not been before. On the mountains and hills, where the water could not reach and where cultivation would be extremely difficult, water will be found and the land will be fertile (cf. Amos 9:13; Joel 3:18; Ezek. 47:1ff.). The verse stands in the same relationship to the two preceding ones as does verse 22 to verses 20 and 21. Hitherto the streams had been in the valleys, and the tops of the high hills had been left to dry under the burning sun. Now all is to be different. "I will open rivers in high places, and fountains in the midst of the valleys: I will make the wilderness a pool of water, and the dry land springs of water" (Isa. 41:18).

To show the abundance of water Isaiah mentions streams, and he strengthens this by adding the phrase "channels of water." It is as though he were seeking to stress the abundance of water that would be found; not merely streams, but even channels of water. This emphasis is further strengthened by the two adjectives that have been used to modify the nouns "mountain" and "hill." Water on the mountains would be remarkable, but they are "high" mountains and they are "lifted up" hills. Isaiah has striven to accomplish the utmost in emphasis,[49] and his words show how great will be the change that God will bring about.

These remarkable changes will be found when there is a great battle. There must first be a period of war and slaughter, and then the blessings will come.[50] By mentioning the falling of the towers the prophet simply carries out the figure. The picture which he here gives is the opposite of that found in verse 17. Some would take the towers in a figurative sense, as signifying the powerful ones on earth, and in particular the haughty Assyrian power. This may be, but it is questionable whether we are to understand this language of one particular slaughter.[51] The prophet speaks of wars and calamities and with them the coming of peace and blessing. This latter is the work of God just as the former is a judgment of God. In all probability the Assyrians are in the picture, as are the forerunners of the judgment that must over-

[49] To both *mountain* and *hill* Isaiah adds epithets, *high* and *lifted up*, and twice uses the word *all*. To the noun *streams* he adds *channels of water*.

[50] E.g. Targ. *rab-r^e-bin*, magnates. S μεγάλους.

[51] If the reference is to the defeat of the Assyrians (Drechsler, etc.) it would point forward to vv. 27ff. If it is to the downfall of the Judahites (Delitzsch, etc.) it looks back to vv. 16ff. and 29:20ff.

take the earth. Whereas some of this language may possibly refer to periods of blessing and peace, in its deepest sense it is a picture of the blessings that the Messiah brings.

26 Again Isaiah begins his verse with "and it shall be," as he had also done in the previous verse. Verse 25 sums up what had been presented in verses 23 and 24, and verse 26 sums up what has been presented in verses 20-25. It presents the results that will come in as a consequence of the things described in these verses (20-25). There will be a glorious restoration in which not merely what has been lost will be restored, but everything will be more glorious than before. Using two poetical names that respectively mean *heat* and *white*, Isaiah speaks of the moon and the sun.[52] The light of the moon (the white) will be as the light of the sun (the heat), which means that it will be as bright as the sun's light. As for the sun, Isaiah mentions not merely that its light will be seven times greater, but in order to make clearer what he has in mind, adds that it will be like the light of the seven days of the week. These blessings are tied up with the healing of the people's wounds.[53] Binding up the breach of the people refers to verses 13 and 14. That which would have broken the people will be bound up by the Lord, and the wounds with which it has been smitten will be healed. These wounds had been received through judgment for its sins. We are not necessarily to understand the prophet as speaking of wounds inflicted by the Assyrian army (cf. 24:23; 60:19b; 19:22).

To what is Isaiah referring by this summary of blessing? Alexander sets forth a generally held opinion when he claims that like previous similes or comparisons the language of this verse is used to set forth the great change in nature or the great revolution in the state of society that will come. He therefore asserts that the language is to be taken figuratively. This is essentially the position of Drechsler, but Delitzsch takes him to task for this and calls the interpretation "hard to understand." Delitzsch holds that the language is no more figurative than Paul's when he speaks of the "corruption" of nature coming to an end. Isaiah, thinks Delitzsch, is not speaking of the new heaven and earth but simply of the glorification of nature which is promised both in the Old and the

---

[52] Horace *Odes* iv.5, 8, *soles melius nitent.* Cf. Aeschylus *Persae* 298.

[53] *in the day of*—the temporal phrase, practical equivalent of a prep., is followed by the inf. const., and then continued by a finite verb.

New Testaments. At that time there will be an alternation between the bright sunlit days and the most brilliant of moonlit nights. This will be the seventh day in the world's week; the sabbath in the world's history. "The light of the seven days of the world's week will be all concentrated in the seventh. For the beginning of creation was light, and its close will be light as well."

There is indeed truth in what Delitzsch says here. At the same time this language must be understood figuratively.[54] Isaiah is using these figures taken from the world of nature to depict the wondrous, catastrophic changes that one day will occur. The great element of truth in Delitzsch's interpretation is that the world's sabbath will finally have come, and the light of the sun will be concentrated to give that light which is adapted to the world's sabbath. The moon and the sun, which now rule the day and the night, will no longer function as they do at present, for the present order of nature will be done away; and "the sevenfold blazing light of the sun" is simply symbolical language to state the truth that the purposes of God with this world will have been completed and the glory of God will shine forth in all its splendor. In reality it will be the eternal sabbath when "the city had no need of the sun, neither of the moon, to shine in it: for the glory of God did lighten it, and the Lamb *is* the light thereof" (Rev. 21:23).

27 Behold! the Name of the Lord cometh from far, burning is his anger, and heavy the uplifted; his lips are full of wrath, and his tongue as a devouring fire.

28 And his breath like an overflowing stream shall divide as far as the neck, to sift the nations in the sieve of ruin, and a misleading bridle upon the jaws of the people.

29 The song shall be to you, like the night of the consecration of a feast, and joy of heart like one marching with the pipe to go into the mountain of the Lord, to the Rock of Israel.

30 And the Lord will cause to be heard the majesty of his voice, and the descent of his arm he will cause to be seen, with indignation of anger and a flame of devouring fire, scattering, and rain, and stones of hail.

31 For at the voice of the Lord Assyria will be broken; he shall smite with the rod.

32 And every passage of the rod of appointment, which the Lord

---

[54] So also Penna, "*Un linguaggio metaforico non insolito*" (24:4; 65:17). An interesting chiasm appears at the conclusion of the verse, *the binding of the Lord the break of his people, and the smiting of its wound he will heal.*

will lay upon him, will be with tabrets and harps, and with wars of shaking it is fought therein.

33 For arranged from yesterday is Tophet; it is even prepared for the king; he has deepened, he has widened; its pyre fire and wood in plenty; the breath of the LORD, like a stream of brimstone, burns in it.

27 The last verses of this chapter serve to answer a number of questions that have been raised. They point out that the destruction to come will begin to manifest itself in the downfall of Assyria. What is the day of great slaughter (v. 25) and the day of God's binding up the wounds of His people? These and other questions have been raised, and Isaiah now proceeds to indicate an answer. The judgment will surely come, he declares, and its first great strokes will fall upon that nation which has exalted itself against the people of God.

To introduce these thoughts Isaiah uses his characteristic "behold!" and therewith immediately directs attention to the Name of Yahweh. Calvin takes this expression as simply indicating the Lord Himself, and thinks that the prophet uses this circumlocution in order to confound the Assyrians and other nations that worshipped gods of silver and gold and ridiculed the Jews because they made no images of their God. More likely, however, the words refer to the revelation of God in His words and deeds. He had said that He could get for Himself a Name, and that He has done; in all His glory and power He comes victorious.

This Name is said to come from afar, for hitherto Yahweh had held Himself apart, as it were, with His aid to His people. The Assyrian nation had been permitted to go its own course, acting as though it were truly sovereign (cf. 18:4). It is not necessary to suppose that the words "from afar" refer to heaven, and certainly not to Mt. Sinai. Nor is it correct to say that Yahweh had become tired of waiting, and so comes to action. "From afar" simply suggests that God comes now to the aid of His people; hitherto He has been removed from them. To Him distance means nothing; at the time of their need He is present with His aid.

burning is his anger—This does not refer to the Name, but seems to be an independent proposition, so that the suffix would then refer to Yahweh. The ascent or uplift refers to the smoke that supposedly arises from the burning fire, for the wrath of God is pictured as a fire and column of smoke; cf. Deuteronomy 29:20; 32:22; Psalm 18:8; 74:1. To express the thought of the vehemence or force of these ascending or uplifted clouds, the prophet speaks of them as "heavy."

Isaiah now continues the description of God's anger, declaring that His lips are full of wrath. This is the first of several independent statements that set forth the anger of the Lord. No words of peace fall from His lips, for they are full of wrath, and only wrath flows therefrom. Possibly there is an intended gradation in that the tongue is next mentioned, and then the breath. The tongue together with the lips speaks forth words; and these are devouring words of wrath, for the tongue burns like a fire that devours. By means of the mouth the pronouncement of judgment is made; and God will utter a severe judgment upon His enemies, which have been attacking His people.

28 Earlier it was said of the Messiah that with the breath of His lips He would slay the wicked (11:4). Here the breath of God is said to be like a stream that overflows. This is the first of three metaphors that Isaiah here uses to carry out his description of the wrath of the Lord. This breath or spirit is like a wadi, a dry river bed that soon fills up with water when the heavy rains fall and then overflows in a flood of raging waters (cf. 66:12 and Jer. 47:2). This flood is deep and reaches to a man's neck, dividing him into two unequal parts. Isaiah has set forth this description of the overflowing wrath of God with figures taken from his eighth chapter (cf. vv. 7, 8 and also 17:12; 28:2). Irresistible is this flood, and it carries everything with it. Against it Assyria cannot stand. Water that rises to the neck is water that can drown; feeling this flood Assyria is in great danger indeed.

There is, of course, a reason why this wrath is so powerful and overwhelming; it is for the purpose of sifting the nations in a sieve of ruin.[55] The Lord is indeed sovereign, and the time has come for Him to sift the nations so that His punitive wrath may fall upon those nations that are deserving of judgment. The sieve that He will use is one that will result in the ruin of the nations that are sifted. We are to take the last clause of the verse as circumstantial. The nations are conceived as wild and strong horses that cannot be contained or restrained, but are now kept in check by means of bridles in their cheeks. They are held back so that they are not able to flee the judgment, and so they bring about their own destruc-

---

55 *lhnph—to sift, swing to and fro. Hiphil* inf. abs. with f. termination; cf. Dan. 5:20.

tion. This bridle is a spirit of deception or blinding which makes the nations that wear it unaware of the true nature of the events in which they are participating. Thus they are restrained from understanding the course of events. It is not necessary to hold that this spirit of blindness came because the nation of Assyria had given itself up to demonic powers (cf. 1 Kings 22:19ff.), for in His providence God had permitted this spirit of blindness to cover Assyria.

29 The twenty-ninth verse is a circumstantial clause and sets forth the existing conditions under which the Lord acts. While Yahweh marches forth to punish the nation which had been His instrument in the destruction of the theocracy, Israel herself is engaged in song. The first word of the sentence is emphatic and sets the key or tone of the entire sentence. Isaiah employs the definite article, *the song*, which is probably to be taken in a generic sense. Hence, the prophet is not speaking of one particular song, as he had done for example in 26:1, but rather of songs and singing as such.

Isaiah's manner of statement is somewhat unusual and forceful. "Song will be to you," he says, by which he means simply that the people will have or possess song. They will be engaged in singing. This singing will be like that which is found in the night in which the feast is sanctified. Of what feast, however, is the prophet speaking? It has been suggested that this first comparison which Isaiah makes is with a New Year's Festival which supposedly derives from a national liturgical festival.[56] With this interpretation we cannot agree, for there is serious question whether such a festival was really ever celebrated in Israel. The high point of the festival was the night, for it was the night in which the festival was sanctified, i.e., celebrated. It would seem that the reference is rather to the Passover, for in the prescriptions for that celebration there is also emphasis upon the night. "It *is* a night to be much observed unto the LORD for bringing them out from the land of Egypt: this *is* that night of the LORD to be observed of all the children of Israel in their generations" (Ex. 12:42). At the close of the 14th of Nisan (i.e., in the evening) the paschal lamb was slain and eaten; and on the 15th began the feast of unleavened bread,

---

[56] Cf. Penna, who also compares the feast in *Gilgamesh* 11:74. Dillmann, however, remarks, *"Da feiert Isr. mit Lobgesängen das Fest seiner Erlösung."* The article indicates the kind of song well known at festivals.

which lasted for seven days. On both the first and last days of the feast there was a sacred assembly (cf. Num. 28:16-25). That songs were sung upon the occasion of the Passover we learn from the New Testament (cf. Matt. 26:30), and hence we may conclude that it was an ancient custom. The New Testament also speaks of the Passover as the feast (Matt. 27:15; cf. John 4:45; 5:1; 18:39; cf. 2:13, 23).

Whether Isaiah actually introduces a second comparison or not is difficult to say. At least it seems to be clear that in the second line of the verse he is alluding to a deep, inner joy of the heart, whereas in the first line he had spoken merely of an outward joy that found expression in the festivals. The procession unto the sanctuary would be accompanied by playing upon the flute (cf. Ps. 42:4; 2 Sam. 6:5, 6). This would be a time of great joy, for one would be approaching the holy God to worship him. The *mount of the Lord* is the mount of the Temple where God's dwelling is, and the *Rock of Israel* is Yahweh Himself.

30 At that time when the remnant of His people will rejoice in His deliverance, He will manifest the greatness of His power in the punitive judgment that falls upon Assyria and the enemy nations of Judah. Isaiah employs a circumlocution, *the majesty of his voice,* i.e., *his majestic voice.* The image is that of a theophany, in which a storm is an accompanying factor. Many commentators think that there is a specific allusion here to the thunder, for the thought is similar to that of Psalm 18:13; 68:8; 77:18-20, etc. This may be, but the heart of the thought is not the storm but the appearance of God. Hence, it is not necessary to understand the *voice* as necessarily referring to thunder.

Together with causing His majestic voice to be heard, the Lord also causes the falling of His arm to be seen. The entire sentence is arranged chiastically and gives a forceful effect. An upraised arm is now brought down in punishment. This lowering of the arm is accompanied by an indignation of wrath and a flame of devouring fire, for the purpose of the action is to destroy. In a most vivid manner Isaiah brings the verse to a close, mentioning what accompanies the descending of the upraised hand. The words stand out vividly: scattering, and downpour, and stones of hail.[57]

---

[57] *nptz*—to break through. The word possibly indicates the breaking of a cloud. *zerem*—pelting, driving rain. For *stones of hail* cf. Josh. 10:11.

31 Now the explanation is given. By reason of the voice of the Lord, Assyria ceases to exist. This does not mean that thunder causes Assyria to cease, but the voice of the Lord; His command expressed in His raging brings to an end the existence of Assyria as a nation. Isaiah had earlier used this word (7:8) in referring to Ephraim's ceasing to be a nation. It would seem that he now reflects upon that passage. Then it was Ephraim that was without power. Ahaz looked to Assyria and Assyria came upon Judah. Now, however, it is Assyria herself that will cease to be a nation. Originally the root of this verb means *to be broken*, and it is used in a figurative sense of the breaking of the spirit through alarm and fear.

In the last clause of the verse Isaiah begins with the noun, *with the rod*.[58] By placing these words before the verb he emphasizes the hardness of the punishment that will fall. The verse then concludes with a statement, *he will smite*. The reference is to the Lord and the object to be understood is Assyria. Thus, the verse states clearly the downfall of Assyria and illustrates the principles of the divine economy which the prophet has been setting forth in this chapter.

32 The general sense of this verse is similar to that of verse 29. God will punish Assyria, and Israel will rejoice in singing. Hence the introductory *and it shall be* connects with what was said in the previous verse about God's smiting Assyria and shows how fully and completely this is carried out. A literal rendering of the prophet's introductory words is *and every passage of the rod of appointment* (lit., *founding, establishment*).[59] The rod that will fall upon Assyria is one that has been determined long in advance. Assyria's downfall is not a "chance" event, but one that had been decreed by God in His counsel.[60] The reference is not, as Drechsler says, to providential determination, but rather to the eternal decrees of God, which are now being carried out in His works of providence. What God does in providence is simply the unfolding or fulfilling of His eternal decree, His eternal purpose

58 *with the rod*—a verbal, circumstantial clause.

59 *whyh*—the common formula of advancing prophetic speech, not to be connected with *every passage; cf.* 14:3. The rendering should be, *and it shall be, every passage, etc., is with drums, etc.,* not *and every passage will be, etc.*

60 *mwsdh*—*foundation; cf.* 28:16, i.e., in the sense of an appointment for punishment. 1Q reads *mwsdw,* clearly preserving the *Daleth,* which should not be emended to *Resh.*

which He purposed before the foundation of the world. This is supported by other passages in which the root *yasad* is found; cf. Habakkuk 1:12; Psalm 104:8. The words exhibit a striking alliteration, which should not be overlooked.

Again Isaiah asserts that the Lord is the one who causes the blows to fall. As in verse 30 he had declared that the Lord would cause men to see the descent of His arm, so now he adds that Yahweh will make the predetermined staff rest upon Assyria. In 30b he stressed the arm of the Lord, but here the staff. God causes this staff to rest upon Assyria, not in the sense that it will lie there inactive, but rather in the sense that Assyria is the object of its smiting. As these blows fall upon Assyria, there will be the accompanying sound of musical instruments, the tabrets and harps. These are the instruments that will accompany the song described in verse 29. A strong contrast is here presented. It is as though with each stroke of the battle a cry of exultation arises in the city of God. On the one hand there falls the punitive rod of Yahweh upon the enemies of Zion, and on the other there is the song of gladness and rejoicing because of deliverance. What is the meaning of this picture? Is it one of the Assyrians being mown down to the tune of the rejoicing Israelites? A musical setting for a slaughter, some have held, is too strong for our taste and also for Isaiah's; and so these words are denied to Isaiah. But have those who object to the truth of this verse really grasped the true significance of what Isaiah is saying? Is Isaiah giving us merely a musical setting for a slaughter in which one group of people simply rejoices over the misfortunes of another? That is far from the truth. The deep meaning is that God's people have been redeemed, and that they will sing His praises and rejoice at the fulfillment of His purposes. They will exult when the evil ones are punished, just as we, in praying "thy kingdom come," are beseeching God for the destruction of all that would prevent the coming of God's kingdom. And so it is here. The enemies of God were being used by Satan to frustrate the purposes of God in the bringing of the Redeemer to earth. Had they been successful there would have been no salvation and all men would have perished. It is a serious and wicked thing to be a tool of Satan, to oppose oneself to the purposes of God and to seek to thwart them. That the Assyrians had done, and for that reason their kingdom must be destroyed. The destruction of enemy kingdoms can only bring joy to the heart of the remnant, not because particular individuals are being punished, but because the opponents of God's work are being destroyed.

In bringing this remarkable verse to a close Isaiah further characterizes the destruction of Assyria as *wars of shaking*. Earlier he had spoken of the shaking of the Lord's hand, and it is that which describes these battles. In them the hand of the Lord shakes and so punishes the enemy. Apparently Isaiah pictures the falling of God's hand upon the enemy with the word *battles*, to stress how great is the task involved in destroying the entire enemy army. In this manner, namely in battles of shaking, does God fight.

33 To support the truth that the staff of punishment had been foreordained, Isaiah explains that Tophet has been prepared from of old. From Jeremiah 7:31, 32 we learn that Tophet was located in the valley of Hinnom south of Jerusalem and was the place where unbelieving Israelites offered up their sons and daughters to Moloch. Here too the refuse of the city was deposited and burned; the fires of consumption burned continually. Thus, the place came to take on the name of Gehenna, i.e., the valley of Hinnom, and was a symbol of the place of eternal torment. Instead of saying that destruction had long been determined upon Assyria, Isaiah remarks that a Tophet has long been prepared. The Tophet is a place of burning; but by merely mentioning the Tophet, Isaiah includes as it were the secondary conceptions of a curse and bann. One may well wonder whether in choosing this figure Isaiah had in mind the practice of Ahaz, who brought the Assyrian upon the scene of the theocracy. Ahaz sinned in that he caused his son and daughter to pass through the fire (2 Kings 16:3); and Ahaz, rejecting the Lord, turned to Assyria for help. In his religious practices Ahaz followed the heathen nations; now, that nation which he had brought upon Judah would itself suffer the punishment of idolatrous and cruel rites. It would itself be consumed at the place where Ahaz had sacrificed. For it Tophet was prepared. Ever conscious of the ascending fires and smokes of this abominable place, Isaiah uses it as a symbol of the destruction to come upon Assyria. He does not necessarily mean that Assyria will be destroyed in this actual place near Jerusalem, but merely uses the name figuratively.

An emphatic passive participle introduces the thought. We translate *prepared*, for the word is used as in 21:5. The root appears also in the twenty-third Psalm, "Thou preparest a table." For His own God prepares a table; for the enemy, Tophet. In each instance it is God who arranges and sets in order. This arrangement has already been made; indeed, since yesterday.[61] Alexander refers to the Jewish tradition, doubtless founded upon this very passage, that hell was prepared on the second day of creation, i.e., the first day that would have had a yesterday. For this reason, they say, God pronounced no blessing upon this day. All that this expression means in this particular context is that Tophet is already prepared. It is not being prepared at this very moment when the prophet speaks but is already waiting for the Assyrian king.

even it for the king is prepared—The language is to be taken in this sense, rather than *even for the king is it prepared*. By using the definite article, Isaiah gives a certain force to the words, *the king*. It is the king *par excellence*, the great king of Assyria, as Rabshakeh also identifies him (36:4). Thus, to take but one example of how the Assyrian kings boasted, Esarhaddon speaks of himself as "the king of the world, king of Assyria." This king who could not conquer enough territory nor extend his realm far enough would receive in his place of death the site that he desired. For him, Tophet has been enlarged. In actual fact the Hinnom valley was little more than a narrow gorge; now it is to be prepared to befit one who exulted in bigness. Isaiah had earlier expressed the same thought, "Hell hath enlarged herself and opened her mouth without measure . . ." (5:14).

A fitting end is prepared. The funeral pyre of Tophet is simply fire, by which Isaiah expresses the truth that the end of the king is a funeral, one that is on a pyre to be burned, one characterized by given over to the burning of fire. This is a pyre that will have a great burning, for there is abundant wood with which it may burn. Above all, however, the breath of the Lord burns in it and this breath is like a stream of brimstone. It is this breath of the Lord that breathes upon the wood and sets it on fire. That this language is to be understood figuratively is clear from its general character. It is not a reference to the precise manner of Sennacherib's death, for example, but simply a statement of the general truth that the Assyrian king who had risen up against the people

[61] Lit., *from yesterday*—the writing with *Shureq* is strange, but cf. Mic. 2:8. *tpth*—with *ḥ* in 1Q. This form appears only here. Drechsler suggests that the ending characterizes the *Nomen unitatis*, a *Tophet*. Delitzsch takes it as a primary form of *tpt*. *mdwrth*—*its pyre*, i.e., its pyre is fire and wood, made of fire and wood.

of God would be brought to everlasting death. In the Bible fire is used to symbolize complete destruction from the presence of the Lord; Christ Himself spoke of the fire of hell. What Isaiah is here teaching is the full overthrow and perdition of the powers that have exalted themselves against the God of Israel and His sovereign purposes.

2. EGYPT IS NO HELP, BUT THE LORD WILL PROTECT JERUSALEM (31:1-9)

1 Alas! those who go down to Egypt for help, and they lean on horses, and trust in cavalry, because it is great, and in horsemen, because they are very strong, and they look not to the Holy One of Israel, and they seek not the LORD.

2 And also he is wise, and brings evil, and his words he removes not, and he rises up against the house of evil doers, and against the help of the workers of iniquity.

3 And Egypt is a man and not God, and their horses flesh and not spirit; and the LORD will stretch out his hand, and the helper will stumble, and the helped fall, and together all of them will cease.

1 Without any particular break in the thought Isaiah continues his denunciation of those who look to Egypt for aid. Delitzsch regards this as the fourth in a series of five woes (chaps. 28–33) uttered against various peoples. Here Isaiah again expresses the grief of heart that is his as he beholds his people placing their trust in that which satisfieth not. He identifies them as those who go down to Egypt, and his use of the participle does not indicate that they are going down for the first time. It simply characterizes those who often do such a thing. With a somewhat similar expression he had earlier identified them (30:2), *they who walk to go down.* Their purpose in going down is to seek help, for they realize full well that they need help (cf. 20:6 and 30:5, 6).

Reliance upon Egypt involves placing one's confidence in what Egypt possessed in abundance, namely, horses and chariots. In contrast to the mountainous country Egypt was ideally a land for horses, a *hippasimos,* as Diodorus Siculus (i.57) aptly characterized it. Classical writers attest to the abundance of horses in Egypt. Thus, Homer, for example, declares that through each of the

373

hundred gates of Thebes some two hundred "men go out with horses and cars."[1]

By means of an imperfect with *waw* consecutive following the participle, Isaiah develops his thought. The people go down to Egypt for help and they rely upon horses, yea, more than that, they place their trust in cavalry. A small country like Judah could support only infantry. Cavalry, therefore, such as that possessed by Egypt, might seem to it to be a great necessity. Deuteronomy 17:16, however, had forbidden a return to Egypt.

Egypt's cavalry is mighty, and the Judahites believe in might and power. They exemplify the one of whom the Psalmist wrote: "Behold! this man has not made God his stronghold, but he has trusted in the abundance of his riches; he is strong in his wickedness" (Ps. 52:7). The horsemen of Egypt also are said to be exceedingly powerful, and Judah regards them too as a fitting object of trust. Isaiah first mentions horses generally, for horses are used to pull the wagons or war chariots and for the riding of warriors. In the second line, however, he breaks down the reference into chariots and horsemen.

The last line of the verse may be rendered by the pluperfect. The Judahites have trusted in Egypt, but they had not trusted in the Holy One of Israel. They have done the one without having done the other. In this verse, as Drechsler has pointed out, Isaiah, by his vocabulary, takes up the thoughts expressed throughout chapter thirty. Cf. 30:2 (go down to Egypt) ; 30:5 (help) ; 30:7 (help) ; 30:16 (horse) ; 30:12 (lean upon) ; 30:12, 15 (trust) .

2 The first words are ironical.[2] Isaiah either means that God also is wise as well as the Egyptians whose wisdom and strength the Judahites sought, or he may mean that God is also wise as well as the Judahites who foolishly are seeking for Egyptian aid. The latter alternative is probably correct. It is as though the prophet said, "Ye claim to be wise, but ye act in folly for ye think that ye can carry on your plans without the knowledge of God (29:15) .

1 *Iliad* ix.383. Compare the relief from the palace of Ramses II at Thebes, which depicts the chariots advancing into battle.
2 König renders by the past, because of the imp. with *waw* cons., *and he was wise.* Note the chiasm, *and he brought evil and his wounds he did not turn aside.* I would render by the present, *and he is wise,* and the chiastic sentences as prophetic perfects to be translated by the fut., expressing a consequence of the wisdom.

But God also is wise, and consequently His purposes come to pass."

The wisdom of God is said to be manifest in that He has brought evil. If the verb is a prophetic future it has reference to evils that God will yet bring. The *waw* consecutive at least shows that the verb expresses the consequences of God's wisdom. Evil here refers to the calamities of war rather than to moral evil. In another respect also is God's wisdom shown, namely, that He does not turn aside His words. He abides by what He has spoken. Herein is a characteristic of wisdom indeed! If one speaks and then later must retract His words, He has evidently spoken without full knowledge. A commentary on the thought appears in Numbers 23:19, "God *is* not a man, that he should lie; neither the son of man, that he should repent: hath he said, and shall he not do *it?* or hath he spoken, and shall he not make it good?" Isaiah's language is picturesque; it implies turning aside words that have been spoken and now stand in the way as hindrances. Such words must be cleared away, for they are seen to be false. Turning aside words is a common feature of human activity; God, however, so the argument runs, inasmuch as He is wise, need not do this.

God's wisdom is not seen in an indiscriminate bringing of evil, but manifests itself in God's rising up against the house (i.e., the family) of evildoers. Corresponding to the actual standpoint of the prophet who speaks, the language now continues with the perfect and *waw* consecutive. The house of Jacob (2:5), a seed of evildoers (1:4), has now become a house of evildoers. God stands up against such in that He turns against the help that the workers of evil provide. These workers of evil are not the Egyptians, but those in Judah who seek help from man rather than from God. The words aptly describe the Judahites, and in the following verses Isaiah shows how he designates the Egyptians. The phrase "help of the doers, etc." means "the help that the doers of evil receive." The word "help" refers to the Egyptians, so that we learn that God will rise both against the help (the Egyptians) and the doers of iniquity (the wicked Judahites).

3 The introductory "and" is to be taken in the sense "and yet," or "for." This verse gives the reason why Egypt will perish and why it cannot be the help that Judah needs. Egypt is man and not God.[3] The distinction is metaphysical, designed to set forth the

---

3 Cf. 10:15, *not wood.*

difference between the Creator and the creature. For this reason the term *'el* rather than *'elohim* is used. Whereas *'elohim* might in certain instances denote beings that were actually creatures, this is not true of *'el*. On the other hand Yahweh is not man but is God (*'el*). Only *'el* (God) can be a help to the theocracy in this time of deep need. As for the horses of Egypt in which Judah wished to place her trust, they are but flesh and not spirit.[4] Here the contrast is not between what is material and what is nonmaterial, but is similar to the contrast just made between man and God. The horses are merely flesh, i.e., they are creatures of flesh and blood; they are not spirit, i.e., not above flesh, not supernatural, not of divine nature. They can do only what flesh can do, not what spirit can perform. Thus, when the Psalmist asks, "What can flesh do to me?" (56:4) he is simply saying that man the creature cannot harm him. The contrast is also brought out in Zechariah 4:6, "Not by might nor by power, but by my Spirit, saith the Lord of hosts." Jehovah and Egypt are set in contrast one to another. One is a true help, the other not; the people of God choose what is not a true help.

In contrast to Egypt the Lord stretches out His hand. A description of Egypt's nature is given, but God is presented as acting. He is powerful, and in stretching out His hand brings about the downfall of both Egypt and the Judahites who trust in Egypt. Egypt the helper stumbles and Judah the helped falls. There is an intriguing gradation between *stumbles* and *falls,* as well as a certain rhyme in the words themselves. Together, all of them, or, as we would say, both of them, will come to an end. The last two words in Hebrew exhibit a striking paronomasia. There is an interesting development in thought between this and the preceding chapter. Chapter thirty teaches that Judah sought help from Egypt and placed her trust falsely. Egypt's help, however, would bring her to disgrace. In the present chapter there is a gradation in the thought. Not only does Judah seek help from Egypt but she also rejects the help of the Lord. It is her unbelief that is here prominent, and it is the Lord who brings her and the country to which she had turned for help to shame.

4 For thus saith the LORD unto me, As the lion growls and the

---

4 Flesh is not yet, as in the NT, associated with sin; it signifies the innate inertia of the creature, apart from God, whereas "spirit" refers to the energy of life in God. Cf. G. Vos, *Biblical Theology,* 1948, p. 257.

young lion over his prey, against whom a multitude of shepherds is called forth, at their voice he is not frightened, and at their noise he is not humbled, so will the LORD of hosts come down, to fight upon mount Zion and upon her hill.

5 As birds flying over, so will the LORD of hosts cover over Jerusalem, cover and rescue, pass over and save.

6 Return unto him (from whom) the children of Israel have deeply revolted.

7 For in that day they shall reject, each one his idols of silver and his idols of gold which your hands have made for you as sin.

8 And Assyria will fall by the sword, not of a man, and the sword, not of a man, will devour him, and he will flee from before the sword, and his young men will become tribute.

9 And his rock shall pass away from fear, and his chiefs shall be afraid of a standard, saith the LORD, to whom there is a fire in Zion and a furnace in Jerusalem.

4 Isaiah now presents Judah's true help. His introductory "for" takes up what has been stated in verses 1-3 and supports it. We may paraphrase, "For in the light of what has just been stated, the Lord Himself speaks." The formula does more than merely introduce words of the Lord. It strengthens and gives authority to the message, a message spoken by the very Lord whom the people of Judah are despising.

The Lord begins His words with a comparison, which, as has often been pointed out, appears also in the *Iliad* xviii.161:

And as from the carcass in no manner are the shepherds dwelling in the field able to drive away the tawny lion.

The definite article is generic; *even as a lion growls, and a young lion over its prey.*[5] The lion is ready to defend its prey and growls against those who would approach to take it away. It would be the task of the shepherds to rescue the sheep or lamb that the lion has stolen. When he hears their voice, however, he is not frightened. This and the following clause are subordinate to the introductory, *when he hears. . . .* We may render, *without being afraid at their voice or humbled at their noise.*

Isaiah compares the Lord to the lion facing the shepherds. He will come down as the Lord of hosts (*tzeva'oth*) to fight (*tzava'*)

---

[5] *growls*—the imp. expresses customary action, *is wont to growl. the lion*—i.e., *lions;* the definite article is used generically.

upon Mt. Zion and its hill. This hill probably refers to all the elevation of the city of Jerusalem. Against the wicked of Judah the Lord will fight, permitting His own army to march on and to destroy the city despite any help that the Egyptians could offer.

5 Verse 5 forms a complement to verse 4, forming as it were the reverse side of the picture. Isaiah changes the comparison to show that from the outbreaking wrath of the descending Lord there appears also the grace of God to His people. God is now compared to birds that hover with outspread wings that they may protect the young.[6] It is probably correct to say that the feminine form of the participle alludes to the care of mothers for their young. God cares for Jerusalem as mother birds watch over their young in the nests. Possibly also the use of the plural stresses the fullness of protection. The lion-like fierceness that must fight against Mt. Zion appears toward the remnant as the motherly love of birds. Although the objects Zion and Jerusalem are here used interchangeably, nevertheless, from the entire context of the prophecy we understand that the wrath of God must bring to naught the physical city of Jerusalem and destroy the theocracy, but that toward His own, i.e., the remnant, the delivering and redeeming mercy of God will be shown.

Just as the Lord of hosts will fight against Zion, so also will the Lord of hosts (note the repetition of these words) exhibit protection over Jerusalem. The central and basic thought of the verse is protection, and is expressed by a finite verb in the imperfect. The concept is then strengthened by two infinitives absolute, and each of these is accompanied by a verb in the perfect with *waw* consecutive in order to complete and fulfill its meaning.[7] In covering or surrounding, the Lord will deliver; and in passing over he will save. Isaiah chooses an expression that calls to mind the Exodus, when the destroyer went through the land (Ex. 12:13; 23:27). As then the destroyer passed over the house of the Israel-

---

6 *he will cover, surround, defend.* This form is probably *Qal,* for the normal *Hiphil* imp. would be *yā-gin,* but the *Hiphil* seems not to occur in this sense. Barth regards the form as having an original *i* in the second syllable and appeals to Ar. *ya-jin-nu;* cf. also *ya-fir-ru* for *yaf-rir.* Cf. Houtsma, *ZAW,* Vol. 27, 1907, p. 57.

7 *whtzyl*—the inf. abs. is followed by the perf. with *waw* cons., which may be regarded as a frequentative with future meaning. Cf. Josh. 6:13 and 2 Sam. 13:19.

ites, so now like birds God passes over His people and delivers them.[8]

As remarked earlier, these two comparisons complement one another. First, God is compared with a strong lion, bold, unafraid, powerful; then with tender and loving birds which protect their nest. But can mere tender birds protect their nest? To support the latter comparison we have the first. He who protects is He who is strong as a lion to accomplish His purposes.

6 Having set forth the sureness of the Lord's protection, Isaiah now commands the Israelites to return to God. Even though their rebellion against Him has been deep, nevertheless, He alone can help and will welcome them if they do return to Him. The form of statement is somewhat difficult. We may render, *Return to him against whom the children of Israel have deeply revolted*, or, *Return unto him against whom men have deeply revolted, ye children of Israel*. Difficult as it is, we prefer the latter interpretation as more faithfully setting forth the meaning of the prophet.[9] He begins with an imperative, *return ye,* for when the nation had rebelled through idolatry it had departed far from the Lord.

In issuing this command is Isaiah disobedient to his inaugural? God had enjoined him to preach in such a way that the people would not return (6:10). Now he orders them to return. An answer to the problem probably lies along the following lines. God had declared that the nation as such, to which so many gifts had been given, would not repent but would be carried into exile. At the same time, the nation would not perish in its entirety. A remnant would return (note the use of the verb in the name of Isaiah's son, Shear-yashub), and through this remnant salvation would ultimately come to the world. In what manner, however, will this remnant appear? Only through individuals returning to the Lord. Isaiah, therefore, commands the entire nation to repent (note that the verb is plural). The whole nation will not repent, but the elect among them will do so. The prophet's command is not in vain; but God will bless it so that the true sons of Israel, the

---

[8] *psh—a passing over.* Penna thinks that there is implicit an allusion to the massacre of the enemies, and that the Lord saves in the massacre. Cf. B. Couroyer, "L'Origine Égyptienne du mot 'Paque'," *Revue Biblique*, Vol. 62, 1955, pp. 481-496.

[9] *in respect to whom they have made rebellion deep;* cf. Judg. 8:15. The phrase is repeated in 1Q. Note the change from 2nd to 3rd person. Cf. Van der Ploeg, *OS*, Vol. 5, 1948, p. 144.

elect according to the promises of God, will hear the command and turn from their evil ways and return to the Lord.

The Hebrew words following the command may be rendered, *with respect to him against whom they have deepened rebellion.* The subject may either be impersonal, and if so would refer to the fact that rebellion against the Lord has been of a deep and serious kind, or the subject may be the Israelites generally. It is difficult to say what is intended, but it may be that the verb is simply to be understood in an impersonal sense. The language suggests an intensification of rebellion. To make rebellion deep, therefore, is to make it heinous (cf. Hos. 9:9).[10] The people are then addressed as *sons of Israel,* and thus attention is directed to their glorious ancestry. The sons of Israel should be truly Israel's sons, and this they may be only when they abandon their course of deep rebellion and return to the Lord. It was this that Jacob had also been compelled to do. He had made deep rebellion in the practices that characterized his earlier life, but there came a time when he was compelled to return to the Lord. Let the sons of Israel do as Israel himself had done. Let them cease being Jacob and become Israel; let them return unto the Lord.

7 Isaiah now proceeds to give the motivation for his command to repent. "Return," we may paraphrase, "for in that day ye will indeed recognize that ye have rebelled and ye will then cast away your idols." The words "in that day" simply refer to the time when God delivers the people. Then, when they see the power of His hand, they will recognize the folly of their own actions, and will reject with contempt the idols of silver and gold that their own fingers have made.

Between the first and the second part of the verse there is an interesting change of person. Those who possess the idols and expect the idols to help them in time of need have received these idols from the human hands that made them. Coupled with confidence in idols is also confidence in human helpers. It is folly compounded. The result is that the whole matter has become sin to

---

10 At the same time, in rebellion against God there is a sinking down, a descent, an abasement.

11 Perhaps there is particular reason for the change of person. The nation that Isaiah addresses is responsible for the idolatry that the people will one day reject. *ḥṭ'*—a second acc., indicating the result, *object of sin,* or, *for sin;* cf. 41:

Israel.[11] It has not brought deliverance, but only sin. In this striking word "sin," the verse is brought to its close.

8 If there is to be a true returning unto the Lord and a wiping out of all the false gods, there must first be the destruction of the power that God has used as the instrument of judgment against Judah. That power is Assyria, but Isaiah is not here speaking merely of the incursions of Sennacherib. It is rather the Assyrian power as such that he has in mind. The Assyrian power must first be done away and then the remnant will enjoy the blessings of full deliverance.

The first verb indicates that Assyria, which now is standing, will fall and cease to be a power. This fall is said to be accomplished "by a sword of one who is not a man" (lit., *by the sword of a not-man*).[12] By using this forceful designation the prophet apparently reflects upon a similar usage that he had already employed in 10:15. What is meant is not merely that the sword is not that of a man, but it is the sword of One who is far more than a man, namely, the Lord Himself. By means of a chiastic arrangement of language Isaiah repeats the thought, "the sword not of a man will devour it." Isaiah employs two different words for "man," but there is here no particular difference in the shades of their meaning. His purpose is simply to show that the sword which caused Assyria to fall was in no wise wielded by a mere man, but was wielded only by the hand of God. Assyria represented the kingdom of man, which would attempt to dominate all the earth. It is significant that the kingdom of man will be brought to an end by the sword of a *not-man*.

From this sword Assyria will seek to flee for its own safety; but it will not be successful, for its young men will become tribute.[13] It

---

24. For the whole verse cf. 2:20 where there is a change of number instead of person.

12 *by the sword*—i.e., not with the sword of a man; cf. v. 3, to which this verse is a contrast. Cf. the similar phraseology of 1:20. The point is not to deny that God may have employed human agents in destroying Assyria, but to lead us directly to the ultimate cause of the destruction (cf. 24:21; 27:1; 34:3 etc.)

13 יֹל—ethical dative of advantage. Note the emphasis upon *sword* in this verse. Drechsler applies the fulfillment to 37:37. He thinks that the army of Sennacherib suffered a complete demoralization and was scattered on all sides and fell into the hands of those who used the occasion for their own advantage.

will taste what it had imposed on others. Throughout its history Assyria had laid tribute on others; indeed, Hezekiah himself was compelled to pay tribute. This state of affairs was to cease; and now Assyria would pay the heaviest of tribute, even its own young men, its chosen ones, those most suitable to fight its battles.

There was no period in Assyria's history, apparently, when the young men of Assyria actually became tribute to Judah. It would seem that the prophet is speaking in wider and grander tones of the final destruction of the power that, were that possible, would have destroyed the theocracy. To say that the young men of Assyria will become tribute is to say that Assyria herself will be completely destroyed.

9 In this verse Isaiah continues the description of the defeated Assyria. Different renderings of the first words are given. Do they mean, *his rock shall pass away from fear* or, *from fear he will pass over his rock?* Perhaps it is not possible to choose either one of these renderings with certainty, although the first may be preferable.[14] The emphasis of the words may then be brought out as follows: *As for his rock, from fear it will pass over.* The rock is not the strength of Assyria, but the place in which he finds protection, his fortress, as in the passage 33:16, "the munitions of rocks." The rocks are unscalable and inaccessible save with the utmost difficulty, and they are also easy to defend. Furthermore, in them there are caves and crevices which serve as protection. This fortress is pictured as passing away from fear. It will not stand impregnable, but overcome with fear will pass over. The rock is thus personified. Isaiah refers not to any specific fortress of the Assyrians, but simply makes a general statement that the strength of Assyria, her place of refuge, will be so overcome with fear that it will pass over the land in flight.

An explanation of the first clause is really provided by the second, when it is stated that the princes of Assyria will be frightened before a standard that God Himself will raise. All that is needed is for the Assyrians to see the raised standard and they fall into fear and panic. The truth of this defeat is attested by the

---

14 *its place of refuge*—cf. Terence *Phormio* v.2, 3: *fugit etiam praeter casam.* König insists that *his rock* must be subj., and designate the king. If *his rock* be taken as subj., there is a very effective chiastic arrangement in 9a. Those who apply *rock* to the Assyrian god appeal to Sennacherib's designation *šadû rabû* (lit., great mountain), line 23.

Lord, of whom Isaiah says that He has a fire in Zion. The reference is to the fire burning continually upon the altar of burnt offering. Parallel to the "fire" is the "furnace" in Jerusalem by which the prophet designates the burning wrath of God. On the altar there is the sacred fire and in Jerusalem the wrath of God's presence, which will consume the enemies of the nation. It may be that there is a particular allusion to Tophet as the furnace of God's wrath wherein the enemies will suffer the flames of vengeance. Of this, however, one cannot be certain. What is clear is that the fire and the furnace belong to the Lord and they are present in Jerusalem, ready to consume the enemies.

It is significant that this verse presents quite an advance over verses 4 and 5. These verses had given the assurance that God would and could protect His people, but nothing had been said about so complete a defeat of the enemy. It was well then that the people were commanded to return to the Lord, for now it is revealed that the fire of God is burning to bring about a complete destruction of the Assyrian. The present verse also prepares for 33:14ff., and reflects upon 30:33.

C. THE CERTAINTY OF THE COMING SALVATION (32, 33)

1. A CONDITION OF TRUE BLESSEDNESS WILL COME (32:1-20)

1 Behold! for righteousness a king will reign, and as for rulers, for judgment they will rule.

2 And a man will be as a hiding place from the wind, and a covert from the rain, as channels of water in a dry place, as the shadow of a heavy rock in a weary land.

3 And the eyes of those that see will not be dim, and the ears of those that hear will hearken.

4 And the heart of the rash will understand to know, and the tongue of stammerers will hasten to speak clear things.

1 Having been delivered, Zion is renewed in righteousness and justice. For her a new era begins, that of God's righteousness. Things are as they should be. Those who have the gift of sight do actually see. Isaiah expresses this thought first in a positive manner (vv. 1-4) and then negatively (vv. 5-8). To call attention to the new state of things the prophet uses his favorite "behold!" and immediately following this word states that the reign will be "for righteousness." The preposition *Lamed* may express the purpose of the reign or the manner of the reign. Hence, we may either translate "for righteousness" or "according to righteousness," as in 11:4. The common English versions give "in righteousness," but this would normally be expressed by the preposition *Beth*.

Whether Isaiah is stating that the king will reign for the purpose of righteousness or according to righteousness is a question that probably cannot be positively settled. In either case the word *righteousness* is placed in the foreground, for the reign of this king is wholly contrary to the reigns of ordinary kings. The prophets had often condemned the lack of justice in Judah, the theocratic nation. The poor were downtrodden and oppressed, and justice had departed from the land. After the judgment, however, there would be a reign in "righteousness and justice" (cf. 9:5ff.; 11:1-5; 16:5). This reign then stands in contrast with all other reigns. In the common English versions the force of the sentence is lost, *a king shall reign in righteousness*. To bring out the true force of the original we may translate, *Behold! according to righteousness there will reign a king*.[1]

Who is this king? Jerome held that the prophecy was concerned with the advent of Christ and His apostles (the princes). Gressmann also maintained that the picture is Messianic. On the other hand many commentators think that a strictly Messianic interpretation cannot be admitted, inasmuch as the picture does not concentrate upon the king as an individual but rather is one of ideal righteousness such as would be found under ideal rulers. These would have to be more devoted than hypocritical Ahaz and more active and energetic than Hezekiah.

For our part we are impressed with the fact that the picture of righteous government herein presented is a result of the great judgment and visitation of punishment described in the preceding chapter. What is here depicted stands in complete contrast to what has gone before. This government is righteous—it is a contrast not only to the haughty pretensions of the Assyrian king but also to the lack of justice and righteousness of the Judean rulers. It is, therefore, a Messianic government. Granted, nothing further is stated about the king as a person, but only the Messiah can reign in righteousness. Insofar as Hezekiah sought to be a righteous king, he may be said to have adumbrated the Messiah; but Isaiah is not talking about a government that is only partially righteous; he is speaking of one that is completely righteous. It is this strong contrast with the actual governments of the prophet's own day that supports the view that this is the Messianic kingdom.

Isaiah wishes to speak not merely of the king but of the entire government, in order to present a contrast to the condition of things earlier described in 1:21-23. He therefore mentions the princes, declaring that they will rule for justice. Both king and princes will be what they should be; the Davidic government will

---

[1] Thus, the clause reaches a climax in *melek*, which is further heightened both by the paronomasia and by the fact that the verb loses its principal accent, being joined to *melek* by *Maqqeph*. This results in the ultima of the verb becoming a closed, unaccented syllable and so being pointed with *Qametz-Ḥatuph*.

be Davidic in the truest sense. Divinely appointed and revealed standards now prevail and are observed in the administration of the government. It is probably correct to say that this is not a Messianic prophecy in the sense that it speaks of the Messiah personally. It speaks of a government, however, that can belong only to the Messiah and be ruled by Him, and in that sense may be labelled a Messianic prophecy. What Isaiah is saying is that a time will come, as a result of the judgment, when there will be a perfectly righteous government. The king will reign according to righteousness and the princes according to justice, the very opposite of what prevailed in Isaiah's day.[2]

2 The first result of the period of blessedness is now stated. At the outset, however, an exegetical question arises. Are we to render, *And each one will be,* or *And a man will be?* Many commentators prefer to take the language in a distributive sense as though it taught that each individual himself would be as a hiding place. We cannot, however, translate *each one of them* and refer to the princes of verse 1; and hence it is perhaps best to translate *a man,* in the sense of men generally. To paraphrase: "And men will be. . . ." When the word *'ish* is to be used in a distributive sense, it is usually connected with a plural verb. The thought seems to be that a man will be like a hiding place, and this man will be upon the throne. Isaiah is probably referring to the protection from violent wind afforded by a great rock. The one on the throne would be such a protection. Instead of oppressing the people in unrighteousness, he would be a protection to them from oppression, a place in which they could hide from the storm which could beat down mercilessly upon those in open, unprotected country.

In the second half of the verse, by means of beautiful figures, Isaiah continues his description of the protection that the man affords.[3] He is also said to be like streams of water in a dry place. Where dryness had been, abundant water will be found. In a land

2 *and with respect to princes*—The prep. practically has the force of rendering the word a *casus pendens.* By mention of the princes, the king is pushed somewhat in the background. Hence, this passage is probably not a direct prediction of the Messiah as a person, but rather emphasizes the fact that the Messianic age will have rulers who reign for righteousness. In this broader sense the passage is a Messianic prophecy.

3 Cf. Vergil *Georgics* iii.145, *speluncaeque tegunt et saxea procubat umbra;* and Hesiod *Works* 588f.

thirsting because of lack of water he will be as a heavy rock which casts a great shadow to protect from the burning heat of the sun. To one living in the Judean countryside, these figures would be rich with comfort and meaning. Floods, storms, and burning heat would constitute dangers; but the man who sits upon the throne will be a protection from all these. It is interesting that the dangers are symbolized by figures taken from the world of nature rather than by allusions to an enemy. The thought is that in the ordinary course of daily life the man on the throne is to be the refuge for the ones over whom he rules.

3 The truth that things will be as they actually should be is now expressed in yet a different manner. The eyes of those who see will be able to see; they will not be smeared over or blinded so as to prevent seeing.[4] At the present time, when the prophet speaks, because of the hardening that God brings upon the nation, its eyes are smeared over and cannot see. The seers, in other words, are blind. In the Messianic age, however, the hardening will be removed and they will see (cf. Isa. 29:10). Furthermore, the ears which hitherto had been stopped up, will hear as they should. The period of hardening (Isa. 6:9, 10) is passed. God, who once had closed the eyes and ears of the nation, now that His purposes of judgment have been fulfilled, opens the eyes and ears so that they may see and hear as they should.

4 Continuing his description Isaiah remarks that the heart of those who are reckless or confused will understand knowledge. The word that he employs refers basically to one who acts hastily, and hence it is used of those who are confused. Inasmuch as such people are not able to employ their reason correctly they find themselves in embarrassment and confusion. Their mind, as it were, has deserted them; and consequently, they act without wisdom. It may be noted that the eyes, ears, and heart, mentioned in this and the preceding verse, correspond to the same organs mentioned both in 6:9 and 10. The heart, here conceived as the seat of the intelligence, will perceive in such a way as to arrive at knowledge (cf. 29:24). Up to this point the people had been in a stupor

---

[4] *be blinded!*—"In this case, however, a contrary meaning (i.e., to look at) seems to be so clearly required, both by the context and the parallelism, that most interpreters, ancient and modern, concur in deriving it from שעע or in supposing שעה to have been sometimes used in the sense of blinding, which the former verb has in Chapter vi.10 and xxix.9" (Alexander).

THE BOOK OF ISAIAH

of confusion, not understanding things as they actually were. Hence, they had turned aside from the Lord and looked to Egypt for help. God, however, will give them understanding, so that they will know things as they are. To possess understanding and knowledge is to live in obedience to God and His commands. Only those who are enlightened of Him can understand so as to know. Knowledge is their possession alone.

A further evidence of the great change is to be seen in that the tongue of those who stammer will speak clear things.[5] Isaiah is not speaking of those who by nature were stammerers in the physical sense, but rather of those who in drunkenness (cf. 28:7, 8; 29:9) were stammering forth nonsense. This will be completely changed. They will possess a fluency of speech such as they never had before, and they will speak what is clear. Their words will come forth readily and distinctly, perhaps even with a certain amount of eloquence. It is well to note the contrast between *nimharim* and *t'maher*. The heart of those who *in haste* have become confused will perceive knowledge, and the tongue of stammerers *will hasten* not to confusion but to the utterance of things that are clear and distinct.

5 There will no longer be called to the fool noble, and the knave will no longer be spoken of as liberal.

6 For the fool will speak folly, and his heart will do iniquity, to do wickedness and to speak unto the LORD error, to starve the soul of the hungry, and as to drink he will leave the thirsty to fail.

7 And as for the knave, his instruments are evil. He deviseth plots to ruin the afflicted with words of falsehood, and when the poor man speaks judgment.

8 And the noble one will devise noble things, and he upon noble things will stand.

5 A third blessing to flow from the Messianic reign appears in that a man will be acknowledged for what he actually is and not for what he appears to be. When men's minds are blinded they do not behold the true character of other men, but judge merely by appearances; when their eyes truly see, however, they will behold the real worth of men. The only true realism therefore is found in salvation. Isaiah uses an expression that might almost be called a

---

5 *clear*—f. pl. of צח, *dazzling, glowing, clear*. The pointing is strange; we should expect *tzaḥ(ḥ)ôt*.

favorite of his, namely, the *Niphal* imperfect, *will be called.* The fool *(naval)* will no longer be called a prince *(nadiv).* The last person on earth capable of serving as a prince is a fool. Nevertheless, because of the perversion of their own hearts, men do not make correct evaluations, and they call a fool a prince. When their eyes are opened they will no longer do this, but will then recognize the fool for what he actually is. The prince *(nadiv)* is one whose character is high and noble, and the word itself comes to designate nobility of position and rank. "Nobility of birth and wealth," says Delitzsch, "will give place to nobility of character." The fool has manifested his greatest folly in his preference of sin over righteousness, and hence the word *fool* comes practically to designate a wicked person.

The precise force of the second part of the verse is difficult to determine, for the exact meaning of some of the words is not known. Corresponding to the word *naval* (fool) in the first half of the verse is the word *kilay,* which occurs only here. Some think it denotes a churl or a niggardly person. If that is the meaning, then the verse teaches that such a person will no longer be regarded as the opposite of what he actually is. He will not be thought to be liberal and free when in reality he is niggardly. Another procedure is to take the word *kilay* in the sense of *crafty,* or *deceitful,* and quite possibly this is the correct reading. The verse then teaches that the man who engages in crafty and cunning plans will not be regarded as the one who possesses wealth or is a noble person.[6]

6 In this and the following verse Isaiah points out the characteristics of the ones of whom he has just spoken. The fool is characterized as speaking foolish things; cf. 9:16. Words that come from his mouth are lacking in wisdom but are full of folly. Isaiah uses an interesting alliteration *(naval—n°valah).* The heart of the fool, moreover, devises iniquity; it plans purposes of evil. The fool is dangerous, then, for his heart is set on accomplishing iniquity, and his mouth speaks words of folly. His entire personality is dedicated to the performance of evil.

There is a reason why the personality is so engaged. It is for the

---

6 נדיב—*generous, noble* (in mind and character). כילי—*knave.* The root *nkl* apparently means *to be crafty, deceitful, knavish;* cf. *nakâlu.* שׁוע—The precise significance of the root *šw'* is not positively known. It seems to be a synonym of *nadib, noble,* and here possibly designates one who is *noble* or *independent.* 1Q gives the verbs in the plural.

purpose (and Isaiah expresses this purpose by means of infinitives) first of all of doing what is unholy or profane.[7] The word translated *profane*, which occurs only here, apparently has to do with sin against Yahweh, doing what is the opposite of His will. A second infinitive expresses the second purpose, namely, to speak against the Lord what is error. What is spoken is not in accord with the truth. Isaiah had already used the word in 29:15. The participle of this root is used of Joseph's wandering in the field (Gen. 37:15). *To'ah* is that which is astray, having wandered from the truth. Our English word *error* well represents the meaning of the Hebrew word. What is spoken is uttered against the Lord, and will cause men to stray from Him.

To complete the picture Isaiah mentions two more matters, introducing the first with an infinitive, and the second with a finite verb. These two matters are stated in chiastic order, "to make empty the soul of the hungry, and the drink of the thirsty he makes to fail." The fool, devising devices of evil, is nevertheless without mercy toward his fellow men. He wars against God and consequently also against men, for love of God and love of man belong together (cf. Matt. 22:36-40).

Isaiah has sought to be exhaustive in his description. In the first part of the verse he has given a contrast between what is inward and what is outward. The first part of the verse also presents the fool as opposed to God, and then in the second part as really opposed to man also. Again there is a division into two clauses for each of the lines that express the purposes of the fool; first, his action and his speech against God, and then a contrast between food and drink with respect to man.

7 Having spoken of the fool Isaiah now states what the *knave* (*kelay*) really is. The word is deliberately chosen to form a word play with the immediately following *kelayw* (instruments). The first word is a *casus pendens,* and we may translate, *and as for the knave, his instruments are evil.* Emphasis is placed here upon the manner in which the knave works. Despite all his planning and cunning what he does is evil; his methods of working are not good.

---

[7] *ḥonep—alienation;* to be polluted, inclined away from the right relation to God. מַשְׁקֶה *—drink.* The word is absolute, introducing a circumstantial clause. The first imp. should be taken as a fut., expressing the reason why at that time the fool will not be regarded as noble. *he causes to lack*—frequentative action.

Setting his heart upon riches, he oppresses all who come in his way. As Alexander puts it, "He that hastens to be rich can scarcely avoid the practice of dishonest arts and of unkindness to the poor." The reason for this is stated in a second clause, "he (and the pronoun is emphatic) counsels plots."[8] He is a man of tricks and plots, always scheming and devising devices to accomplish his ends. Perhaps the word *counsels* (*ya'atz*) is deliberately used, for the knave is one who advises others what to do in order to attain his own purposes. The sentences have been short and emphatic, and somewhat of a climax is reached in the pausal form of the verb *ya'atz* (*he counsels*).

The purpose of these plots is to destroy the afflicted by means of false words, even though the poor man may be pleading his own cause.[9] What Isaiah means is that even when there is a just case for the poor man, and the poor man sets forth his case, the knave has no heart.[10] He is not moved by pleas of pity or of right. He seeks his own riches and his own ends; if the poor stand in his way, they must perish. He is of all men most self-centered and egotistical. His wishes must prevail.

8 Finally, it is necessary to state what the noble truly is. A nation with perverted mind cannot recognize men for what they are. They must therefore be instructed as to the true condition of affairs. They must know what a fool and a knave are, they must also know what a noble is. The construction of this verse is similar to 7a. Again the prophet employs an alliteration.[11] Like the knave, the noble also engages in counselling others, but his counsel is noble in character and quality. What he counsels bears the same exalted character of nobility as the man himself who counsels. Not only does he counsel such things but he also abides by and stands with them. He is habitually engaged in those things that are noble.

In verse 5 Isaiah had mentioned four concepts; of these only three are developed in the subsequent verses; the fourth one (the

8 *loose conduct*—cf. Ar. *ḍamma, to blame,* and Ug. *tdmm(t).* The reference is probably to *shameful acts.*

9 *the poor*—The word is of Egy. origin, from the root *b'n, bad, evil.* It appears also in Ug., *'abynt* (Aqht ii.1.17).

10 The conjunction is emphatic, *even when the poor man speaks judgment.*

11 Note the word order: subj., obj., verb. The *Tiphḥa* gives to the subj. almost the force of a *casus pendens: as for the noble—noble things does he devise.*

sho$^{a'}$) is lacking, evidently being covered by what is said of the noble person.

9 Careless women, arise, hear my voice; trusting daughters, give ear unto my speech.

10 Days upon a year, ye shall tremble, ye trusting ones, for the vintage fails, the gathering shall not come.

11 Tremble, ye careless women, quake, ye trusting ones, strip you and make you bare, and gird on your loins,

12 Mourning for the breasts, for the pleasant fields, for the fruitful vine.

13 Upon the land of my people thorn and thistle will come up, for upon all houses of pleasure—the joyous city.

14 For the palace is forsaken, the crowd of the city left, hill and watchtower have become caves for ever, a joy of wild asses, a pasture of flocks.

9 As a completion to the fourth woe, which began in 31:1, Isaiah adds a section addressed to the women of Jerusalem. His purpose is to show that the present condition and attitude of the women is wrong and deceptive, and to point out what the true condition should be. Although addressing them as women and daughters, he does not have two classes of women in mind. The two words, standing in a parallel relation, are synonyms. As in 3:24 he had spoken to the women, so again he feels the necessity for addressing them. Women are more sensitive and understanding than men; surely the prophet's appeals would have made an impression upon them. This was not the case, however, for they continued on in false trust and security.

For that reason Isaiah addresses them as *careless*. The word is used in a bad sense, and signifies more than carefree.[12] These are women who have a false confidence as to their security and therefore believe themselves to be protected from harm. They are not aware of any approaching danger, and so give no thought thereto. They are at ease in Zion (Amos 6:1) and are not concerned about the true welfare of the city. Quite possibly they were also characterized by a certain arrogance and would not be moved by the earnest pleas and warnings of the prophets. When the

---

12 *careless*—the Gk., Syr., and Vulg. translate *wealthy*, e.g., *mulieres opulentae.* So also Rosenmüller, *"divites, luxuriantes, urbes et vici Judaeae prospere, hilariter ac secure ad omnem copiam et abundantiam pasti."*

women of a country are not concerned about its true welfare, its plight is tragic indeed.

Such women are commanded to arise, to do the very opposite of what they actually are doing. The word is not to be taken in a literal sense, as though Isaiah were speaking to an actual group of sitting women,[13] but is a general command to change the attitude completely. In the present condition of lethargy and indifference the women cannot hear the prophet's voice.[14] They must first throw off their unconcern, and then they can hear what Isaiah is saying. We only hear the voice of God when our hearts are awakened from sleep.

In addressing the women as daughters, Isaiah probably intends to designate them as inhabitants of the city (cf. Ps. 45:12, "daughter of Tyre"). They are daughters who are confident and trusting, for they are secure in their insecurity. An illusory tranquility governs their lives and thoughts. If the women of a land thus have false security and confidence they cannot inspire the men to act rightly and to ward off the dangers that threaten.

10 There is a good reason why Isaiah commands Zion's women to hear his voice. His prophecies of destruction are true. A time of desolation is coming when the vintage will fail and the calamities predicted will be present. When, however, will these things take place? Isaiah designates this time as days upon a year. In itself the expression "days" may indicate either a few days (cf. Gen. 24:55 where it is used of ten days) or many days; but in any case it denotes the days that taken together make up a whole, an entirety, and so, in this sense the word *days* is really to be understood as signifying a year (cf. 1 Sam. 27:7 and Judg. 17:10; Isa. 29:1). The entire expression, therefore, "days upon a year," is equivalent to saying, "in a year or more." Gesenius aptly calls attention to the German expression, *über Jahr und Tag*. The words do not designate the length of the judgment, for Isaiah is not saying, "Ye will tremble for a year or more." Rather, they serve to indicate when the judgment will come. It is as though the prophet had declared, "Within little more than a year ye will tremble." The words are a temporal accusative, and we may bring out their force in English by rendering, *Within a little more than a year.*

---

[13] So Hitzig. Vitringa, Rosenmüller, etc., following David Kimchi, apply the reference to the villages of Judah.

[14] האזנה—note contraction of final *Nun* with the *Nun* of the suffix.

Isaiah again addresses the women as "trusting ones," using a word that forms a contrast to the verb.[15] Now the women are still, quiet, confident; then they will tremble, for trembling is the sign that all confidence and stay have departed. Then they will become the opposite of what they are at present. To represent vividly the judgment Isaiah mentions some of its effects. Among other things the vintage will come to an end, and the gathering in of the grapes will fail. This is a contrast to the present luxurious life of the women of Zion. Wine that gives them pleasure will then fail. The festival of ingathering was one of the most joyful (16:7-10). In speaking of the ingathering, the prophet states clearly that the present luxury is to come to an end.[16]

11 Hence Isaiah addresses the careless women as though the period of lack had already come, and commands them to act the part of mourners. The command, however, contains a change of gender, for Isaiah begins with an imperative in the masculine plural and then continues his imperatives in the feminine singular.[17] Perhaps there is deliberation in this choice of words; perhaps the prophet thus strengthens the command by giving to it a certain variety of expression. Whether this be so or not, there is certainly no good reason for emending the text. The first command is general; it is a command to tremble and is addressed to those who are careless. A complete change or reversal of attitude is demanded, as though the prophet said, "Ye are now unconcerned, but ye must tremble as though ye were greatly concerned."

Using now an imperative in the feminine singular, Isaiah comprehends the women as a unit.[18] The word is used of the shaking of an earthquake. They who are confident, quiet, and trusting are to shake, for their confidence will no longer be present. More than that, they are to engage in the practice of mourning, to strip off

15 *Ye shall tremble* and *trusting ones* occur side by side.

16 The gathering of grapes and fruit harvest occurred at the same time (Deut. 16:13). Compare the description in Isa. 16:7-10.

17 When the writer views the pl. subj. in its totality, he may place related words in the s.; cf. also Isa. 59:12. Note also that m. forms may be used with f. subjects when no particular stress upon the gender is intended; cf. also 1 Kings 8:31; 22:36.

18 *re̱-gā-zāh*—this and the following imperatives are generally regarded as Aramaizing forms of the 2 f. pl. Cf. F. Scerbo, "*Di alcune presunte forme aramaiche in Isaia*" in *Giornale della Società asiatica italiana,* Vol. 16, 1903, pp. 269-273. I have not seen this work.

their clothing from them and lay themselves bare in humility. All the garments and ornaments of luxury are to be taken off, for these are hindrances to a true attitude toward the Lord. The women must be divested completely of their clothes in order that they may put on a girdle of mourning about their loins.[19] It goes without saying that the prophet has no concern for a mere outward appearance of mourning. In commanding the women to gird themselves, he desires that such action be expressive of a true inward condition of repentance.

12 In verse 11 Isaiah commanded the women to mourn; now he describes how the mourning is carried out. His language, however, is quite difficult. We may render the first three words, either *mourning for the breasts*, or *beating upon the breasts*. If we adopt the first of these renderings we are probably to take the language in a figurative sense. The breasts would then stand for the richness of the land, and the mourning would occur because the land was no longer producing with the abundance that once characterized it. The second interpretation, however, would refer to the actual act of mourning, to a beating upon the breasts as a sign of sorrow. It is difficult to know which of these two is correct.

There is also a further difficulty. No pronoun is given and the participle *mourning* (*sophᵉdim*) is masculine.[20] It does not, therefore, at least grammatically, continue the thought of the preceding verse, for it is not a simple description of the women after they have girded themselves. The change of gender is difficult, but possibly we are simply to regard the participle as similar in force to the masculine imperatives of the preceding verse. If that is done we may regard the participle as circumstantial, describing the action of the women when they have girded themselves. It is also possible to take the participle in an indefinite sense, giving a picture of the deepest mourning, for only such mourning would be suitable at the time of judgment. The prophet, if the word be taken indefinitely, has left the women and includes them only as a part of the entire

19 For a scene of women mourning depicted on Ahiram's sarcophagus, cf. *ANEP*, p. 456. The girding in this instance is only for mourning.

20 *mourning*—note omission of the pronoun *they*. The pl. part. thus expresses an indefinite subject. Cf. *Iliad* ix.141. The reference is to the sound of mourning rather than to beating the breasts (Mic. 1:8), for the root *s'pd* plus *'al* designates the reason why one complains (Jer. 4:8; Mic. 1:8; Zech. 12:10). The impersonal m. does not lend itself well to the idea of women beating upon their breasts.

nation. The mourning of which he now speaks is a deep mourning, characterizing the whole nation.

In support of the first interpretation given above is the second clause, "and for the fields of pleasantness." In this and the following clause also the preposition 'al designates the object for which one mourns. It would seem then that the verse really presents three objects for which mourning is made; the breasts, the fields, and the vine. The first word *breasts* is dual in Hebrew, and possibly, as the older commentators have suggested, is figurative for fruitful fields. There is certainly a word play between *breasts* (*shadayim*) and *fields* (*šᵉdey*). The fields of pleasantness would be the fields that produced rich grain, in distinction from the vineyards. Together, the fields and the vineyards provided the bread and wine that made man's life pleasant. The vineyards had been fruitful; and when they were destroyed, the regular life of the nation was brought to an end.

13 What is particularly tragic is that this desolation is to take place on the rich land that belongs to God's people. Using his favorite designation and speaking in God's Name, the prophet refers to the nation as "my people." The land is Judah, the land flowing with milk and honey. Isaiah had just described it as the pleasant fields and the fruitful vine. Now all will be transformed into a desert; the ground will no longer be *'ᵃdamah* (productive), but *shᵉmamah* (barren, desolate): "Your land is desolate," Isaiah had earlier declared (1:7), and it is that condition which he again pictures. The following words should be translated, *as thorn and thornbushes will it come up*. Both the nouns are masculine and are to be taken as circumstantial accusatives. The verb, on the other hand, is feminine, and hence is impersonal.[21] The meaning is that instead of the productive fields and fruitful vineyards, the land of God's people will be covered with thorns and thornbushes. The verb suggests that there is a certain productivity; a

---

21 *thornbushes*—note the asyndetic usage, which is characteristic of this section. In six verses (vv. 9-15a) conjunctive particles occur only three times. Cf. also 27:4. Characteristic of Isaiah had been his use of the two substantives *thorns* and *thistles* (*šāmir wāšayiṯ*). Here, however, he substitutes another word, *qôtz*, which had already appeared in Gen. 3:18. Quite possibly, Isaiah now uses that word to call to mind the thought of judgment. As a result of the fall, thorns (*qôtz*) would grow upon the earth; so, when God visits Judah in punishment, *qôtz* will again grow.

harvest will *come up*. What will come up, however, is the opposite of what the present well-cultivated land produces.

Isaiah now gives the ground for what he has been saying. The thorns will indeed come up, so the thought may be paraphrased, for even upon the houses will they appear. Thorns will cover the entire land without exception. They will come up upon all the houses of pleasure, i.e., upon the places where these houses once stood.[22] When the thorns appear all will be in ruins. These were the houses of the city of Jerusalem in which the trusting and carefree women lived. Pleasure had once ruled in them; now their ruins will have a covering of thorns and thornbushes.

Isaiah adds a phrase in apposition to the "houses of pleasure," and characterizes them as an exulting city. All these houses in which the wealthy inhabitants of Jerusalem found their pleasure and enjoyed the pleasures of life are, taken together, an exulting city.

14 The prophet points out the truthfulness of what he had just said by mentioning individual objects that once had formed the exulting city. What had once been the palace is now forsaken.[23] The palace is the dwelling of the king, probably considered in its entirety; with its downfall there would be the downfall of the kingship also. The presence of this word "palace" makes clear that the reference here is to the downfall of Jerusalem. Isaiah's sentences are short, as though reflecting his own grief over the destruction of the city.

A second short sentence confirms what had been declared in 13b; "the crowded city is forsaken." Isaiah's emphasis falls upon the tumult of the city, a phrase that indicates the great activity, the buzzing and humming that characterize its daily life. What is noteworthy of the first two clauses is that they speak of a city that has been abandoned or forsaken but do not themselves actually mention the city's destruction. Isaiah then mentions two place names, Ophel and Bahan. The first of these is well known; it is the

---

[22] *māśóś—pleasure*. The form is abs., and the following words are appositional, *upon the houses of pleasure—even the joyous city*. Because of *Zaqeph-Qaton*, the following word is not to be regarded as a genitive.

[23] *palace*—note absence of article in the enumerating style of the passage; note also the presence of pause. Penna takes the term *palace* as a practical equivalent of the expressions of 13b. Steinmann also asks, "*Le mot palais désigne-t-il palais de Solomon ou généralment toutes les demeures somptueuses des riches?*" and thinks that the latter sense is more probable.

little hill south of the Temple area in Jerusalem. Possibly, however, Isaiah does not intend to mention a specific geographical location. The term Ophel is used elsewhere,[24] and it may be that there it is merely intended to designate a hill. In close connection with Ophel is the word Bahan, which means to prove or test.[25] Hence, the suggestion has been made that it designates an observation tower (cf. Neh. 3:25-27). But, if Ophel is to be taken as a proper name, and probably it is so to be understood, then it would seem that Bahan is to be similarly interpreted. If this is the case, we simply do not know what is intended. Possibly Bahan is the name of some tower, but of this one can say nothing.

What is noted is that both Ophel and Bahan are to be about caverns, which would seem to imply that they are to encompass caverns within their midst. Into the abandoned towers the beasts of the field will come, and this will be for a time of long duration. The wild asses were noble beasts, living far from mankind, a prize for hunting; they would find their delight in the towers.[26] The expression points up how completely abandoned the city will be. The wild ass lived in remote regions, far from mankind's cities. When wild asses find their pleasure where once there were houses of pleasure, it is clear that the city will have become nothing but a wilderness. There flocks will find their place of pasture, as Isaiah had already predicted; cf. 7:21, 22. Drechsler well brings out the contrast between the first and second parts of the verse, "Palaces there; caves here; the turmoil of blustering life there; the quiet of the wilderness here." And over all there is the stillness of pasturing animals, the opposite of the carelessness of the complacent women.[27]

15 Until the Spirit is poured out upon us from on high, and the

24 E.g. 2 Kings 5:24 (Samaria), Moabite stone, line 22 (Dibon). Penna suggests that here it may not be a topographical proper name, but only a common term to indicate a hill or a fortified ridge.

25 Cf. *ba(h)-hin*, 23:13. The *Qametz* under the conjunction shows that Bahan and Ophel stand in close relationship; cf. 5:30.

26 The wild ass is mentioned also in Gen. 16:12; Jer. 2:24; 14:6 etc. It is of interest to note that in ancient Near Eastern maledictions the wild ass played an important part. Fenshaw speaks of the present passage as a prophetic malediction; cf. "The Wild Ass in the Aramean Treaty Between Bar-Ga'ayah and Mati'el," *JNES*, Vol. 22, 1963, pp. 185-186.

27 Note the paronomasia between *'armôn* and *hᵃmôn*; *nuṭṭāš* and *'uzzāb*; note also *'îr* and *'uzzāb*; *'aḏ-'ôlām*; the alliteration *mᵉśôś* and *mir'ēh*; and the rhyme *pᵉrā'îm* and *'ᵃḏārîm. Caves* and *palace* correspond, and *mᵉśôś* is chosen with reflection upon *bāttēy māśôś* of v. 13.

wilderness will be a fruitful field, and the fruitful field is reckoned a forest.

16 And judgment will dwell in the wilderness, and righteousness dwelleth in the fruitful field.

17 And the work of righteousness will be peace, and the service of righteousness quietness and confidence for ever.

18 And my people will dwell in habitation of peace, in sure places of dwelling, and in secure resting places.

19 And it shall hail in the downfall of the forest, and the city shall be brought low in a low place.

20 Blessed are ye, *who* sow upon all waters, who send forth the foot of the ox and the ass!

15 The condition of the city described in the previous verse will have a termination, and the present verse states when that termination will be.[28] It is when a Spirit from on high will be poured out.[29] Then there will occur a reversal of the present condition, a renewal that is indeed revolutionary, the very opposite of the condition described in 29:10. No longer will a spirit of sleep be poured out upon the people, but the Spirit from on high, the Spirit that is to be contrasted with mere flesh (31:3), the Spirit who brings rich gifts (11:2). This Spirit is poured out from the height of heaven (cf. 24:21), and in a proverbial manner similar to that employed in 29:17 Isaiah represents the change that is wrought.[30] Just as God had poured a spirit of deep sleep "upon you" so now He pours out His Spirit "upon us," and we therefore receive the blessings that He brings.

Far-reaching and all-embracing are the changes that follow the outpouring of the Spirit. As a result of the judgment pictured in verse 13, the land of Judah had become a wilderness; but it shall be changed into a fruitful land.[31] The harvest had failed; the

[28] This is true, despite the presence of the words *'ad 'ōlām*. For similar usages of *'ad 'ōlām*, cf. 1 Sam. 1:22; 1 Kings 1:31; Neh. 2:3; Dan. 2:4, etc. The usage is hyperbolical.
[29] *rûaḥ*—used anarthrously. Gesenius thinks that the Spirit poured out belongs to the Messianic representations. It is God's creative Spirit who brings about what amounts to a new creation (cf. Isa. 24:18; 31:3; 44:3; Ps. 33:6; 104:30).
[30] Penna thinks that the Spirit first works in the physical world and then in the moral.
[31] Note the anarthrous use of *midbār* and *karmel*, but note Dagesh in the *Kaph* of *karmel*. Possibly, the form was originally *wᵉ-hak-kar-mel*, the *He* having dropped out. This would bring the form into conformity with *lak-kar-mel;* the

THE BOOK OF ISAIAH

ingathering had ceased; the fields of pleasantness were no more, and the fruitful vineyard no longer produced. As a result of the carefree and luxurious living of the people of Judah, a sad change had been introduced. Only the Spirit will be able to restore what the sin of man had destroyed. The fruitful land (*karmel*) that the Spirit produces will be far richer and more glorious than any fruitful land that man might cultivate, for the figure of the fruitful land here signifies the rich and true blessings that God through His Spirit gives to renewed mankind.

As for this *karmel* (fruitful land), it is to be reckoned as a forest. What Isaiah means is that what at the present is considered to be a fruitful field will then be regarded as something far more glorious, as a forest where all grows wild. It is another picture of complete reversal, of complete change.

16 Just as the Spirit comes upon the Messiah and endues Him so that He judges with righteousness (11:4, 5), so also when the Spirit is poured out upon the land, judgment and righteousness dwell therein. In what had once been a wilderness, judgment now takes up its abode and makes its dwelling. And in what had once been reckoned a fruitful field righteousness makes its habitation. Isaiah reverts to the thought that he had introduced in his first chapter, "And I will restore thy judges as at the first, and thy counsellors as at the beginning: afterward thou shalt be called, The city of righteousness, the faithful city" (1:26). When the Spirit is poured out upon Jerusalem, she becomes filled with judgment and righteousness, and these make their dwelling within her forever. What wondrous inhabitants! How men strive in their own power to invite these inhabitants to dwell in their land! And how impossible such human strivings are! When justice and righteousness are found, it is because the Spirit has been poured out from on high, for these are the gifts of God alone.

17 Judgment and righteousness are not idle; they work and they produce from their labor. The Spirit gives righteousness and

---

Patah and simple *Sheʷa* might have been carelessly written as a compound *Sheʷa*. Compare the language of this verse with 29:17; also the construction of this verse with 59:14. Note also the close connection of *justice* and *righteousness* with *peace* in 59:8-9 and 9:6. This combination does not occur outside of Isaiah. It is a combination due not to chance, but to the Messianic message of the prophet.

righteousness works a work that is peace.[32] Peace, then, cannot come as the result of efforts of sinful men but by righteousness alone. Furthermore, righteousness has a service to perform, and that service produces certain blessed effects. Isaiah in the preceding verse had spoken both of justice and righteousness; here, however, he mentions righteousness alone, attributing to it all the blessings set forth. It first produces quiet; yet how different is this quiet from the slumber and confidence of the inhabitants of Jerusalem who were lulled into a false security![33] This is a quiet of blessedness, flowing from righteousness, a supreme reposing in the wondrous grace of God. Together with this quiet there is a certainty, so different from the confidence or certainty of the careless women of Zion, for this certainty is founded upon the sure promises of God; it is the work of His own Spirit. And this condition will endure for ever. What a contrast between the 'ad 'olam of verse 14 and that of the present verse! There, the condition of devastation would have an end, being interrupted by the outpouring of the Spirit. The condition described in this verse, however, is produced by that Spirit and will have no end.

18 Isaiah now adds another item in the description of the future state of salvation, and this he does in such a way as to introduce a sharp contrast between that future and the actual present. "There is something tranquilizing," says Alexander, "in the very sound of this delightful promise. . . ." It is a promise limited to "my people," for only those that are the elect will enjoy the blessings herein set forth.[34] To denote the dwelling of God's people Isaiah uses a word that generally denotes a pasturage.[35] Involved is the concept that the people of God are sheep for whom the Shepherd provides. What characterizes this dwelling is peace. No ravenous animals can enter this "pasturage" to destroy the flock. They will dwell in a place of perfect peace.

The "pasturage" is further described by two words of quite similar formation, "dwellings sure." In the word translated "sure" Isaiah uses the root *bṭḥ,* which had appeared in the previous verse and which was also used to describe the women (v. 10). In this

---

[32] The combination *peace* and *righteousness* is Isaianic. Cf. also 48:18; 60:17.

[33] הַשְׁקֵט—the inf. abs. is used as a predicate.

[34] I.e., *God's people,* as throughout the prophecy. Penna, however, refers the possessive pronoun to the prophet.

[35] Isa. 33:20; 34:13; 35:7 in the sense of dwelling; in the sense of pasture Isa. 27:10; 65:10.

word the contrast comes to particular expression. In the present time the women are confident that nothing will happen to them. They have a security but it is false. In the period of redemption and blessing, on the other hand, there will be found a true confidence; their dwellings then will be such that nothing can move or destroy them. Again going back, this time to verse 9, Isaiah takes up the word "carefree." The places of rest will one day themselves be "carefree." Thus the contrast is heightened; at present the women are carefree, and they have no reason for so being, for danger is at hand. In the future their places of rest will be carefree, for then there will be no care to disturb.[36] The goodness of God provides the only security, the only reason for freedom from care and anxiety.

19 The picture of peace is interrupted, for we must be reminded that such peace can come only when judgment has been accomplished. Isaiah, therefore, again mentions the judgment, taking up as it were where he had left off in verse 13. Thus, he turns from the promise of great peace in the future to the near threat of destruction that hangs over Jerusalem. Before the peace can come there must be the hail, a figure of the divine judgment.[37] And hail actually was one of the forces destructive to Assyria (30:30, 31; cf. also 28:2, 17). There is a paronomasia and alliteration between the first two words. The hail will come down in the downfall of the forest (cf. 10:18, 19, 33, 34). The forest falls because of the trees cut down by the axe (for the verb cf. Deut. 28:52; Zech. 11:2). While the forest trees are falling, the hail of punitive judgment will come down. Perhaps the forest is symbolical of Assyria (cf. 10:34), but this cannot be pressed.

In the latter half of the verse the prophet speaks of humiliation or "being brought low." The definite article is employed to point out that this is a particular instance of humiliation, and the position of the word as first in the clause lends emphasis to its meaning. When this great act of humiliation comes the city will be

---

36 In 11:10 $m^e n \hat{u} h \bar{a} h$ is used of the Messiah; of the people, Num. 10:33; Deut. 12:9.

37 Lit., *and it hails, when the forest falls.* What connection, asks Penna, is there between the forest and the city? Perhaps it is the sudden reference to a disaster. Penna thinks that B offers a plausible solution, and assumes that the verse may have been interpolated or out of place. He reads $w^e \cdot y \bar{a} \cdot ra \d{d}$ for the initial word. Delitzsch understands here the city of Jerusalem, which must go through a humiliating punishment (29:2-4; 30:19ff.; 31:4ff.).

brought low. What city, however, is intended? On this question it appears impossible to give a positive identification. Some think that the city is Jerusalem, for in this particular cycle of prophecies the world city is not mentioned at all. This is true, but on the other hand there is the parallelism of the first clause, which appears to refer to the destruction of Assyria. In the light of this parallelism others think that the reference is to the world city from whence stemmed opposition to the people of God. Those who apply the reference to Jerusalem think that there is here a double judgment, striking both the world power and the holy city, which in order to receive true peace must go through the humiliation of judgment. In any case there is an interesting word play between *ya'ar* and *ha'ir*.

20 To conclude the chapter the prophet pronounces the blessings that belong to those who will enjoy God's benisons. These sow by every water, whenever the opportunity arises, and so enjoy the productivity and richness of a most fertile soil. Nor need they watch the animals, for these may roam where they will, unhindered and free from all dangers.[38] These who are blessed are such as sow in the proper places and diligently cultivate their fields in order to reap a good harvest. They are faithful, daily performing their proper duties. Such is the only procedure for those who would truly be blessed. This lesson is as profound as it is needed. The wondrous changes that are to occur are the work of God alone; His purposes will be carried out; the judgment will come, and with it the promised peace. What then is the responsibility of His people? It is to continue in their own work, wisely living for Him. Such are blessed, yea, blessed indeed!

[38] The phrase *senders of the feet of, etc.* means, allowing their feet freedom i.e., to roam where they will. They allow the animals to graze freely, for it is assumed that no harm can befall them.

2. OPPRESSION WILL END, AND GOD'S KINGDOM WILL BE ESTABLISHED (33:1-24)

1 Alas! the spoiling, and thou wast not spoiled, deceiving and they did not deceive against thee! When thou shalt cease to spoil thou shalt be spoiled, and when thou art done deceiving they shall deceive thee.

1 The fifth woe in this series is directed against the enemies of God's people. The enemy is addressed, and possibly Isaiah has in mind Sennacherib as a representative of the Assyrian power. Following the pronunciation of "woe," the prophet uses a participle, so we should render, *Woe to thee, plundering, and thou art not plundered.* The latter clause is really circumstantial, and we may paraphrase, "Woe to thee, thou plunderer, while thou for thy part art never plundered." The enemy evidently boasted that he had not been plundered. He himself plundered, but what he meted out had never been meted out to him. Furthermore, the enemy was one that deceived, but men had not deceived him in turn.[1] In 21:2 the same expressions are employed in reverse order.

This condition of affairs about which the enemy could raise its boast would not continue, however, for when the enemy had finished his work of spoiling, then he himself would be spoiled.[2]

---

[1] A verbal, circumstantial clause with concessive force, *yet they did not deal treacherously.* Penna takes the root *bāḡaḏ* in the sense of depredate, treat with scorn (the enemy) ; he appeals to Isa. 21:2, possibly 24:16, and compares Hab. 1: 13 and Prov. 23:28. For the boasting of the Assyrian cf. Isa. 36:13ff. and the general tone of boasting found in the inscriptions of the Assyrian kings.

[2] The intransitive use of the *Hiphil* is well known; cf. also 2 Sam. 20:18. The normal form of the inf. is *hātēm;* with the addition of the suffix the following changes occur: *hā-ṭēm-mᵉ-ḵā* > *hᵃ-ṭim-mᵉ-ḵā.* Dagesh forte, however, is generally not written in *Mem* when the latter is followed by vocal *Shᵉwa.* The *Milel,* therefore, is a closed, unaccented syllable, in which the *i* vowel naturally appears as *Hireq.* Because of the omission of the *Dagesh,* a *Meteg* is written to emphasize the vowel; lit., *according to thy ceasing as a spoiler,* i.e., when thou hast ceased to spoil.

The completion of the work of spoiling does not lie in the hands of the enemy; he does not determine when he has finished. Rather, when he completes the spoiling that God has determined, then he himself will be spoiled. By placing the active and passive forms of the root in immediate juxtaposition Isaiah produces a striking effect.

The truth is stated in a parallel fashion in that Isaiah addressing the enemy declares that when it has attained unto the limit or goal allotted by the Lord, men will oppress it.[3] Thus the pretensions of the enemy are shown to be nothing. Believing that it was acting in its own strength, it had boasted of its might and power (cf. 10:7ff.). As a matter of fact, it was but an instrument in the hands of the Lord; and when it had plundered as much as He had determined to permit, then its time of plundering would be concluded, and men would turn against it as never before, and would plunder and oppress it.

2 O LORD, favor us; for thee we wait, be their arm in the mornings, also our salvation in time of trouble.

3 From the noise of tumult the people flee: at thy rising the nations are scattered.

4 And your spoil shall be gathered like the fathering of the devourer; like the running of swarms running on it.

5 Exalted is the LORD, because (he is) dwelling on high; he fills Zion with judgment and righteousness.

6 And he shall be the security of thy times, wealth of salvations, wisdom and knowledge; the fear of the LORD, that is his treasure.

2 In contrast with the *hoi* (alas) which introduced the previous verse, this one begins with *'ᵃdonai* (Lord). Isaiah offers a prayer on behalf of his people that God would be their strength, and then gives the prayer of the people themselves. In 30:19 he had prophesied that God would be gracious to the people when they cried unto Him; now he prays that such may be the case. As had also been prophesied (25:9), Isaiah declares in the name of the people, or as speaking on behalf of or as representing the nation, that they had waited in hope for God. He then separates himself from the people, as it were, speaking of them in the third person, and

---

[3] כְּנַלֹּתְךָ—*according to thy finishing*, i.e., *when thou art finished*, probably from a root *nālāh*, related to the Arabic, *nāla, to complete*; cf. Job 15:29. The form stands for *kᵉ-han-lṓ-ṭᵉ-ḳā*. The Dagesh is *dirimens*, and strengthens the vocal *Shᵉwa*.

imploring God to be their arm, the One in whom their strength is found.[4] Every day men need God's strength; when the day breaks in the morning, His strength must be manifested. Hence, the prophet prays that "for the mornings" God will be their strength. Every day the besetting dangers were present; each new day should find present the strength of God (cf. 28:19).

Trouble, however, would increase; and there were yet to be many adversaries. Hence, again the prophet identifies himself with those for whom he prays and urges God to be "our salvation" in the time of affliction. His introductory particle, *'aph, yea,* is emphatic, as in 26:9, for it is in this particular respect, namely, the matter of salvation, that Isaiah prays God may be the nation's strength. In itself the prayer is a refutation of the idea that deliverance can come from man. God must be their salvation, else there will be no salvation.

3 Continuing his prayer to God, Isaiah points out that at the voice of tumult (i.e., the tumultuous voice) peoples flee. His reference is not to thunder but simply to the speaking of God, "For through the voice of the LORD shall the Assyrian be beaten down, *which* smote with a rod" (Isa. 30:30).[5] Cf. also Daniel 10:6 and Revelation 1:10. Among these peoples the enemy Mesopotamia, now represented in Assyria, would be the chief.

Parallel with the thought of God's voice is that of His rising for action. The idea is well exemplified in 30:27, 28. Both voice and rising are simply concomitant parts of God's entering into action against the enemy. Later, in 33:10, God responds to the prayer with the words, "Now will I rise."

4 Using a word that is employed of the gathering of harvest, Isaiah declares to the enemy itself that its spoil will also be gathered (cf. 17:5). It has labored long to acquire this spoil, but, like the grain of the field, so this spoil will be gathered as a harvest and the enemy will not enjoy it. Although the prophecy may be taken as the statement of a general truth, namely, that when the enemy has served its purpose, God will intervene and deprive it of

---

4 The final *Mem* of *zr'm* may be *Mem* enclitic.

5 But cf. Penna, *il rumore è il rombo del tuono. rô-mē-mŭṭ—arising, uplifting.* 1Q *mdmmtk.* The two verbs (perfects) express future action, *will flee, will be dispersed.* This interpretation fits in best with the context.

its power, one cannot help thinking of the sudden departure of Sennacherib from the land.

It is difficult to decide whether in the second clause the genitive is subjective or objective. Does Isaiah wish to say, "like the gathering of locusts" (objective), or "like the gathering that locusts make" (subjective)? If the former, then the reference is probably to the manner in which men gather the locusts for the purpose of destroying them.[6] On this construction the locusts are to be compared with the spoil of the first clause. Even in the present day men gather the locusts for this purpose. The writer has seen in Transjordan, just northeast of Akaba, how the locusts are driven into trenches and destroyed by blowtorches. The point would then be that the spoil is innumerable. Great and vast as the spoil is, it will be carried away completely so that nothing remains for the enemy.

If the genitive is subjective the reference would be to the manner in which the locusts (lit., the devourer) swarm down upon a field and destroy everything. What would then be in view primarily is the haste and greediness with which the locusts gather up all before them. If this interpretation is correct, however, the root *'sp* is hardly appropriate; and hence, we should probably construe the genitive as objective.

The second half of the verse refers to the running about of swarms of insects.[7] In such a manner do men run about collecting the spoil of the enemy. There is no order or arrangement, but, just as locusts run here and there, so men will run to gather up what had been collected by the enemy.[8] These running insects have full mastery of the situation, carrying off all that they can.

5 Seeing the people of Jerusalem victorious, Isaiah breaks out into praise of God, who has manifested His power and is therefore exalted. It is necessary to emphasize this fact, for the Assyrians had thought that they could ascend to God and bring Him down (10:9-11, 15; 36:18-20; 37:10-13, 16-20, 23, 24); but God is exalted,

---

6 חסיל—1 Kings 8:37; Josh. 1:4; 2:25; Ps. 78:46; 2 Chron. 6:28. These passages show that the word indicates a harmful insect which can destroy a harvest. משׁק—construct of *šqq*, with doubling of the first radical.

7 גבים—*swarms* of locusts; cf. *Theologische Zeitschrift*, Vol. 4, 1948, p. 317, where Ludwig Köhler discusses the word.

8 The part. is indefinite, lit., *as the running about of swarms* (is the) *running on it*, or, *does one run on it*. Cf. J. Ziegler in *Biblica*, Vol. 14, 1933, pp. 460-464.

i.e., high so that man cannot reach Him. Isaiah places this word *exalted* first in the sentence and thus emphasizes it.[9] The form implies that God has shown Himself to man to be exalted in the destruction of the enemy. Assyria had conquered many gods, casting them down as she wished. To her Yahweh appeared to be like them; He, however, is different, and in overthrowing them He has shown that He is exalted. He dwells on high, where no mere man can ascend to bring Him down (cf. v. 16). It was from on high that God would pour out His Spirit. A God who dwells on high was something new for the Assyrians. They had never had experience with such a God. Israel's God, however, was no limited, local tribal deity, but the God who dwells in heaven.

Outwardly God has wrought a great victory for His people, and inwardly He has filled the Holy City with righteousness and judgment. These are His attributes displayed in that place where His people are to dwell, and which has been set free from the occupation of the enemy. In the destruction of this foe the power and glory of God are displayed; and in the city itself, once the adversary is removed, the attributes of the true King manifest themselves; the city is filled with justice and righteousness.

6 Addressing the nation as an individual, the prophet continues the thought of the preceding verse. The subject of the first verb is the Lord, so that Isaiah is saying, "And the Lord will be the certainty of thy times."[10] The word that we have translated *certainty* is from the same root as faith, and means *constancy, trustworthiness*. The times of the people were the revolving, changing times, the periods of their history. Throughout the changing scenes of her life, God is the security, the One constancy of the people. Another manner of construing the relationship of the words

---

9 Not, *he has become exalted*. B reads ἅγιος. With the participle שׁכן note omission of the personal pronoun.

10 Thus, the common English versions. This construction has simplicity and naturalness in its favor. The principal difficulty is that the suffix in *his treasure* must then refer to God. God's treasure, on this construction, is said to be *the fear of the Lord*. Yet, the language seems to reflect upon 2:7a. Hence, some would emend the suffix to the feminine to refer to the nation; but the present consonants appear in 1Q. I, therefore, retain the construction and interpret as in the exposition. Many take *wealth of salvations, etc.*, as subject, but this is somewhat cumbersome and does not remove the difficulty occasioned by the masculine suffix. Vulg. reads *et erit fides in temporibus tuis*. B goes its own way.

is to render, *And the strength of salvations, wisdom, and knowledge will be the certainty of thy times.* The rendering given above, however, seems to have the most in its favor. *strength of salvations—* Better, fullness of salvations; the thought is that salvation, in all its fullness and plenitude, will be found in the Lord. The words *wisdom*[11] *and knowledge* may also be construed with fullness, so that the entire phrase reads, *fullness of salvation, wisdom, and knowledge.* It is not grammatically necessary, however, to make them dependent upon "fullness." We may also render, *fullness of salvations is wisdom and knowledge.* Wisdom is the true and correct evaluation of things, whereas knowledge is the true recognition of what things are. It emphasizes the objective, whereas "wisdom" brings to the fore the subjective aspect.

Lastly, we are told that "the fear of the Lord, that is His treasure."[12] There would appear to be a certain gradation. Salvation refers to gifts bestowed from without, wisdom and knowledge to inward gifts, themselves a part of salvation, and lastly, the fear of the Lord, the complete and entire devotion of the whole man to the Lord. This treasure belongs to God, but He brings it to His people. It thus becomes their true treasure, and stands in contrast to the false treasures upon which the nation at present was pinning its hopes.

Prominent in this verse is the final *t* of different words, an effect that seems to be deliberate. Throughout his prophecy Isaiah often strives to produce similarity of sound, and the abundance of final *t*'s in this verse is an instance of such striving. Eight nouns follow one another in a row, and these are arranged in pairs. Three of these pairs stand in the construct relation, and one pair, the third in the list, probably stands in the relation of appositional genitive. In the first and fourth pairs the first word ends in the construct form with *t;* and the first word of the third pair, which is really absolute, also ends in *t,* probably to emphasize a genitival relationship. The final *t* of the second word in the third pair is also significant, for this is the only pair in which both words end in *t.*

---

11 חכמת—*wisdom.* Possibly the *-at* ending is intentional to avoid the hiatus *-māh wā.* Cf. also 35:2 and Ezek. 26:10, where a word appears in the const. before the conjunction.

12 The definite pred. circumscribes the class to which it belongs so that the subj. is identical with it. The pronoun both indicates and gives emphasis to the subject.

That the two words of this pair bear a special relationship is shown by the pointing of the conjunction.

7 Behold! their valiant ones have cried without, the ambassadors of peace weep bitterly.

8 The highways are wasted, the wayfarer ceaseth; he breaks the covenant, despises cities, values not mankind.

9 The land mourneth, languisheth, Lebanon is ashamed, it pines away; Sharon is like a wilderness, and Bashan and Carmel cast.

10 Now will I arise, saith the LORD, now will I be lifted up, now will I exalt myself.

11 Ye shall conceive chaff, ye shall bring forth stubble; your breath, a fire will devour you.

12 And nations shall be burning places of lime; thrones cut up, in the fire they shall burn.

7 In accordance with his custom, Isaiah having presented his message, returns to approach the subject again from a different angle. His purpose now is to show the miserable condition of things, and with his people he weeps over their present plight, bringing us face to face with the subject by means of an introductory "behold!" The following word, 'er'ellam, however, has been the subject of much discussion.[13] It would seem in some sense to refer to the enemy warriors who cry out. Inasmuch as the term in Hebrew is difficult to translate, for its precise significance is not known, we may use a provisional rendering, such as heralds or

[13] Some derive the word from Ariel (29:1) and apply it to the inhabitants of Jerusalem (cf. Fischer, Drechsler). Most of the old translations (Targ., Syr.) took it as a combined form of 'er-eh lām (I shall see for them), which they pronounce as Niphal. 1Q reads hn 'r' lm. Cf. Aq, S, T, and Ibn Ezra; Vulg. ecce videntes, but B evidently derived it from yā-rē' (to fear).

Some render the word heroes; in 2 Sam. 23:30 'rī'ēl is defectively written; and it is argued that 'ar-'ē-li may have been a patronymic, descendant of a lion of God, i.e., son of a hero (Gen. 46:16; Num. 26:17) (cf. König). The suffix could refer to Israel, their heroes, the word being taken as a collective, or the ending itself thought to be collective, like kinnām, Ex. 8:16-18.

Gesenius suggests the pointing 'er-'ē-lim or 'ar-'ē-lim, which would be supported by the variant in 8 mss. 'r'lym. As Gesenius points out, however, if this variant had stood originally in the text, the false explanation of the ancients would never have arisen. Cf. Albright's discussion, JBL, Vol. 39, 1920, p. 138.

Perhaps the wisest course is to adopt in translation a word parallel to the noun in the second stichos. The messengers of peace weep bitterly, the 'er'ellām cry without. This is the only justification for adopting the interpretation given in the text.

heroes. It is quite tempting to see, and quite possibly we should see here, a reference to the haughty and overbearing language of the Rabshakeh who commanded the city of Jerusalem to give itself over to surrender (cf. Isa. 36:13).

The messengers or ambassadors of peace may be those mentioned in 36:3, namely, the ambassadors of Jerusalem who seek peace from the Assyrians, and failing to accomplish their end, cry out bitterly[14] over their failure. Sennacherib had demanded from Hezekiah three hundred talents of silver and thirty talents of gold (2 Kings 18:14b), but this was not satisfactory. Sennacherib broke his word and required the surrender of the entire city (2 Kings 18:17ff.). It was this behavior of the Assyrian king that caused Hezekiah's envoys to cry out in bitterness. Contrary to his own agreement Sennacherib continued to storm the fortified places of Judah (cf. 2 Kings 18:13).

8 Isaiah now describes the condition of Judah as a result of the depredations of the Assyrian. In the previous verse his attention had been concentrated upon the city itself, the men outside crying boastfully, and the ambassadors weeping bitterly. The word "outside" serves as a connecting point for the present verse, for now the prophet takes us without the city to the country itself. No longer could men travel in safety, due to the presence of the enemy; and hence, the thoroughfares were empty;[15] they lay wasted (cf. Judg. 5:6). No longer are there any travellers,[16] they have ceased.

In the latter half of the verse the prophet mentions the reason for this desolation and emptiness, namely, that Assyria has broken the covenant.[17] Isaiah now uses the language of universalism, as he had in 24:5. There he had spoken of the world nations generally as having frustrated a covenant; now he shows that the

---

[14] מר—the adjective does duty as an adverb.

[15] מסלות—roads or caravan paths, not city streets. As Smith says (*Isaiah Chapters XL-LV*, London, 1944, p. 169) this is almost a characteristic word of Isaiah; cf. 7:3; 11:16; 19:23, 40:2; 49:11; 59:7; 62:10. Here he thinks that the reference is to the natural main routes followed by Assyrian armies for centuries.

[16] Lit., *the one passing over (the) way.* Cf. 51:23 and note the phrase '*ōbʰrē derek,* Ps. 80:13; 89:42, etc., and Ps. 8:9, *one passing over (the) ways of the sea.* The phrase is about equivalent to *traveller.*

[17] Cf. 2 Kings 17:14-16 and 17ff. Penna gives a thorough discussion of the phrase. Note that *bʰriṭ* is anarthrous.

world nation *par excellence,* Assyria, has done what is characteristic of the world powers; it has also frustrated the covenant.
The reference here is to Sennacherib's flagrant disregard for the
covenant or agreement that he had made with Hezekiah. In
his marching he had overcome cities without any difficulty, cap-
turing them easily (36:1).[18] What Isaiah describes is an agreement with the actual course of history. One who thus lightly would
break his word and conquer cities is no respecter of human life.
Hence, Isaiah points out that the Assyrian has no hesitation in
offering up human life. Neither moral responsibility (covenant)
nor fear of physical opposition (cities) nor mercy stand in his way.
The short, asyndetic sentences correspond to the rapid blows of the
enemy struck one by one.

9 Continuing with the language of chapter twenty-four, Isaiah
now applies that language, there used in a universal sense, to the
land of Judah itself. In verse 7 he had concentrated upon the city,
in verse 8 upon the land about, but now upon the entire holy land.
The first three words present a striking alliteration, and only in the
second verb is the gender of the subject made clear.[19] With its
inhabitants the land has mourned, and over it all a sense of fading
has taken hold. Life, as it were, has gone out of the whole land.
Isaiah's language is of course figurative, but it expressively sets
forth the sad condition that the coming of the Assyrians has
brought to Palestine. Lebanon, known for its verdure, is now
brown;[20] its leaves have fallen and Lebanon is ashamed; indeed, it
pines away, languishing, as though deprived of vitality. Sharon,
also, known for its excellency of blossoming, has become but a
desert region[21] (cf. 65:10). Sharon lay along the coast of the

---

18 *cities*—1Q reads *'dym,* hence Penna translates, *ha respinto 'i testimoni.'*
But M gives a good sense. The Assyrian, aware of his own might, conquers
cities without difficulty. It is an accurate characterization of Assyria; cf. 10:9;
36:19; 37:12, 13, and Sennacherib's own account, *ANET,* p. 288.

19 *mourneth*—the masculine verb, standing first, almost has the force of an
inf. absolute. When two or more predicates stand together (here, *mourneth,
languisheth*), only the one closest to the modified feminine noun (here, *'eretz*)
is placed in the feminine. Cf. GKC § 145 t.

20 קמל—*has become decayed, moulded.* The *Patah* indicates that the form is
pausal, instead of *qāmēl* (cf. 19:6, and *ḥēṭaz,* 18:5). The two verbs are separated by the intervening subject, and so, like the two verbs of the first clause,
are unconnected. The first statement refers to the land generally, the second
is more specific. *There feels abashed Lebanon; he has become decayed.*

21 נער—*to shake out,* Qal active part., lit., *and shaking* (its leaves) *is Bashan*

Mediterranean; in the winter it was covered with green; the anemone decorated its fields. Assyria's presence, however, has turned it into a wasteland.

A conclusion is reached in the last clause of the verse, and this is the first in a long list of clauses introduced by a conjunction. Bashan and Carmel are also brought into the description; their trees stand bare, the leaves having fallen to the ground. Carmel was known for its foliage and Bashan for its oaks (cf. 2:13). Assyria's fear has dominated the land; and all stands still, cold, and lifeless in the grip of dread. The land has become withered.

10 After his description of the desolation of the land, the prophet introduces the Lord as speaking. The right time for exalted action on God's part has come, and hence the great emphasis of this verse falls upon the word *now*, a word that occurs three times in the verse. Man's kingdom has exalted itself and spread itself over the world; now the time has come for God Himself to take action.

I will arise[22]—The verbs point to a near future of action, the breaking off of a period of inactivity. In a certain sense God's withholding His punitive hand may be described as such a period. He abides His time; He permits evil men and nations to go only so far, and then He stands up for the sake of acting. This first verb not only indicates an arising from a sitting position, but also the intent to engage in action against the enemy (31:2). An emphasis is given to the verb by the following *saith the Lord*.[23]

now will I be lifted up[24]—In the sense of exalting Himself. This

---

and Carmel, probably a circumstantial clause, construed with היה. While Sharon was like an Arabah, Bashan and Carmel were shaking. When the leaves were shaken from the tree it would stand bare. This figurative language describes the condition of Bashan and Carmel.

22 *I will arise*—the verb also contains the idea of determination upon the part of the speaker. God's actions are not haphazard, for He performs them only at the time upon which He has determined. Cf. John 2:4; 12:31.

23 *saith*—the imp. with *Pataḥ* is characteristic of Isaiah, being found in 1:11, 18; 33:10; 40:1, 25; 41:21 (*bis*); 66:9. Note that the form occurs twice in the introductory chapter (1, 40) of each part of the book. Note also the similar structure of each of these verses and the frequentative force of the verb.

24 *I will be lifted up*. The form is *Hitpael*, the *Tau* being assimilated before *Resh*. Possibly, a desire for conformity with 'en-nā-sē' has influenced the writing. The *Qametz* is evidently pausal with *Zaqeph Qaton*, and serves to give a solemnity to the pronunciation. There is no reflection upon any dying-and-rising-God motif such as supposedly was found in the ancient Near East.

word is used of the exaltation of the Servant of the Lord in 52:13. God will now raise Himself up high so that His exaltation in what He is about to do will be known of all men. Perhaps there is an allusion to the phrase "at thy rising" in verse 3, where the same root is found.

I will exalt myself—Again, Isaiah uses a verb that he will later employ of the exaltation of the servant (52:13). In meaning it is a practical synonym of the preceding verb. The prophet produces a remarkable effect in this verse by his introduction of the word *now* before each of the three verbs, by his use of three short independent sentences, instead of the usual gradation accomplished by the use of two verbs of similar meaning, by employing two verbs of practically identical meaning, and by the asyndetic relationship of the verbs.

11 Now Isaiah addresses the Assyrians, confident in the triumph of the Lord. All the enemy's efforts will be in vain, for God's victorious purpose is made known.

Ye are pregnant with chaff[25]—Isaiah does not at all deny that the enemy is active. By addressing it as pregnant, he means that it is full of plans and schemes which it is seeking to carry out. In discharging them, however, it will fail; and all that it will bring forth is as chaff. Likewise, in the actual birth or bringing forth, the enemy will produce nothing but stubble. The entirety of the enemy's purposes, their conception and their accomplishment, is a vanity. They strive and labor to no profit; they will be frustrated, for they are fighting against the Lord of hosts. Hay, chaff, and stubble burn easily; they are readily consumed; they have no endurance, and so it will be with the plans of the enemy; they will readily come to naught.

Your breath[26]—Isaiah uses the word in the sense of panting, as in 25:4; 30:28. The thought is that the breath of the enemy wherewith they pant after or blast against the Lord and His people will be the very means of their own destruction. It is a fire that instead of consuming their enemies, will consume themselves.

---

25 קֹשׁ—note the *Pataḥ* in a pausal form; cf. *baz*, 8:1, and *'aṭ*, 8:6.
26 M is supported by 1Q. It is possible to follow the Targum, *rûḥi kᵉmô, my spirit is like*, since this involves no change of consonants. On the other hand, the change is not necessary; and it is better to keep the address in the second person throughout. For the phrase *a fire devouring* cf. 26:11 and 29:6; 30:27, 30; 33:14.

12 Isaiah then goes on to show the result of what has just been stated. He speaks of "peoples," using the noun in the plural. It is possible that he has reference to the various groups of nationalities that composed the army of Assyria, or it may be that his reference is to the enemy nation generally. Earlier (v. 3) he had spoken of the fleeing of peoples. Perhaps more than any specific reference there is prominent the thought that as a result of God's judgment, peoples, representing the world of man without God, will be forced to abandon their plans of power and to flee. These peoples will be burnings that are as strong and bright as the burnings of lime. An example is given in Amos 2:1, where Moab is condemned for having burned the bones of the king of Edom into lime. The thought is that the peoples will be burning lime, a figure that expresses the completeness of their annihilation.

To emphasize how completely the peoples have lost their power the prophet states that they will be burned like thorns that are cut down.[27] Thorns that are cut up are dry and flammable. Crackling, burning, readily consumed—they are the people that have fought against God.

13 Hear, ye far ones, what I have done, and know, ye near ones, my might.

14 Afraid in Zion are sinners, trembling has seized the impious; who fears for us the devouring fire? Who fears for us the burnings of eternity?

15 Walking in righteousness, and speaking right things, despising the gain of extortions, shaking out his palms from taking the bribe, stopping his ear from hearing bloods, and shutting his eyes from looking at evil.

16 He shall inhabit high places; fastnesses of rocks will be his lofty place; his bread is given; his waters are sure.

17 The king in his beauty thine eyes shall see; they shall behold a land of distant places.

18 Thy heart shall meditate terror; Where is the scribe? Where is the one who weighs? Where is he that counts the towers?

19 The insolent people thou shalt not see. A people deep of lip from hearing, stammering of tongue without meaning.

20 Behold! Zion, the city of our festivals. Thine eyes shall see Jerusalem a secure habitation, a tent that shall not be removed; its

27 *will be burned*—the *Tau* contains a *Dagesh affectuosum*, which renders more emphatic the vowel in the principal pause.

stakes will not be pulled up for ever, and none of its cords will be broken.

21 But there will the LORD be might for us, a place of rivers, streams, broad of hands; there will not go in it an oared ship, and a gallant ship will not pass through it.

22 For the LORD our judge, the LORD our lawgiver, the LORD our king, he will save us.

23 Thy ropes are loosed; they do not hold upright their mast; they do not spread the sail; then there is divided the booty of spoil abundantly; the lame spoil the spoil.

24 And the inhabitant will not say, I have been sick. The people dwelling in it, its iniquity is forgiven.

13 The enemy has been destroyed, the enemy that had exalted itself as at the Tower of Babel to unify man into one worldwide empire in which God would not be recognized, an empire in which man alone was to be exalted. It is right that a pause be made to take cognizance of the greatness of what God has accomplished. For that reason, God Himself commands that men shall hearken and know the might of His work. He addresses those who are afar and those who are near (with reference to Jerusalem), by which terms all men are included.

Although the two imperatives belong to different parts of the verse, nevertheless, in meaning they are not to be separated, for both are needed to show what God's command is in its fullness. God commands that men not merely hear of what He has done, but that they understand its significance. They must realize the meaning of the mighty events that have transpired, attributing them not to chance or to mere happening, but to the great power of the God of Judah. At the same time there is a certain appropriateness in the distribution of the verbs. On the one hand, those that are near are commanded to know. They would not need to hear, as would, on the other hand, those that were afar, who could not see the work of God. Upon those who were near lay the necessity of understanding the meaning of what had transpired at Jerusalem. They would know, for many of them apparently refused to acknowledge the power of the Lord; and they would continue in unrepentance, trembling before His power. Thus, this verse forms an introduction to the following address to the sinners in Zion.

14 Turning to those near at hand, the Lord now addresses the sinners in Zion. Dwelling in Jerusalem itself were Jews who did not see the hand of the Lord in the mighty events of judgment; they were unrepentant, and continued to commit gross sins. At the same time they were afraid and trembled. They were profane and impious. The word is one that Isaiah uses elsewhere (9:16; 10:6; cf. 24:5; 32:6) and refers to those who despise God and treat with scorn and contempt things that are sacred. These were the men who felt no need for God, who neglected His ways and commands, walking secure in their own power, breaking His law, when they felt it was for their own profit. Now, however, not understanding the meaning of what was transpiring, they were afraid and seized with trembling.

These sinful ones are then introduced as speaking. We are to understand the language as spoken at the time of danger, when trembling and fear take hold of the speakers. The words are those of complaint and lamentation. When all was well these men thought they had no need of God; but in a time of trouble and distress, their voice is raised in desperation and in alarm. To bring out the full force of the question, we may render somewhat literally, *Who to our advantage will sojourn? etc.* Often the question is translated, *Who among us will sojourn? etc.*, but this is not correct. "We want to be sojourners," so the thought may be paraphrased, "but who can be a sojourner, so that benefit and blessing will accrue to us?" (cf. Deut. 30:12, 13; Judg. 1:1; Isa. 6:8).[28] In the very word *sojourn* there seems to be implied the idea that the dweller is a guest, who in himself has no right to dwell when the punitive hand of God is felt. All that the Jews can recognize is the devouring fire; and the import of their question may be stated, "Who can dwell together with devouring fire? In Isaiah and elsewhere this devouring (lit., eating) fire is an accompaniment of the divine presence in judgment (cf. 29:6; 30:30; cf. also 31:9, 10, 16-18). Those who cry in despair recognize that the consuming fire is no mere local phenomenon, but that it represents the everlasting punishment of God, for they characterize the fire as "burning places of eternity." Thus, there is brought to the fore the fact that the fire is an inexhaustive abyss of anger, and that the places of burning provide ever fresh sources of punishment. Perhaps there is a certain gradation in the questions, as though the sinners were to

28 לנו—*for our benefit*, ethical dative. גור—*to dwell*, may be used with the acc., *to dwell with someone*, Ps. 5:5; 120:5; Judg. 5:17; Ar. *já-'i-run*, neighbor. Penna renders *chi di noi può resistere;* others, *who can fear;* but these renderings do not suit the context.

ask, "None of us can sojourn with the temporal punishment of consuming fire; surely then none of us can sojourn with those places of burning that are of eternity." If this is the force of the questions it teaches that the temporal judgments of God should prepare and warn of the eternal punishments to follow. Temporal judgments should lead us to repentance. Woe to us if they do not do so.

15 Isaiah himself now gives an answer to the question of the sinners, and this answer he frames very largely in the language of Psalms 15 and 24.[29] The prophet knows; the sinners do not know. To all in Jerusalem the command had come to hear and to know. Those in Jerusalem like Isaiah who loved their God did hear and did know; the sinners, however, did not hear and did not know. Unlike the prophet, they did not know how one could sojourn with the devouring fire. They were rich in ignorance and poor in knowledge; rich in fear and trembling, but poverty-stricken in obedience. Isaiah, on the other hand, was rich in knowledge, for he was also rich in hearkening and obeying.

What the prophet does is describe the man who may dwell with a devouring fire. It would be a mistake here (just as it would be a mistake in Psalms 15 and 24) to assume that the prophet is setting forth the grounds why a man may escape the judgment. Isaiah is not asserting that because a man walks in righteousness, he will be delivered from punishment. Rather, he is merely describing those who do escape the judgment. The ground for the deliverance must be found only in the sovereign, electing love and decree of God, and not in any human merit. This is abundantly shown by many passages in the prophecy. Isaiah's purpose is to characterize those who are the elect, and this he does so that all men may know that the Lord loves righteousness and hates iniquity. It is not doing justice to the genius of prophecy, therefore, to hold that we have here merely a list of various moral virtues that permit one to escape the judgment.

How then does the prophet describe the man who will not feel the judgment? *walking in righteousnesses*—I.e., conducting the en-

---

[29] V. 15 constitutes the prophet's own response to the questions of the sinners. To introduce the concept of two choirs, one chanting the question and the other the response, seems out of keeping with the tremendous earnestness of Isaiah's proclamation. Gunkel's view of a Torah-liturgy is not applicable.

tire course of life in the field of righteousness.[30] The life is a righteous one, conducted in conformity to the righteous requirements of God's law, filled with actions which are right and which flow from a heart that is right with God.

speaking right things—It is possible that the plural form of the noun may serve to indicate the abstract, *righteousness, rectitude.* The contrast is not so much between the speaking of right and the speaking of evil things, as between speaking and acting themselves. The righteous man is one who not merely acts in accordance with the law, but also speaks those things that are straight and right.

despising the gain of extortions—I.e., the gain that extortions bring or produce. Not only will he not receive gain derived in such a manner, but within his heart he despises such gain. It is to be noted that here a particular is introduced that exemplifies the general expression employed at the beginning of the verse. One manner both of walking in righteousnesses and of speaking upright things is the despising of unjustly acquired gain. Isaiah employs a word that in itself denotes such gain. Here the particular is pointed out to show how this gain has been obtained. Allusion is probably made to the practices of judges and rulers who exact from the powerless payments that are not legal (cf. 1:16, 17, 23; 3:14, 15).

shaking out his palms—When others press into his hands the gain acquired from oppression he shakes his hands so that the gain falls to the ground. His action represents an indignant refusal of all such gain and money. The opposite conception is expressed in Proverbs 21:14. If the hands are wrung or shaken then the bribe cannot remain in them. The righteous man not merely speaks against evil, but refuses to take part in it.[31]

stopping his ear—When he hears of plans involving the taking of life or the shedding of blood, he will have no part in such plans, and stops his ear so as not to hear.[32]

shutting his eyes—The righteous one will not look at evil with delight, nor will he desire to become a participator in evil deeds. His organs of receptivity, the eyes, the ears, and the hands, are not

---

[30] *Righteousnesses*—a plural of intensity used pregnantly for *way of righteousness;* cf. *death* in Ps. 13:4. The verb of motion (הלך) may take as its object the place upon which the action is to occur, *walking* (in) *righteousness.*

[31] The use of the pl. is emphatic; cf. Matt. 10:14; Acts 13:51.

[32] *from hearing*—the prep. implies motion or separation away from something. *Ear* is singular, to denote the ear into which evil is whispered.

at the service of evil; and his organs of activity, the tongue and feet, likewise will have no part therein. The man who is to inhabit high places wishes that none of his members be yielded as instruments of unrighteousness.

16 In this verse the apodosis follows. The one who does the things described in verse 15 will be the recipient of the blessings now described. By using the personal pronoun, *he,* Isaiah emphasizes the subject. There were those who dwelt in high places who, because of their wickedness, would be brought down from them. The righteous one, however, will occupy high places, exalted above others, for now he will be high above the reach of the enemy.[33] His dwelling will be one of perfect security. These will not be mere places of sojourning, but actual dwelling places. The wicked speak of sojourning with consuming fire, but the righteous will dwell permanently on high. The lofty place[34] where he lives will be beyond the reach of the enemy, consisting of fortresses built high upon the rugged cliffs of the land. The figure is that of complete inaccessibility and security. High and practically inaccessible are the lofty crags of the Judean mountains. What better picture of the full security that comes to the righteous one (cf. 25:12; 26:5)!

Such a picture, however, in itself is not complete. The top of the crag is not a place where sustenance is found. Is the righteous one, therefore, simply to be placed in an inaccessible place, and left to his own devices? This unspoken question the prophet answers by making clear that the food that the redeemed need will be given to them and water will constantly be available. Unlike the waters which fail, of Jeremiah 15:18, this water is sure and constant. It will never fail nor diminish, but will always be at hand to supply the needs of those who must have it. It is obvious that the figure is not carried through consistently, nor can it be. How can there be a perennial supply of water and abundant food in a fortress of the crags? The language suggests that the gifts of food and water are from God. They are given of grace, and not acquired by human effort. In the reference to food and water there is also an allusion to the richness and fullness of the deliverance that God provides.

---

[33] *heights*—a collective plural possibly used to denote level surfaces; cf. Job 16:19 and Isa. 26:5.

[34] The term *miś-gāḇ,* often employed of God, is appropriate here.

17 Continuing his description Isaiah now addresses the people as a single individual, as he had previously done in verse 6. What is emphatic in his address is the object that the people's eyes will behold, namely, a king in his beauty. In the approach of the Assyrian the theocratic king had been deeply humiliated and brought low into disgrace. At that time, however, when God will destroy the enemy and the sinners in Zion will be punished, then for the righteous, who through God's grace escape the punitive judgment, the king will reign in all the splendor of his royalty. He will be a victorious king, in a sense that was not true of the actual kings of Judah. The king is not Hezekiah nor any mere human king. The whole context refers to something greater than the bestowal of honor that Hezekiah received (2 Chron. 32:23). It is a king of the redeemed Israel, who reigns when the outward enemy has been punished and when the sinners of Zion have been judged. He is and can only be the Messiah.[35] This does not conflict with what is stated in verse 22, that the Lord Himself is king. The Messiah is a manifestation of the rule of the Lord. In the deepest sense the Lord alone is king, but the Messiah is the royal mediator and reigns as is described of Him in this context. The beauty is not merely physical but spiritual. It is the Messiah in the glory of His wondrous reign over His Church that is here in view.

In addition to seeing the king,[36] the people's eyes will also see a land of distances, i.e., a distant land; and thus the prophet includes the entire concept of a kingdom. In the first half of the verse the king is mentioned, for without him there can be no kingdom; but there is also mention of his land. Just as the phrase *in his beauty* modifies *king*, so also does the word *distances* modify *land*. Thus,

---

35 In defense of the Messianic interpretation we may note the following considerations: *a)* The phrase *in his beauty* is never used of God but is perfectly applicable to the Messiah. Cf. also Ps. 45:3. *b)* The reference to the *land of distances* fits in well with the emphasis that the Messiah's kingdom will be universal. Cf. Isa. 26:15. Such a reference, however, is not applicable to Hezekiah's reign. In Isa. 8:9 the Gentile nations are called *distant places on the earth. c)* The anarthrous use of מלך would be strange if Hezekiah were intended, for it is too indefinite. Nor is מלך as it occurs here used absolutely of God. If the reference were to God we should expect a phrase *shall see God*. The mysterious indefiniteness of the emphatic word מלך raises us to the realm of the spiritual. Gone will be the king in sorrow and affliction, and in his stead will be a king ruling over *lands of distances*. In contrast to the sick Hezekiah (Isa. 38) will be a king in beauty.

36 Not to be overlooked is the tenderness expressed by the singular, *thine eyes.* The prophet addresses the nation as though it were an individual.

there is created an interesting parallelism in the verse. It is a land of distances, a land that contains distances, stretching far in all directions. Isaiah creates a contrast with the condition of the land when it had been occupied by the enemy; then it was narrow and confined; now, however, when a king in his beauty reigns, it will be a broad and wide land (cf. 26:15; 32:1ff.). A king in the beauty of his reign, a realm wide and spacious; such is the glorious vision that the eyes of the now oppressed people will one day behold.

18 Isaiah has just spoken of what the eyes will see; he now directs attention to what the heart will think. In the preceding sentence the emphasis had fallen upon what was seen, namely, the king, whereas here it is upon the heart that meditates. What is meditated upon is terror, the remembrance of the former condition of the country when the enemy was dominating the scene. So great is the victory and the redemption, that if the people wish to remember it at all, they must turn their thoughts back to it. They must bring it to mind and meditate upon it.

To support the first statement of the verse Isaiah asks three questions, and these are designed to show how completely every trace of the opposing enemy has disappeared from the people's thoughts. *Where is the one who counts?*—Lit., *a one who counts.* This man had the task of counting money that had been raised, probably by tribute; hence, the counter was a reminder of the presence of the enemy. In the question there appears to be somewhat of a mocking tone, as though to taunt the enemy. Where are now the enemy's representatives who made life so burdensome for the people of God? The second noun refers to the one who weighs the money that has been counted, and the third, *the counter of the towers,* is probably the one who made note of the towers or fortresses that the country under Hezekiah was allowed to possess.

19 The questions that have just been asked imply that the enemy has completely disappeared. This thought is strengthened by the present verse, in which Isaiah tells the people that it will no more see the enemy. The enemy is an insolent people, bold in its opposition to Israel, daring and barbarous.[37] Such a people will no longer be seen but will have disappeared completely from the

---

[37] נוֹעָז—*Niphal* participle of יָעַז. The context would seem to demand a meaning such as *barbarous.*

scene. Furthermore, the people is described as deep of lip. Isaiah's meaning is that the people are too deep of lip to be understood. What is deep of lip is difficult to understand. This people speaks a foreign, barbaric language, not understandable to the Jews (cf. 36:11). It was a "nation whose language thou knowest not, neither understandest what they say" (Jer. 5:15). This would be true, even if the enemy spoke a cognate language of Hebrew. Delitzsch makes the interesting comment that "their language must have sounded even more foreign to an Israelite than Dutch to a German." How degrading to hear in the streets and at the gate of one's own city the harsh and incomprehensible sounds of the unknown language of a boasting conqueror! In speaking, the nation stammers, seeming to mock; and the mocking sounds of the language preclude any genuine understanding.

20 In place of the departed Assyrians God's people are commanded to look at Zion. The imperative is stronger than a mere statement of what is to occur in the future. "In place of Assyria, see Zion!" The king and his land have been mentioned, and now the city itself. Isaiah describes the city as a center of religious gatherings.[38] The phrase harks back to the tent of meeting mentioned in the Pentateuch. There God had met with His people. Later, the Temple became the center of meeting of God with His own. In the deep sense, "our places of meeting" refers to the places where the people were met by God. The gathering together of the people was in order that God Himself might meet with them. In the description, therefore, there is a religious emphasis. Perhaps there is also a tone of longing and fond recollection. The redeemed will love to think of their city as the place where their God met with them.

Abandoning the imperative, the prophet now addresses the redeemed using the future. As in verse 17 so also here he places emphasis upon *thine eyes*. Faith will then have given place to sight, for the people will see Jerusalem, not as it was in the days of the oppression, but a renewed, permanent Jerusalem, a city that cannot be moved. To describe the city the prophet takes his language from that of nomadic life and uses the word that indicates the habitation of shepherd and flocks (cf. Ps. 48:13, 14). This dwelling will be secure (cf. 32:18 where both words are also

---

[38] Isaiah was not opposed to assemblies as such, but only to those that were celebrated apart from God. In the future Zion the assemblies will truly belong to the people; now, God hates "your assemblies" (1:14).

used). Continuing the description the prophet designates Jerusalem as a tent that will not be removed.[39] Travellers in the desert are compelled each morning to pull up their stakes and move their tent.[40] A tent that does not have to be moved is permanent. From the realm of nomadic language this is probably as strong a symbol of permanence as can be found. The dwellers in the former Jerusalem ("Jerusalem which now is") had gone through life as on a pilgrimage, and they had seen the necessity for pulling up stakes and moving their dwelling when the exile came upon them. The stakes, however, will never again have to be pulled up, for the elect will abide in the "Jerusalem which is to come." Nor will the cords that connect with the stakes ever have to be broken. In the nature of the case a tent is not a permanent abode; the language, therefore, makes even more clear the fact of permanence. (Jeremiah 10:20 gives an opposite picture.)

21 Isaiah now presents a contrast to the preceding. Even though it seems to be only a moveable tent, Zion is more stable than the most well-founded cities. Zion will not be moved, but the Lord will be mighty for us (cf. 26:1). There in Zion, the city where God meets with His people as a mighty One, mighty in great deeds whereby He accomplishes His purposes of deliverance and the destruction of His foes, God will be for our benefit.[41] All His wondrous works He does for our good and blessing. Furthermore, He will be a place of rivers, streams broad of hands; i.e., inasmuch as He dwells there, the place will become a place of broad streams like those that surround other cities.[42] He has become to Jerusalem what canals and broad streams have been to other places; and hence, no enemy vessels may approach there. Vessels of war, whether they be rowing ships (lit., ship of oar)[43] or noble ships,[44]

[39] יִצְעָן —lit., *will it wander;* the reference is to the tent's not being moved. Cf. Koran 16:82.

[40] *pegs, pins*—in the plural, the *e* vowel appears to be naturally long, *yᵉ-ṭē-ḏó-ṭāw,* and should be accompanied by *Meteg.* But note the construct plural *yi-ṭᵉ-ḏóṭ.* The *é* of the plural may be merely a stereotyped writing.

[41] Cf. 10:34.

[42] Lit., *the place of rivers, Niles,* i.e., rivers that are like true Niles; cf. 7:18; 19:6. For a discussion of the textual problems and a suggested rearrangement of the text, cf. Penna.

[43] שַׁיִט —*rowing?*, a *hapax legomenon;* 1Q reads *sṭ,* possibly a synonym of *mā-šóṭ.*

[44] צִי —*a ship.* The word is of Egyptian origin, *g³j,* a kind of river ship. Coptic *goi* (cf. Lambdin, *JAOS,* Vol. 73, No. 3, 1953, p. 153).

cannot approach the city, for its defense is the Lord. In his choice of the word *might* (*addir*) there is a play on the use of the same word in the first part of the verse. Inasmuch as the Lord is the *might*, certainly no ship of *might* will cross.[45] These may have been river ships of great beauty. Whatever their precise nature, they could not come into the place where the true *might* of Israel was to be found.

22 Isaiah now gives the reason for the confidence of the people, namely, the presence of the Lord. Three times he uses the word *Lord,* and in each instance places it in the position of emphasis.[46] It makes no great difference whether one renders the three clauses as sentences, *the Lord is our judge,* or whether one takes them merely as consisting of a noun and an epithet, e.g., *for the Lord our judge.* In either case, the emphasis falls upon the *Lord.* By designating God as judge, the people have in mind the period of the judges, when God raised up for them deliverers, who governed the nation. Thus, deliverance and salvation come alone from Him. Perhaps too there is implied a contrast with the present unjust judges of the nation. In that day, the Lord alone will be the judge; and consequently, justice will truly be administered. With the epithet *lawgiver,* there is reflection upon the Messianic promise of Genesis 49:10 and also upon the administration of the government (cf. Deut. 33:21 and Judg. 5:13, 14). The word points to the true head of the people, whether in time of war or of peace. The king was both lawgiver and law executor. "If we subtract from the words of Louis XIV their proud flippancy, the statement 'L'état c'est moi' would most nearly express the idea. This is not from our point of view good politics, but in religion it is not only allowable; it is the only principle on which a truly religious relation can be built, and revelation has made use of this monarchial and King-centered state of affairs to build up its doctrine of the Kingdom of God in the sphere of righteousness."[47] This one is the Law-giver who will rule

---

45 יעברנו—note insertion of *Nun* to prevent hiatus between two vowels, for *ya-'ab̠-rē-hû.*

46 Note in this verse the prevalence of the sounds, *ē-nû.* Jerome rendered *m^e-ḥô-q^e-qē-nû* as *legifer noster.* This would be supported by the frequency with which the word *ḥōq* designates the Law (Ezek. 12:24; 30:21).

47 Vos, *Biblical Theology,* Grand Rapids, 1948, pp. 419f. For the modern concept of sacral kingship, cf. A. R. Johnson, *Sacral Kingship in Ancient Israel,* Cardiff, 1955, and J. de Fraine, *L'aspect religieux de la royauté israelite,* Rome, 1954.

with absolute authority. He is also the king, the true ruler of the theocracy. With the Lord Himself as the occupant of these offices, the people had every ground for confidence and trust.

23 This verse contains an address in the words, "thy ropes are loosened." But to whom is the prophet speaking? It is generally held that he is addressing the enemy. In verse 21 he had said that no ship would come near to Jerusalem; but now one ship has done so, namely, Assyria, and as a consequence has suffered disaster.[48] Drechsler, however, has made out a good case for the position that it is Zion itself that is addressed. In verse 20 Jerusalem was presented under the figure of a tent, and here as a ship. It is a ship in poor condition, tossed about by the waves, and yet, despite all this, a ship that will not go down. Now, at the time when the prophet addresses it, Zion is as a ship whose ropes are loosened.[49] They are not taut and strong as they should be. No longer do men hold upright the support of their mast.[50] (This support appears to have been a crossbeam with a hole in it, and in this hole the mast was placed.) Nor do men spread out the ensign or standard.[51]

The second part of the verse introduces a contrast with the present condition of Jerusalem. At the time that the prophet is speaking, Jerusalem is in a poor condition; but then, when the deliverance will have come to pass, Jerusalem will do valiantly. Isaiah uses an expression, *the booty* or *plunder of spoil,* possibly to indicate the abundance thereof. Abundant spoil will be divided and even the lame will take plunder. The last phrase is added almost as an afterthought, *lame people will take plunder.* Thus, the prophet again emphasizes both the abundance of the spoil and the ease with which it may be taken. Possibly there is an allusion to the constant emphasis of the Assyrian kings upon taking spoil. Assyrian kings always boasted of taking spoil; among God's people even the lame will take plunder.[52]

48 Calvin, e.g., states that Assyria is addressed.

49 *They are loosened*—The root means *to forsake, abandon, let loose.*

50 כֵּן—*kēn,* lit., *base* or *pedestal,* here, *support* or *socket.* Gesenius identifies it with the μεσόδμη (*Odyssey* xv.290), τὰ μεσόκοιλα, the ἰστοδόκη (*Iliad* i.494), and ἰστοπέδα (*Odyssey* xii.51). The word is construct, but apparently has become stereotyped with *Tzere.*

51 The context would require that the word *nēs* here mean a sail.

52 As an example of this boasting cf. the inscription upon the statue of Shalmaneser III, "cities without number I destroyed. I devastated, I burned with fire, causing great loss of life. Their spoil without number I took, his tribute I

24 In this concluding verse Isaiah points out the complete bliss of the inhabitants of the new Jerusalem. His purpose is not to connect these thoughts with those of the preceding, as though to say that participation in the taking of spoil would be so great that everyone will forget his sickness, but rather to state that in the day of salvation there will be neither physical nor spiritual suffering. In the first part of the verse, he declares that no outward ill will overtake the people, and in the second that no inward ill as well will be theirs. Between these two there is really a causal connection. Inasmuch as the people is one whose iniquity is forgiven, it is also one that suffers no external malady. In 24a the people are represented as speaking, "I am sick"; and in 24b, a reason is stated in the third person. The iniquity that the inhabitant had committed has been lifted up, and so no longer is held against the sinner. Isaiah uses the well-known idiom to express the forgiveness of sins.[53] This is the heart of the whole matter; the ground for the peace, security, and blessedness that will come upon God's people. Their iniquity has been lifted up from them, held no longer against them. They are forgiven.

---

received" (*Iraq*, Vol. XXIV, pp. 90-115, lines 33f.) . The thought of the lame or crippled seizing plunder finds somewhat of a parallel in the Era Epic, Tablet V, line 27, "May crippled Akkad cast down the Sutu power" (*a-ku-u kur akkadu ki dan-na su-ta-a li-sam-qit*) .

[53] Lit., *the people—lifted up of iniquity*, i.e., whose iniquity is forgiven. The noun in the gen. (*iniquity*) denotes the respect in which the preceding attribute (*lifted up*) applies.

D. GOD'S SOVEREIGNTY MANIFESTED IN JUDGMENT AND SALVATION: CONCLUSION TO CHAPTERS 28-33 (34, 35)

1. GOD'S SOVEREIGNTY MANIFESTED IN JUDGMENT (34:1-17)

> 1 Draw near, O nations, to hear, and ye peoples, hearken! Let the earth and its fullness hear, the world and all that goes out from it!

1 Time and again Isaiah has uttered his oracles against the heathen nations! Now, as it were, he is to sum up his invectives against them, and because of the importance of the subject, summons both the heathen nations and the earth to hear. He begins with an imperative, *draw near,* commanding the nations to abandon whatever they are doing, and to come near to him that they may hear what he is about to say.[1] They are to come for the purpose of hearing and they are to give ear to the solemnity of his message concerning the future judgment. These two chapters (34 and 35) stand in the same relation to 28–33 as do 24–27 to the preceding chapters 13–23.

So significant and important is the message that even the earth is to hear. Departing from a strict imperative, Isaiah now uses the jussive, "let the earth." Yet the force of the verb is in no sense diminished. The nations are to draw nigh, and the earth as well is to lend its ear to the words of God through the prophet. Employing language reminiscent of the twenty-fourth Psalm, Isaiah speaks

---

1 For this type of summons cf. 1:2, 10; 33:13; 41:1; 49:1. Note the variety—first an imperative and infinitive, then the mere imperative. This is followed in the second line by a jussive. As is pointed out by Mrs. Margaliouth in *The Indivisible Isaiah,* New York, 1964, the proximity of the roots *qrb* and *šm'* is also found in Isaiah 48:16, but nowhere else in the prophets. Cf. also the language in 49:1. The word *offspring (tze-'ᵉ-tzā-'im)* is Isaianic, occuring also in 22:24; 42:5; 44:3; 48:19; 61:9; 65:23, and nowhere else in the prophets.

of the earth and "its fullness, the world and its issue."[2] It is the earth in its entirety, with all its inhabitants, all that belongs to it, that must now obey the prophet. God is about to speak of judgment; the earth must hearken.

2 For the LORD has anger against all the nations, and wrath against all their host. He has doomed them; he has given them to the slaughter.

3 And their slain will be cast out, and as to their corpses, their stench will go up, and the mountains will be melted because of their bloods.

4 And all the host of heaven will consume away, and the heavens will be rolled up like a scroll. And all their host will fade like the fading of a leaf from the vine, and as a fading from the fig tree.

2 In this verse the prophet gives the reason for the summons addressed in verse 1. "There is anger to the Lord," he says, using a form of expression similar to that found in 2:12, "there is a day to the Lord of hosts." What he means is that the Lord possesses anger, but he stresses the word *anger*[3] in that he puts it first in the sentence. The theme of this verse, in other words, is "anger." And this anger of which Isaiah speaks belongs to the Lord, and hence may be used by Him as He sees fit. It is an anger that will have to do with all the heathen nations (cf. the similar sentence structure in 2:12) and a burning of wrath that has to do with all of their host. This expression, *host,* simply refers to all the forces that belong to the nations; Moses had employed the word in a similar sense in Genesis 2:1.

In two simple statements the prophet relates what God will do to the nations. He utters these statements in the past tense, as though the action of God had already taken place, and thus shows how sure he is that these things will occur. He has placed the ban upon the nations, devoting them to a full and complete destruction.[4]

---

2 The meaning is parallel to "its fullness," i.e., all mankind.

3 Dillmann denies to Isaiah the words *qtzp* and *ḥmh*. *Ḥmh,* however, occurs in Isa. 27:4; 34:2; 42:25; 59:18; 66:15; 51:13, 20, 22; 63:3, 5, 6; 51:17.

4 The practice of the ban was used also by the Assyrians (37:11; 2 Kings 19: 11) and is mentioned on the Moabite stone (lines 14-17), which may be rendered: "And Chemosh said to me, 'Go, seize Nebo against Israel.' And I went at night and I fought against it from daybreak unto noon, and I took it and slew all, seven thousand men, boys, women and girls and slaves, for to Ashteroth Chemos I had devoted it, i.e., placed it under the ban."

They had determined upon such a destruction for Judah, but they were not successful. Despite their attempts, a remnant of grace was preserved by the mercy of God. For the nations, however, the ban is complete; there is no escape. The manner in which this ban is placed upon the nations is explained by the last clause of the verse, "He has given them to the slaughter." His sword is prepared in the heavens and will accomplish His purposes. Although the language used is military, describing the slaughter of the enemy on the field of battle, in the nature of the case the destruction is spiritual, accomplished by God's sword. There may indeed be a reflection upon nations perishing in earthly battles, but it is the complete defeat of the enemy nations who have set themselves against God that is in view. "Thou shalt break them with a rod of iron; thou shalt dash them in pieces like a potter's vessel" (Ps. 2:9).

3 The prophet now states the results of God's punitive action. Throughout this verse and part of the preceding he refers to the enemy as "they" or "them." This leads to a predominant emphasis in the Hebrew text upon the *m* sound. Those of the enemy who have been wounded unto death are simply cast out and have received no burial.[5] For an Israelite this would have been a supreme disgrace (cf. Deut. 28:26; 2 Sam. 21:10ff.; Ezek. 32:5ff.).

Isaiah makes his description very vivid. As for the bodies of the slain, he continues, their stench keeps arising. One is reminded of the "foul-smelling fields" (*olentes agros*) of Lucan. The bodies lie unburied on the field, and the stench of these decaying and rotting bodies constantly ascends from the earth. The language makes clear in no uncertain terms the contemptuous defeat of the once arrogant nations that had arrayed themselves against the Lord and His anointed (cf. Joel 2:20; Amos 4:10).

By means of a strong hyperbole, Isaiah declares that the mountains will melt because of the blood of the slain. What he means is that just as the water of a heavy rain washes away the soil, so also will the flood from the corpses flow in such strength that it will cause the mountains to melt. A certain gradation is discernible: first (2b), the declaration that the Lord has given the nations over to slaughter; secondly (3a), the disgraceful nature of the slaughter and the character of it. It is a slaughter that continues. Lastly, the

---

5 ונמסו—*Hophal* imperfect. Note *Qibbutz* in place of *Qametz-Hatuph*. In a closed, unaccented syllable the short *u* may appear either as *Qibbutz* or as *Qametz-Hatuph*. 1Q *ywslku*.

enormous extent of the slaughter is portrayed (3b); a glimpse or foretaste is given in Isaiah 37:36.

4 This verse continues the description just introduced. Not only will the mountains melt, but the mighty changes in the universe brought about by the destruction will apply also to the heavens themselves. All the hosts of heaven, which God Himself had created (Gen. 2:1), will rot.[6] The judgment of God thus affects all creation, both heaven and earth. For this reason, despite the poetic character of the language, we are justified in finding here a description of the final judgment, the very end time.[7] The punishment of the wicked nations, beginning with the defeat of Assyria will culminate in the complete overthrow of all nature. It is this fact that lays the preparation for the mention of Edom as a representative of the peoples that have set themselves in opposition to the chosen of God.

Enlarging upon what he has just stated, Isaiah points out that the heavens, which to man seem enduring, would be rolled up like a scroll or book.[8] Even the mountains were regarded by man as eternal (Ps. 90:2), and the heavens might be thought of as abiding forever. The heavens, however, were an expanse, spread out by God; and so they might also be rolled up together as one rolled up an ancient scroll. The same fundamental thought, expressed in different words, is given by the Psalmist: "They shall perish, but thou shalt endure; Yea, all of them shall wax old like a garment; as a vesture shalt thou change them, and they shall pass away" (Ps. 102:26). As for the host of heaven they will fade and wither as a leaf upon the vine withers. The withering of grass and flowers is

---

[6] and they will moulder away—the root mqq means to rot, fester, decay. Cf. 3:24; 5:24. 1Q reads והעמקים יתבקעו, and the valleys will cleave asunder. Note the plural verb, and also the chiastic arrangement. In v. 4a we have host of the heavens, whereas in 4b heavens and their host. For the expression cf. 24:21, and note Gilgamesh i.5.28, kima ki-iṣ-ru ša ⁱⁱA-nim.

[7] Gesenius, however, interprets of political revolutions by which the most powerful kingdoms fall, being represented as the last day. Cf. 2 Pet. 3:12; Matt. 24:29; Rev. 6:12-14, for the description of the last judgment. Cf. Koran, Sura 81:1. The exegetical question, therefore, is whether the judgment herein depicted is a forerunner of the final judgment or whether it is that final judgment itself. The description goes beyond that given in 13:10, 13.

[8] Scripture speaks the language of daily life, which, despite the advances in astronomical science, is still in use today. The definite article in kassēper determines the class. The word receives a certain emphasis in being placed first, as a scroll, the heavens will be rolled. Both 4a and 4b end with hšmym.

employed elsewhere by the prophet as a symbol of that which passes away (cf. 40:6-8 and also Ps. 103:15, 16). The figure is striking and forceful. The rich colorful leaf of the vine loses its color and strength, and falls from the vine to earth. So will the host of heaven, supposedly strong (note the force of the word *host*), fade and vanish away.[9] All created things, even the most powerful, are wholly without strength and power when the breath of God's judgment blows upon them. The Lord alone is supreme in power and the Lord alone reigns.

> 5 For my sword is drunken in heaven; behold! upon Edom it shall come down, and upon the people of my curse for judgment.
>
> 6 The LORD has a sword; it is filled with blood; it is smeared with fat; with the blood of lambs and goats, with the fat of the kidneys of rams, for the LORD has a sacrifice in Bozrah, and a great slaughter in the land of Edom.
>
> 7 And wild oxen will come down with them, and bullocks with bulls, and their land will be drunken with blood, and their dust will be fattened with fat.

5 God now speaks, giving a reason for the severity of the judgment just described. His sword is drunken, not with the blood of the slain but with wrath and anger.[10] Wrath has so filled the sword that it will swagger forth, drunken, to execute vengeance on the enemies of God. This sword is in heaven, waiting the command of the Lord to action. It is conceived, as it were, as lying in rest, ready to do the Lord's bidding when He calls. It is a sword that has been patient; and wrath and anger have overcome it, so that it is drunk with them. Hence, the longer the delay the more severe will be the judgment. In Genesis 3:24 the Lord had placed a sword that turned every way, to guard the way to the tree of life. The sword had won a great victory for Gideon, when the people cried out, "The sword of the Lord and of Gideon" (Judg. 7:20; cf. also Josh. 5:13). What God relates here of His sword is based upon the song of Moses (Deut. 32:41-43).

Abruptly God calls attention to the action of the sword. "Behold!" He cries, for now, after long waiting, the sword is falling

---

9 Note the homogeneous structure of the three verbs, ונמסו (v. 3); ונמקו and ונגלו. In the third verb *Holem* is used (as in *Ayin-waw* verbs) to avoid a repetition of *Qametz*. Cf. P. Wernberg-Møller in *ZAW*, Vol. 71, 1959, p. 63.

10 *rwh* expresses the idea of drinking to the full; cf. 16:9. Here, the *Piel* is to be rendered, *was drunken;* Vulg., *inebriatus est.*

upon Edom. Suddenly, the sword is present. As an example of its
action, Edom is mentioned, just as in 25:10-12 Moab had been
used as an example. Like Moab, Edom was also an inveterate
enemy of Israel (cf. 11:14 where both of them are named together). Drunken with wrath, it will come down from heaven to fall
with great vengeance upon Edom. Edom is also described as *the
people of my ban* and so ripe for judgment. Justice will finally be
executed upon those who are under the divine ban. Justice is
administered from heaven; the sword comes down, and so earth,
under the divine curse, is punished.

6 Continuing without any connecting word, Isaiah declares that
the Lord has a sword full of blood. He focuses attention upon the
sword and then makes two statements concerning it. It belongs to
the Lord, and it has become full of blood. The force of this can
best be seen by a literal rendering, "A sword to the Lord; it is filled
with blood." In the Old Testament a great battle is often compared
to the slaughter of sacrifice (cf. Jer. 46:10; 50:27; 51:40; Ezek.
39:17-19 and also Rev. 19:17, 18). This sword has struck the animals
of sacrifice and as a result is covered with their blood. If anyone
should take offense at the boldness of the language, he should
remember the warning of Calvin: "It is therefore necessary that the
judgments of God should be set forth as in a lively picture, that it
may not only make a deep impression in their dull minds but may
encourage believers by holy confidence, when they learn that the
pride and rebellion of their enemies cannot at all hinder them
from being dragged like cattle to the slaughter, whenever it shall be
the will of God." The blood-red sin of rebellion demands a blood-
red punishment of judgment.

Having been dipped in the fat of the animals the sword has also
become smeared.[11] Fat and blood simply refer to the animal
substances that are offered in the sacrifices. The terms are taken up
again in 6b, and Isaiah identifies what blood and fat he has in
mind. It is the blood of lambs and goats and the fat of the kidneys
of rams. Although these were sacrificial animals, it is clear that the
language is symbolical. The lambs were the fattest and most plump
of the animals, and the goats were males. Under these figures it

___

11 *hdśnh*—it is smeared, for *huṭ-daš-še-nāh.* In two other verbs, *u* is placed in
the prefix when the *Tau* is assimilated to the first radical; cf. Deut. 24:4 and
Lev. 13:55, 56. It may be that where the *Hitpael* has genuine passive significance, the tendency was to employ the vowels of the passive.

would seem that the prophet is referring to the inhabitants of the nation itself.

To explain these statements the prophet adds that the Lord has a sacrifice in Bozrah and a great slaughter in the land of Edom.[12] The sacrifice here refers to the actual act of slaying. What was slain was under the ban; and according to Leviticus 27:28, whatever was under the ban was holy of holiness to the Lord. The objects to be sacrificed belonged to the Lord and it was His right to engage in this action of sacrifice. By means of the parallelism Isaiah points out that the sacrifice is a great slaughter. Bozrah is mentioned as a leading city of Edom, but the slaying will actually fill the entire land.

Why is Edom mentioned at this point? In chapters 13–23 she had not been mentioned; but here she is introduced as an example, just as Moab is in chapter twenty-five.

7 This verse continues the description. As a result of the smiting of the sword the wild oxen will fall.[13] (Cf. Habakkuk 2:22 for the use of the verb.) The Hebrew word *r⁽ᵉ⁾emim* refers to a wild animal (Job 39:9ff.) that has strong horns (Deut. 33:17; Ps. 22:21; 92:10). In Ugaritic it seems to indicate the buffalo, and in Hebrew the wild oxen. So all-embracing and widespread is the slaughter that together with the lambs and goats, the ordinary animals of sacrifice, the wild oxen also will fall. Likewise bullocks together with the bulls will fall. These were animals of strength and also of great rage. Possibly they symbolize the leaders of the nation, men strong and powerful, determined in their purpose, but nevertheless objects of the avenging sword of God.

The land that belongs to these animals will become drunken from their blood, and the dust of their land will become fat. All-devouring and all-consuming is this sacrifice, yet it is a genuine sacrifice. The description is given in the language of the religious cult. Sacrifice was worship of the Lord; and whereas in itself the sight of slaughter was revolting, nevertheless in the sacrifice the God of Israel was honored and glorified. So it will be even in the judgment. The sword will fall in equity and justice, for none can say that justice is lacking; and inasmuch as this judgment is here

---

12 *Bozrah*—probably to be identified with the modern el-Buseira, 25 miles southeast of the Dead Sea. Cf. Gen. 36:1 and 1 Chron. 1:44; Amos 1:12; Jer. 49:13, 22 and Isa. 63:1.

13 *wyrdw*—lit., *and they will come down*, i.e., *fall*. Cf. 32:19; Hag. 2:22.

pictured in terms of sacrifice, God will be glorified even in the punishment of the wicked. Even in the judgment of vengeance to come upon the reprobate the honor of God will shine forth brightly. He who really takes offense at what is here related has no true conception of the heinous character of sinful rebellion against the Holy One of Israel.

8 For the LORD has a day of vengeance, a year of recompenses for the cause of Zion.

9 And her streams will be turned to pitch, and her dust to brimstone; and her land will become burning pitch.

10 Day and night it will not be quenched; for ever will its smoke go up; from generation to generation it will lie waste; for ever and ever there will be no one passing through it.

8 By means of the introductory "for," Isaiah connects this with the preceding section and gives further explanation as to what has just been stated. Using a form of statement that he has already employed in verse 6b and in 2:12 and 22:5, the prophet declares that the Lord possesses a day of vengeance. This period is further characterized as a year of recompenses, i.e., a year in which full recompenses will be made for the sins of God's enemies.[14] Both expressions, "day" and "year," are simply used to designate a period when God will carry out His purposes of vengeance, which consist of His executing deserved and merited punishment upon those who have transgressed His commands.[15] It is not mingled with malice and evil as is the case with human vengeance. It is a quality that in God is divine and praiseworthy and in the execution of which God is honored and glorified. Furthermore, it is a day and a year that exist for the cause of Zion. By means of taking vengeance and carrying out recompenses, God will prosper the cause of Zion, the city of His elect people.[16] Throughout the years Zion has had a legal cause with the heathen nations. Her rights have completely been trampled in the ground. Her case has gone unheard. Now, however, her God intervenes on her behalf. What He does is to further her cause. Among the nations Edom in particular stands out as one that from early times had treated Zion with injustice.

[14] *recompenses*—the plural serves to heighten the word's force.
[15] The prophecy of Nahum exemplifies this truth as it is applied to Nineveh.
[16] König, however, interprets, "for the quarrel of the Edomites with Zion." This does not seem natural.

9 Hitherto the prophet has spoken of the enemy itself, and now he turns to the enemy's land. Judgment brings great cataclysmic changes.[17] The streams of Edom, her rapidly filling wadies, will be changed to pitch. Using the language of the downfall of Sodom and Gomorrah the prophet applies it to Edom herself, adding, however, the mention of pitch.[18] Not only the liquid, but also the dry land, the dust, will be affected. Thus, the prophet includes the entire land, and then sums up by saying that Edom's land will become burning pitch.[19] In this latter sense he refers to the earth or ground of Edom rather than to the nation as a political or geographical entity. These figures show that a devastating judgment has fallen upon the land (cf. Jude 7).

10 "The remarkable gradation and accumulation of terms denoting perpetuity can scarcely be expressed in a translation" (Alexander). An attempt, however, should be made; and hence we shall render:

> *Night and day it is not quenched;*
> *For ever its smoke keeps ascending.*
> *From generation to generation it will burn,*
> *For ever and ever there is no one passing through it.*

By night and day the land burns with pitch and bitumen, yet it does not extinguish itself; it continues to burn. Throughout the night the brightness of its flames rises to heaven, and during the day those flames are not diminished. It is a continual and eternal burning. The smoke that accompanies the burning persists in ascending with no cessation. In this verse eternity is denoted four times, and in each instance the expression that denotes it is at the head of the clause in the position of emphasis. When one generation has passed away and another comes, it beholds the same constant burning. It is an uninterrupted burning that endures forever, and so the land can have no travellers; no one will pass

---

[17] *wᵉ-ne-he-p̄ᵉ-k̞û.* Note omission of *Dagesh lene* in *Kaph.* This is because the preceding *Shᵉwa* is vocal. The *Sᵉgol* takes the place of compound *Shᵉwa* under *He.* In nonpausal forms of the finite verb without accusative suffixes, a short vowel (here *Patah*) in a near open syllable is dropped to *Shᵉwa.* A preceding compound *Shᵉwa* must then be changed to its homogeneous short vowel, thus: *ne-hᵉ-p̄ak̞* > *ne-h̞ᵉ-p̄ᵉ-k̞û* > *ne-he-p̄ᵉ-k̞û.*

[18] Jer. 49:18 states expressly that Edom will be destroyed like Sodom and Gomorrah.

[19] *bʿrh*—the vocalization is probably to be explained as due to pause; otherwise we should expect *bō-ʿᵃ-rāh.*

through it. This last clause, like the others, must be taken in a figurative sense. Attempts to show that there are deserted towns in Edom, or that the travellers there are few in number, have nothing to do with the meaning of the prophecy. What Isaiah is picturing under the usage of figurative language is a full destruction of the ancient enemy of God's people, a destruction that will endure for ever so that Edom will no longer be a country able to oppress and harass the Israelites.[20]

11 And there will inhabit it the pelican and porcupine, and the crane and raven shall dwell in it. And he will stretch upon it the line of desolation and the stones of waste.

12 As for her nobles, and there is no one there, they will still call a kingdom, and all her chiefs will be cessation.

13 And her palaces will come up thorns, nettles and brambles in her fortresses. And it will be a habitation of jackals, a court for ostriches.

14 And desert creatures will meet demons. And the shaggy beast will call to his fellow. Surely there the night demon reposes, and finds for herself a resting place.

15 There will the arrow snake make its nest and lay, and hatch, and father into her shadow; surely there will the vultures be gathered, each with her mate.

16 Seek ye from the book of the LORD and read. One of them is not lacking. One another they miss not; for my mouth, it has commanded; and his spirit, it has gathered them.

17 And he has cast the lot for them, and his hand has divided it to them by line. For ever will they hold it as a heritage; to all generations they will dwell therein.

11 Great strength is given to the description by a change of the figure. Having pictured Edom as a continual burning, never to be extinguished, Isaiah mentioned that no one would ever pass through it. Thus he introduced the concept of emptiness and waste and of a land devoid of inhabitants. It is this latter concept that he now takes up. No human inhabitants are to be found, but nevertheless there will be inhabitants who have received the land by inheritance from those who had once lived there. The human dwellers of Edom have left the land to those who are mentioned in this verse. These are the pelican,[21] the porcupine, the owl, and the

---

20 Cf. 2 Pet. 3:7, 10, 12.

21 *qā-'āṭ*—indicates a bird (Lev. 11:18; Deut. 14:17), pelican or screech

raven. Very similar is this description to that which Isaiah had earlier given of Babylon (13:21f.). The pelican builds its nest in deserted places; cf. Zephaniah 2:14 and Psalm 102:6. In the second noun we have reference to a rolling, an animal that rolls itself up, hence, probably the hedgehog or porcupine, an animal that also likes deserted places.[22] The third noun refers to a bird that inhabits deserts, possibly a bird with a strident note. It may be an owl. Of this, however, one cannot be sure.[23] Finally the raven is mentioned, a bird that lives in deserted walls.[24] All serves to give a picture of lonesomeness and desolation; only wild and solitary birds are to be found.

Concluding the verse, Isaiah points out that God (for God is evidently to be understood as the subject of the verb) performs His work with precision and thoroughness. He stretches out the plummet line and the stone attached to the end of the line, that the demolition may be carried through completely.[25] Taking language from Genesis 1:2, the prophet shows how great the desolation will be, for he speaks of the line as one of desolation and the stones as those of waste. Not without purpose does Isaiah use the plural, for it lends a certain emphasis. This is to be the end attained; the land will become a desolation and waste so that it can no more receive inhabitants.

12 Asyndetically Isaiah introduces another subject to stress the desolation of the land.[26] What, however, is this subject? According to Alexander, the prophet is now speaking of Edom's caves. He points out rightly that the word *ḥorim* may mean holes or caves, and also that Edom was full of caves, remarking that the original

---

owl? Cf. Bochert, *Hierozoicon*, II:454-62. B ὄρνεα; Vulg. *onocrotalus*. Cf. the pointing in Lev. 11:18; Deut. 14:17 when the word receives the definite article. The effect of the article is similar to that of pause.

22 קפוד—*the curly one;* cf. 14:23. The root means *to roll up, gather together.*

23 וינשוף—The word designates a bird (Lev. 11:17), and the present passage would indicate that it inhabits desolate or waste places. B ἴβεις. Possibly it is an owl.

24 *raven*—B κόρακες. The meaning of this word is better attested than that of the others; cf. Gen. 8:7; 1 Kings 17:4, 6.

25 *line of desolation*—Note aspiration (i.e., omission of *Dagesh lene* from *Tau*) despite the immediately preceding *waw*, which closes a syllable.

26 In 1Q, however, the conjunction is written. Possibly the conjunction strengthens the expressions; your nobles *are by no means there.* Cf. Leo Prijs, "*Ein 'Waw der Bekräftigung'?*" *Biblische Zeitschrift*, Vol. 8, No. 1, Jan. 1964, p. 106.

inhabitants were known as *troglodytes* or inhabitants of caves. Thus, according to Alexander, the prophet is saying that the whole country will be a kingdom of deserted caverns.[27]

There is difficulty, however, in this interpretation, for the verse mentions a kingdom and princes, and these do not fit in well with the mention of caves. It is preferable, then, to take the word, as do the majority of expositors, as meaning *nobles*. Such a translation agrees better with the remainder of the verse. At any rate the word receives emphasis, being first in the sentence, and has absolute force, so that we may translate, *As for her* (i.e., *Edom's*) *nobles, etc.*

and there are none there—Emphasis here falls upon the word *there,* for Edom is a place where the pelican and the porcupine dwell, not where the nobles of the kingdom live. As far as the nobles of Edom are concerned, so runs the argument, there are no longer any there at all who proclaim the kingdom. Some expositors think that Edom had an elective kingdom in which the nobles could call their ruler. For this, however, there is really no evidence. Others take the words *to call the kingdom* as meaning to proclaim the kingdom or to call a king. Another view refers to the calling of someone to the kingdom, and still another is that there will no longer be a kingdom. The phrase is confessedly difficult, but the following is a possibility: "As for the nobles, there is none there that they call a kingdom." In other words, the object of the verb is found in the words "and there is none there." All the former nobles of Edom have disappeared, and there are none at all remaining who might constitute a kingdom. The language is abrupt and not entirely free from difficulty, but the above seems to be as devoid of difficulty as any of the other suggestions.

By way of gradation Isaiah declares that all the princes of Edom are ceased. Not only are there no nobles, but all of the princes also are gone. Evidently the point of pride as far as Edom was concerned was in its rulers. Genesis 36:40-43 mentions the chiefs of Edom in which the aristocracy apparently culminated. The greatest of disgrace and humiliation for Edom would be to be deprived of her rulers, and it is just that humiliation which she will have to undergo. Her rulers will be cessation; they will no longer exist.

[27] The term "Horites" is now seen to refer to the Hurrians, and the ancient interpretation "troglodyte" should be abandoned.

13 This verse gives the result of the desolation. With respect to the palaces of Edom, a reminder of her once great grandeur, there will come up thorns.[28] The once sumptuous palaces, filled with mankind, now give place to thorns. It is difficult more forcefully to describe the desolation. Likewise Edom's fortified places will give way to nettles and brambles. Can there be a more useless and profitless vegetation? Yet the palaces and fortresses will not be completely devoid of inhabitants. Jackals will have their pasturage there, and it will be a grass plot or court for ostriches. The second part of the verse corresponds to the first. In place of the palaces will be the pasture; instead of the fortresses, the grass plots or courts.[29] Edom will still have places of dwelling, but they will be the very opposite of what they previously had been.

14 Using language in part taken from chapter thirteen, Isaiah continues his description of the desolation.[30] In place of the once festal gatherings there will be meetings of another kind. The wild animals of the desert will then meet one another.[31] They will be the only inhabitants of the once glorious kingdom of Edom. Borrowing again from the thirteenth chapter, the prophet states that demons in goat form (*sa'ir*) will call one to another.[32] The desolation of Babylon will overcome Edom also. There also, in just that place, so suited to the presence of the powers of darkness, is the Lilith; there she has taken her rest and found a place of repose.[33] In Assyrian and Babylonian mythology Lilitu appears as a feminine night demon (cf. also Tobit 8:3). The thought here seems to be similar to that expressed in Matthew 12:43. Lilith is a

28 *and will come up*—f. singular. The noun *sirim, thorns*, is evidently regarded as f. in this instance; cf. Brockelmann, 50 c. *her palaces*—acc. of respect; *and there will come up in respect to her palaces thorns*, i.e., *thorns will come up in her palaces*. For a discussion of the nouns denoting animals, etc. cf. the commentary on 13:21ff.

29 *ḥtzyr—settled abode or haunt*, corresponds to *fortresses* of 13a. Opposite the enclosed fortresses is the open *haunt* of ostriches, etc. 1Q, however, reads *ḥtzr*.

30 For discussions of many of the nouns of this verse cf. the notes on 13:21ff.

31 את—despite the absence of the article with both nouns, the *notum accusativum* is here necessary to distinguish subject from object.

32 *will call*—the word probably reflects upon v. 12. In Edom no one will proclaim a kingdom, only the satyrs will call to one another. Perhaps a particular nuance (against?) is intended by על instead of אל. Cf. the call of the seraphs in 6:3.

33 1Q reads לילית, and Vulg., importing Greco-Roman mythology, *ibi cubavit lamia et invenit sibi requiem*.

440

demon that wanders about through the desert places. In itself the word simply means "Nocturnal." Alexander thinks that the mention of a demon here would be out of place in a list of animals. In answer, however, it is probable that the *sa'ir* does actually refer to a demon in goat form. Isaiah is using this language in order to point out how great is the desolation of Edom. Only the powers of evil can find rest here.

15 It is not without purpose that the first word is "there." The prophet is again directing attention to Edom, the place where these wild creatures will live. The English translations are in error at this point, for the word that KJV renders "great owl" refers to the arrow snake, taken to be a kind of small snake native to Arabia and Africa, which could rush on men from a tree or other ambush and seriously wound them.[34] This snake makes its nest and lays its eggs, hatching them and gathering them into her shadow.[35] The thought is that the snake protects the young, covering them as do the birds with their wings. As in 30:2, so here the shadow is a symbol of protection.

To show how forbidding and desolate is this land Isaiah states that only there do the vultures gather, coming one after another, as though from flight. Three clauses (14b, 15a, and 15b) begin with the word "there." There in Edom, the once noble country, there and nowhere else, will the doleful creatures of the wasteland find their home.

16 What the prophet has declared may seem strange and difficult to believe. Edom, the inveterate enemy of Judah, so prosperous, so strong, so powerful—can it be that Edom will have the weird inhabitants that Isaiah has just mentioned? Is there any control of his words? Is there any means of attesting their truthfulness? There is indeed such a means, the only means by which the truthfulness of any message may be attested; and Isaiah invites, rather, he commands, men to use this means. It is the book or writing of the Lord, and Isaiah enjoins men to search in this writing. Then they will be able to compare the prophecy with its fulfillment and to see that

---

34 *arrow snake*—cf. Ar. *fiq-qâ-za, arrow snake,* B ἐχῖνος, Vulg. *ibi habuit foveam ericius,* which reflects *qpwd;* found in 1Q.

35 מלט—*Piel, to lay,* i.e., let the eggs slip out. *dgr—to gather as a brood. dywt*—cf. Deut. 14:13, where the word occurs in connection with the buzzard; cf. also Lev. 11:14.

all that the prophet had prophesied had in actuality come to pass.

Isaiah uses a preposition, *from upon*. One often speaks of writing upon a book (cf. Josh. 10:13; 2 Sam. 1:18). Now men are commanded to read *from upon* the book, i.e., to read the writing that is found upon the book. The immediate reference is to this particular prophecy. In commanding men to search the writing he desires that they look at the writing to see whether this prophecy is true. At the same time, in speaking of the writing or book of the Lord, as several commentators have pointed out, Isaiah has more in mind than this particular prophecy. He is in effect referring to this prophecy as a part of a whole. It is part of an actual Scripture, of a book written down, so that men may turn to it and find therein the reference to this prophecy. Isaiah appeals to written words of God as the authority by which men are to judge the truthfulness of His message. When one finds the prophecy in the Scripture he is to read, and by reading will be able to verify the truthfulness of what Isaiah has predicted.[36]

The prophet himself has no question but that his words will be fulfilled; and hence, using a prophetic perfect, he positively asserts that not even one of all the animals that he has mentioned will fail.[37] They will all be there in Edom as its inhabitants just as the prophet had predicted. It is as though Isaiah had commanded to read in the book and so to discover mention of every one of the animals to which he had referred. What he means by this statement is that the prediction will most assuredly be fulfilled. The thought is strengthened by the additional comment, *one another they miss not*. Difficult as this phrase is, it simply is a way of saying that all of the animals mentioned will be present. None will be lacking; one will not miss the other.

Confirmation of this truth is given by the assertion that God has spoken it. *My mouth* refers to Isaiah's own mouth. "I have myself spoken this prophecy," we might paraphrase him as saying, "and have spoken it truly." Indeed, in view of the lack of belief the

---

36 Fischer believes the reference to be to Isa. 1–34 and in particular to chap. 13, where vv. 20-22 give a similar description of wild beasts. Hence, the present prophecy would be an extension or application of that in chap. 13. This is improbable, for it appeals to what has been said about Babylon to support what is now being said about Edom.

37 *'aḥat*—f. used as a neuter, although at the end of the verse the f. becomes prominent. A stateliness is given to the language by the three pausal forms and the fully written מהנה.

prophet's own mouth is said to have commanded. Isaiah was a spokesman for Yahweh, and in Yahweh's Name had the right to command. In reality it was Yahweh who commanded through him. The command has reference to the presence of the animals in Edom. This is supported and explained by the last clause of the verse, "His Spirit has gathered them"[38] (cf. Isa. 63:14; Zech. 4:6). The Spirit, God's Agent in the carrying out of His purposes, will gather together the animals, as Isaiah has commanded. The spoken word is accompanied by the working of the Spirit, who makes the word effective. This is the true biblical picture of the word, a picture that is contrary to the common notion that in the word itself there resides a particular efficacy.

17 In 16a the command had been given. This was followed by the gathering of the animals in 16b, and now there follows the division and measuring of the land (17a) according to which they will have possession of the land of Edom for ever (17b). The expressions are evidently taken from the partition of the land of Canaan (cf. Num. 26:55, 56; Josh. 18:4-6). God had once partitioned Canaan and allotted it to Israel, and now in similar fashion allots Edom to the creatures of whom the prophet has been speaking. They will be the eternal heirs of the land. God causes the lot to fall for their benefit, and it is His own hand that divides[39] for them[40] by the line. The division will be exact and precise, as it should be, for it has been measured by the measuring line. Inasmuch as God Himself has made the allotment, it cannot be changed by man at will. It is a permanent arrangement which will endure for ever.

The prophet regards the animals as the heirs of this land, which is the place of their dwelling. To emphasize the eternity of this inheritance he places first in both of the two final clauses the words that refer to eternity. This is the same procedure that he had earlier employed in verse 10. From that verse he takes two expressions to emphasize the concept of eternity. These two expressions, *unto eternity* and *for generation and generation,* bring to the fore the fact of the complete and never ending desolation that will overcome this inveterate enemy of the people of God.

---

38 ורוחו—*his spirit*; the noun is here evidently construed as masculine.
39 חלקתה—*has divided it*, for hil-lᵉ-qaṭ-hā.
40 להם—used generally, although the reference is to feminine objects.

SPECIAL LITERATURE

Wilhelm Caspari: "Jesaja 34 and 35," *ZAW*, Vol. 49, 1931, pp. 67-86.

G. B. Gray, *ZAW*, Vol. 31, 1911, pp. 123-127, discusses the question whether the Edomite monarchy was elective, Isa. 34:12-14.

Marvin Pope: "Isaiah 34 in Relation to Isaiah 35; 40-66," *JBL*, Vol. 71, 1952, pp. 235-243.

C. C. Torrey: *The Second Isaiah*. Edinburgh, 1928, pp. 279-295.

Edward J. Young: "Isaiah 34 And Its Position in the Prophecy," *WThJ*, Vol. 27, No. 2, 1965, pp. 93-114.

2. GOD'S SOVEREIGNTY MANIFESTED IN SALVATION (35:1-10)

1 There will rejoice for them the desert and wasteland; and let the
    wilderness rejoice and blossom as the rose.
2 It shall surely blossom, and let it rejoice, yea, with joy and shout-
    ing, the glory of Lebanon shall be given to it, the splendor of
    Carmel and Sharon; they shall see the glory of the LORD, the splen-
    dor of our God.

1 Isaiah delights in contrasts. In the preceding chapter he has
described how the once rich and luxurious Edom has become a
desolate wilderness, the habitation of doleful creatures. Now, he
points out that what was a desert will become a place in which rich
flowers are springing and luxuriant growth covers the ground. It is
a contrast similar to that found between chapters ten and eleven.
As a keynote to the entire theme, the verb appears first. The
wondrous revolution is one that is characterized by rejoicing. In
contrast to the gloom of the preceding chapter there stands out the
joy that the new order of things introduces. In the Hebrew the
verb has a suffix, "them"; and if this be retained, we are to
understand the prophet as referring to those who will inhabit the
wilderness.[1]

The desert and dry land represent the land devastated by the
enemy. It is a land that will now come to life, bursting forth in joy
as a living creature. To carry out the figure, Isaiah employs a

---

[1] *they shall rejoice*—Kennedy would delete the final *Mem* as "a retrospective
dittogram" from the next word, thus obtaining the simple imperfect *yā-śi-śû,
wilderness and desert shall rejoice*. It has also been conjectured that final
Nun has been assimilated to the following *Mem*, which is then written double.
This supposition is questionable. Final *Mem* occurs in 1Q, and it may be the
suffix, *shall be glad for them*. Inasmuch as the verb is intransitive, the suffix
would really express an indirect object. We should expect *yᵉ-śi-śûm*, but even
1Q has no *yod*. Cf. GKC § 47, note. The inf. construct is *lā-śûś*; cf. Deut. 30:
9. The verb occurs seven times in the latter part of Isaiah 61:10; 62:5; 64:4;
65:18ff.; 66:10, 14.

jussive, "and let rejoice," appealing to the Arabah.[2] The reference is to the region south of the Dead Sea reaching to the Gulf of Akaba. Evidently Isaiah has in mind primarily Judah, but his purpose is not thus to restrict himself. He is referring to all that has become desert through the depredations of the ecumenical empire of man. The waste world will become like an earthly paradise, for a whole reversal of conditions will set in.

Instead of remaining in Arabah, the land is to rejoice and to sprout or blossom like the rose. Isaiah uses a word whose precise meaning is not known.[3] A good case can be made out that it is some kind of crocus, but this is not certain. Whereas the common translation *rose* may not be precisely correct, it is far more beautiful than crocus. Alexander remarks that the poetry, if not the botany, is superior; and inasmuch as we do not know the exact force of the Hebrew word, we may abide by the common English rendering.

The language of this chapter is unusually beautiful, for under the figure of a barren land now clothed with luxuriant flowers, such as Palestine itself, where during the winter months the hillsides and fields are covered with the red anemone, the prophet sets forth the truth that God has prepared a place for those who love Him. A period of great blessing will have come to the Church, which is perhaps foreshadowed by the return of the Jews from exile, but above all which finds its realization in the saving work of the Lord. In this land of wondrous delight and beauty there is peace and blessing, for it is Immanuel's land, and its blessings are for those who have been redeemed by the King Himself.

2 This verse continues the description of the future change. An infinitive absolute introduces it, and then follow two verbs that were used in the previous verse. Through the infinitive absolute particular emphasis is given to the first verb, and this emphasis points to the abundance with which the earth in those days is to

---

2 *wᵉṭāḡēl—and let rejoice.* The jussive form introduced into a prediction indicates the concurrence of the prophet and his approval of what is foretold.

3 חבצלת—asphodel? It occurs only here and in Song of Sol. 2:1. Cf. Akk. *ḥab(a)ṣillatu.* Not a reference to plants generally, but a definite plant, the exact identity of which is not known. Not the rose (Luther, Kimchi, Ibn Ezra) nor lily (B, Vulg., Targ.) nor narcissus (Saadia, Abulwalid). On the basis of the Syriac *ḥamᵉtzaloyto'*, colchicum (autumnal), the word is thought to designate a crocus. *BH* reads *Beth* instead of *Kaph;* i.e., the desert would blossom *with* the rose. 1Q, however, supports M.

446

produce. As in the preceding verse the thought of rejoicing stood first and occupied the center of attention, so here emphasis falls upon flowering or shooting forth. Although the two verbs are taken from verse 1, nevertheless they here appear in chiastic order. First the shooting forth, and then the rejoicing is mentioned. The concept of rejoicing (again a jussive) is strengthened by two nouns that may be construed as accusatives of specification, *in respect to rejoicing and shouting.*[4]

Indeed there is reason for this command to the desert to break forth into such great rejoicing, for the glory that belongs to Lebanon will be given to the desert. Lebanon's glory consisted in her beautiful trees and magnificent vegetation. What made Lebanon glorious would also be given to the desert. In itself the desert could not produce such glory; and hence the glory must be given to it. It is God and He alone who can give this glory to the desert, and so the very verb *is given* points to the grace of God. All the rich blessings of salvation are gifts of God. Together with this glory the beauty of Carmel and Sharon will also be given to the desert. It is Mount Carmel to which Isaiah here refers. With the words Lebanon, Carmel, and Sharon, he includes the great western part of the country: the mountains belong to Syria proper, Carmel is in Palestine, and Sharon is the plain that extends along the western coast. In 33:9 Isaiah had also mentioned these three places, there in contrast to the Arabah. Here again the same relationship is introduced, but this time, not to the disparagement of these places but to their honor. The desert will be so transformed through God's work, that it will become glorious and honorable like these three places.

The pronoun *they* is somewhat difficult to construe, but possibly we should refer it to the desert and dry land mentioned in the first verse.[5] There would appear to be a reason for making the pronoun emphatic. It is as though Isaiah said that they, the desert and dry land, which no one could believe would ever change, have now received the precious gift of luxuriant verdure and vegetation such as had characterized Lebanon, Carmel, and Sharon. In the change

---

[4] *rejoicing*—the const. before the conjunction; cf. also 33:6; Ezek. 26:10 and Isa. 51:21. *ran-nēn—shouting;* a verbal noun (*Piel* inf. const.).

[5] Some have sought to identify the subject with the three geographical names, but there is no reason for thus limiting it. B inserts ὁ λαός μου (my people), but this is questionable, and as Penna suggests, may be due to a desire to have inanimate beings see the glory of God.

that has come over them they will see the glory of the Lord, the splendor of the God whom Isaiah loves and whose prophet he is. The picture, in other words, is symbolic of the great change that God's grace will introduce, and in the performance of this work the true beauty, glory, and honor of the God of Israel will be made manifest.[6]

> 3 Strengthen the sinking hands, and the tottering knees make firm.
> 4 Say to the hasty of heart, Be firm, fear not, behold! your God, vengeance is coming, the retribution of God; he is coming, and may he save you.

3 In view of the change to come over the desert and dry place, Isaiah as a prophet of the Lord encourages the inhabitants of Judah unto mutual strengthening.[7] His command is general, but is addressed to the people themselves. They are to make firm the hands that are now sinking and to make strong the knees that are tottering. Vitringa points out that hands and knees are mentioned to combine the ideas of action and endurance. Hands that are sinking because their owner is frightened and fearful cannot do the things that they should.[8] Knees that shake and are tottering cannot endure, nor permit a person to stand erect and firm as he should. Fear takes strength from a person, and at this time there was reason for fear. Over the face of the earth spread the wings of that great bird of prey, Assyria. For Judah there seemed to be no future. Doom and destruction appeared certain. The ancient order of things must surely pass away, and the promises made to the fathers go by the board. It was a time of fear and trembling. But such fear was really a sign of disbelief; there was no reason for it. God had promised, and His promises would come to pass. The blessings of redemption would be brought about, for God is true. It is a time, therefore, for strength and boasting in the Lord. If there are among the people those whose hands are now sinking and

6 Cf. comments on 6:3, and note 40:5, 9; 60:1. Hengstenberg asserts that to see the glory of the Lord is to behold Him in the full glory of His nature. Such a revelation took place in Christ, the brightness of God's glory and the express image of His person, who revealed the glory as of the only-begotten of the Father (John 1:14; 2:11). The emphasis of the present verse, however, is upon the miraculous change, which of course is possible only because of the work of the Messiah.

7 Some take the words as addressed to the prophets. Surely they are included in the address.

8 *hands*—note that dual nouns may be modified by f. pl. adjectives.

whose knees are tottering, strengthen them, make them strong. And this is to be done only by calling to mind the ancient promises of God, and looking to the future when He will have accomplished His redemption. To state this command, Isaiah uses his familiar chiastic arrangement of words. The combination of verbs found in this verse also appears in the command to Joshua as he takes up his work of leading the Israelites into the land of promise. For the great work that God had for him to perform, he was charged by means of these two verbs, *be strong and of good courage.* In a time when it seems that that work is to fail and the land of promise will be taken from the people the same command comes. The attitude of Joshua is the only one that will suffice at such a time, and one can have only this attitude when he realizes that the God who had been with Joshua is also at all times with His people.

4 The prophet now describes men by their inward condition, whereas in the preceding verse he had merely mentioned the outward manifestation of that condition. The hasty of heart are those who in their inmost thoughts are impatient with the apparent delay in God's fulfillment of His promises. They would hasten along the work of God, in that they think in their heart that He is too slow and that He delays His redemption. In Judah there were doubtless such people, and this inward attitude may in large measure have explained why their hands were sinking and their knees tottering. Such an attitude was in fact a dissatisfaction with God's purposes and His method of carrying them out. To such people there is need for being strong and fearless. In His own time and manner God will fulfill His Word.

All who are hasty of heart Isaiah commands to behold their God![9] Indeed, they are to behold Him in a specific way. He is coming to bring vengeance. The prophet's language has been subjected to various constructions, but it would seem that the meaning may most naturally be brought out by construing the words, "Behold! your God, in vengeance He comes."[10] The thought is that

---

[9] *your God*—a *Pashta* disjoins this from the following word.

[10] *nāqām*—may be taken as a *Ḥal* acc.; as *vengeance* (i.e., *in a state of vengeance*) *he will come.* König, however, renders, *behold! your God; vengeance will come, the recompense of God.* But the pronoun אוה would refer to *God,* rather than to *recompense.* Whereas the syntax is difficult, I prefer the construction set forth in the exposition. Influenced by the *Manual of Discipline,* 5:25, Wernberg-Møller (*VT,* Vol. 69, 1959, pp. 72f.) would render, "Behold, to you vengeance will come, the recompense of God will come, and your

God is coming in vengeance and for the purpose of executing vengeance. To say that God is coming does not suggest that He is far away and must travel to be on hand. It is merely a forceful manner of stating that God will be on hand at the moment when He is needed. He comes to the aid of His people to execute vengeance on His enemies. In 40:10 Isaiah uses a similarly constructed phrase.

The terse language is difficult to construe. Possibly the following paraphrase represents the thought. "Behold! your God, in respect to vengeance He comes; indeed the recompense of God will take place." This arrangement of the words appears to contain the least difficulty. On this construction the words *the recompense of God* are really explanatory of *vengeance*. It is God who will recompense to men the reward of their doings. Thus Paul writes, "Seeing it is a righteous thing with God to recompense tribulation to them that trouble you" (2 Thess. 1:6). The words bring to the fore the fact that the recompense to be visited upon the enemy is not the work of man but of God Himself.

In the final clause the reference is to God and refers to a work of salvation that He will perform in the future. It is a deliverance not only from outward foes but also from personal enemies. More deeply than that, however, it is a deliverance from man's greatest foe, sin and its consequences. It is a spiritual salvation, such as only God can accomplish. In the Old Testament salvation is connected with the coming of the Lord.[11] When salvation will have been accomplished, then God will be present with His people.

5 Then will be opened the eyes of the blind, and the ears of the deaf will be unclosed.

6 Then shall the lame leap as a hart, and the tongue of the dumb shall shout, because waters have burst forth in the wilderness and streams in the desert.

5 Both this and the following verse begin with *then*. It is the word that indicates the Messianic time of salvation when the blessings to be described will appear. When God comes and saves His people then they will experience a great change. Just as the

---

salvation." This is not supported either by the versions or by 1Q, which latter strongly supports the rendering herein adopted.

11 *and may he save you—Hiphil* jussive. The imperfect would be *yô-ší-'ª-ḵem*. The jussive form is regular and there is no need for emendation.

desert itself is changed into something other than what it formerly was, so will the people themselves be changed. Old things will have passed away indeed, and all things will have become new. One evidence of the remarkable change is that the eyes of the blind will be opened.[12] Likewise will the ears of the deaf be unclosed.[13] The reference is not specifically to the miracles of healing that our Lord performed, although these miracles are themselves a part of the means by which the change is accomplished. Rather, the entire emphasis of this chapter is that when the Lord comes He will bring about a radical change in the world. Just as the desert will no longer be a desert but will blossom like the rose, so also will the blind see. All these expressions simply indicate in beautiful fashion how far-reaching and thoroughly radical will be the change that the coming of the Lord accomplishes. Our Lord Jesus Christ did reflect upon this passage (Luke 7:22) as an evidence of His Messiahship. In the performance of His mighty miracles Jesus Christ showed that He was divine, but the present passage teaches far more than that these miracles will be performed. It teaches a complete, all-embracing, radical change.[14]

6 Continuing the description of the powerful change, Isaiah remarks that the lame, who now must shuffle along, will then leap as a hart for joy. When the lame man at the Beautiful Gate was miraculously healed, he leaped up (cf. Acts 3:8).[15] The thought expresses a vigorous contrast to the previous condition of the lame person. Also emphasizing this contrast is the thought that the tongue of the dumb will shout. No more will the dumb be silent; he will not merely speak, but he will shout aloud for joy.[16]

There is a reason for this reversal of condition. In the wilder-

12 פקח is used 20 times, 19 for the opening of the eyes and once (42:20) for the opening of the ears.
13 Note the chiasm in the verse and the paronomasia between the two verbs.
14 Blind and deaf are mentioned as representatives of weak and sinful humanity (cf. John 5:3). And yet they themselves will also receive the blessings of this promise. Those who are physically blind and deaf are intended. Yet in a wider sense are included those who are spiritually blind and deaf. (Cf. Isa. 29:18; 42:18; 43:8; 56:10 and Isa. 6:10; Matt. 15:14; John 9:39; Eph. 1:18; 2 Pet. 1:9.)
As to the fulfillment we may note Matt. 11:5; 15:31; 21:14; Mark 7:37; and John 9:39. Even now, however, we see but as in a glass darkly. When Christ returns, then shall we see, and this prophecy will receive its deepest fulfillment.
15 Cf. also Acts 8:7; 14:10; John 5:9; Heb. 11:12.
16 Cf. Matt. 12:22.

ness, where no water was, water has burst forth, and streams in the Arabah where all was dryness. These are further symbols of the great change to come. God's work produces joy in His people. There is an allusion to Exodus 17:3ff. and Numbers 20:11. Water in the desert is a figure of salvation.

> 7 And the parched ground shall become a pool, and the thirsty land springs of water, in the habitation of jackals, their lair, green grass for reed and rush.
> 8 And there shall be a highway and a way, and it shall be called the way of holiness, and there will not pass through it the unclean, and it will be for them; the traveller and the fools will not err.

7 To the weary traveller in the wasteland[17] nothing could be more cheering and refreshing than to find water. When the salvation of God comes, there will be found a pool of water. Indeed, the dry thirsty land will have become springs of water. By using the plural Isaiah makes the figure more powerful. The land itself longs for a drink of water; it is thirsty and no water is at hand. Now, however, not merely will there be a trickle of water, but actual springs gushing forth. In the wilderness are the dwellings of jackals which destroy and steal. Now, however, the waters themselves, which bring blessing, will be in the very dwelling of the jackals.[18] Here in place of reeds and rushes there will be green grass. Here will be ample water to supply their needs. Water is here seen as a fructifying, life-giving element.

8 The desert is barren and without water, and hence, unable to sustain the growth of luxuriant verdure; and it is also without means of communication, without roads (cf. Ps. 107:4). Not only will it cease to be barren, but there will also be there a highway over which God's people may travel in safety. As in 34:14b, 15a, and

[17] šrb—probably *parched ground* or *burning heat;* B, Vulg. (*et quae erat arida*), Syr. But it is not to be connected here with the name of the Babylonian deity *šarrabu.* It stands in parallelism with *tzimmā'ón, thirsty ground,* which supports the meaning given above, as also does the usage in 49: 10. The appeal to *širâb, mirage,* is to me questionable. But cf. the philological discussion in Gesenius.

[18] רבצה—lit., *her lair.* Plural designations of animals of either gender may be joined with the f. singular. Hengstenberg erroneously refers the suffix to Zion, supposing that Zion has been changed into a garden of God. Drechsler refers the suffix to *waters* (cf. Job 14:19). The construction that seems to be most free of difficulty would be, *in the habitation of jackals, even their lair.*

15b, so here also Isaiah places his emphasis upon the word *there*. In that place of desolation there will now be what deserts do not normally have, namely, a *highway*. By means of a hendiadys the prophet speaks of a highway, i.e., a way that is cast up. Job 12:24 mentions a *wilderness without a way,* and Jeremiah 18:15 *a way that is not cast up.* Here then is no mere faint track in the desert, such as is usually found, but a prepared, cast up way, whose existence can be detected without any difficulty.

It is no ordinary road of travel, but one of holiness, on which pilgrims will travel to the Holy City; nothing impure or unholy can enter upon it.[19] Perhaps the figure is taken from the presence of "holy" ways in antiquity on which cultic processions were found. In Thebes, for example, there was a way that connected the temples of what are now known as Luxor and Karnak. On such a way whatever was ceremonially unclean could not pass over. The unclean of which Isaiah speaks, however, are unclean not merely in a ceremonial manner, but also because they are out of conformity with the Law of the Holy One of Israel.[20] The unclean one does not belong to the Holy One. Only the redeemed who are God's own people shall cross over the desert on this way. What a contrast with the present! Now foreigners and strangers occupy the highways and byways of Judah; the land is no longer the possession of its own inhabitants. Then, however, in crossing the desert the way that leads to the city of Holiness will be reserved for God's people. By means of a circumstantial clause, Isaiah emphasizes this fact. "The unclean shall not pass over it inasmuch as it belongs to them, i.e., the redeemed."[21]

The last thought of the verse may be expressed thus: "They who travel the way, even though fools, will not go astray."[22] Isaiah does not mean that there will be fools who will walk on this highway; he is simply using a figure taken from the present. The way will be so clearly marked, so well constructed and so easy to follow that even fools would not go astray thereon. Again, the contrast with the actual condition is vivid. One who travels in the desert without

---

[19] *lāh—to it* (f. also in 1Q), referring to the collective *highway* and *way*.

[20] They are not necessarily degenerate Israelites and unworthy ones; cf. 32:5 (Penna). All who walk on this highway are unworthy.

[21] A circumstantial clause, *since it is for them,* i.e., as their own possession. The m. pronoun, as also the m. suffix *-ennû,* apparently refers to the first word of the hendiadys, *maslûl,* and not to the collective expression.

[22] Lit., *the walker, goer* (on) *a way;* i.e., *traveller.*

guide or without knowing the way that he must go, may very easily lose his way. The path is sometimes obliterated by the sand; it is not clear-cut and well defined. The way of holiness, however, is one that does not lead astray; it leads to its destination. "The circumstance that even the foolish cannot miss the way, indicates the abundant fulness of the salvation, in consequence of which it is so easily accessible; and no human effort, skill or excellence is required to attain the possession of it" (Hengstenberg). One cannot overestimate the grandeur of this description! How many there are who wander in life, not knowing its meaning, not knowing their destination, not knowing where they are going. How blessed are they who know the Way, the Truth, and the Life, who through God's grace are in that holy way that leads with unerring sureness to the city where the Holy One of Israel reigns in solemn majesty and glory!

9 There will not be there a lion, and a ravenous beast will not ascend it, nor be found there; and redeemed ones will walk there.

10 And the ransomed of the LORD will return and come to Zion with shouting, and everlasting joy upon their head;· gladness and joy will overtake them, and sorrow and sighing will flee away.

9 As Isaiah had earlier said (30:6), the desert was the home of dangerous animals. He who travelled in the wilderness had much to fear. Would the mere presence of a raised highway[23] be a sufficient protection from these animals? Perhaps in itself it would not be, but this highway is the way of holiness and those who journey on it will do so in perfect safety. Although the lion might be one of the chief terrors that met the wayfarer, on this highway no lion will ascend from the surrounding desert. The statement is categorical, a complete denial.

The following clause emphasizes the ravenous character of wild beasts. We may bring out the full force by rendering, *nothing ravenous of beasts,* i.e., no ravenous beast, none that tear and devour will ascend unto this way.[24] Those who walk or travel there will be the redeemed, and they alone. What a contrast to the conclusion of the preceding chapter! There, the inhabitants of Edom will be removed from their land, and only the doleful creatures of the desert will have occupation. Here, all obstacles

---

23 The f. suffix probably refers to the collective *highway* and *way*. The variety of gender is effective.

24 *ravenous beast—pᵉritz* is in the construct governing the noun, *ḥay-yôṭ.*

and hindrances will be removed from the land and only the redeemed, the rightful heirs of the promises, will walk in their land. The redeemed are those that have been delivered out of the hands of the enemy. Isaiah refers not merely to a physical deliverance, such as return from the exile, but, as the whole context shows, to a greater, even a spiritual deliverance. We may see the fulfillment of this prophecy in our Lord's words, "Be of good cheer, I have overcome the world" (John 16:33).

10 In this final verse the prophet sums up the promises of restoration and renewal. The ransomed of the Lord who have been far from Zion will now return in joy and thanksgiving. These ransomed are the ones whom the Lord has redeemed by delivering them from their bondage (cf. Deut. 7:8; 13:5; 2 Sam. 7:23; Mic. 6:4). There is no need, however, to eviscerate the word "ransom" of its meaning. It surely does designate those who are redeemed, but it is a different word from that used in the preceding verse. Hence, we may simply take it as meaning what it says. It refers to the redeemed as those who are "ransomed of the Lord," i.e., for them the Lord has paid a ransom. Alexander calls attention to the rendering of an old French version, *"ceux-la desquels l'Éternel aura payé la rançon."* This is entirely correct. For these redeemed ones the Lord has paid a ransom. In back of this word lies the idea of the payment of a price.

In their returning they will come to Zion. It seems quite likely that the basis of this manner of speech is actually the thought of a deliverance from the land in which the Israelites had been taken captive. Isaiah had predicted the coming of a hostile enemy and the carrying off of captives. The deliverance from that captivity would consist in a return to the land of promise. At this point, however, Isaiah is not merely predicting a return to Palestine from Mesopotamia. Although that return doubtless lies at the basis of this form of language, nevertheless, what the prophet has in view is a return to God in Jesus Christ, a spiritual turning unto God. "Ye turned to God from idols," writes Paul to the Thessalonians (1 Thess. 1:9). It is such a returning that is in view here. The whole tenor of the chapter has to do with a salvation from what is unclean and defiles. The highway in the desert is no mere physical road and it certainly is not the modern railway connecting Egypt with Palestine. It is the way that leads unto life eternal. As Good-will in *Pilgrim's Progress* said unto Christian, "Look before thee; dost

455

thou see this narrow way? That is the way thou must go: it was cast up by the Patriarchs, Prophets, Christ, and his Apostles; and it is as straight as a rule can make it: This is the way thou must go."

These ransomed ones will walk on the way with shouting, for they will know that the burden which would have precluded their entrance into the Holy City has been removed. They are not numbered among the unclean but among the ransomed of the Lord. On their heads, resting as a crown (cf. Ps. 8:6), will be an everlasting joy. In remarkable alliteration Isaiah expresses the thought that rejoicing and gladness will overtake them. During the time of oppression, rejoicing and gladness had been removed. There is no joy when one is in the thraldom of sin. Now, so long separated from them, rejoicing and gladness, as it were, pursue and overtake them to accompany them on their way to the Holy City.[25] On the other hand, the sorrow and sighing that had been their ever present companions now flee away. They do not merely depart; they flee, for they cannot be present with rejoicing and gladness. What a striking and blessed climax to the preceding chapters, 28–34! How glorious, how filled with eternal bliss, will be the future for God's redeemed! Isaiah has not yet risen to the heights of the New Testament revelation, although he will do so later. But he is preparing for the heart of the whole matter, the blessed thing that God will do to bring about these gifts for His own. He is pointing forward to the saving work of the Servant of the Lord. Behind all the beauty and the glory, the joy and gladness that rest upon the ransomed like a crown, is the suffering and death of God's Servant, Jesus the Christ.

25 It is also possible to construe *rejoicing* and *joy* as objects; *they* (i.e., the redeemed) *will overtake rejoicing and joy.*

IV. THE CONNECTING BRIDGE BETWEEN CHAPTERS 1—35 AND 40—66 (36—39)

A. THE CONCLUSION OF THE ASSYRIAN PERIOD (36, 37)

1. SENNACHERIB AND THE FIRST ATTEMPT OF THE EMPIRE OF MAN TO DESTROY THE KINGDOM OF GOD (36:1-22)

1 And it came to pass in the fourteenth year of King Hezekiah that Sennacherib the king of Assyria came up against all the fortified cities of Judah, and he took them.

2 And the king of Assyria sent Rabshakeh from Lachish to Jerusalem unto King Hezekiah with a strong army, and he stood by the ascent of the upper pool in the way of the field of the fuller.

3 And there went out unto him Eliakim the son of Hilkiah who was over the house, and Shebna the scribe, and Joach the son of Asaph the recorder.

1 With this thirty-sixth chapter we have reached a section of historical narrative which forms a connecting link or bridge between the first and second parts of the prophecy. Up through chapter thirty-five Isaiah had been dealing with the Assyrian period. At times, however, his eye had pierced beyond the circumscribing horizon that confined his own day, to the successor of Assyria, the later representative of man's empire, Babylon. Assyria's last great representative was Sennacherib, and so in chapters 36–37 he deals with that king. He proceeds then to face the future, and in chapter thirty-nine introduces Babylon, the kingdom that was to loom in the background during the latter part of his ministry. Chapters 36–37 look back to the Assyrian period, and chapters 38–39 point forward to the ascendancy of Babylon. In this beautiful manner, Isaiah bridges the gap between the two periods that form the background of his ministry.

The opening of this chapter is similar to that of chapter seven, the other chapter whose principal events also transpire at the "ascent of the upper pool in the way of the field of the fuller." Once before, Judah in the person of her king had stood at that spot of infamy, for there Ahaz had rejected the Word of God and had turned to Assyria. Assyria had come and had overrun Immanuel's land. In Judah, however, a new king had arisen, Hezekiah, a man of different stripe from Ahaz. He was a believer, and he too would be faced with decision at the same spot. Would he turn to the Lord for help, or would he simply rely upon the power of man? Was he another Ahaz?

The date of the events to be related is the fourteenth year of the reign of Hezekiah.[1] In distinction from Jerusalem, Sennacherib[2] turned his attention to all the fortified cities of Judah and captured them. Chronicles (2 Chron. 32:1) relates that the king encamped against these fortified cities and purposed to win them for himself. Lachish and Libna appear to have been exceptions. At least at the time when Sennacherib turned toward Jerusalem they had not been captured. The first verse is probably intended as an introductory, summary statement. In 37:8 the king is still warring against Lachish. For Sennacherib's own account of the invasion of Judah see the translation, Appendix III.

2 Cf. 2 Kings 18:14-16 which inserts three verses between verse 1 and the present verse. Cf. also 2 Chronicles 32:2-8. It would appear that Hezekiah had sent to the Assyrian king, again seeking his alliance and acknowledging his error in having renounced the treaty with Assyria. At the same time Hezekiah also took measures to protect the city's water supply. In answer to Hezekiah's request the Assyrian king Sennacherib sends the Rabshakeh to Jerusalem.[3] This is not a personal name, but the name of an office, which was evidently military; and here the Rabshakeh is a military official. In addition to the Rabshakeh, the account in Kings mentions the Tartan and Rabsaris, two other officials.

These men were sent from Lachish (the modern Tell ed-

1 According to Assyrian chronology Sennacherib's invasion of Palestine occurred in 701 B.C. Cf. "The Reign of Hezekiah" (Appendix I).
2 *Sennacherib came up*—cf. 7:1. The Assyrian name is ᵐᵈSîn-aḫḫê-errîba (Sin has increased the brothers), i.e., the god Sin has granted a substitute for the brothers that have died.
3 רב שָׁקֵה—lit., the chief cupbearer (*rab-šaqû*). Evidently the word refers to some official of military rank. Cf. the Hittite *GAL.GEŠTIN* (wine-chief). In The Annals of Muršiliš II, Nu-ua-an-za-aš is named as the *GAL.GEŠTIN*.

Duweir), southwest of Jerusalem, where Sennacherib at that time
was stationed (cf. 2 Kings 18:17 and 2 Chron. 32:9) and against
which he was laying siege. It was to Lachish that Hezekiah had sent
his own envoys (2 Kings 18:14). Sennacherib sends his men to
Jerusalem, but specifically to Hezekiah the king. The language of
the text carries us on the journey, as it were, first to Jerusalem, then
to the king, the real object of the mission.

Emphasis is placed upon the great army that accompanies the
Rabshakeh.[4] Possibly, however, this is to be taken in a somewhat
relative sense. Rabshakeh was sent more for the purpose of persuad-
ing the king than of actually occupying the city. He stood, i.e.,
halted, and took his stand at the base of his operations, at a place
where meetings may frequently have been held. Here it was that
Ahaz had rejected the Word of the Lord and the true King and
had turned to the Assyrian. Now, the Assyrian is here on this spot,
a reminder of Judah's faithlessness. In the background of the
entire episode stands Isaiah, the faithful prophet of the true,
promise-keeping God of Israel.

3 According to 2 Kings 18:18 the additional information is given
that the Assyrian king's envoys called out to Hezekiah, and in
response to this the representatives of the king came out. For a
discussion of the individuals involved and their offices, see the
comments on Isaiah 22:20ff. It is of note that Eliakim here
appears as Shebna's successor and that Shebna has an inferior
position. Shebna's office is that of scribe or writer, possibly a secre-
tary, although it is not possible to determine precisely what the
exact functions of this office were. Among the officials mentioned is
Joach, the son of Asaph, the recorder. Again, the exact significance of this office is not known, but see the comments on 22:20ff.
It is of interest to note that the father of both Eliakim and Joach is
mentioned, but to the name of Shebna, which stands between these
two, no father's name is added.

> 4 And Rabshakeh said unto them, Say now unto Hezekiah, Thus
> saith the great king, the king of Assyria, What is this confidence
> which thou hast trusted in?
> 5 I say, surely, the word of lips is counsel and strength for the war;

---

4 *with a great army*—the noun is in the const. before its adj.; cf. 1 Kings
10:2 and 2 Kings 6:14. For a recent discussion of the location cf. Gilbert Brunet,
"*Le Terrain aux Foulons*," in *RB*, Vol. 71, No. 2, April 1964, pp. 230-239.

now in whom hast thou confided, that thou hast rebelled against me?

6 Behold! thou hast trusted upon the stay of this broken reed, upon Egypt, which if a man leans upon it, then it comes in his hand and pierces it; so is Pharaoh, the king of Egypt to all who trust upon him.

7 And when thou sayest unto me, Unto the LORD our God we trust, is it not he whose high places and altars Hezekiah turned away, and he said to Judah and Jerusalem, Before this altar ye shall worship?

8 And now, exchange pledges, I pray, with my lord, the king of Assyria, and I shall give to thee two thousand horses, if thou art able to give for thyself riders upon them.

9 And how wilt thou turn aside the face of one governor of the least of my master's servants, when thou hast trusted for thyself upon Egypt for chariots and horsemen?

10 And now, is it without the LORD I have come up against this land to destroy it? The LORD said to me, Go up unto this land and destroy it.

4 Rudeness characterizes the Rabshakeh. Part of his title is Rab (chief, great one) ; but he is not great, for he is a man of rudeness. Immediately he commands the envoys to speak to Hezekiah, and in referring to the king does not even deign to designate him as king of Judah. Here is no courtesy, not even the sham courtesy that characterizes so much of diplomacy. Here rather is a blunt, impolite command. On the other hand, the Rabshakeh has no hesitation in referring to Sennacherib with the stereotyped monotonous phrase that the Assyrian kings themselves employed to designate themselves, "the great king, the king of Assyria."

An insulting question begins the message, a question containing a shade of depreciation. *What kind of a trust,* we may render. More than that, however, there is the tone of astonishment. It is as though Rabshakeh had said, "What has happened to you that you place your confidence in a reed as weak as Egypt? What kind of an object is that to trust in?" Rabshakeh speaks in the singular; he by-passes the three envoys and is concerned with the king alone.

5 Continuing with his insulting speech the Rabshakeh gives it as

5 1Q reads אמרתה. Hence, RSV, *do you think?* Cf. M. Weinfeld, "Cult Centralization in Israel in the Light of a Neo-Babylonian Analogy," *JNES,* Vol. 23, No. 3, p. 206.

his opinion (*I say*)[5] that the counsel and strength for war of Hezekiah is mere word of lips, i.e., vain talk. The Judahites have taken counsel and amassed strength, but all of this is no more than mere pretension and empty words. It will not avail against the might of Assyria. Another construction of the Rabshakeh's words is also possible. "Your confidence," we might paraphrase him as saying, "is mere word of lip. What is needed for war is counsel and might."[6] Of these two views the latter appears to have more in its favor.

Returning to his questioning, Rabshakeh then asks who it could possibly be that was worthy of trust so that Judah would rebel against Assyria. He speaks in the first person as though Hezekiah had rebelled against him personally.

6 Rabshakeh answers his own question, and calls attention to the answer with a *behold!* It is as though he had said, "You do not answer, but I tell you in whom you trust." He characterizes Egypt as a staff which is a broken reed.[7] Egypt was a land of reeds, so that the designation is particularly appropriate. What is in mind is the *arundo donax*, which grows along the banks of the Nile. To trust in a reed is foolish for it cannot support one; but to rely upon a reed that is bruised is more foolish, for it is no support at all. Such was Egypt and Pharaoh. Such a reed would only go into one's hand[8] and pierce it, so that the one who trusted in Egypt would come off worse than before. Later, Ezekiel takes up the same figure (Ezek. 29:6). This had happened to all who had put their confidence in Egypt. Consider Ephraim, "And the king of Assyria found conspiracy in Hoshea: for he had sent messengers to So (i.e., Sais) king of Egypt, and brought no present to the king of Assyria, as he had done year by year: therefore the king of Assyria shut him up, and bound him in prison" (2 Kings 17:4). Egypt had never proved to be an advantageous ally.

7 Suppose, however, that Judah trusted in Yahweh its God? Should Egypt prove to be false, would not Yahweh be a true support? The thought is: "And if thou shouldst say unto me, etc.,

---

6 *counsel and might*—this combination is Isaianic and speaks for the Isaianic origin of this section.

7 *the broken reed*—another Isaianic expression; cf. 42:3.

8 *then it comes*—the perf. with *waw* cons. has the force of introducing an apodosis.

461

then it is to be answered, etc."9 Rabshakeh had heard of Hezekiah's religious reform, how he had removed the high places and called men to worship before the altar of the Lord. He had sought for a centralization of the worship of Yahweh (cf. 2 Kings 18:4; 2 Chron. 31:1).10 Not really understanding the true nature of the situation, the Rabshakeh is actually reproving the king. The reference to the Lord is disparaging. Certainly, the Rabshakeh implies, He whose high places Hezekiah had removed could be of no help to the people at this time.

8 The time has come for a conclusion of the argument. *And now,* as a result of what I have been saying, *strike a bargain.* The verb means to exchange pledges, to engage with, to undertake together a common enterprise. The one with whom Hezekiah is to engage is none other than the master of Rabshakeh, the king of Assyria.11 Alluding to the paucity of horses in Judah, Rabshakeh declares that he will give to Hezekiah two thousand horses if Hezekiah on his part could provide two thousand men capable of serving as a cavalry.12 It was a tempting offer, for at that time Judah thought she could find safety in horses (cf. Isa. 30:16). In disobedience to the earlier promises (Deut. 17:16; 20:1) she looked to Egypt for horses (Isa. 31:1, 3). But Judah's cavalry could not stand up against the might of Assyria.

9 Rabshakeh believes that he has good grounds for continuing his argument and pressing it home. Inasmuch as matters are in such a condition, how can Hezekiah possibly turn away the face of one governor?13 Everything that is demanded must be granted. Hezekiah cannot refuse even one governor. Whatever is proposed

9 2 Kings has the plural, which fits better with *we have trusted.*
10 Note the order *Judah and Jerusalem* as in 1:1 and 2:1, and cf. the discussion of this phrase in note 13 to chap. 1. high places—these apparently were originally Canaanitish places of worship. During the time of Isaiah they had become centers of idolatrous worship which stood in opposition to the service of the Temple. As the name *bāmāh* suggests, they were often erected upon hill tops. Cf. *New Bible Dictionary,* Grand Rapids and London, 1962, pp. 525f.; W. F. Albright, "The High Place in Ancient Palestine," Supplement to *VT,* Vol. 4, 1957, pp. 242-258; A. von Gall, *Altisraelitische Kultstatten,* 1898; L. J. Vincent, "La notion biblique du haut-lien," *RB,* Vol. 55, 1948, pp. 245-278, 438-445.
11 *the king of*—a noun in the const. may take the definite article. It is also possible for the noun to be absolute.
12 *and I shall give*—the imp. with cohortative *He* expresses determination.
13 *one prefect*—the noun is in the const. before the numeral *one.*

to him, he must accept; he can reject nothing! Surely if the Assyrian king himself would demand, Hezekiah would be forced to grant his demand. But the same applies even to the governors of the smallest, most insignificant of the king's servants. Even their demands Hezekiah must grant! He can turn none of them away. It would be difficult to express more cogently the complete dependence of Hezekiah upon Assyria. And yet, Judah trusted in Egypt with respect to horses and chariots.[14] The last words of the verse show the utter futility of what Judah was doing.[15]

10 As though to add to the fear and dismay of the Judahites, the Rabshakeh announces that he has come up against Jerusalem with the help of the God in whom they claimed to trust. It need not be assumed, as some have done, that the Assyrian actually had knowledge of Isaiah's prophecies respecting Assyria. Rather, this is a bold stroke, a daring attempt to terrorize the Jews. Even their God is against them and on the side of the attacker. Rabshakeh makes no pretense about his purpose in coming against Jerusalem. He is to destroy Jerusalem, and in this attempt he believes the Lord is with him. Indeed, he claims that the Lord commanded him to go up and to destroy Jerusalem. Possibly also the Rabshakeh, seeing how events were going, actually believed that the God of the Jews had deserted them and that all things were now on his side.[16]

11 And Eliakim and Shebna and Joach said unto Rabshakeh, Speak now unto thy servants in Aramaic, for we understand it, and do not speak unto us in Judean, in the ears of the people that are upon the wall.

12 And Rabshakeh said, Is it unto thy master and unto thee that my master hath sent me to speak these words; is it not unto the men who sit upon the wall to eat their own dung and to drink their own urine with you?

13 And Rabshakeh stood and cried with a loud voice in Judean, and he said, Hear the words of the great king, the king of Assyria.

14 Thus saith the king, Let not Hezekiah deceive you, for he is not able to deliver you.

14 לך—*for thyself*; the ethical dative of advantage after an imp. with *waw* consecutive.
15 *with reference to*—the *Lamed* introduces a loose connection with the verbal idea.
16 Penna aptly calls attention to an inscription of Cyrus, in which he claims that the god Marduk is with him; cf. *ANET*, p. 315b.

15 And let not Hezekiah cause you to trust in the LORD, saying, The LORD will surely deliver us, this city will not be given unto the hand of the king of Assyria.

16 Hearken not unto Hezekiah, for thus saith the king of Assyria, Make with me a blessing, and come out unto me and eat, each one his vine and each one his fig tree, and drink each one the water of his well.

17 Until I come and take you unto a land like your land, a land of corn and wine, a land of bread and vineyards.

18 Lest Hezekiah seduce you, saying, The LORD will deliver us. Did the gods of the nations deliver each his land from the hand of the king of Assyria?

19 Where are the gods of Hamath and Arpad? Where are the gods of Sepharvaim? and when was it that they delivered Samaria from my hand?

20 Who among all the gods of these lands is there who delivered their land from my hand, that the LORD should deliver Jerusalem from my hand?

21 And they kept still, and did not answer him a word, for it was the commandment of the king, saying, Ye shall not answer him.

11 Realizing that the words of the Rabshakeh will only cause terror and consternation in the hearts of the men who hear them, the envoys of Hezekiah request the Rabshakeh to speak in Aramaic.[17] Their command is polite; nevertheless, it is a command. At that time, Aramaic would be understood by the envoys; and it is assumed that Rabshakeh himself could speak it.[18] It was even at this time the common language of diplomacy. At the same time, the common citizens and soldiers would probably not have been able to understand it. Inasmuch as the northern kingdom was no longer in independent existence, the Hebrew language could now rightly be called "Jewish." Some of the older commentators (e.g., Gesenius, Hitzig) thought that the word "Jewish" was an indication of late date, and presupposed a time long after the downfall of Israel. This does not necessarily follow. Even though the ten tribes had only been in captivity for a few years, there had been hostility between Judah and Israel throughout

---

17 ויאמר—the verb is singular with a plural subject. This idiom is sufficiently common in Hebrew, and there is no need to place the verb in the plural.

18 שמעים‎—lit., for hearing are we; i.e., "when we hear the language we understand it." The subj. follows the part. in order that stress may rest upon the idea that the part. conveys.

their history. It is quite possible that since the time of the great schism under Jereboam the son of Nebat, the southern kingdom began to designate its language by the term "Y^ehudith."

That Aramaic was widely used in the eighth century before Christ can no longer be doubted. We may note the Aramaic inscriptions of Sefire as an example of the use of this language.[19] That the Rabshakeh was able to speak Hebrew is a tribute to his learning and knowledge. The Jews were dealing with a man who knew how to employ psychology well to accomplish his own purposes.

12 Rabshakeh's reply bristles with haughty disdain. Apparently Eliakim had acted in the capacity of an ambassador for Hezekiah, for Rabshakeh employs the singular, as though speaking to one man alone. Rabshakeh, however, would seize the situation and be master of it. No mere ambassador of Hezekiah was going to lay down the terms in which the message would be presented. "My message," he says in effect, "is not for thy master (i.e., Hezekiah), nor is it for thee." Rabshakeh makes a forceful contrast between "thy master," and "my master," which the following rendering seeks to bring out. "Is it unto thy master there hath sent me my master?" The message of Sennacherib was to be addressed to the ordinary men of the city, who were then sitting on the walls in order that they might know the severity of the famine to come. An interesting change of prepositions occurs. In the first question, Rabshakeh uses the word "unto" ('el). Now he employs another preposition, "concerning" ('al). He is not sent unto Hezekiah, but with respect to the people on the wall. His message concerns them. Apparently a number of the inhabitants out of mere curiosity were at the time seated on the wall to hear what was going on. Rabshakeh refers to them merely as representative of the inhabitants. It is possible, however, that he makes an allusion to men ready to defend the city, and so suggests that the cruelest kind of famine and hardship will overtake them. Ordinary food will be so lacking that the men will be compelled to eat[20] their own filth.[21]

---

[19] Cf. J. A. Fitzmeyer, "The Aramaic Inscriptions of Sefire I and II," *JAOS*, Vol. 81, No. 3, pp. 178-222.

[20] *to eat*—We may paraphrase, "with respect to the fact that they must eat, etc."

[21] *their dung.* The two terms translated *dung* and *urine* are found combined only here and in 2 Kings 18:27. The Q^ere sought to modify the ex-

The expressions are revolting, but the Rabshakeh probably chose them purposely to paint the famine in its most revolting and disgusting form. He speaks with assurance, as though his master Sennacherib had control of the situation. But he does not know the entire truth, for God's purpose was not to destroy the people entirely (cf. Isa. 30:20).

13 Translating his haughty words into haughty action, Rabshakeh now addresses the people themselves. This was as effective a humiliation as can be imagined. Hezekiah's officials are by-passed completely, and Rabshakeh acts as though they are not present. Whether the first verb means that he simply raised his voice or whether it suggests, as is probable, that the Rabshakeh took a particular position from which to speak, may be difficult to determine. At any rate, we may be sure that he stood in such a position as to focus attention upon himself. In this position and in these words the voice and attitude of Satan are manifest. It is the kingdom of man, unregenerate, self-sufficient man, that now speaks, confident that Yahweh is merely a god like other gods and can be embraced in man's empire. To heighten the infamy Rabshakeh raises his voice, and speaks in the language that the inhabitants of Judah would understand. He is about to lay down an ultimatum.[22]

14 Nevertheless, Rabshakeh is not speaking in his own name or by his own authority. What he says is the message of the king, and he reminds his audience of this fact. In his inaugural vision Isaiah had seen the King, the Lord of hosts; and it was that King to whom Isaiah was seeking to turn the people. Now, the world power commands the city of God to listen to its king, not Yahweh, but the man who sat upon the throne of the would-be ecumenical empire.

To hearken to such a king is to listen to words of falsehood and

---

pressions with *their filth* and *the water of their feet*. As far as the *Kᵉtiv* is concerned the consonants should probably be pointed *ḥar-'e-hem* and *šēy-nēy-hem*. The suggested pointing (e.g. *BH*) *hᵃ-rā-'ē-hem* introduces a naturally long *Qametz* in a distant open syllable, and for this there seems to be no evidence. Syriac has *ḥar-yo'*, Ar. *ḥur*, Amharic *ḥa-ru*.

22 *the words of*—In 2 Kings 18:28 we have *dᵉ-ḇar, the word of*. The singular conceives of the following command as a unit, whereas the plural of Isaiah calls attention to the ultimatum as a number of explanations and individual statements.

deceit. The force of the language may be expressed as follows: "Let not Hezekiah engage in deception upon you."[23] Rabshakeh uses the dative case, as though to suggest that Hezekiah might arouse hopes that would deceive. "Hezekiah," so we may paraphrase, "will seek to arouse in you (or, for you) a hope of deliverance. This is treacherous and deceptive, for he is not able to fulfill his promises and to bring deliverance." Thus, Rabshakeh accuses the king of entertaining illusions as to his own power and position. Insofar, however, as Hezekiah's confidence reposed in Yahweh, as Yahweh's will had been expressed through the prophet Isaiah, his assurance that the city would be saved was justifiable, nor would one be deceived who placed his trust therein.

15 As a particular instance of the manner in which Hezekiah would supposedly deceive the people, the Rabshakeh singles out the thought of placing one's confidence in the Lord.[24] "May he not cause you to trust in the Lord." That, of all things, would be most deceptive. Wicked men regard confidence in God as the height of folly. One thing certainly cannot save, Rabshakeh would say, and that is to place one's confidence in Yahweh. And yet, the Rabshakeh has accurately analyzed the true nature of the religion of Hezekiah; it was a confidence reposed in the God of Israel,[25] a confidence that Yahweh would remember His promises and not permit His city to be delivered into the hands of the king of Assyria. Nevertheless, Rabshakeh was wrong. In His own time, God would permit His city to be delivered into the hands of another representative of the world kingdom, even Nebuchadnezzar; but it was not His will for Jerusalem to fall into the hands of the first nation in the world empire. That haughty nation boasted of its plans and purposes, but it would not carry them out as far as Jerusalem was concerned. Seeking to be worldwide, it nevertheless, at each step, was subject to the power of Yahweh, the God of Israel. Jerusalem was to be delivered up, not when Assyria desired it, but when Yahweh was ready.

16 Rabshakeh now gives the particulars of his demands. He first repeats his prohibition not to hearken unto Hezekiah, for he well

---

23 *he will deceive*—If this form is intended to be a jussive, it is written with naturally long *Ḥireq*.

24 The negative אל has a tone of depreciation or dissuasion when used with the jussive.

25 The confidence is emphasized by the use of the inf. absolute.

understands that if the people listen to their own king, they will pay no attention to the king of Assyria.[26] He then turns to a positive message. There must be no hearkening unto Hezekiah and no trusting in Yahweh's power to deliver the city; but there is something that the king does demand, and this demand is strengthened by "Thus saith the king." Rabshakeh speaks as though there were no other king. When the king of Assyria speaks, all men are to hearken. He first requires that they make a blessing with him. The language is difficult, for the word "blessing" is not used in this sense elsewhere in the Old Testament. It would seem that the Rabshakeh intends that the inhabitants are to enter into a relationship with the Assyrian king that would be a blessing for both parties. In other words, he probably means simply that they should conclude an agreement with the king, or enter into peaceful relationship with him.

The willingness to conclude such a pact will be shown by the willingness of the people to come out from the city to the envoy and then to return to their own manner of living.[27] We need not necessarily think that people had forsaken their homes and sought protection within the walls of the city, although some may have done this. But the Rabshakeh's words simply promise a return to the normal manner of life, if the people will surrender to him. The vine, fig tree, and water from the well signified the abundance of daily life, forming a sharp contrast with the prospects offered in verse 12; and the boasting words of the Rabshakeh imply that the Assyrian king had the power of granting these.

17 A certain frankness appears now in the language of the Assyrian envoy. The condition of normal living that he promises is not to continue forever, but only until the Assyrian king comes and takes the people away.[28] It has been supposed by some that Sennacherib must first conclude his Egyptian compaign and then return to take the people away. Whether this is actually the case or not, is difficult to say. What the Rabshakeh means is that if the

26 המלך—in 1Q the article is omitted; cf. v. 8.

27 צאו—expresses the consequences of the condition contained in עשו, thus, make etc., and ye shall then go out. These consequences are continued by the following imperatives.

28 באי—my coming and I shall take; i.e., until I come and take. The construction of an inf. with a prep. is continued, not by a second co-ordinating inf., but by a finite verb in the perf. with waw consecutive. B renders accurately ἕως ἂν ἔλθω καί λάβω.

people will submit to him they can continue on in their accustomed mode of life until the Assyrian king is ready to take them into exile.

Rabshakeh's description of the land of deportation is interesting. He wishes to make it clear that this land will be as sufficiently productive as the Jews' own land. His language is not necessarily ironical; indeed, in part it may be true. What he desires to convey to the people of Jerusalem is the thought that the land to which they will be deported is one that can compare with their present land in productiveness. Such a condition would also benefit the conqueror. Apparently, later, some Jews were content to remain in that land, for Daniel was among those who did not return to Palestine when the opportunity was offered.

18 Apparently Rabshakeh is aware of the hold that Hezekiah had over his people, for again he must warn against Hezekiah's deceiving them.[29] Isaiah had already prophesied that the Assyrian would speak in the haughty manner here represented; cf. 10:9ff. Rabshakeh's reasoning is clear. If the gods of other cities were not able to deliver those cities, why should it be thought that Yahweh, the God of the Jews, would be able to deliver Jerusalem? To Rabshakeh all gods were alike; all were equally impotent before the king of Assyria. There was but one who did according to his will, one who could carry out his purposes, not the gods of the nations, nor Yahweh of Jerusalem, but the great king of Assyria. Penna suggests that this is not necessarily a denial of the power or capability of God, but simply an assertion that this is no time to expect miracles. But it would seem that the Rabshakeh is confident that the God whom the Jews worship is no more able to save than were the gods of the nations round about.[30]

19 The sense of these questions may either be, "Where now are the gods of these various lands? What has happened to them, for since I have attacked their countries they have disappeared," or else, "Where were the gods of the various lands at the time that I attacked them?" The latter sense is probably to be preferred. In other words, the Rabshakeh is not asking what has become of the gods of these different countries, but where they were at the time

---

[29] *seduce—Hiphil* 3 m.s., usually derived from סות, *to incite, allure, instigate.*
[30] Hitzig appears to be correct in his assertion that in vv. 7, 10, Rabshakeh denied God's will to save, whereas here he denies God's power.

when they should have defended their lands. When he attacked, those gods should have been present to deliver; but they were not. Where, then, were they? The sense is really the same as that expressed in 19:12, "Where then are thy wise men?" Just as these gods were not present at the time when help was needed, so Yahweh also will not be present to help when Jerusalem needs that help. Sargon had occupied the Syrian city of Hamath in 720 and Tiglath-pileser had entered Arpad in 740. Both of these are mentioned in 10:9. Sepharvaim was probably in north Syria, but its identity is not certain.[31]

The remainder of the sentence is best understood as containing an elipsis. "And where were the gods of the other nations, that they should have delivered Samaria from my hand?" In 10:11 Samaria had also been mentioned in connection with Jerusalem.

20 Rabshakeh lays his emphasis upon the word *my hand*. The hand or power of the Assyrian king was uppermost in his mind. Against that power no god could stand. "Who among all the gods of these lands," he asks, "delivered their land from my hand? All of these lands that I have conquered," so we may paraphrase, "had gods; but at the decisive moment, each of these gods proved impotent to deliver." Rabshakeh gives expression to the widespread belief of antiquity that deliverance from a foe was the business of a god. Inasmuch, therefore, as no one of all these gods was able to deliver his land, Yahweh cannot deliver Jerusalem. In the eyes of Rabshakeh, Yahweh is on a par with all the gods of antiquity. The devils believe and tremble; but the Rabshakeh, blinded by the power of the Assyrian king, thinks that the God against whom he is to fight is as impotent as the gods that are the creation of men's hands.

21 Rabshakeh's address to the men on the wall did not have the desired effect. The verb probably refers to the three envoys in the first place, but it is not clear that a reference to the men on the walls is entirely excluded. Hezekiah, however, was unwilling to stoop to reply to insults such as those which had been heaped upon his

---

31 Some have sought to identify Sepharvaim with the Sibraim of Ezek. 47:16, but this is doubtful. The locality was conquered by the Assyrians, and its inhabitants sent to colonize Samaria after the deportation of the Israelites; cf. 2 Kings 17:24, 31; 18:34.

God. There are times when the best answer to blasphemy is a disdainful silence, and this seems to have been such a time. A reproof would have fallen flat before the Rabshakeh. History would show that even at this moment, Yahweh, whom he despised and denied, was in actual control of the entire situation. Rabshakeh, in his boasting and haughtiness, is not successful.

22 And there came Eliakim the son of Hilkiah who was over the house, and Shebna the Scribe and Joach the son of Asaph the Recorder unto Hezekiah with rent garments, and they made known to him the words of Rabshakeh.

22 At the same time the three envoys are unhappy and express their mourning by means of the rent garments.[32] In such a state they approach the king. The rent clothes would be a sign of distress not merely over the message that must be brought to the king, but also over the fact that God had been blasphemed, and that Jerusalem was threatened.

32 Lit., *rent of garments;* i.e., *with rent garments.* The gen. expresses the area in which the rent is found.

471

2. THE FAILURE OF THE FIRST ATTEMPT TO DESTROY THE KINGDOM OF GOD (37:1-38)

1 And it came to pass when the king Hezekiah heard, that he rent his garments and he covered himself with sackcloth and he came to the house of the LORD.

2 And he sent Eliakim who was over the house and Shebna the scribe and the elders of the priests covered with sackcloth unto Isaiah the son of Amoz the prophet.

3 And they said unto him, Thus saith Hezekiah. A day of anguish and rebuke and contempt is this day, for the children are come to the birth, and there is not strength to bring forth.

4 Perhaps the LORD thy God will hear the words of Rabshakeh, whom the king of Assyria his lord hath sent to reproach the living God, and he will rebuke the words which the LORD thy God hath heard, and thou shalt lift up a prayer on behalf of the remnant that is found.

1 The narrative continues without interruption. At the official report of Rabshakeh's speech, Hezekiah also puts on sackcloth and enters the Temple. It is true that in ancient times a king in need would enter a temple; but Hezekiah goes to the Temple because it is the dwelling of the "living" God, and there he may pray. Prayer was connected with sacrifice; and hence the Temple, the place where sacrifice was offered, was most suitable for approaching God. The veil of the Temple had not yet been rent in twain. Hezekiah knows the right thing to do in time of need. Rending his clothes and putting on sackcloth represent a true penitence and contriteness of heart, and in this condition he would go to seek the face of the Lord. Happy the nation that has such a ruler.

2 Hezekiah's piety is truly exemplary, for not only does he himself engage in prayer, but he also seeks the Word of God through the mouth of the prophet (Deut. 18:18). In the envoy that he sends, Joach is not mentioned (cf. 36:3, 11, 22), but instead the elders of the priests. The reference is not to the personal age, i.e.,

472

the eldest of the priests, but rather to the chiefs or heads of the sacerdotal groups.

Hezekiah does not send to Isaiah merely to procure his participation in the lamentation, but rather to learn what the Word of God is in this given situation. In this particular time of distress Isaiah was the only one to whom the king might turn.

The nobility of Isaiah may possibly be seen in that the king sends an envoy to consult him, an envoy that even included the priestly leaders. That it was not Isaiah in his private capacity who was to be consulted is apparent from the designation employed, *the prophet.* Hezekiah desired to hear the prophet speak as mouthpiece of God. Hence, he surrounds his request with the reverence and dignity that is due the prophet as a spokesman for God. In reality Hezekiah is approaching the King, the Lord of hosts; and therefore he sends in a formal and respectful manner.

3 In accordance with Hezekiah's command, the envoys speak unto Isaiah. There is no need first to record the giving of the command, for they themselves state that they are speaking what had been enjoined upon them. As Alexander observes, "the details of the command are to be gathered from the record of its execution."

In language similar to that of 22:5, Hezekiah describes the day. It is first a day of anguish. The word used implies not only trouble from without, the oppression of the Assyrians, but the whole distress and pain of heart, manifesting itself both in external and internal anguish, which the tragic situation involved. By *rebuke* or *correction* there is reference not so much to the blasphemies of Rabshakeh as to the rebuke of God Himself, for the calamities that enemies might inflict were regarded often as punishments from God. Hosea employs the word in a similar sense; cf. 5:9. Cf. also Psalm 149:7. It is furthermore a day of *contempt* or *contumely,* in that now the theocratic nation is contemned of Yahweh. What a contrast this forms to Isaiah's cry in chapter one, "They have contemned the Holy One of Israel" (v. 4). For a contemning of Yahweh, such as Judah had been guilty of, leads in time to Yahweh's contemning His people. What is meant is clearly expressed in Deuteronomy 32:18ff.; cf. also Jeremiah 14:21 and Lamentations 2:6. Perhaps these words are an acknowledgment that Hezekiah had been foolish in earlier submitting to the Assyrians. Possibly, however, they simply point out that the whole policy of yielding to Assyria, begun by Ahaz, was now bearing its fruits. In gaining Assyria, Judah became an object of contempt in Yahweh's eyes. Whereas on the part of many the day may have been one of distress because of the presence of the Assyrians, for Hezekiah the distress was probably deeper. He saw that the real calamity lay not so much in the presence of a physical enemy as in the displeasure of the Lord that now was being visited upon the nation. It is a spiritual need, and Hezekiah turns to Isaiah, the only one to whom he could turn and the only one from whom he will receive spiritual help.

The king compares the present situation with that of a pregnant woman who is about to bear and yet is unable to do so. The children about to be born have come to the place of breach, i.e., the mouth of the womb (cf. Hos. 13:13); but there is not the strength to bring them forth. The emphatic word in the last clause is "strength."[1] We may render, *sons have come to the birth, and strength, it is not present for the bringing forth.*[2] The metaphor pictures extreme distress, need, and suffering, and above all the fact that the intervention of extraordinary help is needed. In reality it is a cry of utter acknowledgment that God's help is required. If the womb does not open so that the child can be born, the child will die and probably the mother also. So, unless strength is at hand to deliver Judah, she too will perish.

4 Hezekiah's words probably reveal also a certain amount of shame at the policies that had been followed, such as the trust that Judah had placed in the weak reed of Egypt. Hence his "perhaps." It is a word in which hope is expressed. "Perhaps, despite our sin and folly, the true God will hear our prayer, and take cognizance of the plight in which we are." To hear the words of Rabshakeh would be not merely to hear them spoken but to take notice of them with intention to punish. Such a hearing on God's part is sometimes mentioned in a good sense, as in Exodus 2:24; 3:7, where God has heard the cry of His people in bondage and has come down to help them. Here, however, God hears the blasphemous words for the sake of punishing the one who utters them.

There is restraint and reverence in Hezekiah's designation, "Yahweh thy God," for it acknowledges that Isaiah stands in a

---

1 *strength*—The absolute אין always follows the word negated.
2 *lēḏāh*—a *Qal* inf. const. with feminine ending for *le-ḏeṭ*. Cf. also *dē-'āh;* Ex. 2:4; Jer. 13:21; Hos. 9:11.

peculiar relationship to God. He was God's mouthpiece, who spoke forth the words that God commanded him. Furthermore, he was a faithful servant of his God, whom he loved as "the Holy One of Israel." Hezekiah does not mean to imply that Yahweh is not his own God nor that He is no longer the God of the nation, but he does recognize that in a particular and unique sense, Yahweh is Isaiah's God. Perhaps too, his language implies that he and his people have not been as faithful to God as has Isaiah.

At least Hezekiah does recognize that the God of Isaiah is the living God, and he purposely employs this designation to set forth the contrast with the blasphemy of Rabshakeh.[3] This blasphemy had consisted in the fact that Rabshakeh regarded Yahweh as simply one god among many. Hezekiah, however, knows that He is the living God; and henceforth, all other gods are dead, i.e., nonexistent. It is therefore the hope of the king that the living God will rebuke in that He will punish for the words of reproach that He has heard.[4]

Hezekiah further states specifically what he desires Isaiah to do. He is to lift up a prayer on behalf of the remnant present. The language signifies more than the mere utterance of a prayer; it has reference to the expressions, "to lift the voice" and "to lift up the heart." Isaiah is thus commanded earnestly to lift up unto God the desire of his heart on behalf of his people. It was thus to Isaiah in his capacity as prophet that Hezekiah turned. Like Abraham, he was a prophet, whose prayer was effective (cf. Gen. 20:7).

It is not perfectly clear what Hezekiah had in mind in speaking of the remnant, but it would seem that the word is here used in a sense different from elsewhere in Isaiah. Here it probably refers to Jerusalem in distinction from the remainder of the country, inasmuch as only Jerusalem now remains. Or, it may be taken in a general sense to indicate all who remain.

5 And the servants of King Hezekiah came unto Isaiah.

6 And Isaiah said unto them, Thus ye shall say unto your lord, Thus saith the LORD, Fear not before the words that thou hast

---

[3] Thus David also had spoken against the blasphemy of Goliath, 1 Sam. 17:26, 36.

[4] *and he will rebuke for the words*—i.e., on account of the words of Rabshakeh, God will rebuke. The rebuke will probably take the form of chastisement, so that Drechsler's rendering, *Züchtigung vornehmen,* correctly brings out the thought.

heard wherewith the soldiers of the king of Assyria have blasphemed me.

7 Behold! I am about to place in him a spirit, and he will hear a report and will return unto his land, and I shall cause him to fall by the sword in his land.

5 The verb of this verse need not suggest that· it describes something subsequent to what has just been stated. Rather, this is parallel to the preceding. The thought can be brought out in English by rendering, *So the servants came to Isaiah.* The verse therefore is not mere repetition, but gives the whole thought in succinct and compact manner and so prepares for the following verse.

6 Isaiah's reply is authoritative, simple, direct, and encouraging, and contains a striking contrast. "Thus ye shall say" forms a contrast with "Thus the Lord has said." The messengers are to repeat what God has already told His prophet. It is authoritative for it is spoken by God. It is thus not merely Isaiah's own opinion with which we have to do. The message is simple and practical, immediately commanding the king not to fear. In similar manner Isaiah had once spoken to Ahaz (7:4; note also 41:10, 14). As in that case, so here also, there is no ground for fear. The blasphemous words have been spoken by the soldiers of the Assyrian king.[5] In so designating them Isaiah probably uses a tone of disdain. They are really young men, not the highest officials of the Assyrian. Only soldiers, young men at that, have spoken words of blasphemy. These words have been directed against God Himself.

7 Isaiah now gives the reason for his utterance. The blasphemous words have been spoken, but the Assyrian king is powerless against the King of glory. God will act in that He will place within the king a spirit that will cause him to return to his home. Elsewhere also, Isaiah has spoken of the giving of a "spirit." In 19:14 he declared that Yahweh had mingled a perverse spirit in the midst of Egypt, and again in 29:10 he remarks that Yahweh has poured out a spirit of deep sleep. In the present instance the word does not mean "intention" or "will" but rather seems to refer to a compulsion or power sent by God which influences a man's conduct and thought. The reference is not to anything specific, such as

---

5 אשר—*with which.* The instrument of the action is here regarded as its remote object.

fear or terror, but rather simply to a general impulsion placed in the human mind by God, compelling to action.[6] "Then shall the Assyrian fall with the sword," Isaiah had earlier said (30:8, 9), "not of a mighty man; and the sword, not of a mean man, shall devour him: but he shall flee from the sword, and his young men shall be discomfited. And he shall pass over to his strong hold for fear, and his princes shall be afraid of the ensign, saith the LORD, whose fire is in Zion, and his furnace in Jerusalem."

Sennacherib is also said to hear a report. The word simply means, *That which is heard.* Often it is thought that the reference is to Tirhaqah's approach, but the news of that approach simply led Sennacherib to send messengers to Hezekiah demanding his surrender (cf. vv. 9ff.). It would seem more likely that the report was one that came to the king from some other part of his vast empire, such as Nineveh or Babylon.

The phrase "and he shall return" is to be closely connected with what precedes, so that we are to understand the returning to Nineveh as a consequence of what Sennacherib hears. It is to be noted that at this point Isaiah says nothing about the great catastrophe that will soon fall upon the Assyrian army. The reason for this may quite possibly be due to a desire to strengthen the faith of Hezekiah. It is not necessary at once to tell the king everything. Sufficient for him if he knows that God will take the enemy king from the land. If he will believe the plain Word of God that Sennacherib will return to his own land, his faith is indeed strong. Later he will see the wondrous power of God in bringing about the downfall of the army, and the event that the Lord will use to turn the Assyrian from Judea.

One final detail is added to complete the picture. It does not follow that Isaiah is asserting Sennacherib's death immediately upon his return to Assyria. Isaiah's purpose is not to recount everything concerning the king but only those details which it is essential for Hezekiah to know. As a matter of fact Sennacherib was not killed for twenty years or so later. What is important is not the time but the fact of his death.

> 8 And Rabshakeh returned and he found the king of Assyria fighting against Libnah, for he had heard that he had fled from Lachish.

6 Calvin interprets of a wind or whirlwind which God used to drive Sennacherib away.

9 And he heard concerning Tirhaqah, king of Ethiopia, saying, He
has gone out to fight with thee; and he hearkened, and he sent
messengers unto Hezekiah, saying:

8 It is of interest to note that nothing is said about a report
given to Rabshakeh. We are left to infer that Hezekiah's refusal of
his demands had been conveyed to him. Thus, the narrative gains
in strength, relating simply that he returned. Rabshakeh alone is
mentioned as the principal representative of the Assyrians. He
went to Libnah, for word had come to him that Sennacherib had
decamped from Lachish.[7] Although Sennacherib himself in his
inscription does not mention Lachish, a relief in the British
Museum shows the king besieging that city (see *ANEP*, pp.
129-132). Evidently thinking that Rabshakeh could bring about
capitulation upon Hezekiah's part, Sennacherib continued his
work of attack, now turning his attention to Libnah, a village
mentioned several times in the Old Testament (cf. Josh. 10:
29, 31ff.; 12:15; 15:42; Jer. 52:1). It was of significance as a city
of refuge. Libnah was probably situated in the Shephelah at the
mouth of the Vale of Elah, and is generally identified with Tell
es-Safi (cf. the Alba Specula of the Crusaders), although Tell Bor-
nat, somewhat further south, has also been proposed as the site. It
would thus appear that having escaped from Lachish, Sennacherib
was marching toward the north; and Rabshakeh went to meet him
on his northward march, a march that was possibly undertaken
with Jerusalem as its goal.

9 Abruptly a change of subject is introduced. It is Sennacherib
who hears about the approach of Tirhaqah. Tirhaqah was the
most famous ruler of the twenty-fifth dynasty (the so-called Ethiopian dynasty), who succeeded Shabataka in 690 B.C. and reigned
until 664 B.C. It has been held that Tirhaqah was born about 710
B.C. and thus would not have been able to command an army in
701. This argument is not necessarily conclusive, however (see
Appendix I, "The Reign of Hezekiah"). In all probability
Tirhaqah is here called king proleptically. One cannot be certain of
the date of his birth; for one thing his father Pianki died in 710
B.C. Inasmuch as the chronology of the time is so complicated, it
seems the part of wisdom simply to acknowledge that we do not yet
know all the facts.

---

[7] Cf. the order in Josh. 10:29-32.

Scripture does not say whether Tirhaqah actually had set out against Sennacherib; it merely relates that the latter had heard that such was the case. At any rate, this very rumor, whether true or not, was sufficient to cause the Assyrian king to send envoys to Hezekiah with renewed demands for surrender. It does not cause him to abandon his campaign and return to Nineveh. If Tirhaqah were approaching, it would be necessary to have Jerusalem on his side; a hostile Jerusalem at his rear might indeed cause a serious threat, and Sennacherib therefore immediately takes action to bring Hezekiah around.

10 Thus ye shall speak unto Hezekiah the king of Judah, saying, Let not thy God in whom thou trustest deceive thee saying, Jerusalem will not be given into the hand of the king of Assyria.

11 Behold! thou hast heard what the kings of Assyria have done to all the lands to devote them to destruction, and thou, wilt thou be delivered?

12 Did the gods of the nations deliver them, which my fathers destroyed, Gozan and Haran, and Rezeph, and the children of Eden which were in Telassar?

13 Where is the king of Hamath and the king of Arpad, and the king of the city Sepharvaim, Hennah and Ivvah?

10 Sennacherib mentions Hezekiah as king of Judah, thus paying a certain amount of respect, for his intention now was not to destroy the nation's confidence in Hezekiah but rather Hezekiah's confidence in God. Sennacherib concentrates upon the point that Rabshakeh had already made in 36:18-20. Inasmuch as Yahweh had given Hezekiah advice contrary to that of the Assyrians, Yahweh was "deceiving" Hezekiah. Hezekiah, however, had placed confidence in Yahweh, and manifested this confidence by the assertion that Jerusalem would not be destroyed. The words "Jerusalem will not be given into the hands of the king of Assyria" are best construed with the preceding "trusting," and thus represent the thought of Hezekiah, rather than the statement of God. The King James Version prefers the latter construction, and the Revised Standard Version is even stronger. Hezekiah's confidence, of course, was based upon the revelation that God had given to him through His prophet Isaiah. Quite possibly also the reply to the Rabshakeh had made it clear that Hezekiah was trusting in his God to deliver him and Jerusalem.

11 Sennacherib then calls attention to defeats that Hezekiah

479

would know about. By the introductory word "behold!" he implies that these defeats were indeed well known and indisputable. It is as though he has said, "You know well enough what my ancestors have done." He adds effectiveness to his statement by using the personal pronoun, "thou." The word is emphatic and implies that at least Hezekiah knew of these things, even if some of the ordinary citizens of his country did not. Sennacherib attributes to his ancestors what Rabshakeh had attributed to Sennacherib himself.

The king uses a term that expresses the complete destruction of an enemy territory. From the religious standpoint the enemy land is regarded as unclean and must therefore be placed under the ban and dedicated to destruction.[8] It was this attitude that Sennacherib's ancestors had toward the lands that they conquered. Believing that they were fighting in the strength of Asshur their lord, they regarded these lands as devoted to destruction and did not rest content until they had thoroughly destroyed them.

What reason would there then be for Hezekiah to think that he could be delivered, when all these other lands had been destroyed? Implied in this question is also the thought that the god of Hezekiah was not as powerful as the gods who were with Sennacherib. The Assyrian king is perfectly willing to regard this as a contest of the gods, a warfare between Yahweh and his own deities.

12 To justify the question that concluded the preceding verse, Sennacherib immediately asks another. The gods of the nations that were destroyed were not able to save them, he reasons; why then should you be delivered? Thus there is implied that the God of Hezekiah was no more powerful than the gods of the nations. Sennacherib's list of nations is shorter than that of Rabshakeh, and it is notable for its omission of Samaria. Gozan is mentioned also in 2 Kings 17:6 and 18:11 as a river by which the exiles were placed. The term Guzana is found on Assyrian texts as the name of a location south of Nisibis and east of Haran. Haran is well known because of its connection with Abraham (cf. Gen. 11:31; 12:5; 27:43); it is situated on the river Balikh. Reseph has been identified with the Akkadian Rasappa, and is possibly to be identified

---

[8] Thus Ashurbanipal, e.g., states his purpose with respect to Egypt, *a-na da-a-ki, ḫa-ba-a-te ù e-kem mât Mu-ṣur il-li-ka ṣiru-uš-šu-un*, for the sake of killing, plundering and taking away the land of Egypt he came against them (first campaign).

with the present Rusafe between Palmyra and the Euphrates. The
sons of Eden (i.e., *Bene Eden*) is along the middle Euphrates, and
Telassar is in Mesopotamia, the word evidently referring to a
district.

13 Like Rabshakeh the king asks some rhetorical questions. Instead, however, of inquiring where the gods of certain lands were,
he uses the word "king." The answer to these questions is that these
kings have now disappeared; at one time they resisted the Assyrian,
but they are now conquered, and have vanished from the scene. Of
particular interest is the manner in which Sennacherib speaks of
Sepharvaim. He does not ask, "Where is the king of the city of
Sepharvaim?" but rather, "And a king of the city of Sepharvaim,
where is he?"[9] The last two cities (cf. 2 Kings 18:34; 19:13) are
unknown. Evidently the king does not deem them worthy of having possessed a particular king. If there was a king of these cities,
where is he now?

> 14 And Hezekiah took the letter from the hand of the messengers and
> he read it, and he went up to the house of the LORD, and Hezekiah
> spread it out before the LORD.
>
> 15 And Hezekiah prayed unto the LORD, saying:

14 Up to this point no mention has been made of letters, and it
is impossible to state whether the communication had been
confined to letter or whether it had also been delivered orally.
Quite possibly it had been uttered orally or read to the king by the
envoys. At any rate, Hezekiah now receives the letter from the
messengers. This seems best to agree with 2 Chronicles 32:16, 17,
which makes mention both of Sennacherib's servants speaking
against the Lord, and of the Assyrian king writing letters. The
word translated *letters* is plural, possibly because the sheet was
folded into several pages. The plural word, however, like the
Latin *litterae*, simply designates a letter.[10] Hezekiah first read the
letter, and then had recourse to the one source of true help, his
God. He spread out the letter before the Lord, not that the Lord

---

9 לעיר—*and a king to the city Sepharvaim*, i.e., with respect to the city.
Where is a king who would identify himself with the city Sepharvaim? Possibly,
however, the *Lamed* may be rendered *from*.

10 Lit., *the books*, possibly a roll of papyrus or parchment; cf. Jer. 36:2.
For examples of letters written in cuneiform, cf. *ANET*, pp. 482-490. For the
Mari letters cf. Claus Westermann, *Grundformen prophetischer Rede*, 1960,
pp. 82-91.

might read it, but by way of supplication. Isaiah does not state how Hezekiah did this, whether he himself was prostrate on the floor of the Temple and placed the letter before him, or whether he placed the letter on the altar. The action is symbolical, in which the king places before God all his need; it is furthermore an action of childlike trust, for the king is confident that God will come to his aid. It goes without saying that God knows our needs before we make them known to Him; indeed, He knows them better than we ourselves (Matt. 6:8). But God would have His own come to Him with their problems and perplexities. Hezekiah acted as a true child of God should act.

15 The prayer that Hezekiah offered on the previous occasion is not recorded; at that time it was sufficient to state that the king had entered the Temple. The renewed demand, in the form of a written communication from Sennacherib himself, caused Hezekiah to understand that the Assyrian king would seek to depose him. Instead of immediately answering the letter, the king really prays that God will provide the answer. How different Hezekiah's action is from that of Ahaz! The latter will not ask for a sign in obedience to the prophecy given by God. He would rather rely upon human defenses, such as the aid of Tiglath-pileser. Hezekiah, however, betakes himself to prayer. But we are not to think of the king as an impractical dreamer. Hezekiah prayed, as he should have done, for in the last analysis, only God could help. At the same time in 2 Kings 20:20 we read of his practical activities, "and how he made a pool, and a conduit, and brought water into the city. . . ." Here then was a faith that manifested itself in works.

16 O Lord of hosts, God of Israel, who dwelleth between the cherubim, Thou art the God alone of all the kingdoms of earth, thou hast made heaven and earth.

17 Incline, O Lord, thine ear and hear; open, O Lord, thine eyes and see, and hear all the words of Sennacherib which he hath sent to reproach the living God.

18 It is true, O Lord, the kings of Assyria have laid waste all the lands and their land.

19 And hath given their god in the fire, for they were no gods, but the work of the hands of men, wood and stone, and they have destroyed them.

20 And now, O Lord, our God, save us from his hand, that all the kingdoms of the earth may know that thou art the Lord alone.

16 This prayer is the outpouring of a truly adoring heart. Hezekiah immediately addresses God as Yahweh, the Name of redemption and covenant, the Name that identifies the true God as the God of Israel. He then adds the epithet "of hosts," a combination of words frequent in the prophetical books but rarely occurring in the historical ones. Here the word calls attention to the almighty power of God. Next, Hezekiah identifies His god as the "God of Israel." Here is a king speaking to his God, a king who, unlike his Assyrian enemy, boasts not of himself, but of his God. Hezekiah chooses his introductory words so as to pay the highest honor to the God whom he worships.

The next phrase is difficult. Literally translated, it is, *who sits the cherubim*, or *the sitter of the cherubim*. Hezekiah is not intending to identify God with the cherubim, but probably is referring to the dwelling place of God between the cherubim over the ark of the covenant. Thus the God of Israel manifested Himself as Israel's God. The cherubim were winged-like figures that overspread the mercy seat of the ark of the covenant in the Holy of Holies. By means of the reference to the cherubim Hezekiah is in no sense entertaining crass thoughts of God. He well knows that God is not limited or bound to a specific locality; he does not place God in the category of the idols whom Sennacherib worships. But God Himself had chosen the Temple to be His dwelling place that He might be in the midst of His people. The Temple then signified to Israel that God was in her midst. In making this reference to the cherubim, Hezekiah is merely reminding himself that God is present with him in the beleagured city of Jerusalem. Sennacherib thought that he had shut up Hezekiah in Jerusalem "like a bird in a cage" (See Appendix III), but God was with Hezekiah in that city. Sennacherib's boastings were vain indeed.

That the king did not entertain false notions of the God whom he worshipped may be seen from the following phrase, "Thou art He, the God." In thus using the definite article before "God" Hezekiah is asserting that His God is the true one. The whole phrase simply means, "Thou art the true God" (cf. 2 Sam. 7:28; Isa. 43:25; 51:12, etc.). To this the king adds the word, "alone," and thus exhibits as strong an affirmation of true monotheism as can be found anywhere in Scripture. This monotheism, however, expresses itself in a particular matter. It is with respect to all the kingdoms of the earth that God shows Himself to be the only true God. Hezekiah really uses a circumlocution for the genitive case. What he means is that as far as all the kingdoms are concerned the God of Israel, Yahweh, is the true God; and so the gods of these kingdoms are nothing but vain idols, incapable of acting for their welfare.

Then follows a noble affirmation of the fact of creation. This is denied to Isaiah by Duhm and others who are under the influence of a certain theory of the development of Israel's religion. But it must be remembered that Israel did not in her own strength attain unto her ideas of God; rather these conceptions were made known to Israel by God. There is no reason why Hezekiah might not have spoken as he did; what he says is simply based upon the fact of creation revealed in the first verse of Genesis. In his prayer Hezekiah inserts the personal pronoun, as though to say, "Thou, and no other; thou alone, hast made heaven and earth." It is through the creation that Yahweh is seen to be the true God. "For all the gods of the heathen are idols, but the LORD made the heavens" (Ps. 96:5). By this reference to the creation Hezekiah intends to understand that God who has created all things will continue His work, not allowing it to be destroyed by an enemy such as the Assyrian king.

17 With this verse the petition to God begins. It is expressed in five imperatives, commanding God to incline, twice to hear, to open (His eyes), and to see. This does not mean that God is ignorant of what the Assyrians are seeking to do; it is tantamount to saying, "Act as though thou didst see and hear." The imperatives imply an effective, accompanying action. "Incline (lit., stretch) thine ear, and act as one whose ear has heard what is transpiring."

It is not merely to the contents of the letter that the king had spread out before him that the imperatives are intended to refer. Rather, Hezekiah desires the Lord to take into cognizance the entire situation in which Hezekiah and his people then found themselves. Hezekiah in faith believed that God had inclined His ear, else he would not have entered the Temple to pray. What he means by these commands is that he would earnestly beseech God to take notice of the situation. Often in prayer we urge God to hear us, not that we believe He does not hear, but simply to express our importunity and the need that God give to us an answer. ". . . We frequently speak in such a manner," says Calvin, "as if we thought that God was absent or did not attend to our afflictions." Hezekiah mentions both the ear and eyes, for he wants God wholly to notice the condition of affairs.

The reason for the prayer is clearly stated. Sennacherib has sent to blaspheme the living God, and it is the blasphemous words directed against the living God that Hezekiah wishes God to notice. It appears then that the king's first and primary concern was not for the welfare of himself and his country but for the glory of God. Sennacherib had blasphemed God in uttering his reviling words. He himself evidently thought that Yahweh could not punish these words. To him Yahweh was but the national God of the Judahites, impotent to defend his honor. But Hezekiah knows that the God who dwells between the cherubim is actually the Creator of heaven and earth, and to blaspheme that living God is to incur His wrath. Hezekiah is concerned for the honor of God. He shows himself a true and good king of the theocracy.

18 The first word may be rendered, *to be sure, indeed, true* (German, *allerdings*). The word is a concessive particle, and acknowledges the truth of what Sennacherib had been saying, namely, that he had conquered the lands round about. He did indeed conquer them, Hezekiah admits. The following words, "all the lands and their land," have occasioned much difficulty. The parallel passage in 2 Kings reads "all the nations and their land." Various expedients have been proposed to solve the difficulty, but quite probably Isaiah simply means "all the nations of the lands and their land."[11] It is a usage similar to that found in Genesis 6:11, 12, which speaks of the earth as corrupt, instead of saying that the inhabitants of earth were corrupt. Thus, Hezekiah is acknowledging that Sennacherib and his hosts have laid waste the inhabitants of the lands and their lands themselves.

19 Hezekiah continues his description of what the Assyrians have done.[12] Not only have they wasted the inhabitants of the lands and their land but they have also given their gods into the fire. They have simply consigned the idols of these nations and lands to the fire to destroy them. This they could do, Hezekiah explains, for these gods were simply no gods at all but the work of men's hands, wood and stone. Hezekiah very clearly asserts that a true God cannot be the work of men's hands. That which men have made is

---

11 Rosenmüller, "genies et terram earum. *Eadem metonymia Genes,* VI 11. 12. I Sam. XIV, 29. terra *pro* terrae incolis ponitur."

12 *wᵉ-nā-ṭón*—the inf. abs. may continue the narration indicated by a finite verb and may also take a direct object. Cf. also Isa. 22:13.

no god, and hence the Assyrians could easily consign them to the fire. Furthermore, these idols were material, made of wood or stone, and hence no gods. The true God is not material but spiritual.

20 The introductory word "now" introduces the conclusion of the prayer, and seems to have logical force. "Now," we may paraphrase the thought, "inasmuch as what has just been stated is so, do Thou act." Sennacherib has blasphemed the God of Israel and he has destroyed many nations; God, therefore, should arise to vindicate His Name and to deliver His own people. Hezekiah addresses God as Yahweh, for Yahweh is the One who delivered Israel from Egypt and chose her to be His people. This Yahweh is our God, in distinction from the gods of other nations. Perhaps in the utterance of the words "our God" there is an expression of hope and confidence. Hezekiah knows that the gods of the destroyed lands could not have helped; but the God of his people was the living God who could do what to dead idols was impossible.

The prayer itself is simple and direct, "save us from his hand." It is a confession of human impotence, a recognition of the true nature of the situation, and a complete casting of oneself and one's hope on Yahweh the God of Israel. It is also a prayer of faith and confidence, uttered in the assurance that God can do what must be done. As Calvin points out, the king now rises above the fear with which he has struggled; he is sure that his God can deliver. The hand of Sennacherib signifies his power. Hezekiah well realized that he was actually in the power of the Assyrian king. That he himself had made this possible probably tortured his soul, but he knows that One can free him from that power.

Hezekiah's concern, however, is not primarily for himself but for the honor of God's Name. He desires deliverance so that all the kingdoms of the earth may know that God is Yahweh alone. The last words are capable of a double construction. They either may be rendered, *that thou, Yahweh, art the only one,* in which case they call attention to Yahweh as the alone true God, or they can be rendered, *that thou art Yahweh alone,* in which case they call attention to the import of the name Yahweh with all its rich significance. Either of these constructions has much to commend it, although it may be noticed that the Masoretic accentuation supports the first. To say that "thou Yahweh art alone," is to say that

there is no other God besides Yahweh. Hezekiah's exclusiveness
must be noted. He is not willing that Yahweh should share a place
with other gods. He would reject all other gods and hence all other
religions. He was not willing that everyone should worship as he
saw fit. Yahweh was not one God among many; He was alone, the
only God beside whom there was no other. Revealed religion is
exclusive; God demands absolute obedience and submission, for
Yahweh is alone.

21 And Isaiah the son of Amoz sent unto Hezekiah saying, Thus
saith the LORD, God of Israel, In that thou hast prayed unto me
concerning Sennacherib the king of Assyria,

22 This is the word that the LORD hath spoken concerning him, There
hath despised thee, hath laughed at thee to scorn the virgin daughter of Zion; after thee has the daughter of Jerusalem shaken her
head.

23 Whom hast thou reproached and blasphemed? and against whom
hast thou lifted up the voice and raised on high thine eyes unto
the Holy One of Israel?

21 God begins right away to answer the prayer in that His prophet sends a message to Hezekiah. Oftentimes the prophet went
directly to the person concerned, but here he chooses to send the
reply to Hezekiah by a messenger. Quite probably this reply was in
writing; at least its contents and form would seem to suggest that
such was the case. If this is so, it may be that Isaiah deliberately
chose thus to write so that the written Word of God would stand in
contrast to the blasphemous fleeting word of the Assyrian king.

It is not without significance that Isaiah designates Yahweh as the
God of Israel. This corresponds to what the king himself had
uttered in his prayer and assures the king that he is now receiving
the Word of the God who is truly "our God." The concluding
words of the verse contain the protasis, the apodosis following in
the subsequent verses. In the protasis we may note that both the
fact of Hezekiah's prayer and its content are stated as well as the
Source to which the prayer is directed, "Inasmuch as thou hast
prayed unto me concerning Sennacherib the king of Assyria."

22 There now follows, written in poetic parallelism, one of the
most majestic and stately of Isaiah's prophecies. He introduces and
describes it as a word that Yahweh has spoken, thus calling attention to its character as a verbal or propositional revelation. The
message begins with a verb in which the reaction of God's people to

Sennacherib is clearly depicted. To bring out the force, we may render, *There has despised with respect to thee; there has mocked with respect to thee.*[13] Thus the verb sets forth the general proposition, and the specific particular follows. Israel's despising and her mocking have channeled themselves toward Sennacherib. Isaiah identifies the nation as the virgin, daughter of Zion.[14] The people are a virgin and a daughter, who belong to Zion, for Zion is the dwelling place of Yahweh. By the term "virgin," the prophet probably alludes to the inaccessibility of Zion, which will not be touched by the "base ruffian and infamous robber" (Calvin; cf. 23:12).

In the second line of the parallelism, the first words, "after thee," lend color to the description. It is as though the prophet had said, "After thee, as thou art running away, Jerusalem shakes her head in scorn."[15] It is an act of depreciation, as though to say, inasmuch as he is what he is the enemy must flee; he cannot do otherwise. He is not able to carry out his evil designs. The inhabitants of Jerusalem, in other words, simply look with scorn upon the attempts of Sennacherib.

23 Jerusalem's disdain is a sign of her faith. She knows her God but Sennacherib does not. Her boasting, therefore, is in the Lord. In verses 4 and 17 the verb "to reproach" has occurred; now it appears again. Whom does Sennacherib think that he has reproached and reviled? Does he think that he has been uttering boastful words against an empty vanity like the gods of the nations whom he and his fathers had conquered?[16] Those gods had disappeared, for they were no-gods; they had never really been on hand. Now, however, Sennacherib is face to face with a situation entirely new to him. He is dealing with the living God. Whom does he think he has reviled? It is a pertinent question and very relevant.

---

13 Drechsler notes that *bûz* is generally used with the acc. rather than with the dative, and *bāzāh* the opposite; *she has shown contempt with respect to thee.*

14 For the explanation of this construction cf. footnote 22 to chapter 23.

15 Note the anarthrous usage of ראש and its emphatic position before the verb.

16 Rosenmüller well interprets, "Do you not know, O miserable one, to whom you have brought injury? do you not know how great a crime you have committed?" (*nescis, O miser, cui convitiatus sis? ignoras, quantum scelus conmiseris?*).

This blasphemy was not done in a quiet manner, but in the open. The voice was raised in defiance and the eyes were lifted up to heaven where God dwelt. Sennacherib, as it were, would look God in the face when he uttered his blasphemies. His contempt for God was great, for it was founded on an ignorance of God. The devils believe and tremble. Sennacherib did not believe, for he did not know enough to believe, and therefore he did not tremble. He was boastful instead. Boasting blasphemy based upon ignorance can only lead to destruction.

What is particularly tragic in the whole picture is that Sennacherib lifted up his eyes to the Holy One of Israel. Isaiah himself had once seen this Holy One seated upon a throne, high and lifted up. But Isaiah's sight had caused him to cry out in dismay over his own sin; Sennacherib lifts up his eyes but does not see the Holy One of Israel. He is blind; he knows not the true God. His sin therefore is the greater; his blasphemy is directed against that One whom Isaiah reverenced and served.

24 By the hand of thy servants thou hast mocked the Lord, and thou hast said, By the multitude of my chariots I have ascended the height of the mountains, the sides of Lebanon, and I cut off its high cedars, the choice of its cypresses, and I came to its extreme height, the forest of its Carmel.

25 I dug wells and I drank waters, and dried up by the sole of my foot all the streams of Egypt.

26 Hast thou not heard from afar (that) I have done it; from days of old that I have formed it; now have brought it to pass, that fortified cities should become laying in waste, ruinous heaps?

27 And their inhabitants, short of strength, are dismayed and confounded; they are the herb of the field and the greenness of grass, grass on the roofs, even blighted before it has grown.

24 Isaiah now answers the questions that he has just raised. For the sake of emphasis he places first the words, *by the hand of thy servants.* The reference is to the blasphemous approach of Rabshakeh and the messengers, and stands in contrast to *the Lord.* Isaiah deliberately chooses a word that sets forth the power of God. Sennacherib has sent forth his *servants* to blaspheme the one who was truly *the Master.* The passage does not deny that the king himself had blasphemed, but it points out the height of his iniquity in that it shows him as willing to use servants to blaspheme the true God, and thus more clearly to express his reproach and contempt for God.

and thou didst say—Isaiah now sets forth the basic thought that has guided all of Sennacherib's actions.[17] The king relied alone on material might. In his language the word "multitude" is prominent. Sennacherib has a multitude of chariots, and therefore is sure that he can do as he wishes. He does not realize that he is but an instrument in the hands of the Almighty God, the true *'adon,* but is deceived into thinking that his own power and weapons can accomplish his desires. There is an interesting alliteration between *rov* and *rikbi* (*multitude of my chariots*), and the chariots are singled out for mention because they well represented the wealth of the army in fighting power. Sennacherib himself in his inscriptions spoke of chariots. Chariots would of course be most suitable for use in a flat country (cf. Judg. 1:19; Isa. 22:7), but that thought is not here in view. An army rich in chariots is a powerful army, and only for that reason are they mentioned. The king does not intend to reflect upon the actual method by which the Lebanon mountains are ascended. The chariots were an occasion for boasting, for the king stresses the pronoun, *I.* It is as though he said, "I have ascended the Lebanon, I and no other. No one else deserves praise for this feat." Likewise in his own inscriptions Sennacherib is quite lavish with the use of the first person pronoun. His glorious army has made it possible to ascend the very height of the mountains, even the extremities of Lebanon. No peak was too high, no pass too difficult for him.

The following clauses are not coordinate but subordinate, and probably express purpose, *that I might cut down.* By the phrase, *the height of its cedars,* is simply meant *its high cedars.* This arrangement of the words lends a particular emphasis to the concept of height. In the following words the same construction appears; *the choice of its cypresses* means *its choice cypresses.*[18]

By means of figurative language the king now sets forth the actual goal of his journeys. He would go to the height of its extremity (i.e., to its extreme height) and to the forest of its fruitful field (i.e., a forest that forms a fruitful field). But to what does the language refer? In what sense is it used? For one thing, the constant employment of the preterites in this and the following

---

17 In summing up Sennacherib's thought the prophet seems to reflect upon the actual language that the Assyrian kings used.

18 *choice of*—the noun in the const. before a partitive gen. conveys an attributive idea.

verse supports the idea that the events described have actually occurred in the past.

If, however, Sennacherib is speaking of something that is past, what does he have in mind? He himself did not ascend the heights of the Lebanese mountains with chariots. It would seem rather that in these words the spirit of Assyria is set forth, the spirit that is convinced that it can conquer all things. Lebanon stands for the highest and most inaccessible of places; evidently the term is broadly used to cover all the western coast lands, and in this sense it may be said to be figurative. Sennacherib is boasting that he has taken the western lands, and that no obstacle is too great for his power and might.

25 Again Sennacherib calls attention to himself. His military excursions were not without difficulties, for he and his armies had to go into waterless wastelands. Such wastelands, arid as they were, were nevertheless no obstacle for the Assyrian king. He dug water when it was necessary and drank it. Just as high mountains and the extremities of Lebanon had been no hindrance to his armies, so also the dry, parched desert land could not keep water away from him. Whenever the earth, in one form or another, stood in his way, he overcame it and made it subservient to his purposes. One man, the Assyrian king, stands against nature, confident that he can always overcome it.

Consequent upon the king's digging, he dried out all the Niles of Egypt with the soles of his steps or footprints. He is not referring so much to his troops as to an action of his own, for he continues to take the credit for himself. The Niles are the streams of the Delta, the great obstacle to anyone who would take Egypt. For Sennacherib, however, the Niles are no obstacle. He simply treads upon them and dries them up. His confidence is further seen in the word "all" which he uses before "the Niles." Not one of the many streams of the Delta can stand in his way. In its entirety the country is affected by his presence. Sennacherib mentions different parts of the landscape in order to show the completeness of his power; heights of the mountains, the deserts, and the rivers. He speaks of the north (Lebanon) and the south (Egypt) to show how all-embracing his work was. And his description would have been filled with meaning for the people of Jerusalem. Before them stood a world conqueror.

26 It was wrong for Sennacherib to act boastfully. In God's

491

hands the Assyrian was but an instrument, designed from of old to carry out God's purposes of punishment toward His chosen people. It became the Assyrians therefore to act with great humility. Instead, they acted as though they had control of the entire situation and were doing according to their own will. In place of acknowledging the sacredness of their task and giving glory to God, they boasted as though all had been done in their own strength and by their own might.

This was foolish, for they should have known of God's purposes. The question with which this verse begins is really addressed to the Assyrian. At the same time it is intended for Hezekiah and the people of Judah that they too may know the meaning of the events that are transpiring. All should have heard concerning these things, for they were not esoteric matters to be learned only by long and laborious investigation. Rather, they had already been proclaimed by the prophets, and they were truths out in the open. They should have been heard. Included in the question also is an element of surprise that anyone could be ignorant of these well-known truths.

What is transpiring is not something new, but was present in the eternal counsels of God. *from afar*—I.e., long ago.[19] God has not recently devised this plan, but accomplished it from afar, away off, i.e., from eternity. What the Assyrian has done in climbing Lebanon, obtaining water from the desert, drying up the Niles, etc. is something that God long ago had determined upon. The thought is made particularly vivid by the language, "I did it." Parallel to this expression is the statement, "from days of old, and I formed it." Included in these verbs is the thought of the devising of the plan. It was performed by God in that it was His work, and it was formed by Him in that He devised it.

It is perfectly true that in themselves the words "from afar" and "from days of old" do not indicate eternity. Nevertheless, it is the context that shows that the reference is to the eternal counsel of God. The entire Old Testament militates against the conception of a God who is subject to time and space. The things that occur on this earth are the outworking of a purpose and plan that God devised in eternity before the foundation of the world. Yahweh did not devise this plan somewhere early in Israel's history; He devised

19 למרחוק—*from afar*. In this combination the *Lamed* either indicates specification, *with respect to being from afar,* or else it is used as a synonym of *min, from.*

it in eternity.[20] What Sennacherib is now doing and has been doing is simply the carrying out of the eternal purpose of God. God has foreordained whatsoever comes to pass, and that is also true with respect to Sennacherib and the Assyrian invasions.

Now, however, the time has arrived for God's plan to be executed; and for that reason, Sennacherib is permitted to come to Palestine. The suffix of the verb refers to the plan of God. Now God has brought it to pass, in order that fortified cities be laid waste in desolate heaps.[21] The fortified cities are those of Judah and elsewhere that feel the attack of the Assyrian. They are to be changed into the very opposite of what they now are, namely, into ruined heaps. Sennacherib himself speaks of turning cities into ruins.[22] In other words, the work of devastation which Sennacherib has accomplished and is accomplishing in Palestine and which the other Assyrian kings before him have accomplished is the carrying out of God's eternal plan. God had determined that this devastation must go on even until Jerusalem itself should finally perish. But God's decrees are not capricious; there was a reason for this work of the Assyrian. In all of this God was showing Himself faithful to His wondrous promise of salvation. The theocracy had now sunk so low that it was a blemish. It must suffer the humility of exile and live as a servant, that God might again bring it into its land and give to it the Messiah. At the same time God was teaching the world a lesson through the destruction of Judah and the haughtiness of the Assyrian (and the later-following Babylonians). That lesson can be simply and clearly stated. Even when God's own people sin they must be punished. God is no respecter of persons. He once drove the Canaanites from the land that He might carry out His plan of redemption; now, Israel herself is a Canaanite as

---

20 ויצרתיה—*so have I formed it.* After a preceding isolated portion of the sentence, particularly when it designates time, *waw* cons. may thus be translated. Perhaps the *waw* is emphatic, "Indeed, I have formed it." Cf. *Biblische Zeitschrift*, Vol. 8, 1964, p. 106.

21 ותהי—the weak *waw* here expresses purpose after a preterite. The following inf. may be translated periphrastically, *what there is to lay waste*, freely, *that you might be laying waste*. The whole construction may be taken as a passive, *that fortified cities might be destroyed as desolate heaps.* This construes the *ú-ṭe-hi* as third person. The inf. is followed by an acc. of the product before the proper obj., i.e., *to lay waste fortified cities into desolate heaps.*

22 E.g., in the second campaign (against the Kassites), Sennacherib speaks of turning the cities into ruins (*u-še-me kar-miš*). In the sixth campaign, "To mounds and ruins I turned (them)" (*a-na tilli ú kar-me u-tir*).

far as sin is concerned, and hence she too must be put out of the land that the purposes of redemption may be fulfilled. In executing God's will Sennacherib was a haughty, sinful instrument. He did not learn from Israel, nor did he pay attention to the purposes of God as these had been made known through the prophets. And hence, Sennacherib will fail. He will fail in that he himself will not conquer Jerusalem and also in that he will die.

27 This verse connects immediately with the preceding in thought. Isaiah has just described the effect of the destructive force of the Assyrian might on the cities themselves. Now he turns to the consequences of that power on the inhabitants of the cities. Actually, the words *and their inhabitants* are to be connected in thought with *I have caused it to come* in the preceding verse. God's action, in other words, brings it about that the inhabitants of the cities that the Assyrians lay waste are themselves short of hands. It is for the sake of emphasis that the inhabitants are mentioned first. In his boasting the Assyrian claimed: "And I have put down the inhabitants like a valiant *man*..." (cf. Isa. 10:13, 14).

The words *short of hand* indicate a condition of powerlessness. The hand cannot reach the necessary length to accomplish what it desires. Cf. Isaiah 50:2; 59:1 and also Numbers 11:23. The expression does not imply that the hands are weak or that they have been mutilated, but simply that they are too short to accomplish what is necessary. The two following verbs actually serve to explain the expression. The people are broken and so not able to continue; they are confused, in that they do not understand what has taken place.

Isaiah compares the Assyrian onrush to the eastern Sirocco, which brings harmful consequences to both plants and animals. As herbs of the fields and green grass cannot withstand the strength of the destructive wind or storm, so were the people of the conquered nations. In Scripture mankind is often compared with grass; cf. Isaiah 40:6-8; Psalm 37:2; 90:5, 6; 103:15, 16. And Isaiah had earlier spoken of the failing of grass, and the lack of any green thing (cf. 15:6). The *grass of the roofs* is grass that "withereth afore it groweth up" (Ps. 129:6). The oriental roof is flat and has no depth of earth; before the scorching sun and the violent wind, such grass cannot live any length of time.

As the last words of the text stand, they are to be translated, "as a field before the standing corn." This would suggest that the field, i.e., the corn growing in the field, before it has come into the stalk, is weak and easily destroyed. All the comparisons herein employed serve to show how fragile and weak were the inhabitants of the cities that the Assyrians had conquered.[23]

28 And thy sitting down and thy going out and thy coming in I know, and thine exciting thyself against me.

29 Because of thine exciting thyself against me, and thy arrogance has come up into my ears, I will put my hook in thy nose, and my bridle in thy lips, and I will cause thee to return by the way by which thou camest.

30 And this will be the sign to thee: eat this year that which groweth of itself, and the second year that which springeth of the same; and in the third year sow ye and reap, and plant vineyards, and eat the fruit thereof.

28 God through His prophet now addresses Sennacherib directly. His words show that He is fully acquainted with all that the Assyrian does. The phrases *thy going out and thy coming in* are commonly used in the Old Testament to express the entirety of a person's activity. For the sake of fullness and emphasis, however, an additional phrase is here added, *thy sitting down.* (Cf. Deut. 28:6; 1 Kings 3:7; Ps. 121:8, etc. Ps. 139:2 speaks of "downsitting and uprising.") The actions of the Assyrians are in no sense hidden from God. God's knowledge therefore is more than mere acquaintance. Indeed, the verb "know" is used with pregnant sense. It implies a previous action with respect to the Assyrian (cf. Ps. 139, which is really a commentary upon the verb "know"). God has foredetermined all that the Assyrian will do. In the deepest sense He is acquainted with all Sennacherib's ways. Nothing that the Assyrian king does can come as a surprise to God, for God Himself decreed the actions of the king.

Almost as an afterthought there is added the statement, *and thine exciting thyself against me.* In these words Isaiah comprehends the purpose of all Sennacherib's actions. This king was directing his movements against the Lord, Yahweh, the God of Judah. Isaiah, by the mere statement of the situation, shows how great a folly it is to set oneself against God, for one is not acting as a sovereign, independent power, but rather as subject to God and

---

[23] For a discussion of the text in the light of 1Q, cf. Greenberg, "Text of the Hebrew Bible," *JAOS*, Vol. 76, No. 3, 1956, p. 164; Millar Burrows, *BASOR*, No. 111, 1948, p. 23; No. 113, 1949, p. 28.

under His control. Even the plans of men to overthrow the Most
High are predetermined of Him and are in His hand. How purposeless then were the machinations and actions of Sennacherib!
Indeed, how purposeless are the efforts of all wicked men to oppose
God! And how great is the comfort that comes to God's own when
they realize that He knows all that wicked men are doing. What a
wealth of comfort and assurance in those words: *I know!*

29 Again God refers to the exciting of oneself against Him and
adds mention of the confidence that accompanies it. In other
words, in Sennacherib's action there was manifested an arrogance
against God. Sennacherib was sure of himself, confident that he
could carry through what he had undertaken. This had come up
into God's ears—a strong way of saying that God had heard of it
and knew about it. It was not something of which He was ignorant; and hence, He must take action against it. "The more furious-
ly wicked men rise up against God, and the more outrageous the
violence by which they are actuated, so much the more is he wont
eventually to set himself in opposition to them" (Calvin).

Sennacherib's sin requires that he be stopped. God will treat him
as He would a horse or ox that must be halted. God will place
His hook in the nose of the king, thus to subdue and to tame him
and to treat him as His prisoner. There are illustrations on the
Assyrian monuments that depict the prisoners being led by a cord
or rope attached to a ring in the nose or in the upper lip.[24] From
this time on Sennacherib will be compelled to cease his boasting,
and will be led about as a beast with the bridle. He will be the
Lord's prisoner, restrained in his movements, compelled to abandon the siege upon Jerusalem and to return to his land. Thus, as
God's prisoner, he will be caused to return to his land by the same
way by which he came.

What must not be overlooked is the wondrous mercy of God to
His people. It was God's purpose to save the world through a
Redeemer. When His own nation, the theocracy, became so wick-
ed that it must be destroyed, God permitted the Assyrian to appear
upon the scene. It was His purpose to use the Mesopotamians as
instruments to carry out His work of punishing the theocracy.
Hence, He first permits Tiglath-pileser III to do his work, and then
Sennacherib. But there had been godly sorrow upon the part of

---

[24] Illustrations depicting the binding of prisoners are found in *ANEP.*

Hezekiah. Hence, God is willing to allow a respite. The real reason why Sennacherib was not allowed to destroy the theocracy lies in Hezekiah's reformation. God had not abandoned His ultimate purpose, but He holds it off, that His people may truly turn from their sins. Sennacherib is not to carry out the work of destruction. He must return to his own land, not having accomplished his desire toward the theocracy. Thus, God's mercy is manifest, and His people should have turned toward Him. But Hezekiah was followed by Manasseh, and wickedness once again soon prevailed. It was best for the world that the theocracy be destroyed; and finally that was done, but not by Sennacherib. How closely related are sin and judgment! Repentance keeps the judgment at bay; but unless that repentance is genuine, the judgment will surely follow. How well for His people that God's sovereignty shines forth in these verses!

30 Isaiah continues in the second person, but now addresses his remarks to a different object. His speech is still address, but he no longer speaks to the Assyrians. It is Hezekiah to whom he now turns. Furthermore, the character of the language completely changes. In the preceding verse it had been that of threat, a declaration of the humiliation of the Assyrians; now it becomes language of comfort to the king of Judah. Isaiah uses a well-known formula to express the truth that God will give a sign that the prophet's words are true. It is a sign that has reference to Hezekiah, and is for his benefit. In itself the sign is simply a pledge or an attestation that something promised will come to pass.

The present language must be compared with the sign offered to Ahaz. Ahaz had been granted the opportunity of choosing a sign but had refused. Therefore, the Lord took matters out of his hand and gave a sign to the people, to be fulfilled in the birth of the Messiah. Now, however, God simply states what the sign will be. With respect to Ahaz, we are led to expect that the sign will either be a miracle or something extraordinary; in the present instance it is not particularly necessary that the sign should be a miracle.

The essence of the sign is expressed by the concept "eating." Isaiah uses the infinitive absolute in place of the imperative or a finite verb, for the infinitive absolute brings out well the essential nature of the sign. It is not the eating this year or the next, but eating in itself that constitutes the sign. That eating is expressed differently in the various years to follow, but the mention of the years is not of the essence of this particular sign. At the same time the concept "eating" is not undefined. It is not an eating that has already taken place, but one that is to occur in the future. Hence, we may legitimately translate, *ye shall eat.* This is shown by the context, and in particular the words, "this to thee the sign." Furthermore, the words *this year, the second year, the third year* show that the sign has reference to something that has not yet taken place.

A first definition or limitation of the concept of eating is found in the words *this year.* Isaiah uses the definite article, so that the phrase *the year,* like the common *the day,* is to be understood in the sense *this year,* i.e., the particular year in which Hezekiah was then living, the current year. It was one in which the people had been hindered from carrying out the regular occupation of sowing, for the Assyrian was present in the land; and for that reason they were dependent upon the *saphiᵃḥ,* i.e., what has been poured out or spilled accidentally and so springs up of itself. It is grain that has not been planted on purpose, but may have fallen into the ground from the previous harvest. That the nation was compelled to eat such grain was evidence that its land was in a sad condition.

In the second year, i.e., the year following the one just described, the people were to eat *shaḥis,* i.e., grain that springs up of itself, having come from the grain of the first year, the *saphiᵃḥ.* This would imply that the condition of things had not improved. In the third year, however, the people were to sow and harvest as usual, signifying that the period of calamity and danger would be over. Isaiah now turns the prediction into a command, using a row of imperatives, *sow* and *harvest, plant* and *eat.* Thus he expresses the fullness of normal agricultural operations. Furthermore these imperatives lend confidence to the nation. There is to be no hesitation in going about normal work, no holding back for fear of a return of the Assyrians. So sure will the fulfillment of the prophecy be that the people are commanded to carry out their tasks. Here in these imperatives there is a definiteness that is lacking in the infinitive, and thus a striking contrast is formed between the imperatives and the infinitive. The word "eating" expresses the idea of monotonous regularity and sameness; on the other hand, the imperatives bring out the idea of variety and fullness of activity. The first two imperatives are significant, for they point out that the work of sowing will be followed by that of enjoying the fruit of the labor. What is sown will be harvested; it will not fall into the hands of the Assyrians nor will it perish. Sowing will result in harvesting, as should be the case. Variety further appears in that Isaiah uses a third imperative and then concludes again with an infinitive absolute. *Plant vineyards*, he commands, *and eat their fruit.* The thought then is that if they plant their vineyards they can enjoy the results continually. As the description of the sign had begun with the concept *eating,* so it also concludes. In the conclusion, however, the concept is a more blessed one, for now it is an *eating* that will continue in joy and satisfaction without end. The eating in a condition of temporary calamity and devastation gives way to eating in a condition of restoration and joy.

So far the actual language of the sign itself is clear enough. In what sense, however, is it to be applied to Hezekiah's time, and in what sense would Hezekiah have understood it? Some have applied the first year to the past; the second year they have regarded as the current one in which Isaiah utters the prediction, and the third as the following year. Others have placed the first and second years in the past, as though Isaiah were teaching that for two years the people had been eating the *saphiᵃh* and *shahis*, but that now in the year ahead, things would be better.[25] It would be difficult, however, to show that the infinitive absolute should be rendered by the past, and also there is no warrant for taking *the year* as referring to the year before last. Such a meaning would be without parallel.

It is far more in keeping with the grammar to take the passage as predicting that for two years the people will eat what had not been normally sown, and then in the third year they would return to the regular course of life. A problem arises, however. Why is the period of blessing set so far in the future, when as a matter of actual fact the humiliation of Sennacherib's armies seems to have taken place in the very near future (cf. v. 36)? A number of scholars have held that the year during which Isaiah spoke this prophecy was a sabbatical year, to be followed by the year of Jubilee. During these years the regular sowing of seed was suspended (cf. Lev. 25:4, 11). Hence, this sowing in the nature of the case would not be resumed until the third year. There is no evidence that this was a sabbatical year; and yet, in itself, that does not seem to be a sufficient objection to such a view. More serious, it seems, is the contrast intended between the first two years and the third. The first two years are those in which there is no sowing, not

---

[25] The word *sāpiᵃh* is used of the harvest from the fallow ground of the sabbatical year, Lev. 25:5.

THE BOOK OF ISAIAH

because of normal conditions (and the sabbatical year would be such), but rather, in the light of the context, because there was affliction from without which prevented such normal sowing. Furthermore, if Isaiah were speaking during a sabbatical year, he would simply be telling the people what they knew already; and it is difficult to understand how the normal course of events could be regarded as a sign. A sign must at least be something definite and striking; the normal course of events could in this instance hardly be so designated.

Others have thought that the prophet was using a proverbial manner of speaking, to indicate that the situation would progressively improve for the Judahites. On this construction it would not be necessary to press too closely the details. But against this it has been rightly objected that the language is not that of proverbial speech. The prophet does, as a matter of fact, seem to be giving a definite prediction of what will come to pass.

Is there then any explanation of this difficult language? One cannot be dogmatic, but the following is suggested as a possibility. When Isaiah spoke to Hezekiah (i.e., this year) the people were suffering the effects of Sennacherib's presence. Isaiah had earlier predicted that this would be a difficult time (7:21-25). It was the period of briers and thorns. Suppose also that it was autumn, as Delitzsch has suggested, and that the new year would very shortly begin. Even though the humiliation of Sennacherib might take place very soon (and verse 6 implies that such was the case) the condition of devastation and suffering brought about by the Assyrian's presence would continue for a time. It would not be changed overnight. Hence, it would be perfectly true that during the second year (the year that would shortly begin) the nation would continue its unnatural diet. In the third year, however, there would be sufficient time for people to go about their own work as in normal times. We need not suppose that the eating of *shaḥis*, attributed to the second year, would necessarily last an exact year of 365 days. It is sufficient to know that during this year, indeed, for its greater part, the abnormal condition would continue; and then gradually, as the effects of the Assyrian's presence were removed or disappeared, the change to normal life would take place. This explanation, set forth with hesitation, is not free from difficulty; but it may be that such is what Isaiah intended.

31 And the remnant of the house of Judah which is left over will take root below and will make fruit above.

32 For from Jerusalem will go forth a remnant, and the escaped ones from mount Zion; the zeal of the LORD of hosts shall do this.

33 Therefore, thus saith the LORD unto the king of Assyria, He will not come unto this city, and he will not cast there an arrow, and not will a shield come before it, and he will not cast up a mound against it.

34 In the way in which he has come, in it will he return, and unto this city he will not come, saith the LORD.

35 And I shall cover over upon this city to save it, for my sake and for the sake of David my servant.

31 Isaiah continues the thought of the preceding verse by showing that when the normal order of life returns, what is escaped from Judah (i.e., what remains after the depredations of the Assyrians in the land) will again take root like a plant and will send forth fruit. By means of this well-known figure (cf. also Isa. 11:11) the prophet shows that Judah will again become a prosperous nation. Again, she will flourish and be successful as a people. The contrast between *downward* and *upward* is striking. By reaching down into the earth she brings forth her fruit above.[26]

32 Isaiah now proceeds to explain the words *rest* and *left over* of the preceding verse. There was to be a remnant from Jerusalem; this is a fact that should be known from prophecy, and what has just been stated is therefore in accord with what had already been determined by God. This verse is essentially Isaianic in its form as well as content. From Jerusalem and Mount Zion the remnant will go out until it covers the entirety of the land (cf. Deut. 30:1-10).

What is to be accomplished will be through the zeal of the Lord of hosts. It is a wondrous deliverance, in reality typical of the greater deliverance (and a forerunner thereof) that the Messiah was to accomplish. For that reason Isaiah uses the formula that he had earlier employed with respect to the birth of the Messiah (cf. 9:6). Truly this salvation is of significance, for in the present preserving of a remnant there appears the earnest that ultimately, in God's own time, the full salvation from the archenemy of mankind and from sin will take place. In that a remnant will go out from Jerusalem there is seen a renewal, probably also an increase of

[26] The language speaks of a complete restoration, just as the opposite thought of wiping out or destroying root and fruit indicates a total destruction. Cf. Gevirtz, *VT*, Vol. 11, No. 2, 1961, p. 150, note 1.

God's people. It is a sign of hope, of encouragement, a pledge that the Messiah will come.

33 The prophet is now ready to give the conclusion to the entire message, a conclusion that concerns the Assyrian king. It is a positive, definite assertion that the king will not come unto this city (Jerusalem). Not only will he not enter, but not even an arrow will be shot there.[27] The remaining portion of the verse carries out the principal thought. There will be no approach with shields, nor will there be earthworks cast up about the city. It is very interesting that Sennacherib himself makes no mention of having conquered Jerusalem. All he states is that he shut up Hezekiah like a bird in a cage, and that he did lay siege to the city.[28] It would seem that Sennacherib himself is referring to a previous time, possibly to the approach of Rabshakeh or even earlier. Isaiah's prophecy is that from this time on the Assyrian will not attack Jerusalem, and that prophecy was fulfilled (See Appendix III, "The Invasion of Sennacherib," and Appendix I, "The Reign of Hezekiah"). Sennacherib will no longer have power to hurt; he can do nothing more against Jerusalem.

There is no reason to suppose, as Knobel suggested years ago, that the plague had already broken out, and that Isaiah was really doing little more than engaging in shrewd guessing. The introductory words, *Thus saith the Lord,* show that we have to do with genuine prophecy. In his inaugural call Isaiah asserts that a remnant will return. To this fact he has reverted, and now comes out clearly summing up all that has been said before. This is the climax, as it were; the Assyrian will not enter Jerusalem. Such definiteness is what might be expected.

34 A further thought is added to what has just been stated. Not only will the king not come unto Jerusalem, but instead, he will return unto his own land, and that by the very way in which he had come. There is an interesting assonance in *ba' bah* (*he has come in it*), which is weakened by the substitution in Kings of

27 Iwry, *JAOS,* Vol. 81, No. 1, 1961, p. 29, interprets the act of shooting an arrow as one of sympathetic magic.

28 In the "Apology" of Hattusilis, the king speaks of the goddess Ishtar as having shut up Urhitesupas in the city of Samuhas like a pig in a sty; *"na-an-kam I-NA ᵘʳᵘ ŠA-MU-HA ŠAH GIM-an ḫu-u-um-ma EGIR-pa iš-tap-pa-aš."*

yavo' (*he will come*). On the king's retreat he will not turn aside to attack Jerusalem.

35 It would be a mistake to assess Sennacherib's withdrawal as a mere happening of chance. God Himself was at work, protecting Jerusalem in such a manner that He would save it. God Himself would see to it that Sennacherib should not touch Jerusalem. This He would do for two reasons; for His own sake, and also for the sake of David His servant. He would save the city for His own sake, as Hezekiah had prayed (v. 20). In the deliverance of Jerusalem the world would see that God was true to His promises, and that He was able to deliver His own from the hands of a mighty oppressor.

Furthermore, the deliverance will be for David's sake, not that David himself was personally deserving and hence merited so great a deliverance of his city, but because of the promises made to David. Isaiah refers to the promises found in 2 Samuel 7 in which God swore to establish for ever the throne of His kingdom (cf. 1 Kings 11:13, 34, 36; 2 Kings 8:19). Isaiah had earlier spoken of David, and the mention of David here is no evidence that the text in Kings is earlier than that of Isaiah (see Appendix II, "The Nature and Authorship of Isaiah 36-39"). Note such passages as Isaiah 9:6; 7:2, 13, 17; 16:5; 22:22. But why mention David at this point? For one thing Hezekiah was similar to David and is compared to him (2 Kings 18:3). Hezekiah is a son of David, sitting upon the throne at a crucial time, when it appeared that the Davidic dynasty would be completely destroyed. Was the kingdom of man, represented by Sennacherib, to triumph, and the kingdom of David to go under? This was the question at hand. That the kingdom of David might be saved, God intervened. In delivering Jerusalem God showed that He intended to abide by the promises that had been made to David.

36 And the angel of the LORD went out and he smote in the camp of the Assyrians a hundred and eighty and five thousand, and they arose early in the morning, and behold! all of them were dead corpses.

37 And Sennacherib the king of Assyria journeyed and went and returned, and he dwelt in Nineveh.

38 And it came to pass while he was worshipping at the house of Nisroch his god, that Adrammelech and Sharezer his sons smote him with the sword; and they escaped to the land of Ararat, and Esarhaddon his son ruled in his stead.

36 With this verse Isaiah begins to state the fulfillment of his prophecy. It is a fulfillment not merely of the message that the prophet has just uttered, but of all his prophecies that have pointed to an Assyrian defeat, for, although an ecumenical kingdom would arise in which man was to be exalted and God ignored, and although that kingdom would finally overcome and bring to an end the theocracy, nevertheless, in its first attempts against Judah, namely, the Assyrian phase of its existence, it would not be successful. Even to this kingdom of man God was merciful, giving it an opportunity to learn that He was in control, and through its defeat, to desist from attack against God's people.

Isaiah begins his statement in straightforward prose, employing the language of battle, *and there went out the angel of the Lord.* This verb is used of setting out to battle, for the angel is setting out with hostile intent against an enemy. He who went out was an angel belonging to Yahweh, the God of Israel. The phrase is not a substitute for Yahweh himself, nor does it simply designate a messenger, but an angel. The language calls to mind the destroying angel of Exodus 12:12, 13, 23, and of 2 Samuel 24:1, 15, 16. Emphasis in all these passages falls upon the Lord as causing the destruction; and yet He does this through His angel, whom He sends for this purpose. From this we learn the seriousness of the situation and its significance in the history of redemption. This was a conflict between the spirit of Babel, which would unite all men into a universal human kingdom, and the progress of God's kingdom. In its initial attempt against God's people this world kingdom must be defeated and that roundly, that all might know that Yahweh was truly the God of heaven and earth and able to deliver His people. Sadly, neither the Mesopotamians nor the inhabitants of Judah learned this lesson; and hence, in His providence, Yahweh permitted the Babylonians finally to overthrow Jerusalem. The angel then is a messenger sent to do God's will.

To the account in Isaiah, 2 Kings 19:35 adds the words "in that night"(!) which would seem to refer to the night of the day in which Isaiah had delivered his message. At any rate, the smiting of the Assyrians occured immediately after that message. As the angel at the time of the Exodus smote the Egyptians, so now the angel smites in the camp of Assyria 185,000 men. Why these men were smitten and not the entire army we are not told. A remnant must return in haste to Assyria where the king is to receive a greater punishment in his death. Even the humiliation of thus returning

504

does not bring the wicked king to repentance. At the time of the Exodus the smiting is attributed directly to Yahweh Himself; here it is the angel who smites.

It is impossible to give the precise location of the Assyrians at this time. The last biblical reference to them would place them at Libnah, but it may be that they had turned themselves toward Egypt in order to meet the approach of Tirhakah. This may possibly be referred to by Herodotus, who recounts that Sennacherib had been compelled to retreat from Pelusium because of field mice which the god Vulcan had sent to deliver Sethos his priest, and the Egyptian king. From this tradition it would appear that the disaster occurred in Egypt. Quite possibly, the Assyrians had actually reached the Egyptian border in their endeavor to resist the Ethiopian king.

The verb "to smite" implies the smiting with a disease; but what this disease may have been we cannot tell.[29] The destruction of the Assyrian army is not to be accounted for on naturalistic terms but as the result of a supernatural, miraculous action of God performed through His angel. With one stroke or blow, as it were, the angel brought death into the camp. No mere natural phenomenon accomplished this, but only the sovereign power of the one true Lord, who controls heaven and earth. At this crucial moment the world must know that He who reigns in Jerusalem is unlike other gods; He alone is the living, the true God.

When those who remained alive arose in the morning, they saw that all the rest were dead bodies. Among these who remained was the boastful King Sennacherib. Before him lay his army of dead corpses. The language is forceful, *and behold! all of them, corpses, dead ones.* No doubt remained; nothing could be done; a Power greater than Assyria had acted. All was sudden; no disturbance or cry had awakened the king. Throughout the night he and his men had slept, awaking in the morning as usual, ready to go about their business. But, behold! all of them were dead corpses.

37 This was no place for Sennacherib. The gods of Arpad and Sepharvaim and the other places might not have been able to withstand him; but now he has felt the power of Yahweh. He leaves, and his departure is told in short, rapid terms. *And he set out, and he went, and he returned.* Many commentators have been struck by the similarity between the description of Sennacherib's

---

[29] *and he smote*—note the retention of the *He* with *waw* consecutive.

hasty departure and that which Cicero gives of Cataline, "he went away, he departed, he escaped, he fled away."[30] Sennacherib had probably already heard a report from home, but now the urge is within him to return immediately. Now there is no longer cause for delay. He cannot stand against the God of Judah. To Nineveh he must return and dwell in his own capital. This last verb implies that he continued to live there for some time. As a matter of fact it was about twenty years until he was slain.

38 This verse relates what happened to the king about twenty years after his return to Nineveh. It begins in the style of true narrative, *and it came to pass.* Emphasis is placed upon the fact that it was the king himself who was praying, for the personal pronoun is employed. Hezekiah had prayed, and his God had heard him and delivered him from peril. Sennacherib also prayed, but his god did not hear him nor did he deliver him from any peril. Rather, while he was in the very act of praying, his sons slew him. His god was Nisroch,[31] and Hezekiah's god was Yahweh. As Hezekiah had gone into the house of his God, so Sennacherib went into the house of his god.

As he was engaged in this act of devotion, his two sons slew him with the sword, and then were compelled to flee to the land of Ararat, the Urartu of the cuneiform documents, the section of Armenia about the Arasse river. The kingdom passed to Esarhaddon, and thus Sennacherib is out of the picture. He could no longer harm the people of God. The first major attempt of the kingdom of man to destroy the kingdom of God ended in complete failure.

---

[30] *Abiit, excessit, evasit, erupit (In Catilinam* ii) .

[31] *Nisroch—*a corruption (intentional?) of Marduk. Cf. P. Dhorme, *RB,* Vol. 19, 1910, p. 510. *Adrammelech—*possibly represents *Ašur-šum-ušabši. Sharezer—Šar-uṣur.*

B. INTRODUCTION TO THE BABYLONIAN PERIOD (38, 39)

1. THE GODLY HEZEKIAH (38:1-22)

1 In those days Hezekiah was sick unto death, and there came unto him Isaiah the son of Amoz the prophet, and he said unto him, Thus saith the LORD, Command thine house, for thou art about to die, and thou wilt not live.

2 And Hezekiah turned his face unto the wall, and he prayed unto the LORD.

3 And he said, Ah! now LORD, remember now that I walked before thee in truth and with a perfect heart, and that which was good in thine eyes I did; and Hezekiah wept with great weeping.

1 This and the following chapter serve as a transition to introduce the latter portion of the prophecy (chapters 40—66). At the outset a difficulty emerges, namely, the relationship that these two chapters sustain to the preceding. The introductory words, *in those days*, would seem to refer to the events just described, namely, those of the fourteenth year of Hezekiah. If this were so, inasmuch as Hezekiah reigned for twenty-nine years, and inasmuch as he is promised fifteen more years of life, his sickness is believed by many to have taken place in the year of Sennacherib's invasion, the fourteenth year of his reign. On the face of it, there would seem to be no difficulty in this position.

What causes the difficulty is the fact that Sennacherib's invasion occurred in the year 701 B.C. If Hezekiah began to reign in 727 B.C. (or thereabouts) and in 701 he was promised fifteen more years of life, he would have lived to 686 B.C. If, however, he reigned a total of 29 years, beginning in 727 B.C., he must have ceased reigning in 698 B.C. Conceivably he might have lived on after he had ceased reigning, but the text in Kings implies that death brought an end

507

to His reign and that Manasseh reigned in his stead (cf. 2 Kings 20:20, 21).

If the phrase *in those days* has reference to the times of Merodach-baladan, described in the subsequent chapter, then the account of Hezekiah's sickness is definitely to be placed earlier than the invasion of Sennacherib. Merodach-baladan was first king of Babylon from 721-710 and then again for nine months in 703 B.C. 39:1 begins with the words *at that time*, which also is a general reference. It would seem that had Hezekiah already experienced the presence of Sennacherib, he would not have shown his treasures to the Babylonian king. Indeed, would not Sennacherib have demanded many of those treasures as tribute? Probably, therefore, in the light of such considerations, we are to understand the events of chapters 38-39 as having taken place before those of chapters 36-37.

In those days, therefore, is a general expression, pointing to the time of Hezekiah's life when he had relations with the Mesopotamian countries. More precisely then this, one cannot indicate the time. What the sickness was that befell the king, we are not told. It was, however, so severe that it would issue in death. Possibly the infinitive suggests that the sickness was such that Hezekiah was about to die. In John 11:4 a similar phrase is employed to indicate a sickness that actually resulted in death.[1] Unless there is special intervention, Hezekiah will die.

That the sickness was serious is also seen from the fact that Isaiah comes to the king and announces that he is to die. Isaiah's appearance is also an indication that God has not forsaken the king. A man who is about to die must be ready in every respect. Hezekiah was in a right relation with God. But a man about to die must also have his affairs in order.

Command thine house—Lit., *Command with respect to thine house* (cf. 2 Sam. 17:23). Hezekiah is to give those orders that will result in the affairs of his house being set in order. They were to be commands for the best interests of his house. The thought is that the king must leave his financial and business affairs in order, so that undue burdens will not devolve upon his heirs; but he must also see that his house itself, i.e., his heirs, have received from him instruction in the way in which they should walk. A man leaves his house in order, not only when the proper wills and testaments have

---

1 αὕτη ἡ ἀσθένεια οὐκ ἔστιν πρὸς θάνατον.

been executed, but also when he has instructed his family in the ways of the Lord.

Isaiah gives the reason for his command; Hezekiah is to die and not to recover from his illness. This last part is not superfluous, for it intensifies the first statement. It is as though the prophet had said, "You are going to die, and there is no hope of your living again after this sickness." Thus this last phrase lends a certain amount of emphasis. "You will die and there is no escape therefrom."[2] In the ordinary course of events, there can be no hope. Only a miraculous intervention of God could deliver the king's life; and this God would not do, unless first the king turned to Him in supplication. Thus, Hezekiah must learn how fully his life lay in God's hands. It is in this way that the apparent difficulty between Isaiah's prophecy of death and the addition of fifteen years of life is to be reconciled. Vitringa stated the matter beautifully when he said, "According to natural causes he (i.e., Hezekiah) would have to die, unless with His aid God should intervene beyond the ordinary; God, however, had decided not to intervene, unless at the supplication of the king and the trials of his faith and hope. Moreover, in cases of this kind (Gen. 20:3) the condition is not expressed, in order that God may call it forth as voluntary."[3]

2 The sad news drives Hezekiah to seek the Lord in supplication for his life. Hezekiah did not want to die; and his conduct has sometimes been contrasted with that of Paul, who declared that to depart and be with Christ was "far better" (Phil. 1:23). But the comparison is hardly just. Paul had a far fuller revelation of the glory to come than did Hezekiah; Paul knew the risen Christ and understood the work of Christ; Hezekiah belonged to the Old Testament economy. God had not yet spoken in a "Son." Furthermore, it is quite possible that Hezekiah at this time had no heir. Manasseh was twelve years old when he began to reign (2 Kings 21:1). If Hezekiah was to live yet fifteen years, and if Hezekiah's death and the termination of his reign coincided, then Manasseh would not be born for three years. If such were the case, Hezekiah

---

[2] The opposite combination appears in Gen. 42:2; 43:8; Num. 4:19.

[3] *"moriendum illi esset secundum causas naturales, nisi Deus sua ope praeter ordinem interveniret; erat autem Deo statutum non interveniere, nisi ad supplicationem regis eiusque fidei et spei experimenta. Reticetur autem in eiusmodi casibus conditio, ut Deus illam tanquam voluntariam eliciat"* (Com. in loc.).

may have been concerned about an issue. Indeed, inasmuch as he
was a godly king (2 Kings 18:3) his concern was far deeper. If he
were to die without issue, how could the Davidic dynasty culminate
in the advent of the Messiah? Hezekiah could well be facing the
same temptation that came to Abraham when he was commanded
to offer up his son (Gen. 22:1). He turns to the wall then, not
acting childishly, as some commentators suggest,[4] but merely to be
alone so as to speak to his God without disturbance. Possibly his
action is also a dismissal of Isaiah; he turns to the wall that he may
undisturbedly speak to God and pour out his grief unto the One
who holds in His hand the issues of life and death. The wall is not
that of the Temple, but of Hezekiah's own room; the text pictures
a man seeking to shut out all impressions of the outside world and
to concentrate his thoughts upon God alone.

3 This verse contains the words of the kings's prayer, a prayer
that ends in strong weeping. *Ah!*—An ejaculation expressing the
sorrow and anguish of Hezekiah's soul, and entreating the pity of
the Lord.[5] Hezekiah prays to the covenant God of his people, the
One who formed them into a nation at Sinai. He enjoins God to
call to mind (remember) his manner of life.[6] In Old Testament
times longevity was regarded as a blessing; if this prayer occurred
in the fourteenth year of his reign, he would have been only 39
years of age. But Hezekiah's desire is not merely for a longer life;
quite probably he is concerned because it appears that he is to die
without an heir. His manner of life has been lived *coram Deo,*
and has been steadfast, without hypocrisy or wavering. He is not
pleading his merits before God, as though to claim that he was
deserving of salvation, but is merely pointing out the tragedy that
would seem to occur if a theocratic ruler who had lived his life
righteously before God should be taken without heir.

a perfect heart—I.e., a whole heart, that in its completeness is devoted to the Lord. Hezekiah's service to God was not half-hearted.
the good in thine eyes I have done—Hezekiah does not set

4 E.g., Hitzig; cf. Ahaz' attitude, 1 Kings 21:4.
5 אנא—a particle of entreaty; *ah! now.* The word is *'ān-nā'* and not *'on-na'*,
and should have a *Meteg* with *Milel*. The principal stress must be on the
penult, since *Qametz* cannot stand in an unaccented, closed syllable. Before
the Tetragrammaton, the word receives a major accent (as distinguished
from *Meteg*). In Gen. 50:17 and Ex. 32:31 a conjunctive accent replaces the
Meteg.
6 *this that*—the clause introduced by אשר is the direct object of the verb.

himself up as the judge of what is good. God alone is to say what is good, and what God has declared to be good Hezekiah has done. In line with the ancient promises expressed in Exodus 20:12; Deuteronomy 5:30 and 30:16, Hezekiah would claim a long life for himself. The thought that this life might be brought to a sudden end is too much for the king, and he breaks out in strong crying.[7]

4 And the word of the Lord was unto Isaiah saying,

5 Go! and thou shalt say unto Hezekiah, Thus saith the Lord, the God of David thy father, I have heard thy prayer, I have seen thy tears, behold! I am about to add upon thy days fifteen years.

6 And from the hand of the king of Assyria I shall deliver thee, and this city, and I shall cover over upon this city.

4 Immediate answer is given through the prophet. Calvin comments, "What interval of time elapsed between the Prophet's departure and return we know not," and states that only after "long and severe struggles" was the Lord's Word brought to the king. But in the parallel passage 2 Kings 20:4 we read, "And it came to pass, afore Isaiah was gone out into the middle court, that the word of the Lord came to him, saying. . . ." The passage is instructive as to the light that it shed upon the manner of prophetic revelation. To Isaiah, as he has departed from the king and persumably is on his way to his own house, walking amid the throngs of the city, the Word of the Lord comes in clear, distinct speech. It does not necessarily follow that the Divine speech was heard by the physical ear of the prophet any more than in his inaugural vision he should have heard the voice of God with the physical ear. There was a genuine hearing with the inner ear and the speech was audible to none but Isaiah. The speech, however, did not originate with the prophet, but was spoken by God. It was objective speech, coming to the prophet from God Himself.

5 There is a certain dignity in the command to Isaiah. In place of the imperative, God employs the infinitive absolute. Isaiah was going *from* Hezekiah; he is now to go *to* him and to speak unto him. The message is introduced by a full identification of God as Yahweh, who is the God of David, Hezekiah's father. The Lord Yahweh to whom Hezekiah had complained is the God who knew David. David, as Calvin well remarks, is not mentioned here as a private individual, but as the king who in his posterity was to

7 *with great weeping*—this clause has adverbial force.

511

see an everlasting kingdom. The Seed of David, who should bring to accomplishment the kingly blessings, was Christ. Hezekiah is reminded that David is his father, and therefore, that he himself is a legitimate ruler upon the Davidic throne, an heir to the promises that God had made to David. Nor can there be any greater comfort than the knowledge that God is faithful to the word of promise and salvation which finds its fulfillment in Christ the Savior. If Hezekiah were to die without issue, the Seed of David would not be born.

God has heard the king's prayer. The prayer does not move God to change His purposes, for He is the unchangeable one; but God now reveals to Hezekiah what His purposes were. By revealing to the king only a part of what was to occur, God causes Hezekiah to turn to Him completely, seeking aid only from Him and so acknowledging that only in Yahweh, the God of David, are deliverance and help to be found. Hezekiah's prayer had been accompanied by tears, for it flowed from a heart deeply moved to express itself in strong emotion. Then follows the gladdening announcement that God, who alone can lengthen a man's life, will add to all the days of Hezekiah fifteen years.[8]

6 Whatever the exact time of the utterance of this prophecy, it was clear that the Assyrian king was upon the horizon. We need not assume that Sennacherib was actually in Palestine at the time, although that may well have been the case. At any rate it is necessary to tie up this promise with that of the preceding verse, in order that Hezekiah may know that during the fifteen added years of his life he will reign in safety, and Jerusalem will not fall to the Assyrians. During this time God Himself will cover over the city with His protection so that the enemy cannot conquer it.

7 And this shall be to thee the sign from the LORD, that the LORD doeth this word that he hath spoken.

8 Behold! I am about to cause to return the shadow of the steps which has gone down on the degrees of Ahaz with the sun, backward ten degrees; and the sun returned ten degrees on the degrees which it had gone down.

8 behold! I (am he who) will add—The change of person is striking; the verbal form is the 3 m.s. Hiphil and not the participle.
A somewhat formal parallel appears in the Apology of Hattusilis, "For Hattusilis, the years are short; he will not live. Give him now to me that he may be my priest. Then indeed he will live (nu-wa-ra-aš Tl-an-za)."

7 Hezekiah had asked the Lord for a sign (cf. 2 Kings 20:8; Isa. 38:22), and so exhibited in his attitude a marked contrast from that of Ahaz. To Ahaz God had offered a sign, but Ahaz had rejected it. God, therefore, took from Ahaz the choice of a sign, and Himself gave one, a sign of comfort to believers, but one that forbode disaster to Ahaz and to his people. Hezekiah, on the other hand, realizing the severity of the test that is upon him, wishes a sign to strengthen his faith. Again God chooses the sign, but the sign that He gives is one of blessing. It is a sign for the benefit and blessing of the king (the "unto thee" is an ethical dative of advantage), and it is a sign that comes from the Lord.[9] It originates with Him and is of His choosing. It is the pledge that God will perform the thing that He has spoken.

8 Like the sign given to Ahaz (7:14) this one also is introduced with *behold!* It is therefore a sign of significance. Isaiah's account, however, is shorter than that given in 2 Kings (20:9b-11), where the king is asked to choose whether he desires the shadow to go forward ten degrees or go back ten degrees. Realizing that the normal thing is for the shadow to go down ten degrees Hezekiah asks that it return backwards, and his desire is fulfilled. Isaiah also mentions the sun returning, using slightly different language to speak of the same thing. We cannot agree with Stade, Marti and others who think that the longer version given in Kings is simply a later intensification of the miracle.[10] It is a fuller account, which fact perhaps indicates that the account in Isaiah is the earlier. There is no reason, however, for doubting the reliability of what is related in Kings.

At the outset an exegetical question arises as to whether Isaiah is speaking of a sun dial or of steps in general.[11] Does the word rendered *steps* refer to the scales or degree markers of a sun dial? This is essentially the position adopted in the Targum, Jerome,

---

[9] *ʾăšer—that*, in place of *ki*, e.g., Ex. 3:12. These two words can loosely connect dependent with independent clauses.

[10] Duhm believes that additions have been made to the text in 2 Kings 20:8-11. Marti also asserts that the choice given to Hezekiah as to whether the shadow should advance or retard ten degrees is a later intensifying of the miracle. Stade (*ZAW*, Vol. 6, 1886, pp. 184ff.) developed this argument. Even if the text of Kings is expanded, there is no reason for doubting that the choice actually was presented to Hezekiah.

[11] Delitzsch states that "steps of Ahaz" was a name that he gave to one of his sun dials.

and in Symmachus. On the other hand B, the Syriac, and Josephus take the word in its actual sense as referring to steps. Those who adopt this latter position often assume that there was some kind of pillar or obelisk that would cast a shadow, and that in this instance the shadow cast would descend the stairs. Thus, the entire staircase served as a kind of dial itself. Perhaps the question cannot be answered with certainty. It has been maintained that a sun dial would not have been known as early as Hezekiah's time, but Herodotus declares that the Babylonians invented the sun dial (ii.109). Quite possibly Ahaz might have had a sun dial introduced into Jerusalem as he had also brought in the Damascene altar (cf. 2 Kings 16:10ff.). In either case, however, whether the reference is to an actual sun dial or merely to a flight of steps used to tell time by the position of a shadow, the event was a true sign and equally wonderful.

A question arises as to the translation of the first part of the sentence, and the question revolves around the point whether *tzel* (shadow) is to be regarded as a construct or an absolute. As the Masoretic pointing stands, the word is to be taken as a construct. Perhaps, however, it is better to take the following word, not as a genitive, but as an accusative, thus obtaining the rendering "Behold! I am about to cause the shadow to turn back with respect to the steps (or, along the steps) which it has gone down, etc." The word *steps* is then best construed as an adverbial accusative. The antecedent of the relative may either be *the shadow* or *the steps* (degrees). Isaiah is then either speaking of the shadow that has gone down or of the degrees that have gone down. Possibly the first of these is to be preferred. The words *on the degrees of Ahaz by the sun* refer to the place (whether a dial or the steps) where the shadow falls. The phrase *by the sun* stresses the fact that the shadow could not be changed merely by human will or power but only through the sun. It is best to construe this phrase with the verb *had gone down*. Thus, the entire thought is that God will cause the shadow which by means of the sun had gone down backward on the steps (degrees) of Ahaz to turn back the steps (degrees) ten steps (degrees). While we really know very little as to the exact nature of this instrument, it would seem that there were at least twenty degrees. This follows from the fact that a choice had been given to Hezekiah whether the shadow should advance or decline ten degrees. Conceivably there were 24 degrees, each one representing a half hour; or there may have been 48 degrees, each indicating a quarter of an hour. On this point one cannot be sure.

The fulfillment of the promise is related very simply. Isaiah merely declares that the sun returned ten degrees (or steps). The passage in 2 Kings states that God "brought the shadow ten degrees backward, by which it had gone down in the dial of Ahaz." There is no conflict, however. One passage focuses attention upon God's moving the shadow, and the other upon the sun. From this we may at least learn that God used the sun to produce the result, a thought that is supported by the usage of *by the sun* earlier in the verse.

Those who would regard this account as mere saga or legend have perhaps unwittingly spoken a word in defense of the true interpretation. For they regard the story as a miraculous one but do not believe that it actually occurred. And indeed the story is one in which a miracle is involved. Whatever the method by which God accomplished this result, we may discern here an act performed by the supernatural power of God in the external world, contrary in its appearance to the ordinary providential working of God, and designed to be an attestation or sign of the redemptive purposes of God. Inasmuch as the sign fits this definition, we may rightly say that it was a miracle. How God performed this miracle is another question; whether by mere refraction or by laws unknown to man, one cannot say.[12] It is well to remember the words of the Westminster Confession, "God in His ordinary providence maketh use of means, yet is free to work without, above, and against them, at His pleasure" (V:III). This sign, so unusual, was a pledge to the fearful yet believing king, that God would fulfill

---

12 ". . . it may have been simply through a phenomenon of refraction, since all that was required was that the shadow which was down at the bottom in the afternoon should be carried upwards by a sudden and unexpected refraction" (Delitzsch). 1Q adds עֲלוֹת.

It is thought that the device consisted of two sets of steps each facing a wall whose shadow fell upon the steps. As the sun arose, the eastern steps would be in the wall's shadow, which, as the day advanced, would grow shorter. On the other hand, during the afternoon, the steps facing west would more and more be in the shadow. According to 1Q, the steps were of the עֲלוֹת (upper chamber) of Ahaz. Possibly it was mid-day when Isaiah spoke. The shadow had just descended the eastern steps and now was ready to ascend the western steps. Instead, however, the shadow again ascended the eastern steps ("Behold, I am causing to return (i.e., to ascend) the shadow of the steps which had gone down (during the morning) on the steps of Ahaz, namely, the sun, etc.").

the promise of life that He had made, and in the deeper sense, would be true to the promises of salvation made to David, Hezekiah's father (cf. v. 5).

9 A writing of Hezekiah king of Judah when he was sick and he lived from his sickness.

10 I said in the pause of my days, I shall go into the gates of the grave, I am deprived of the rest of my years.

11 I said, I shall not see the LORD, even the LORD in the land of the living; I shall not behold man again with the inhabitants of the world.

12 My dwelling is departed and uncovered from me, like the tent of a shepherd; I have rolled up, like the weaver, my life; from the thrum he will cut me off; from day to night thou wilt finish me.

13 I awaited the morning; as a lion, so will he break all my bones: from day to night thou wilt make an end of me.

14 Like a swallow or a crane, so I chirp: I moan like a dove; my eyes are weak on high; O lord, I am oppressed, be surety for me.

9 The parallel account in Kings omits these verses, but the genuineness of the song is unquestionable. As David, the king whom he so closely resembled, had written songs of praise to God, so also does Hezekiah. The song is called a *writing*, but in its form it does resemble the *miktam*. It is a writing that claims Hezekiah as its author and derives from him. The time of composition is also given; it is the general period of Hezekiah's sickness and recovery. At the same time, not each section or stanza of the Psalm reflects the same period. Thus, in the first five verses (strophe one) the period reflected is that which is described in verses 2 and 3, namely, the period when the king was sick and had not yet heard the gracious news that he would be healed.

10 Hezekiah begins immediately with an expression of his melancholy thoughts as he contemplated death. The introductory words, *I said*, set forth or introduce the thoughts that had possesssed the king. Several commentators believe that the first word *I* is without particular emphasis; in this they see a similarity to Qoheleth, and argue for a late date for the Psalm. This conclusion does not necessarily follow. It may be that there is an emphasis falling upon the personal pronoun, to point out that the king was such a one as might not expect anything else but death. Yet even if there is no particular emphasis upon the word, the fact that the

separate personal pronoun is used does not in particular indicate a late date.[13]

The third word of the verse gives the time when the king uttered his thoughts. It was when a pause or period of cessation had entered the days of his life. There is question as to the precise significance of the word *d⁰mi*, for it is not found elsewhere in the Old Testament.[14] In the light of the context, however, it would seem to apply to a period in life of the king when that life was about to come to a close. It should be noted that the position of the word lends it a particular emphasis. At this time, when a pause had entered into the vigorous and full life of the king, then, at that time, did he fear death. Indeed, this is one of the leading thoughts of the passage; cf. vv. 12, 13. In speaking of *my days,* the king simply has reference to his period of life, the days that he is to live upon this earth.

Probably the verb is to be construed with what precedes, the following words then serving as a mere adverbial modifier. Thus, we may render, "In the pause of my days I shall go to the gates of Sheol." Some break at least is intended between the verb and the following, for the verbal form is in pause. The thought is, "I shall go from the days of my life to the gates of Sheol."[15]

In the gates of Sheol expresses the destination to which Hezekiah believes he must go. It is not merely Sheol, but its gates that find emphasis.[16] The mention of the gates suggests the impossibility of return. Once the gates have closed on the person who has entered, there is no possibility of escaping or returning through them to the days of this life. The thought of finality, of the absolute conclusion of this life, breaks in upon the king.

The second member of the parallelism may be rendered, *I am deprived* of the remainder of my years. This deprivation is to be considered as a punishment, a consideration that would add to the king's bitterness of spirit. In the normal course of events Hezekiah might have expected a longer life, but now he feels that because of his sins, God is taking away from him what would ordinarily

---

[13] Brockelmann thinks that the pronoun has no particular emphasis, *op. cit.,* § 34b. Green also, *op. cit.,* § 246:1a. Drechsler, however, comments, "*Der Nachdruck liegt auf* אני, *anzudeuten: ich, ein Solcher, für den schon etwas Anderes nicht mehr übrig zu sein schien.*"

[14] דמי—*likeness, half, midst.*

[15] *I must go*—the form practically expresses a cry of despair.

[16] *Sheol*—cf. chap. 14, footnote 20.

remain of his life. It should be noted that the verb *I am deprived,* like *I am going,* is separated from what follows by a disjunctive accent. The emphatic member of the verse is the phrase, *in the pause of my days.* To exhibit the parallelism, we may print it as follows:

I said

In the pause of my days
> a. I shall go into the gates of Sheol.
> b. I shall be deprived of the remainder of my years.

11 Like the preceding verse, this one also begins with an *I said;* but here the personal pronoun is missing. The king's complaint is that he will no longer see God in this life. The *land of the living* does not refer to Palestine but to life itself, the abode of the living, in distinction from the gates of Sheol. To see God is not to see Him as He is, nor to behold His essence, which man cannot see, but to see Him as He is displayed in His works of creation. "For the invisible things of him from the creation of the world are clearly seen. . . ." (Rom. 1:29a). But in particular Hezekiah may have reference to worshipping God in the Temple. "When shall I come and appear (lit., be seen) before God?" (Ps. 42:2b; cf. also Isa. 1:12; Ps. 63:3). To see God is to rejoice in Him, in His works, and as one approaches Him in worship. Why, however, does the king employ the term Yah?[17] This word had already appeared in 12:2 and 26:4. That the word Yah is employed twice is not an error. Rather, it gives a peculiar force to the thought, as though the king were saying, "I shall not see Yah, even Yah in the land of the living." Thus a certain gradation or intensifying of the thought is introduced, and this is accomplished by means of the modifying phrase, *in the land of the living.* From these two passages we learn that the word is used to designate God as the One worthy of trust who can deliver from fear. Perhaps Hezekiah realizes that without Yah there can only be fear, and death can then claim him. If he could see Yah, he would not have to fear death. It may be, however, that we cannot say precisely why the king chose this expression. His utterance may merely mean that he will no longer be able to see the almighty God as he had done in times past. The intimate fellow-

---

17 In 1Q יה is written only once. *BH,* appealing to S and Syr., suggests that יה יshould be read יהוה (Yahweh).

ship of worship on this earth would no longer belong to Hezekiah.

If he would be deprived of fellowship with God on this earth, so also would he lose the companionship of man. In the light of the parallelism, the words *inhabitants of ḥadel* serve to designate the place of man. They form a parallel to *land of the living.* As in the land of the living Hezekiah will no more see Yah, so among the inhabitants of *ḥadel* he will not see a man.[18] Yah is in the living, I am among the inhabitants of *ḥadel.* In the first line there is manifested the true piety of the king, whereas the second line shows his humanity. It is a natural feeling to want association with other men, and it is the deprivation of this association that grieves the king. "We were born," says Calvin, "for the purpose of performing mutual kind offices to each other"; and that Hezekiah desired to serve his fellow men is amply apparent from what Scripture records of his life.

12 Hezekiah now expresses the same essential thought by means of two different figures. To express the first picture Hezekiah uses a term with the Aramaic significance *dwelling,* and uses this term figuratively, referring to the body as man's place of abode. This verse is not introduced by an *I said,* but instead there is an easy and natural continuation of the preceding. Of this dwelling Hezekiah complains that it has departed (the idea of forceful removal is present; cf. 33:20), and has been removed from him. He speaks as though this had already taken place, and that he is a man bereft of life, which has gone from him (cf. 2 Cor. 5:8). The king compares his life to a tent belonging to the shepherd.[19] In the first place the tent, in contrast to the permanent palace of a king, is a temporary abode; secondly, it is the tent of a shepherd, used only for passing purposes, easily erected and easily removed. Possibly Hezekiah is reflecting upon the tents of the shepherds, similar to the black tents of the present-day Bedouin, which can so easily be removed and moved about. When one place has been

18 חדל —it is sometimes thought that the word is an intentional variation of חלד; cf. Ps. 17:14; 49:2. Drechsler, however, interprets it of the underworld. He asserts that it arises from the concept of ceasing to act and to suffer (cf. Job 14:6; Ps. 39:5), and first denotes death, then the kingdom of the dead (cf. Job 3:17). By means of a word play it thus forms a contrast to חלד.

19 *rō'i—belonging to a shepherd, pastoricius.* The word might also be rendered, *my shepherd.*

depasturized, the shepherd may move to another, there again to erect the temporary dwelling. Once the tent has been taken down and removed the place knows it no more; so it is with the king's life.

In the second figure the king declares he has rolled up his life like a weaver. As the weaver when he has completed his work rolls up the cloth on the roller so that all that remains is to cut it off from the thrum, likewise Hezekiah has finished all the responsibilities of life and has nothing more to do than to await the coming of death. The king thus attributes to himself the cause of death; he himself has brought his death about; and yet ultimately he recognizes that his death is in God's hands, and that God is the true agent thereof.[20] Thus, he passes over from the first to the third person as the subject of the action. It is God who is to cut him off from the thrum. The word *dallah* (*thrum*) is placed first and so is made emphatic. It refers to the ends of the threads that fasten the web to the beam.

To express the suddenness and shortness of time involved, Hezekiah uses a somewhat proverbial manner of speech in asserting that *from day unto night thou dost bring me to an end*. The thought is that in the morning one did not expect anything untoward to occur, and by evening, when darkness had come, the event had already taken place (cf. Job 4:20). Having begun with the first person, the king changes to the third and concludes with a transition to the second. The last phrase of the verse, therefore, is a prayer, addressed directly to God Himself. The verb is used of the completion of a work (cf. 1 Kings 7:51; Neh. 6:15) and of the passing of time (Isa. 60:20). The time of Hezekiah's life has been completed, rounded out, filled full (cf. Gal. 4:4).

13 Returning to the first person, the king declares that he has waited till morning.[21] Throughout the entire night the king looked

---

[20] Note in both vv. 12 and 13 the ellipsis of God as the subject. This occurs in poetic use although it is also found in prose.

[21] שׁוּיתִי —lit. *I have been like, resembled;* In Ps. 131:2 we may possibly render, *I have smoothed* (i.e., composed) my soul. Hence, some would supply נפשׁי (*my soul*) here, as Gesenius, who translates, *I have sought to soothe myself* (*ich suchte mich zu beschwichtigen*). For support he appeals to the Arabic where the concept "smooth" is applied to what is still. *'an-nafsu-l-mut-ma-'innah—soul (that art) at rest* (Koran 89:27). Hence we may understand the Vulg. *sperabam (I awaited) usque ad mane.*

Following the Targ., some emend the text to read *šiw-wa'-ti, I have cried.*

upon Yahweh as upon a lion, expecting Him to act as such. Hezekiah was constantly mindful of the presence of Yahweh, his God (cf. Job 7:4; 30:17). He compares his death to the breaking of all his bones. It is an utter crushing and destroying such as a lion would wreak upon its prey. The death that God sends him is like the attack of a lion who breaks all the bones of its prey. In mentioning the bones the king refers to a destruction that is thorough and complete. He closes the verse with a repetition of the thought with which the preceding verse closed, thus strengthening and confirming what he had previously said. Drechsler is correct when he points out that the repetition of these words gives a good effect elegaically.

14 Hezekiah begins the verse by comparing his sufferings to the moanings of certain birds, the swallow and the crane. The two nouns are related asyndetically, perhaps to show the strong contrast between the sounds of the two birds. The swallow gives forth a murmuring, softer sound, whereas the crane makes a louder, creaking noise.[22] Like the sounds of these birds, so the king chirps, muttering his sounds in mourning calls of grief, longing for help. Like the mournful sound that the dove makes, so does Hezekiah mourn (cf. Isa. 59:11; Ezek. 7:16; Nah. 2:7).

Yet the king has not abandoned all hope. His eyes have become weak, but he has lifted them up on high, hoping that God will take notice of him. Indeed, it is this looking up that has weakened his eyes. Thus he gives another picture of his great despair. Yet he cries out to God, addressing Him as *'ᵃdonay* (sovereign Lord). This is the word that Isaiah himself so often has used to set forth God as the One who can carry out His remarkable purposes. Hezekiah appeals to God as One who has all power, the only One who can help him. Briefly he states the condition that has befallen him. Oppression has come to him.[23] It is an impersonal construction,

---

König holds to the literal meaning of the root, *I acted till morning like a lion (ich machte es bis zum Morgen dem Löwen gleich),* i.e., in roaring from pain. If the language can bear this meaning it yields a good sense and forms a suitable parallel to the opening clause of v. 14, but the כֵּן of v. 13 seems to refer to the manner in which Yahweh will break his bones.

22 עָגוּר seems to be the name of a bird and hence should not be interpreted as an adjective (cf. Jer. 8:7).

23 *there is oppression to me*—impersonal. As this form is pointed, it is not a noun, *'oś-qāh* (oppression, so BDB). GKC, § 48 i note, takes it as an em-

which sets forth briefly and fully the completeness of despair that rests upon the king. Hence, he prays earnestly, *be thou my surety*.[24] It is a command to take Hezekiah's part, to take the condition and cause of the king into His own hands, to make it His affair. The prayer is similar to that of the Psalmist, "Be surety for thy servant for good: let not the proud oppress me" (119:122). Hezekiah has faced his desperate condition and has had resort to prayer. He has reached the point described in the prose narrative in verse 3, which relates his praying to God. The following verses therefore treat of his deliverance, and correspond to the prose account, verses 4-8, which mention Isaiah's ministry.

15 What shall I say? and he will speak to me and himself hath done it; I shall go softly all my years for the bitterness of my soul.

16 Lord, upon them they live, and as to everything in them is the life of my spirit, and thou wilt recover me and make me live.

17 Behold! to peace my bitterness, and thou hast loved my soul from the pit of destruction, because thou hast cast behind thy back all my sins.

18 For Sheol will not praise thee, nor death praise thee; they that go down to the pit shall not hope for thy truth.

19 The living, the living, he will praise thee; like me today; father to sons will make known with respect to thy truth.

15 The verse before us is beset with difficulties, and the interpretations are numerous. Calvin, for example, believes that Hezekiah is continuing in his grief and lamentations. On the other hand, it seems more likely that this verse represents a change of standpoint, and that the king is now beginning to give utterance to his gratitude for the deliverance experienced. Like David in 2 Samuel 7:20 (cf. also Gen. 44:16), so Hezekiah by his question *What shall I say?* gives expression to his gratitude at the change of events. How can he suitably praise and thank God for what has been done?

One must not overlook the conjunction that introduces the third word of the verse. It ties up the thought with the prayer uttered in the preceding verse, and also points toward the answer to that prayer. No sooner had the king besought the Lord than the Lord

---

phatic imper. (but can *Qametz - Hatuph* stand in a distant open syllable?). As it stands, the form must be 3 f. s. perfect.

24 *go surety for me, take on a pledge for me*—the term "arabon" is used even today in Arabic in the sense *pledge* or *deposit*.

spoke to him with words of assurance. How then can Hezekiah
fittingly praise such a God of mercy? What the Lord had said to
Hezekiah was a promise, an assurance that He would restore life to
the king. Furthermore, not only did He speak a word of comfort,
but He performed it. Here the personal pronoun is emphatic, for
Hezekiah would gratefully give to God all credit for His healing.
One may call to mind the words of Balaam, "hath he said, and shall
he not do it? or hath he spoken, and shall he not make it good?"
(Num. 23:19b). Here is the comforting assurance that belongs to
all of God's people, "God has spoken and He Himself has performed His Word." Hezekiah's utterance, *he has said*, reflects upon
the verb *to say* in verses 4 and 5, whereas the *and he has done* calls
to mind the *will do* of verse 7.

As a consequence of God's faithful dealing, Hezekiah describes
how he can now live the remainder of his life. Indeed, 15b is really
an answer to the question that had introduced 15a. He will go
slowly step by step, thus living a quiet, peaceful life; and so his
entire course of life will be an answer to the question how he shall
praise his God.[25] Events have humbled the king and brought him
low. He cannot live proudly and haughtily, but must walk in
humility before his God all his days. It will be a long life, for the
king speaks of *all my years*. He has heard the message of Isaiah
that God will add fifteen years to his days. Unlike Ahaz, who
proudly rejected a message from God, Hezekiah acknowledges the
truth of the message and gratefully speaks of the remainder of his
life as *all my years*. Once the people marched in solemn procession to Zion (Ps. 42:4). Now Hezekiah uses the same verb that had
described the solemn procession of the people to apply to his own
manner of life. He too will walk solemnly, quietly, humbly, unto
Zion. His life will be lived before God.

There is a reason for this resolve, and that reason is found in the
words, *on account of the bitterness of my soul.* This was the
bitterness that his soul had experienced in the thought that he had
been mortally sick. Ever would the anguish of that experience be
before him. One who had experienced so great a deliverance could
only walk quietly, step by step, before his God.

16 Again a verse filled with difficulties. Penna can say that it is
the most enigmatic verse of the entire song, and he gives several

---

25 אדדה—generally regarded as a contracted form for *'et-daw-deh,* a *Hitpalpel*
from *dādāh, to walk* deliberately, i.e., at ease.

examples of proposed translations. We shall endeavor to expound
the words of the text as they stand. Hezekiah begins by addressing
God as *'ªdonay* (the Sovereign One). The word is well chosen, for it
fits in with the idea of keeping men in life, a work that belongs to
God alone.

The second word, *'ªleyhem* (upon them), contains a suffix that is
to be construed as a neuter. It refers to the speaking and performing of God mentioned in the preceding verse, the promises of
grace and the works of power and blessing. They are, as Delitzsch
points out, "the gracious words and gracious acts of God. These
are the true support of life . . . for every man, and in these does
the life of his spirit consist. . . ." In this context the two verbs
said and *did* occur together in verses 7, 16, and 25. The action
represented by these two verbs is that which in the creation constituted man the creature. In the first chapter of Genesis, the
thoughts *and he said* and *and he made* are partners.

We may render the verb impersonally, *men live.* As the creative
word and the creative deed had brought the creatures into existence, so their power alone can preserve the creature in life and
also bring about a renewal of life. In the remainder of the first part
of the verse, the emphasis falls upon the word *all.* It is a striking
word, for Hezekiah has been faced with death; now he can say
that everything in his life is preserved by the word and power of
God. Through them—again the reference is to God's words and
deeds of grace—the life of the king's spirit is preserved.[26] Perhaps
the word *spirit* (*ruªh*) is somewhat stronger than *nephesh* would
have been, in that it points to the active principle of a man's
life. Hezekiah will live, and he will live actively. The thought of
death is completely past.

Lastly, the king expresses a correlative thought by means of two
verbs. Addressing God in prayer, he states that God will both make
him recover and also cause him to live again. The first verb, used
of physical prowess in youth (cf. Job 39:4), here refers to the
renewal of bodily powers in the recovery of Hezekiah.[27] More
than that, God will restore to the king his life in all its fullness and

---

[26] בהן—this suffix is found elsewhere only in 1 Sam. 31:7 and Ezek. 42:14.

[27] ותחלימני —*and thou shalt restore me to health; cause me to be healthy,
strong.* The force of the verse as it stands is, "O Lord, upon them (thy
words and deeds) do men live, and completely in them is the life of my spirit
(or, and through them to the whole life of my spirit) ; and thou shalt make me
healthy and cause me to live."

strength. The latter verb is actually an imperative, but it may have future force. Hezekiah has expressed some profound truths in this verse. He begins by addressing God as the Sovereign One. Then he declares that by God's gracious words and deeds men live. Next he makes specific this general truth, applying it to himself. Through these wondrous things the very life of his own soul is preserved. Finally, in prayer, he addresses God as the One who gives him strength of recovery and keeps him in life.

17 Events have turned out differently than the king had expected, and so he exclaims, *behold!* It is a matter deserving of praise and also wonder, for God has dealt so bountifully with him. One might have thought that events would result in the death of the king, that his bones would truly have been broken as a lion breaks bones; but actually everything has worked itself out for peace. What is expressed in these words is the same truth that the New Testament writer sets forth, "nevertheless afterward it yieldeth the peaceable fruit of righteousness unto them which are exercised thereby" (Heb. 12:11b). The king's condition had been one of bitterness, indeed, one of great bitterness; and he employs an expression to show the extremity of the bitterness.[28] This bitter condition, however, has been changed into peace and fullness of being.

Emphasis now falls upon the pronoun, *yet thou.* The thought is that despite the bitterness that had befallen the king, God had loved him. He had been in the very pit of destruction and yet God had so loved him as to bring him out of it.[29] This love was manifested in that Yahweh had cast all of Hezekiah's sins behind His back to get rid of them. The figure is one that is clearly understood. What one does not want he throws away behind him. It is that which God had done. Hence, He would no longer see or remember the sins of the king. Forever they would be out of His sight. As always in the Scriptures a close connection between sins and death is found here. Hezekiah was a pious king, a great reformer in Israel; yet he realized that his sins were the cause of death. When God had cast his sins behind His back, then Hezekiah knew that there would be life for him and that he was one truly loved of God.

---

28 *(it was) bitter to me, bitter*—cf. the repetitions in vv. 11 and 18. Whether the first word is to be construed as an impersonal verb is difficult to determine.
29 *be-li*—lit., *wearing out,* figuratively *destruction.*

18 In this verse the king expresses a strong reason for his gratitude to God for deliverance, and also alludes to the reason why God will keep him in life. God desires that men should praise Him, and He will add to Hezekiah's years that Hezekiah also may praise Him. As a dead man, the king would be robbed of the privilege of exalting God in praise; hence, his deep gratitude for God for the extension of his life. Using the technical device of *continens pro contento* he speaks of Sheol, by which he means those who are in Sheol. The dead are conceived as a unit; all of them are in the grave. Death itself is mentioned by the king as the equivalent of Sheol. When death overtakes a man, that man becomes an inhabitant of Sheol. To speak of death's not praising God is to say that those who are dead will not praise God. A certain poignancy is given to these words in that they are a prayer and so are addressed to God.

Does Hezekiah intend to assert that death brings about annihilation so that the dead have simply ceased to exist? In particular, is his fear of death and Sheol a fear that he himself will be annihilated and pass into an oblivion so that he will no longer be? Or does he suggest that at death the soul falls asleep and so can no longer praise God until the resurrection? These questions, we believe, must be answered in the negative. Hezekiah has been deeply conscious of his sins. To this he has just made allusion, rejoicing that God has cast them behind Him. He knows that his sins are the cause of his death, and he looks upon this death as a punishment for them. Furthermore, he looks upon God as one who does punish him, who will fall upon him as a lion does upon its prey, and will break his bones. To go into such a death would mean an eternal separation from the God whom he wants to praise; if such a death overcomes him, then indeed he will no longer be able to praise God. It is death conceived under this aspect and Sheol regarded from this standpoint that are uppermost in Hezekiah's mind. One who is so wicked that his sins are to be swallowed up in death is hardly fit to praise God. It is in this sense also that we are to understand certain expressions in the Psalms and in Ecclesiastes. Thus, "The dead shall not praise thee, nor those that go down into silence" (Ps. 115:17), and "In death there is no remembrance of thee; in the grave who shall praise thee? (Ps. 6:5). Sheol and the grave are real places, however. They are filled with inhabitants, as Isaiah elsewhere has taught. Hezekiah is not speaking of that which does not exist; he is not giving assent to any

526

doctrine of annihilationism or of soul sleep. His words are deeper and more penetrating. He is concerned with the question of one's sins depriving him of the privilege of praising God. The form of the statement is significant (18a). Hezekiah places the negative first, then the subject, and finally the verb. *For it is not true, Sheol (that) it praises thee.* Emphasis falls upon the negative. In the corresponding line, the word *death* is introduced without a connective; but in English we may bring out the sense by inserting *nor; nor death, doth it praise thee.*[30]

Less emphatic is the negative of the second part of the verse (18b). Those who hope are those who have something for which to hope. They are yet in earthly life and are hoping for the blessing of the eternal state. Those, however, that go down to the pit, i.e., those who, because of their wickedness, are cut off from the land of the living, do not hope. The object of hope is said to be *thy truth;* the path of hope for the dead does not lie unto God's truth. The truth of God's promises cannot be hoped for by the dead. As a living person the king will see the fulfillment of these promises, but the death of the wicked will cut him off from them.

19 Those who praise God are the living, and in this verse the king sets forth a strong contrast to what has just been stated. In contrast to Sheol and death he speaks of the living one who lives again. The word *ḥay* is repeated, and we may bring out the force by rendering, *the living one, even the one who lives again, he it is who will praise thee.* Emphasis is given also to the personal pronoun. It is the one who lives again who is to praise God. Having made this general statement, the king points to himself as an example. He himself is a living one, who indeed lives again, for he has heard the promise of the prophet, and he praises God. Only such are the ones that praise God, not those that go down into the pit in death.

In the second line there is an exegetical question. Is the word *father* subject or object? Is Hezekiah saying, *a father to sons will make known,* or *he will cause a father and sons to know?* Perhaps it is not possible to decide positively, but what is clear is that the words *father to sons* are in an emphatic position. They imply a continuity of life, for the father will tell his children of the truth of

---

[30] *death*—the power of the negative is extended to include the second clause.

God's promises. Whereas this was probably not yet possible in Hezekiah's case, for as yet he seems not to have had sons, nevertheless, his utterance of these words is an expression of his belief that God would grant to him a seed and that he would live to tell that seed of the promises that God had made and that He fulfills.

> 20 The LORD to save me. And my songs we shall play all the days of our life at the house of the LORD.

20 These words form a conclusion to the entire beautiful prayer of thanksgiving. Probably we may understand the elipsis in the first part of the verse as signifying, *The Lord is present to save me.* It is also possible that some verb is to be understood, such as *came, was ready,* etc.[31] At the time of the king's great need, when above all else he required deliverance from death, the Lord intervened to bring him salvation. The result of this salvation is that the king would sing with the choir his own songs.[32] He did indeed restore singing to the worship of God (2 Chron. 29:30). In speaking of *my songs* the king probably has reference to songs of thanksgiving and deliverance which he himself has composed. Yet the king, in the transition from singular to plural, wishes to identify himself with others who also sing, namely, the choir. The singing was religious worship of praise, for it was to be conducted in the Temple as long as the singers lived. A preposition is used before *the Temple,* and this preposition signifies the elevation of the Temple, as though to say, *up to the Temple.* "We shall ascend to the house of the LORD, and there sing my songs all the days of our lives." Again, the king mentions the word *life,* a word now filled with precious meaning to him, for he recognizes how wondrous a gift from God life is. Isaiah was to tell the king (2 Kings 20:5, 8) that on the third day he would go up to the Temple, and it is this thought that brings to a close his remarkable prayer.

> 21 And Isaiah said, Let them take a cake of figs and let them rub it upon the boil and he will live.
> 22 And Hezekiah said, What is the sign that I shall go up to the house of the LORD?

21 In the account in 2 Kings, this verse and the following occur immediately after the announcement that God will add fifteen

---

[31] *The Lord is ready to save me*—the prep. with the inf. expresses an aim, tendency, or direction.

[32] נְגִינָה—properly, the music of stringed instruments.

years to the king's life, and for that reason, some commentators believe that the verses are out of place in their present position in Isaiah. It should be noted, however, that the account in Kings does not include the psalm of Hezekiah; furthermore, there is added material found in Kings including the conversation about the sun dial. It would be expected, then, that in the book of Kings the verses should occur where they do. That Isaiah has placed them after the psalm of praise does not indicate that they are misplaced; they merely serve to bring about a suitable conclusion to the entire account.

Through Isaiah the prophet, God had announced to the king a lengthening of his life; through Isaiah God also commands a means of healing to be employed. Isaiah gives the command that a cake of pressed and probably dried figs should be taken and smeared over the sore, so that Hezekiah will live. Possibly this mass would have been mixed with milk or some liquid and then applied. What the precise effects of the figs would be is difficult to say. Some have thought that they would be harmful and would impede recovery;[33] on the other hand, others have maintained a different opinion. Evidence has now come from Ras Shamra showing that figs (*dblt*) were used in healing.[34] But it was not the figs themselves that would heal the king. God is often pleased to use means in the performance of His works, and that He does in this case. What brought healing to Hezekiah was the Word of God, the Word that is powerful and efficacious. Apart from the promised Word, the figs would not have healed the king. He was in such a state or condition that no mere medicine could have preserved his life. For Hezekiah supernatural intervention was needed and this was given. The figs were but a means to show that God's power was at work.

Isaiah's command was that the cake of figs should be pressed or squeezed over the sore. What the precise nature of this sore is one cannot say. It may have been a boil or an eruption, for the Hebrew word seems to imply such. It is the word that is used of one of the plagues of Egypt, referring to the "boils, breaking forth." Possibly it was simply a manifestation of an internal wound, of so serious a nature that death would result. At any rate, when Isaiah had been obeyed, the king would live.

[33] Particularly some of the rabbinical interpreters, and even Grotius.
[34] Cf. C. H. Gordon, *Ugaritic Literature*, 1949, p. 129; *Ugaritic Manual*, 1955, p. 146.

22 Hezekiah's question is to be understood as uttered in connection with his healing. He uses the word *sign* anarthrously, as though to ask, What kind of a sign will the Lord give to me? The question is asked in reference to the promises of Isaiah (2 Kings 20:5) that on the third day the king will go up to the house of the Lord. The question was not evidence of a lack of faith, but the opposite. Having heard the promise, Hezekiah also asks what sign there is that the promise will be fulfilled.

SPECIAL NOTE ON THE POSITION OF VERSES 21, 22

Jerome was one of the first to notice a difficulty with respect to the position of these verses. *"Hoc prius legendum est, quam oratio Ezechiae, sive Scriptura, quam nunc interpretati sumus, ante enim cataplasma vulneri impositum est, et prius signum ab eo petitum futurae sanitatis, quam gratias ageret Domino, quod dicitur fecisse sanatus."*

Modern criticism has no hesitation in asserting that these verses are out of place and that they belong before v. 7. To support this position the following considerations are advanced.

1. In 2 Kings these verses appear after 20:6 where they seem to belong naturally. In v. 9 Isaiah apparently answers Hezekiah's question concerning a sign.

2. After the psalm was inserted in its present position some later writer made two minor additions.

3. V. 21 was probably at first a marginal note to v. 5 and v. 22 to v. 7, and both were attached by a later hand to the song of Hezekiah.

4. The glossator found no account of Hezekiah's being healed and so inserted the gloss that is now v. 21. Furthermore, he thought it important that Hezekiah had asked for a sign, and so inserted the gloss that is now v. 22.

5. V. 22 really forms an introduction to v. 7.

6. That this account is derived from 2 Kings is shown by the mention of approach to the Temple.

It will be noticed at once how much of the above is mere assumption. How, for example, can one possibly know that some glossator considered Hezekiah's asking for a sign so important that he felt the need of inserting a marginal gloss as the present twenty-second verse? (". . .*und weiter schien ihm zu V. 7 erwähnenswert, dass Ezeckias erst nach dem Zeichen gefraght hat (2 K. 20, 8), daher die Glosse V. 22."* —Fischer).

In 1Q the copyist inserted v. 21 immediately after v. 20. He began the following line, however, with chap. 39 v. 1, and continued vv. 21 and 22 at the side in the margin. B also includes these verses after v. 20.

The only argument that vv. 21, 22 belong before v. 7 is that v. 21 contains a question that is answered in v. 7. But if the verses are out of place, how did they come to be omitted before v. 7 and placed where they now are? Especially pertinent is this question if the passage before us is based upon Kings. Why, then, would these verses have been omitted?

In 2 Kings 20:7 the language continues in narration, but here in the afterglow of lyric effect the poetically inspired mood of Hezekiah mentions the two points that are of dramatic nature, the command and the question. These two points were the climax of the entire episode.

Alexander suggests that Isa. 38 is the original form of the narrative, in which the content of vv. 21 and 22 was added somewhat as an afterthought, and that in rewriting them, the prophet placed them in their natural order. This accounts for the difficulties as well as any hypothesis, and possibly it is correct.

2. The Babylonian Exile Announced (39:1-8)

1 At that time Merodach-baladan the son of Baladan king of Babylon, sent a letter and a gift unto Hezekiah, for he had heard that he was sick and had regained strength.

2 And Hezekiah rejoiced over them, and he showed them the house of his treasure and the silver and the gold and the spices and the good oil and all the house of his implements and all which was found in his storehouse; there was not a thing which Hezekiah did not show them in his house and in all his kingdom.

3 And Isaiah the prophet came unto King Hezekiah and he said unto him, What did these men say, and whence did they come unto thee? And Hezekiah said, From a distant land they came unto me, from Babylon.

4 And he said, What did they see in thy house? And Hezekiah said, All that which is in mine house they saw, there was not a thing which I did not show them in my storehouses.

5 And Isaiah said unto Hezekiah, Hear the word of the Lord of hosts.

6 Behold! the days are coming that there will be taken up all that is in thy house and which thy fathers have gathered unto this day to Babylon, there will not be left a thing, saith the Lord.

7 And of thy sons which go out from thee which thou wilt beget, they will take, and they will be eunuchs in the palace of the king of Babylon.

8 And Hezekiah said unto Isaiah, Good is the word of the Lord which thou hast spoken. And he said, That there may be peace and truth in my days.

1 This chapter is written in prose and recounts the sending of an embassy from the Babylonian king, Merodach-baladan. These events are dated by the general phrase, *at that time*, which evidently refers to the time of Hezekiah's sickness and his recovery. Upon the horizon lay the threat of Assyria, and the congratulatory embassy of Babylon apparently seemed to Hezekiah a way out of the danger. The name Merodach-baladan is a transcription of the

cuneiform, Marduk-apal-iddina, i.e., *The God Marduk has given a son*.[1] He had been a ruler of Bit-Jakin, which lay on the coast of the Persian Gulf. With the help of the Elamites he had taken possession of Babylon as early as 721 B.C. and succeeded in reigning there until 710 B.C. when he was driven out by Sargon II. After the death of Sargon, he again conquered Babylon in 703. First, however, he seems to have engaged in psychological preparation for ruling. At this time or shortly after, when he again occupied the throne of Babylon, he sent his messengers to Hezekiah. If this were the case, then the sickness of the king and the embassy of Merodach-baladan would fall in the year 703, and so would be earlier than the approach of Sennacherib. Merodach-baladan succeeded in reigning only nine months before he was defeated by the Assyrians. This was in the first campaign of Sennacherib, who describes his enemy as king of Karduniash and speaks not only of his defeat but also of the defeat of the troops of Elam. In the light of what Hezekiah did for the Babylonians, it is interesting to note that Sennacherib remarks that he entered Merodach-baladan's palace and also his treasure house and took away precious treasure. The purpose of the envoy to Hezekiah may have been to gather aid for a rebellion against Sennacherib.

The Babylonian king sent a letter of congratulation.[2] Having heard of the sickness and recovery of Hezekiah, Merodach-baladan wished to send his greetings;[3] yet his purpose was obviously political. The second half of the verse is explanatory of the first. It evidently presents the account of the sickness that had come to the Babylonian king. He had heard that Hezekiah had been sick and had become strong again. At least at this point no mention is made of the miraculous recovery of Hezekiah (but cf. 2 Chron. 32:31). What the amount of tribute was we do not know.

[1] We first hear of Merodach-baladan in the inscriptions of Tiglath-pileser, who refers to him as King of the Sea Country. He claims royal descent and mentions as an ancestor Eriba-Marduk (782-762). Under Sargon II he made himself ruler of Babylon with help from Elam. Merodach-baladan continued to rule until 710. In 703 he casts out Marduk-zakir-šumi from Babylon and again becomes king, trying with the Arabs to incite the Assyrian vassal states to rebellion. This was also the purpose of his writing to Hezekiah. Sennacherib, however, took Babylon away from him, and he fled to Elam. Only in the Scripture is the father's name given as Baladan.

[2] ספרים—cf. 37:14; *a letter*, not *letters*.

[3] *and he had heard*—the phrase serves as a parenthesis, to set forth the specific circumstances that led to the principal action of the main sentence.

2 To Hezekiah the arrival of the envoys brought joy. It was an honor thus to be noted by the king of distant Babylon. But Hezekiah, it would seem, had forgotten the God who had brought him to recovery. He was rejoicing, for here there seemed an opportunity of withstanding the approaching Assyrian. Hence, he was willing to show the envoys what weapons and resources he possessed.[4] Silver and gold, because of their great value, are usually mentioned first in an itemized list of wealth. Sennacherib also mentions them first, but reverses the order, gold, silver. The spices were used for fragrance and for salves. Likewise, the *good oil*, i.e., oil of fine quality, served for salve and ointment. The *house of his utensils*, probably an arsensal, is also known as the house of the forest of Lebanon; cf. 22:8. Whatever the king had collected and placed in his storehouses was also opened and displayed to the Babylonian ambassadors.[5] The words of the text are all-embracing. Everything, without exception, was shown to the Babylonians.[6] It was a foolish move, and some of this treasure would soon be sent to the Assyrians against whom it was designed to serve. Indeed, from this time on, it would seem, access to Judah became a prime desire of the Mesopotamian powers, until finally Jerusalem was completely destroyed.

3 As usual, Scripture goes to the heart of the matter, and here merely relates that Isaiah went to the king. Doubtless, as Vitringa suggested, this was at the divine command, and Isaiah was acting in his capacity of prophet and not as a private person. It is certainly not likely that the king had summoned him; for that matter, the king probably would not have wished to see him, for the presence of Isaiah was a reminder of the will of God.

In revealing all his treasures to the Babylonians Hezekiah had manifested an amount of vanity and pride. He seems to have forgotten the promises of God, and was willing to join with a human power to throw over the yoke of Assyria. His action, there-

---

[4] Cf. Akk. *bit nakāmti* or *nakānti*. In Hebrew the word seems to mean house of spices; thus, Vulg. *cellam aromatum*, also Aq and S. The Targ. however, renders *treasure house (bēt gnzwhy)* as do the Syr. and Saadia. B merely transliterates. All the disjunctive accents are found in this verse.

[5] *he showed them*—Note the S^egol under *He*, which sometimes occurs in the *Hiphil* perf. of *Lamed-He* verbs.

[6] It must be remembered that this occurred before the demands of Sennacherib were made.

fore, was on the same plane as that of Ahaz. He is willing to defend the theocracy and so to procure the fulfillment of the Messianic promises through human means; he is not acting like a theocratic king, but like a king of one of the heathen nations. It was necessary, therefore, that Isaiah intervene, for as a faithful prophet it was incumbent upon him to remonstrate even with kings when they no longer acted in a theocratic manner. It is no accident therefore that the description, *the prophet*, is appended to the word *Isaiah*. Isaiah approached Hezekiah as an accredited prophet of the Lord.

His questions are not for the purpose of obtaining information, but rather to bring the king to a realization of the enormity of what he had done.[7] The questions focus Hezekiah's attention upon the two important points of *a*) intercourse with the east and *b*) glory in material pomp and display; and in his answer Hezekiah also goes to the heart of the matter. At the same time Hezekiah actually answers only Isaiah's second question. He does not tell the prophet what the men had said. The approach of Isaiah must have caused the king to recognize his folly in turning from God and leaning upon men and might. He speaks clearly and directly, concealing nothing of what he had done and said. The king is both humble and honest; for him it must have been difficult so to reply.

In the answer there is a certain gradation, "the men who have come have come from afar, yea, they have come from Babylon." Babylon was to be the center of opposition to the kingdom of God; indeed, even at the time of Hezekiah there was already manifest in Assyria what in time would culminate in Babylon under Nebuchadnezzar. In his weakness Hezekiah had listened to an appeal from the very heart of the enemy. He should not have looked to the east and least of all to Babylon.

4 Isaiah's question is in preparation for the prophecy that he is about to utter in verse 6. Some commentators think that there is still manifest a certain amount of pride in the reply, for the king speaks of all that is in his house. Rather, it would seem, Hezekiah, convicted of his folly by the approach of Isaiah, simply speaks the

---

7 *do they come*—the imperfect may here be translated by the present, for in the mind of the speaker the action is regarded as not yet completed. On the other hand אמרו refers to an action that in the speaker's mind is regarded as entirely completed.

full truth, hiding nothing. It was necessary that he should tell what had occurred.

5 The verse is self-explanatory, but it should be noted that there is a certain emphasis and solemnity which lends dignity to the language. The message to follow is not the word of the prophet, not the mere pious advice of a devout man, but a word that comes from or has been spoken by the Lord of hosts. As has often been remarked, the words *of hosts* are omitted in the parallel account in Kings, but their presence lends a certain force to the message. Hezekiah would go to the Lord of hosts in prayer, when he should receive the message of the Assyrian envoys (37:16).

6 Just as Hezekiah had shown the Babylonian envoys everything in his house and the Temple, so everything that was in his house and in the Temple would be taken away into Babylon. This is the first time that the Babylonian captivity is thus expressly mentioned by Isaiah. We must not think that Hezekiah's folly was the cause of this captivity. It was not the cause, but rather the occasion. As early as the Pentateuch we read that Israel will be taken from her land (cf. Lev. 26:33; Deut. 28:64-67; 30:3). There were earlier prophecies of a captivity, but here we should note that the emphasis falls upon the house of David going into captivity.

Isaiah states the prophecy in general terms. *Behold!*—By means of this introductory word attention is focused upon the subject of the prophecy, and that subject is expressed in the term *days are coming*. No further identification or qualification of these days is given. Actually, this prophecy began to find fulfillment in the carrying away of Manasseh (2 Chron. 33:11) but was completely fulfilled during the reign of Zedekiah (2 Chron. 36:18). The language is that of predictive prophecy; the days in which the captivity is to occur have not yet appeared; they are in the future.

In describing what is to take place during the days that will come, the prophet uses a passive that may be rendered, *there will be lifted up*. What belongs to the king and his house will be taken away from him. With this verb there is construed the accusative of place, *to Babylon*. All will be taken away in the direction of Babylon.[8] The purpose of lifting it up from Jerusalem is that it

---

[8] Dillmann thinks that the passage does not refer to the Babylonian exile, for, he says, it mentions only the deportation of the king's house and treasure,

may be taken to Babylon. Isaiah first mentions all the king's own property, *all that is in thine house,* and then speaks of all that the ancestors of Hezekiah had acquired that was still present in Jerusalem at the time of Isaiah's speaking. Particular emphasis is given to the prophecy by the negative statement with which the verse concludes. Everything will be taken; absolutely nothing is to be left.

It is of import to note that Babylon is mentioned as the destination to which the property of the king will be taken. In Isaiah's day, and at this time particularly, Babylon was not a powerful nation. Merodach-baladan reigned but a short time in 703 B.C. Assyria was in the ascendancy, and Babylon was seeking Hezekiah's help in opposing the power of Assyria. How could Isaiah be so sure that Babylon would be the destination of the captivity and not Assyria? In his own unaided wisdom and knowledge he could not have guessed this. That he mentions Babylon is evidence that he spoke as an inspired prophet of God. Were one to rely merely upon human sagacity, one would likely predict that Assyria would take away the house of David. So striking is this prediction that some writers are compelled to speak of its author as a postexilic writer. Whether in so speaking modern commentators are motivated by a desire to do away with predictive prophecy is not for us to say; but one thing is surely clear: whether these commentators are motivated by such a desire or not, they do as a matter of fact remove true predictive prophecy from its rightful position. The results of this procedure are serious in the extreme. If this passage is the work of a postexilic writer then it is of no historical significance as a prophecy. If it is a genuine prophecy, then it points out how significant were the actions of Hezekiah, and how tragic it was that God should raise up a nation like Babylon to bring the theocracy to an end.

7 At the time when this prophecy was uttered Hezekiah had no children. The present prophecy, however, refers not so much to his own children as to descendants. In 38:5 David had been called the father of Hezekiah. Nevertheless, the close relationship of these descendants to the king is brought out in the words *that shall go forth from thy loins,* and this is further strengthened by the addi-

---

not of the people, nor does it mention the destruction of the city or the Temple.

tional words, *which thou shalt beget*. Isaiah is intent upon strengthening the thought that there is a close connection between these descendants and the king himself. They are his very own, begotten of him. Thus there would come into fulfillment the words of the promise, "Thy sons and thy daughters shall be given unto another people, and thine eyes shall look, and fail with longing for them all the day long: and there shall be no might in thine hand" (Deut. 28:32).

Not of their own volition do these descendants go to Babylon. They will be taken; again the passive is employed, thus showing that a force greater than the Judeans will take them away. The destiny that awaits them is that of being eunuchs in the palace of the Babylonian king, and this finds fulfillment in the words of Daniel 1:3, 4, 6; 2 Chronicles 33:11; and 2 Kings 24:12-16. Whether the word *eunuchs* is to be taken in a strict sense, as Codex Vaticanus does, or whether the word should have a wider application at this point is difficult to decide positively.

Again we must notice the mention of Babylon. If the events described in this and the preceding chapter occurred about two years before those depicted in chapters 36–37, why did Isaiah place these chapters after 36–37? This question is addressed in Appendix II. The prophet mentions Babylon, for he is preparing the reader for the fortieth chapter. What is presented in that chapter has as its background the events described here. It is against the dark background of despair presented in this chapter that Isaiah can utter his gracious words of comfort with which the fortieth chapter begins.

8 Hezekiah's true piety manifests itself in his willingness to obey God's word spoken through the prophet. He acknowledges that God's word is *good*, and uses the word in the sense of *just* or *right*. It is a word that is *just* for it has declared what is true; at the same time it is a word that is gracious, for it was far milder than it might have been. Hezekiah further pays a certain amount of tribute to Isaiah, for he acknowledges that Isaiah has spoken the word of the Lord. The language is a tacit acknowledgment that the prophet has done his duty. He has been a faithful messenger of Yahweh, declaring His word at a difficult time. Both men now stand out in a favorable light. On the one hand there is the faithful and courageous prophet; on the other the true-hearted king, ready in humility to acknowledge that what God has spoken is right.

A further statement is added, introduced by the words, *and he said.* These words simply constitute a general utterance of the king made with respect to his own relation to the punishment to come upon his descendants. They furthermore point out one reason why the king should have regarded the Lord's word as good. "The word of Yahweh is good," so we may paraphrase the king's thought, "for in my days there will be peace and truth." There is no egoism in this thought, as Penna seems to think, for the king is not attributing these blessings to his own merit. In reality the words constitute a childlike acknowledgment of the truth of the prophecy and also of the mercy with which it is intermingled. Surely he would be thankful that in his own days the punishment was not to be visited. At the same time his very language shows that he considered the mitigation of the punishment a blessing for himself, and yet regarded the woes pronounced upon his descendants as a misfortune of his own. "There will be peace and truth at least in my days," we may paraphrase this thought, "but I am not spared the misfortune of the knowledge that my descendants will go into captivity."

During the remainder of his own reign there would be peace. At that time the shadow of Sennacherib hung over the world, and Hezekiah would have to feel the force of this conqueror. Nevertheless, there would not be war for Jerusalem. Hezekiah would not have to lead his armies, nor would he see his people go into captivity. Likewise there would be steadfastness and truth, not of human character, but the truth of God which would bring the blessing of grace to the people. The mercy of God would not be removed during Hezekiah's lifetime. Thus the chapter closes on a note that reveals the goodness of God. Yet the enemy is on the horizon. The power of Mesopotamia, the representative of the worldwide kingdom of man, is growing stronger and stronger, and at the appointed time will strike against the little kingdom of Judah. If it should succeed, the promises of God would go by the board. It is no ultimate and final comfort to know that in Hezekiah's day alone there will be peace and truth. What about the future fortunes of the people of God? What ultimate comfort can be given to "my people"? The answer to these questions is reserved for the chapters that follow.

Appendix I

THE REIGN OF HEZEKIAH

A.

At the outset we encounter a chronological problem. Both Isaiah 36:1 and 2 Kings 18:13 state that in the fourteenth year of Hezekiah Sennacherib came up against all the fortified cities of Judah and seized them. This campaign of Sennacherib took place in the year 701 B.C and hence the year of Hezekiah's accession would be 715 B.C., a date that several modern scholars are accepting. According to 2 Kings 18:1, 2, however, Hezekiah began to reign in the third year of Hoshea of Israel and reigned for 29 years in Jerusalem.[1] Inasmuch as Israel, the northern kingdom, fell to Shalmanezer in 721 B.C. (2 Kings 18:9ff.) this would mean that Hezekiah began to reign six years before the downfall of Samaria, i.e., in 727 B.C. In the light of this passage, therefore, Hezekiah cannot have begun his reign in 715 B.C. A further difficulty also emerges. According to 2 Kings 16:1 Ahaz began to reign in Judah at the age of twenty and reigned for sixteen years. This was in the 17th year of Pekah. Pekah was followed, in the twelfth year of Ahaz, by Hoshea, who reigned for nine years (2 Kings 17:1). Thus, Ahaz would reign for four years after the accession of Hoshea, or until three years before the attack of Shalmanezer.

Complicated as are the various problems with respect to the dating of Hezekiah's reign, what concerns us now is the question of reconciling the data given above. If Hezekiah began to reign in 715 B.C. how can we square this with the statements that he was on the throne before the downfall of Samaria? To this problem various solutions have been proposed. Albright, for example (*BASOR,* No. 100, p. 22, n. 28, and No. 130, p. 9), would date the reign of Hezekiah from 715-686. This of necessity rejects the passages that synchronize the reigns of Hezekiah and Hoshea

---

[1] Hoshea was king of Israel when Shalmanezer began to besiege it. This was Hoshea's seventh year and Hezekiah's fourth. Three years later, in Hoshea's ninth year and Hezekiah's sixth, Hoshea was carried captive (2 Kings 18:9, 10). Cf. Hayim Tadmor, "The Campaigns of Sargon II of Assur: A Chronological-Historical Study," *Journal of Cuneiform Studies,* Vol. 12, 1958, pp. 22-40, 77-100.

as well as the attribution of Shalmanezer's coming to Samaria to the fourth year of Hezekiah (2 Kings 18:9).

Bright also (*A History of Israel*, n.d. p. 259) is willing to disregard 1 Kings 18:1ff. Such a solution, however, is too facile. Rowley has pointed out ("Hezekiah's Reform and Rebellion," *Bulletin of the John Rylands Library*, Vol. 44, No. 2, p. 410) that the synchronisms between the reigns of Hezekiah and Hoshea are made more than once and at different points of the two reigns, and hence he rules out the possibility that incorrect transmission of a figure could explain the discrepancy. As Rowley and others have indicated, the rejection of 2 Kings 18:1ff. involves something far more serious than the rejection of an error in the transmission of a figure. What it would actually involve is the assigning of the downfall of Samaria to the wrong reign. The synchronisms are tied up with the statement of Shalmanezer's attack. They are supported by all the textual evidence, form an integral part of their contexts, and hence, cannot this easily be disposed of.

In his commentary Edward J. Kissane (*in loc.*) proposes an emendation of the numeral in Isaiah 36:1 and 2 Kings 18:13. In place of "fourteenth" he would read "twenty-sixth."[2] The number fourteen, he asserts, has been obtained by inference from Isaiah 38:5, where Isaiah is commissioned to tell Hezekiah that God has added fifteen years to his life. The argument is that if Hezekiah reigned 29 years, and lived fifteen years after his recovery, the sickness must have occurred in his fourteenth year.

In reply it may be said that even if this line of argumentation were valid, at most it would explain the presence of the numeral "fourteenth." It does not grant warrant for substitution of the words "twenty-sixth." Indeed, no manuscript evidence permits such a substitution. This amounts to a rewriting of the text for which there is no justification. The problem cannot be solved in such a manner.

Nägelsbach (com. *in loc.*) simply interprets the figure as referring to the fourteenth year after Hezekiah's sickness. This also is not warranted, for the text, both of Isaiah and of Kings, explicitly refers to the fourteenth year of the king, not to the fourteenth year after his sickness.[3] The meaning is that in the fourteenth year of Hezekiah's reign, Sennacherib seized the Judean cities.

A far simpler attempt at solution would substitute "twenty-fourth" for "fourteenth" in 2 Kings 18:13. This actually involves merely the substi-

---

[2] Oppert had proposed to read 29 and Rawlinson 27.

[3] C. Schedl, "*Textkritische Bemerkungen zu den Synchronismen der Könige von Israel und Juda*," *VT*, Vol. 12, No. 1, Jan. 1962, pp. 112ff., identifies the fourteenth year as 714 B.C. The date is correct, he holds, but is in the wrong place, having originally introduced the account of Hezekiah's illness and the embassy of Merodach-baladan. Textual evidence, however, does not support this.

tution of עשרים for עשרה. Indeed, it may be that the substitution of only one letter is involved, ם for ה. In the ancient pointed script (Phoenician) the two letters would have appeared as ૫ (m) and ૩ (h). While these letters are obviously easily distinguishable, nevertheless, they are sufficiently similar so that if one had been carelessly written, the other might have been substituted for it. If we adopt this solution, we would bring Hezekiah's revolt to 703 b.c., two years before Sennacherib's invasion, and most of the difficulties would be cleared up.[4]

At the same time there is no extant manuscript evidence to support this emendation. Even 1Q is in agreement with M. The substitution of ה for ם therefore, if there were such a substitution, must have crept in at a very early date. If this emendation is legitimate, the 24th year of Hezekiah could be 701 b.c. and the beginning of his reign would be 727 b.c. If this does not solve all the difficulties, it at least indicates that the major points in Hezekiah's life may be understood. Certainly we must abandon the attempt to place the beginning of Hezekiah's reign in 715 b.c. The scriptural evidence is too strong against such a position.

B.

A second difficulty has to do with the nature of the account itself. As the text in Isaiah stands, it gives two attempts of Sennacherib to demand Jerusalem's surrender (namely, Isa. 36:1–37:8 and Isa. 37:9-38). In the first attempt the Assyrian king sends the Rabshakeh to taunt the people of Jerusalem and to tell them that unless they make an agreement with Sennacherib, he will take them into exile. With respect to all this Isaiah declared that God would cause Sennacherib to hear a rumor and to return to his own land where he would be slain. On the return of the Rabshakeh he finds Sennacherib warring against Libnah, and Tirhaqah of Ethiopia is said to be ready to fight against him. Thereupon, the Assyrian king again sends messengers to Hezekiah, demanding Jerusalem's surrender. Again Isaiah declares that Sennacherib will not come into the city of Jerusalem but will return by the way that he came. The angel of the Lord then smote the camp of the Assyrians; Sennacherib departed and was finally slain.

It is argued that instead of a continuous narrative containing two successive events (i.e., the two attempts of Sennacherib to threaten Jerusalem)

---

[4] Rowley, *op. cit.*, p. 413, suggests that the 24th year could be the year of the revolt (703 b.c.). This would make Hezekiah's year of ascendancy 727 b.c., which would fit in with the statement that Hezekiah began to reign six years before the fall of Samaria. The principal difficulty, however, is that the 24th year (assuming that this emendation is correct) is declared, both by Isaiah and by Kings, to be the year of Sennacherib's invasion. Between the revolt and the Assyrian king's arrival in Palestine some time must have elapsed, but possibly Isaiah and Kings are speaking of the initiation of Sennacherib's march.

what we really have is a composite account, with two versions of the same occurrence. In other words Sennacherib sent only once to Jerusalem, and not twice as the Scripture teaches. Sennacherib's conduct is said to be improbable. Hezekiah had already defied the Rabshakeh. Now that help from the Ethiopian Tirhaqah was at hand, can we really think that the mere sending of a letter would have been sufficient to induce Hezekiah to surrender?[5] Furthermore, the two incidents exhibit a close parallelism which suggests that they are two versions of the same event. It is also said that the two narratives differ in significant respects. Skinner, for example, lists the differences as follows:

1) a. The demand for surrender is backed by military force.
   b. The demand for surrender is simply presented by means of a letter.
2) a. Hezekiah sends a deputation to Isaiah.
   b. Hezekiah takes the letter to the Temple.
3) a. Isaiah waits to be consulted.
   b. Isaiah spontaneously intervenes.
4) In each instance Isaiah gives different answers.
5) a. A rumor is said to cause Sennacherib to leave.
   b. There is a miraculous destruction of the Assyrian army.

Skinner himself thinks that only in the last two points is the divergence of material importance, and shows that these divergences are really not very significant. It will, however, be necessary to examine the entire question of the unity of the passage.[6]

First of all we must say a word about the account found in 2 Chronicles 32. Both Kings and Chronicles stress the reform of Hezekiah and the advent of Sennacherib. Kings lays more emphasis upon the experience with the Assyrian king, whereas Chronicles in accordance with its purpose, to exalt the Davidic line,[7] stresses the reform. Chronicles does, however, state the central facts of the campaign and presents several additional details.

The date of Sennacherib's invasion is not mentioned, but we are told that his design was to conquer the cities for himself (v. 1). In response to this Hezekiah makes preparations (vv. 2-8). Sennacherib sends his servants against Hezekiah and against all Judah that was in Jerusalem

---

[5] This reasoning, found in Skinner's commentary, for example, is presented, even though it is widely held that the mention of Tirhaqah is but an anachronism. Inasmuch as we do not believe that the mention of Tirhaqah is an anachronism, we shall have to return to this argument later.

[6] L. Honor, *Sennacherib's Invasion of Palestine*, concludes that it is not possible to reconstruct the course of events.

[7] Cf. my discussion of this point in *Introduction to the Old Testament*, Grand Rapids, 1958, pp. 393f.

(vv. 9-11). It is true that nothing is said of an army's being sent to Jerusalem, but the word עבדיו quite likely denotes military men. It would seem that Chronicles is simply compressing what Kings and Isaiah relate, for it gives only the main ideas of Sennacherib's generals. This seems to be substantiated also by the statement of verse 16, "And yet more did his servants speak against the Lord (who is) God, and against Hezekiah His servant." Apparently Chronicles does not deem it necessary to report all of the blasphemous speeches of Sennacherib's envoys.

Hezekiah turns in prayer to the Lord for help (vv. 20-23), accompanied by Isaiah. This is really not in conflict with the accounts of Kings and Isaiah. 2 Kings 19:2ff., and Isaiah 37:2ff., relate that Hezekiah sent messengers to Isaiah beseeching him to pray ("wherefore lift up thy prayer for the remnant that are left"—2 Kings 19:4b; Isa. 37:4b). In response to this request Isaiah gives a reply. We may infer that Isaiah did indeed pray, and that his response was the answer to his prayer. It is perhaps reading too much into the text to assert that "Isaiah joins the king in the Temple and both resort to prayer."[8] 2 Chronicles 32:20 simply states that both Hezekiah the king and Isaiah the prophet prayed concerning this. Nothing is said as to where they were when they prayed, nor even that they were together. Chronicles simply remarks that two people prayed; one was the king Hezekiah and the other the prophet Isaiah. It does not recount any word of deliverance uttered by Isaiah but merely relates that the Lord delivered Hezekiah from Sennacherib, by the sending of an angel who cut off the leaders of the Assyrian army. No mention is made of any tribute paid by Hezekiah to Sennacherib.

How shall we evaluate this account in Chronicles? De Moyne (*Mélanges rédigés en l'honneur de André Robert*, 1957, pp. 149ff.) holds that Chronicles used only 2 Kings 18:26-34 and 19:8-37. Many scholars, however, think that 2 Kings gives two variant traditions and that Chronicles fuses them into one (cf. Rowley, *op. cit.*, pp. 400f.). But it is not necessary to maintain such a view. The writer of Chronicles has a didactic purpose; he desires to point out how God delivered the king Hezekiah from Sennacherib and how by a miracle He brought the presumptuous Assyrian to humiliation. It was not his purpose, therefore, to relate all the details of the twofold embassy of Sennacherib, but merely to give a summary account such as would suit his purpose. What he relates is in agreement with the facts, and does not conflict with what Kings and Isaiah recount.

(1) Returning to the more extended narrative we may consider the alleged differences between the two embassies of Sennacherib noted above. First, then, the actual nature of the demand for surrender. In the first account it is said to be supported by force, whereas in the second it is presented only by a letter. Is it likely, so the argument runs, that when the army of Sennacherib could not have brought about a surrender,

8 Rowley, *op. cit.*, p. 399.

he would have sent a mere letter in which he repeated his demand?

Sennacherib sent three leaders with a large army (בחיל כבד, lit., a heavy force). They did not immediately attack Jerusalem, but engaged rather in psychological warfare, declaring plainly to the men on the wall that Hezekiah could not deliver them, and commanding them to make an agreement with the Assyrian king. When Hezekiah heard this message he sent his servants to Isaiah, who announced that God would bring about deliverance.

Now it must be noted that no answer is given to the envoys of Sennacherib. The men on the wall did not answer the taunts of Rabshakeh, for Hezekiah had commanded them to keep silence (2 Kings 18:36; Isa. 36:21). Nor is there any mention of any official reply being given to Rabshakeh at this point. Very abruptly the text states that Rabshakeh returned (2 Kings 19:8; Isa. 37:8). The only clue to a reason for Rabshakeh's action lies in the words, "for he (i.e., Rabshakeh) had heard that he (i.e., Sennacherib) was departed from Lachish" (2 Kings 19:8b; Isa. 37:8b). Possibly, therefore, we may assume that Isaiah's message was delivered to the Rabshakeh and the Rabshakeh, hearing that Sennacherib had departed from Lachish, may have felt that he was not in a position to attack Jerusalem. Driver (*Isaiah: His Life and Times,* New York, p. 79) comments, "The troops at his disposal were apparently not sufficiently numerous to enforce submission, and he was obliged to return to his royal master with the report that his mission had proved unsuccessful." At this point we learn that Sennacherib heard that Tirhaqah had gone out to make war with him. Hence, he again sends messengers to Hezekiah. Why does he do this? It could very well be that he became alarmed, fearing a possible coalition of Tirhaqah's troops with those of Hezekiah, and realizing that a mistake had been made in allowing Jerusalem to go unscathed.

At any rate, he sends messengers unto Hezekiah boastfully demanding surrender. They did not stand before the walls to taunt the people, but presented the Assyrian king's message to Hezekiah in a letter. Hezekiah took the letter into the Temple, and spread it out before the Lord, praying for deliverance. Isaiah then sent to Hezekiah and prophesied that Sennacherib would not take the city. Again we are not told of any message given to the messengers or even of their departure. Modern scholars seem sometimes to make a contrast between the sending of an army and the sending of a letter. Scripture, however, seems to make clear that there were actually two embassies, the first presenting its message orally, the second by means of writings.

Between the accounts of the two embassies there are certain similarities.

(a) In both instances the demands are the same, couched in boastful, taunting language.

(b) In both instances Isaiah prophesies deliverance.

(c) No account of a reply to Sennacherib's envoys is given in either case.

There are, however, sufficient differences to make it clear that we do not have two variants of the same episode.

(2) A word must be said about Hezekiah's consultation of Isaiah. When Hezekiah hears the demands of the Rabshakeh he rends his garments, puts on sackcloth, and goes to the Temple (2 Kings 19:1; Isa. 37:1). Then he sends an embassy to Isaiah the prophet commanding Isaiah to pray. Following the demands of the second embassy Hezekiah spreads out the letter before the Lord in the Temple and prays. Isaiah then sends unto him (2 Kings 20:1ff.; Isa. 37:21ff.) giving him a message of comfort.

The differences here would seem to point to two different events. In the first instance Hezekiah sends what amounts to a formal embassy to Isaiah; in the second Isaiah sends a message (possibly through a disciple) to the king. Isaiah, obeying a specific command of God, went personally to Ahaz (7:3) and also to Shebna (22:15). Later, he went personally to Hezekiah (38:1 and 39:3). In the present instance, however, we first read of an embassy sent to Isaiah and then of Isaiah's sending to the king. Is there any reason for this?

Hezekiah had voluntarily submitted to the Assyrian yoke and a tribute had been imposed upon him (2 Kings 18:14-16, omitted in Isaiah). Sennacherib, however, apparently is not satisfied with this tribute but demands full surrender of Jerusalem. In submitting to Sennacherib Hezekiah had been disobedient to God's will, for Isaiah had made it abundantly clear that Assyria was but an instrument used of God to punish His people. It would not be expected that Isaiah should immediately approach the king as he had approached Ahaz. That Hezekiah had to send envoys to Isaiah may be a tacit acknowledgment that Hezekiah had done wrong and that he was now realizing that fact. His rending of the garments and wearing sackcloth also may be an indication of genuine regret for what he had done.[9] At any rate, Isaiah's reply is somewhat terse.

Following the second embassy, however, quite a different situation prevails. Now there is no mere outward rending of the garments but a turning to God in true dependence. In genuine humility and contrition Hezekiah betakes himself to the Temple in prayer. He now acts as a theocratic king should act, not merely seeking a message of hope from the prophet, when he himself has given no true acknowledgment of sin. He acknowledges by his action that God is his true help, and beseeches God to save His people.

[9] The envoys also had rent their clothes, which may simply have been an indication of despair and sadness, possibly of rage at what had happened. Cf. Matt. 26:65; Job 2:12.

Hezekiah's prayer is answered in that God speaks to him through Isaiah. It is an answer filled with comfort and one that contains the ancient promises made to the fathers. God will not forget His faithfulness to send Christ the Redeemer (2 Kings 19:30, 31, 34; Isa. 37:31, 32, 35). Isaiah does not come to Hezekiah personally, but sends his message by means of a messenger. Could it be that, just as Sennacherib had sent a letter to Hezekiah, so also Isaiah now sends the divine message by means of a letter? At any rate, whether this be so or not, Isaiah's message is full of comfort, and presents a striking contrast to the terseness of the earlier message. There is therefore a perfectly good reason why Hezekiah in one case sends to Isaiah and why Isaiah, in the second instance, sends his message to Hezekiah. What is related on this question does not support the position that there are two traditions of one event, but rather there were two separate embassies.[10]

(3) In each instance, it is argued, Isaiah gives different answers. This, however, does not prove two traditions but merely shows that in each case Isaiah answered in such a way as best to meet the situation. The first reply is simply a command not to fear and an announcement that Sennacherib will return to his land and there die by the sword. The second answer is stated to be a direct answer to Hezekiah's prayer (2 Kings 19: 20; Isa. 37:21), and may be expected to be concerned with what Hezekiah had prayed for. Is Isaiah to be allowed no individuality? Why must his response on these two occasions be identical? Each response well applies to the occasion of its utterance. The diversity therefore argues for the genuineness of the narrative as it stands rather than for the presence of two traditions.

(4) In one instance the deliverance of Jerusalem is attributed to a rumor, whereas elsewhere it is said to be the result of a miraculous deliverance. But may not both these explanations be true? Skinner, appealing to H. Schmidt, uses Bismarck's example in the Prusso-Austrian war of 1866. Bismarck desired to conclude peace without taking Vienna, fearing that Napoleon might intervene on Austria's side. Before this could be accomplished, however, he learned that cholera had broken out in some regiments. Under the influence of both considerations, therefore, he besought the king immediately to bring the war to an end.

In 2 Kings 19:7 (Isa. 37:7) the Lord states that He will place a ru^ah in Sennacherib, i.e., a divinely given power or drive that will cause the king to act. Furthermore, he will hear a rumor (not of Tirhaqah's advance, but of something at home; see com. *in loc.*) and as a result will return. This is presented, both in Kings and Isaiah, as prophecy. On the other hand, both Kings and Isaiah relate that the angel smote a vast

10 What has been set forth above also deals with the question why Isaiah "waits to be consulted" whereas in the other account he "spontaneously" intervenes.

number in the Assyrian camp, thus causing the king to abandon his efforts and to return to his own country.

There is no reason why Sennacherib may not have heard a rumor and determined to return home, and why the plague may not have struck his camp, clinching, as it were, his decision.

As the accounts stand, then, both in Kings and in Isaiah, they are unified and consistent. Leaving out of account for the time being 2 Kings 18:14-16, we may interpret the events (based on Isaiah) as follows. Sennacherib sends the Rabshakeh with a large army to Jerusalem. Rabshakeh does not attack Jerusalem, but converses with Hezekiah's envoys, who ask him to speak in Aramaic, so that the men on the wall will not understand. They desire negotiations to be carried on through purely diplomatic channels. In defiant disdain, however, Rabshakeh blurts out his coarse speech in Hebrew so that all may hear and understand. The envoys of Hezekiah then report the message to him. Upon hearing it, he puts on sackcloth, enters the temple, and calls for Isaiah, who announces that God will cause Sennacherib to return to his own land.

Rabshakeh then departs and finds Sennacherib at Libnah. A report concerning Tirhaqah evidently caused Sennacherib to send messengers to Hezekiah with a letter, which Hezekiah spreads out before the Lord in the Temple. Isaiah assures Hezekiah that Jerusalem will not be taken. An angel attacks the camp of Sennacherib, and he returns to his land.

We conclude, therefore, that this account is a unity. Nevertheless, it contains many difficulties, and to these we must now turn our attention. In the first place it is necessary to give some attention to the relation of 2 Kings 18:14-16 to the remainder of the account. Why the material contained in these verses is omitted in Isaiah is difficult to say, save that it evidently did not serve the prophet's purpose to include it. Isaiah wishes to stress the fact that the enemy of God's people, despite his blusterings and boasting, is overthrown by God Himself. To accomplish this purpose there really is no need to recount Hezekiah's lack of faith. If Hezekiah had continued steadfast, refusing to pay the tribute that Tiglath-pileser III had imposed upon Ahaz, he probably would have been in a stronger position. His confession of error, however, led to the approaches of the king upon which Isaiah does place his emphasis.

Sennacherib himself has left an account of his relations with Hezekiah, and it will be necessary to consider this account in the light of what is related in Scripture.[11] In his third campaign, directed against what he calls the Hittite land (*a-na* *ma'Hat-ti lu al-lik*) he came to the West. Lule, king of Sidon, fled, and all his domain was subdued. Sennacherib placed on the Sidonian throne a man named Tuba'lu and imposed tribute upon him. Most of Judah's neighbors were compelled to pay tribute, but Sidka of Ashkelon was rebellious, and the Assyrian king carried him to Assyria,

11 The text is found in Daniel David Luckenbill, *The Annals of Sennacherib*, Chicago, 1924.

reinstating his predecessor Sharru-lu-darri. Sennacherib continued victoriously in Philistia. The king of Ekron, Padi, had been loyal to Assyria; but the people had handed him over to Hezekiah, "the Jew," who had imprisoned him like an enemy. At the approach of Sennacherib they feared and called upon the Egyptian and Ethiopian forces for aid. Near Eltekeh, however, they were defeated; and Padi was reinstated.

Turning his attention to Hezekiah ($\check{u}$ ^{m}Ha-za-ki-a-u ^{mat}Ia-ú-da-ai) the king states that he took 46 of his walled cities together with smaller cities and great plunder. Hezekiah himself he shut up like a caged bird in Jerusalem, diminished his land and imposed a tribute of more than thirty talents of gold and 800 talents of silver.

What relationship does this account bear to that in 2 Kings? Some scholars believe that it is impossible to reconcile the accounts upon the assumption that both are describing only one campaign, and hence conclude that there were actually two campaigns. This position has been set forth recently by Professor John Bright in *A History of Israel*, Philadelphia, pp. 282-287. Bright believes that the author of Kings has telescoped the accounts of two campaigns, one having occurred in 701 (2 Kings 18:13-16) and the other later (2 Kings 18:17—19:37). In the interval between the campaigns, it is assumed, Tirhaqah backed a rebellion in the West; and this brought back the Assyrian king. At first glance this solution appears to remove the difficulties, but in reality it does not do so.

In addition to what has been remarked above about the unity of the text both in Kings and in Isaiah there are further remarks that must be made.

(a) 2 Kings 18:13 with its mention of the fourteenth year clearly refers to the events described in verses 16ff. and Isaiah 36:1. The Isaianic account must be assumed to be the earlier (see above). Inasmuch as 2 Kings 18:14-16 was not integral to Isaiah's purpose he omits those verses. But it is clear that Isaiah intends to connect the events of 36:2ff. with the invasion that occurred during the fourteenth year of Hezekiah. To assume that the biblical writers were confused or ignorant of their material is to adopt a view of Scripture contrary to that of Scripture itself. It should further be noted that the verb *wayyiṭpᵉśēm* is in agreement with what Sennacherib himself states. It is strange that Isaiah would allow 36:1b to stand if it really were in conflict with the account of deliverance to follow.

(b) When did this second campaign take place? Sennacherib himself says nothing about a second campaign. If it were placed shortly after 701 B.C. as Rawlinson suggested, it meets with some difficulties that are generally urged against placing the campaign in 701, for example, the mention of Tirhaqah.[12]

---

[12] Rowley has effectively answered the view that the second campaign could have taken place a year or so after 701 B.C. (*op. cit.*, pp. 407-408).

APPENDIX I

Advocates of the two-campaign theory, therefore, generally place the second campaign some time after the ascension of Tirhaqah, 687/6 B.C. Bright, for example, suggests that news of Assyrian reverses and promises of aid from Egypt may have moved Hezekiah to rebel and this brought Sennacherib a second time to the West. All of this, of course, is mere assumption, for which there is no extant evidence. Had there actually been such a campaign, it is difficult to believe that Sennacherib would not have mentioned it, particularly when he was victorious over so strong a foe as Tirhaqah and the Egyptians. Furthermore, it may well be questioned whether Hezekiah was still on the throne after the accession of Tirhaqah. If Hezekiah began to reign in 727 B.C. he reigned for 29 years (2 Kings 18:1) until 698 B.C. Even if Hezekiah assumed the throne in 715 B.C. his reign would terminate in 689 B.C., probably two years before Tirhaqah's accession.[13] From 2 Kings 20:21 it would appear that Hezekiah's death terminated his reign and that Manasseh was not a co-regent but occupied the throne after the death of Hezekiah. If, however, the supposed second campaign be placed before the death of Hezekiah, we really have not escaped the difficulties alleged against referring 2 Kings 18:17ff. to the year 701. On the other hand, if the second campaign belongs after the accession of Tirhaqah, the problem of Tirhaqah (to be discussed later) is satisfactorily cared for, but fresh difficulties have been added.

The supposition, therefore, that there were two invasions of Sennacherib really does not solve the problem of the relationship between the biblical and Sennacherib's account. We need not be surprised that Sennacherib does not mention his final defeat and the calamity that befell his armies. The style that he exhibits on his monuments is somewhat boastful, and it is to be expected that he would have little or nothing to say about his reverses.

As is well known, however, Herodotus preserves a tradition that probably has bearing upon the situation. He relates (ii. 141) that when Sennacherib (Σανααριβον) entered Egypt the Egyptian warriors refused to come to the aid of their king Sethos. Sethos therefore entered the inner sanctuary, lamenting his fate. In a dream the god appeared to him, giving him encouragement, and Sethos therefore collected what men he could find and made his camp at Pelusium (Πηλουσίῳ). During the night a multitude of field mice devoured the enemy's quivers and bow strings as well as the thongs of their shields. On the following day, the enemy, having no arms with which to fight, fell in great numbers. Whatever may be the precise significance of this tradition, it does seem to support the view that the enemy host was defeated.

In 2 Kings 18:14 the payment of a tribute is mentioned, and then follow the details of Sennacherib's negotiations with Hezekiah. A different order, however, appears in Sennacherib's own account, where the army

---

13 Cf. Rowley, *op. cit.*, p. 413.

is first sent against Jerusalem and the tribute later imposed. But 2 Kings 18:13-16 is short and compact, and the added details mentioned in the following verses are not given by Sennacherib at all. Inasmuch as Sennacherib's account really serves as a parallel only to 2 Kings 18:14-16, there can hardly be any contradiction. Furthermore, as we shall see, the Assyrian account, as was often the case in Assyrian annals, is not given in strict chronological order.

A minor divergence in the amount of tribute imposed appears in that Scripture speaks of 300 talents of silver whereas Sennacherib mentions 800. Both agree in mentioning thirty talents of gold. Competent scholars, however, have suggested that the Assyrian and Hebrew talents may not have been the same and that consequently, there is no contradiction.[14]

More important is the question why, if we follow the biblical order, did Hezekiah first yield (2 Kings 18:14-16) and then rebel (2 Kings 18:17ff.; Isa. 36:2ff.). According to 2 Kings 18:14 Hezekiah sent to Sennacherib at Lachish saying, "I have sinned." The usage of *hata'* in the sense of rebellion is well attested. Sennacherib himself uses such language of those at Ekron who were not rebellious (*la ba-ail hi-ṭi-ti*). Hezekiah had fought against the Philistines and, according to Sennacherib, had taken prisoner Padi, an Assyrian sympathizer. Now, however, Sennacherib was at hand; and at Eltekeh he defeated Philistine resistance supported by Egyptian aid. This would appear to have been sufficient to cause Hezekiah to act in weakness and to seek surrender.

But was Sennacherib actually at Lachish at this time? Scripture clearly affirms that he was. 2 Kings 18:14 states that Hezekiah sent to the king of Assyria at Lachish, and 2 Kings 19:8 (Isa. 37:8) speak of his having departed from Lachish, statements that fit in very well with 2 Kings 18: 14, 15. In his own account Sennacherib makes no mention of Lachish, but a relief in the British Museum pictures him there. He is seated upon his throne receiving the spoils that had been taken at Lachish. A short, four-line inscription in cuneiform clearly mentions Lachish as the site that has delivered the booty to Sennacherib. The inscription may be rendered as follows: "Sennacherib, king of the world, king of Assyria, sat upon the nimedu-throne and reviewed the booty (which had been taken) from Lachish (La-ki-su)."[16] Whether Hezekiah's submission to Sennacherib preceded or followed the battle of Eltekeh cannot be

---

14 Cf. particularly J. Brandis, *Das Munz-Mass und Gewichtswesen in Vorder-asien*, 1866, p. 98. Other literature is cited by Rowley, *op. cit.*, p. 415. It is possible, but not likely, that Sennacherib exaggerated. Also it has been suggested that in transmission the Hebrew figures may have been corrupted. Again, this is very questionable.

15 The Rabshakeh was sent from Lachish (2 Kings 18:17; Isa. 36:2).

16 Cf. James B. Pritchard, *Archaeology and the Old Testament*, Princeton, 1958, pp. 19ff.

determined with certainty.[17] At any rate, Sennacherib now appears as master of practically everything except Jerusalem, and it is readily understandable that in a moment of doubt and weak faith Hezekiah might have written to the king as he did.

Tribute was demanded and paid, probably being sent to Nineveh,[18] although Boutflower held that it was sent to Lachish.[19] To provide this tribute Hezekiah took the silver from the Temple and stripped the gold covering from the Temple doors, a procedure that must have taken some time. Apparently this was satisfactory to Sennacherib, for he did not displace Hezekiah from the throne. This was strange indeed. We might well have expected that Hezekiah would have been deposed, and a king submissive and favorable to Sennacherib placed upon the Davidic throne. With lesser enemies the Assyrian king had dealt more ruthlessly. Why this leniency with Hezekiah? It was a mistake in tactics that could not later be overcome. But "the sceptre shall not depart from Judah," and in this tactical error of Sennacherib we may discern the hand of God, carrying out His matchless purposes of redemption. Hezekiah was not deposed, nor was Jerusalem occupied.

A change of attitude now takes place. Sennacherib apparently learned that Hezekiah was no longer in a submissive spirit; hence he sends the Rabshakeh, demanding complete surrender. At any rate Sennacherib regretted this mistake. It is also quite possible that there had been no indication of a change on Hezekiah's part, and that the sending of Rabshakeh was simply a determination on the part of Sennacherib to rectify his tactical blunder. If this were so, it would explain the consternation that filled Hezekiah's heart. Whether or not there had been actual evidence of a change in Hezekiah's attitude, the mission of Rabshakeh is to be regarded as an effort of Sennacherib to accomplish what he should have accomplished at the start.

At the same time the mission of Rabshakeh is a strange one. It amounts to a blustering threat of what will happen. It is an attempt by psychological methods to unnerve Hezekiah and his city. At the moment Sennacherib himself cannot come to take Jerusalem, for he is engaged in the Philistine territory; but he sends the envoy as a second-best.

When the envoys return to Sennacherib they find that he has departed from Lachish and is warring against Libnah, northwest of Lachish (2 Kings 19:9; Isa. 37:9). A new element now enters the picture. Word came that Tirhaqah, king of Ethiopia, intended to fight with Sennacherib.

17 Cf. Rowley, op. cit., p. 417, for literature.
18 Included would probably be the return of Padi and the implements of war. Reference to this latter is made in the Rassam Cylinder, the text of which is given in Luckenbill, op. cit., p. 60.
19 Journal of the Transactions of the Victoria Institute, 1928, p. 208, and Hans Schmidt, Die Schriften des Alten Testaments in Auswahl, 2, II:ii, 1923, p. 17.

The first mission to Hezekiah had not been successful as far as the Assyrian is concerned, but now there is need for another. If he must be engaged in battle with the Ethiopian king, certainly it would not be well to leave Jerusalem unconquered in the rear. Hence, Sennacherib now sends envoys to Hezekiah to seek to accomplish what his force under Rabshakeh had not been able to bring about.[20]

Jerusalem, however, was not captured, a fact that is substantiated by Sennacherib's own account. Sennacherib heard a rumor, not of the approach of Tirhaqah, although that interpretation is possible, but in all probability a rumor of disquietude at home. Added to this the angel of the Lord visited the camp and destroyed great numbers of the Assyrian host. Sennacherib, therefore, returned to Assyria, as Scripture relates. Thus, it can be seen that the scriptural account as it stands is perfectly reasonable and self-consistent.

Two more difficulties, however, remain, to be noticed. Both 2 Kings 19:37 and Isaiah 37:38, it is said, imply that Sennacherib was actually slain shortly after his return to Assyria. As a matter of fact, however, it was some twenty years after his return before this took place. Sennacherib's death is generally placed in 681 B.C., and in that year his successor Esarhaddon began to reign. But the purpose of the biblical writers is not to give a detailed history of Assyrian events. For them it is enough to state that death did overtake the king. In the final revision of his book Isaiah simply added this summary note.

A second difficulty, however, is far more serious. This is the mention of Tirhaqah, king of Ethiopia (2 Kings 19:9; Isa. 37:9). At this time, namely, 701 B.C., Tirhaqah was not yet the king, but only became king some ten or more years later. He was not in the direct line of descent, being a nephew of Shabaka. It has often been assumed that he is called king proleptically, just as Nebuchadnezzar is in Daniel 1:1. Indeed, that is probably the answer to the problem. In itself there can be no objection to such a usage. Now, however, it is asserted that, inasmuch as Tirhaqah was born about 710 B.C., such a solution is not possible. For, if 710 or thereabouts were the birthdate of Tirhaqah, he would have been only 9 or 10 years old in 701, and hence could not have led an army against Sennacherib.[21] For this reason the mention of Tirhaqah is often thought to be an anachronism.

But how could such an anachronism have crept into the text? The manner in which the king is mentioned both in Kings and in Isaiah makes it difficult to believe that it is an anachronism. "And he (i.e., Sennacher-

[20] There is no reason to think that the force sent with Rabshakeh was a gigantic army. It was a large force and evidently Sennacherib thought it sufficient to cause Hezekiah to surrender.

[21] M. F. Laning Macadam, *The Temples of Kawa*, chap. 1, "The Inscriptions," London, 1949.

ib) heard concerning Tirhaqah, the king of Ethiopia, saying, Behold! he has gone out to fight with thee." How could such a verse find its way into the text by accident? It is needed to explain Sennacherib's action in sending envoys to Hezekiah. Without this verse that action finds no explanation.

1Q supports the Masoretic text, save that it reads אל in place of על. B also lends its support, Θαρακα Βασιλεὺς Αἰθιόπων. From the textual standpoint, therefore, it is difficult to understand how the mention of Tirhaqah can be an anachronism, for the verse in which his name occurs is an integral, even essential, part of its context.[22]

Who was Tirhaqah? Tirhaqah belonged to the 25th Egyptian dynasty, which is generally designated the Ethiopian.[23] To this dynasty there belonged at least three Pharaohs, Shabaka, Shabataka and Tirhaqah. The succession apparently did not pass from eldest son to eldest son, but from brother to brother and nephew to nephew. Shabataka was the brother of Tirhaqah and his predecessor, and Shabaka was the uncle of Shabataka, a younger brother of Piankhi, the father of Shabataka. Thus:

PIANKHI----------SHABAKA (younger brother of Piankhi)

SHABATAKA (nephew of Shabaka)

TIRHAQAH (brother of Shabataka)

Tirhaqah is thought to have ascended the throne in 690/89.[24] At the age of twenty he came from Nubia to be associated with Shabataka his brother.[25] That he was co-regent with Shabataka for six years is very questionable.[26] If, however, at the time of his association with Shabataka

---

[22] Kings has אל in place of על and also omits הנה. These are the only variants in the part of the verse that deals with Tirhaqah.

[23] It must furthermore be noted that Sennacherib himself speaks of the king of Maluhha (Ethiopia) coming to the aid of the men of Ekron (lines 73-81).

[24] Macadam believes that this year was actually the beginning of a co-regency with Shabataka, and that the actual coronation occurred six years later. It is questionable, however, whether this really was the case. Cf. Jozef M. A. Janssen, "Que sait-on actuellement du Pharaon Taharqa?" in Biblica, Vol. 34, 1953, pp. 23-43. Note the discussion on p. 26.

[25] Albright claims that Macadam has "proved convincingly that Tirhaqah was then co-regent with Shebteko for six years before the death of the latter." BASOR, No. 150, April 1953, p. 9. As the subsequent discussion will show, this is a judgment that cannot be established.

[26] The evidence for this statement is found in the following inscriptions (as given in Macadam, op. cit., p. 28):

a. Stela, Year 6, "I had departed from her (i.e., his mother) as a youth of twenty years when I came with His Majesty to Lower Egypt" (lines 50, 51).

Another Stela also dated year 6, states that Tirhaqah "came north to Thebes in the company of goodly youths whom His Majesty King Shebitku had sent to fetch from Nubia" (lines 17, 18).

he was twenty years of age, he would have been born in 710/9 B.C. and hence at the time of Sennacherib's campaign in 701 B.C. a mere lad of nine years, not able to lead an army. For this reason the mention of Tirhaqah is thought by many to be an anachronism.[27]

Serious question, however, may be raised as to the correctness of this chronology. The first problem concerns the length of Shabaka's reign. Macadam attributes to him twelve years, namely 708-697; but the evidence shows that his reign was longer. Leclant and Yoyotte appeal to a statue in the British Museum and derive therefrom a minimum of x days plus 13 years plus 9 months and 11 days of reign.[28] Even then, if we assume two years of co-regency between Shabaka and Shabataka, this would bring Shabaka's accession to 711, at least 1 year plus x days before the supposed birth of Tirhaqah, the son of Pianchi. Pianchi, let it be remembered, was also the father of Shabaka and had died in 712 B.C.

Macadam gives fifteen years to Shabataka. But there are very few monuments from this time, a fact that would point to a fairly short reign. Leclant and Yoyotte even suggest that our ignorance of the length of Shabataka's reign really renders quite vague any absolute chronology of the Cushites. They present the following chronological table:

Shabaka	715-701 (or sooner)
Shabataka	701-689
Tirhaqah	689-664

If then it was 701 or earlier that Tirhaqah in his twentieth year came to be with Shabataka, he might have served in the army and led a division against Sennacherib. If this were the case, he would have been called "king" proleptically. Hence, we cannot say that the mention of Tirhaqah is an anachronism. The chronology is difficult, and we must await further light to understand the solution of many problems. We do know enough, however, to see that Scripture is not in error in its mention of Tirhaqah.

I cannot agree with Albright that "In these inscriptions it is repeatedly stated that he first came to Nubia to be associated with his brother Shebteko when he was twenty years old" (op. cit., pp. 8, 9). On only one inscription is the age given; a second inscription merely states that Tirhaqah came to Thebes with goodly youths and that he had beheld a temple as a youth in the first year of his reign (cf. Macadam, op. cit., p. 15).

27 Rowley, op. cit., p. 420; C. Schedl, op. cit., p. 117.

28 "C'est inexactment que le tableau de M. Macadam donne à Shabaka douze années de règne, puisque l'an 15, 11 Paôni en est connu par la statue du Brit. Mus. 24429, d'où un minimum de x jours + 13 ans + 9 mois 11 jours de règne" (Notes d'histoire et de civilisation Éthiopiennes), Jean Leclant et Jean Yoyotte, Bulletin de L'Institut Francais D'Archéologie Orientale, Vol. 51, 1952, p. 25. This assumes that the Ethiopians made the second year of a king begin with the New Year following the accession. Each one of the supposed co-regencies has little to support it.

Appendix II

THE NATURE AND AUTHORSHIP OF ISAIAH 36-39

As is well known these four chapters are practically identical with 2 Kings 18:9—20:19, the principal divergence being the omission in Isaiah of Hezekiah's acknowledgment of repentance (2 Kings 18:14-16). What is the relationship that the two accounts sustain one to another? It might be held that both were taken from a common source. This is a possibility, but the theory is not widely held, and there is no actual evidence to show that such was the case.

By far the greater number of modern critics hold that the original narrative is found in 2 Kings and not in Isaiah. To support this position attempts are made to demonstrate that Isaiah could not have written these chapters and also that the author of Kings must have written them. The view set forth in this commentary is that Isaiah is the original author, and to defend this position we must note the arguments advanced against Isaianic authorship.

(a) In these chapters there is mention of the death of Sennacherib (Isaiah 37:38), an event that occurred in 681 B.C. It is held to be improbable that Isaiah was still alive at that date. Dillmann even goes so far as to say, *"Die 37³⁸ gemeldete Ermordung Sanheribs i.J. 681 (was nach 37⁷ nicht etwa ein späterer Einsatz sein kann) fällt weit über Jesajas Lebenzeit hinaus, u. führt sogar in Verbindung mit 37⁷ in eine Zeit, wo man von der grossen Zeitentfernung zwischen der Heimkehr Sanheribs u. seiner Ermordung kein Bewusstsein mehr hatte."* If, however, Isaiah's call occurred in 739 B.C., and assuming that he was twenty years of age at the time, he would be 78 years old in 681. If his call occurred when he was a few years younger, he would still probably be in his seventies. What is unheard of in this, that a man in his late seventies should write? Many men of eighty have strong intellectual power. Think of Sir Winston Churchill, Herbert Hoover, or Douglas MacArthur. Isaiah could well have mentioned the death of Sennacherib and could easily have edited his prophecies, giving them their final form.

In this connection we must notice the testimony of 2 Chronicles 32:32, "Now the rest of the deeds of Hezekiah and his gracious acts, lo! they are written in the vision ($h^a z \acute{o} n$) of Isaiah the prophet, the son of Amoz, and in (lit., upon) the book of the kings of Judah and of Israel." What is of interest here is the mention of the *hᵉzôn* of Isaiah, by which the Biblical book is clearly intended (cf. Isa. 1:1). Dillmann summarily dismisses this verse with the apodictic statement, "*Aber diese Vorstellungen eines so späten Schriftstellers über Jes. als Geschichtschreiber können nicht mass-gebend sein.*" The testimony of Chronicles, however, cannot be thus cursorily tossed aside.

Wholly apart from the fact that modern scholarship is tending more and more to acknowledge the trustworthiness of Chronicles, the question must be raised how the tradition of Isaianic authorship came to be accepted. Even if one grant a late date such as 300 B.C. to Chronicles, how did this tradition begin? For the redaction of Kings is said by many to have come from about the time of Jeremiah. Nevertheless, in the space of a little over 200 years, Isaiah's stature as a historian supposedly rose to such a degree that it completely overshadowed the true course of events.

For the verse in Chronicles clearly has reference to the canonical book of Isaiah. Furthermore, the verse plainly attests that the account of Hezekiah is written in the vision of Isaiah. The final words of the verse are difficult, but possibly the force of עַל is that the deeds of Hezekiah that were written in the vision of Isaiah had been inserted in "the book of the kings of Judah and Israel" or else that the entire vision of Isaiah had been inserted. Probably the former is intended, but one cannot be certain. At any rate, the author of Chronicles is stating that the acts of Hezekiah written in the vision of Isaiah were then placed in another book. This is interesting and trustworthy testimony to the fact that Isaiah first wrote these words.

Another testimony in Chronicles is also of significance. 2 Chronicles 26: 22 states, "And the rest of the deeds of Uzziah the first and the last, did Isaiah the prophet the son of Amoz write." Here the reference is not to the canonical book of Isaiah but to an independent work. Isaiah did not include this history in his "vision," for it was obviously not germane to his grand purpose of centering his early message around the reigns of Ahaz and Hezekiah. But the significance of the reference is that Isaiah is seen to be a history writer. For him to have written of the deeds of Hezekiah, therefore, is in accordance with what we know of Isaiah.

(b) A second objection has to do with the material contained in these chapters. The miracle of the sun dial, and the loose connection of chapters 38 and 39 with the preceding, are said to show that the narrator was no contemporary of the events that he describes but that he lived long afterwards. Likewise the predictions in 37:7 and 38:5 through their definiteness show that they were uttered after the event.

The words *yᵉhûdît* (36:11, 13) for Hebrew and *bêṭ nᵉkôṭôh* for treasure-house (39:2) are thought to be unlikely words to have been used in Isaiah's time. In 37:4, 35; 38:3, 5 there are several thoughts and expressions that are said to be characteristic of the Deuteronomistic author of

Kings. 37:19b, "for they are not gods, but the work of men's hands, wood and stone," is thought to apply better to a later age. 36:7 is said possibly to contain an anachronism. In addition to these considerations Dillmann also points out that the events described in Isaiah 36, 37 are not found in Sennacherib's own account, and he also thinks that there may be a double account of the events. On these last two points cf. Appendix I, "The Reign of Hezekiah."

(c) The inversion of the chronological order of events is said to be characteristic of the writer of Kings, who would complete one narrative before taking up another one that was somewhat contemporary. The sickness of Hezekiah, it is argued (e.g., Kissane), follows the account of Sennacherib's invasion yet was chronologically prior to it. Actually it followed the invasion of Shalmanezer. Isaiah, it is held, simply maintains the order of Kings, but does not mention the invasion of Shalmanezer. This and one other argument are thought by Kissane to be conclusive.

(d) A comparison of the two texts (i.e., Isaiah and Kings) is held to show that Kings is the earlier of the two accounts.

Before we proceed to a direct answer to these objections there are a few considerations that must be noted.

(1) It is clear that the author of Kings was acquainted with the canonical work of Isaiah, a fact that is seen from a comparison of 2 Kings 16:5 with Isaiah 7:1. The former passage was obviously written with the latter in view.

(2) The style of Isaiah 36–39 is prophetical and stands out from the ordinary style of Kings, just as do the narratives concerning Elijah that begin abruptly in 2 Kings 17:1. Quite possibly the author of Kings also took these Elijah sections from some earlier prophetical work.

(3) There is a similarity between chapter 36 and chapter 7 of Isaiah that is generally not stressed by the "critical" scholars, for these two chapters deal with historical events in the lives of the two kings Ahaz and Hezekiah, whose lives formed the pivotal points of Isaiah's earlier ministry.

(a) Both of these chapters begin with a historical notice concerning the approach of an enemy. Compare carefully the form of 7:1 and 36:1.

(b) In both of these chapters Isaiah is described in the third person. If Isaiah could thus have written of himself in chapter 7, he could also have done the same thing in chapter 36. Sometimes Isaiah used the first person, as in chapters 6 and 8:1ff.; at other times he employed the third person. Surely there can be no objection to this procedure. Sennacherib, Hezekiah's great enemy, did the same thing, using both the third and first persons. Moses wrote of himself in the third person.

(c) In neither of these chapters is the initiative of the king toward

Assyria described, although both kings did approach Assyria. This fact we learn from 2 Kings.

(d) The chapters serve to contrast the attitude of the two kings. Ahaz is hypocritical, self-satisfied, and confident that Yahweh's help is not needed. On the other hand, Hezekiah willingly sends to Isaiah for help.

(e) In both instances Isaiah commands the king not to fear:

Isaiah   7:4   fear not

Isaiah 37:6   fear not from before

(f) In both chapters there is mention of the "ascent of the upper pool, unto the way of the fuller's field" (7:3 and 36:2). This is a genuine Isaianic touch that serves to connect the two passages.

(4) The prominence of Isaiah in chapters 36—39 is quite striking. If the passage is original with Kings or even if the author of Kings took it from some earlier source, why does he give so much prominence to Isaiah? This is the more striking when we note the manner in which Kings deals with the reign of Ahaz. In his short treatment of Ahaz' reign not a word is said about Isaiah. Indeed it is not characteristic of the author of Kings to say much about the prophets. The treatment of Elijah and Elisha forms an exception, but this is because the days of Elijah and Elisha were unique in Israel's history. Apart from this, however, the author deals with the reigns of the kings and only incidentally mentions various prophets. The prominence given to Isaiah in connection with Hezekiah is unique and contrary to the author's custom. It points to the fact that the Hezekiah section is not original in Kings.

(5) Isaiah did as a matter of fact include historical sections in his prophecies. Cf. e.g., 6:1; 8:1-4; 7:1ff.; 20, etc. That he should include such historical background in connection with Hezekiah's reign is in keeping with this practice.

(6) The purpose of Isaiah 36—39 must be kept in mind. If Isaiah is not the original author, we are left without a sufficient explanation of the purpose of these chapters. If Isaiah is the author, however, the position of the chapters in his book becomes very clear, for these chapters serve a double purpose, on the one hand pointing back to the Assyrian period and on the other, looking forward to the latter portion of the prophecy, when Babylon hovered in the background. They thus serve as a conclusion to 1—35 and as a transition to 40—66.

As our exposition has endeavored to show, Isaiah's early ministry centers about two prominent kings, Ahaz and Hezekiah. With chapter 25 his prophecies revolving about Hezekiah begin, the conclusion to this section, 34—35, roughly corresponding to the conclusion of the first section, 24—27. At this point Isaiah introduces his historical account, written, as Delitzsch long ago pointed out, in usual biblical historical style, omitting those matters that were not immediately relevant to his purpose. Thus, he deals with the approaches of the Assyrian king, carrying the history on to the completion of the matters about which he had prophesied.

Chapter 38 evidently reverts to a time previous to the events just described, although to precisely what time it is difficult to say. It is most unlikely that Merodach-baladan would have sent an envoy while Sennacherib was in Palestine, harassing Jerusalem. On his prism inscription Sennacherib claims that he defeated Merodach-baladan in his first campaign.

Why, however, are these matters not recounted in chronological order? Why do the events of 38–39 precede those recorded in 36–37? The answer would seem to be that this arrangement was intentional. 36–37 form the key and conclusion of the preceding Isaianic prophecies, whereas 38–39 are the key and presupposition of the following prophecies.[1] 36–37 look backward; 38–39 forward. It would appear then that Isaiah himself deliberately arranged the chapters as we have them in order thereby to connect the two great parts of his book.[2] This explains why Isaiah first related the events concerning Sennacherib and then those that had to do with Merodach-baladan. The inversion therefore is not to be explained as due to the author of Kings. Nor, despite Kissane, does the book of Kings contain any inversions similar to this one.

(7) One final point must be noted before we take up the various ar-

[1] This sentence is based upon Schegg, quoted by Delitzsch in an appendix to Drechsler's commentary, *"Die c. 36-37 stehen voran, weil sie der Schlüssel und die Ergänzung der vorausgegangenen jesajanischen Weissagungen sind, die c. 38-39 folgen, weil sie der Schlüssel und die Voraussetzung der von c. 40 an folgenden Weiss. sind"* (p. 395).

[2] It is often argued that, inasmuch as Hezekiah reigned 29 years, and he was promised 15 years more life after his sickness, the sickness must have occurred in his 14th year. From this it is concluded that chapters 38–39 must recount events that took place previous to those of 36–37. But if the 14th year refers to Hezekiah's sickness it cannot be 701 B.C., the year of Sennacherib's invasion, for that would carry his reign to 686 B.C., which would cause tremendous difficulty as far as the chronology of the seventh century is concerned, and also ignores the clear teaching of Scripture that Hezekiah reigned before the downfall of Samaria. We suggest the following as a provisional outline of Hezekiah's life, for it entails less difficulty than any other construction and is most in accord with the statements of Scripture.

727-6	Hezekiah's accession.
723-1	Siege and capture of Samaria.
711	Hezekiah's sickness
701	Sennacherib's invasion
696	Hezekiah's death.

On this arrangement the accession year (part of 726) is not counted as the first year of Hezekiah's reign.

guments one by one. Isaiah 37:23 and 2 Kings 19:22 mention the Holy
One of Israel. In both cases the phrase appears in a prophecy uttered by
Isaiah. This phrase is characteristic of Isaiah and is what we might expect
in one of his prophecies. Indeed, there is no reason for denying either the
genuineness or the authenticity of this prophecy. But if this is a genuine Isaianic prophecy it was obviously taken over by the author of
Kings. And, inasmuch as this prophecy forms an integral part of its
context, if it were taken over by the author of Kings, so was the rest also.
Certainly, this prophecy cannot have originated with the author of Kings
and then only later have been inserted in Isaiah. For it is true prophecy,
wholly different in style from the history of Kings, and the words, "the
Holy One of Israel," while characteristic of Isaiah are certainly not characteristic of the writer of Kings. In fact, apart from this one occurrence,
the phrase does not appear in Kings at all.

With these preliminary considerations in mind we may briefly note
the objections that have been raised against the Isaianic authorship
of 36–39.

(1) With respect to the miraculous, we cannot dismiss it because it is
miraculous. Why cannot the all-powerful God of Scripture have intervened in human history by performing miraculous deeds? Let the critic
answer that question before he rules out accounts in Scripture that mention God's miracles.

(2) We have discussed above the relationship between chapters 36–37
and 38–39. How does it follow from the arrangement of these chapters
that the author must have lived long afterwards? Those who raise that
objection give no evidence to support their statement. And why cannot
definite predictions such as 37:7 and 38:5 have been uttered before the
event? The Old Testament is full of definite predictions that were
uttered before the event (e.g., Gen. 15:13-16). But the modern view of
the Old Testament, based upon naturalistic presuppositions, really rules
out genuine predictive prophecy.

(3) Cannot the words יהודית and בית נכאת have been used by Isaiah?
The adverb יהודית occurs only 6 times in the Old Testament. Five of
these instances have to do with Sennacherib's envoys addressing the men
on the walls, namely, Isaiah 36:11, 13; 2 Kings 18:26, 28; 2 Chronicles 32:
18. The only other occurrence is Nehemiah 13:24. Sennacherib himself
uses the Gentilic ^mIa-ú-da-ai (Col. ii, 76; iii, 18). In the light of these
facts Dillmann's contention seems very weak.

The phrase בית נכאת is found but twice, namely, in the parallel passages Isaiah 39:2 and 2 Kings 20:13. Apart from that the word נכאת
(spices) appears in Genesis 37:25 and Genesis 43:11. In Ugarit (Krt ii.
2.25) the word nkyt is used in the sense of "treasury." In Akkadian the
phrase bit nakamti occurs, and this removes the objection that bêt nᵉkôt
would have been an unlikely word to have been used in Isaiah's time.

(3) Perhaps the strongest argument for the priority of Kings is derived from a comparison of the two passages. Driver, for example (*Literature of the Old Testament,* Edinburgh, 1909, p. 227), claims that Kings has the fuller details, and that Isaiah is evidently an abridgment. He further asserts that the narrative as it stands in Isaiah shows traces of having passed through the hand of the compiler of Kings.

One or two general remarks may be made. A shorter work is not necessarily to be regarded as an abridgment of a longer one. The shorter work could be earlier, and the later one could be an expansion. The author of the shorter work may deliberately have omitted certain matters of which he had knowledge but which were not immediately germane to his purpose. A later writer may not merely have expanded the text of an earlier work but may also, for one reason or another, have included material that did not appear in the earlier work. It is not always possible to tell from these considerations alone which work is the earlier. It must be remembered that Isaiah (as witness the first chapter) knew the book of Deuteronomy. This is a sufficient explanation why Deuteronomic "influence" at times may appear in chapters 36—39. It also explains why the language may at times be similar to that which is characteristic of Kings.

Furthermore, it is not always possible to explain variations. Semitic style did not at all times seek to give nor did it claim to give a verbatim account of what it reported. A good example of minor variations may be seen in a comparison of Rameses' Hittite Treaties. Variations in the Gospel accounts also illustrate the same principle. This in no way militates against the scriptural doctrine of verbal and plenary inspiration, for this doctrine merely teaches that Scripture faithfully presents what it purports to present. It does not claim that duplicates of one account must be slavishly identical.

Our purpose in what follows will merely be to show that there is nothing in these two accounts of Sennacherib's invasion that precludes Isaiah from being the original author. To explain each variation would probably be impossible, and we shall not attempt it. Delitzsch has salved the consciences of all future expositors of Isaiah by his remark, "But the task of pronouncing an infallible sentence upon them all (i.e., upon all the variations) we shall leave to those who know everything."[3]

(1) Driver calls attention to the fuller details given in 2 Kings 20:4, 9-11 as over against Isaiah 38:4, 7-8. In Isaiah 38:4 1Q follows M, as do the Greek mss. also. Can one really say that Isaiah 38:4 is an abridgment of 2 Kings 20:4, and not that 2 Kings is an expansion? It is wiser on this verse to reserve judgment. With respect to Isaiah 38:7, 8 and 2 Kings 20:9-11 there is additional material in 2 Kings. Again 1Q follows M, as

3 *Op. cit.,* II, p. 85n.

do the Greek versions. It is just as possible to regard 2 Kings as an expansion as it is to consider Isaiah an abridgment.

(2) Driver also compares Isaiah 36:2, 3a, 17, 18a with 2 Kings 18:17, 18a, 32. Here again in each verse, Kings supplies additional details. But, as pointed out elsewhere (Appendix I) the entire account of Hezekiah's acknowledgment of sin is omitted in Isaiah, for it is not germane to his purpose. This omission in no sense proves the originality of Kings. As for Isaiah 36:17, 18a the same remark holds good. Obviously, Kings is a fuller text; but does that prove it to be the original?

(3) In Hezekiah's prayer, the reference to David is thought to show the hand of the compiler of Kings. This reference (Isa. 37:35b) is said to be a motive without parallel in Isaiah. If, however, this explanation is correct, why is there no reference to David in Isaiah 38:6 where Kings and 1Q both have such a reference (similar to the one in Isa. 37:35b)? It should be noted that this is the only historical section in Isaiah in which such a reference might be expected. Note also 38:5. Hezekiah was similar to David, and hence the mention of David (see also the exposition). Of course there are many references to David in Kings; that is a historical work. Such references are not necessary in a prophetical book; but where Isaiah deals with the one king who was similar to David, we may very well expect that he should mention him. To claim that such mention shows the hand of the compiler of Kings is to make an assertion for which there is no evidence.

(4) Driver appeals to phrases such as *in those days,* 38:1, and *at that time,* and claims that the narrative surrounding the prophecy (37:22-32, which Driver attributes to Isaiah) seems to belong to a writer of a subsequent generation, for this writer attributes the successes against Hamath, Arpad, and Samaria to Sennacherib, whereas they were achieved by earlier kings. First of all, phrases such as *at that time* and *in those days* were not the property of any one particular writer. They are used for introducing historical material; and inasmuch as Isaiah is writing historical material at this point, there is no reason why he may not use them.

As for the attribution to Sennacherib of the successes against Hamath, Arpad, and Samaria, Driver does not accurately state the case. In 36:18 Rabshakeh speaks in the name of the Assyrian king as such. He does not necessarily intend to attribute these successes to Sennacherib individually. This is proved by Sennacherib's own statement in 37:11-13. It is passing strange that the "hand" of the compiler of Kings would so have blundered as to attribute the downfall of Samaria to Sennacherib, when this same "hand" so clearly attributes its downfall to others, and that in the preceding chapter (2 Kings 17). Furthermore, if the prophecy of Isaiah be divorced from its context, it becomes devoid of significance.

There are certain points in the variations where the preference should go to Isaiah as containing the better text.

APPENDIX II

(1) In 2 Kings 18:20 *'āmartā* is not preferable to Isaiah. If the second person is to be retained, we should expect *dibbartā*.

(2) In Isaiah 36:7 the singular verb is probably original, inasmuch as Hezekiah is addressed throughout. The plural does not necessarily go better with the plural suffix in *our God*, for a single individual can speak of *our God*. A positive decision is difficult.

(3) In Isaiah 36:14 the omission of *from his hand* is probably original, for the appearance of the phrase in 2 Kings 18:29 is probably altered from that in Isaiah 36:20.

(4) Of particular interest is a comparison between Isaiah 36:17 and 2 Kings 18:32, for the latter contains additional materials. The addition in 2 Kings 18:32 is not necessary, for the text of Isaiah is sufficiently clear. Here the shorter reading should be preferred as original. Nor is the additional material in 2 Kings 18:33 necessary. Isaiah is more concise and well rounded. It is questionable whether Kings could here be the original.

(5) Isaiah 37:2 and 2 Kings 19:2. The order of words in Kings, *unto Isaiah the prophet, son of Amoz*, is declared by Delitzsch to be inadmissable. It is certainly contrary to the normal order; cf. Isaiah 38:1; 1 Kings 16:7; 2 Kings 14:25; Jeremiah 28:1; Zechariah 1:1, 7. Dillmann acknowledges it to be unusual (*ungewöhnlich*) and thinks that it arose through adding the words *son of Amoz* that were originally omitted. In this instance the text of Isaiah is to be preferred.

(6) Isaiah 37:9 and 2 Kings 19:9. Although 1Q here supports Kings, there is good reason for believing that Isaiah is original. The words *and he heard* are repeated, to show that Sennacherib, as soon as he heard of Tirhaqah, acted. Thus, Vitringa, *Simul intellexit, simul misit nuncios*. Delitzsch acknowledges this, but thinks that the second occurrence was changed from *and he returned*. This is a point that cannot be proved one way or the other, but the force of the Isaianic text certainly supports the position that it is original.

(7) Isaiah 37:14 and 2 Kings 19:14. Here the singular suffixes of the two verbs in Isaiah agree and form a certain harmony, *and he read it and he spread it out*. This fits in well with the singular sense of letters (*epistolae*). It is a constructio ad sensum. Kings by its use of the plural suffix, *and he read them*, apparently has tried to make the suffix agree with the plural noun, in which 1Q also agrees. The singular, however, is certainly to be preferred. Delitzsch also acknowledges that Kings made the change.

(8) Isaiah 37:16 and 2 Kings 19:15. In the prayer Kings omits the designation *of hosts*, but its presence is surely original. It serves to designate Yahweh as the God of power, a most necessary designation at this point (see exposition). Furthermore, the addition of this epithet is reg-

ular both in Kings and Isaiah; cf. Isa. 37:32; 39:5; 1 Kings 18:15; 2 Kings 3:14.

(9) Isaiah 37:24 and 2 Kings 19:23. *Servants* is to be preferred to *messengers*, for the latter would seem to be due to the influence of verses 9, 14, where mention has already been made of messengers. *By the multitude of my chariots* is to be preferred to the reading of Kings, *rkb rkbi*. In Kings the suffix is missing in the first word, so that there is not an exact repetition. Nor does the repetition of the word in Kings give a good sense, by *the chariot of my chariots*, i.e., by my best chariots. That is questionable. Many commentators prefer Kings, *min qtztzh*. But it is difficult to tell. *R* easily passes into *L* in many languages. 1Q is faint, but seems to read *mrwm*.

(10) Isaiah 37:32 and 2 Kings 19:31. This verse is clearly original with Isaiah. 37:32 is of similar construction to Isaiah 2:3, and 37:32b is similar to Isaiah 9:6b.

CONCLUSION

(a) From a comparison of individual words and phrases it is not always possible to decide whether Kings or Isaiah should be given the preference. In a very few instances (possibly 2 Kings 19:17 and 23) the text of Kings may be preferable. Nevertheless, there are certain unmistakable marks of Isaiah in these passages which support the position that the text of Isaiah is original. These have been discussed in the immediately preceding comparison of the two texts.

(b) The author of Kings was acquainted with the canonical prophecy of Isaiah.

(c) The prophetical style of Isaiah 36—39 stands out in marked contrast from the historical style of Kings.

(d) The similarity between Isaiah 36 and Isaiah 7 is striking.

(e) The prominence of Isaiah in chapters 36—39 is certainly out of keeping with the ordinary method of writing employed in Kings.

(f) Isaiah included historical material in his prophecies.

(g) 2 Chronicles 32:32 states that Isaiah wrote the deeds of Hezekiah in his prophecy.

(h) If Isaiah is not the original author, these chapters have no apparent purpose. On the other hand they form an integral portion of the prophecy of Isaiah.

(i) The designation "Holy One of Israel" appearing in these chapters is characteristically Isaianic.· It is found nowhere else in Kings.

(j) The objections to the Isaianic authorship are not cogent and can easily be answered.

In the light of these considerations we may safely assume that Isaiah is the author of chapters 36—39.

Appendix III

THE INVASION OF SENNACHERIB

Translated from the Assyrian text as given in Daniel David Luckenbill, *The Annals of Sennacherib*, Chicago, 1924; the translation herein given is fairly literal and as much as possible follows the word order of the original.

Column II

Line

37 In my third campaign I set out against Hatti.
    As for Luli, the king of Sidon, the awe-inspiring splendor
    of my lordship overwhelmed him and far away

40 in the midst of the sea he fled and disappeared.
    Sidon the Great,[1] Sidon the Small
    Bit-Zitti, Zaribtu, Mahalliba,
    Ushu, Akzib, (and) Akko
    his cities, strong (and) fortified supplied with food[2]

45 and drink (i.e., well provisioned) for his garrisons,
        the awe-inspiring weapons of Aššur[3]
    my lord overwhelmed them and they bowed at my feet.
        (i.e., submitted to me)
    Tubalu[4] on the royal throne
    over them I placed, and gifts due to me as overlord[5]
    yearly without cessation I imposed upon him.

50 As for Menahem, the Shamsimurunite,
    Tubalu, the Sidonite,
    Abdiliti, the Arvadite,
    Uru-milki, the Gublite (i.e., from Byblos)
    Mitinti, the Ashdodite,

---

1 Cf. Josh. 11:8.
2 Lit., places of food and drink.
3 Lit., the terror of the weapons of Aššur.
4 Ethbaal?
5 *Biltu* and *mandattu belutiya* may be taken as a hendiadys.

55 Budu-ilu, the Beth-Ammonite,
   Kammusunadbi, the Moabite,
   Aaramu,[6] the Edomite
   all kings of Amurru,[7] splendid gifts,
   their weighty show piece, fourfold[8] before me

60 they brought and kissed my feet. But Sidqa,
   the king of Ashkelon who had not submitted
   unto my yoke—the gods of the house of his father,
      himself, his wife,
   his sons, his daughters, his brethren, the seed of
      the house of his father,
   I deported and unto Assyria I brought.

65 Sharruludari, son of Rukibtu, their former king
   over the populace of Ashkelon I placed and
   the payment of tribute, a gift of alliance
      due my lordship I imposed upon him.
   He did the labor.[9] In the course of my
   campaign Beth-Dagon, Joppa,

70 Banaibarka, Asuru, cities
   of Sidqa, who had not bowed quickly
   unto my feet, I besieged, I conquered, I took
      away their spoil.
   The officials, the nobility and the populace[10] of Ekron
   who had thrown Padi their king, lord of a
      sworn treaty, with Assyria[11]

75 into iron fetters and
   unto Hezekiah the Judean
   gave him over—like an enemy
      they committed sacrilege.[12]
   There became afraid the Egyptian kings
   the bowmen, charioteers (and) horsemen

80 of the king of Ethiopia, an army without number,
   when (-ma) they called upon (them), they came to
      their aid

6 Cf. *Yô-rām* in 2 Sam. 8:10.
7 Lit., kings of Amurru, all of them.
8 Lit., unto the fourth.
9 Lit., he pulled my ropes.
10 I.e., the common people.
11 Cf. Gen. 14:13.
12 I.e., they had put in prison one who had been in a relationship of oath with Assyria.

in the plain of Eltekeh.
The battle line being drawn up in front of me

Column III

1   they sharpened their weapons.[13] With the trust of Aššur
    my lord, I fought with them and brought about
    their defeat. The Egyptian charioteers and princes[14]
    together with the charioteers of the king of Ethiopia

5   alive in the midst of the battle I captured.
    Eltekeh (and) Timnah
    I besieged, I conquered, I took away their spoil;
       unto Ekron
    I approached, and the officials (and) nobles who
       devised the crime[15]
    I slew, and on poles round about the city

10 I hung their bodies. As for the ordinary citizens
    the perpetrators of sin and infamy[16] I counted (them) as spoil.
    The remainder of them (who were) not guilty of sin
    and contempt, who had no punishment due them;
    I ordered their release. Padi their king

15 from the midst of Jerusalem I brought out and
    as lord on the throne[17] over them I placed and
    the tribute (due to) my lordship I imposed upon him.
    And (as for) Hezekiah the Judean
    who had not submitted unto my yoke—46 of
       his strong

20 walled cities and the small cities
       that are in their environs
    which were without number by piling up
    siege ramps, bringing near battering rams, the
       battling of foot soldiers, mines, sap works
    and supplements of siege, I besieged (and
       conquered)

---

13 *ú-ša-'a-lu* ^ú*kakkê* ^{meš}*-šu-un.*

14 Lit., sons of the kings.

15 Lit., who caused sin to be.

16 In a private communication G. Lindsay Russell points out that in this
context there are three forms of action determined by the degree of guilt.
   (a) *kiṭa šubšu*—those who devised the crime—death and impalement.
   (b) *ēpis anni u gillati*—perpetrators of the deed—deportation.
   (c) *lā bābil hiṭiti u gulluti.ša aransunu la ibšu*—those who did not
       take part in the crime—freedom.

17 Lit., in the throne of lordship.

200,140 people, young and old, male
    and female

25 horses, mules, asses, camels,
    oxen and small cattle which were without
      number from their midst
    I brought out and counted as spoil. Himself,
      like a bird in a cage
    in the midst of Jerusalem, his capital city,
    I shut up. Earthworks against him I raised,

30 I prohibited exit from his city;[18] his cities
    which I had plundered from the midst of his
      land I cut off and
    to Mitinti king of Ashdod,
    Padi king of Ekron and Silli-bel
    king of Gaza I gave and thus I reduced his land.

35 Beyond the former tribute, the gifts of their land
    imposts, presents (due to) my lordship I added and
    imposed against him. As for Hezekiah himself
    the awe-inspiring splendor of my lordship
      overwhelmed him and
    the Arabs[19] together with his crack troops which he
      had brought in for the purpose of strengthening

40 Jerusalem, his capital,
    took leave. Together with the 30 talents of gold
    800 talents of silver, costly stones, antimony,
    large pieces of sandu (red?) stone, ivory couches,
    ivory arm chairs, elephant hide, ivory,

45 ebony, boxwood, all kinds of valuable treasures
    together with his daughters, his concubines, the male
    and female musicians into Nineveh my capital
    he sent to me, and for the payment of tribute
    and the performance of servitude he sent his
      messengers.

[18] Lit., the exit of the gate of his city I turned into a taboo.
[19] The term may refer to irregular troops.

Bibliography

Abarbanel, Don Isaac; also Abravanel; cf. Rosenmüller.

Abulfeda; cf. H. O. Fleischer, *Historia anteislamica arabice edidit, versione latina auxit.* Lipsia, 1831.

Albright, William F., *Archeology and the Religion of Israel.* 1942.

——, *Geschichte und Altes Testament.* Tübingen, 1953.

Alexander, Joseph Addison, *Commentary on the Prophecies of Isaiah.* 1846. Grand Rapids, 1953.

Allis, Oswald T., *Prophecy and the Church.* Philadelphia, 1943.

Alt, Albrecht, "Ägyptisch-ugaritisches," *Archiv für Orientforschung,* 15, 1951.

——, "Galiläische Probleme," *Palästinajahrbuch,* 1937.

——, *Kleine Schriften,* II. Munchen, 1953.

——, "Menschen Ohne Namen," *Archiv Orientální,* 18, 1950.

Amarna Text. J. Knudtzon, *Die El-Amarna Tafeln.* Aalen, 1964.

Amr el-Quais, *Moallaka;* cf. W. Ahlwardt, *The Divans of the Six Ancient Arabic Poets.* London, 1870.

Anderson, Robert T., "Was Isaiah a Scribe?" *JBL,* 79, 1960.

Annals of Mursilis, text in Sturtevant and Bechtel, *A Hittite Chrestomathy.* Philadelphia, 1935.

Anspacher, Abraham S., *Tilgath Pileser III.* New York, 1912.

Arias Montanus, Benito, *Polyglot Antwerp,* 1569-1573.

Avigad, N., "The Epitaph of a Royal Steward from Siloam Village," *Israel Exploration Journal,* Vol. 3, No. 3, 1953.

Baedeker, *A Handbook of Palestine and Syria.* 1912.

Baker, S. W., *The Albert Nyanza, Great Basin of the Nile and Exploration of the Nile Sources.* London, 1871.

Barnes, A., *Notes on Isaiah,* I. New York, 1840.

Bea, A., "Ras Samra und das Alte Testament," *Biblica,* Vol. 19, 1938.

Begrich, Joachim, "Sôfer und Mazkir," *ZAW,* Vol. 58.

Béguerie, La *Vocation d'Isaiae,* Études sur les prophètes d'Israel. Paris, 1954.

Bentzen, Aage, *Jesaja,* Band I, Jes. 1-39. Kobenhavn, 1944.

——, *King and Messiah.* London, 1955.

Berry, G. R., "Messianic Predictions," *JBL,* 45, 1926.

Bewer, Julius A., *The Literature of the Old Testament.* New York, 1940.

Biblia sacra iuxta versionem simplicem quae dicitur Peschitta, II. Beirut, 1951.

Biblical Archaeologist, The. New Haven, Connecticut.

Bijbel in Nieuwe Vertaling. Kampen, 1952.

Birkeland, H., *Zum Hebräischen Traditionswesen.* Oslo; 1938.

Blank, Sheldon H., *Prophetic Faith in Isaiah.* New York, 1958.

Bleeker, *Kleine Propheten,* II.

Böhl, Franz, *Nieuwjaarsfest en Konigsdag in Babylon en Israel.* 1927.

Boutflower, C., *Journal of the Transactions of the Victoria Institute,* 1928.

Brandis, J., *Das Munz-Mass und Gewichtswesen in Vorderasien.* 1866.

Bratcher, Robert G., *The Bible Translator.* July, 1958.

Breasted, J. H., *Ancient Records of Egypt,* Vol. II.

Bright, John, *A History of Israel*. Philadelphia, 1959.
Briggs, Charles A., *Messianic Prophecy*. New York, 1886.
Brockelmann, *Hebräische Syntax*. Neukirchen, 1956.
Brunet, Gilbert, *"Le Terrain aux Foulons," RB*, Vol. 71, No. 2, 1964.
Bruno, D. Arvid, *Jesaja, eine rhythmische und textkritische Untersuchung.* Stockholm, 1953.
Bultema, Harry, *Practische Commentaar op Jesaja*. Muskegon, 1923.
Burrows, M., Trevor, J. C., Brownlee, W. H., *The Dead Sea Scrolls of St. Mark's Monastery*, I, *The Isaiah Manuscript and the Habakkuk Commentary*. New Haven, 1950.

Calvin, *Commentarii in Isaiam prophetam*. Geneva, 1570.
Campbell, Roderick, *Israel and the Covenant*. Philadelphia, 1954.
Cappellus, Ludwig, *Critica Sacra*. 1650.
Caspari, Carl Paul, *Jesajanische Studien*. Leipzig, 1843.
Caspari, Wilhelm, "Jesaja 34 and 35," *ZAW*, Vol. 49, 1931.
Castellio, Sebastian, *Biblia Sacra*. 1531. Frankfurt, 1669.
Ceriani, A. *Translatio syra Pescitto Veteris Testamenti*. Milan, 1876.
Chafer, Lewis S., *Systematic Theology*. Dallas, 1947-48.
Cheyne, T. K., *The Prophecies of Isaiah*, I. 1868. New York, 1888.
Childs, B. S., *Myth and Reality in the Old Testament*. Naperville, 1960.
Chrysostom, *Hermeneia*, in Migne, *Patrologia*.
Churgin, P., *Targum Jonathan to the Prophets*. New Haven, 1927.
Cocceius, Johannes, *Opera Omnia Theologica*. Amstelodami, 1701.
Condamin, Albert, *Le Livre d'Isaie*. Paris, 1905.
Contenau, G., *La civilisation phénicienne*. 1928.
Cooke, G. A., *A Textbook of North Semitic Inscriptions*. Oxford, 1903.
Coppens, *La Prophétie de la 'Almah*. Bruges, Paris, 1952.
Cordero, M. Garcia, "El Santo de Israel," *Mélanges Bibliques rédigés en l'honneur d' André Robert*. Paris, 1957.
Couroyer, B., *"L'Origine Égyptienne du mot 'Paque,'" Revue Biblique*, Vol. 62, 1955.

Dalman, Gustav, *Jerusalem und seine Gelände*. Gütersloh, 1930.
Dathe, Johann August, *Opuscula*, ed. E. F. Rosenmüller. Lipsiae, 1796.
DeBoer, P. A. H., *Second-Isaiah's Message*. Leiden, 1956.
De Fraine, *L'aspect religieux de la royaute israelite*. Rome, 1954.
Delekat, L., "Die Peschitta zu Jesaja zwischen Targum und Septuaginta," *Biblica*, 38, 1957.
Delitzsch, Franz, *Biblical Commentary on the Prophecies of Isaiah*. 1866. Grand Rapids, 1949.
De Vaux, R., *"Titres et Fonctionnaires Égyptiens a la cour de David et de Salomon," RB*, Vol. 48, 1939.
Dhorme, E., *L'evolution religieuse d'Israel*. Bruxelles, 1937.
Dillmann, August, *Das Prophet Jesaia*. Leipzig, 1890.
Diringer, *Le Iscrizioni Antico-Ebraiche Palestinesi*. Firenze, 1934.
Döderlein, Christoph, *Esaias*. Altsofi, 1825.
Dougherty, R. M., *Nabonidus and Belshazzar*. New Haven, 1929.
Drechsler, Moritz, *Der Prophet Jesaja*. Stuttgart, 1849.
Driver, G. R., *Canaanite Myths and Legends*. 1956.
————, *A Treatise on the Use of Tenses in Hebrew*. 1892.

BIBLIOGRAPHY

————, *Von Ugarit nach Qumran.* 1958.
Driver, S. R., *Isaiah, His Life and Times.* New York.
Duhm, Bernhard, *Das Buch Jesaia.* 1892. Göttingen, 1922.
Dussaud, R., *des Religions de Babylonie et d' Assyrie.* Paris, 1945.

Eaton, J., "The Origin of the Book of Isaiah," *VT,* 9, 1959.
Edelkoort, A. H., *De Christusverwachting in het Oude Testament.* Wageningen, 1941.
Eichhorn, Johann G., *Die hebräische Propheten.* Göttingen, 1819.
Eitan, I., "A Contribution to Isaiah Exegesis," *HUCA,* 12-13, 1937-38.
Engnell, Ivan, *The Call of Isaiah.* Uppsala and Leipzig, 1949.
————, *Studies in Divine Kingship in the Ancient Near East.* Uppsala, 1943.
Erman, A., *The Religion of the Egyptians.*
Euting, Julius, *Sinaitische Inschriften.* Berlin, 1901.
Ewald, H., *Die Propheten des alten Bundes erklärt.* Stuttgart, 1840-41.

Fahlgren, K. H., *Nahestehende und entgegengesetzte Begriffe im Alten Testament.* Uppsala, 1932.
Feldmann, Franz, *Das Buch Isaias,* I, II. Münster, 1926.
Fenshaw, "The Wild Ass in the Aramean Treaty Between Bar-Ga'ayah and Mati'el," *JNES,* Vol. 22, 1963.
Finkelstein, Louis, *The Commentary of David Kimchi on Isaiah.* 1926.
Fischer, Johann, *Das Buch Isaias.* Bonn; 1, 1937, II, 1939.
Fitzmeyer, J. A., "The Aramaic Inscriptions of Sefire I and II," *JAOS,* Vol. 81, No. 3.
Fleming, W. B., *The History of Tyre.* 1915.
Frankfort, Henri, *Kingship and the Gods.* Chicago, 1948.
Friedrichsen, A., *Hagios-Qadosh.* Oslo, 1916.
Frost, S. B., *Old Testament Apocalyptic.* 1952.
Fullerton, K., "Studies in Isaiah," *JBL,* 38, 1919.

Gadd, C. J., *Ideas of the Divine Rule in the Ancient East.* 1948.
Galling, Kurt, *Textbook zur Geschichte Israels.* Tübingen, 1950.
Gehman, H. S., "The 'Burden' of the Prophets," *JQR,* Vol. 31, No. 2, 1940.
Gesenius, Wilhelm, *Der Prophet Jesaia.* Leipzig, 1820, 1821.
Gesenius, Kautzsch, Cowley, *Hebrew Grammar.* Oxford, 1910.
Gevirtz, "West-Semitic Curses," *VT,* No. 11, 1961.
Gill, John, *Body of Divinity.* 1771. Grand Rapids, 1951.
Ginsberg, "Some Emendations in Isaiah," *JBL,* 69, March, 1950.
Ginsburg, C. D., *Prophetae posteriores.* London, 1911.
Goetze, A., "The So-Called Intensive of the Semitic Language," *JAOS,* Vol. 62, No. 1, 1942.
Gordon, C. H., "Homer and the Bible," *HUCA,* Vol. 26, 1955.
————, *Ugaritic Literature.* 1947.
————, *Ugaritic Manual.* 1955.
————, *Ugaritic Textbook.* 1965.
Gray, G. B., "Kingship of God in Prophets and Psalms," *VT,* Vol. 11, 1961.
————, *The Prophecy of Isaiah.* Edinburgh, 1926.
Green, *Hebrew Grammar.* New York, 1898.
Greenberg, "Text of the Hebrew Bible," *JAOS,* Vol. 76, No. 3, 1956.
Grelot, P., "La denière étape de la redaction sacerdotale," *VT,* 6, 1956.

Gressmann, *Altorientalische Texte zum Alten Testament.* 1909.

Grotius, Hugo, *Annotata ad Vetus Testamentum.* 1644.

Guillaume, A., "The Dead Sea Scrolls of Isaiah," *JBL,* Vol. 76, 1957.

Gunkel, Herman, *Die Schriften des Alten Testaments,* 2. Abteilung, 2. Band. 1921, 1925.

Guthe, Hermann, *Geschichte des Volkes Israels.* Tübingen and Leipzig, 1904.

Haller, Max, *Die Schriften des Alten Testaments,* II, 3. Göttingen, 1914.

Hammurabi; cf. A. Deimel, *Codex Hammurabi.* Romae, 1930.

Hanel, J., *Die Religion der Heiligkeit.* Gütersloh, 1931.

Hattusilis, *Apology;* cf. Sturtevant and Bechtel, *Hittite Chrestomathy.* Philadelphia, 1935.

Heidel, A., *The Babylonian Genesis.* 1951.

————, *The Gilgamesh Epic.* 1946.

Heidel, W. A., *The Day of Jahweh.* New York, 1929.

Held, Moshe, *Studies and Essays in Honor of Abraham A. Newman.* 1962.

Henderson, Ebenezer, *The Book of the Prophet Isaiah.* 1840. London, 1857.

Hertzberg, H. W., *Der erste Jesaja.* Kassel, 1952.

Herzfeld, E., *Altpersische Inschriften.* 1938.

Hill, G., *A History of Cyprus,* I, 1940.

Hillers, *Treaty-Curses and the Old Testament Prophets.* Rome, 1964.

Hitti, P. K., *History of Syria.* New York, 1951.

Hitzig, Ferdinand, *Der Prophet Jesaja.* Heidelberg, 1833.

Hölscher, G., *Die Profeten.* Leipzig, 1914.

————, *Geschichte der israelitischen und jüdischen Religion.* 1922.

————, *Die Ursprünge der jüdischen Eschatologie.* Giessen, 1925.

Holwerda, B., *De Wijsheid die Behoudt.* 1957.

Honor, L., *Sennacherib's Invasion of Palestine.* 1926.

Hooke, S. H., *Palestine Exploration Fund, Quarterly Statement for 1935.*

Hoonacker, A. Van, *Het Boek Isaias.* Brugge, 1932.

Huffmon, Herbert, "The Covenant Lawsuit in the Prophets," *JBL,* 78, 1959.

Hummel, Horace, "Enclitic Mem in Early Northwest Semitic, Epecially Hebrew," *JBL,* 76, 1957.

Hvidberg, "The Masseba and the Holy Seed," *Interpretationes (Mowinckel Festschrift).* Oslo, 1955.

Hyatt, James P., *Prophetic Religion.* New York, 1947.

Ibn Hisham, ed. Wüstenfeld, *Des Leben Mohammeds.*

Ilgen, Karl David, *Die Urkunden des jerusalemischen Tempelarchivs in ihrer Urgestalt, als Beitrag zur Berichtigung der Geschichte der Religion und Politik.* 1798.

Interpreter's Bible. New York, Nashville, 1952ff.

Jacob, Edmond, *Theologie de l'Ancien Testament.* Neuchâtel, 1955.

Janssen, J. M. A., "Que sait-on actuellement du Pharaon Taharqa?" in *Biblica,* Vol. 34, 1953.

Jastrow, *Hebrew-Babylonian Traditions.* 1914.

Jenni, "Das Wort 'ōlām im Alten Testament," *ZAW,* Vol. 65, 1953.

Jennings, F. C., *Studies in Isaiah.* New York, 1950 .

Johnson, Aubrey R., *Sacral Kingship in Ancient Israel.* Cardiff, 1955.

Keizer, P., *De profeet Jesaja.* Kampen, 1947.

BIBLIOGRAPHY

Keilschrifturkunden aus Boghazkeui, 1916, 1921.
Kennett, R. H., *Ancient Hebrew Social Life and Custom as Indicated in Law, Narrative and Metaphor.* 1933.
Kimchi, David; cf. L. Finkelstein.
Kissane, E. J., *The Book of Isaiah.* New York, 1926; Dublin; I, 1941, II, 1943.
Kittel, Gerhard, ed., *Theologisches Wörterbuch zum Neuen Testament.*
Kittel, Rudolf, *Biblia Hebraica,* 3rd ed. Stuttgart, 1937.
Kline, Meredith, "The Intrusion and the Decalogue," *WThJ,* 16, Nov., 1953.
————, *Treaty of the Great King.* Grand Rapids, 1963.
Knobel, August W., *Der Prophet Jesaja.* Leipzig, 1872.
Köhler and Baumgartner, *Lexicon in Veteris Testamenti Libros.* 1953.
Köhler, Ludwig, *Theologie des Alten Testaments.*
————, "Syntactica, II, III, IV," *VT,* III, 1953.
König, Eduard, *Stylistik.*
————, *Syntax.*
————, *Das Buch Jesaja.* Gütersloh, 1926.
Koppe, J. B., 1779-81, editor of Lowth's commentary on Isaiah.
Koran, ed. Mavlana Muhammed 'Ali. Lahore, 1951.
Kraus, Hans Joachim, *Psalmen.* Neukirchen, 1958.
Kroeker, Jakob, *Jesaia der Altere (Cap. 1-35).* Giessen, 1934.

Ladd, George E., "Apocalypse, Apocalyptic," *Baker's Dictionary of Theology.* Grand Rapids, 1960.
Lagrange, M. J., *"Apocalypse d'Isaie (xxiv-xxvii),"* *RB,* Vol. 3, No. 2, 1894.
Lambert, W. G., "Three Unpublished Fragments of the Tukulti-Ninurta Epic," *Archiv für Orientforschung,* 1957.
Landsberger, Benno, *Sam'al.* Ankara, 1948.
Le Clant, Jean, and Jean Yoyotte, *Bulletin de L'Institut Francais D'Archéologie Orientale,* Vol. 51, 1952.
Lidzbarski, *Ephemeris üfr semitische Epigraphik,* I, 1900.
Liebmann, E., "Der Text zu Jesaia 24-27," *ZAW,* Vols. 22-25, 1902-1905.
Lindblom, *Prophecy in Ancient Israel.* Oxford, 1962.
Lohmann, Paul, "Das Wächterlied Jes. 21:11-12," *ZAW,* Vol. 33, 1913.
————, "Die selbständigen lyrischen Abschnitte in Jes. 24-27," *ZAW,* Vol. 37, 1917-18.
Löw, I., *Die Flora der Juden,* I-IV, 1924-34.
Löwth, Robert, *Isaia.* London, 1779.
Luckenbill, D. D., *The Annals of Sennacherib.* Chicago, 1924.
————, *Ancient Records of Babylonia and Assyria.* Chicago, 1926.
Ludwig, Emil, *The Nile.* New York, 1937.
Luther, *Luthers Werke, Deutsche Bibel,* II. Band, I. Hälfte. 1528. Weimar, 1960.
Luzzatto, Samuel David, *Il Propheta Isaia volgarizzato e commentato ad uso degl' Israeliti.* Padova, 1855.

Macadam, M. F. L., *The Temples of Kawa.* London, 1949.
Margaliouth, R., *The Indivisible Isaiah.* New York, 1964.
Marti, Karl, *Das Buch Jesaja.* Tübingen, 1900.
Maurer, *Commentarius in Vetus Testamentum,* I. Lipsiae, 1835.
McClain, Alva J., *The Greatness of the Kingdom.* 1959.
Meyer, Ernst, *Der Prophet Jesaja,* Erste Hälfte. Pforzheim, 1850.
Michaelis, J. H., Halle Bible with annotations, 1720.

THE BOOK OF ISAIAH

Milik, J. T., "*Il Rotolo frammentario di Isaia*," pp. 246-249; cf. also pp. 73-74, 204-225, *Biblica*, 31, 1950.

Moallaka, see Amr 'l-Quais.

Möller, Wilhelm, *Die messianische Erwartung der vorexilischen Propheten*. Gütersloh, 1906.

Mowinckel, Sigmund, *He That Cometh*. Nashville, 1954.

————, *Jesaja Disciplinen*. Oslo, 1926.

————, *Psalmenstudien II, Das Thronbesteigungsfest Jahwäs und der Ursprung der Eschatologie*. Christiana, 1922.

Munch, P. A., *The Expression bajjöm hähū*. Oslo, 1936.

Murray, J., *Romans, NICNT*. Grand Rapids, 1959.

Musil, Alois, *The Northern Hegaz*. New York, 1926.

Nägelsbach, Carl W. E., *Der Prophet Jesaja*. Leipzig, 1877.

Noth, *History of Israel*. London, 1958.

Nöttscher, F., "Entbehrliche Hapaxlegomena in Jesaia," *VT*, 1951.

Nyberg, H. S., *Hebreisk Grammatik*. Uppsala, 1952.

Oesterley, W. O. E., *The Doctrine of the Last Things*. London, 1909.

Oppenheim, A. Leo, "Assyriological Gleanings," *BASOR*, No. 103.

Orelli, Konrad von, *The Prophecies of Isaiah*. Edinburgh, 1899.

Orlinsky, Harry M., "Studies V," *Israel Exploration Journal*, 4, 1954.

————, "The Treatment of Anthropomorphisms and Anthropopathisms in the Septuagint of Isaiah," *HUCA*, 27, 1956.

Ottley, R. R., *The Book of Isaiah According to the Septuagint*. I, 1904, II, 1906.

Pallas, Svend Aage, *The Babylonian 'akitu' Festival*. Kobenhavn, 1926.

Pap, L. I., *Das israelitische Neujahrsfest*. Kampen, 1933.

Paulus, Heinrich Eberhard Gottlob, *Philologische Clavis über das Alte Testament*. Jena, 1793.

Pedersen, J., *Israel*, I, II. London, 1926, 1947.

Penna, Angelo, *Isaia* (La Sacra Biblia). Torino, Roma, 1958.

Pentecost, J. Dwight, *Things to Come*. 1958.

Perles, *Analecten zum Alten Testament*, 2 vols.

Pfeiffer, *Introduction to the Old Testament*. New York, 1948.

Poidebard, A., *Un grand port disparu: Tyr*. 1939.

Poole, M., *Annotations Upon the Holy Bible*. London, 1688.

Pope, Marvin, "Isaiah 34 in Relation to Isaiah 35; 40-66," *JBL*, Vol. 71, 1952.

Prijs, Leo, "*Ein 'Waw der Bekräftigung,'*" *Biblische Zeitschrift*, Vol. 8, No. 1, 1964.

Pritchard, James, *Ancient Near Eastern Texts*. Princeton University, 1950.

Procksch, Otto, *Theologie des Alten Testaments*. Gütersloh, 1950.

Rahlfs, A., *Septuaginta*, II. Stuttgart, 1935.

Ranke, H., *Die aegyptischen Personennamen*. 1935.

Reichel, Carl Rudolf, *Der Prophet Jesaias*. Leipzig and Görlitz, 1755-1759.

Reider, J., "Etymological Studies in Biblical Hebrew," *VT*, Vol. 2, 1952.

Reventlow, Henning Graf, "*Das Amt des Mazkir*," *Theologische Zeitschrift*, Vol. 15, 1959.

Ridderbos, J., *Jesaja in Het Godswoord des Profeten*, 1932.

————, "Jahwäh malak," *VT*, 4, 1954.

BIBLIOGRAPHY

Ringgren, Helmer, *The Prophetical Consciousness of Holiness.* Uppsala, 1948.

———, *Word and Wisdom,* 1947.

———, *Messias Konungen.* Uppsala, 1954.

Robertson, Edward, "Isaiah xxvii:2-6," *ZAW,* Vol. 47, 1929.

Robinson, *Studies in Old Testament Prophecy.* 1950.

Rosenmüller, E. F., *Scholia in Vetus Testamentum.* Lipsiae, 1791-93.

Rost, P., *Die Keilschrifttexte Tiglatpilesers,* III. Leipzig, 1893.

Rowlands, E. R., "The Targum and the Peshitta Version of the Book of Isaiah," *VT,* 9, 1959.

Rowley, H. H., *The Relevance of Apocalyptic.* London, 1944.

———, *The Faith of Israel.* 1956.

———, *The Zadokite Fragments and the Dead Sea Scrolls.* Oxford, 1952.

Rudolph, Wilhelm, "*Jesaja 23, 1-14,*" *Festschrift Friedrich Baumgärtel.* Erlangen, 1959.

———, "*Jesaja 24-27,*" in *Beiträge zur Wissenschaft vom Alten Testament.* Leipzig, 1908.

Saadia; see Gesenius' commentary for Saadia's exposition. Cf. also S. Landauer, *Kitab al-Amanat.* Leiden, 1880.

Sabatier, P., *Bibliorum sacrorum latinae versiones antiquae,* II. Paris, 1751.

Saggs, H. W. F., "The Nimrud Letters," *Iraq,* Vol. 21, Part 2, Autumn 1959.

Scerbo, F., "*Di alcune presunte forme aramaiche in Isaia,*" in *Giornale della Società asiatica italiana,* Vol. 16, 1903.

Schilling, S. Paul, *Isaiah Speaks.* New York, 1958-59.

Schmidt, *Der Ewigkeitsbegriff im Alten Testament.* 1940.

Schmidt, Hans, *Die Schriften des Alten Testaments.* 1921, 1925.

———, *Die Thronfart Jahves.* Tübingen, 1927.

Schmidt, Sebastian, *Commentarius super illustres prophetias Jesaeae.* Hamburgi, 1702.

Scott, R. B. Y., "Isaiah xxi:1-10; The Inside of a Prophet's Mind," *VT,* Vol. 2, 1952.

Schräder, *Die Keilschriften und das Alte Testament.* 1883, 1903.

Seeligmann, I. J., *The Septuagint Version of Isaiah.* Leiden, 1946.

Sellin, E., *Israelitische-jüdische Religionsgeschichte.* Leipzig, 1933.

Sievers, Eduard, "*Zu Jesajas 21:1-10,*" *Karl Marti Festschrift,* 1925.

Skinner, J., "Isaiah," *Cambridge Bible.* Cambridge, 1925.

Smend, R., "*Anmerkungen zu Jes. 24-27,*" *ZAW,* Vol. 4, 1884.

Smend, R., and A. Socin, *Die Inschrift des Königs Mesa von Moab.*

Smith, George Adam, *The Book of Isaiah.* New York; I, 1888, II, 1890.

Stamm, J. J., "Ein Vierteljahrhundert Psalmenforschung," *Theologisches Rundschau,* 23, 1955.

Steinmann, J., *La Prophète Isaïe.* Paris, 1950.

Stenning, J. F., *The Targum of Isaiah.* Oxford, 1949.

Strachey, Edward, *Hebrew Politics in the Times of Sargon and Sennacherib.* London, 1853.

Stummer, F., *Einführung in die lateinische Bibel.* Paderborn, 1928.

Sukenik, Eleazer, *Otzar Hammegilloth haggenuzoth.* Jerusalem, 1954.

Tadmor, H., "The Campaigns of Sargon II of Assur: A Chronological-Historical Study," *Journal of Cuneiform Studies,* Vol. 12, 1958.

Tallqvist, *Die assyrische Beschwörungsserie Maqlu.* 1895.

Talmon, S., *Annual of the Swedish Theological Institute*, Vol. I, 1962.

Targum, see Stenning, J. F.

Thiele, Edwin F., *The Mysterious Numbers of the Hebrew Kings*. Grand Rapids, 1965.

Thomas, D. Winton, *Documents from Old Testament Times*. 1958.

Torrey, C. C., *The Second Isaiah*. Edinburgh, 1928.

Trapp, John, *Commentary on the Old and New Testaments*. London, 1867.

Umbreit, F. W. C., *Jesaja*. 1841.

Van der Flier, A., *De Profeet Jesaja*. Zust, 1931.

Van Dorssen, J. C., *De Derivata van de stam 'mn in het Hebreeuwsch van het Oude Testament*. Amsterdam, 1951.

Van Imschoot, *Theologie de l'Ancien Testament*. Tournai, 1954.

Van Til, Cornelius, *The Defense of the Faith*. Philadelphia, 1955.

Van Zyl, A. H., "Isaiah 24–27; Their Date of Origin," in *New Light on Some Old Testament Problems*. Papers read at 5th meeting of Die O. T. Werkgemeenskap in Suid-Afrika, 1962.

Varenius, August, *Commentarium in Isaiam*, Pars I-III. Rostochi, 1673.

Verhoef, P., *Die Dag van der Here*. Den Haag, 1956.

Vincent, *Jerusalem de L'Ancien Testament*. Paris, 1954.

——, "La notion biblique du haut-lien," *RB*, Vol. 55, 1948.

Vischer, *Die Immanuel Botschaft im Rahmen des königlichen Zionsfestes*. Zollikon-Zürich, 1955.

Vitringa, Campegius, *Commentarius in librum propheticum Jesaiae*. Leavadre, 1724.

Volz, Paul, *Das Neujahrsfest Jahwes*. Tübingen, 1912.

Von Rad, Gerhard, *Old Testament Theology*, 2 vols. New York, 1962, 1966.

——, "The Origin of the Concept of the Day of Yahweh," *JSS*, 4, April, 1959.

Vos, Geerhardus, *Biblical Theology*. Grand Rapids, 1954.

Vriezen, Th. C., *Hoofdlijnen der Theologie van het Oude Testament*. Wageningen, 1954.

Wade, G. W., *Old Testament History*. New York, 1908.

Weinfeld, M., "Cult Centralization in Israel in the Light of a Neo-Babylonian Analogy," *JNES*, Vol. 23, No. 3.

Weiser, Artur, *Einleitung in das Alte Testament*. Göttingen, 1949.

Welch, Adam, *Kings and Prophets of Israel*. London, 1953.

Westermann, C., *Grundformen prophetischer Rede*. 1960.

Winckler, H., *Die Keilschrifttexte Sargons*. Leipzig, 1889.

Whitcomb, J. C., Jr., *Darius the Mede*. Grand Rapids, 1960.

Widengren, George, *Religion och Bibel*, II, 1943.

Wilson, Robert Dick, *A Scientific Investigation of the Old Testament*. Chicago, 1959.

Wiseman, Donald J., *Chronicles of the Babylonian King*. London, 1956.

——, "Secular Records in Confirmation of the Scriptures," *Victorian Institute*, 1954.

——, *Vassal Treaties of Esarhaddon*. London, 1958.

Wright, G. E., *Biblical Archaeology*. Philadelphia, London, 1957.

——, *Isaiah*. Richmond, Va., 1964.

Wright, William, *Arabic Grammar*. Cambridge, 1967.

BIBLIOGRAPHY

Young, E. J., *Introduction to the Old Testament*. Grand Rapids, 1958.
————, *My Servants the Prophets*. Grand Rapids, 1954.
————, *The Study of Old Testament Theology Today*. London, 1958-59.
————, *Studies in Isaiah*. Grand Rapids, 1954.
————, *Thy Word Is Truth*. Grand Rapids, 1957.
————, *Who Wrote Isaiah?* Grand Rapids, 1958.
————, "Adverbial *u* in Semitic," *WThJ*, XIII, 2, May, 1951.
————, "Isaiah 34 and Its Position in the Prophecy," *WThJ*, Vol. 27, No. 2, 1965.

Ziegler, J., *Isaias* (Septuaginta Vetus Testamentum graecum). Göttingen, 1939.
Zwingli, *Zwingli's Sämtliche Werke*, 14. Zürich, 1959.

Index of Scripture

26:8	193	88:1	237	131:2	520
28-34	456	88:11	186	132:13, 14	214
30:4	213	89:42	411	137:1	21
31:5	189	89:3	216	137:7	135
32:4	177	89:8	143	138:2	185
32:28-32	327	89:10	342	138:12	228
33:6	399	90:2	431	139:2	495
33:12	222	90:5, 6	494	139:3	105
34:22	159	90:10	137	139:20	278
37:2	494	90:17	218	145:1	185
38:7	64	91	212	148:7	233
39:5	519	91:9	204	149:7	473
40:8	326	91:13	233		
42:2b	518	92:8	241	**Proverbs**	
42:4	367, 523	92:10	434		
44:22	226	95:10	65	3:6	211
45:3	421	96:5	484	4:10	333
45:12	393	96:13	14	4:11	333
45:13	142	102:1	223	4:22	342
48:3	166	102:6	438	5:11	219
48:8	245	102:14	353	7:10ff.	138
48:13, 14	423	102:26	431	7:16	24
49:2	519	103:15, 16	432, 494	8:11	221
51:6	219	104:3	14	11:6	211
51:18	99	104:8	135, 369	16:6	216
52:7	374	104:26	233	17:3	287
54:5	187	104:30	399	21:14	419
54:8	185	105:39	98	22:7	152
54:9	309	106:5	222	23:28	174, 404
55:6	65	106:13	218	25:4	245
56:4	375	106:15	173	25:19	176
63:3	518	106:38	156	27:24	323
63:6	193	107:3	170	29:8	281
66:3	218	107:4	452	31:21	129
68:8	367	107:27	35		
72:6	228	110:1	204	**Ecclesiastes**	
72:10	142, 145	112:8	207		
74:1	364	115:7	526	1:13	218
74:12	167	118	303	5:17	103
74:13	233	118:19	205	7:27	251
74:14	233, 235	118:19, 20	205	7:29	219
75:5-10	210	118:22	303	8:9, 11ff.	218
75:6b	59	119:122	522	9:7ff.	103
77:15	186	119:176	252		
77:18-20	367	120:5	417	**Song of Solomon**	
78:12	186	120:7	168		
78:46	407	121:4	239	1:9	111, 351
80:9ff.	241	121:8	495	2:1	446
80:13	411	124:8	301	2:8, 9	72
87:3	99	125:2	85, 204	3:1	446
87:4	242	129:6	494	7:3	117

2:11	148	9:9	340	**MARK**	
2:11b	75	9:14	251		
2:34	148	10:4	116	1:11	224
3:4	138	10:5	194	2:6	59
3:5	97	10:6	339	3:29	104
3:12	178, 268	10:8	251	6:2b	28
3:13	32	10:34	402	7:6	319
		11:2	402	7:11	141
HABAKKUK		11:7	251	7:22	450
		11:10	402	7:37	451
1:4, 13	172	12:3	301	9:45b, 46	201
1:5	314	12:10	395		
1:12	369	13:2	30	**LUKE**	
1:12b	134	13:4	54		
1:13	404	13:7	232	2:34	288
2:1	70, 73	14:4	85	3:22	224
2:2	343	14:16	48	3:30	112
2:4	172	14:21	129	12:10	104
2:7	291			19:43	308
2:22	434	**MALACHI**		21:20	308
3:12	74				
3:13	135	1:11	48	**JOHN**	
3:16	350	2:7	151		
				1:14	448
ZEPHANIAH		**MATTHEW**		2:11	448
				2:13, 23	367
1:5	35, 77	3:4	54	4:22	45
1:5a	88	3:17	224	4:45	367
1:14	193	5:3	327	5:1	367
2:1	315	6:8	482	5:3	451
2:9	222	8:29	181	5:9	451
2:11	173	10:14	419	9:39	451
2:14	438	10:21a	16	11:4	508
3:8	354	11:5	45	11:11	227
3:9	79	11:13	142	12:31	168, 180
		12:22	451	16:33	455
HAGGAI		12:32	104	18:39	367
		12:43	440	21:7	55
2:14	222	13:21ff.	440		
2:22	434	15:8	319	**ACTS**	
		15:9	320		
ZECHARIAH		15:14	451	1:7	14
		15:31	451	2:10, 13	206
1:1, 7	564	21:14	451	3:8	451
1:2	69	21:42-44	303	4:26, 27	179
2:9	204	22:36	390	8:7	451
3:9	303	23:6	27	8:30	326
4:6	375, 443	23, 37	279	13:51	410
5:3	159	23, 37, 38	104	14:10	451
8:10	83	24:29	431	14:14ff.	14
8:13	45	24:30	14	17:18	279
9:3	140			25:20	34

INDEX OF SCRIPTURE

Index of Persons

Aaramu, 567
Abdiliti, 566
Abel, 231
Abimelek, 143
Abimilki, 143
Abishai, 120
Abraham, 37, 330, 475, 480, 510
Achimit, 51
Adam, 154, 158
Adonijah, 240
Ahab, 118, 144, 182
Ahaz, 14, 89, 94f., 99, 222, 225, 255, 262f., 277, 284, 302, 314, 321, 324, 335, 337, 343, 351, 368, 370, 385, 458, 474, 476, 497, 510, 513-515, 523, 535, 540, 546, 557, 559
Ahijah, 53, 62
Ahimiti, 52
Ahiram, 395
Ahishor, 107
Alexander the Great, 121, 127, 143f., 229, 237f., 241
Amos, 87
Amoz, 556f., 564
Antigonus II, 32
Ariel, 306f., 310-312, 410
Artaxerxes III Ochus, 144
Asa, 182
Ashteroth Chemos, 429
Ashurbanipal, 80, 144, 480
Assur, 568
Azuri, 51f.

Baal, 191
Baal-Perazim, 292
Bacchus, 298
Balaam, 523
Baladan, 533
Baruch, 260
Basilus, 276
Belshazzar, 81
Bismarck, 547
Budu-ilu, 567

Cataline, 506
Cebriones, 120
Ceres, 298

Chemosh, 429
Churchill, Winston, 556
Cleopatra, 49
Cyrus, 60-62, 73

Daniel, 14, 67, 89, 192, 258, 260, 294, 469
David, 57, 99f., 106f., 109, 113f., 119f., 144, 221, 292, 305f., 308, 312, 355, 475, 503, 511f., 516
Deborah, 14

Elah, 118
Eliakim, 111-119, 459
Elijah, 54, 558f.
Elisha, 559
Elu-eli, 144
Enoch, 260
Ephraim, 461
Eriba Marduk, 533
Esarhaddon, 25, 52, 58, 144, 145, 290, 371, 506
Ethbaal, 144
Ezekiel, 121, 124, 130, 153, 228, 231, 260, 461

Gedaliah, 118
Gideon, 432
Goliath, 475

Habakkuk, 70
Hannah, 223
Hanum, 57
Hattusilis, 502, 512
Helena of Adiabene, 109
Hezekiah, 52, 56, 88f., 98, 100, 108f., 111, 114, 119, 255, 262, 302, 314, 319, 335, 358, 382, 385, 411f., 421f., 458-464, 467-470, 472-475, 477, 485-487, 492, 497, 409, 502f., 506-514, 516-527, 529f., 532-554, 556-560, 563-565, 567-569
Hilkiah, 112f., 115f.
Hiram, 121, 144
Hoover, Herbert, 556
Hosea, 54
Hoshea, 540f.
Hyrcanus, John, 187

597

Ia-ma-ri, 52
Ibn Janah, 170
Ipu-wer, 16
Isis, 298
Ishtari, 502
Istanu, 189

Jacob, 38, 241f., 330
Jaman, 51
Jamani, 58
Jehoiakin, 112
Jeremiah, 15, 32, 38, 50, 82f., 93, 134, 163, 256
Jeroboam, 62, 465
Jesse, 74
Jezebel, 144
Joach, 118f., 459, 472
Job, 92, 231
John, 173, 182f.
John the Baptist, 54
Jokin, 112
Jonah, 109f.
Joseph, 65, 119, 179
Joshua, 241, 292
Jotham, 118

Kammusunadbi, 567
Khnumhotep, 24

Libnah, 542
Lilitu, 440
Lillith, 440
Lule, 548
Luli, 566

MacArthur, Douglas, 556
Malachi, 151
Manasseh, 508f.
Marduk, 73, 192, 252, 463, 506, 533
Menahem, 566
Menua, 24
Merodach-baladan, 98, 252, 508, 532f., 537, 545, 560
Micah, 107, 263, 278
Mitinti, 566, 569
Mohammed ib Mudaffir, 116
Moses, 13, 42, 53, 56, 232, 251, 558
Mot, 192
Mursilis II, 458

Nabonidus, 81

Nahum, 32, 268, 435
Napoleon, 547
Nebat, 465
Nebuchadnezzar, 88f., 94, 114f., 134, 163, 308, 310, 467, 535, 553
Nehemiah, 112
Nisroch, 506
Noah, 157, 175
Nu-ua-an-za-as, 458

Obadiah, 118
Ochus, 19
Omri, 182
Onias, 49
Osiris, 298

Padi, 551f., 567-569
Paul, 58, 157, 173, 178, 278, 302, 362, 450, 509
Pekah, 540
Peter, 115, 286
Pharaoh, 26f., 53, 116, 119, 337, 461
Piankhi, 16, 19, 554f.
Plato, 351
Psammetichus, 16, 19
Ptolemy, 49
Pyrrhus, 129

Rabsares, 458
Rabshakeh, 115f., 117, 371, 411, 458-462, 464-472, 474f., 478, 481, 489, 502, 543f., 545f., 551-553, 563
Ramses II, 374, 562
Rukibtu, 567

Sargon II, 19, 48, 51f., 58, 62, 80, 87, 145, 470, 533, 540
Sarpedon, 120
Sennacherib, 52, 62, 87f., 100f., 119, 144, 187, 255, 262, 371, 381f., 404, 411f., 457-460, 465, 477-483, 485-491, 493-497, 499f., 502f., 505-508, 512, 533f., 540-556, 558, 560-564
Sepharvaim, 470
Sethos, 505, 550
Shabako, 16, 26, 56, 58, 553-555
Shabataka, 554f.
Shalmanezer, 51f., 144, 426, 540f., 558
Shamash-shum-ukin, 62
Sharru-lu-darri, 549, 567
Shebitku, 554

Index of Authors

Aeschylus, 231, 362
Albright, William F., 80, 305, 410, 462, 541, 554f.
Alexander, Joseph A., 54, 73, 127f., 148, 164, 168, 196, 198, 265, 271, 279, 290, 310, 339, 371, 384, 391, 401, 436, 439, 441, 446, 455, 473, 531, 548
Arrian, 128
Augusti, J. Chr. W., 174
Augustine, 325
Avigad, N., 108, 118

Baedeker, 109
Baker, S. W., 21
Barnes, 60, 198
Barth, Karl, 283, 356, 378
Bea, A., 234
Begrich, J., 119f.
Bentzen, Aage, 143, 159, 161, 164, 179
Blank, Sheldon H., 288
Bochert, 341, 438
Boutflower, Charles, 552
Brandis, J., 551
Breasted, J. H., 119f.
Bredenkamp, 172
Bright, 541, 549
Brockelmann, 108, 265, 440, 517
Brunet, G., 459
Bruno, 143
Buhl, F., 71
Bultema, Harry, 41, 192
Burns, R., 198
Burrows, Millar, 495

Caesar, Julius, 96
Calvin, John, 41, 54, 95, 132, 149, 157f., 159, 172, 179f., 183, 206, 212f., 229, 271, 364, 433, 477, 484, 486, 488, 496, 511, 519, 522
Caspari, William, 444
Cheyne, T. K., 157
Cicero, 96, 334, 506
Cobb, W. H., 84
Cocceius, Johannes, 273
Condamin, Albert, 71
Contenau, G., 145

Cooke, G. A., 81
Couroyer, B., 379
Culver, R., 181

de Boer, P. A. H., 13
de Fraine, J., 425
Delitzsch, Franz, 30, 54, 73, 82, 117, 127, 132, 142, 173, 207, 241, 253, 256, 259, 264, 272, 283, 286, 333, 340, 349, 355, 361-363, 371, 373, 389, 402, 423, 500, 513, 515, 524, 559f., 562, 564
de Vaux, R., 119f.
Dhorme, E., 60, 62, 506
Dillmann, August, 13, 21f., 24, 64, 66-68, 71, 98, 127, 134, 137, 140, 143, 164, 191, 199f., 204, 207-209, 212, 218, 221, 225, 251, 267, 270, 288, 301, 304, 329, 331, 366, 429, 536, 556f., 558, 561, 564
Diodorus Siculus, 23, 127, 132, 373
Doederlein, Christoph, 52
Dougherty, R. M., 67
Drechsler, Moritz, 25, 28, 30, 46, 51, 54, 66, 76, 79, 87, 94, 98, 117, 123, 136, 151, 154, 156, 160, 165, 168, 171-173, 176, 182, 185, 189, 195, 213, 222, 236, 241, 247, 255, 257f., 264f., 273, 281, 298, 300, 308, 315, 330, 349, 361f., 368, 371, 374, 381, 398, 410, 426, 452, 475, 488, 517, 519, 521, 560
Driver, S. R., 65, 135, 176, 199, 244, 276, 545, 562f.
Duhm, Bernhard, 14, 18, 22, 47, 49, 56, 71, 73, 75, 79, 111, 135, 148, 150, 164, 178, 185-187, 190f., 201, 204, 207, 223, 233, 253f., 265, 338, 484

Edelkoort, A. H., 38
Ehrlich, 71
Eichhorn, Johann G., 235, 277
Eitan, I., 25, 83
Eliezer of Beaugency, 283
Ephraim, S., 117
Epiphanius, 304
Eusebius, Emesenus, 304
Ewald, H., 142, 207, 209

601